Great
Pets!

Great

An extraordinary guide to usual and unusual family pets

Pets!

By Sara Stein

WP WORKMAN PUBLISHING COMPANY, INC.
NEW YORK

To Igor and Ralf

Who hated to have me
leave out the vampire bat
and wanted you to know
the following:
vampire bats bite toes
and noses painlessly,
have an anticoagulant saliva
and can lap up
their own weight in blood.

Published simultaneously in Canada by Saunders of Toronto, Inc.

Library of Congress Cataloging in Publication Data

Stein, Sara.
Great Pets!

SUMMARY: A guide to more than fifty housepets suitable even for city families. Includes animals of many classes, construction tips and training information.
1. Pets–Juvenile literature. [1. Pets]
I. Title.
SF416.2.S7 1976 636.08'87 75-44012
ISBN 0-911104-71-2
ISBN 0-911104-72-0 pbk.

Workman Publishing Company, Inc.
231 East 51 Street
New York, New York 10022

Created by Media Projects, Inc.

Illustrations: Sara Stein
Book Designer: Bernard Springsteel
Cover Photograph: Robert Weinreb
Photographs: Robert Weinreb (photo on page 78, used with the permission of Dick Frank)
Manufactured in the United States of America

First printing, September 1976
1 3 5 7 9 8 6 4 2

Many Thanks

To the Orbans and their poor dog Kiddoy, who got so nervous posing for the cover of this book that he walked off camera and vomited. To Mr. Chapin, the gentleman goat farmer in the wonderful hat. To the Humane Society of New York and their emotionally balanced kittens. To Fish and Cheeps and the parakeet. To Bruce Kyff, whose wolf spider really does eat mealworms from his fingers. To Mrs. Meade, who drove 20 miles through a snowstorm to deliver 10 children into the coils of a 150-pound python, and to the python who was delivered into the hands of 10 children; and to Rick, who first had to extricate the python's front half from an 80-gallon fish tank filled with exotic goldfish.

And to Igor's skunk; Billy's raccoon; Scott, Catherine, Christopher, Beverly and Stephen Inness' bunnies; Mrs. Reiner's salamander; Mrs. Caddell's fat cat; Garrett's shaggy dog; and Anne's Joe-Joe.

And to the New Canaan Nature Center for saving that tiny turtle from a snowy road in the middle of December.

And to The Pet Shop for boarding a tortoise so it was available to bite my toes, ordering out-of-season lizards that no one has bought, and chasing after the two parakeets that escaped in the confusion.

And to my children, for taking after me.

To guests and relatives who may have suffered from my love of animals, specifically: for Ringo, who sat on the chandelier and dropped his droppings on the Thanksgiving dinner, I apologize. For Pest, who chewed through the freezer cord and cost us a side of beef, I apologize. For escaped crickets who chirped in the night, for snakes who fell from rafters, for geese who hissed at relatives, for tortoises who got stuck behind the washing machine, for goats who ate cigars and cats who ate hamsters; and for all the animals who make the weekly grocery list read "mealworms, overripe banana, crickets, chow, hamburger, seed, spinach, mice, bone meal, kidney, hay. . . ," I apologize. But I'm not really sorry. And after reading through this book, I think you will understand why.

Contents

First Words

From time to time in my life, I have wanted to make a pet of nearly every animal imaginable. At 10, I saved up my allowance for a horned toad. At 25, I had a monkey. At 30, I raised a coyote. At 35, my husband prevented me from buying a wallaby. And right now I am resisting everything from a kinkajou to a burro.

Why aren't these animals in this book? Because they are too difficult or not worth the trouble. The horned toad died for lack of ants, and the monkey died of dysentery. The coyote grew up wild. Wallabies are nervous, kinkajous sleep all the time and burros are unresponsive. For these animals and hundreds more, the work is too great, the reward too little, and the guilt at failure too high a price to pay. The realistically chosen pets in this book should be enough to satisfy the whims and talents of any animal lover.

Everyone's idea of a pet is somewhat different. Whether your idea is a wild chipmunk who comes each afternoon for food, or a caterpillar kept overnight, or a lizard who lives in a homemade desert, or a mouse who rides in a pocket, or a parrot who falls in love with you, or a dog who does what you tell it, or just a gaggle of geese in the yard, you'll find it here.

But before you rush out to get a pet, use common sense. There is a summary included for each of the permanent pets in this book. The summaries tell you at a glance the diet and pet costs, housing, care, special problems and life span of each pet. The summaries also tell you how tame you can expect a pet to become.

Use the summaries to help you compare one animal with another. Use it to check your expectations: don't get an animal that requires more care than you want to give; don't get an animal that will love you less than you wish, and don't get an animal that will bore you within a month. Be honest with yourself; we have been honest with you.

Each summary includes initial costs for pet, housing and equipment, and ongoing costs like food or medical care. It has been very difficult to be accurate. Prices for pets vary with availability, with where you live, and even with the quirks of individual stores. For instance, a lizard might cost $6.00 in the summer when it is easy to catch and ship, and $16.00 in the winter when it is hard to come by. Small parrots are cheaper in California, where they are bred in outdoor aviaries, than in Connecticut, where shipping prices must be included.

Equipment like tanks, lights and water dishes steadily rise in price. We've aimed toward higher rather than lower prices. You may be able to save money by shopping at a discount store.

Food, especially seed and grain, and materials, especially lumber, are also going up. Our estimates may be accurate now, but they won't be for long.

Prices for homemade housing are based on all new materials. Many of the animal homes could be made of scrap wood or old containers and parts found in thrift shops. The illustrations are very basic. It won't matter if you change dimensions or construction a little to suit the materials you find, as long as you meet the requirements of space, environmental controls, and ease of cleaning.

Sooner or later, with any pet you choose, you'll run into a problem for which we have no sure answer. When a pet gets sick, or behaves strangely, who can help? Zoos and nature centers are often both informed and reliable. Like you, they are faced with the difficulties of maintaining animals under artificial conditions of captivity. They too have sick snakes, lethargic lizards and nervous birds. Don't be afraid to call and ask for advice.

Surprisingly, the best resource of all might be your own neighbors. In our small community, there is a naturalist who is an expert on snakes and amphibians; tropical fish collectors who know about aquarium problems and fish diseases; an advertising executive who breeds exotic birds; a teen-ager who keeps dozens of different lizards; plus pigeon racers, rabbit breeders, goat milkers, chicken farmers, dog trainers, and raccoon, skunk and flying-squirrel owners. The combined knowledge of all that experience is there for the asking in our neighborhood, and maybe in yours, too.

Veterinarians are trained to care for cats and dogs. They are not trained to care for boas or gerbils, and except in rural areas, they can't help you with a goose or a goat, either.

For the most part, pet stores can't help you. A pet store is a business, not a service. Pet store dealers are not experts in nutrition, environment, disease, animal behavior, natural history, or even the scientific names of the pets they sell.

Pet books are not, on the whole, reliable. I have read books that tell me snakes split their skin along the belly before they shed, that rats turn cannibal if they are fed meat, and that a dog will stop chasing cars if water is thrown on him. I haven't observed any of these statements to be true.

Yet no matter what resources are at hand, you may find, as I have, that you never get the same answer twice. Much of the time, answers contradict my own experience. The best advice may be to experiment. Listen, read, try this, try that, and wait and see. For instance, we often offer a delicatessen of foods to new pets. Individuals differ enormously: we have several parrots who stick with spinach, apples and a variety of seeds, but we have another who eats meat, eggs, cheese and pizza.

We have raised the heat in a terrarium to see whether it increases a lizard's appetite. We have stopped a puppy's training for a while, to see if a rest increases his enthusiasm for learning commands. We have tried a new toy for a screaming parrot, a cave for a nervous spider, a sleeping shelf for a restless snake, more exercise and a swim in the bathtub for an irritable iguana.

Occasionally, the results are dramatic and immediate. The parrot quit screaming when he got a new toy, and the iguana stopped snapping at us. Other times we weren't sure what effect our experiments had on the health, disposition or ultimate fate of a pet. So, like veterinarians, pet store dealers, zoos and other pet book authors, I can't tell you everything either.

You may also run into problems with equipment, food and housing. Commercial cages may not be designed well for cleaning, or for removing and replacing your pet. Many are badly made, too. We've tried to give you practical homemade alternatives.

Other commercial products may not be much better. Manufacturers make siphons that barely bend, water bottles that leak, exercise wheels that jam, and thermostats that kick off when an airplane flies overhead. They also manufacture many things you definitely don't need: dog rainboots, hamster treats, parakeet mirrors and snake-carrying bags.

On the other hand, there are things you do need that are hard to find: a good soaking dish for a snake, lab chow for rodents, cork rafts and smooth stones for turtles, large perches for parrots, and tiny harnesses for ferrets. We've tried to give you either clues on where to look or directions for how to improvise.

Pets in the Wild

Pets In The Wild

CHART: FAVORITE FOODS

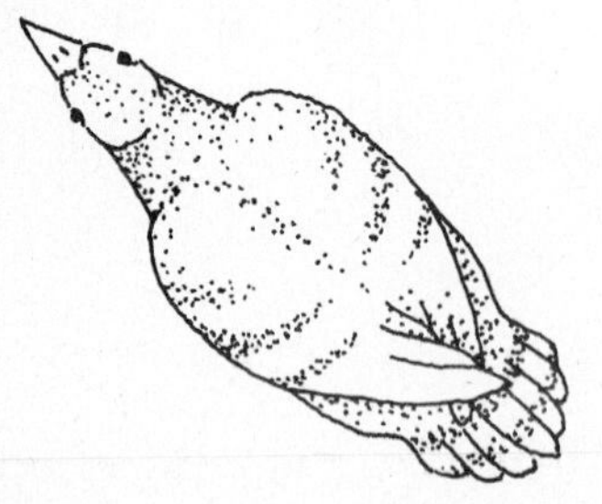

Pigeons: Broken-up stale bread or crumbs.

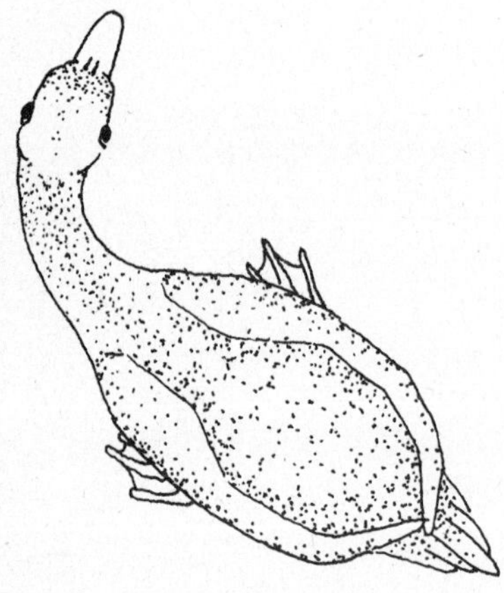

Ducks: Broken-up stale bread, cracked corn.

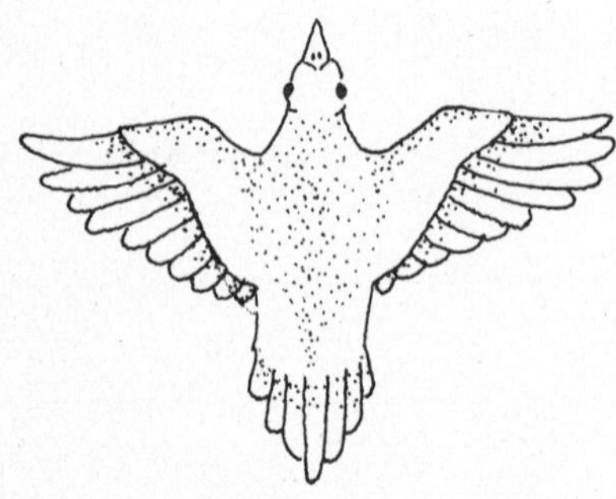

Songbirds: Commercial birdseed, sunflower seeds, suet (raw beef fat), peanut butter, bacon grease.

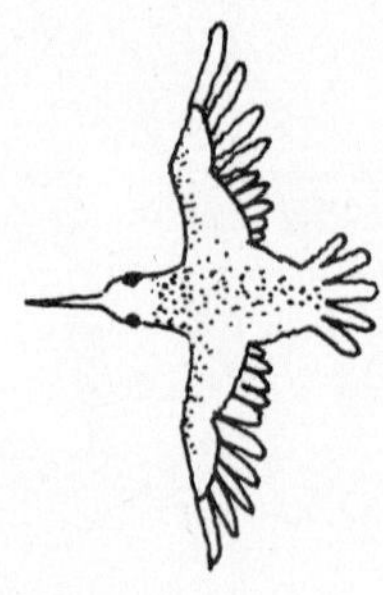

Hummingbirds: Sugar-water, honey-water.

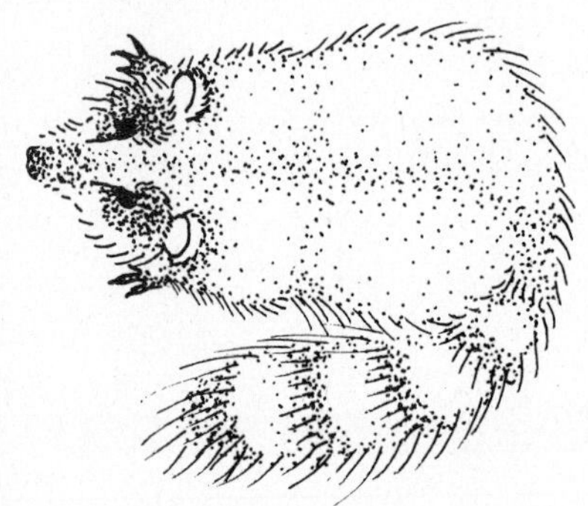

Raccoons: Raw eggs in the shell, meat scraps and bones, fish, canned cat or dog food.

Squirrels: Peanuts in the shell, other nuts, popcorn raw or popped.

Chipmunks: Sunflower seeds, peanut butter.

Opossums: Raw eggs in the shell, meat scraps and bones, canned cat or dog food.

Rabbits: Raw greens and vegetables.

Skunks: Apples, canned cat or dog food.

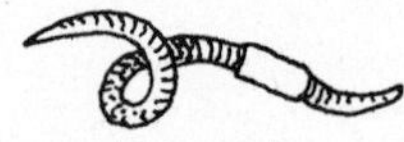

Earthworms: Organic fertilizer.

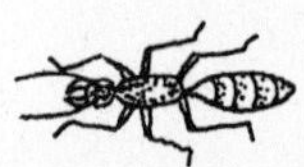

Ants: Cake and cookie crumbs, sugar, bits of raw meat or fruit.

It's not hard to imagine that long before the first animal became a pet, some prehistoric child used to throw his bone to the edge of the forest and stay to watch some prehistoric jackal, ears pricked, toes set to run, snatch it for a snack. That cave child was already treading along the path of pet owner. That jackal was already nosing itself into a collar.

Soon the same jackal (or the same squirrel, or the same crow) came every day. And soon the child became fond of the animal, and came to think the animal was fond of him. And eventually, his great-granddaughter fashioned the first collar, and her great-great-grandson built the first fence, and his great-great-great-grandnephew wove the first cage.

Just because the fruit of their affection and ingenuity is now available in every pet store, there is no reason for you not to start again at the beginning. There is no reason not to make friends with

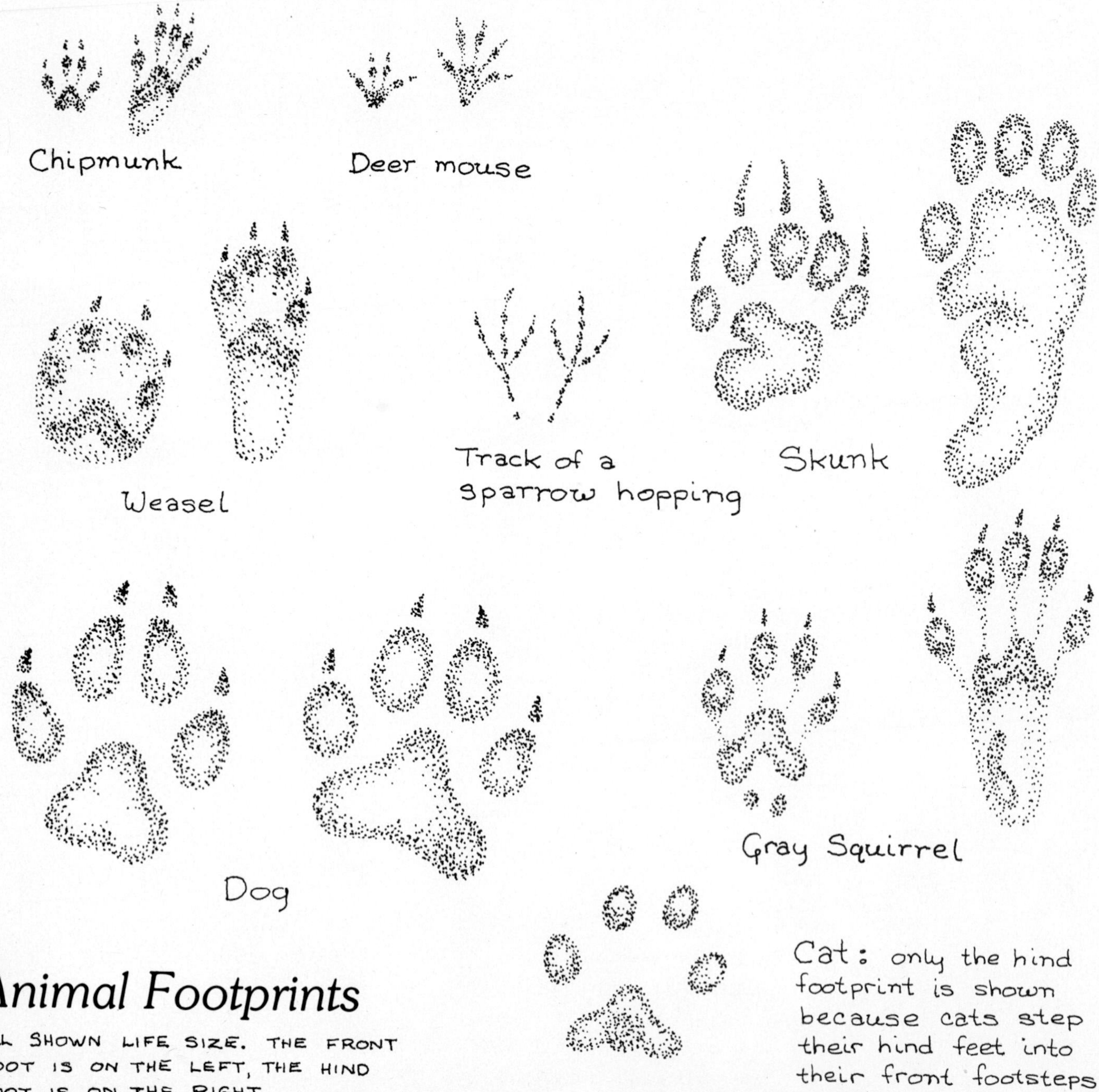

Animal Footprints

ALL SHOWN LIFE SIZE. THE FRONT FOOT IS ON THE LEFT, THE HIND FOOT IS ON THE RIGHT.

animals in the wild.

A wild animal is considered to be any animal who lives in nature by its own resources. If its resources include an ability to locate people scattering bread crumbs in the park, or garbage cans with ill-fitting lids, that does not change the fact that it is a wild animal. Pigeons, mice and ants, all of whom have found living quarters as close to city dwellers as window ledges, baseboards and sidewalk cracks, are all wild creatures. Squirrels, ducks and many other birds live happily in city parks. Beyond the city in even the closest suburbs, chipmunks, skunks, raccoons and opossums are common.

This chapter tells you how to make friends with these and other animals by feeding them the foods they prefer. But a caution: wild animals bite if you try to pet them or hold them; occasionally a wild animal may carry a disease you can catch. Feed the animals, watch them, but only touch if we suggest it.

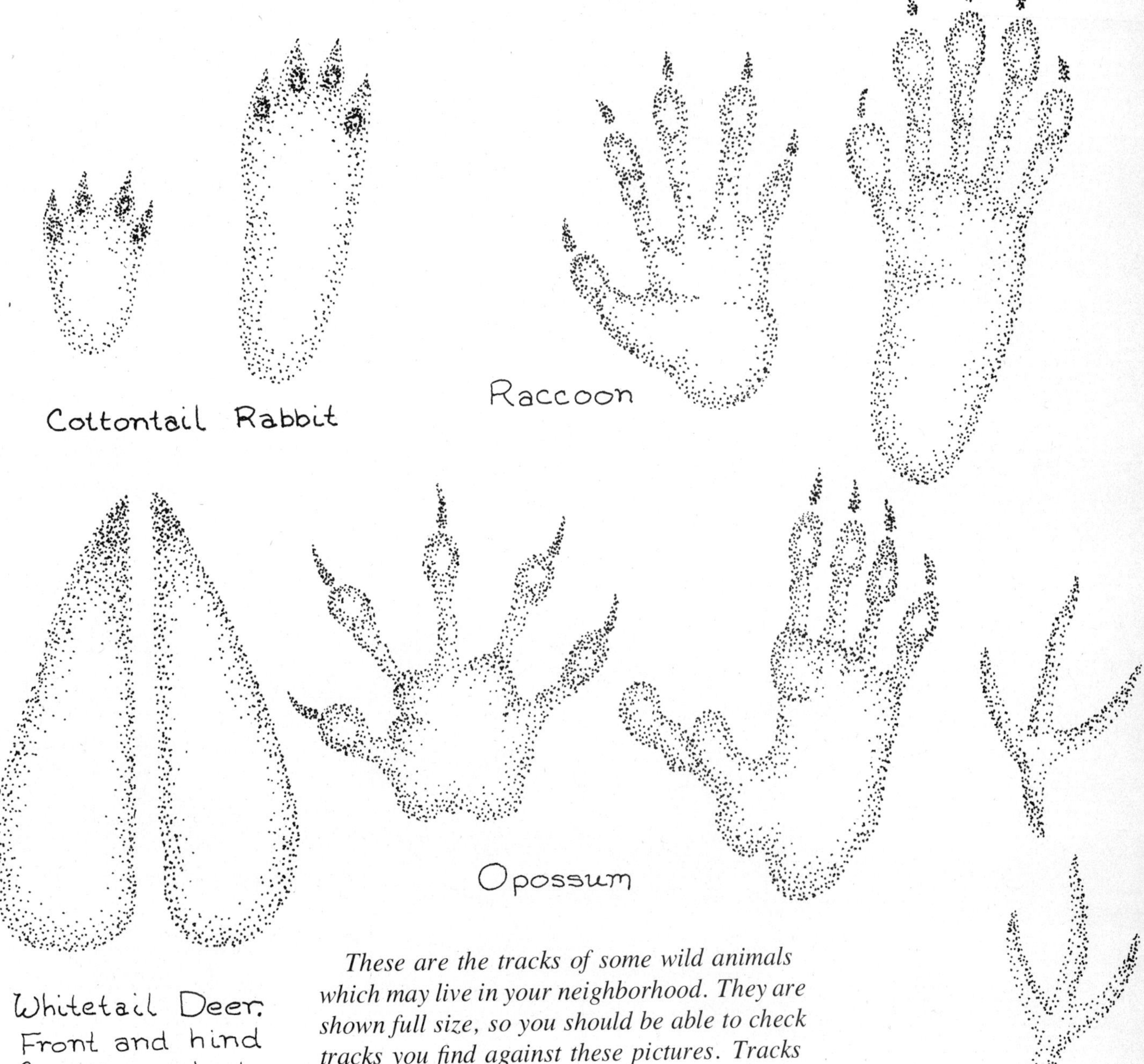

These are the tracks of some wild animals which may live in your neighborhood. They are shown full size, so you should be able to check tracks you find against these pictures. Tracks may be found in mud or sand, but the smallest ones, like those of deer mice, are easiest to see in the snow in winter.

Pigeons In The Park

Every city has its pigeons, and these rather silly, strutting show-offs are creatures of habit. Go to the park or square where you see pigeons. Watch until you find out what time of day a flock of them arrives. This is likely to be morning, not late in the afternoon. Pigeons take off from work early, retiring to their home roosts long before sunset. Bring a bag of old bread with you and feed the birds.

Go to the same place at the same time every day, and the flock will soon learn to expect you and your food. After a while they will not be afraid of you. The boldest of them (when you have found it, why not give it a name) will come to perch on your

shoulder or arm to peck at the crusts and crumbs you offer. Little by little, other individuals will follow suit, and you will get to recognize quite a few pigeons by their colors, and by their personalities.

Pigeons recognize one another too. Although the flock might seem to you a disorganized bunch of birds, it is actually a structured society. Most adult males are mated for life to a hen. The most aggressive cock has fought for and won the most favorable roosting spot in the flock's sleeping area, and the best nesting spot too. He shares both with his hen. You might be able to recognize this bird as the one who flies down to feed first, the one who pecks at his food most vigorously.

In the wild flocks of the city park, some pigeons will have iridescent neck plumage, while others will be quite plain. Many people think the more colorful pigeons are the males, but in fact you can't tell a pigeon by its feathers. If you like knowing which are males and which are females, watch your flock during the months of February through July when courtship is in progress. The males are the ones who are strutting, puffing, bowing, fanning, gurgling, cooing and chasing. The females are the

Pigeons gather when bread is offered.

ones who are getting chased. If you have identified the boldest cock, you can recognize his wife too. She is the more modest bird he is showing off to.

After a rain you may be able to watch pigeons drinking from puddles. Believe it or not, you're seeing something unique among birds. Only pigeons and their relatives drink without throwing their heads back to swallow the water.

If after all your observing, pigeons still seem like silly birds to you, feel justified. They are living relatives of the dodo. The dodo, a flightless giant extinct now for 200 years, looked like a huge squab (baby pigeon), with pathetic little wings and an oversized horny beak. They were not at all bright and would stand around and allow themselves to be clubbed to death by humans for food. Several other members of the family—the extinct passenger pigeon and the nearly extinct crested pigeon—were wiped out by the same trusting behavior. Most other animals have wisely learned to distrust us.

Ducks On The Pond

Wild ducks—mallards and others—can be tamed the same way as pigeons. Do it while they are nesting in late spring and early summer, because they are bound to stay in a relatively confined area during nesting time. Ducks will eat bread, but the proper food if you want to give them a good diet is cracked corn (available in feed stores, and in some pet stores). Watch first to see where ducks come up to shore. Leave some corn or bread there and go away (wild ducks are scared of strangers). Keep leaving food in the same place.

Ducks and geese come looking for handouts.

After a few days, watch the ducks from a distance. Gradually, as the days pass, move closer and closer. You should finally be able to watch the ducks from only a few feet away if you sit still so they are not alarmed. At last they will demand food each day, and will eat it right from your hand.

If you are very lucky, you may discover the nesting site of a pair of ducks and be able to keep an eye on the eggs. A man I know who has made friends with many nesting ducks has even found ways to improve on nature. He lives far north near a salt-water pond which is the summer home of many ducks. Some of the babies hatch while the weather is still too wet and cold—a few die of exposure on their first swim. Of the ones who survive, many more are eaten by gulls. Some even drown. Although they are covered with down, it takes weeks for real feathers to grow. Newly hatched ducklings are not very buoyant and not very waterproof. Adult ducks are covered with 11,000 oil-covered feathers which keep their bodies totally dry and surrounded by a buoyant layer of air, even during a deep dive.

The man I know builds a chicken-wire enclosure

One side of this duckling enclosure is bent down so the mother duck can get in and out. The pan is for water.

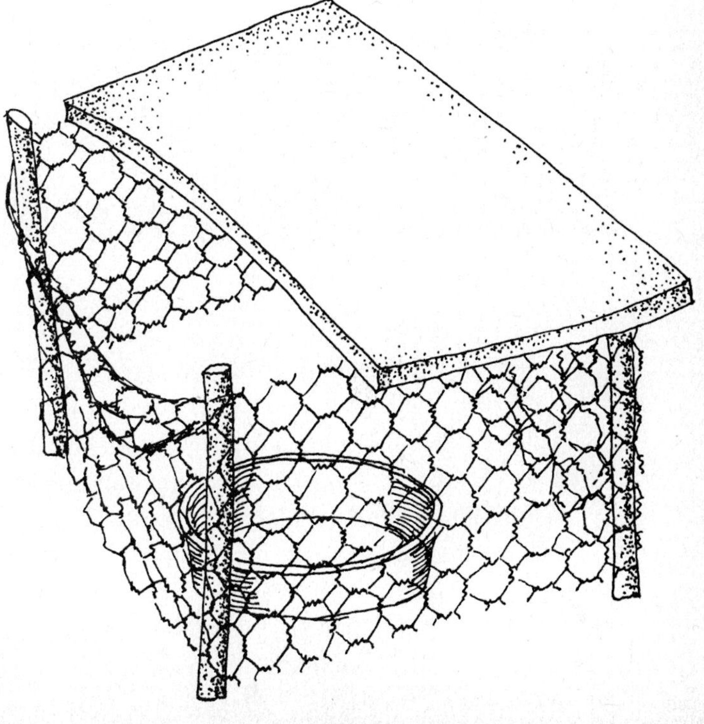

around the nest and sometimes even a roof. The fence is too high for the ducklings to climb over, but the mother can fly in or scramble over the fence with the help of her wings. Since she can't take her babies out onto the pond to eat weeds, the man has to feed them with chick mash (available in pet stores and feed stores). He must also give them water. He keeps them penned until they are several weeks old (too big to die from exposure or to interest gulls) and then lets them go. The mothers have never abandoned either their nest or their babies, and he has increased the flock of wild ducks.

A word of caution: in many states an enclosure such as this one is illegal because these animals are wild and should be left alone. The enclosure built by this man is on his own property and is his way of taking care of the baby wild ducks that make their home on his pond. Check the laws in your state with the local game warden.

A Kindly Stepmother

A naturalist named Konrad Lorenz has gone the limit—he has become a mother duck. This is easier than it sounds. Ducks and many other animals have critical periods early in their lives during which a particular event triggers a lifelong habit. In ducks, the first sight and sound of the mother triggers in the hatchlings an instinct to follow her. Once the image of the mother duck is imprinted in their minds, the babies will unerringly waddle or swim after her wherever she goes.

What Lorenz discovered is that if the first quacking, waddling creature the hatchlings see is a human—in his case, an elderly plump man with a beard—the ducklings will forever after waddle or swim after that elderly plump man with a beard.

And that's not all. Lorenz can also convince unhatched ducklings that it is time to break their shells. Unknown to man, ducklings have been speaking with their mothers from inside their shells for thousands of years. And for thousands of years, each baby has awaited its mother's answering quacks before venturing into the world. Lorenz has learned not only to mother his flock of ducklings across meadows and down village streets, he has learned to talk (or quack) his babies into hatching in the first place.

Birds At The Birdfeeder

You can attract birds to eat at your birdfeeder whether you live in the city or in the country. But there will be differences in which birds you can attract. To find out what each bird looks like and where it is heading, get a copy of Roger Tory Peterson's *Field Guide to the Birds*, or a similar birdwatcher's guide. Buy one published for your part of the country, as well as one for areas north of where you live. During spring and fall migration, birds may fly in flocks of thousands, over obstacles as tall as Mount Everest, along routes as long as from the northern tip of North America to the southern tip of South America. Birds may reach speeds as high as 60 miles per hour, covering as much as 400 miles a day. The largest migrating flocks ever seen by man were those of the passenger pigeon, now totally extinct. The birds blackened the sky in flocks stretching in a swath a quarter-mile wide for a distance of two miles.

Most wild songbirds won't tolerate interference with their nests, but many can be attracted with food. Lately some naturalists have complained that feeding birds during the winter satisfies their appetites so well that they don't bother eating harder-to-find insect eggs and larvas. They think bird feeding during the winter might contribute to plagues of leaf-eating caterpillars the following spring. You might check with the Audubon Society for their opinion, especially if you have had local caterpillar problems.

In the winter birds need high-energy fatty foods to help them produce enough body heat to keep warm in the cold weather. They look for grubs and larvas or raw suet and peanut butter. The easiest feeder of all is a nylon net bag filled with lumps of suet—the crackly dry fat from beef. You may be able to get it free if you know a butcher, but if not, it is inexpensive even at a supermarket. See page 308 for instructions on making birdfeeders.

Some Possible Visitors

Feeding stations that contain seed will attract many kinds of birds. Illustrated are some who might visit your feeder.

The Lovely Hummingbird

If you live in the suburbs or in the country, even that fairylike jewel of birds, the hummingbird, can be encouraged to come to your home for dinner. As bee balm attracts bees, so the trumpet vine attracts hummingbirds. The flower is not too easy to find even in nurseries, though I've seen it offered recently in flower catalogs. If you can get the plant, a hummingbird on the terrace late in a summer afternoon dipping into the vine's deep-orange flowers is a beautiful thing. Hummingbirds also favor lantana, a pretty flowering plant that does well outdoors.

Hummingbirds also accept substitutes for nectar. Find a small, empty, well-rinsed medicine bottle. Wrap a wire around its neck and hang it from a nearby bush or in a potted plant. Tie a bright red ribbon around it because that will make it look like a flower to the hummingbird. Red is supposed to be their favorite color. Now mix up some sugar or some honey in water until it tastes nice and sweet to you. Keep the bottle filled with the sweetened water. If there are hummingbirds around you, especially if they have already noticed pots of bright flowers on your patio or a flower bed in your yard, they will come to hover over the bottle and sip the sugar water. They seem to come mostly late in the afternoon, just before dusk. If you watch carefully you'll notice that hummingbirds not only fly forward and hover motionless in the air, they are also the only bird in the world that can fly backward. You won't see more than the blur of the wings' movement, as they flap at the rate of 50 times per second!

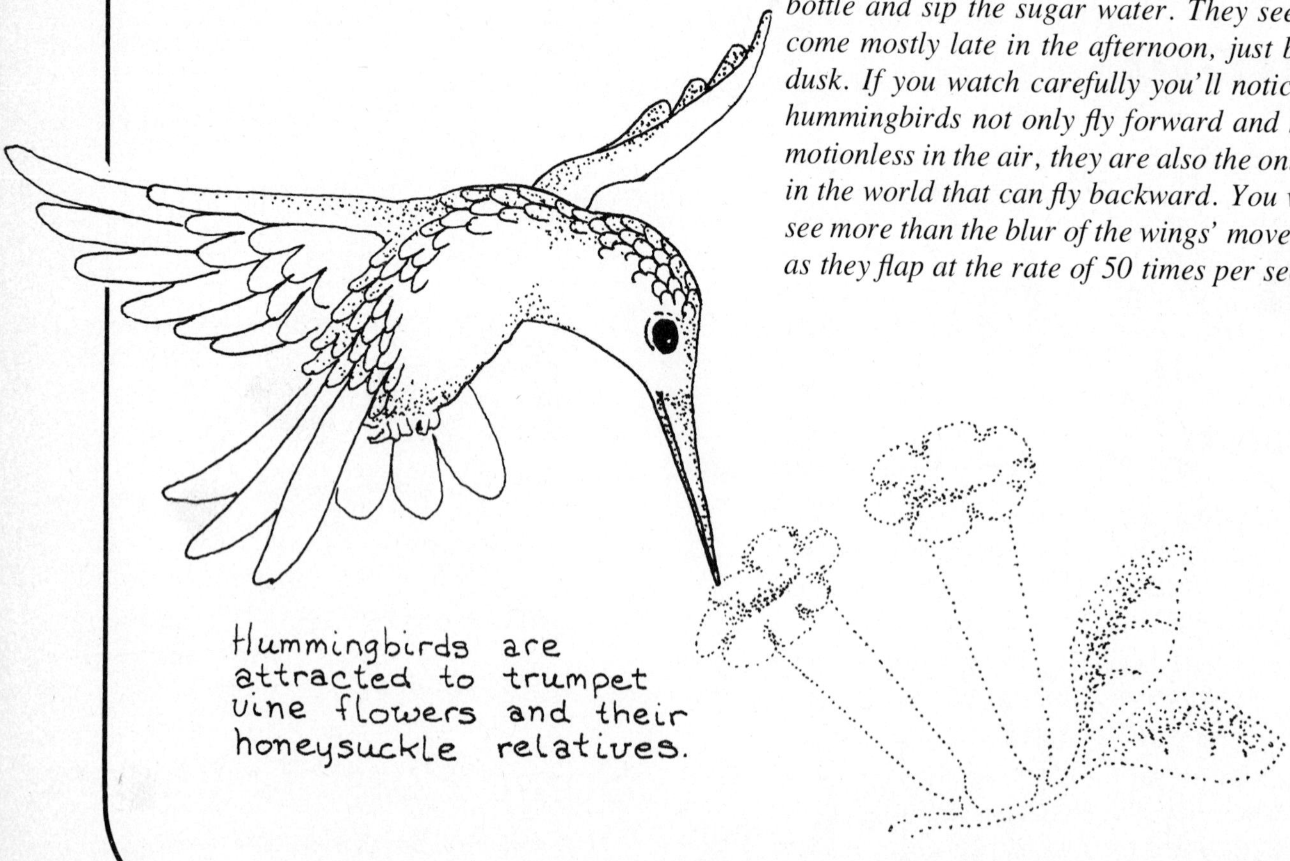

Hummingbirds are attracted to trumpet vine flowers and their honeysuckle relatives.

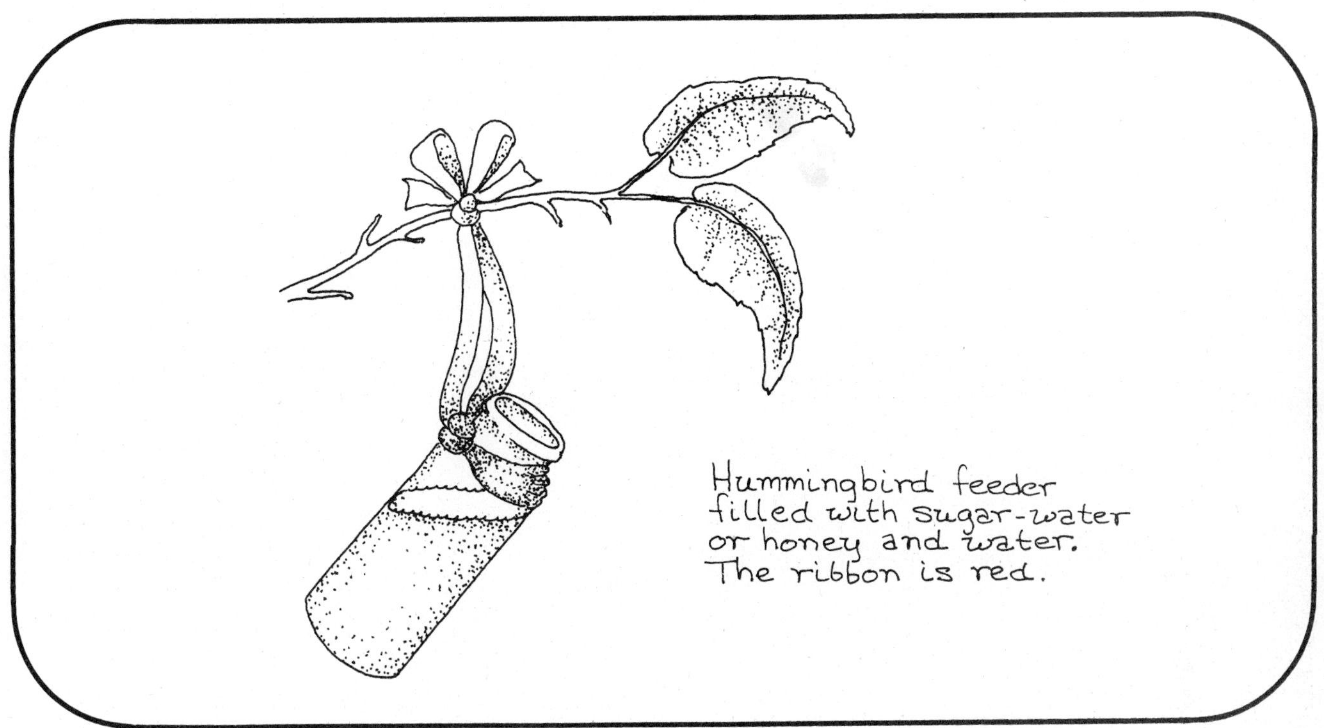

Animals In The Yard

Other wild creatures that tend to live around the haunts of people may eventually happen into your life. Here are a few you may meet in your backyard.

Raccoons

You might look out the window one night and see a raccoon finishing the sandwich you dropped by mistake that afternoon. Since the bold raccoon is not one to turn down a reliable meal, you can get it to come and eat near your house every evening simply by leaving food out. If you have a dog, keep it in after it gets dark, since it may attack the raccoon and vice versa. Continue to leave food out every evening for the raccoon you've noticed. Bread or canned dog food is fine, but if you want to make it completely faithful to you, give it a raw egg right in the shell every couple of days—that's a favorite. Leave out a pan of water too. Raccoons love to wash their food before they eat it, and their hands afterward.

A young raccoon we knew came every evening to our friend's terrace for his dinner. As he grew older, he took a wife and raised a family. Soon the babies came for dinner every night too. Although it would have been unwise to let the adults into the house—they get angry fast and bite hard even if they are very accustomed to humans—the babies were trustworthy for the first few months of their lives. They loved to play with people and were allowed inside for short periods. They wrestled, scampered around, rolled on their backs to have their bellies rubbed, and poked into everything with their clever hands. Of course they also knocked things over, were not housebroken, were unhappy to be asked to leave, and were convinced that every move toward them was a game of tag. They also discovered it was as much fun to wash

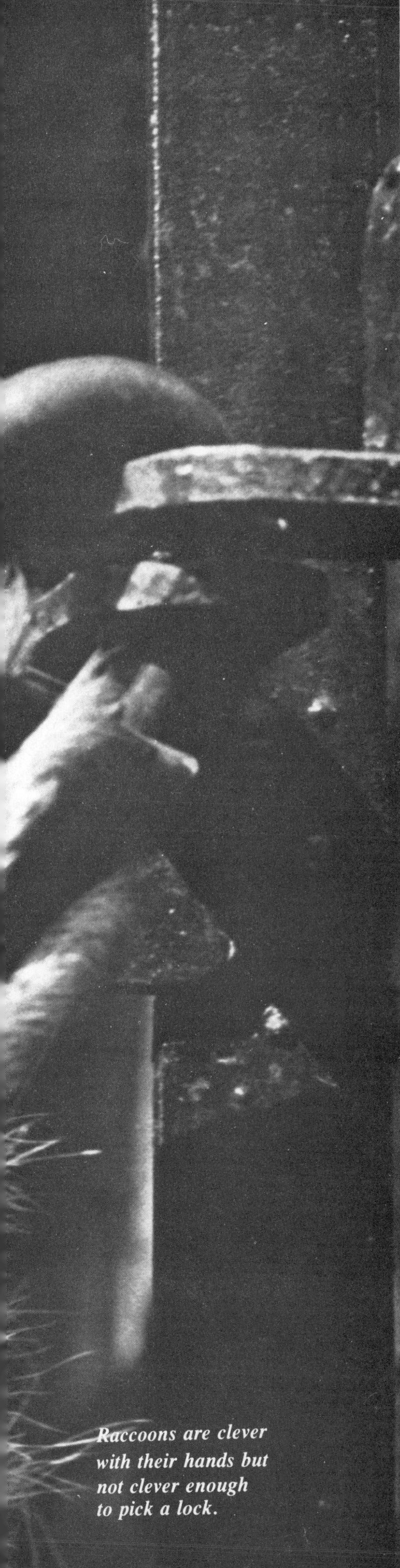

Raccoons are clever with their hands but not clever enough to pick a lock.

their hands and food in the toilet as in a mountain stream. So if you are very easygoing, you might invite a baby raccoon into your house; but if you aren't, don't.

Squirrels

The designs of many birdfeeders are squirrel-proof. But that seems unfair, because squirrels need to eat too. And squirrels are in some ways more fun. If you make a move near the window while birds are feeding, they may fly away. If you open the window while a squirrel is feeding, it may walk in to see if you have even better food in the cupboard.

Right in the middle of New York City there once lived a squirrel who every morning at ten o'clock leaped from its tree onto the ladder of a fire escape. It climbed to our fourth-floor window and fussed on the sill until we opened it. Then it would hop in, sit up and wait for its breakfast. This was not an unusual squirrel; probably any squirrel who becomes accustomed to your birdfeeder will sooner or later venture into the house through the window if you let it. A warning: squirrels can be very destructive if they get stuck in the house and can't figure out how to get out again. They are also quick to bite.

If you're going to try making such close friends with a squirrel, keep your birdfeeder on a kitchen

Unattended peanuts often attract squirrels.

window sill. Before you open the window, be sure your kitchen door is shut so the squirrel won't venture farther into the house. Open the window; put some food right on the window sill so the squirrel doesn't venture too far in at first—it will probably snatch something and pop right out the window again. Little by little, the squirrel will become braver and you will be able to watch it eat every day. When you want the squirrel to leave, shoo it by waving a towel at it. *Don't* try to catch it—squirrels bite hard and if rabies is even suspected in your area, you'll have to receive a painful series of rabies shots.

Chipmunks

Chipmunks are far too nervous to come inside like squirrels and raccoons. However, since they always use the same paths, once you have spotted a chipmunk's run you can leave food on it and have a pretty good chance of watching it eat dinner. We have one trained to look on a certain rock on summer afternoons for its daily treat of sunflower seeds. The chipmunk must watch for us, as it never fails to hop onto its rock if we come outside.

Opossums

I'm convinced, admittedly with little supporting evidence, that opossums get up later than raccoons, and long after my bedtime. I've seen plenty of possums (short for opossums) ambling across the road when I'm on my way home from a party at two in the morning, but we've never caught one in the act of raiding the garbage. Yet possums love to live near garbage pails and you should be able to catch one in the act. The best sight of all would be a mother with her babies—she has as many as 12 or 13, one for each of the teats the babies cling to while finishing their embryonic development inside her marsupial pouch. When the babies are old enough, they ride on their mother's back. The mother curls her tail down toward her head, and the babies curl their tails around her tail to hold on. Then they all raid the garbage together.

Opossums

Opossums (usually referred to informally as possums) are among the most primitive of mammals. In fact, the first mammals, who evolved from warm-blooded and probably fur-covered reptiles 180 million years ago, may have looked and behaved much like today's possums.

Like the possums they would have been nocturnal—a good way of avoiding day-hunting, flesh-eating reptiles (reptiles' eyes are not adapted for seeing in poor light, and few can hear well enough to stalk their prey by ear). Like possums, the first mammals would have relished eggs—an easy food to come by in a world populated with egg-laying reptiles. And like possums, the first mammals would have been small—small enough to be inconspicuous, to find a variety of homes, and to hide out from predator reptiles.

The success of the possum is due to the fact that it never bothered specializing. It's not a fussy eater. The possum still eats eggs and whatever other dead animal meat or live insect food is available. It's still small enough to live inconspicuously out in the forest or as close to man as 100 feet from the henhouse. But possums do have a serious problem caused by their low metabolism rate: they move slowly. They have a hard time making it across busy streets in time to avoid any oncoming cars. They also sleep deeply and "play possum," a comatose state produced by fear that makes them look so dead that predators ignore them.

Baby opossums make affectionate guests.

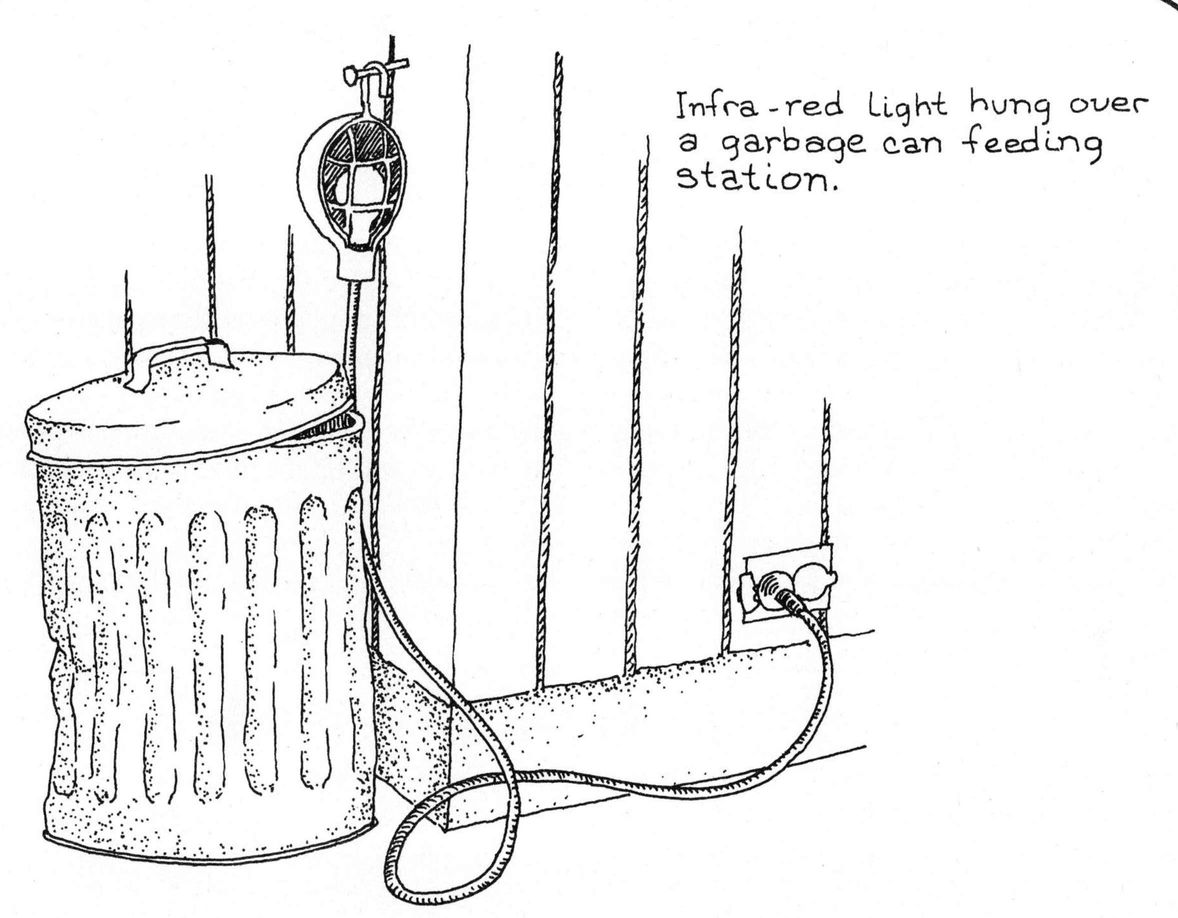

To Some It's Dinner

Quite by accident we discovered a feeding station which attracts neighborhood birds, chipmunks, squirrels, raccoons, mice and skunks. It is truly ingenious. Put your garbage in a can with an ill-fitting lid. Leave something enticing sticking out. Soon the local raccoons will learn to lift the lid and dump the garbage out. Before you know it, a large variety of wildlife will discover your garbage.

Now get yourself an infra-red bulb (photographer's darkroom light) with an extension cord. Find the nearest outlet and run the cord to it. Hang the light by a nail attached to the side of whatever wall or surface is nearest. At night turn off the lights in the house, turn on the red light and watch the animals. You can see them in the red light but they will not be bothered by it at all. Even the following morning you might see a chipmunk inside a peanut butter jar, blue jays in scrambled egg leftovers, and other birds also investigating this new-found delicatessen. Of course, you will have to pick up the garbage that gets tossed around.

Perhaps you will discover for yourself a way to by-pass the garbage pail altogether. We found one way. We fed our dog outside and we neglected to clean extra food out of its dish. Soon there were two dinner shifts—dog at seven, skunk at ten. The dog didn't like the arrangement, and the skunk didn't like the dog. It ended in the usual dog-meets-skunk-spray-in-the-face disaster. We feed the dog indoors now.

Earthworms By The Dozens

We discovered a wonderful way to make an earthworm farm which you might like to copy. We bought a bag of organic fertilizer to fertilize the lawn and garden and forgot to put the bag away where it belonged. It was left out on the lawn so long that eventually there was a big rainstorm. Then when we tried to pick up the bag, it was in such bad shape, it disintegrated.

It became too much trouble to scoop up the fertilizer, so we left the heap there for a year. When we finally dug down with a shovel under the fertilizer, there were dozens of earthworms, all grateful that we had fed them so well.

Earthworms can be used for fishing or redistributed into the garden, where they will aerate the soil and do the flowers or vegetables a lot of good. If you have ever wondered why earthworms come up out of the ground after a rainstorm, the answer is so simple it escapes most people—it's so they won't drown!

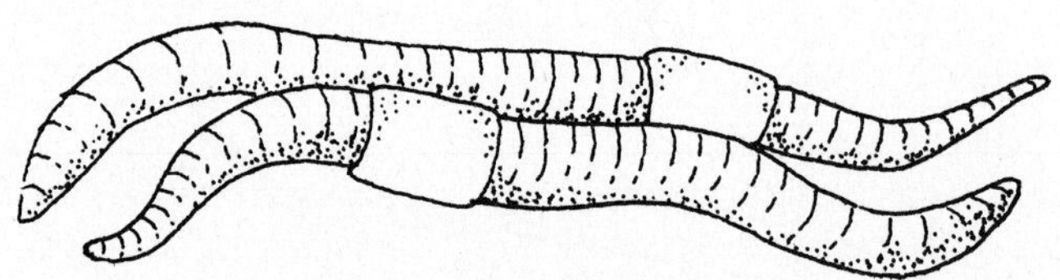

Each of these earthworms is fertilizing the other.

Ants Everywhere

On a summer afternoon, when it's too hot to be running around, find an ant hill and do some ant watching. Drop a bit of food—some grains of sugar or cookie crumbs—close to the nest. Wait. Sooner or later some ant will stop acting like it's in a terrible rush to get nowhere and will start to pull the food towards its nest.

Now try moving some of the food to about three feet away from the nest. Wait. Sooner or later the ants will stop looking like they don't know which end is up and will start to move in a double line to and from the source of food, each carrying the largest piece possible back to the hill.

Now try another experiment. Put a bit of a leaf right on top of the entrance into the ant hill and wait. Sooner or later the ants will stop acting like they are working against one another and remove the leaf. With a small stick, gently knock a little sand from the top of the ant hill down into the hole. Wait. Sooner or later the ants will start to emerge, each with a tiny grain of sand in its mandibles, and rebuild until the hill looks as undisturbed as when you first came upon it.

If by mistake you step on an ant hill or knock over the mound, the results are instantaneous. The ants will scurry like crazy all over the place, each carrying an oval white pupa in its mandibles. Because the ants are upset they will bite, so it is best to stay back and out of their way. Sooner or later the ants will stop running around like crazy and start moving in the same direction. If you watch long enough, you will see them excavate down to their entrance hole, carry their pupas back under the earth, and reconstruct the hill all over again.

The next morning, when all the ants have settled into their new home, feed them again.

Worker ants have found the entrance hole to their partly destroyed nest and struggle to carry their cocoons back.

Overnight Pets

Overnight Guests

(WHERE-TO-FIND CHART)

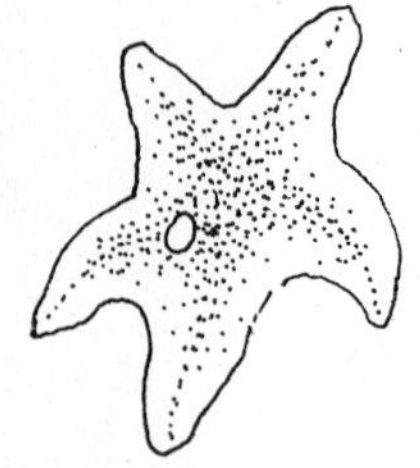

Sea urchins / ***Starfish***: Ocean, under water in rocky areas at lowest tide.

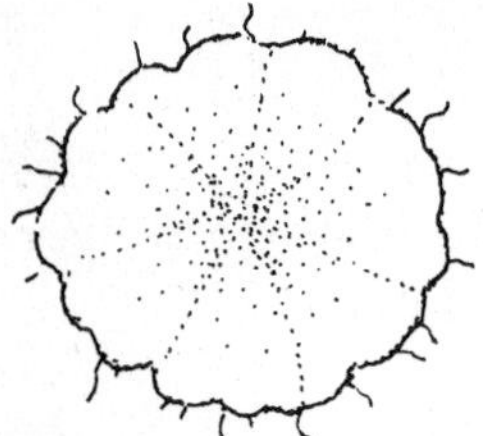

Jellyfish: Ocean, floating near or on surface.

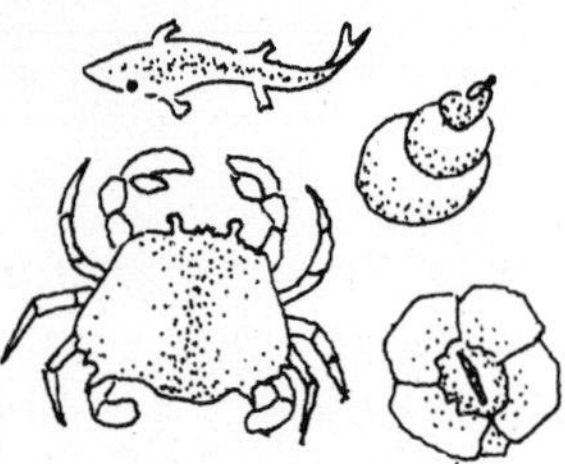

Baby fish / ***Snails*** / ***Crabs*** / ***Barnacles***: Ocean, tidal pools during low tide.

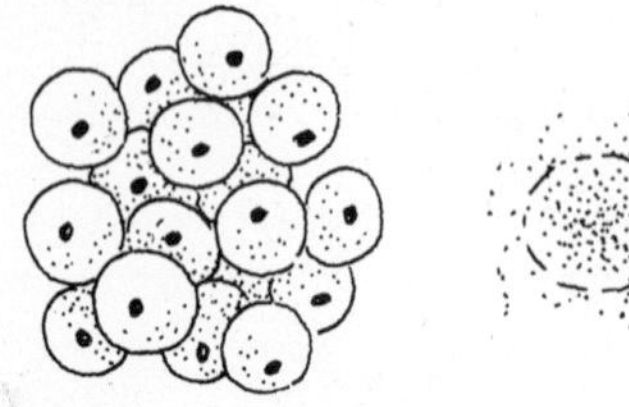

Frog eggs: Pond, floating close to shore in shallow areas.

Spider eggs: In or near spider webs; or close to ground along foundation walls, or bottom edge of clapboards and shingles.

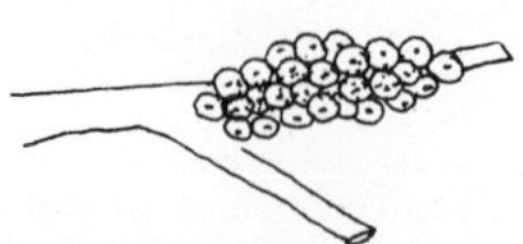

Salamander eggs: Pond, attached to sticks or debris under water close to shore.

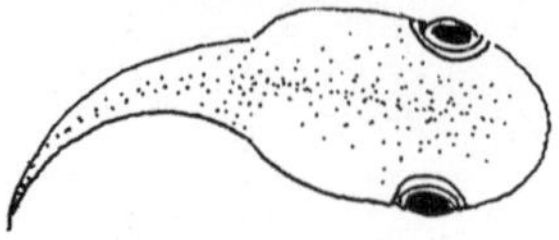

Tadpoles: Pond, along bottom in shallow areas.

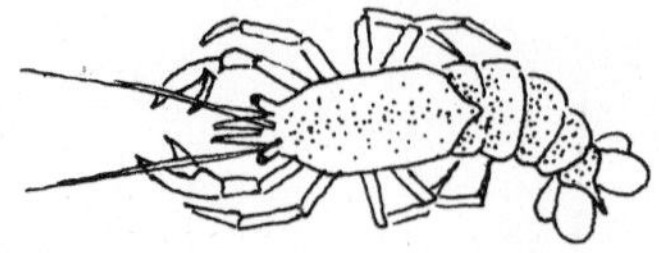

Crayfish: Pond, lurking under overhanging banks, under submerged rocks or logs, buried under mud.

Fresh-water snails: Pond or stream, clinging to rocks or logs below water surface.

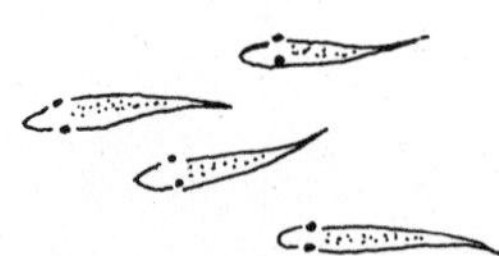

Minnows: Pond, in schools in protected shallow areas close to shore.

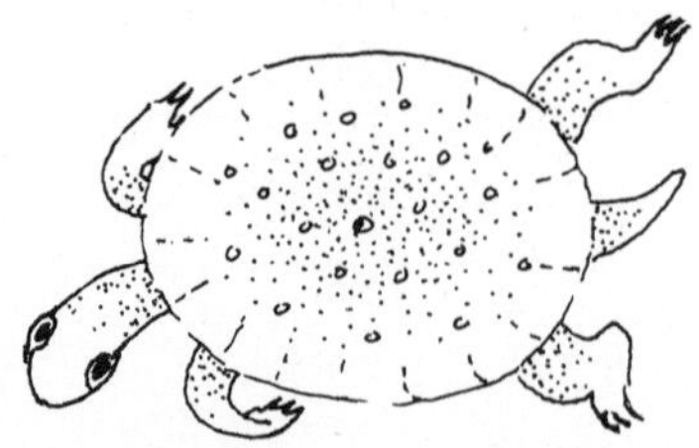

Water turtles: Near or in fresh water. Sunning on rocks or logs. Crossing road between bodies of water.

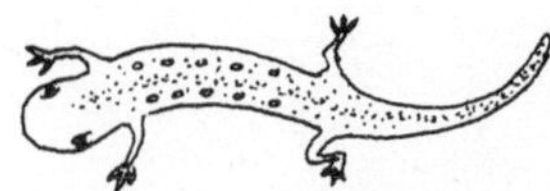

Newts (salamanders): Pond, in deep or shallow water.

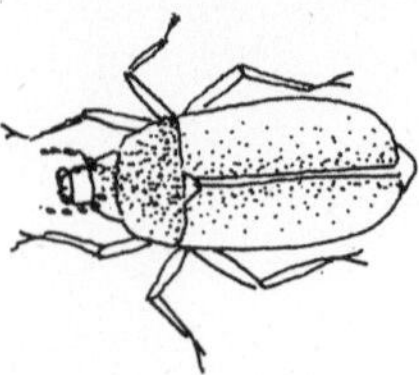

Beetles: Under rocks and logs, in burrows under soft earth.

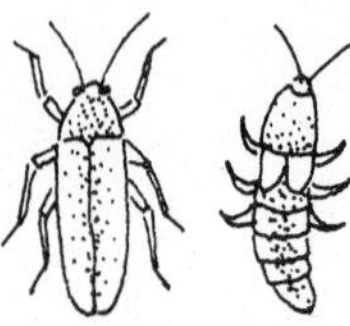

Fireflies: Open areas near shrubbery or woodland.

Glowworms: On the ground under shrubbery.

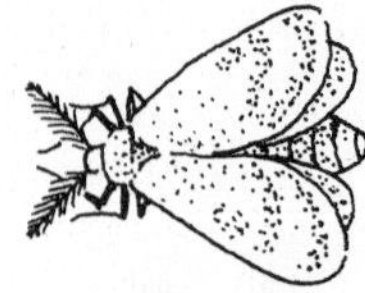

Moths: On window screens outside lighted rooms, around outdoor lights.

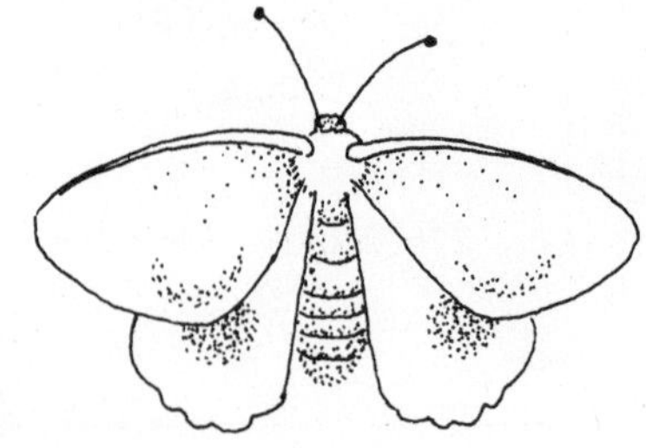

Butterflies: In open meadow, woodland clearings or other open areas where flowers are in bloom.

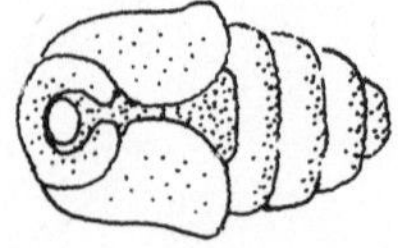

Chrysalises: Hanging from twigs in leafy growth.

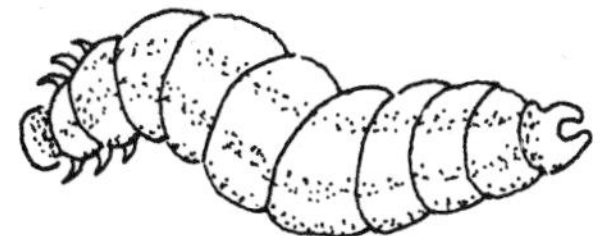

Caterpillars: On trees and shrubs, toward branch tips, often under leaves. Hanging by threads from tree branches. On tree trunks.

Cocoons: Inside curled or bent leaves. Under dead bark. Along twigs. On undersides of rocks and fallen logs.

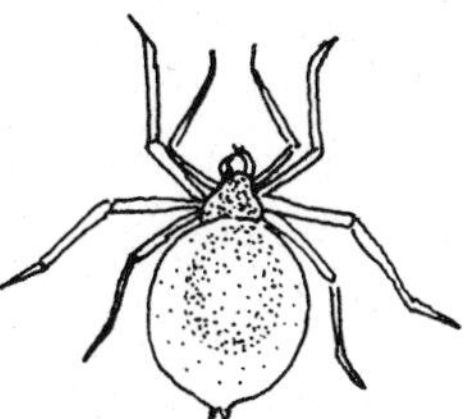

Spiders: In or near webs around outdoor lights, hose outlets, house corners, window frames.

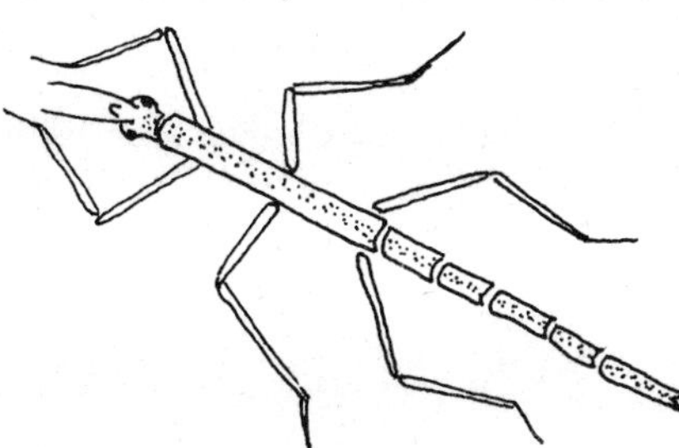

Walking Sticks: Immobile, along smaller branches of trees and shrubs.

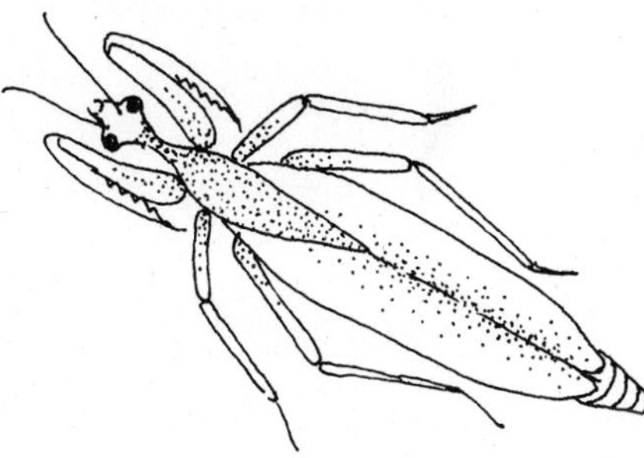

Praying Mantises: In flower gardens where plants are infested with aphids. In meadows.

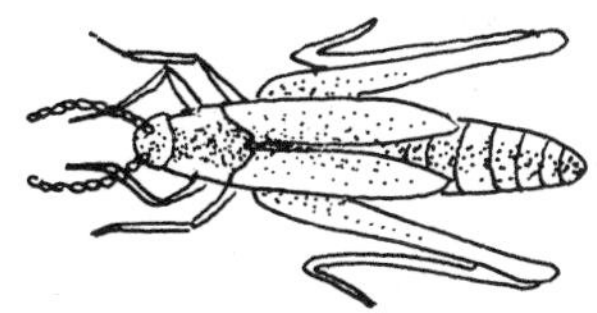

Grasshoppers: On ground in open rocky or dirt areas, on grass stalks in meadows.

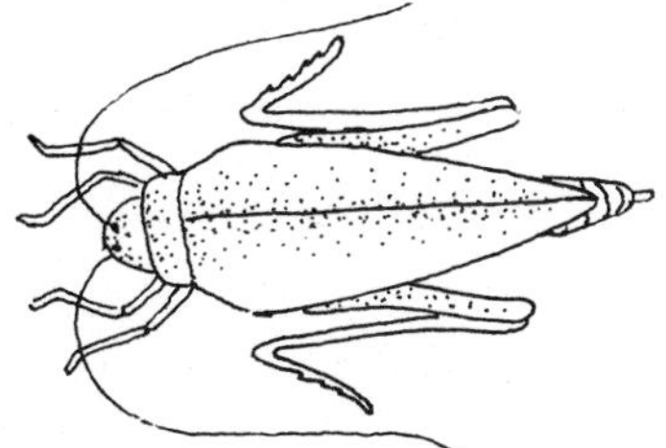

Katydids: On grass stalks in meadows.

Tree frogs: Clinging to roots, trunks or branches of trees and shrubs near water.

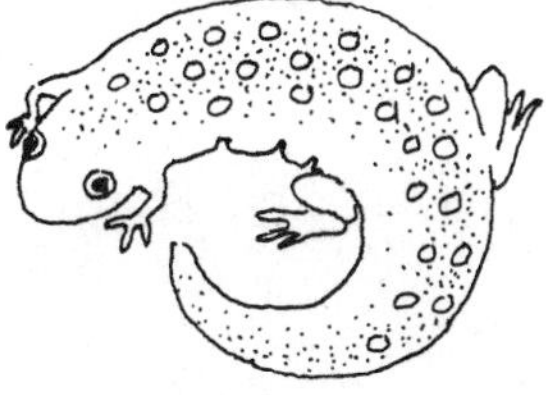

Salamanders: In moist woodland, under stones, rotting logs, exposed tree roots. After rain, walking in open.

Toads: In sunny areas near rock steps, walls, house foundations. Same areas at night.

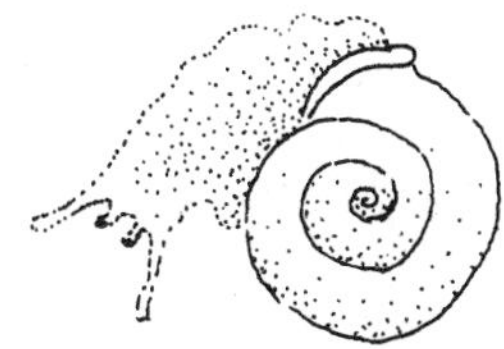

Land snails: Damp areas among grass along foundation walls. Under exposed tree roots, logs, stones.

Snakes: In sunny areas atop rocks, on low leafy branches, along roadways.

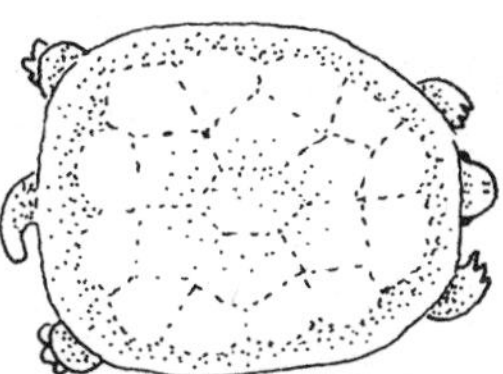

Land turtles: Walking in woodland, crossing roads.

Deer mice: Trapped in drawers, kitchen pails, dog-food bags. Running along the base of rock walls or other protected paths.

Chipmunks: Eating on or running along rock walls, exposed tree roots, or rock formations at the edge of woodland.

Many pets you happen upon can't live with you for long. You can't give them the kinds of food they must have or special environments they must live in. But if you start a kind of hotel for animals—a stopping place for overnight pets—you can watch them for a while, and then let them go. You won't feel too sad letting them go because you know you'll be able to find other pets another day.

The different sorts of homes in Chapter 12 can be the rooms in your hotel. The most useful are the vivariums. Other useful temporary cages are a cake-pan cage, a bug house, and a cheesecloth-covered jar. You will not have to worry about meals because your guests will not be staying long enough to need to eat.

There are a few animals in this chapter that could live with you longer. In those cases, we give you the numbers of the pages that tell you how to house and feed them.

Beachcombing

Salt-water aquariums are very complicated things. The water needs to be kept as cool as the ocean the creatures are accustomed to, and filled with much more oxygen than fresh-water ponds—or fresh-water aquariums. Splashing waves and pounding surf add a great deal of air to ocean water. Ocean creatures depend on high levels of oxygen dissolved in their water. There are really no salt-water animals you can keep as permanent pets without a lot of experience and expertise. But luckily, anything you find in a salt-water tidal pool is

Beachcombing along rocky coastal areas.

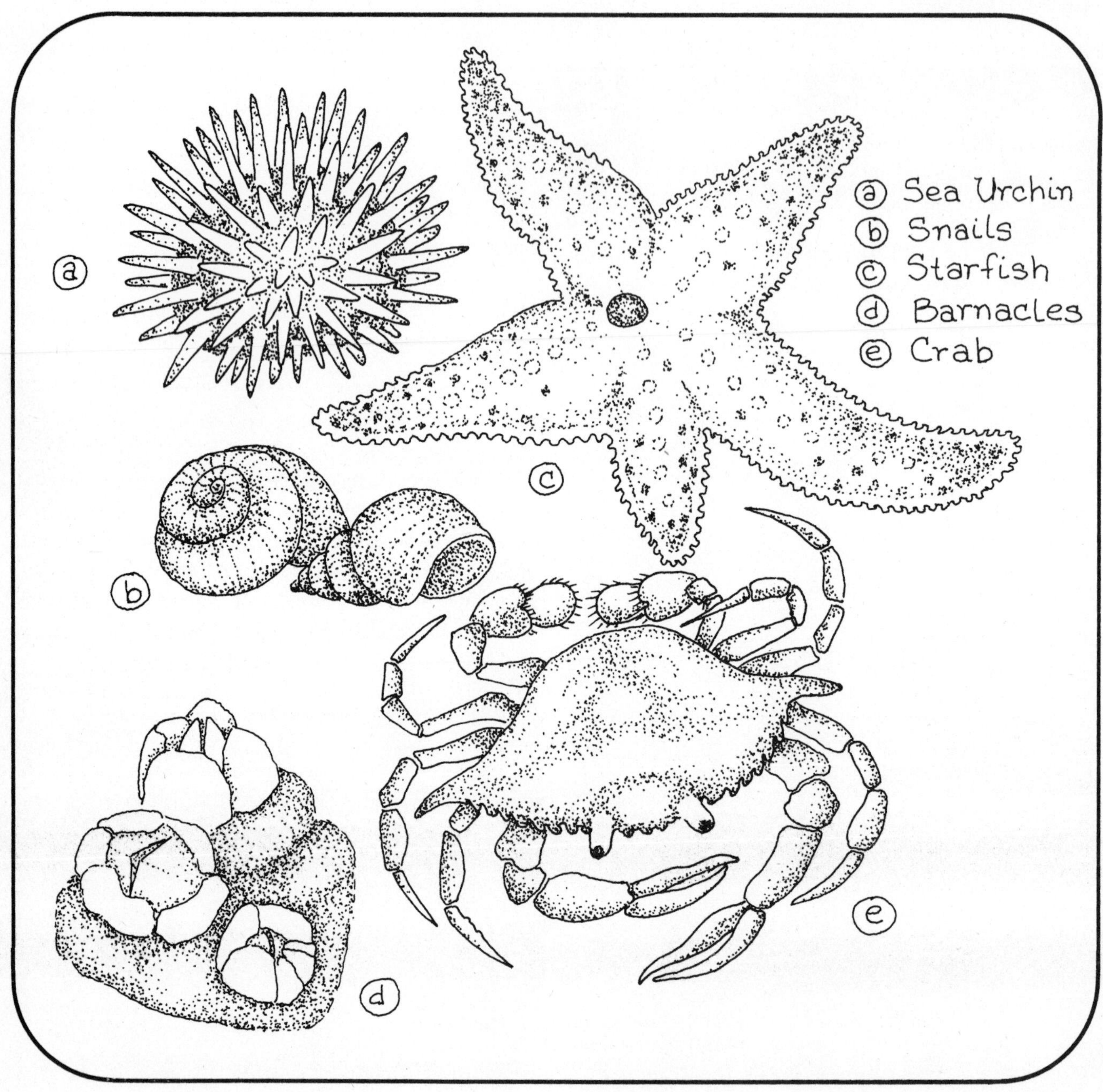

accustomed to sun-warmed and stagnant water during the 12 hours between high tides. Tidal pools form when high tides fill crevices and depressions in rock with sea water. As the tide recedes, the water is left behind, to be renewed only at the next high tide. Tidal-pool creatures will live for a night in ocean water, either in a bucket or in a tank. But you must get the animals back to their natural homes the next morning.

Go to a rocky area of the shore at low tide. Wear sneakers to protect your feet from sharp barnacles and watch out for extra-slippery moist rocks. Bring two buckets with you. One will be the container to collect overnight pets in, and the other is for extra ocean water. You will need a net to catch the pets. You can use the kind of net that pet stores sell for moving fish from tank to tank(see page 329) or you can make your own out of any netlike cloth (cheesecloth, gauze, tulle) and a bent wire coat hanger.

At low tides in rocky areas you may find sea urchins and starfish, both of whom will live for a while in stagnant ocean water. Jellyfish can be found almost anywhere, but many have poisoned tentacles that sting like nettles, or leave an itchy rash. You may find small fish, a variety of snails, and baby crabs. There will almost undoubtedly be barnacles, but it is impossible to pry them off rocks without crushing the animal inside. Instead, look for a small, portable stone with barnacles on it. The

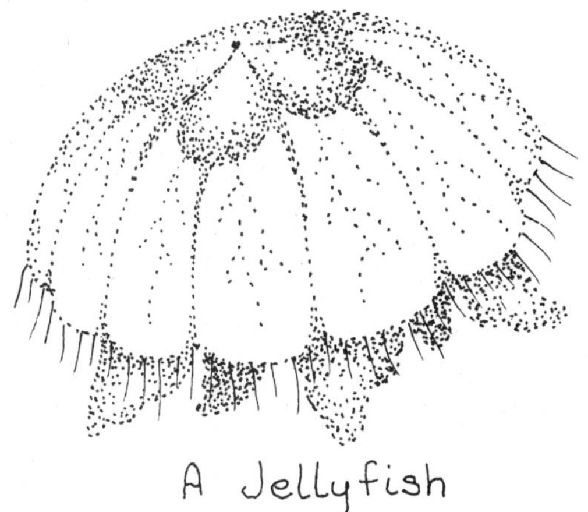

A Jellyfish

barnacles may look dead to you, but if you wait patiently they will open and you will see their tiny tentaclelike cilia waving about in the water, pulling particles of food into their mouths. Barnacles fooled naturalists for a long time. Their shells led naturalists to believe they were mollusks, relatives of clams and snails. But barnacle larvas, when they were discovered, were obviously crustaceans; the barnacle is a relative of crabs and lobsters.

Collect the animals you want in one of the buckets. Add some of the plants that grow in the tidal pool, especially ones that are attached to small stones.

Bring the creatures home in the bucket, but don't forget to fill the other bucket with ocean water. Fill a jar about halfway up with the clean ocean water. Pick the stones and plants out from the other bucket and put them in the tank too. Now you should be able to recapture your pets with the net and add them to the tank. At first nothing much will happen, but after a while the barnacles will open and the snails will move. If you have found a small crab try feeding it a tiny bit of hamburger.

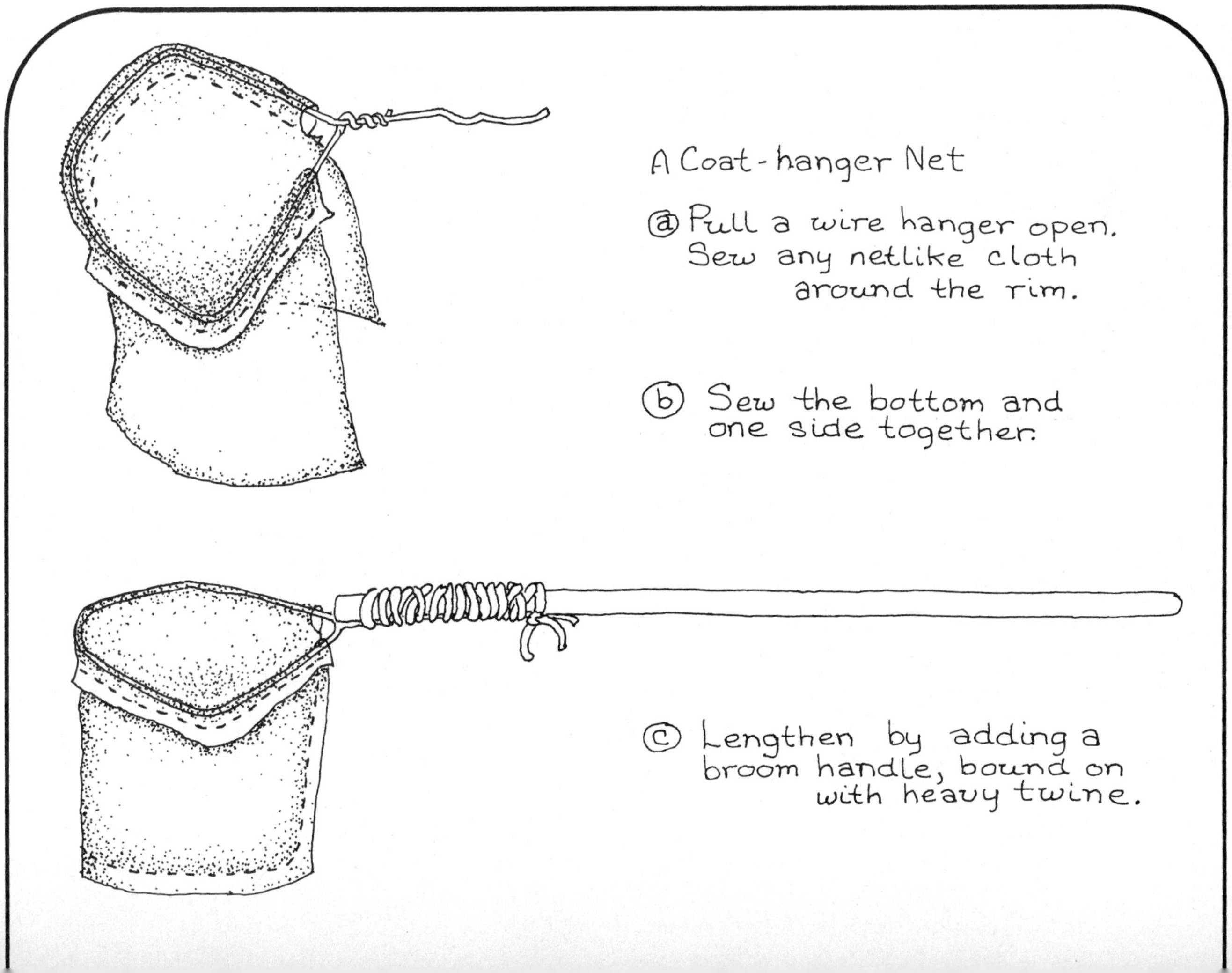

A Coat-hanger Net

ⓐ Pull a wire hanger open. Sew any netlike cloth around the rim.

ⓑ Sew the bottom and one side together.

ⓒ Lengthen by adding a broom handle, bound on with heavy twine.

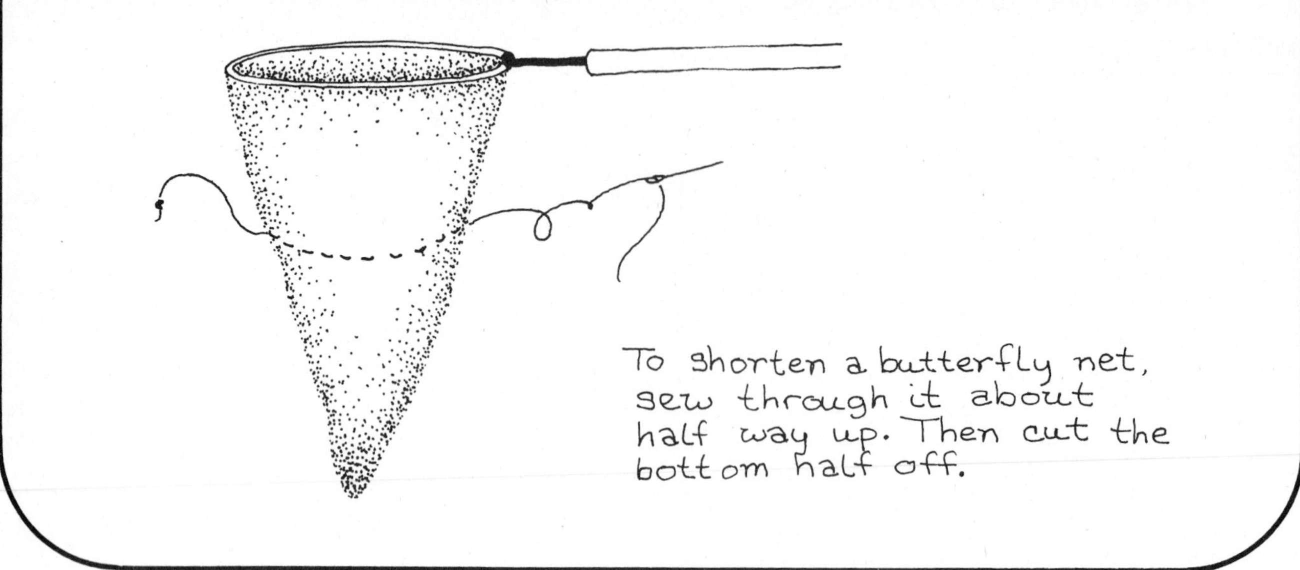

Pond Hunting

Fresh-water pond creatures can stay with you longer than salt-water animals. But the more stagnant the water you look in, the better, because the animals who live there will already be adjusted to a small amount of oxygen in their water. Stagnant ponds are low in oxygen; rushing streams are high in oxygen.

To go pond hunting you will need two buckets, a plastic freezer container with a top on it, and a net. Although there are collecting nets that are made for water hunting, you may have a hard time finding one. It is easier to find a butterfly net and shorten the mesh so that it is shaped like a shallow scoop, or use the coat-hanger net on page 39. A long stick or a broom handle tied to the net to lengthen it might be handy too. Another kind of net to use for pond hunting is a window-screen sieve.

Fill both your buckets with clear pond water before you begin hunting. Keep one bucket to put the pets you find in. Since this will also get full of weeds and mud, keep the second bucket of clear water to fill the aquarium or jar you set up at home.

Ponds are more difficult to see into than tidal pools, especially after you have tried to catch something and muddied the water. If it is early spring, take a good look for frog's eggs before you do anything else. They are masses of jelly with dark spots in them—round spots if the eggs are young, more and more tadpole-shaped as the eggs mature. The egg masses float and tend to be within arm's length of the shore.

Check along the length of old branches and twigs sticking up from the water too. Salamanders attach similar jellylike egg masses to sticks under the water.

Look along the edges of the pond for fresh-water crayfish. They are bottom animals, and since they

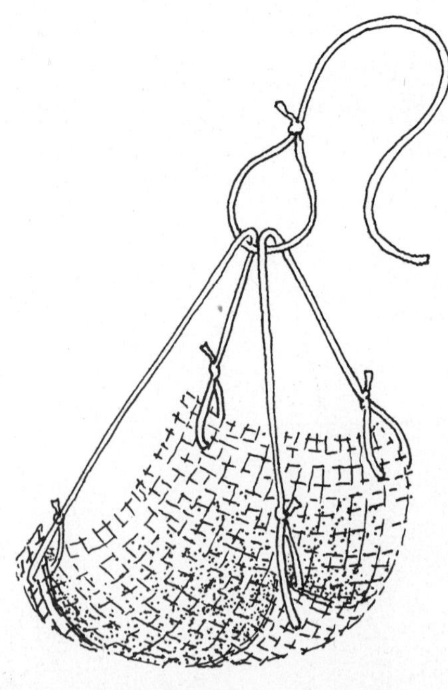

A Screen Sieve

are more or less mud-colored they are rather hard to see unless they move. They also tend to hide under stones. With a long stick lift a stone or prod the mud here and there. If you see a crayfish, try to catch it in the net. Another technique is to simply drag your net across the bottom, swishing it through the water as you bring it up to clear some mud out of it, and see what you catch. You may bring up water snails this way too.

By now you have probably heard the plops of several frogs getting back into the water fast. You could have caught them with your hands while they were still on shore, but you can catch them with the net just as easily. Look for their noses sticking up from the water and swoosh the net from in front of them.

A variety of creatures can be tempted to the surface of the water with bread crumbs. If you can swim well enough to make this a safe adventure, find a rock that sticks out into deeper water or lie on the end of a dock if you're lucky enough to have one. Sprinkle bread crumbs on the water and watch carefully to see who comes to eat. Small fish will almost certainly nibble. You may also get newts, small brown salamanders who hatch in the water, emerge to live on land for a while and go back to the water again to breed as adults. If you are very lucky, baby turtles will come to eat too. Keep feeding until you feel there is a good chance that a swoop of the net will get you something, and then give it a try. The creatures are very fast. It may take you a while to catch one.

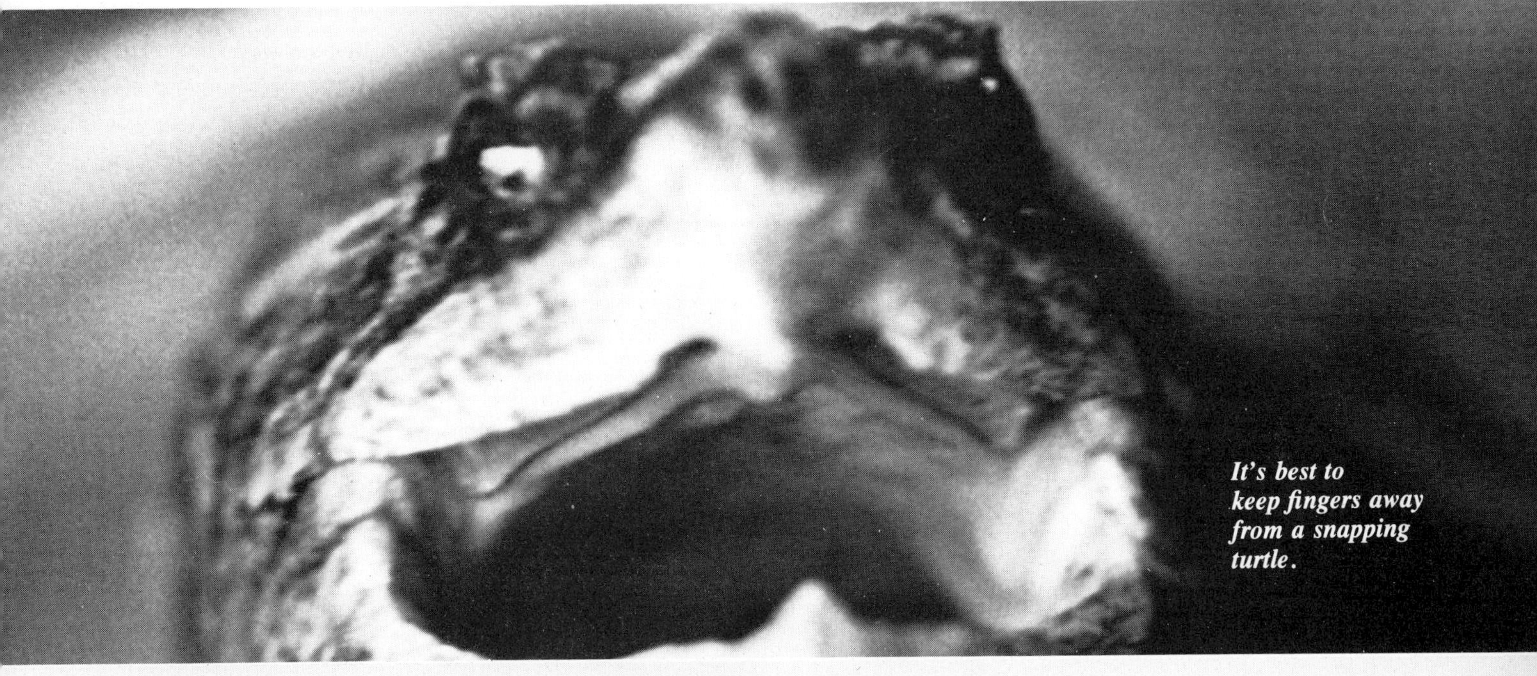

It's best to keep fingers away from a snapping turtle.

Baby spotted turtles may be found in and around a pond.

You can put a toad on a table to watch since it can't jump as far as a frog.

Sometimes it also works to fish for newts, crayfish and baby turtles by attaching meat to a fish hook. The hook will be too big to hurt them—they are caught simply because they hold fast to the meat long enough for you to pull them toward the surface. Net them while they are still under the water. Meat to these creatures includes earthworms, slugs, and for some, insects, but bits of raw beef or chicken taste good to them too.

As you catch the animals put them immediately in the bucket you have reserved for collecting. Remember to keep one of the buckets aside with only clean pond water in it. The frogs you find you will have to keep in the plastic container with the lid on for now. They will jump out of the bucket if you put them in there.

If you already have an aquarium set up at home, you're all set (see page 323). If you don't, pour the clean pond water into your tank once you get home. Now, with a ladle or cup little by little start to empty out the bucket that has your pets in it. Remove any weeds you can by hand. As you get toward the bottom, you will be able to see better what pets are in there and scoop them out one by one with a small net.

You can move your frogs into the aquarium too, but you will have to cover it or they will jump out. Let adult frogs go after a day. If you have found frog eggs in the course of your pond hunt, you can raise them until they are frogs (page 113). When the tadpoles have become frogs, you'll have to let them go too, because from then on they need to catch and eat more insects than you can provide. Crayfish, baby turtles, newts and water snails can all become permanent rather than overnight pets if you wish in Aquarium Pets.

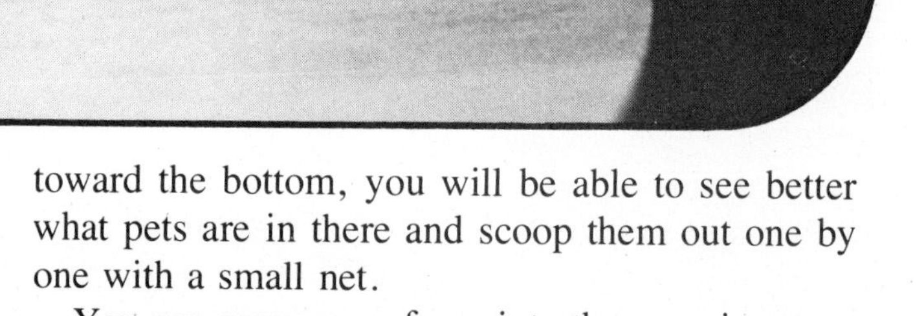

Newt

Bug Collecting

Various sorts of insects can stay in your hotel for a few days. To collect them, you will need a jar with a lid, a piece of cardboard that is big enough to cover the top, and a butterfly net. Or you can hunt just with your hands and the jar, but that is harder. Any of these insects can stay in a bug cage (page311)or in a jar covered with cheesecloth held on by a rubber band (page 311).

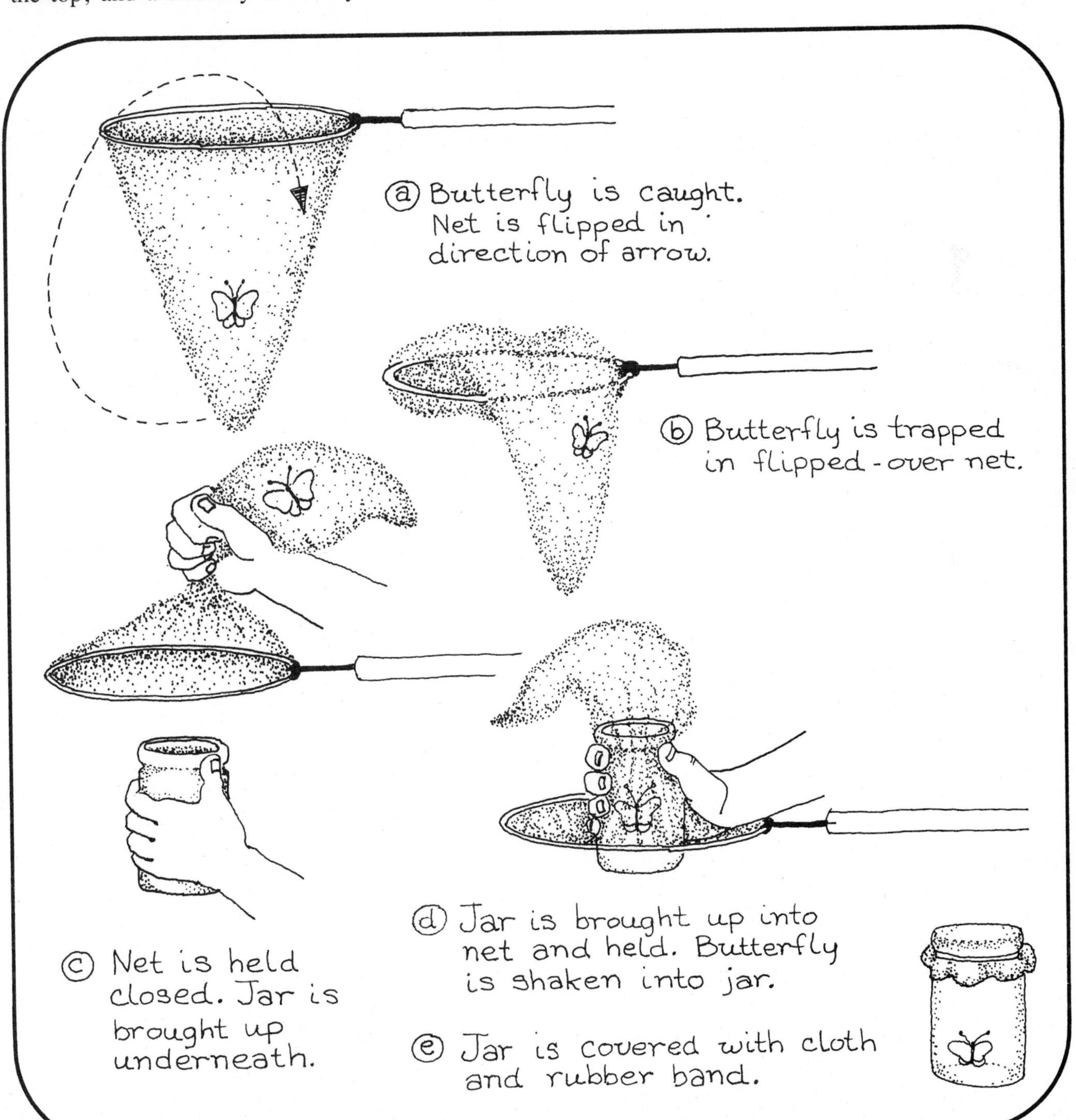

Beetles

Many kinds of beetles live on the ground or under it. You can often find them by lifting rocks or rotting logs. Put a jar over the beetle when you find it and slip the cardboard under the opening. Turn the jar upright so that the beetle falls to the bottom, and put the lid on. You can try feeding beetles on raw hamburger meat. If you observe them eating (most likely at night), you could keep them several days. If not, let the beetles go after a day.

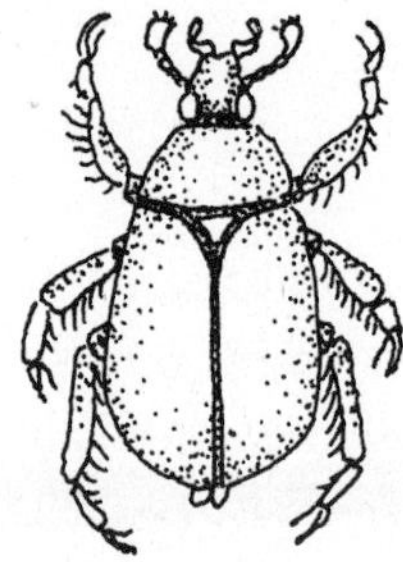

A Beetle

Fireflies

August is the time for fireflies and glowworms, both of whom are actually beetles. Like all beetles, fireflies spend "childhood" as grublike larvas,

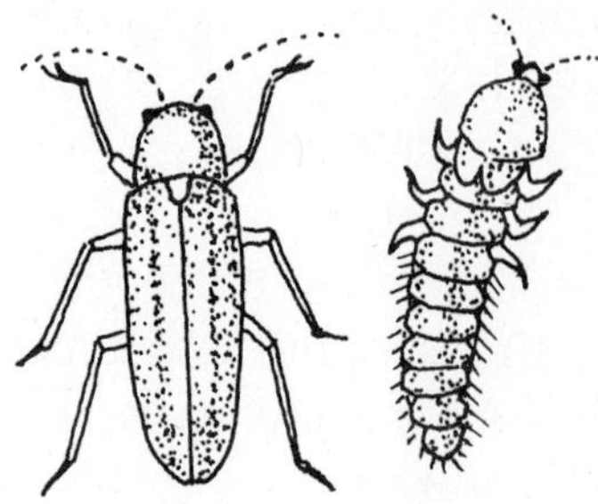

Firefly, Glowworm

then rest for a while as hard-shelled pupas and usually emerge as winged adults. Glowworms are the exception; they are the wingless adult females of certain sorts of fireflies. Glowworm males are ordinary flying fireflies. In other kinds of fireflies, both males and females fly. The flashes are signals, lighting the way from male to female in mating season. Both males and females light up by a reaction between two chemicals called luciferin and luciferase. You will not be able to notice it, but actually male and female signals are different, allowing the two sexes to recognize one another.

To catch fireflies you need only your own hands, because fireflies fly slowly and predictably, and glowworms can only crawl. Of course, you will need a jar to put them in, too. You can't miss seeing fireflies, but if you wait until it is really dark you will have trouble grasping them because they

The Netting Technique

To use a net, sweep it in an arc around you over the top of the grass and end the sweep with a twist of your wrist to flip the net over into a pouch to the side of the metal rim. The creatures you have swept up will be caught in the pouch. Look at what's in the pouch before you try to get anything out. If there's a bee in there, flip the net open and let everything out. Try again. If you catch only one or two insects you want, you can carefully slip your hand into the pocket of the net and gently pick the creatures out. If you have caught many insects, or very small ones like leafhoppers and ladybugs, don't try to pick them out one by one. Instead, follow the directions in the illustration and then quickly get the jar lid on.

Don't try to keep butterflies even if you catch them. They will beat their wings against your bug house and damage themselves too much. Grasshoppers, katydids, praying mantises, walking sticks, ladybugs, and leafhoppers can all live in a bug house for a few days.

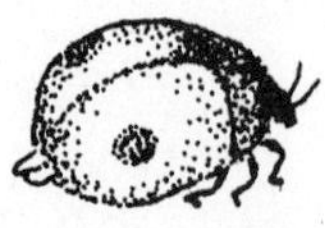

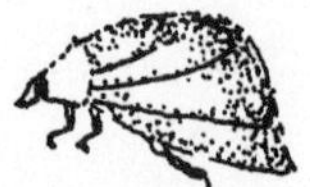

Ladybug, Leafhopper

light up only briefly and are invisible in between their bursts of light. Luckily, they begin to fly about at dusk; if you go out then, you can spot a firefly when it lights up and still be able to track it with your eyes when it turns off. Keep your eye on one firefly at a time. Catch it carefully in midair with your hands and put it in your collecting bottle.

Look for glowworms down on the ground under shrubbery. They stay lit for longer than the winged fireflies, and they also tend to light up when you disturb them. So if you see a glow and then it disappears, run your hand lightly along the ground where you think you saw it. There is a good chance of her lighting up again so you can catch her.

When you have caught as many of these insects as you want, replace the top of the collecting bottle with a piece of cheesecloth held on with a rubber band so they will have enough air circulating. You can watch them for that night, but let them go the next day. Most will live only for a few days longer and females must hurry and lay their eggs to produce more fireflies for you to enjoy next year.

Butterfly Versus Moth

The popular names "butterfly" and "moth" have no particular scientific basis. However, in popular terms, butterflies fly in the daytime, have a curled-up tubular proboscis for sipping nectar, and have slim, knobbed antennas. Their caterpillars (larvas) don't spin cocoons, but form hard shells (they are called chrysalises) in the pupal stage. The moths are mainly nocturnal (except sphinxes and relatives), don't have obvious mouth parts (though some eat pollen), and have feathery, fringed antennas. Their caterpillars (larvas) spin cocoons in the pupal stage.

Caterpillars

Before a moth is a moth (or a butterfly a butterfly), it is a caterpillar. Caterpillar is the popular name for moth or butterfly larvas. The larva is the first stage in these insects' lives, the form in which they hatch from their eggs.

The caterpillar hatches from the egg looking much like an adult caterpillar, only smaller. As it eats and grows it may shed its skin several times, but it still looks like a caterpillar. To turn itself into a lovely flying creature, every cell in its body will actually move to another location within its body or else disintegrate completely, only to be rebuilt into totally new cells and structures. The change is so drastic the caterpillar must go into an outwardly lifeless-looking state—called the pupal stage—while its body self-destructs and reconstructs.

While in the pupal stage the insect is called a pupa. But because its shape, its organs, its chemistry, its very cells are all becoming something else, it is hard to say what a pupa is. It is not a caterpillar, it is not a moth or butterfly, it is a mass becoming a body.

Most caterpillars that will become moths spin a silken cocoon around their bodies to protect themselves while they are pupas. The larva of the silk moth spins a continuous thread 1,000 feet long. It takes 25,000 cocoons to make one pound of silk cloth—and a ton of leaves to feed the caterpillars!

Caterpillars that will become butterflies develop a shell-like skin underneath their caterpillar skin, which is then shed. In the pupal stage a butterfly is called a chrysalis. The hard skin protects the developing pupa and is broken only when the butterfly splits it and climbs out. At first the butterfly's wings are folded and limp; the butterfly unfolds them and they instantly harden in the air.

Caterpillars, unlike moths, do eat a lot. If you find caterpillars on leaves that they are eating, you may be able to feed them on fresh leaves from the same plant or tree. You can even get a small medicine bottle of water, put a twig of leaves from the tree into it, and put the whole thing into your bug house(page 311) for the caterpillar to eat. Get a new twig from the same kind of tree when it has eaten those leaves. If your caterpillar doesn't eat, let it go within a few days.

It is hard to feed a caterpillar enough to keep it, but the common woolly bear, who will grow up to be a yellowish-brown tiger moth, eats so many sorts of vegetation that it is a good candidate for a longer-staying guest. If you have found a caterpillar who has finished most of its eating, or if it will eat what you offer, you may be lucky and see it prepare for the drastic changes that will turn it into a moth or butterfly.

Moths

You will find a variety of moths, different ones at different times during the spring and summer, on the window outside a lighted room at night. The light—electric, oil lamp or candle, and way back in history, the caveman's fire—attracts moths, assuring that male and female get together. In some

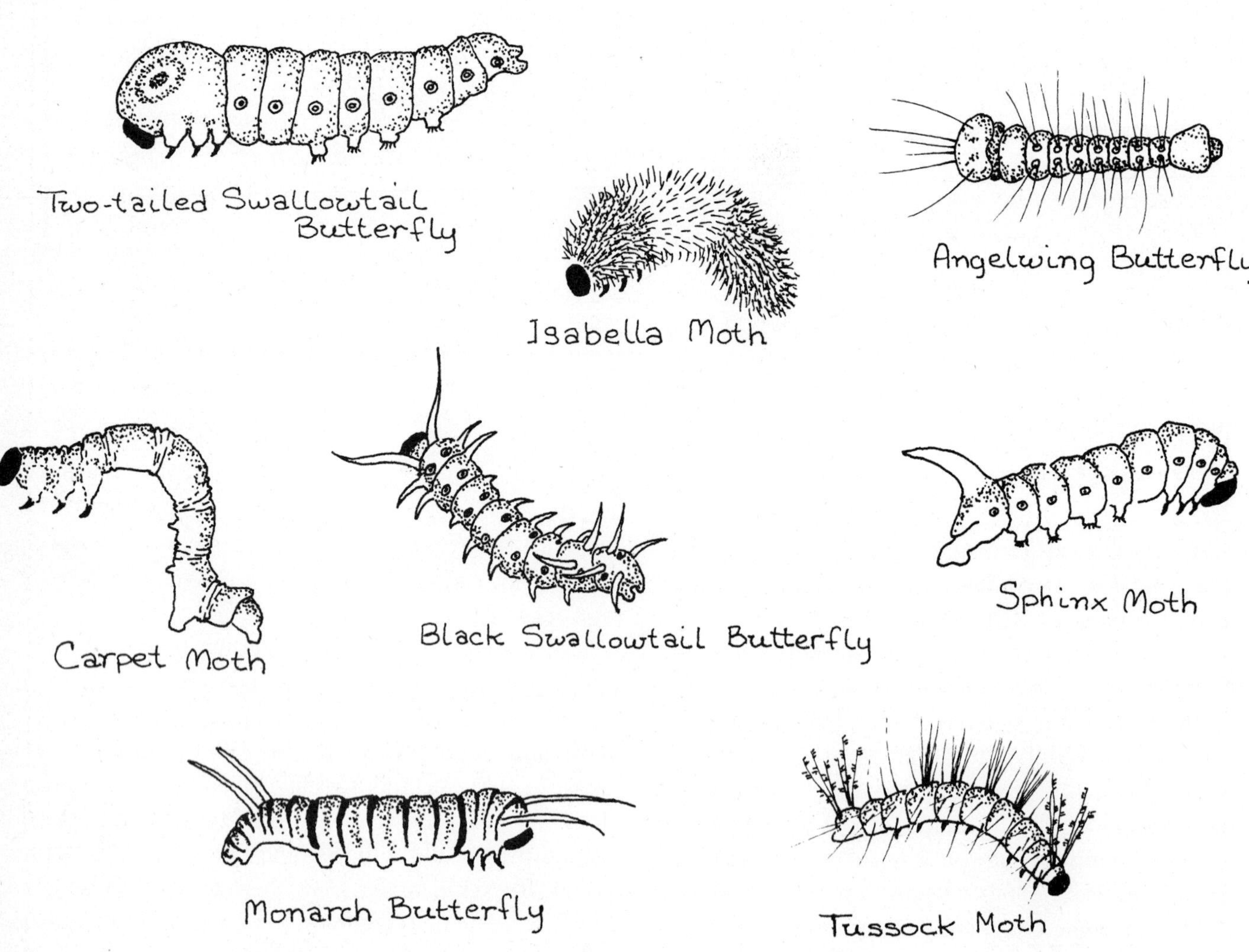

EACH OF THESE CATERPILLARS MAY CHANGE COLOR OR DETAILS WHEN IT SHEDS, SO IT IS HARD TO IDENTIFY FOR SURE.

METAMORPHOSIS OF A MOTH

(a) A caterpillar hatches from its egg.

(b) It eats and grows, shedding its skin four times.

(c) The caterpillar begins to spin its cocoon. The silk comes from its mouth.

(d) A finished cocoon secured to a twig.

(e) Inside the cocoon, the caterpillar skin is shed revealing a new pupal skin

(f) The pupa. Under the two flap like folds, wings are developing.

(g) The pupal skin splits and the moth climbs out. Its wings look small and shriveled.

(h) The moth pumps fluid from its body into its wings to expand them. Metamorphosis is finished.

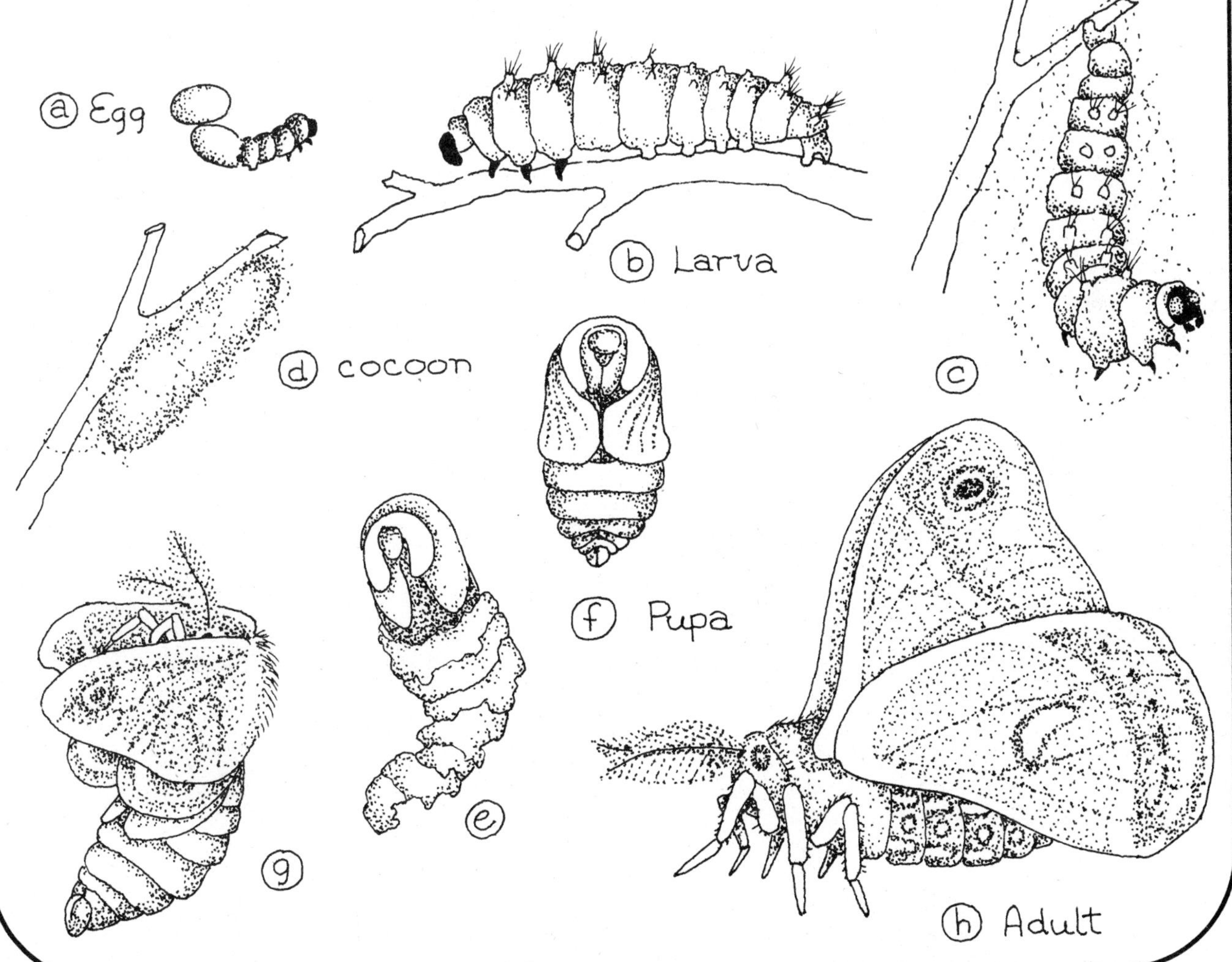

species of moths, the female emits an odor to attract males, too. A male hawk moth can smell a mate from as far away as six miles.

If moths come to your window, try to catch one by using a jar as a net. If you can scoop one up, cover the top quickly with a piece of cardboard. Although moths are easy to catch in your hands, you will rub the tiny colored or iridescent scales from their wings and bodies and they will not be pretty anymore.

Moths may have a very short life—sometimes only a day or two—so it's best to let your moth go before the following morning so it gets a chance to live in freedom, to mate, and if female, to lay eggs. Don't bother trying to feed it. Butterflies sip nectar from flowers, but most moths don't eat at all. Not even clothes moths eat; the damage to wool is done by the moth larvas when they hatch from eggs the female moth lays in woolen fabrics.

Constructing a Cocoon

Cocoons themselves aren't exactly pets because there is no creature to be seen until it emerges from its cocoon. But you can, if you are careful, remove a cocoon and watch the pupa slowly develop into the insect it will become. You can't remove a chrysalis's skin (pupal stage of the butterfly) without injuring the pupa.

Make an artificial cocoon first, by putting a layer of cotton into a small matchbox and keeping a second layer of cotton to put over it. Then carefully remove the thin cocoon with your fingers, helped if necessary with small scissors and tweezers, to reveal the pupa underneath. The pupa is still very soft, so be careful when you pick it up. Place it on the bottom layer of cotton, cover it with the second layer and close the matchbox.

Every few days, check the pupa. You will see that little by little the shapeless body is developing into an adult insect—either male or female. Its legs begin to form, the wings on its back, the eyes and antennae. Generally it will also change from white or pale tan to the color of the adult it is growing to be. As it changes, you may be able to guess what sort of insect it is becoming. But watch out—moths are not the only insects that make cocoons. If you can see that a pupa resembles a wasp or hornet, take the cover off its box before it is quite finished and put the box under a rock outdoors. That way it will be able to get out of its artificial cocoon, and you won't get stung by the baby you raised. Let any insects go when they have grown up so they can lead their normal lives.

Spiders

Spider eggs are easy to find and fun to raise. The egg cases are round. You will find them in spider webs in the grass, in windows, in corners of your basement, or near the foundations of your home.

Carry the egg case gently in your hand and put it in a matchbox. When the babies hatch take them outdoors in the box, then let them climb out. You will be able to watch the hundreds of tiny spiders

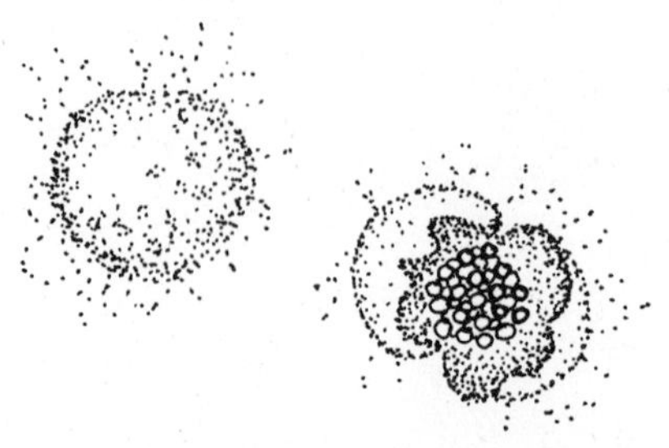

Spider egg case with web still clinging; egg case opened to show eggs inside.

emerge to spin their first webs and start their new lives.

Walking Sticks, Praying Mantises, Katydids and Grasshoppers

All of these make interesting guests. August is the best time of the year to look for walking sticks on tree branches and all the others in meadows. Take a jar or plastic freezer container with you. Walk very slowly and watch very carefully. Each of these creatures is camouflaged in a different way. Walking sticks look like a twig of a tree. They almost never move. Praying mantises and katydids are colored green to match the meadow grass. Some grasshoppers are mottled tan or gray to be invisible against rocks or bare dirt.

If your eye can't see these insects in the grass, you can try a wholesale sweep with a butterfly net.

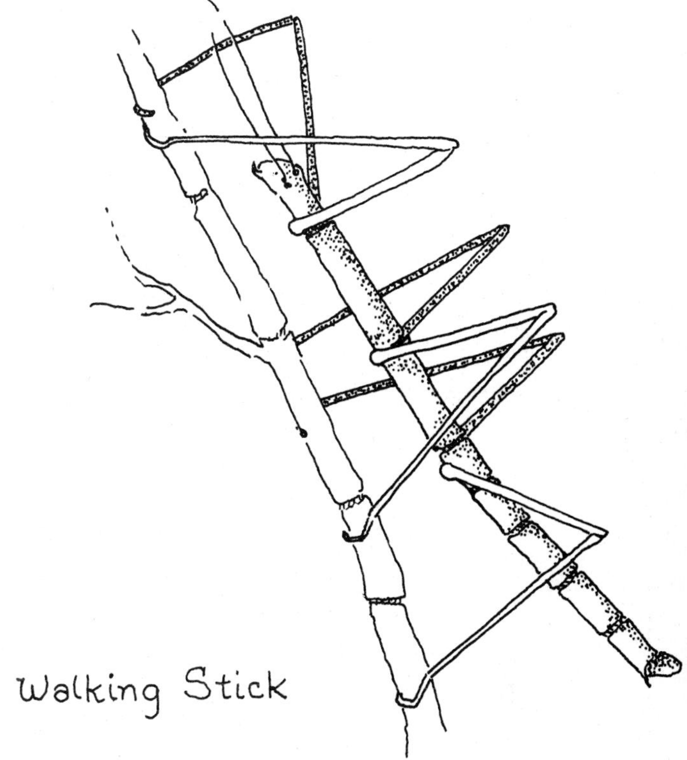

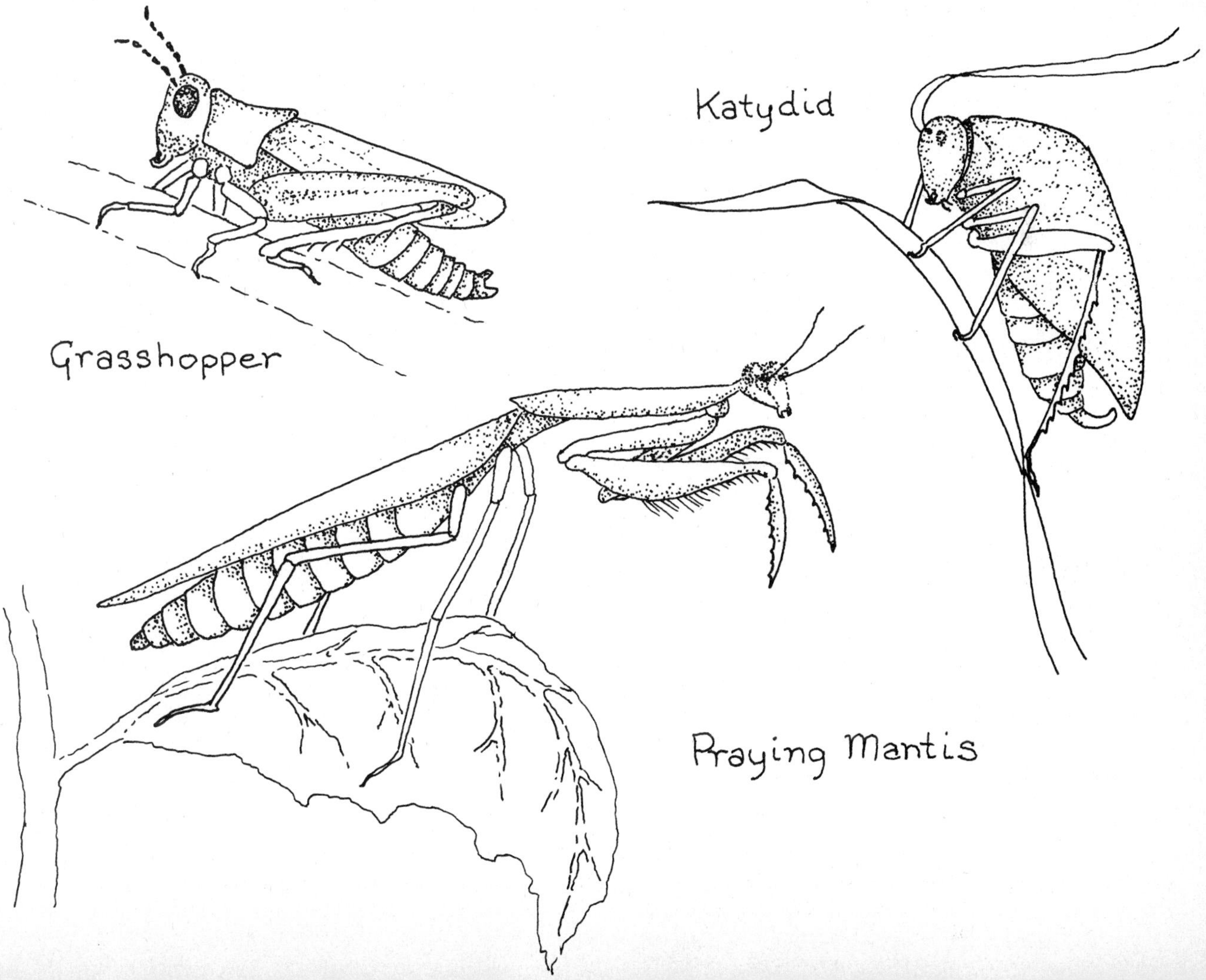

Grasshopper

Katydid

Praying Mantis

Praying Mantis Egg Cases

Praying mantis egg cases, hard to find in nature, can be bought by mail. They are sold because the adult insect is valuable as a predator of aphids and other garden pests. In fact, mantises are so valuable that in many states there is a fine for killing one. You can send for the catalog that lists these egg cases from Edmund Scientific Co., 701 Edscorp Building, Barrington, N.J. 08007, or watch for ads in the gardening section of newspapers or in gardening magazines.

During the winter the egg cases must be kept either outdoors or in the refrigerator for the winter to provide the dormant period they require before hatching. When spring comes, or when you remove them from the refrigerator, put them in a bug jar (page 311) where a hundred or more babies will hatch within a few weeks.

Unlike moths and hornets, praying mantises and all their grasshopper relatives do not go through larval or pupal stages. The babies are called nymphs and are tiny replicas of the adult insect. The nymphs will shed their hard skins many times in order to grow to adult size. You may keep the nymphs in your bug jar for a day to watch them, but then let them go outdoors so they can feed on the live insects they need. You will be rewarded by seeing your praying mantises from time to time outdoors, where they will grow to a hefty four inches while voraciously ridding your garden of small nuisances.

Amphibians

Tree Frogs

These thumbnail-sized acrobats are a lot of fun to watch. They are among the smallest of frogs, especially adapted to living in trees by clinging with suction-cup pads on the ends of their toes. The best time to find tree frogs is on a spring night when you can hear them saying peep-peep-peep. Arm yourself with a flashlight and a jar with a top, and follow the sound. As you come closer, the peep-peep will stop. Stand quietly and wait. When the peeping starts again, move closer. Keep this up until you are very close to the noise. Then start searching with your flashlight. If you find the tree frog, catch it with your hands and put it in the jar to take home.

The tree frog can live in your moist woodland vivarium (page 316) for a week or so, and may even be able to find some small insects there to eat. The supply is limited, however. If you are intent on keeping tree frogs longer, page 84 tells you how to breed colonies of fruit flies as food.

Salamanders

Salamanders can usually be found under rocks and rotting logs in woodlands. You may have to turn over a lot of logs and stones before you find one. Sometimes they will emerge just after a rain, when they are sure to be able to keep themselves moist. Then your hunting may be less work.

Salamanders, like tree frogs, can live for a while in your woodland vivarium, where their skins can stay moist. But they will tend to stay hidden most of the time. Try to keep tabs on where the salamander spends its time so you can find and release it before it starves to death. Like tree frogs, a sala-

Tree frogs can also be kept as permanent pets. *See page 85.*

mander can stay with you longer if it has a supply of fruit flies, or if you can find garden or house plant sprigs covered with a meal of aphids. Put the whole aphid-infested sprig in the vivarium.

Toads

Toads are very common amphibians and very easy to catch. They will look nice in a desert vivarium. They need water, which you can put in a jar top sunk into the sand so it won't tip. Some people have succeeded in feeding a toad by jiggling a bit of hamburger meat on the end of a broom straw to make dinner look alive. It will be fun to see if this works. But you will still not be able to keep the toad for long simply because you will not have the patience to feed it the dozens of insects an adult toad may eat in a single day. By the way, don't worry about handling toads. They may urinate in your hands when upset, but neither their urine nor their bumpy skin causes warts. The toad's bumps are skin glands that secrete an irritating substance. The poison can make a dog's mouth foam for hours, but it doesn't hurt human skin.

Mollusks

Snails

As you look for salamanders, tree frogs and toads you're likely to find land snails. They are mollusks, not amphibians, but they share similar environments. Land snails can stay in a jar covered with cheesecloth and will eat lettuce. If you want to keep a land snail longer than a few days, page 78 tells you how. Fresh-water snails, by the way, can live permanently in an aquarium .

Garter snakes are harmless reptiles who would rather not have too much attention.

Water snails rarely poke their heads out when they are not in the water.

memorizing the poisonous than the harmless varieties; and don't hunt before you are sure you can identify all the poisonous ones. A visit to a local nature center or natural history museum is helpful.

Once you have studied up on these reptiles, wait for a nice hot sunny day for your hunt. Snakes like to sun themselves in the open. Bring an old pillowcase and a rubber band with you. It is the best way to carry your snake around after you've caught it.

To use a snake strap, lay the noose on the ground in front of the snake's head, pull on the cord to tighten it as the head comes through and the noose is just behind the head. The advantage to a snake strap is that it is longer than your arms so you don't have to be as close to the snake to capture it. The less close you are the less chance there is that it will be frightened by you.

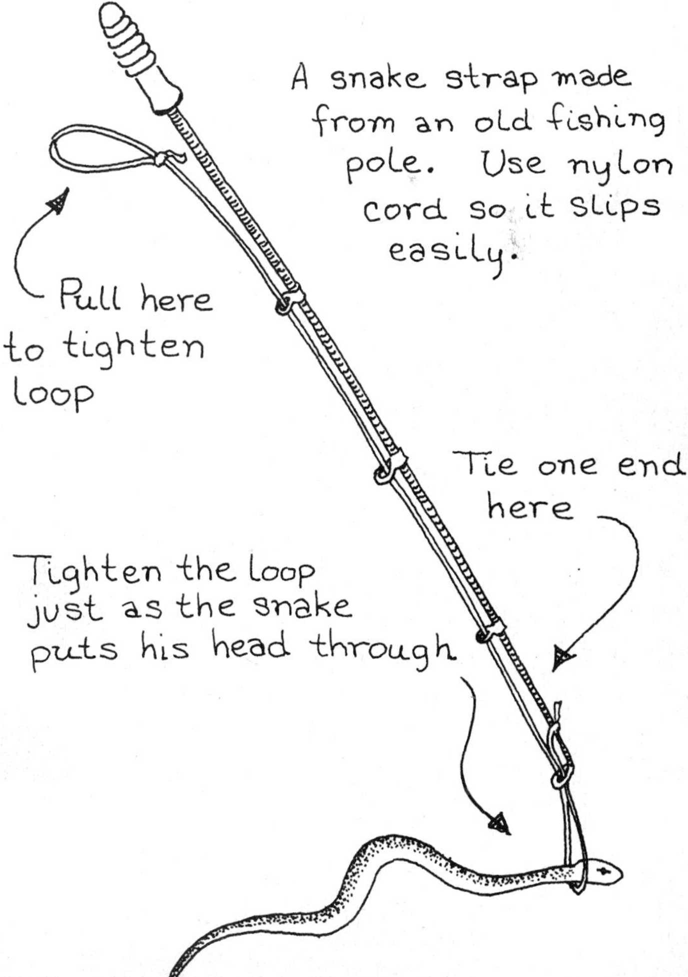

Reptiles

Snakes

Among the common and harmless snakes you may happen upon are the garter snake, ring-neck snake, hog-nosed snake, green snake, rat snake, black snake, and king snake. If you're not familiar with your local snakes, study a field guide before you go snake hunting. Pay more attention to

You have to be fast to catch snakes because they will slither back into their hiding places under rocks and tree roots quickly if they sense you coming. Don't catch them by stepping on them. Your foot could easily tear their skin. Move slowly and very softly. Catch the snake with your hands by grasping it behind its head (or use the illustrated snake strap). Any of the snakes mentioned would be safe for a week in your desert vivarium (page 313).

Snakes can do without food but don't forget to provide a crockery dish of drinking water for your guest. It will begin to suffer from hunger in about a week, and that is the time to let it go. Try to release it in the same place you found it.

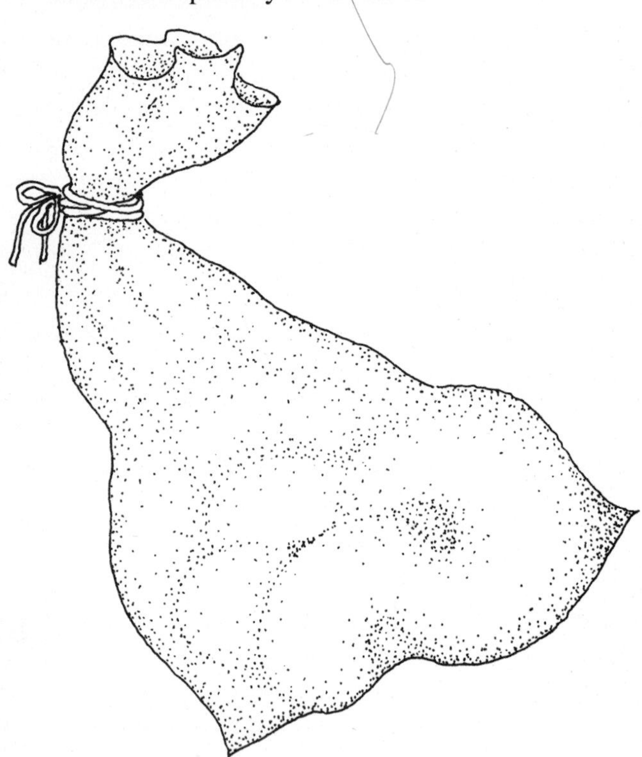

A Snake In A Pillowcase

Box Turtles

A box turtle is a woodland tortoise (not a water turtle) that could be a wonderful permanent pet if there didn't happen to be a law against it. There aren't enough box turtles left for you to keep one in captivity. If you do find a box turtle, you'll recognize it by its hinged shell, which can close its front right up from the belly. You could keep it for a few days in a desert vivarium (page 313), feeding it lettuce, raw hamburger or mealworms. But you must let this tortoise go, and exactly where you found it, too.

Baby box turtles fit nicely on a silver dollar.

Birds

The most tempting, and often most disastrous, overnight guest is the adorable fledgling (young bird) that has fallen from its nest. Our maternal and paternal instinct to feed that gaping mouth is nearly as strong as the parent birds'. But we usually end up killing a baby that might have had a better chance without our love.

If you find a fledgling who has tumbled from its nest and can't fly, the kindest thing to do is return it to its nest if you can, or leave it where you found it if you can't. Some birds only recognize their baby if it is in the nest; but many mother birds know perfectly well where a fallen fledgling is, and will help it to find a hiding place on the ground and continue to feed it until it can safely fly. The biggest enemy to fledglings, besides people who try to rescue them by bringing them home as pets, are cats. If you have to leave a fledgling on the ground, try to convince nearby cat owners to keep their pets home for a few days so the bird will be safe.

Of course, if someone brings you a fledgling and can't remember exactly where they found it, you will have to try to feed it. Try mushed ripe banana or other soft fruits, raw hamburger, bits of earthworm, or bread soaked in egg yolk or milk. Be prepared for failure.

Small Mammals

Deer Mice (White-footed Mice) and Chipmunks

These two small mammals don't take to captivity, but may be watched for a few hours. The only way to catch these small mammals is to trap them. A Havahart® trap, available at hardware stores, is a special patented device that doesn't harm animals. It is a wire-mesh box with a bait platform in the middle and a trap door at each end. The bait platform releases the trap doors when the animal steps on it. Havahart® traps come in various sizes—the smallest one, which costs under five dollars, is the right size for chipmunks and mice.

Chipmunks are active during the day, and deer mice mostly at night. They will both come to traps baited with peanut butter. If you have caught a mouse or a chipmunk and want to do more than just observe it inside the trap, have a wire cage (page 338) ready. Put the trap into the cage. Put in something else that will serve the animal as a good hiding place—a box with a small hole in it, or a sock, or a toilet-paper tube. Open the trap and get the top back on the cage quickly. When the animal comes out, it will very likely go into the hiding place you have provided. It should be safe then to reach in and take the trap out. Sometimes mice and chipmunks are too nervous to eat, but you might try a few sunflower seeds or some peanut butter and see what happens. A very young animal might be calm enough to be able to stay with you for a week or so, but neither of these animals makes a happy or even a trustworthy pet.

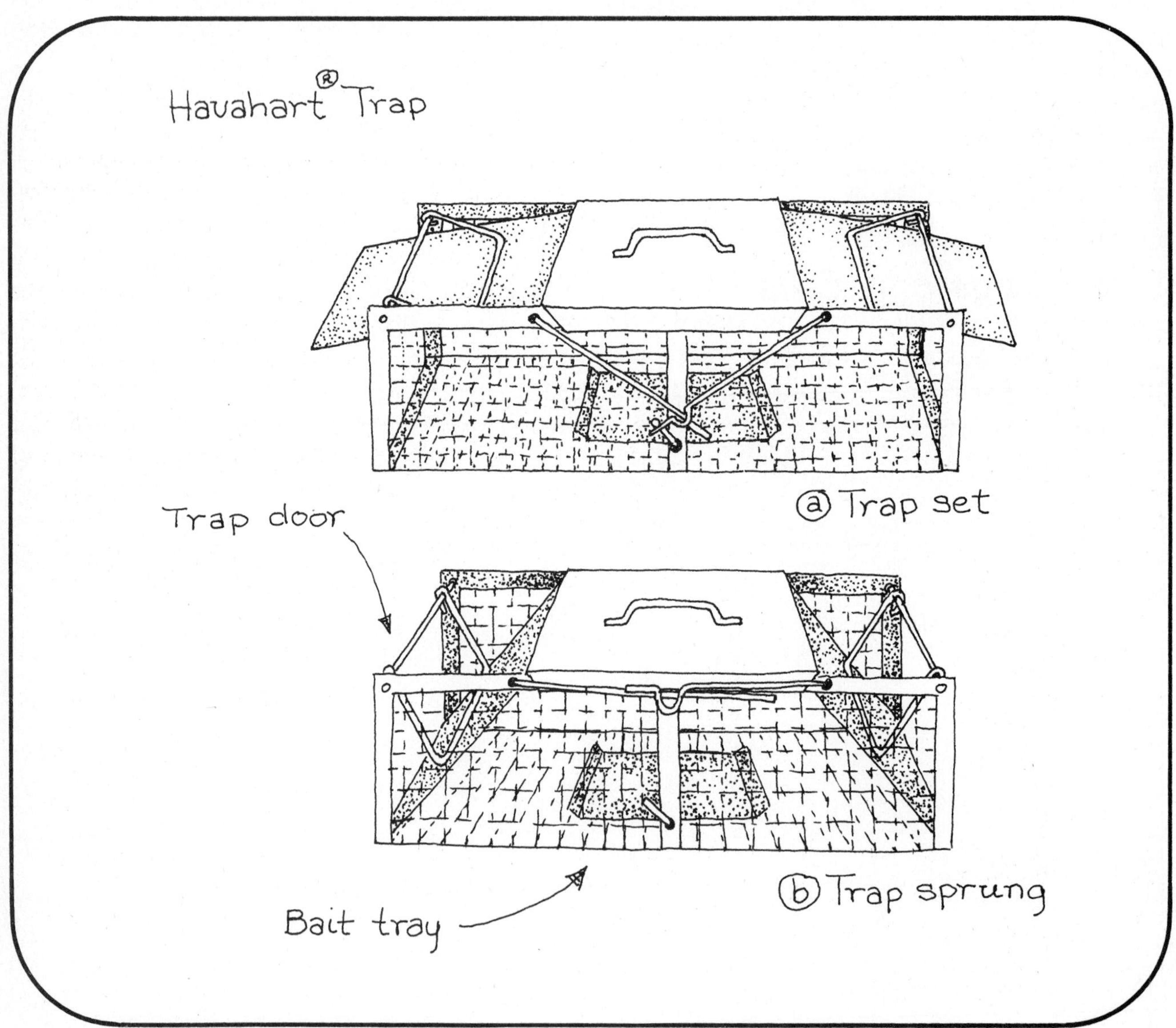

Shrews

By accident you may catch a shrew in your trap. A shrew looks like a longish mouse with a shortish tail. They are among the tiniest mammals in the world, the smallest weighing in at only $^1/_{14}$ of an ounce. To make up for size, however, the shrew is as fierce as it is voracious. Some have poisoned saliva with which to kill their prey.

There is no hope at all of keeping a shrew for even a few hours. The shrew needs to eat nearly three-fourths of its body weight in insects and other

Short Tailed Shrew

live prey each day. It can starve to death within hours. When frightened, a shrew may collapse and die of shock within minutes. If you find a shrew in your trap one morning, open the trap instantly and cover it with leaves or a rag so the animal doesn't die of fright before it can figure out how to escape.

Stray Dogs and Cats

Last but not least of the mammals that might come your way is the stray dog or cat. If you come upon a stray, first try to find out if it is someone's lost pet. Look for a collar or tag. Check with the local A.S.P.C.A. to see if a pet answering this one's description has been reported lost. Sometimes lost pets are advertised in local newspapers, announced on local radio stations or posted on bulletin boards in stores or supermarkets. If there are no such ads by the owner, you as the finder might advertise.

Even if you can be absolutely sure you have found an abandoned animal, strays can be a problem. Usually children beg to keep the stray while adults resist. Then the dog whines, the cat mews; adults say, "Well . . . maybe just for tonight." After one night of the cat purring over its warm milk or the dog snuggling into bed, the overnight guest has become a permanent pet.

Now for the bad news: this is the worst of all possible ways to acquire a family dog or cat. Stray animals are almost always neglected animals—either not cared for long enough by their own parents or not socialized by loving humans, or both. By the time they end up at your door, it is too late to repair the damage. The dog may be stubborn, the cat nervous. This doesn't mean you shouldn't try to find a good home for such pathetic creatures. But a good home is one in which there are no children. Adults have the time and patience to indulge their pet's eccentricities. Put an appealing ad in the local newspaper or harden your heart and take the stray to an adoption shelter. If you want a good family cat, read chapter 9. If you want a dog, read chapter 10. Consider strays as overnight pets only.

Vivarium Pets

VIVARIUM PETS

DESERT IGUANAS

Cost:
$12.00 to $15.00, or may be captured in the wild.

Housing:
10-gallon tank, screen top, incandescent and fluorescent lighting fixtures—$40.00
Gravel for flooring—$1.50

Special Requirements:
Desert environment, high temperature, ultra-violet light.

Diet:
Raw spinach and other greens, mealworms—25¢ per week.

Care:
Feed and pick up droppings and leftover food daily.
Mist with plant mister twice a week.

Tamability:
Become calm with handling, take food from fingers. Not affectionate.

Life Span:
Three to four years, but could be longer with excellent care.

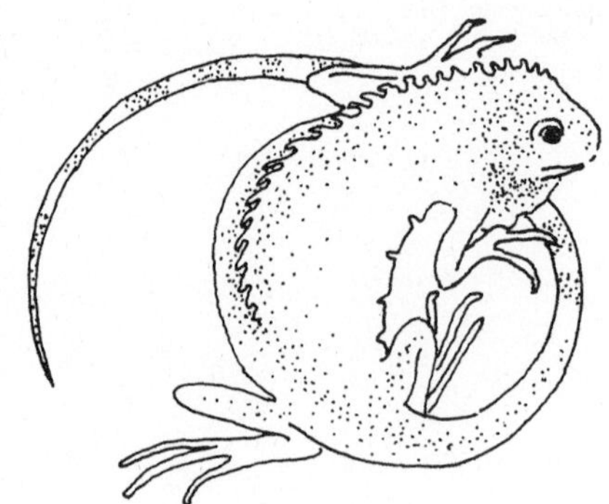

COMMON IGUANAS

Cost:
$3.00 to $4.00 for a six-inch baby (not counting tail).
Higher for larger specimens.

Housing:
18-gallon tall tank, screen top, incandescent and fluorescent lighting fixtures, crockery soaking dish—$54.00
Optional gravel for flooring—$1.50

Special Requirements:
Humid environment, high temperature, ultra-violet light.

Diet:
Soft ripe fruits, leafy vegetables, mealworms or other insects, raw hamburger—50¢ per week.

Care:
Feed, clean up droppings and leftover food, clean and refill water dish daily.
Let out for exercise several times a week.
Clean tank and replace flooring material as needed.

Tamability:
Become calm with handling, eat readily from fingers. May enjoy petting under chin. Bite when annoyed.

Life Span:
20 years in the wild, but five more likely in captivity. Many iguanas die within a year from lack of proper care.

CAROLINA ANOLES

Cost:
$1.00, or may be captured in the wild.

Housing:
5½-gallon tank, screen top, fluorescent light fixture, potted plant—$30.00
Gravel for flooring—$1.50

Special Requirements:
Ultra-violet light. Drink from water droplets only.

Diet:
Mealworms or other insects—25¢ per week.

Care:
Feed, sprinkle water for drinking on plant daily.
Rake up droppings and water plant weekly.

Tamability:
Become calm with handling, may accept food from fingers. Not affectionate.

Life Span:
Two to three years.

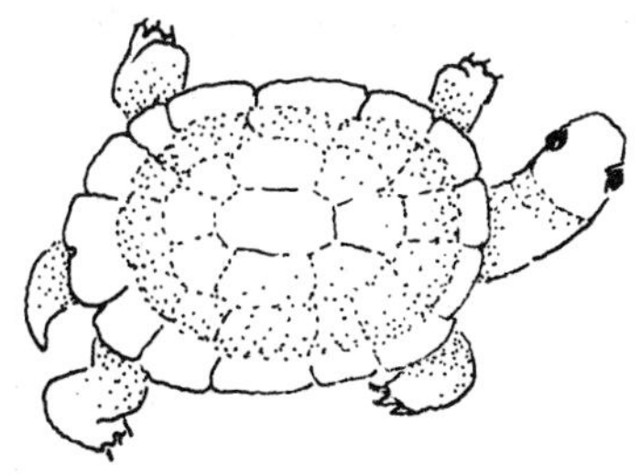

LAND TORTOISES

Costs:
Red-footed tortoise—$6.00
Greek tortoise—$8.00
Elongated tortoise—$10.00

Housing:
10-gallon tank, fluorescent light fixture, crockery water dish—$32.00
Optional incandescent light—$7.50
Gravel for flooring—$1.50

Special Requirements:
Desert environment, high temperature, ultra-violet light, cleanliness.

Diet:
Dark-green leafy vegetables, ripe fruits, raw hamburger, chicken or fish—50¢ per week.
Supplement with calcium.

Care:
Feed, pick up droppings and left-over food, clean and refill water dish daily.
Take out of cage for exercise once or twice a week.

Tamability:
Become very accustomed to humans, but don't like handling. May recognize owner and beg for food.

Life Span:
Many tortoises die in captivity within months from improper care. With good care, 10 to 25 years.

TARANTULAS

Cost:
$12.00 to $25.00, depending on size and species, or may be captured in wild.

Housing:
5½-gallon tank, screen top, incandescent light fixture—$18.00
Optional gravel for flooring—$1.50

Special Requirements:
Desert environment, high temperature.

Diet:
Live crickets or other large insects—25¢ per week.

Care:
Check water daily and replenish if necessary.
Feed two or three times a week.
Remove insect carcasses and droppings as necessary.
Clean up webbing weekly.

Tamability:
Become calm with handling. Do not bite unless startled, teased or cornered.

Life Span:
25 years, but may be less in captivity.

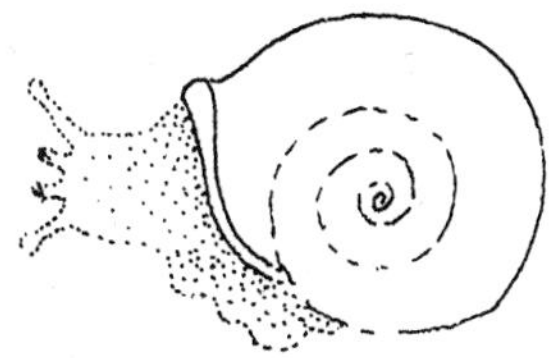

LAND SNAILS

Cost:
Collect in wild.

Housing:
Cheesecloth-covered jar (50¢ for cheesecloth if you don't have any around).

Special Requirements:
High humidity.

Diet:
Discarded outside leaves of salad greens (no cost).

Care:
Wash out jar and replenish leaves daily.

Tamability:
Not tamable.

Life Span:
Three to five years.

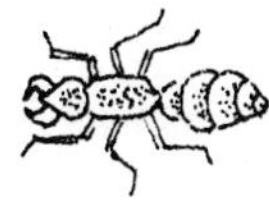

ANTS

Cost:
Worker ants are included in the cost of a commercial ant farm, or worker ants and queen may be collected in wild.

Housing:
Homemade glass-and-wood ant vivarium—$4.00.
Or commercial ant farm—$9.95

Special Requirements:
Soil from home nest area or commercial substitute to build nest in (included in price of commercial ant farm).

Diet:
Dead insects, cake crumbs, fruit, nuts, honey (no cost).

Care:
Feed and remove leftover food daily.

Tamability:
Not tamable.

Life Span:
Workers die within a few months. Queens live several years and continue to produce new workers during their lifetime.

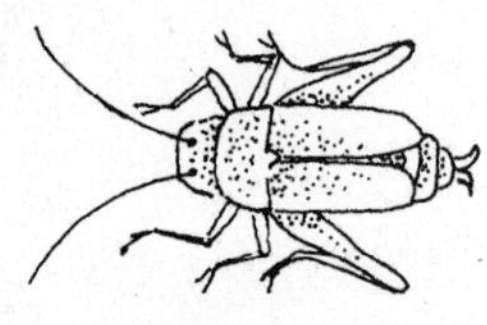

FIELD CRICKETS

Cost:
Collect in wild.

Housing:
Cheesecloth-covered jar or screen-and-can cage—50¢ to $1.00.

Special Requirements:
None.

Diet:
Moist bread and cereals, soft fruits, soft sweet vegetables (no cost).

Care:
Feed and clean cage daily.

Tamability:
Not tamable, but chirp at night.

Life Span:
A year or less.

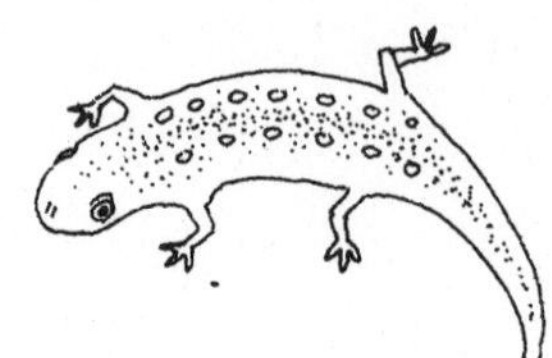

SALAMANDERS

Cost:
$1.50 to $3.00, depending on size and species, or collect in wild.

Housing:
5½-gallon tank, glass cover—$10.00
Optional filter system for large species—$6.00

Special Requirements:
Moist woodland or semi-aquatic environment, high humidity.

Diet:
For small species, home-raised fruit flies (no cost).
For large species, commercial shrimp pellets—20¢ per week.

Care:
Ventilate tank daily.
Feed large species daily, replenish fruit fly colony for small species weekly.
Mist plants, clean filter, or wash soaking dish weekly, depending on type of woodland or semi-aquatic set-up you use.

Tamability:
Not tamable.

Life Span:
Three to four years.

TREE FROGS

Cost:
$1.00, or collect in wild.

Housing:
5½-gallon tank, glass cover, crockery soaking dish—$12.00

Special Requirements:
Moist woodland environment, high humidity.

Diet:
Home-raised fruit flies (no cost).

Care:
Ventilate tank daily.
Replenish fruit fly colony weekly.
Mist plants and wash soaking dish weekly.

Tamability:
Not tamable.

Life Span:
Three to four years.

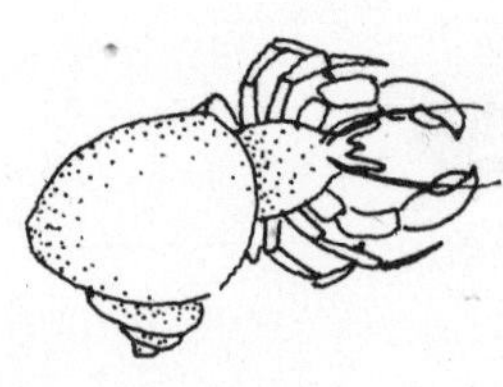

HERMIT CRABS

Cost:
$1.00 to $5.00, depending on size, or collect in wild.

Housing:
Medium-size homemade cake-pan cage, crockery water dish—$8.00
Or 5½-gallon tank, screen top, crockery water dish—$13.00

Special Requirements:
Bark or substitute for climbing, assortment of shells for crab to choose from as it grows.

Diet:
Raw leafy vegetables and greens, raw meat or fish—25¢ per week.

Care:
Feed, replenish water and clean up leftover foods daily.
Wash cage once a month.

Tamability:
Not tamable.

Life Span:
Two years or more.

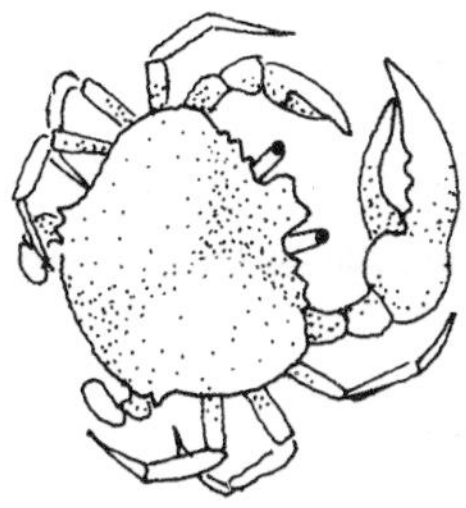

FIDDLER CRABS

Cost:
$1.00, or collect in wild.

Housing:
5½-gallon tank, screen top, crockery water dish—$13.00
Gravel for flooring—$3.00

Special Requirements:
Deep, damp sand to burrow in.

Diet:
Raw leafy vegetables and greens, raw meat or fish—25¢ per week.

Care:
Feed, replenish water, clean up leftover foods daily.
Either wash and sterilize or replace sand monthly.

Tamability:
Not tamable.

Life Span:
Two years.

This chapter is devoted to small but otherwise miscellaneous pets who need special environments to live in. Their world is a vivarium. A vivarium is any container, like a tank or jar, which re-creates a suitable land or semi-aquatic environment for an animal.

Tanks and jars, because they are enclosed by glass walls, can be made into miniature environments quite different from the inside of your home. Birds and mice, although they live in cages, must still get along with your household thermostat, your dry winters and humid summers. But a desert iguana won't eat unless the temperature is 90 degrees in its world, a tree frog can't breath if its skin gets dry, and an anole drinks only dewdrops. Because each of these animals needs such a special environment, we don't recommend trying to keep any but salamanders and tree frogs together in the same vivarium.

Vivariums make it possible to keep representatives of much of the animal kingdom as pets. Frogs and salamanders, for instance, are amphibians, descended from the first fish who learned to walk on land. Their early life is most often spent living like fish in the water, sometimes breathing through gills. Although they develop lungs as adults, most of their breathing is done through their moist skins. A dry frog or salamander quickly suffocates.

The lizards in this chapter look similar to salamanders, but they are reptiles, a completely different branch of the animal kingdom. Tortoises are reptiles too, and extraordinary ones. Their shells are actually bone covered with a thin horny layer similar to the stuff fingernails are made of. At some time in ancient history, more than 200 million years ago, the backbone of the tortoise's ancestor began to grow outside its skin to form a covering over its back. Most of the tortoise family can pull themselves into their shells for protection, and one,

Agatha, a desert iguana, loves clinging to hair.

the box turtle, can shut the door behind as well. The door is a hinged section that closes neatly up against the top shell.

At about the same time the tortoise was creating its shell, the world's most numerous, and some say most successful, group of animals was evolving. This group is called the arthropods; the families within it are crustaceans like the hermit crab, arachnids like the spiders, and insects like ants and crickets.

The habits of these million species, more than all the species of every other animal group put together, can barely be believed. The common hermit crab not only finds a mollusk shell to shelter its unclothed tummy, but attaches to it a bit of live sponge. The sponge grows to cover the shell, effectively disguising the crab from enemies. Spiders spin webs, build trap doors, twirl lassoes at their prey, construct underwater homes and manufacture parachutes on which they float for miles. Ants not only build cities but farm crops and raise livestock.

Moving on from arthropods to mollusks, even the common land snail, an unassuming mollusk, can do extraordinary things. In 1846 an Egyptian land snail was glued to a piece of cardboard and sent to the British Museum as a natural history specimen. In 1850 the cardboard was soaked in water to melt the glue so the specimen could be remounted. The snail crawled away—after four years without food, water or exercise. It had managed this feat by sealing the moisture in its body from the air with a hardened mucus plug at the shell entrance, according to the habit of snails in a dry season, and by lowering its food and air needs as other animals do when they hibernate.

None of these pets is the sort that follows you about the house or nudges you for affection. The reward is in being able to share a little in a captive life made possible by the special world of a vivarium.

A Lizard Tail

The best pet lizards, iguanas and anoles, share one thing in common: If you catch them by the tail, or sometimes even if you just press on it, the tail comes off. It isn't your muscles which have pinched off the tail but the lizard's own muscles. Pressure stimulates muscles between each vertebra to contract suddenly, parting the skin and bone at the same time that other muscles close off the artery to prevent bleeding. It is a clever device—the tail keeps wiggling for a few minutes, fooling a predator into thinking it has caught something interesting. The lizard, meanwhile, is long gone and will soon have grown a new tail, although not as pretty as the original one.

Lizards shed their skins at intervals, but not in one piece like snakes do. The skin peels off in ribbons that run down the length of the lizard's body. They may shed only once or twice a year or as often as every month. When and how they shed is controlled by chemicals in the body, called hormones, and not by rate of growth. No one knows exactly what triggers the hormones that cause the lizard's body to shed.

Desert Iguanas

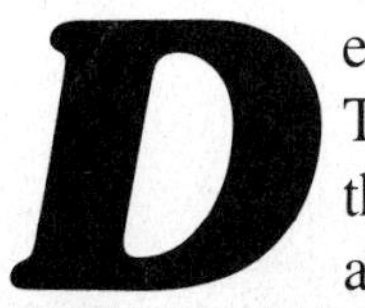

Desert iguanas are handsome lizards. Though they are able to move fast, they don't scurry and only occasionally leap. Their bodies grow to about five inches, but the tail can be twice that length, making the adult a full 15 inches long. They are colored a brownish gray, with mottled markings and stripes that resemble the background of their native Southwest American desert environment.

In nature, the desert iguana's life is ruled by extremes of temperature only a handful of animals have managed to cope with. They live in burrows, from which they don't emerge until late in the morning when the desert has heated up. As the temperature rises to heights that would kill other reptiles, they may seek shade, but only return to their burrows as the heat approaches 115 degrees. By late afternoon they are out foraging for food again. They are probably most active, and most comfortable, at from 90 to 100 degrees.

Our desert iguana is named Agatha. We don't really know her sex and haven't found a way to tell. She just looks female to us and that is how I will refer to her. Outside her vivarium Agatha enjoys walking about, climbing up arms and nestling under hair. If she is warmed up enough to be hungry, she eats mealworms from our fingers, chewing on them at length before she swallows. The chewing seems not to break the worms up at all, but only to get them headed in the right direction. She attacks spinach like a small dinosaur, ripping off great mouthfuls of vegetation and chomping realistically. I say "realistically" because at other times she may stand so still for so long one isn't sure she is real. This "freezing" is probably a protection against predators. Were she that still against brownish-gray ground, she would be invisible.

In the vivarium, Agatha has a daily routine that reproduces to some extent a natural life. At night she sleeps in the shade and coolness of a slanted rock cave. She climbs her branch during the day to bask in the heat and light above. When she is hungry, she actually takes a stroll to her food dish to see what's there.

Housing

Set up the desert vivarium shown on page 313, including the screen top. A 5½-gallon tank is sufficient, but a 10-gallon tank would give more walking space and could be decorated in a more interesting way. Arrange rocks to form a shaded hiding place. Provide a leaning branch so the lizard can get close to the heat and light when it needs to bask. You will need a jar top to serve dinner in, and recently we have discovered our lizard likes to soak in a crockery dish of water sunk into the gravel. We don't know that this is necessary, just that she likes it.

Equip the vivarium with a thermometer as suggested on page 316. Use the ultra-violet light set-up described on page 316 and the incandescent fixture described on page 316 for heat. Both fixtures fit together on the top of a 10-gallon aquarium. If you have a smaller tank, you'll have to take off one fixture each time you need to use the other. Raise the temperature to at least 90 degrees, preferably as high as 100 degrees, by using the incandescent fixture during the several hours of the day that include feeding time. The heat raises the lizard's activity level enough to make it an eager eater. Use the Vita-Lite the rest of the day; it will keep the temperature of a 10-gallon tank near 80 degrees. At night, heat the tank only if room temperatures drop below 65 degrees.

Clean the vivarium of leftover foods after every feeding. Pick up dry droppings from the surface of the gravel as you notice them. There won't be many and there is no smell.

Food and Water

The rule with any relatively unusual pet is: offer a delicatessen. Several books describe the desert iguana as exclusively vegetarian. One prescribes a diet of dandelion leaves and blossoms. Agatha eats spinach and mealworms—seven at a meal. She loves ants. There are reports of these iguanas eating desert cactus blossoms, various insects, the meat from dead animals, and even mouse droppings. Our best advice is to try several kinds of leafy vegetables, hamburger meat, soft fruits, and both mealworms and crickets (available at pet stores). When your lizard has shown its preference, you can give it only the two or three things it likes, offering other choices once in a while just in case it changes its mind. If your lizard refuses to eat anything at first, raise the heat in the vivarium to 110 degrees, and try again.

Agatha eats best if food is offered every other day. The amount eaten seems to have more to do with the temperature in her vivarium and how frequently we let her out for exercise than with any routine daily need. If she is kept warm and allowed to exercise, she eats a small leaf of spinach or about seven worms per meal. If the mealworms are offered with spinach, she eats only the worms. So we offer spinach for one meal, worms for the next. Since mealworms dig into the sand, die and begin to smell, put them in a jar top to prevent escape.

Mealworms are the larvas (or grubs) of a small beetle. They will live for weeks—without changing into fat-shaped pupas and then into adult beetles—if you keep them in the refrigerator.

No one, not even naturalists, has observed a desert iguana drinking water. That does not mean they don't need water, it only means we don't know how they obtain it. Agatha was definitely dehydrated when we got her—her skin loose and dry. Although vegetation provides water, some lizards can also absorb water through their skins. We spray Agatha with a plant mister several times a week. And recently she has taken to soaking herself in a crockery dish of water, as I mentioned before.

Our Agatha

No doubt the healthiest desert iguanas would be ones you caught wild in America's Southwestern deserts. But when we first got Agatha from a local pet store, she was almost as immobile as a statue. If she raised her foot, it might stay raised for 10 minutes, leading us to think she was the only creature in existence who could double as a robot.

We wondered how such an animal could survive in nature, unless her immobility was a ruse to convince a predator she was already dead. In fact, Agatha looked dead every morning. She fell asleep in assorted postures that suggested a crushed rib cage and broken limbs. Sometimes all four legs were stretched straight behind her flattened body—the picture of a lizard just emerged from under a truck tire. We would turn on her incandescent sun. Five minutes passed. An eye opened. A head lifted. A paw assumed a normal position. Her chest raised from the ground. She was alive. Sooner or later (usually after a good 10 minutes) the heat would fill her body with enough life to half-heartedly nibble on a spinach leaf.

Luckily for Agatha we didn't think any lizard should act this way. If we had thought this was normal desert iguana behavior, Agatha would eventually have died from vitamin deficiency and dehydration. The pet store had advised room temperature, no water, vegetarian diet. So you can see you'd better do your own research. In this case, several different books on reptiles and desert animals gave us clues about sunlight, water and a delicatessen approach to diet. Now Agatha doesn't at all resemble the dried-up, lethargic lizard we brought home. She has turned into a perky, plump worm-gobbler.

Common Iguanas

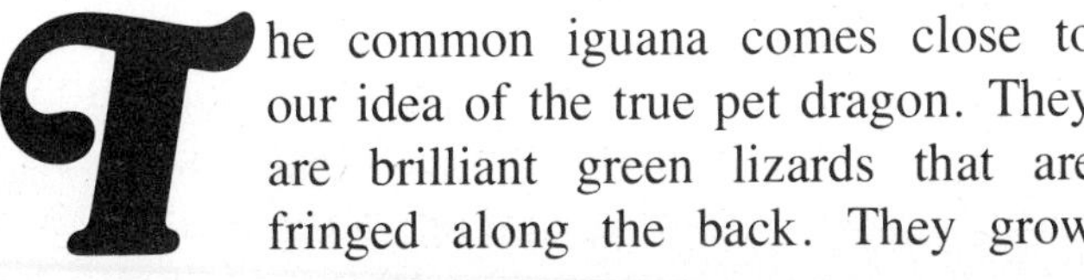

The common iguana comes close to our idea of the true pet dragon. They are brilliant green lizards that are fringed along the back. They grow to be six feet long. In their native Central America, they are hunted and eaten as stew. Iguanas climb trees well and can jump far. But they forage for food on the ground, and plop into rivers and lakes

Bubbles, a common iguana, has a tail twice as long as her body.

when frightened. They can even swim.

Housing

Even as a baby, the common iguana needs more space than the other lizards we suggest. The minimum is an 18-gallon "tall" tank. The base size is the same as a 10-gallon, so any lights you already have will fit. Even this large a tank doesn't allow the exercise these very active lizards need. Let your iguana out in a warm (70 degrees or over) room every day.

An iguana's environment needs to mimic a hot moist jungle. There are no two ways about it. If you don't provide a hot jungle, your iguana will die. A hot desert environment can be turned into a hot jungle environment with the addition of a few plants or a swimming pool. Sink a crockery dish into the gravel. It should be big enough for the iguana to climb in, not just to drink from. Sink three-or-four-inch-wide pots of plants—two will fit into an 18-gallon vivarium. We used ivy. The leaves are too tough for the lizard to eat, and the tendrils can be trained along the basking branch. Rocks may not be necessary, but we included them in case they're needed for shedding skin against.

Use the Vita-Lite® (page 316) to keep the temperature 80 to 85 degrees during the day. If you have trouble maintaining that temperature, use the incandescent fixture as well (page 316). It can go down to 70 degrees at night. As the vivarium heats, water from the pool and plants will raise the humidity. Warmth and humidity without ventilation, however, invite bacterial and fungal infections which could do your iguana in. Don't close off air with the plastic cover that comes with some tank lights. Use a mesh screen top instead.

Droppings (which may smell) and old food have to be picked up daily. The swimming pool has to be washed and refilled every day too.

If you have success with your young iguana, it will grow up to be a big iguana. By the time its body (not counting the tail) is 10 inches long it will be too large for its tank. But by this time it will also be a less delicate creature, less demanding in its environmental needs. We know an iguana who has lived free for years in the front window of a dry-cleaning store. The window is filled with plants; their damp soil provides enough humidity. The window is lit with incandescent bulbs and they provide enough heat. The iguana is four feet long and pleased with itself.

Vivariums themselves should never be placed by a window. The temperature fluctuates too much and the sun can heat this closed-off space to killing heights. At the moment we are trying to work out our iguana housing problems by filling a bathroom with plants and keeping the thermostat at 80 degrees. This should certainly be enough room for our very active lizard.

Food and Water

The common iguana is a voracious eater of soft fruits and leafy vegetables. Ripe bananas, strawberries, pears, plums and peaches are all good. Grapes cut in half are liked too. Leafy vegetables include the darker lettuces like romaine, and other dark-green leaves like watercress and spinach.

Try meat and insects too, no matter what books and pet stores tell you about iguanas being exclusively vegetarian. Bubbles, our iguana, eats ants, raw hamburger and hard-boiled egg yolk. We go very easy on the hamburger, as the first time we gave it to her it made her droppings smell bad. That might mean she wasn't digesting the meat well. We've given her only pill-sized bits a couple of times a week since then. Use a cereal-sized bowl or saucer to hold the food. This won't keep things neat—it's just a way to satisfy the iguana's taste for rummaging through its food. Bubbles is fed once a day, outside her vivarium to cut down on cleaning problems. She accepts food from our fingers.

Bubbles spends a lot of time in her swimming pool. She used to drag food into it and eat there. She also drinks from it. Her combination of aquatic habits is not hygienic, so we wash the pool well every day and so should you.

Carolina Anoles

The Carolina anole, a common native to our Southern states, is another lizard that can live in a dry vivarium. If you live in the Southeast, by all means catch your own on the fences, logs and branches where anoles love to bask in the sun. Otherwise buy them in pet stores during the warmer seasons.

The anole shares one thing in common with a chameleon: it can change its color. The range of color is not nearly so dramatic and no patterns are possible, but an anole can change within three minutes from brown to a bright grass-green. The off-white belly stays off-white.

The color change only camouflages the lizard by accident. If it is lucky enough to be in the right place when a color change happens, it will be camouflaged among the scenery. Color change is triggered by temperature. At 50 degrees an anole is always brown. As the temperature rises to 70 degrees and beyond, it turns bright green if it is in the shade or the dark. In bright light it still stays brown. Above 86 degrees it turns pale green and stays that way regardless of light. The color changes help to regulate the lizard's body temperature. The brown is a dark color—it absorbs heat. The green is a light color—it reflects heat. Besides heat and light, emotions too can make an anole change color. In a fight, the winner turns green, the loser fades to brown. Our Cuban anole, a large relative of the Carolina, turns brown when you bother him, green when you give him a grape.

Anoles are much faster in their movements than desert iguanas, and more sudden in their decisions. We've lost a few anoles by carrying them around on our head or shoulders outdoors. While we thought they were happily resting they actually had their eye on a leafy branch above. The leap to freedom is so quick and light, you can't feel it happen. There was a transient fashion in the last century for wearing an anole on a woman's lapel. The anole was attached by a little chain collar to a pin in the lady's dress. This seems like a cute idea, but no one sells lizard leashes these days.

The male anole can fan out the skin at his throat, a feat he employs both to attract a female and to warn off a rival male. When light shines through the fan of skin, it appears bright red. No smarter than other lizards, a male anole will make great displays of head nodding and throat fanning at his own reflection in a mirror.

Perhaps because of its ability to change color, anoles are often called chameleons by circuses and pet stores, but they aren't. Anoles are not even near relatives to that curious, curly-tailed African lizard. True chameleons come complete with dragon horns

Anoles can change colors but they aren't camouflaged.

and pop eyes that move separately from one another. Their tails curl like a spiral and can hold on to branches like monkeys' tails. Their tongues are sticky and longer than their bodies. A chameleon can catch a fly by extending its elastic tongue and then retracting it complete with stuck-on fly into its mouth.

In case this description makes you want to bypass the common anole and get to the wonderful chameleon, you will find them for sale. But they do not live more than a year in captivity. Because of this, it seems a shame to encourage pet stores to sell these animals—resist buying one so you won't have to watch it die before its time.

Housing

The vivarium for an anole can be the same as for a desert iguana, but at least one plant should be added. Choose a low, leafy variety, and one that will do well with water sprayed on its leaves. An African violet is a good choice. Sink the pot into the gravel so the plant looks like it's growing there. The plant will be used as a watering station, since anoles drink from droplets only.

The incandescent light won't be necessary. Use only the Vita-Lite® which will keep the heat high enough and also provide the equivalent of natural sunlight.

Anole droppings are rather small. Use a fork to rake the sand clean once a week.

Food and Water

Carolina anoles eat many kinds of insects. They are so agile and quick that in the summer you can put them on the window screen and watch them leap on flies and moths that have accumulated there. You can catch spiders or unwelcome insects like cockroaches for them. During the winter, rely on store-bought mealworms, served up in a jar-lid platter. The largest male anoles might tackle a store-bought cricket too, and spiders who live in the house all winter are welcome dinners. Anoles only eat their meat alive, so raw hamburger, while just as healthy, will not do. They don't eat vegetables.

Giving a Carolina anole water is a slight problem. In nature, anoles drink dewdrops or raindrops from the leaves. A pet anole cannot learn to drink from a water dish. Water has to be sprinkled into the vivarium each day, but since water droplets sink quickly into the gravel or drip off the rock, your anole may not have time to drink before the drops disappear. That's the reason for the small leafy plant suggested for this vivarium. Spray the plant daily with a mister, or sprinkle water onto it with your fingers. The natural wax on the leaves will keep the water in droplets for the lizard to lap from.

The Cuban Knight

We are experimenting now with a Cuban anole, sometimes called a Cuban knight. She came to us in just about as poor condition as Agatha, the desert iguana, and we have not had her long enough to know what to advise other owners. So far, she does not eat the live insects which are supposed to be her only diet. She accepts both mealworms and hamburger meat when force fed—although she can spit things out when she finds them disgusting. Force feeding—literally forcing food into an animal that refuses to eat—is done by pulling the lizard's throat flap gently downwards while holding the upper jaw in the other hand. Another person has to pop the food inside the gaping mouth. The only food the Cuban knight grabs on her own is peeled red grapes, and this is most unusual for a carniverous lizard. She does drink from a water dish.

Land Tortoises

All tortoises are turtles. Turtles who live on land are usually called tortoises, but are otherwise hardly different from water turtles. Tortoises, like all the turtle clan, have become a big ''no'' in the pet market since it was discovered that this family of reptiles can carry a bacteria called salmonella. Salmonella causes diarrhea in humans—only unpleasant in adults but often very serious to young children and infants. However, both land tortoises and water turtles checked by the Department of Health are on the market. Land tortoises make particularly good vivarium pets if care is taken about their environment. The elongated, the red-footed and the Greek tortoise are good choices. Pet stores may sell young ones three or four inches long, or adults who may be five or six inches.

Tortoises are among the most ancient reptiles, and how they evolved is still a mystery. The earliest fossil tortoise, a full 200 million years old, is virtually identical to the Galapagos Island tortoise of today except it weighed close to one ton. In other words, no one has dug up a fossil yet that shows a pretortoise reptile just beginning to develop a bony shell, only a perfectly finished tortoise who, except for its gigantic size, would look normal today. As an aside, this is also true of another reptile, the snake. No one has yet found a fossil snake with little tiny legs—a missing link

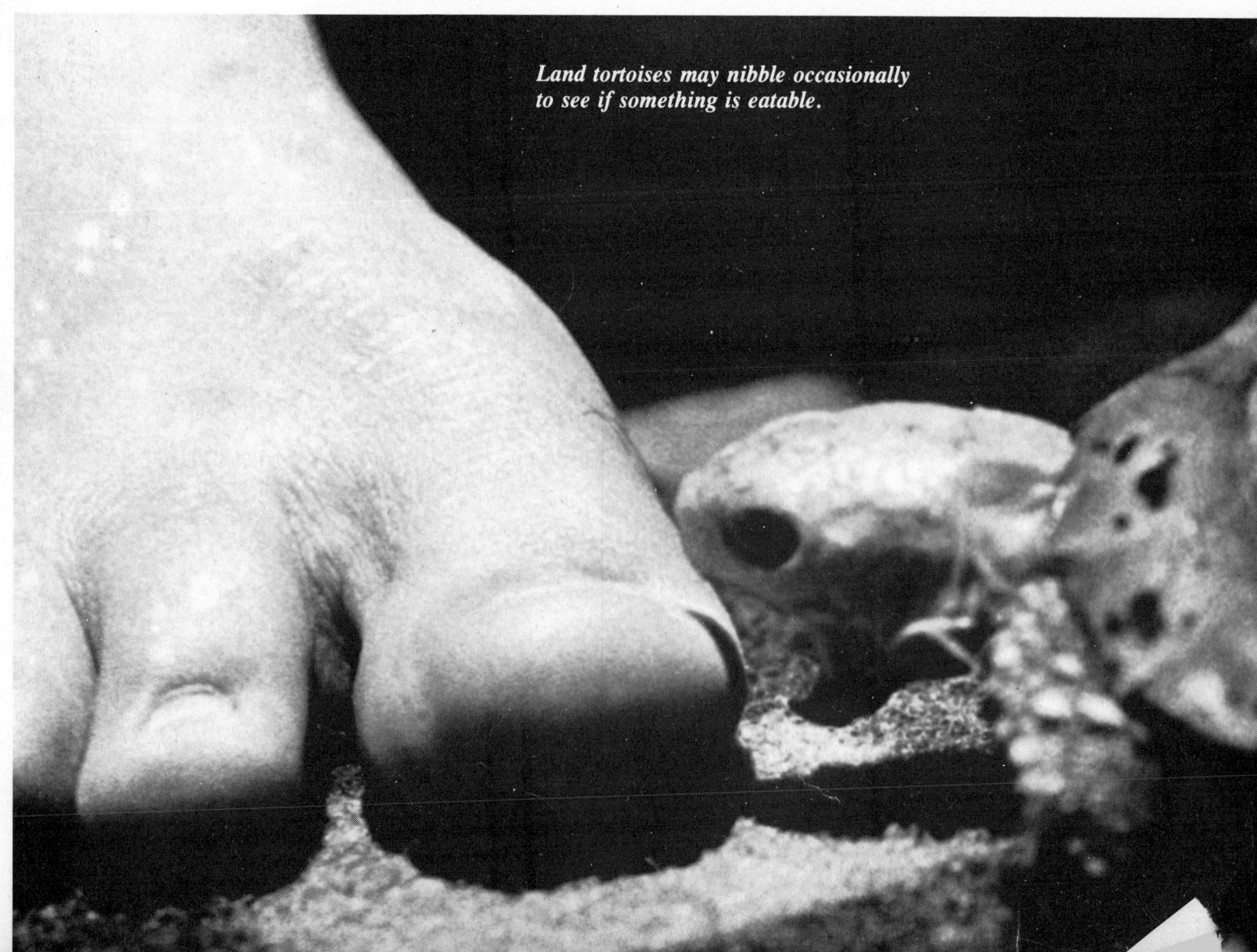

Land tortoises may nibble occasionally to see if something is eatable.

connecting a lizard to a serpent. The only snake fossils found are ordinary legless snakes.

Claims for tortoise age records are extraordinary—over a century and a half. Allowing for exaggeration and the fact that such claims have not been proven, scientists still think the tortoise is the longest lived of all animals.

Housing

Dryness is normal for these tortoises, all of whom come from very dry climates. The desert vivarium (page 313)is a proper home; the 10-gallon size is better than the 5½-gallon. Tortoises don't climb, so you won't need a branch. The screen top is not necessary either. The leaning rock is a good idea because it provides a shaded corner, but be sure there's enough room for the tortoise to walk behind it and get out again. To prevent a leaning rock from falling on a clumsy tortoise, glue a small block of wood to the tank floor with epoxy glue. Position it out from the wall as a wedge for the rock to rest against. Push sand over it so it's not visible. Sink a water dish into the sand with the rim barely above the surface. Tortoises lean down to drink.

Because tortoises look indestructible, people often fail to keep them warm enough. But the tortoises one buys are young and delicate, and usually succumb to respiratory disease if kept in an unheated vivarium. Daytime temperature should be 80 degrees, with normal room temperature (65 to 70 degrees) at night. An 80 degree temperature can usually be obtained with just the Vita-Lite®(page 316).Tortoises must have this ultra-violet light unless you are supplementing their diet with ready-made vitamin D foods like cod liver oil. If the Vita-Lite®doesn't keep the vivarium warm enough, add incandescent light as needed (page 316).

Pick up droppings as they occur, and remove leftovers after each meal. Change the water and

wash the water dish daily.

Once a tortoise has survived infancy, its health is less of a worry. Adult tortoises over five years old can live free in a home or apartment as long as they have access to a warm spot, like a sunny corner or a radiator. Keep a low pan of drinking water available all the time. In really warm areas like Florida or southern California, people keep adult pet tortoises all year long in a fenced yard. They have been known to learn to nudge their owner's feet when they get hungry.

Food and Water

Tortoises are about as omnivorous as we are—they eat fruits, vegetables, meat and even eggs. Offer a selection of dark leafy vegetables like spinach and romaine lettuce, ripe fruits like tomato, pear, banana and chopped apple. Corn on the cob is a favorite. Include raw hamburger in the diet and try snacks of raw fish when you have it for dinner, or raw chicken. Although a tortoise can go for weeks without food, that does not mean it should. Feed your tortoise once every day. A reluctant eater can sometimes be encouraged by dyeing a light-colored food like banana with red or yellow vegetable dye.

Tortoises need extra calcium if they are to grow well in captivity. There are several ways to provide it. Sprinkle bone meal (sold at plant stores as a fertilizer) over the hamburger meat, or pulverize egg shells to sprinkle on it. You can even pound up the cuttlebone sold for birds in pet stores. Two times a week is often enough for the calcium additive.

If you don't use the Vita-Lite® for a vitamin D supply, you'll have to mess with cod liver oil. The oil contains vitamin D, so the tortoise doesn't have to manufacture its own. Occasionally a tortoise will open its mouth and let you put a delicious drop right in. More often, it will merely consent to eat its hamburger with a drop of cod liver oil on it. A drop a day is recommended.

A tortoise will drink from a dish sunk into the gravel so that its rim is almost level with the surrounding surface. It doesn't lap the water, but drinks with a sucking and swallowing movement. Be sure the water's deep enough for it to get its snout in.

Illnesses

If your tortoise gets a respiratory disease, the symptoms are inactivity, a runny or bubbling nose and noisy breathing, which you can hear if you lean your head close. Keep the temperature at 80 or even 85 degrees.

Use a powdered form of Terramycin® (available from a veterinarian) or a bird antibiotic (available from pet stores). Following the recommended dosage for birds, dissolve the medicine daily in the tortoise's drinking water. To be sure the tortoise gets enough, sprinkle about half the same quantity on its food. If the antibiotic is in tablet form, you will have to crush it with a spoon first.

Tarantulas

Another of the larger vivarium pets is both interesting and useful. It is interesting in that it is a large spider called a tarantula. It is useful in that it keeps unwanted guests away. In fact, we recently read of a jewelry store owner who keeps a tarantula in his window display at night. He used to be robbed frequently; he's never robbed anymore.

People's fear of the tarantula is due not only to some deep-seated and ancient horror of the beast but to a totally unfounded belief that tarantulas are deadly poisonous. This is not so. Tarantulas, like most spiders, secrete a salivary fluid that is injected through their fangs into their victim. The saliva contains digestive enzymes. The enzymes digest the prey from the inside out, reducing the tissues to liquid. The spider then sips its dinner neatly from the undigested shell. Its secretions definitely kill insects and even young birds and mice, but its bite causes only local pain and swelling in humans. The malicious rumor that tarantulas are deadly to all probably came from a mix-up between the American tarantulas and some European spiders who are the real bad guys.

Our tarantula measures five inches from toe to

Mary the tarantula feels comfortable resting on a knee.

toe. She is a painted tarantula, native to our Southwestern deserts, and though she's not as large as some of the South American varieties, her bright-orange stripes make her the most colorful member of the family.

We've named our tarantula Mary. How do we know she is a girl? We don't—it's a guess. Male tarantulas have special complicated mouth parts that are simpler in females, but we have not been able to find a picture that makes the differences clear. Both sexes have a hole (or vent) behind where their eight legs emerge. The female lays her eggs through the vent. The male picks up a package of sperm from his vent with his special mouth parts and inserts the package into the female's vent to fertilize her eggs before they are laid.

Mary, like all American tarantulas, has eight eyes, eight legs, a little pair of mouth parts called pedipalps on either side of her mouth, and fangs. She allows us to pick her up and walks freely on us. She has never bitten, reserving her bites for potential dinners only. We use caution basic to animal handling, however. We don't bother her when she is hungry or when she is molting. Hunger makes anybody grouchy. Molting's worse. In a spider, molting is much more complicated than simply climbing out of a tight skin. Each molt is accompanied by radical cell destruction, construction, and rearrangement inside the spider's body. After a molt, and there may be as many as nine in some species, a spider is a different creature inside as well as outside. During the final molt in a male or female spider's life, its internal reproductive organs are manufactured. It's enough to make anyone want to bite.

For some spiders, growing up to sexual maturity means the approach of death. Females may die after their eggs are laid, and in a few spiders the male is killed and eaten after mating. But tarantulas continue their adult lives for a long time, living frequently to the ripe old age of 25.

When we pick Mary up, we do so from behind using two hands as scoops. No animal likes being cornered.

Housing

Our tarantula vivarium is about the same as the desert iguana's. Mary has a rock to hide under, gravel under her feet and an incandescent sun in her sky. The Vita-Lite® isn't necessary. The incandescent light is used to heat her environment when the house is cold. Seventy to 75 degrees is a good average daytime temperature. At night you can let the temperature drop to the 60s. The light bulb serves to keep the vivarium dry too, so it is used even in hot humid summer weather. The temperature will climb but the dryness is more important. Don't be fooled by the apparent immobility of a resting tarantula—a screen top is necessary. Tarantulas can jump out of a tank in a twinkling.

Water is kept in a small dish sunk to its rim in the gravel. We were told to keep a bit of sponge in the water dish. Our tarantula strokes it with her pedipalps but we don't know whether she's drinking or washing her face. In case that's how she drinks, we don't dare remove it. The water is changed several times a week to keep it clean.

Though tarantulas do spin they don't inhabit webs like other spiders, but live instead in burrows under rocks. Mary spins a neat case around the shell of her finished dinner and pushes it to a corner of her cage away from the entrance of her rock burrow. She similarly encases her own weekly bowel movement. Both prey and bowel movement can be picked out by hand whenever you notice them. Stray webbing gets left about on the surface of the gravel and is removed with a fork. We thought plants would look well in her home, and at first had an array of cacti and succulents in small sunken pots in the gravel. The job of keeping them free of webbing was too annoying, so we made her home simpler.

Food and Water

Tarantulas hunt insects and small animals like baby birds and mice. They can leap as far as three feet when attacking prey. Mary does fine on store-bought crickets, usually three or four a week. She either drinks or bathes or both at her water sponge. We've had her for over a year now, and she appears to be in excellent health.

A greater problem than keeping Mary in good health is keeping the crickets alive. She won't eat them dead. Crickets sold for food must have food of their own to survive. Keep them in a coffee can, with holes punched through the plastic lid for ventilation. Sprinkle corn meal in the bottom for them to eat, and add a slice of apple or potato for both food and moisture. Keep the can in a warm place—near a radiator in winter. With this method, we just

A Wolf Spider

barely manage to keep the crickets alive for one week's food supply.

Plumb out of crickets one day and suspecting Mary was hungry, we caught two wolf spiders for her dinner, a large one and a small one. They're similar to tarantulas in that they hunt and leap on their prey. We put both wolf spiders in Mary's cage. In a twinkling, the large wolf spider leaped upon the small one. In another twinkling, Mary leaped upon the large wolf spider. It was nature in the raw.

But the event gave us the idea that if you can't afford a tarantula, you can catch a large wolf spider instead. They hang about under baseboards in the house, in basements, and outside near foundations, coming out mainly in the evening to hunt. It is not hard to catch one in a jar and then slip the lid under the opening. A large wolf spider will eat crickets. A friend of ours found a wolf spider living behind a piece of scrap lumber in his basement. Instead of capturing it he taught the spider to come out for dinner. He feeds it mealworms from his fingers.

Molting Mary

At the beginning of one summer, Mary suddenly refused to eat. Three weeks went by without a cricket. She acted sluggish but was jumpy when touched. Her owner swears she kicked him. Then she began to turn blue. Her normally pinky-beige glow faded to a leaden hue, and her hair dropped out. We called several vets, one of whom had once examined a tarantula with a sore toe, but none of them had advice to offer. It was time for summer vacation, so we left Mary to board at our friendly neighborhood pet shop with our commiserations. "Don't feel bad if she dies," we said. "We know she is very sick."

All summer no one had the nerve to call and find out Mary's fate. When we got back, we went gloomily to the pet store to hear the bad news. Just as we thought, our friend held out to us a plastic bag with Mary's remains. We caught a glimpse of dried legs, an abdomen, fangs. Then he pointed to the shelf. There was Mary, bigger, brighter, hairier than ever. She had molted. We don't know yet if that was Mary's final, grown-up molt, but if she ever stops eating and turns blue again, we'll at least know what to expect. The plastic bag of spider exoskeleton worked well as a show-and-tell item in school.

Land Snails

Even a mollusk can be a pet. The ordinary garden snail, a relative of all the seashell creatures and of clams and mussels, eats well and stays healthy in captivity. Look for snails in the grass along a damp wall or foundation, and in the woods under rocks and rotting logs or at the base of trees.

A snail is such a common, taken-for-granted, everyday critter, few people ever wonder how it gets its shell. The snail makes it—rapidly when it is young and growing fast, slowly as it approaches its natural size limit. Take a magnifying glass and look carefully at your snail's shell. Between the spiral grooves, you'll see the shell is a series of tiny bands. Each band represents a thin layer of a special fluid secreted by the snail. The fluid hardens on exposure to air, forming a new band at the shell opening. The shell begins at the center of the always clockwise spiral pattern. As the snail grows it adds new layers at its shell opening to accommodate its size.

In hot dry weather a snail may shut itself up completely. It seals its shell entrance with an air-hardened substance. Thus protected from loss of moisture, it can estivate (spend dry hot weather inactive) for several months.

The part of a snail's body that makes contact with the ground is called a foot. Its mucus-smoothed, wavelike motion isn't very efficient. Snails really are the slowest animals; the slowest moving about 23 inches per hour.

The long stalks on top of the snail's head are tipped with light-sensitive pigment and serve as eyes. The shorter stalks more toward the front of its head are touch-sensitive feelers. Both move in every direction and can be retracted into its head.

Land snails leave a mucous trail behind them.

Housing

A snail prefers a climate more moist than your home. A jar-sized vivarium (page 311), naturally humidified by the moisture in a lettuce leaf, takes care of that. Ventilation is essential; don't substitute a pierced jar lid for the cheesecloth top suggested on page 311. Never leave a jar vivarium in sunlight. Even one hour of sun heats up the inside like a greenhouse and kills your pet in short order. Snails prefer damp shade anyway.

Every day, remove snail and food from the jar and rinse the jar out well with fresh tap water. You may have to use a sponge too, since the mucous trails left by the snail are quite gooey and hard to clean. The black spots are droppings. Dry the jar so there is no extra moisture to invite decay. Put in a fresh lettuce leaf for humidity, plus whatever other snack is on the day's menu.

Food and Water

Small as it is, a snail has a mouth equipped with powerful teeth, called radula, which chomp through even tough vegetation. In captivity the easiest diet to feed a snail is lettuce, but it wouldn't hurt to offer other leafy vegetables like spinach and watercress. You'll be able to watch your snail eat its way along the edge of a leaf or chomp holes in the middle. If you remove the lettuce and look at the chomp marks carefully, you can actually see the pattern of tiny teeth.

Snails don't drink. They get their water from the leaves they eat. Be sure these leaves are replaced before they dry out.

Ants

Ants are among the few insects who are truly social. Each colony is composed of three kinds of ants: a queen, winged males, and wingless sterile female workers. Most colonies keep only one queen. As winged males and new winged queens come to maturity, they fly from the nest to mate. Sometimes these flights happen all at once over a wide area and the sky is filled with "flying ants," coupling in the air and then falling to the ground still attached to one another.

The males have a short life. They fly, mate and die. Mated queens, however, immediately dig small nests of their own. They bite off their wings if they have not fallen off by themselves, lay their first eggs and raise them to adult workers. Then the workers take over the running of the new colony.

Workers, all the crawling ants you are likely to see, extend the nest, keep it clean, protect it from enemies, forage for food and water, and bring back the liquefied meal in their crops (stomachs) to feed to the larvas in the nest. Ants who have been out foraging also share their regurgitated food with ants who have been too busy in the nest to go out, and with the queen, who for the remainder of her long life—as much as 15 years—will be too busy laying eggs to take care of herself or her offspring in any way.

Getting the Ants

You can buy ants from Uncle Milton Industries, Culver City, California 90230, but the colony won't contain a queen. If you'd rather try for a long-lived colony plus the chance to see eggs develop through larval and pupal stages into full-grown ants, you will have to hunt your own. You will need a white cloth about the size of a pillowcase, two jars with lids, a pair of tweezers, a pointed hand trowel and a friend.

Many common species of ant make good pet colonies. The smallest red ants may be too little to see well but the larger rust or black dirt-dwelling species are fine. Look for a small ant hill that is built in soft dirt or sand that is easy to dig up. The structure of the nest can go quite deep into the soil and the queen either is already in, or soon will depart to, the deepest recesses. She's the one you're after.

Lay the white cloth next to the ant hill. Bravely take your spade and in one deep scoop lift the ant hill and the soil under it onto the cloth. Ants will be all over the place in a second, some dragging oval

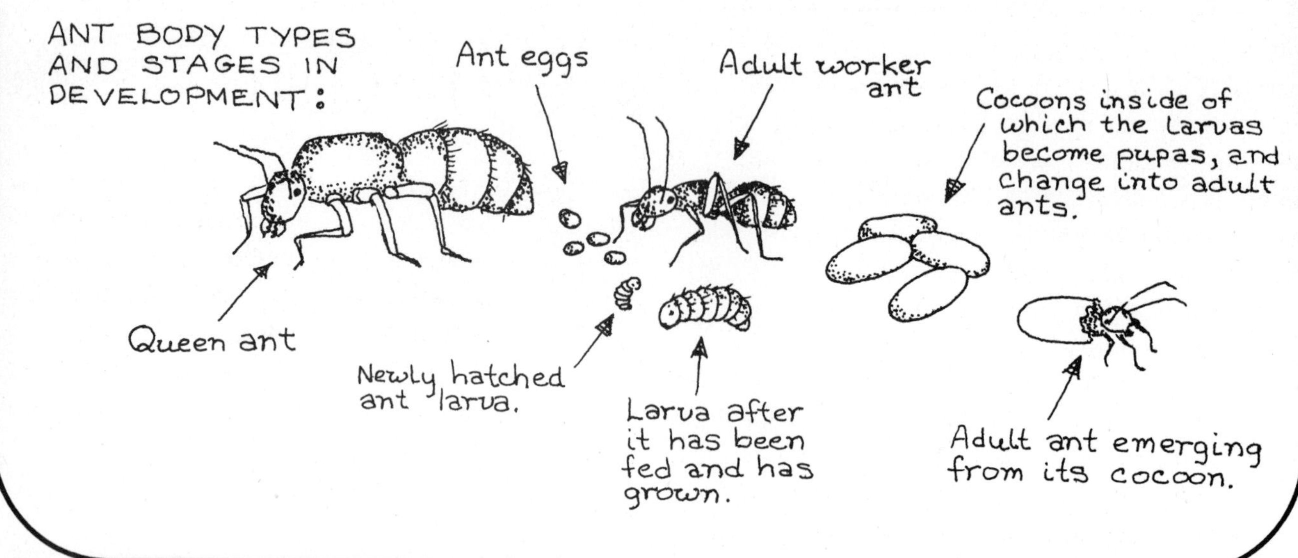

white pupas with them. Now look for the queen. She may be larger than any of the other ants, but not necessarily. Another clue is the size of her thorax (the portion of the body between head and abdomen, or what we would think of as the chest). The queen's thorax is larger than the other ants'. If you see a group of ants dragging another ant around, that may well be the queen. The ants are attempting to get her back into the deep part of their nest. If you don't see the queen, take your time about picking up other ants before you start to search the nest.

Use the tweezers to pick up a few dozen ants and put them into one of the jars. Do it carefully so you don't crush them. If you can, identify by body type the important types of ant that make up a colony. A colony is more effective if it is fully equipped with workers as well as eggs, pupas and larvas. Eggs, pupas and larvas exude chemical substances appreciated by mature members and important to the organization and daily work of a colony. Put each of the pupas the ants are carrying in the other jar to protect them from the overexcited ants. Later, add eggs and larvas you find as you excavate the nest. Your friend should be helping you with all this.

When you have the ordinary ants you want safely in one jar and some pupas in another, start to excavate the nest for the queen, some eggs and some larvas. By this time the queen will be at the very bottom of the nest. Dig carefully, following along tunnels with the point of the trowel. If you find the queen, put her in the same jar with eggs, larvas and developing pupas.

If you don't find the queen in this nest you have a choice. Either settle for this generation of ants and the next that will develop from the eggs, or throw out your catch and start again on another nest. You can't use a queen from another nest, as she will be murdered by the colony.

If you haven't added soil to your ant vivarium yet, you have time to do it now. Soil from near the nest will be appreciated. Add some soil from the nest itself if you can. It will smell like home to the ants.

There are two ways to transfer your ants into the vivarium without getting ants all over the house. The first is to refrigerate them in the jars for a few hours until they move sluggishly and are easy to handle. The second way is to dump them from the jar into a sinkful of water. They won't drown, but they'll be easy to pick up from the surface of the water—gently—with tweezers. Once in the vivarium, the ants will usually set right to work to build a new home.

Watching the industry of ants is exhausting. Some ants excavate whole cities hundreds of feet in extent and housing half a million individuals. Your labors in catching the ants can't begin to match the industry you're about to witness.

Housing

An ant colony is kept in a tall narrow glass vivarium filled with soil taken from the vicinity of its nest or with an artificial substitute. Since the ants have only a narrow space in which to work, many segments of their tunnels and rooms will run along the glass. One can see the construction and the builders themselves as they work. Instructions for making an ant vivarium are on page 323,or you can buy one in a pet department or order one by mail from Uncle Milton Industries (see page 79).

The homemade ant house has cardboard sides to keep light from the ants' tunnels except while you are watching them. The commercial ant houses don't come with cardboard sides. Add your own by cutting shirt cardboard to fit. Attach the cardboard at the top of each side with masking (freezer) tape.

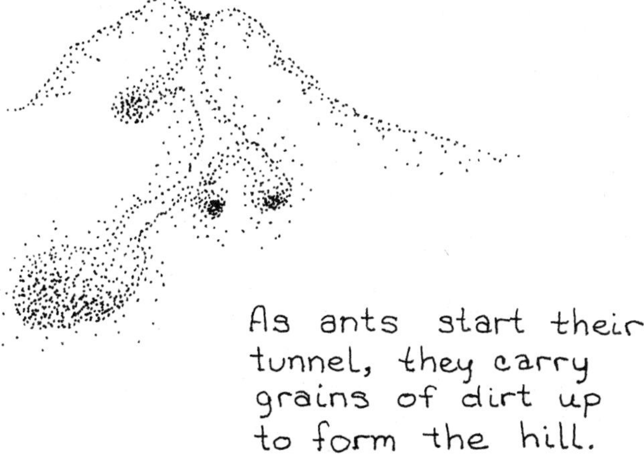

As ants start their tunnel, they carry grains of dirt up to form the hill.

Food and Water

Since captive ants can't forage for food, you have to feed them. Ants eat a balanced diet of dead insects and sweet food. Dead mealworms or flies will do for the insect food. Tiny bits of nuts, cake crumbs, sweet breakfast cereals, honey and fruits are suggested sweets. Water is necessary to an ant environment. A good way to provide both water and honey is to keep a small square of sponge moistened with honey-water in the feeding area. Replenish the sponge with a few drops of water and a drop of honey each day.

Remember ants have tiny stomachs. Try not to overfeed them. Ants will store their food if there is too much for them to eat. Don't give them a surplus for storage, since it can decay, get moldy and ruin the colony. Clean up leftovers and add new food by reaching in through the hole with tweezers.

Field Crickets

The cricket, another insect, has been kept as a pet for centuries in China, where a tiny bamboo cage was designed for it, complete with sliding door. A cricket in a cage, like a cricket on the hearth, was considered good luck in China, as it was in Europe and in America. For people who didn't want the live pet, cricket doorstops and cricket doorknockers provided a substitute. The real thing is easy to keep.

Only the male cricket sings. The sound is made by a process called stridulation, in which one surface is rubbed against the other. It's the male grasshopper who "fiddles" by rubbing his leg against a wing. The cricket uses only his wings. He leans forward, lifting his wings above his back. A scraper under the upper wing rubs against a file on the lower wing. You can produce a similar sound with the back of a knife (which acts as the cricket's scraper) against a regular metal file. It won't sound as pretty as the cricket's chirp, but it's the same idea.

Crickets sing, like birds sing, to announce their whereabouts to female crickets and to warn other males off their small territories. You can recognize the male cricket because he has no ovipositor, the long tube used for egg laying that sticks out the rear end of females. Young crickets can't sing either. A young cricket's wings aren't yet big enough to cover his back. In the North, most field crickets are mature with full wings by late July or August. I think Southern crickets may come to maturity in several batches during the warm months but I am not absolutely sure.

A cricket in captivity can live through the winter and occasionally into spring and summer. His chirping is pleasant but persistent during the night. If it drives you crazy, you may have to lock him out of your bedroom.

Catching a Cricket

Pet stores sell a tan-colored cricket as live food, but this species is difficult to keep alive more than a

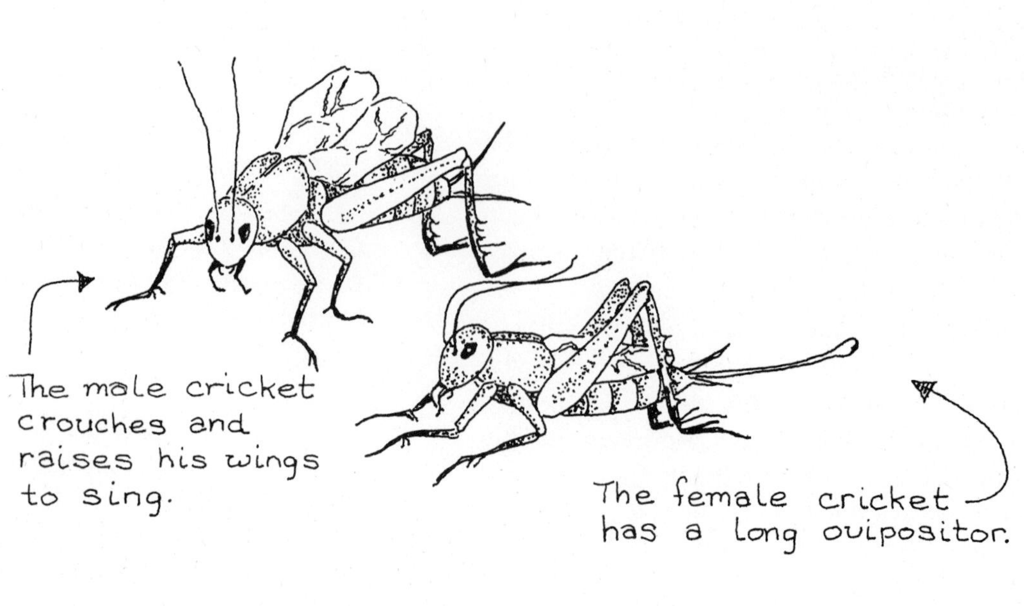

week or so. If you have no other choice, you can give it a try, following the suggestions for keeping a tarantula's dinner alive on page 76 . The dark-brown or black field cricket is a much better pet, and sings better.

Wait until August, when crickets are full grown and chirping. At nightfall arm yourself with a flashlight and a jar. Listen for the crick-crick of a cricket. Favorite haunts of crickets are typically dark and damp, often close to a source of food. Look for them on the damp earth at the base of a foundation, especially where garbage pails are kept, or in other dampish spots in long grass, at the base of rocks or the trunks of trees. We've had our best success at the base of a well near a compost heap where rotting vegetation, dripping water, protective grass and a masonry wall made a fine world for crickets.

When you locate the sound, walk slowly toward it. When the sound stops, stop walking; wait until you hear the chirp resume and then proceed again. The sound of your footsteps will make the cricket stop singing over and over again. But sooner or later he will chirp again, even when you are inches away. When you're quite sure you're almost stepping on him, turn on your light and start searching, pulling grass or leaves apart with your hands until you find him. Clamp your hand over him loosely. Then gently close your whole hand around him. Don't ever pick a cricket up by a leg—their legs come off easily. Let the cricket drop from your hand into the jar. Then turn the light on him and make sure you have found a male. Remember that he's been singing in order to get a lady friend to join him, and if she's arrived you may have caught her instead of the male.

Housing

The bug jar or the screened cage, both on page 311, are excellent homes for a cricket. The humidity has to be kept high by keeping a small square of moist sponge at the bottom of the vivarium. The vivarium should be rinsed out every day to get rid of leftover food and droppings. Dry it so there aren't puddles, but don't forget to rinse out and replenish the moistened sponge. While you're cleaning the vivarium, you can keep the cricket in an empty jar or can.

Food and Water

Once safely home and settled into a cage, your cricket might be hungry. Crickets eat a large variety of foods. Bread moistened with milk is enjoyed, as are soft foods like banana, cooked sweet potato, tomato and moistened cereals. Drinking water isn't necessary.

Salamanders

Because salamanders have the same general body shape as lizards, people often think they are reptiles. But salamanders are amphibians, hatched in the water as tadpoles, living only part of their lives in moist land areas, and going back to the water to mate and lay their eggs. Salamanders don't have scales as reptiles do; their skins are smooth and always damp.

There are several common salamanders you might easily find in the woods in the eastern half of this country. Elsewhere they are more rare. Occasionally salamanders are offered for sale in pet stores during the spring and summer in all parts of the country.

The morning after a rain you may find salamanders walking about, but ordinarily they shy away from the dry outdoors and stick to their damper hideouts. Their native haunts are in woodlands, under rocks and rotting logs. Turning rocks and logs will eventually uncover one if you are persistent enough.

Catching a Salamander

Salamander species are often very local and you will have to look at a field guide to amphibians for your area of the country to see which kinds live near you. The most dramatic are the larger species like the black and yellow polka-dotted salamander, six or seven inches long. If you catch a young one, you could have it as a pet for 25 years—its normal life span.

Another larger salamander is the yellow or light-olive blotched tiger salamander, who at 13 inches is the largest salamander you will find on land in the world. It would still look meager compared to the largest water-dweller—the giant salamander of Japan who measures five feet, weighs over 20 pounds, and may live for 50 years.

Smaller species include the marbled salamander and the striped two-lined salamander. Both can be found on land. The common newt, another small species, is a brown water creature in its adult stage but a bright-red spotted beast when in its juvenile land-dwelling stage. These youngsters are called red efts.

Housing

The moist woodland vivarium on page 316 is a suitable home for salamanders. If you find one of the large species like the yellow polka-dotted salamander, you'll have to add a sunken crockery dish for it to soak in, or instead make one of the other semi-aquatic environments suggested on page 319.

Salamanders are most unlikely to climb out of their home unless there is an obvious route, like a leaning branch. They can't climb glass walls. When weather is humid, you can remove the glass top to give ventilation. When the weather is dry, remove the top once a day and wave fresh air into the vivarium before replacing it.

The semi-aquatic vivarium needs no top. No misting is necessary in a semi-aquatic tank, but mist once a week if you are using a sunken water dish in a woodland vivarium. Clean the bathing dish if you have one at least once a week, and refill it with fresh water.

Any of the salamanders can share their home with other salamander species or with tree frogs.

Food and Water

The smaller salamanders can eat only small insects. These are very hard to collect. The easiest substitute for wild bugs is a fruit fly colony, in which adult flies continue to lay eggs, the eggs become larvas, the larvas hatch into adult flies, and the whole process starts all over again. This whole life cycle takes only ten days. See the Box on page 84 for instructions on how to start a colony.

The large salamanders will eat shrimp pellets, a fish food available in pet stores. Drop food daily on the surface of their bathing pond.

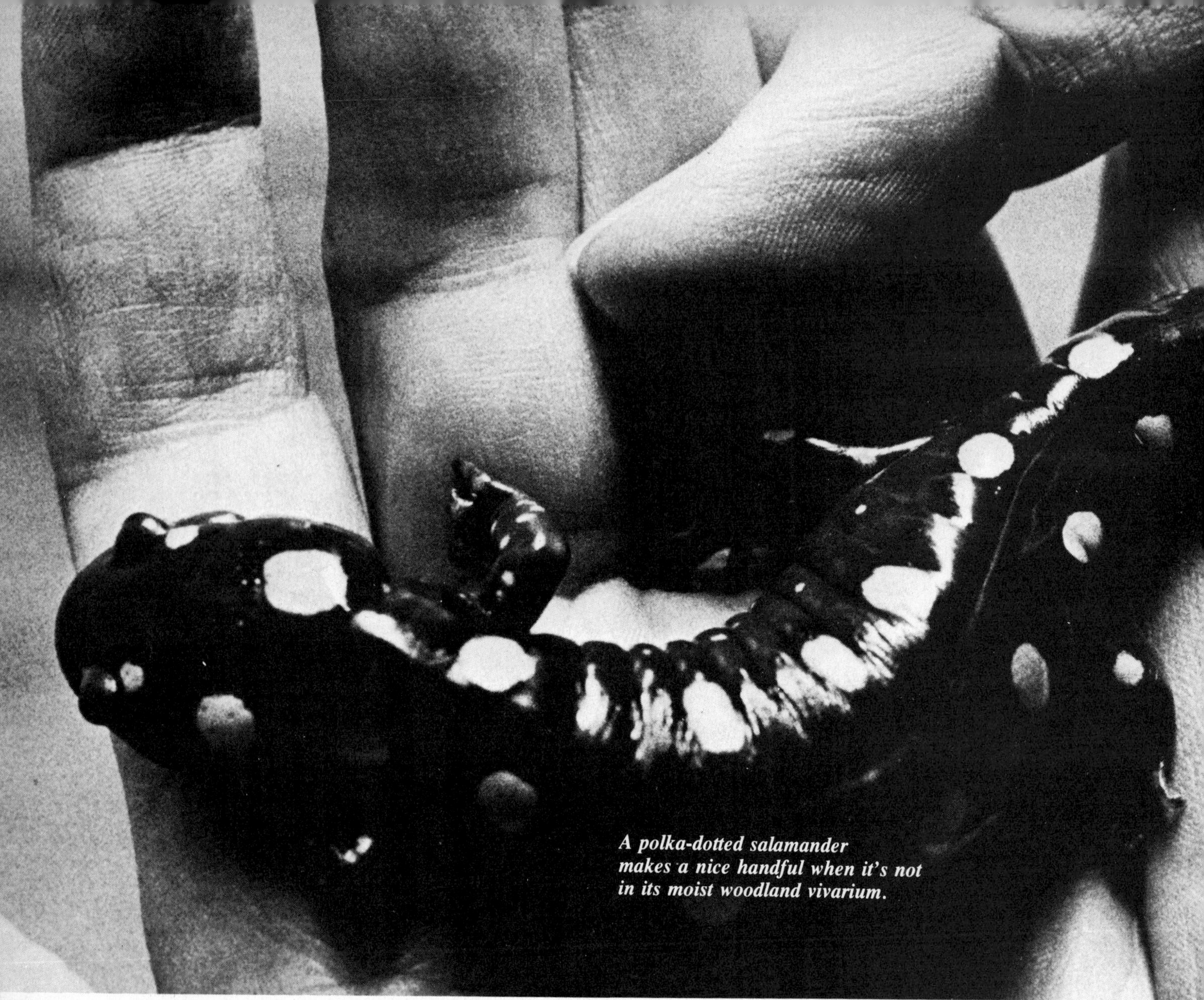

A polka-dotted salamander makes a nice handful when it's not in its moist woodland vivarium.

Colonizing Fruit Flies

Start a fruit fly colony in warm weather when the flies are abundant. Use a baby-food jar as the container. Moisten the bottom. Crush a little overripe banana into the bottom of the jar. Wait until it begins to attract fruit flies—the tiny, slow-flying critters that hover over decaying fruit. Don't let either the fruit or the bottom of the jar dry out. When fruit flies have been swarming over the jar for several days, you can put the jar in the vivarium. Eggs will be laid in the fruit, and more flies will be available soon. Each adult female lays 3,000 eggs!

To keep a fruit fly colony going outside the vivarium, use a larger jar, like a mayonnaise jar. Instead of putting the fruit directly in the jar, put it in two small containers such as bottle caps. Put the filled bottle caps in the bottom of the jar.

Once some adult flies are inside, cover the jar with a thin cloth held in place with a rubber band. Each week you can remove one of the bottle caps to the vivarium, where a new crew of flies will hatch. Replenish the jar with another fruity bottle cap.

A few flies might escape when the top is open, but on the whole they prefer to stay where their dinner is. They aren't aware that they are about to become dinner themselves.

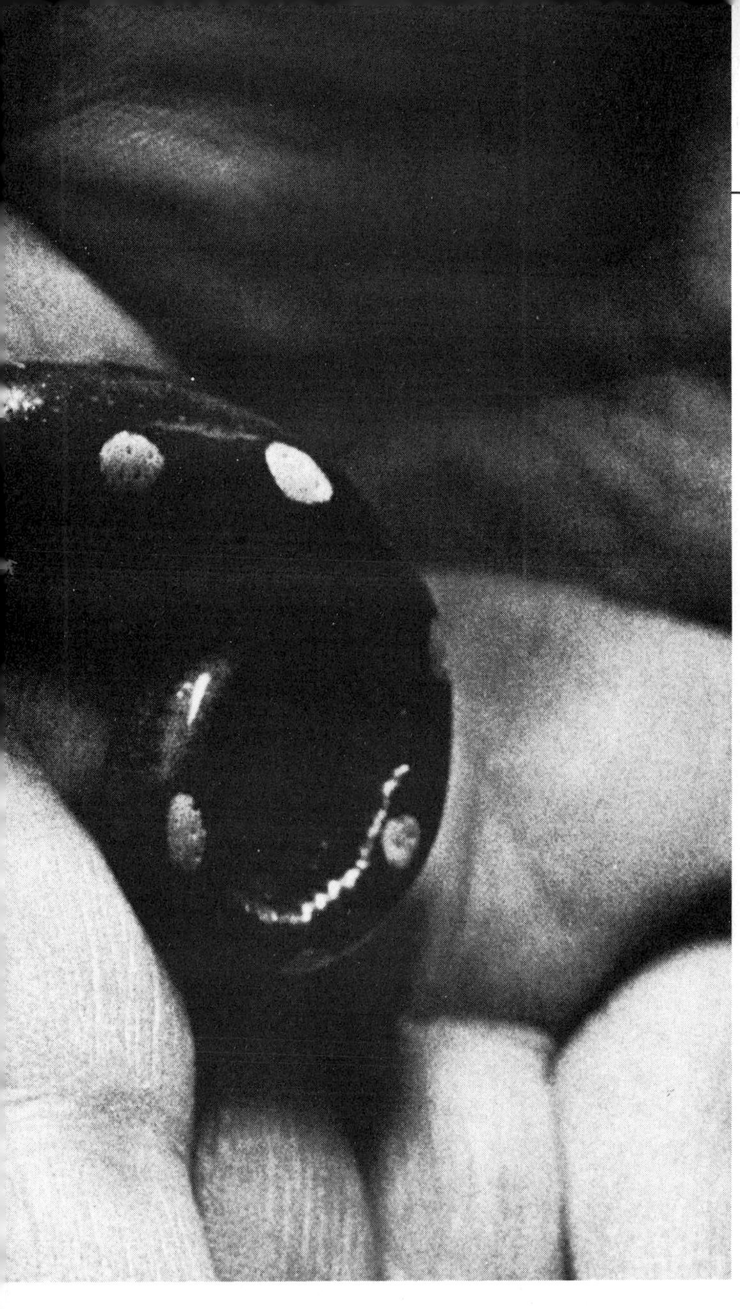

Tree Frogs

The spring peepers of the East and the Pacific tree frogs of the West are both tiny, arboreal (tree-dwelling) frogs whose long toes are equipped with sucking disks that cling to trunks and branches. No bigger than a thumbnail, these amphibians are noisemakers all out of proportion to their size. The male's mating call is enormously amplified by an inflated throat sack, which looks very much like a bubble-gum bubble. It's only by following the sound that you have a chance of finding these tiny, shy creatures.

Catching a Tree Frog

In mating season, most likely April, as evening falls you will hear a chorus of peeping from every damp spot around. The sound is a high-pitched peep-peep-peep, and is coming from the throats of the male tree frogs. Take a flashlight and a jar with a lid and follow the sound. As with cricket hunting, your footsteps will temporarily make the tree frogs stop their peeping. They will start again if you stop

A fruit fly colony in a baby food jar.

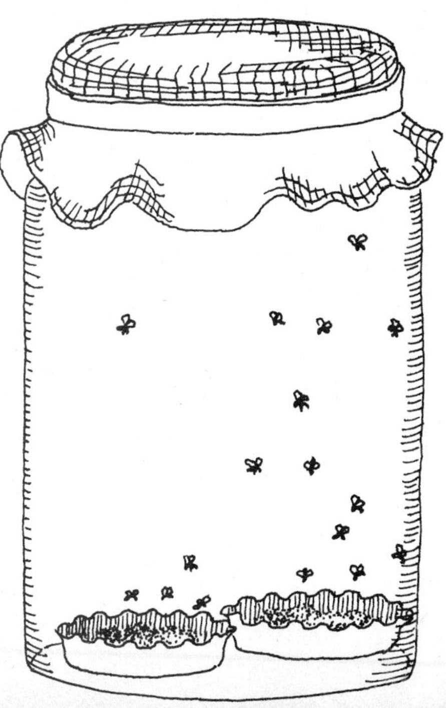

A fruit fly colony in a cloth-covered jar. Each bottle cap will contain eggs which hatch and grow into flies in the vivarium.

walking. When you're close to a particular peep-peep, turn on your flashlight and examine the tree trunks near you. Once you see a tree frog it is not hard to catch it in your hands. Transfer it to the jar and close the lid. Try to get your peeper into his vivarium soon so his breathing pores don't dry out.

Housing

Tree frogs would probably do best in one of the semi-aquatic vivariums suggested on page 319, but may also be kept in a moist, woodland vivarium. They can live with any of the salamanders. Add branches for the frogs to cling to.

A glass cover is absolutely necessary—tree frogs are acrobatic jumpers and climbers; their suction pads allow them to climb glass walls. If a tree frog escapes from its moist vivarium into the dry house air, it will surely die. Amphibians do much of their breathing through their moist skins. A dry frog suffocates. Toads are one of the few amphibians who can live in dry areas entirely by moistening their own breathing pores with mucus produced in the bumps or "warts" on their skin.

Other than water changes or filter cleaning in your semi-aquatic vivarium, the only maintenance is ventilating the vivarium by carefully removing the glass top and waving fresh air in every day. If you are using a woodland vivarium, mist once a week.

Food and Water

Feed tree frogs fruit flies, exactly as for small salamanders. If you can get a look at the frogs feeding, you'll notice they catch insects on the wing with their long, sticky tongues. Misting takes care of water requirements.

Hermit And Fiddler Crabs

Few crustaceans (lobsters, crabs, shrimp), have become popular as pets, but lately the hermit crab (or tree crab) has attracted so many admirers that a beauty contest is being held to choose Miss Crustacean U.S.A. It would seem hard to say one crab is more beautiful than another, but with the hermit crab, the choice is possible. Although the creature itself is nothing much to look at, it clothes itself in a mollusk shell and becomes as lovely as the shell it chooses. One crab I know of lives in a Venetian pearl shell. Behind the hermit crab's hard-shelled head and claws, its body is completely soft. It is shaped in a spiral, twisted to fit snugly in a discarded mollusk shell. It can pull its body almost completely into this borrowed house, and it is probably the excellent protection the shell provides that has allowed several species of hermit crabs to leave the water and live on land. Some even climb trees, and are popularly known as tree crabs.

Fiddler crabs are less dramatic, but still satisfyingly peculiar. The males of this thumbnail-sized species have developed a super big claw—usually the right one—that they wave about comically both to entice females and to threaten other males. They scuttle on the beaches at low tide, picking up anything that might be edible, and waving frantically at real or imagined dangers. The sight of a tiny fiddler crab holding a cigarette butt aloft on a North Carolina beach is among my favorite memories.

Fiddler crabs are among those animals who have an incredible internal clock. For instance, they change colors—dark in the daytime and light at night—but they do it by the clock, regardless of how light or dark you make their quarters. In nature, they burrow into their holes during high tides and scramble out to look for food during low tides. Even when kept as pets thousands of miles from their native seashore, they still emerge from their burrows at low-tide time. Since low tides come at

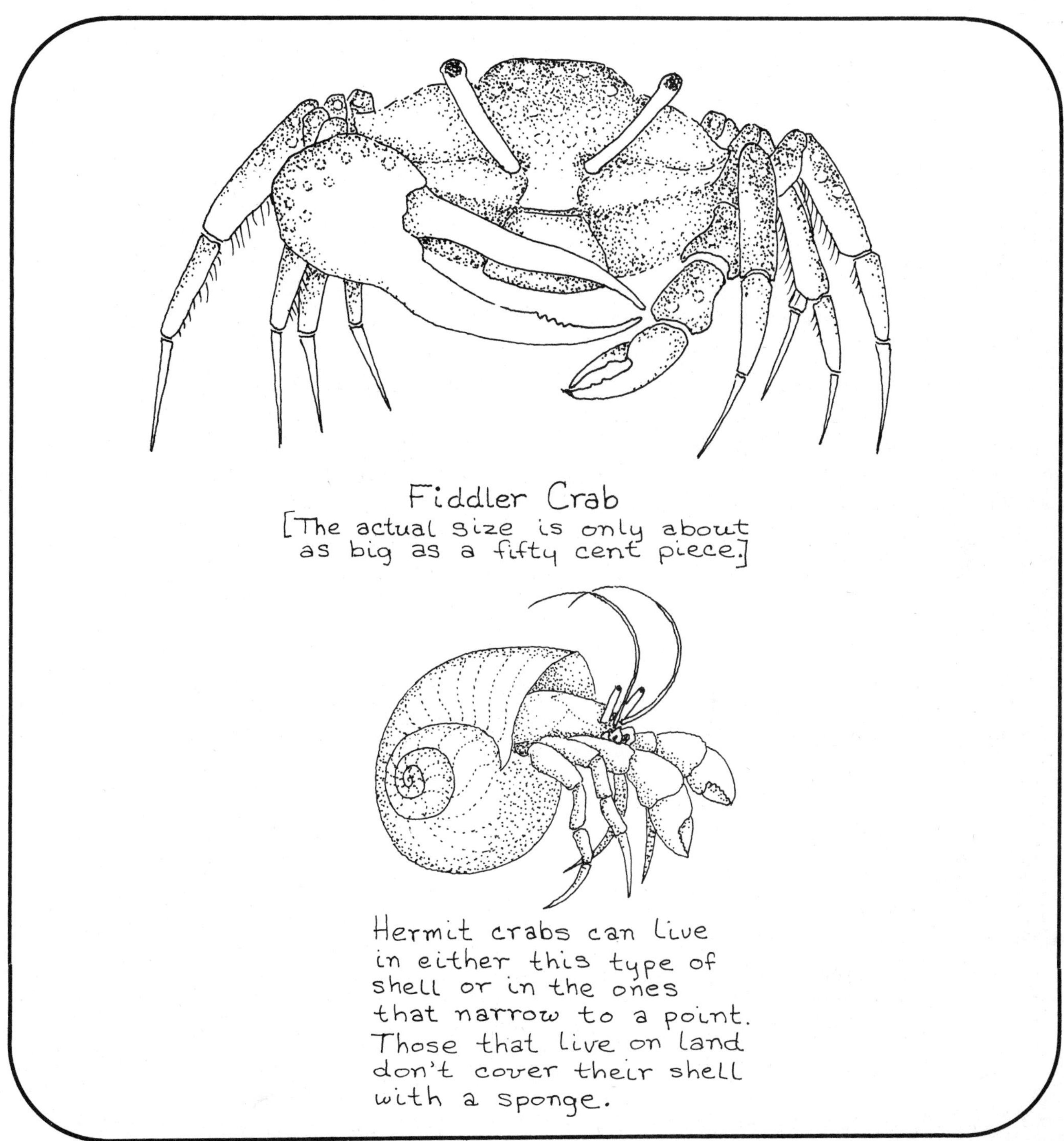

somewhat different times each day, this is a remarkable feat. Even more remarkable, you could live in Ohio and still know, by your fiddler-crab-clock, precisely when low tide is in the area where your pet was originally caught.

Choosing a Crab

Both crabs are quite common—hermit crabs along almost any shore, and fiddler crabs from temperate to tropical beaches. Both are also available in pet stores from time to time. Under the name of tree crabs, hermit crabs are often advertised in the mail-order section of magazines.

Housing

Hermit crabs must have an assortment of new

shells to choose from as their bodies grow. Depending on which species of hermit you have, the shells might be as small as little snail shells or as large as an orange. It is best to provide a whole pile of snail-shaped or pointy-shaped shells. Pet hermit crabs will fuss with this pile, pushing the shells here and there, trying this one and that one on for size.

These crabs enjoy climbing and would be happier with a wire-mesh cage, like the cake-pan cage on page 339 than with a tank. If you'd rather use a tank, provide large pieces of bark or a slanted surface of wire-mesh hardware cloth for climbing.

Fiddler crabs need moist sand in which to live and dig their burrows. Use a 5½-gallon tank, filled with at least six inches of sand to provide enough digging space. In nature, burrows may be as much as a foot deep. Keep the sand moist—about the consistency of seashores after the tide has gone out. Don't flood the sand, since fiddler crabs are air-breathing and can drown.

For either pet, be sure to use a cover—the cake pan, or a screen top to fit the tank. Sink a small water dish into the sand for drinking water. The top of a glass preserving jar would be about the right size.

Clean the cage of leftover foods every day, and refresh the water dish. Moisten the fiddler crab's sand as necessary.

The moist sand that the fiddler crab requires is somewhat difficult to keep clean. A safe routine would be to remove all the sand every month, rinse it well, and bake it in the oven at 300 degrees for at least an hour. The heat will kill bacteria and help prevent decay in the damp sand.

Food and Water

Like most crabs, both hermits and fiddlers are scavengers, which means they eat almost anything. Lettuce, spinach, seaweed or water plants provide their vegetable needs, but it is best to offer small bits of raw hamburger or raw fish—even dog or cat food—also. Cleanup is more of a problem with meat than with vegetables.

Both crabs need fresh water to drink, although the fiddler crab may satisfy at least part of its thirst by filtering water from the moist sand.

Straining pond water with sieves and nets.

Aquarium Pets

AQUARIUM PETS

Comet Goldfish

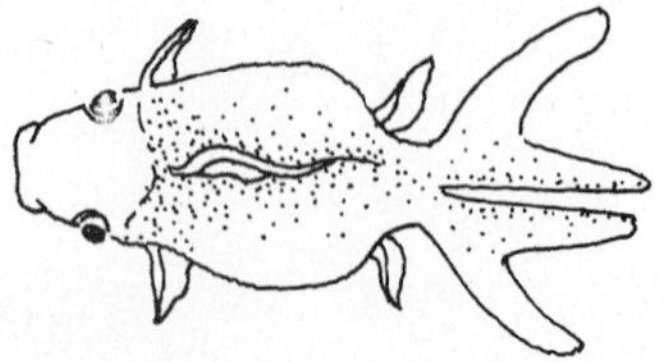

Fantail Goldfish

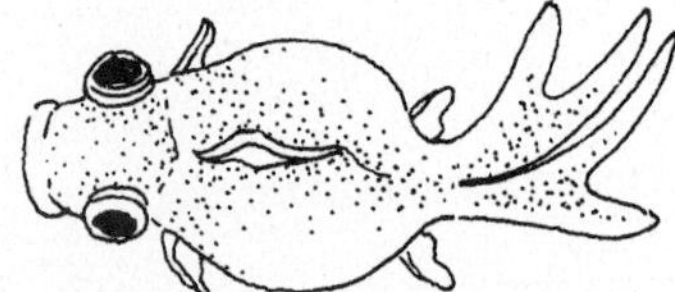

Black Moor Goldfish

GOLDFISH

Cost:
Comet goldfish
small/39¢ large/70¢
Fantail goldfish
small/49¢ large/$1.49
Black Moor goldfish
small/59¢ large/$2.00

Housing:
5½-gallon tank, filter system—$13.00
Or 10-gallon tank, filter system—$15.00
Optional gravel, plants—$2.00

Special Requirements:
None.

Diet:
Commercial granular or flake goldfish food—15¢ to 30¢ per week, depending on quality of food.
Optional supplement, lettuce, water plants, brine shrimp, Tubifex worms—10¢ per week.

Care:
Feed once or twice a day.
Clean filter box once a week.
Refresh water by siphoning four times a year.

Tamability:
Come for food at signal; may eat from fingers.

Life Span:
Three to four years average, but can be as long as 10 years.

COMMON GUPPIES

Cost:
70¢ a pair.

Housing:
5½-gallon tank, filter system—$13.00

Special Requirements:
None.

Diet:
Commercial granular or flake guppy food—10¢ to 30¢ per week depending on quality of food.
Optional supplement, brine shrimp and Tubifex worms—10¢ per week.
Gravel, plants—$2.00

Care:
Feed once or twice a day.
Clean filter box once a week.
Refresh water by siphoning four times a year.

Tamability:
Come for food at signal.

Life Span:
Two to three years.

WATER TURTLES

Cost:
$2.00.

Housing:
10-gallon tank, fluorescent light fixture—$27.00
Optional filter system—$5.00

Special Requirements:
Dry land area as well as deep water area, ultra-violet light.

Diet:
Commercial shrimp pellets or canned cat food—30¢ per week.
Supplement with calcium, raw fruits and vegetables, raw meat or earthworms.

Care:
Feed, clean up leftover foods daily.
Clean optional filter box weekly, or clean tank weekly.
Refresh water in filtered tank by siphoning four times a year.

Tamability:
Become calm, but don't enjoy handling. May come for food at signal.

Life Span:
Most baby turtles die within months from improper care. With good care, up to five years.

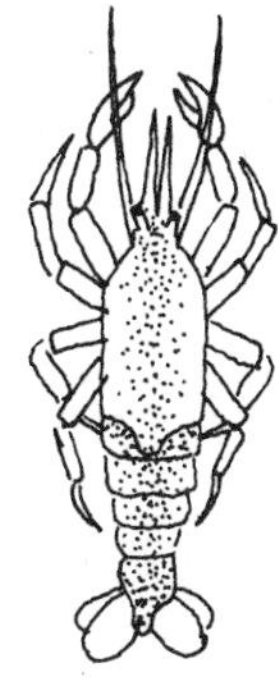

CRAYFISH

Cost:
$1.00.

Housing:
5½-gallon tank, filter system—$13.00
Optional gravel, plants—$2.00

Special Requirements:
Rock to hide behind.

Diet:
Leftover vegetable and meat scraps (no cost).

Care:
Feed daily.
Clean filter box once a week.
Refresh water by siphoning four times a year.

Tamability:
Not tamable.

Life Span:
Five years.

TADPOLES

Cost:
50¢ for bullfrog tadpole, or collect these or other tadpoles in wild.

Housing:
5½-gallon tank, filter system—$13.00
Optional gravel, plants—$2.00

Special Requirements:
None.

Diet:
Leftover salad greens, raw meat scraps (no cost).

Care:
Feed daily.
Clean filter once a week.
Refresh water by siphoning four times a year.

Tamability:
Not tamable.

Life Span:
Become frogs within weeks, or in the case of bullfrogs, one to two years.

WATER SNAILS

Cost:
50¢ to 75¢, depending on size, or collect in wild.

Housing:
5½-gallon tank $8.00
Optional gravel—$1.00
Water plants—50¢ to $1.00

Special Requirements:
None.

Diet:
Algae that forms on tank walls (no cost), or water plants—6¢ per week.

Care:
Supply fresh-water plants several times a year if no algae in tank.
Refresh water by siphoning four times a year.

Tamability:
Not tamable.

Life Span:
Three to four years.

Water pets live in aquatic vivariums called aquariums. A few of these water pets are in-between pets. A turtle can swim in a semi-aquatic vivarium as easily as it can swim in an aquarium. A red eft will eventually leave the land and take to the water, just as a tadpole will eventually leave the water and take to the land.

Ideally, almost all the characters in this chapter can fit into a single tank. A large goldfish, a small turtle, a couple of bullfrog tadpoles, a garbage-collecting crayfish, and an algae-eating snail can live together in an aquarium just as they might share a small pond in nature. You might give yourself still more pleasure by letting a whirligig beetle or a water strider skim across the water. These insects aren't exactly pets: you can't feed them their natural food and they may eventually get eaten by an enterprising goldfish. But here we have a fish (a goldfish or a guppy), a reptile (a turtle), an amphibian (a tadpole or a salamander), a crustacean (a crayfish), and a mollusk (a snail). Might as well add an insect too.

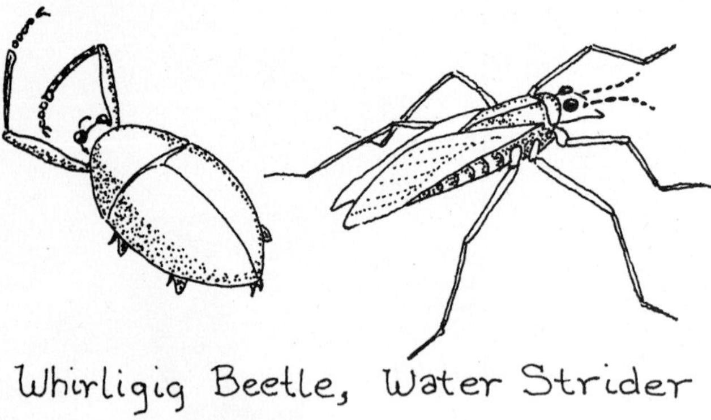

Whirligig Beetle, Water Strider

Fish Facts

Since you can't climb into an aquarium to make friends with a fish, you have to be content with what contact can exist between you from either side of a glass wall or a watery surface. Most of the time that means just watching. Some of the things a fish does—those constant gulping motions, for instance—may look inane to us, but they have a purpose. Other things a fish does are remarkable but unnoticed—not slamming into rocks in the dark, for instance. Watching is more fun when you know a little more about fish.

Fish gulp all the time because that's how they breathe. The gulped water is pushed from their mouths out through their gills (the flapped slits just behind the fish's head), where tiny blood vessels absorb dissolved oxygen from the water. The water is then flapped back out by the gill flap, and the next gulp of fresh water pushed in. Goldfish are among the fish that can survive in stagnant water low in oxygen. They can gulp air directly. When you see your goldfish coming to gulp at the top of the tank at other than feeding times, it is gulping air to push through its gills. Goldfish normally breathe that way some of the time, but if they start to do it often, your water may be too low in oxygen. Check your filter to be sure bubbles are coming from it, or get a stronger pump. More likely than filter problems, it may be time to replenish the water (page 328).

Goldfish are quite nearsighted but they possibly can see colors. Fish as a whole don't hear sound waves very well but they can feel vibrations keenly. When you tap on a tank the vibrations hit the fish like shock waves. The shock makes it acutely nervous and uncomfortable. Don't tap fish tanks. A fish can smell with pits that look like nostrils on its snout. More marvelous is the fish's sense of taste; it is located in taste buds similar to those on your tongue, but these may be scattered all over the fish's body. In other words, a fish can taste its dinner long before it gets into its mouth.

Beyond sight, hearing, touch, taste and smell, fish have a sixth sense which is almost beyond our ability to imagine. Look at the side of your goldfish. There is a line, called the lateral line, running the length of its body. Inside the line is a canal filled with fluid, connected by many other smaller canals to the fish's entire body surface. These canals sense the movement of the water. If water flow is interrupted by an obstacle—another fish, a rock, a bump in the mud—it bounces back, causing ripples. You can see the bounce-back ripples where water touches a rock, or when you toss a pebble into the water. The same movements exist underwater. Fish can read the complicated patterns set up by both bottom contours and the movements of other creatures. They can feel the shape of the water around them. Even in pitch-black darkness or muddy waters, fish don't bump into one another, or into rocks or plants or sand bars.

Breeders have changed the normal streamlined shape of goldfish; the fantails and Moors are not good examples of a fish built to swim fast. But using the kind of goldfish called the comet as an example, you can see that the narrow body, pointed toward the nose, is made to cut through water. Mucus glands under a fish's scales coat the body with a slippery substance that cuts down on friction.

A fish moves through water the same way a snake moves along the ground. Its body and tail curve to form a loop. The rear edge of the loop pushes against the water. The fish is pushed forward. You can see the way the movement works more easily in a snake, and even feel that backward push by putting your hand against the rear edge of a snake's loop. The fish moves so fast it's hard to see.

A goldfish's top (dorsal) fin helps to hold it upright. You can see how this works by holding your hand flat (and perpendicular to the floor) in the water like a fish. It's hard to tip your hand sideways, easy to wiggle it forward. When a goldfish is swimming slowly, it raises its top fin to keep from tipping. Its side fins move about to stabilize the fish too. But when it swims fast, the fish folds its top fin down to streamline itself. It keeps its side-fins tucked flat too, except to help it when it needs to change direction or put on the brakes.

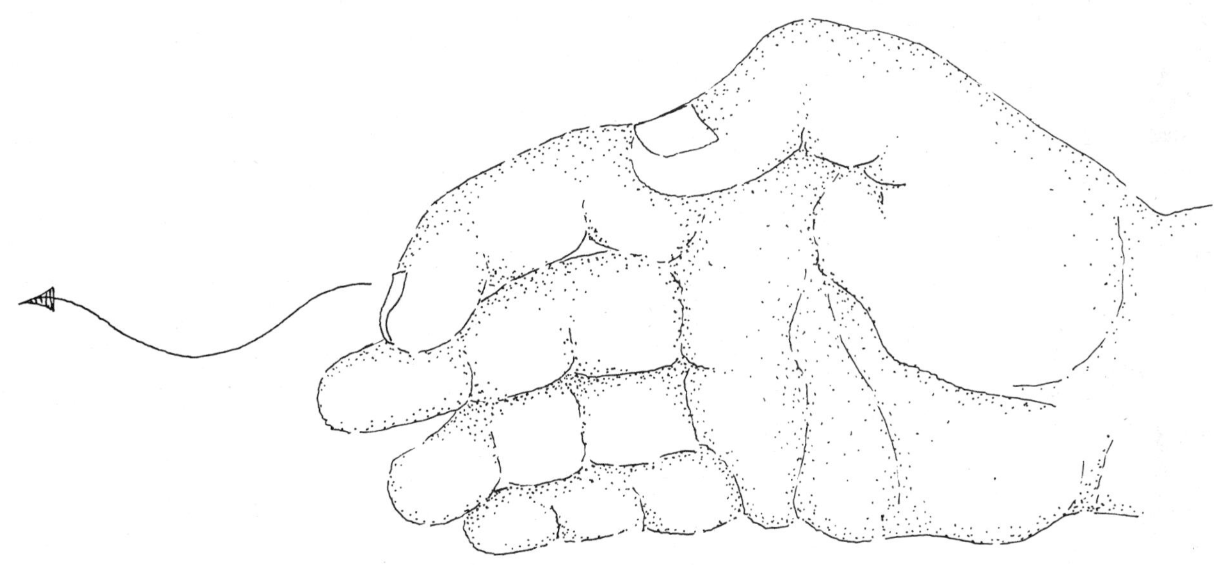

This is how to swim your hand like a fish.

Swim Bladder

You don't see fish having trouble staying near the bottom or top of the tank. They don't fall to the bottom as you do after a jump, or float to the top as you do after a dive. Fish have a swim bladder inside their bodies that constantly adjusts their buoyancy. You can fool around with a plastic bottle in a bathtub to see the way the air-filled swim bladder works.

Fill the bottle two-thirds full of water and screw the top on. The bottle is the fish, the air the swim bladder. If the bottle floats to the top, add some water. If it sinks to the bottom, pour a little water out. Keep adjusting the air until the bottle floats submerged. That's the condition of a fish. If it needs to float higher, it will take more air into its swim bladder to decrease its density. If it wants to float lower,

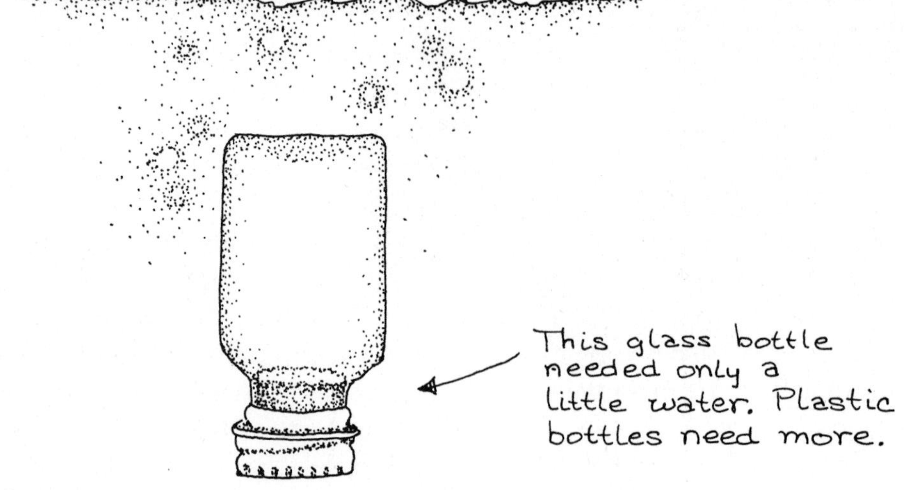

A bottle will float under the water like a fish if you carefully adjust its weight by adding water.

it will let air out to increase its density. Balloonists and submariners maneuver up and down the same way.

It was the swim bladder, by the way, that ultimately allowed the first fish to leave the water. The air-containing bladder evolved over millions of years into lungs. The lungfish that still exist today use lungs instead of gills, coming up to the top of the water to breathe.

Some species are born with gills but lose them entirely, just as many salamanders do. The mudskipper is a fish who not only breathes through lungs but also climbs mangrove trees along the shore to hunt for insects. It lives in mangrove swamps in the Pacific, and in Asia in the Indian Ocean, leaving the water for hours at a time to climb trees with its limblike front fins. A naturalist has told me how he can never get used to coming to a swampy shore and startling dozens of fish who drop from the trees with a splash back into the water's safety.

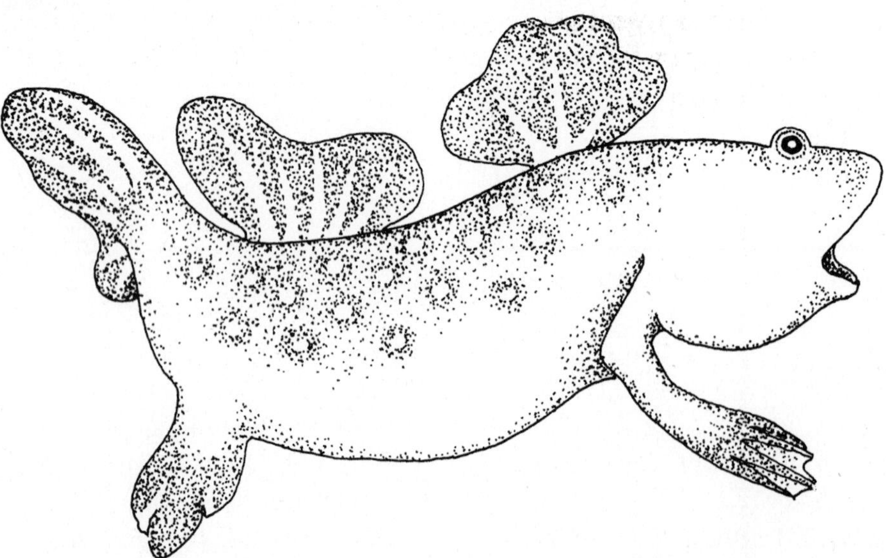

Fish that can walk on land like the mudskipper and this relative, the mudhopper, look like a cross between a fish and a salamander.

Goldfish

The goldfish was bred from the common carp of Asia long ago. The whole carp family is hardy and adaptable, and the goldfish can live a long life — up to 50 years—in captivity. Although most goldfish no longer resemble the bulky, brown, bewhiskered carp, one large Japanese breed, the koi, has kept the typical carp whiskers and can live year-round in outdoor pools.

Choosing a Goldfish

There are several types of goldfish to choose from. The common goldfish, the 39¢ variety, is the comet. It is pleasingly plain: fish-mouthed, fish-shaped, and fish-tailed. The next fancier model is the fantail, who is sometimes called a veiltail. This is actually a two-tailed fish, the result of a mutation. In the best specimens, the two tails grow to be four or five inches long. Fantails have a shorter, plumper body than comets. Between their fat bellies and their waving tails, they swim rather clumsily.

Both the comet and the fantail goldfish come in common gold, a rare silver color, orange, red, white, black, and speckled or spotted combinations of any of these colors. When goldfish are speckled and splotched in orange, white and black, they are called calicos.

The grumpy (or sometimes sad) look of the black Moor goldfish appeals to me most of all. These fat, goggle-eyed fan-tailed creatures come only in black, but the black may look metallic and lightens to a golden gleam along the belly. In a tank of goldfish, black Moors definitely act more curious and aggressive than other types.

There are still fancier breeds of goldfish—the bumpy-headed lionhead, the bubble-eyed celestials. Both are gargoyle grotesques, and both need heated tanks. They are fancy-looking but not too hardy.

Unless a fish is nearly dying, it's difficult to tell whether it is healthy or not. When you go to buy fish, look first at the condition of the tank as a whole. If dead fish are floating about, or if the tank looks dirty, don't buy fish from that tank.

After the tank checkup, pick out the individual fish you like. Larger fish are hardier than smaller fish. Look at the fins and tail for signs of splitting or shredding. Check that the scales look smooth—no injuries, no junky white patches. Watch how it swims—not tilted, not head downward, not noticeably slower than other fish. Memorize how the fish looks so that when the clerk is standing by, net in hand, you don't have to go through the choosing all over again.

Your fish will be handed to you in a plastic bag, usually about one-third filled with water, and either tied at the top or held with a rubber band. The air in the bag will only last the fish about an hour, after which it will slowly start to suffocate. If you are buying several fish, ask for separate bags so each gets more air. Get home within a half-hour.

Do not dump your fish into the prepared tank immediately upon getting home. Put the whole sealed bag in the tank and let it float there for a half-hour. There is always some temperature difference between the water in the bag and the water in your tank. Floating the bag brings the water there to the same temperature as the tank, giving the fish time to get used to it. After the half-hour, cut the bag open and let the fish swim out.

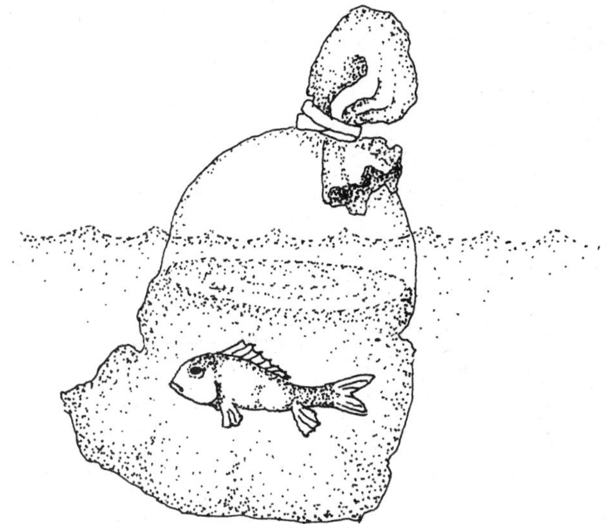

Floating the fish in its bag to let it adjust to the water temperature in the tank.

How To Net a Fish

There are times you'll need to move your fish. You may want to get it into a larger tank, take it to school for a day, or get it out of the way while you clean the tank or change the landscape.

Before you net a fish, fill a jar with water from the fish's tank. Use the square-shaped net sold in pet stores. Don't chase the fish with it. It swims faster than you can maneuver the net. It also gets panicky and can hit its head on the glass wall. Fish react less nervously to a potential enemy who approaches from underneath rather than from behind, so move the net slowly until it is under the fish. Then just raise it to the surface. As you lift the net above the water, close the net above the fish with your other hand so it can't leap out. Turn the net upside-down over the mouth of the jar and release your hand so the fish drops out.

When you put your fish back into a tank, remember to float the jar (a jar one-third full of water will float upright) for a half-hour before releasing the fish into the tank.

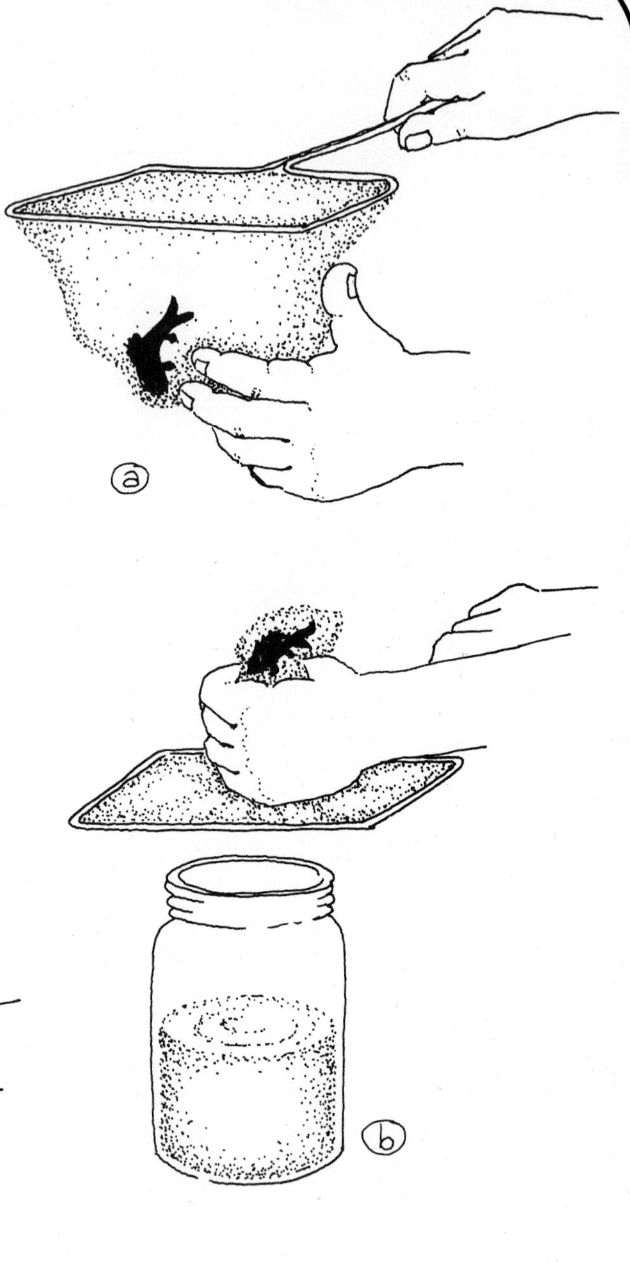

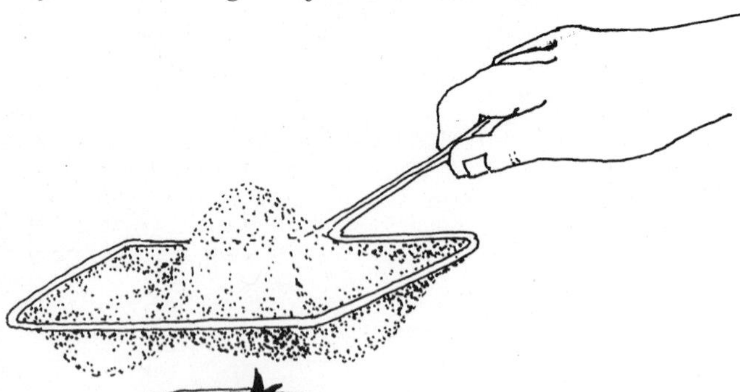

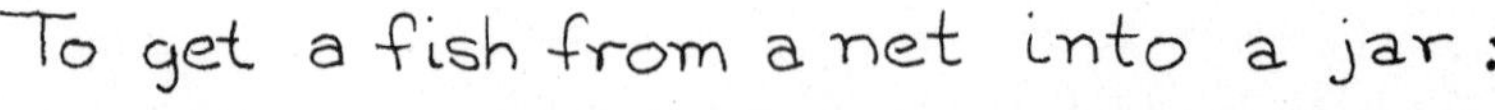

ⓐ Hold the net closed above the fish
ⓑ Turn the net upside down over the jar
ⓒ Let the fish drop into the jar.

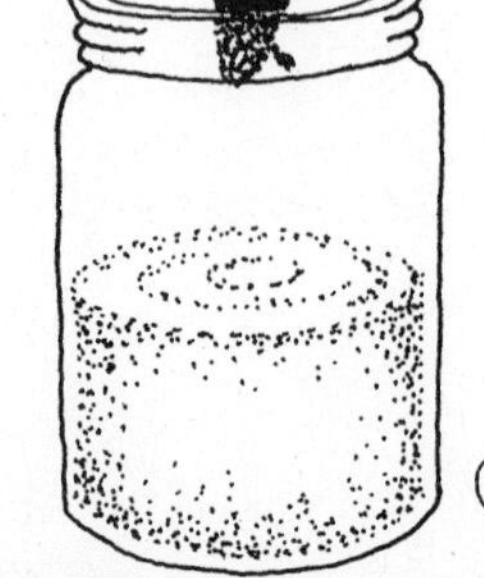

Goldfish are interesting to watch and make unobtrusive pets.

Housing

Before you bring a fish home you'll have to set up a tank for it to live in. Find a place for the tank that doesn't vary much in temperature—no sun, no drafts from cold windows, no air conditioning that will be turned on and off, not too close to heaters either. If you don't already have a tank set up, get it ready two days before you get the fish so that the water can get to room temperature. Although goldfish can deal with warm or cool water, like all fish they are cold-blooded. They have no way to regulate their internal temperature. As the water around them warms up or cools down, their body takes a while to adjust to the change. If the change is fast, they can't keep up. Fast temperature changes have killed millions of pet goldfish.

Fishbowls, the traditional home of fictional and cartoon fish, can be fish killers. The round shape with its narrow top and small opening provides very little water surface. It is at the surface that air comes into contact with the water, allowing oxygen

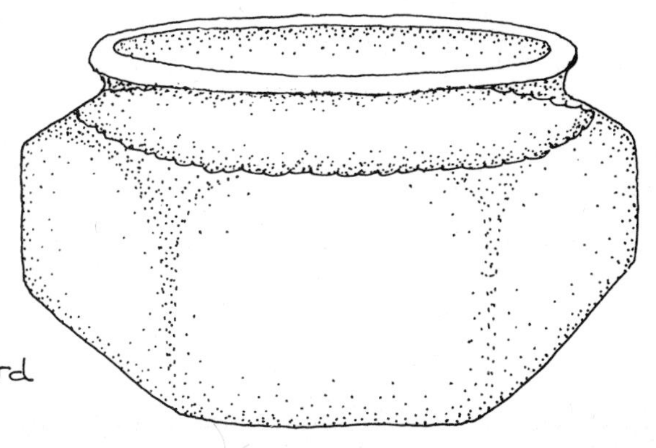

from the air to dissolve into it. The greater the surface in relation to the total amount of water, the more dissolved oxygen is available for fish to breathe. Even though stagnant-water fish like goldfish are able to gulp air directly at the water surface, this is designed as an emergency measure, not a way of life. Fish in round fishbowls slowly suffocate to death. One type of fishbowl is flat and circular with a surface broad enough to provide oxygen, but it is hard to see the fish except from directly overhead. Ordinary tanks may not be as appealing as bowls, but they are best for viewing, and for health.

The basic aquarium set-up on page 323 is fine for goldfish. A 5½-gallon tank is too small for more than one or two baby (two- to three-inch) goldfish. A 10-gallon tank can hold a half-dozen small fish. But none of the six will grow much. To grow a nice big healthy pet, plan to have only one or two fish for a 10-gallon tank. When they are between four and five inches long, they should go into an 18- or 20-gallon tank. True, the fish will look rather small in there at first, but the extra swimming will increase their appetite and the fish can grow to their dramatic maximum of seven inches—not counting the tail.

Do not use glass gravel in your aquarium. Goldfish pick up gravel as they search for leftover food. The glass gravel cuts their mouths.

The only other adjustment that need be made to the basic aquarium set-up is to not include the more tender plants (see page 326). Goldfish eat plants. The commonest plants, anachris (elodea) and cabomba, will be a total loss. Tough varieties like creeping Charlie, Brazilian sword, and banana plants are not so delicious.

Follow cleaning procedures on page 328 to keep your tank in top condition.

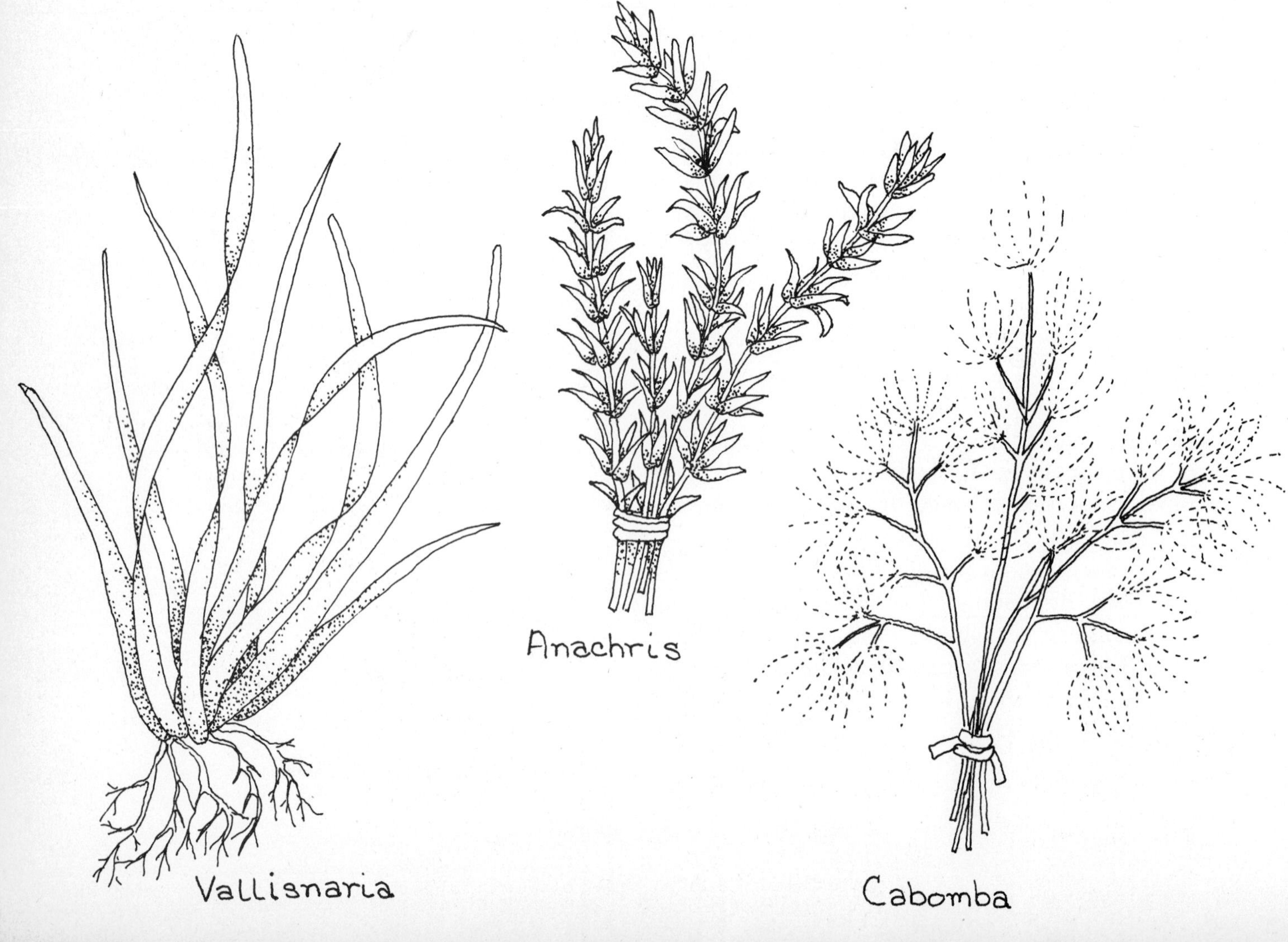

Food

Goldfish eat both meat and vegetables. Dried goldfish food, sold either in grains or flakes, contains such goodies as shrimp and flies, along with dried vegetables, grains, and the same soybean additive that has worked its way into so many human foods. For goldfish over four inches, the same food comes in small pellets. The pellets make bigger mouthfuls for bigger mouths.

Nutritionally, dried food is adequate but rather a bore. Not being fish ourselves, we don't know for sure that they feel emotions, but a goldfish encountering live prey seems to act idiotically happy. The most convenient live prey are brine shrimp. They are a tiny salt-water crustacean sold live in pet stores (they come in a cup of salty water). To feed brine shrimp to your fish, catch a few shrimp in a fish net, then dump them in the tank. This avoids getting salt water in a fresh-water tank, which can be dangerous. The rest of the brine shrimp can be kept in their container of salt water in the refrigerator, where they will live for a week or more.

Another live food available in pet stores is the Tubifex worm, which also lives in salt water but is an inch or more long. A three- or four-inch goldfish would relish a whole worm. You may have to cut the worm up for baby fish.

In the summer, experiment with insects you find. A fly, ant or inchworm can be placed on top of the water. Try spiders too, and small earthworms or big ones cut to suit. Once you have a goldfish eating from your fingers like Big Al, our pet, you could try bits of raw hamburger too. Less reliable eaters might leave the meat to rot in the bottom of the tank.

As for vegetables, buy tender anachris plants: they are an all-time goldfish favorite. Keep them growing in a big jar full of water. Feed your

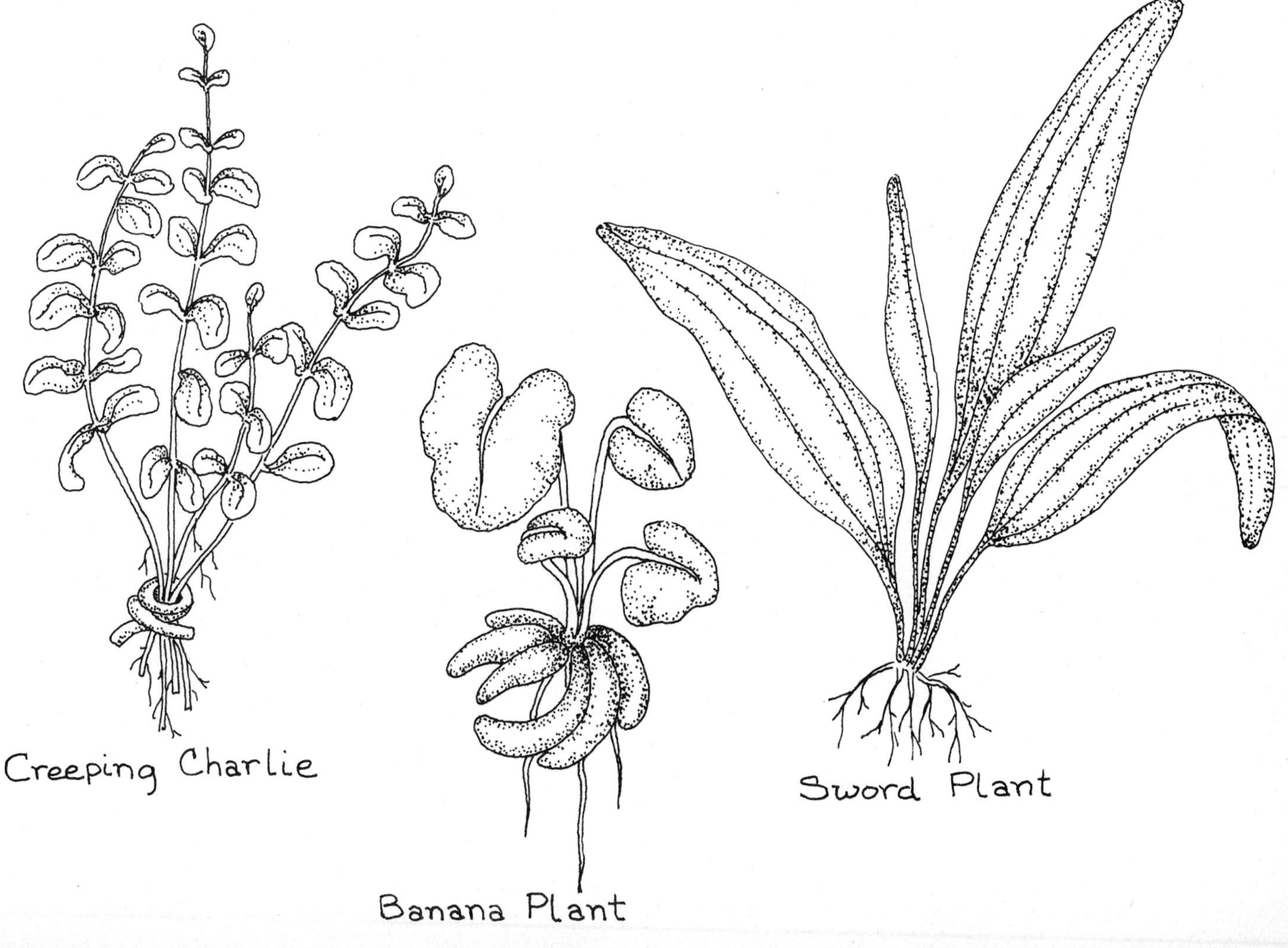

goldfish a sprig a week. Take the stem from the water after the leaves are nibbled off. Lettuce is often eaten too, but try to remove uneaten bits before they start decaying.

Since a pet goldfish acts so enthusiastic about its dinner, you'll tend to feed it too much and too often. Overfeeding kills goldfish, but not because they overeat. Although goldfish scrounge about looking for in-between-meal leftovers, any stomach has its limits. The food they can't eat sinks to the bottom and begins to decay. The decaying process requires oxygen, the same oxygen your fish needs to breathe. If your fish doesn't die from bacteria that reproduce in decaying matter, it may slowly die of suffocation.

Put only a few flakes or grains of food in the tank at a time. Watch to see that they are all eaten, then add a few more. When your fish isn't eating anymore, it's had enough. This is the best way to tell how much to feed your fish. If you decide to feed your fish twice a day, judge the amounts needed at each mealtime the same way.

Aquaria Planaria

If you have too little space for an aquarium, but still want a water pet, you can keep planaria. Planaria are tiny flat worms that live in ponds and streams everywhere. Look for them on the undersides of rocks.

When you look closely, planaria seem to be cross-eyed. The outside edge of the "eye" is really only a slight depression in the worm's head. The cross-eyed "pupils" are small spots of light-sensitive pigment—too simple an arrangement to be called an eye at all.

Keep planaria in fresh water in any sort of jar lid or in a glass cup. Be sure not to let the water evaporate entirely. Feed the worms a few times a week with a crumb of raw hamburger or other raw meat.

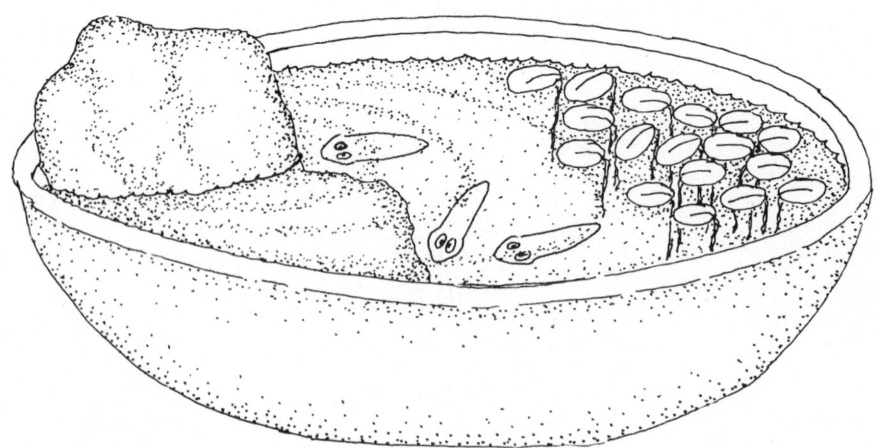

The actual size of a planarium is 1/4 inch or less. These three are at home in a glass preserving jar top decorated with a stone and the tiny leaves of duckweed. Duckweed grows wild on ponds in most of the country.

Illnesses

Fish sicknesses tend to be unpleasant to see. Two common ones are tail rot, in which tail and fins begin to shred and fall apart, and ich, which sounds like what it is—icky white fungal patches that form on the fish's body. Both of these, and many other fish diseases, are cured by patent medicines sold in pet stores.

Unfortunately, many other fish disorders are not visible. By the time the fish begins to keel over on its side, skulk at the bottom, or trail long threads of excreta behind, it may be too late to save it. When it is obvious that a fish is sick, get it out of the tank and into a jar fast. That just might save your other fish, if you have any, from infection. Then find out what you can from the pet store. Better yet, ask a neighbor who is a tropical-fish collector. He is likely to know more. Do whatever is suggested, but be prepared for the fish to die.

Once something is wrong with a fish, be hard on yourself about the condition of the tank. Check to see that it is clean and the filter is working properly. Test the water temperature and quality: when did you last add in some fresh water? As a last resort, empty the whole tank, wash it with salt, rinse it, and leave it to dry for a week. Then begin all over.

Meet Big Al

Big Al is our six-inch comet goldfish. We trained him to eat from our fingers and here's the method we used: we fed Big Al at the same times every day and in the same spot. Before dropping the food, we tickled the water with our fingers. Within a week, the tickle brought him dashing to the surface, mouth gaping. It was only another week until we could drop a food pellet directly into his greedy maw.

Then Al made up his own trick. His small fish brain made the connection between the humans on the other side of the glass and mealtime. As he became hungry, he moved to a front corner of his tank. There he did an agitated dance, made up of jerking, grouchy-looking dashes back and forth. The constant motion drove us crazy, so of course we fed him. He is no longer a mere fish; Big Al is a pet.

Guppies

Guppies are my only concession to tropical fish—and I'm not going to go into the fancy guppies that need heated tanks. Tropical fish are usually beautiful, but I consider them collector's items, not pets.

Common guppies are fun to have around because they are forever mating and having babies. Fish babies are called fry, as in "small fry." With the proper set-up, you can achieve a natural fish population that will survive for many generations. Guppies can live in the same tank with any of the creatures in this chapter except for larger goldfish, who occasionally eat small fish.

Choosing Guppies

A single guppy is too inconspicuous to bother with. Neither male nor female grow to much longer than an inch and a half. Start with a pair. The female has a plump belly, with a small black spot towards its rear. The black spot (a "gravid" spot) is actually a bunch of eggs and will eventually be a bunch of babies (see Breeding). The male's body is slimmer and smaller, although longer in the tail, and often marked with very bright spots of orange, red, green or blue. In a typical tank of mature guppies, many of the females are already pregnant. To speed things up, choose a large female with a large spot. Obviously, choose the prettiest male you can.

Housing

Guppies are less tolerant of low temperatures than goldfish. It might be helpful to keep a thermometer in the basic aquarium (page 324) so you can check that the water doesn't get below 60 degrees on winter nights. If there is no such place in your house, use the incandescent lamp suggested for desert vivariums on page 316. If algae is encouraged to grow by the extra light, take it out and heat the tank with an aquarium heater and thermostat

from a pet store (see page 327).

To establish a natural environment in which a proportion of guppy fry survive to adulthood, you have to provide hiding places. An area of thickly planted grass like Vallisnaria should do the trick. A few rocks surrounding the planted area will darken it for even better hiding.

Food

Feed guppies once or twice a day, using the same technique suggested for goldfish to avoid overfeeding (see page 102).Guppies eat more of a meat diet than goldfish, so you can't use the same food for both. Guppy food is dried insects, shrimp and so on, plus some cereals. It comes in flakes or grains, both sized smaller than goldfish food. When fry are born, an even finer, almost powdery food must be fed to them until their mouths grow large enough for adult food. You can try newly hatched brine shrimp for guppies, or cut up Tubifex worms. Both are appreciated and nutritious. Gup-

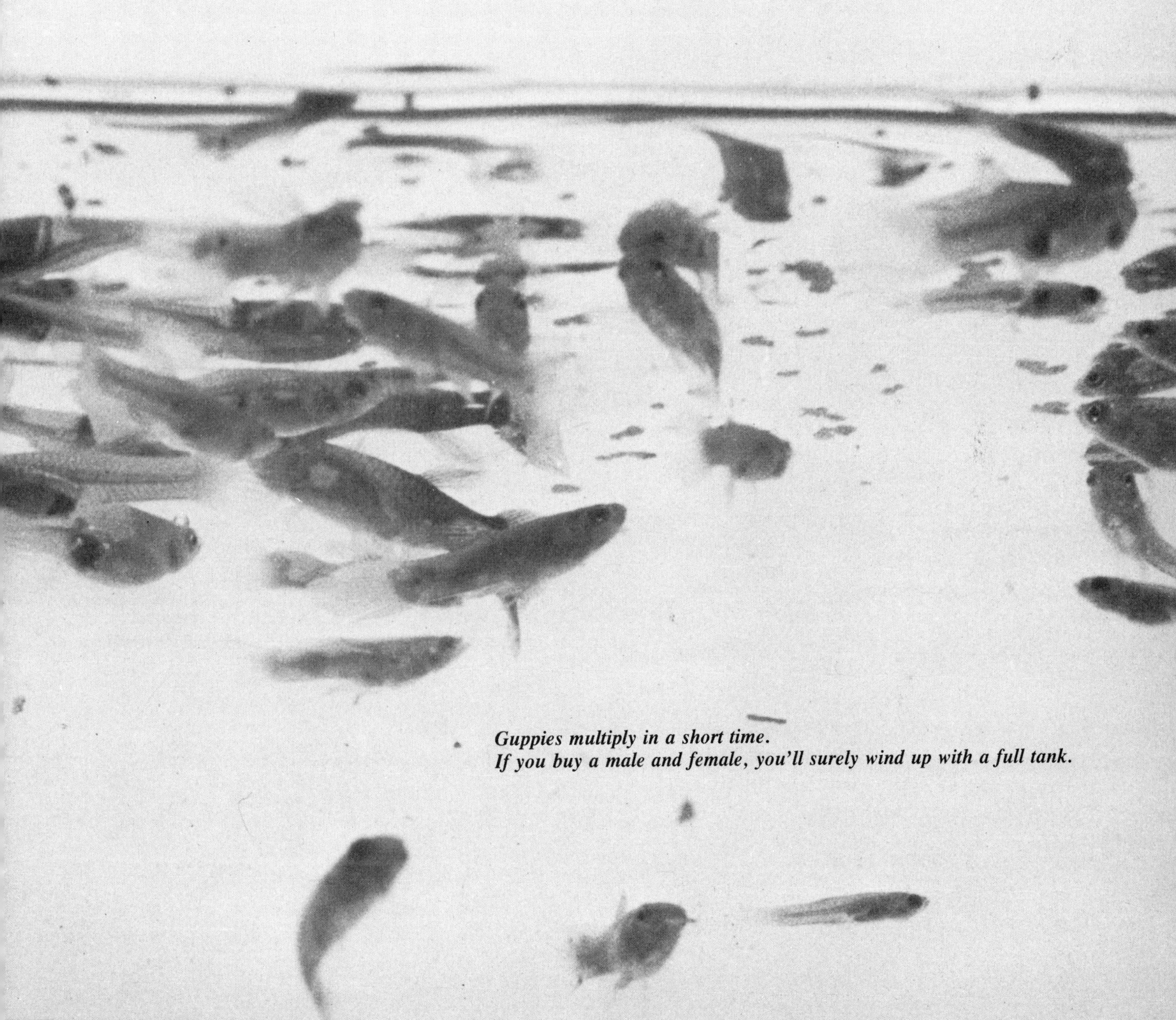

Guppies multiply in a short time.
If you buy a male and female, you'll surely wind up with a full tank.

pies don't bother much with vegetables.

Breeding

Male guppies pursue female guppies relentlessly. They vibrate their bodies to get attention, and even back up toward the female to show off their pretty tail spots. When the female allows it, mating is achieved through a long organ called a gonopodium. You can see the male's gonopodium trailing along under his body, an almost transparent tube one half inch long or longer. The sperm (male reproductive calls) are ejected through the gonopodium.

Unlike many other fish who fertilize (unite their sperm with) the female's eggs after they are laid in the water, guppies fertilize the eggs inside the female's body. She doesn't use all the sperm the male has put inside her at once. Once fertilized, she can produce a batch of fry every month for the next four months, doling out stored sperm as needed. The eggs develop into fry completely inside the female's body. As her gravid spot grows larger, look at it carefully through her transparent belly. You can see the tiny gleaming eyes of the fry staring out at you.

By the last day or so of her one-month pregnancy, the female begins to spend much of her time areas in which to give birth. She will prefer the planted area for the big event.

Each fry is expelled within its own transparent bubblelike membrane. The bubble seems to pop out of the mother's belly. Within seconds, the fry has stretched its body, broken the bubble and swum off among the plants.

Depositing her fry in a reasonably safe area is the mother guppy's last responsibility toward the next generation. Once born, the fry are considered food by their parents. Both will gulp them down for breakfast, lunch and dinner. Nevertheless, in a heavily planted aquarium enough will survive to assure future generations.

If cannibalism is too much for you, net the parents and get them into another tank within minutes of the birth in order to save all the fry. Of course, eventually you will face the same predicament over and over again. The chore of separating the sexes is difficult and the fry may mate before you can tell male from female. It may be better to leave their fate to nature.

As time goes on, the females will have fewer babies (see Box). Smaller fry will be eaten, larger ones will survive. In general the guppies will be smaller as adults and will take longer to become sexually mature. Finally you will have a rather natural fish population which can go on and on.

Make Room for Guppies

Nature has devised automatic birth control—it is possible for the first group of guppy fry to be as many as 50 or 60. As normal crowding occurs, the number of fry per birth will be reduced to a couple of dozen. As the environment changes with crowding—less food, less oxygen, fewer private places to give birth—hormones in many fish cause fewer eggs to ripen, or cause the body to reabsorb eggs or even to abort.

In guppies, another effect of crowding is that most—even all—the babies will be female. The scarcity of males is still another form of natural birth control. How the sex of babies is controlled is another mystery science will answer some day.

Turtles

Scientists don't distinguish between turtles and tortoises, but other people think that tortoises are land animals, whereas turtles must live where they can get into the water. Like the land tortoises in the previous chapter, the water turtles are temporarily difficult to come by because they can be carriers of salmonella, an intestinal illness that causes diarrhea. Hatchling turtles found in pet shops now are checked by the Department of Health. They are most likely the red-eared turtles (so called because of red markings on either side of their heads), bred on turtle farms for the pet market.

Other turtles you might find in a pet store are the painted turtle, with a red to yellow stripe down its black carapace, or the more rough-shelled green-backed cooter turtle. Both these turtles are caught in the wild, so there is the chance that you too might find one. These three common American turtles live primarily in the water.

In the spring and summer you often find turtles ambling across a road near water. They are usually water turtles out for a walk or heating and sunning themselves on the hot black macadam road. More than likely the turtles are moving from their usual pond to a different one to find a mate or to lay eggs. These short migrations help spread the turtle population. Help a turtle across the street if you wish, but don't take it home as a pet unless it is under five inches or you have a 50-gallon tank. These water turtles need swimming space. Your pet store turtle will too if it lives long and grows that big.

Choosing a Turtle

Hatchlings, up to a month old and usually from one to two inches, have an incredibly high mortality rate in captivity. So the bigger the baby you can find, the better off you are.

Squeeze the shell of the turtle between your thumb and finger, especially the rear portion. If the shell is soft, the baby is already suffering from malnutrition. Look at the turtle's eyes. Puffy eyelids, which are quite easy to notice because they are pale and partly or completely cover the turtle's otherwise round eye, mean eye infection. Look at the skin on the legs and neck. White patches are a fungal infection.

Look for a turtle who is moving about quickly and swimming well. Turtles who have been kept too cool are sluggish, and sluggish turtles can't digest their food. Buying a pet who suffers from indigestion is at the least a bad start, and sometimes fatal.

The sex of your turtle is unimportant, since you won't be able to breed it. Breeders breed outdoors, on ponds with either sandy or leafy shores and plenty of good nesting sites.

Housing

The basic aquarium on page 323 can be adapted for a turtle home by adding a dry land area to the water environment. Lower the water level a few inches so the turtle can't climb out of the top of the tank, and float a raft on the water for the turtle to climb up on. The raft can be made of a piece of thick cork or cork bark. Some florists keep cork bark around for training plants on; some home-decorating centers might give you a sample of the thick rough cork used to cover walls. If you can't get cork, look for a fireplace log. A rounded section of log with the bark still on can be cut to the tank's width for an adequate land area. Logs don't float as well as cork. Cut accurately so you can jam the raft against the tank sides to hold it in place.

Using shallow water and the smallest size corner filter there is another way to make a land area. Fill the tank to just above the top of the filter. Find a large smooth stone with sloping sides that will stick out from the water. The smoothness is important. Turtle shells are more tender than they look and turtles can develop sores from scraping against rough stones or bricks. The slope is important too. Turtles are rather clumsy climbers.

Other part-land, part-water environments are the

semi-aquatic vivariums on page 319.

Whatever land area you devise, it should be dry. Turtles may love the water, but they must dry off completely between swims to kill fungus growth. Turtles will come up onto the land area for hours to dry, warm up, and bask in artificial sunlight.

Use the fluorescent Vita-Lite® bulb (page 316) for both a heating and a basking light. Turtles need ultra-violet rays for manufacturing vitamin D, and turtles need heat too. Like many reptiles, they are too slowed down by temperatures under 75 degrees to either eat or digest well. Keep the light on all day. During the night, you can let temperatures drop to 60 degrees or lower with no trouble.

The tank filter will keep the water reasonably clean. If the water does begin to smell or if you can see debris collecting at the bottom, siphon the water off (see page 328), wipe the tank well, and refill. Though not as effective as a filter, a bubble stone can be used if your water level is too low for a filter.

To save on tank space and to make a more lively world, you may want your turtle to share a tank with goldfish; you can do this. The deep-water tank arrangements won't bother the fish, and the light won't either. Be on the lookout for fish-chasing by your turtle—yours might enjoy teasing its tank mates. Also, calcium-containing materials necessary to your turtle's diet will kill goldfish. The problem is easily solved by feeding your turtle

Plaster of Paris Molds

Another method of giving calcium to turtles is to mix up some plaster of paris. Mix it with the recommended amount of water (found on the package) and let it harden in some sort of mold. This can be an ice-cream carton, a plastic bag or a hole you have scooped out of damp sand, as in the illustration. When hardened, the plaster can be sunk in the aquarium where turtles will nibble it as they wish. (If your turtle is sharing an aquarium with goldfish, don't use this method as a calcium supply.

Molding A Plaster Block In Sand

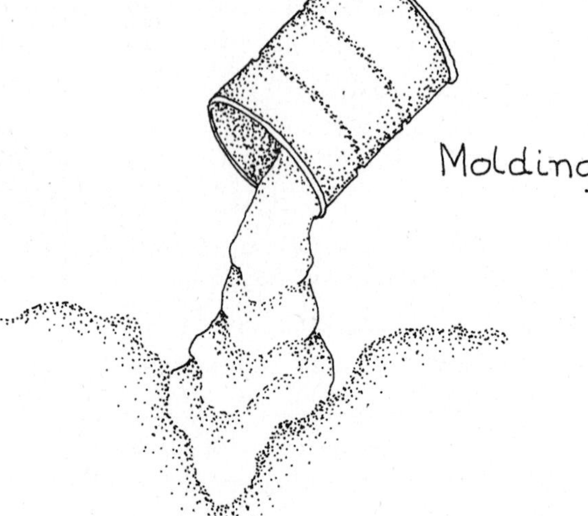

1. Mix plaster according to directions on package. Pour into a hole scooped in sand.

2. When plaster is cool and hard, lift from sand. Rinse before putting in turtle tank.

Water turtles have shiny shells when they are wet.

separately in a shallow bowl outside the tank. It only takes five to ten minutes for a turtle to finish its meal.

Food

Turtles are more or less scavengers. In ponds they eat water weeds, dead fish, live water snails, live insects, and whatever else comes along. In spite of the fact that pet stores may sell ant "eggs" (really pupas) or dried flies as turtle food, turtles can't survive on either.

Feed your pet on a dried or pellet food that is made of many different ingredients. Also offer it vegetables in the form of water plants like anachris, or romaine lettuce, raw spinach, or watercress. Try bits of fruit to see what happens. Chopped-up apple may work well. When you buy fish, cut off a shred or two and offer it raw. Do the same with raw chicken and raw beef, all in bite-sized bits. Turtles think earthworms are delicious too. All food must be fed to the turtle in the water; it is unable to swallow food on land.

Beside this delicatessen approach to mealtimes, turtles need additional calcium. Calcium deficiency is among the causes of soft shell, a killer disease of thousands of baby turtles. A turtle also needs extra calcium to continue growing its shell as its body gets larger.

Calcium comes in lots of forms: crushed oyster shell, sold at pet stores; powdered calcium carbonate, sold at drugstores; bone meal, sold at garden stores; or eggshells from the garbage pail. You can crush the eggshell with a hammer. Sprinkle calcium on the water surface once a week.

Turtles are as intelligent as fish—which is to say not very. The limit of their learning capacity may be the old come-for-your-dinner trick. A turtle is not shocked by tapping the way a fish is, so if your turtle doesn't share a tank with fish, you can rap on the tank edge to teach it to come for its food. Teach the trick by feeding at the same time and in the same place each day. First signal with a tap, then feed.

Illnesses

Most turtle problems arise because there's something wrong with food or housing.

Infected eyes are caused by bacteria that grow in dirty water. The eyelids swell and the turtle may not even be able to open them. Ask a vet for an antibiotic eye ointment. Put it on the turtle's eyes three times a day with the flat end of a toothpick. Carefully lift the upper lid first with the same dull toothpick end, because the ointment can't help if it's outside the eye. Don't expect the turtle to cooperate with the treatment. Grasp its head firmly from underneath with thumb and forefinger so it can't withdraw it into its shell. If it pops its head in the minute you touch it, turn it upside-down. This often makes a turtle put its head out in an effort to push itself upright again.

Fungal infections, white patches on the skin, happen when a turtle can't get itself dry. Perhaps its basking area is not really out of the water, or you have not used a Vita-Lite® bulb, or you have not been keeping it on all day. Mend your ways. Then buy an ich remedy from the pet store. It should be the kind that contains a dye called malachite green, the most effective fungal remedy in this case. Fix up a separate bath container in a bowl. Fill it with three cups of water, add several drops of ich remedy and a teaspoon of salt, mix well, and add the turtle. Let him soak there for 10 or 15 minutes twice a day. Make the bath solution fresh each time.

Respiratory infections look about the same in turtles as they do in us—runny or bubbly nose, noisy breathing (put your ear close to listen), no appetite, lots of snoozing. Even though you don't know whether your turtle has a virus cold that antibiotics won't help or a bacterial pneumonia that antibiotics will help, use antibiotics. The antibiotic tablets sold for birds work well on reptiles. The tablet is dissolved in water according to the proportions recommended for birds on the package. The turtle has to live in the medicated water for the next week, or until he gets better. But once the antibiotic is dissolved in water, it only stays active for about a day. The solution has to be made fresh each morning. It will waste less antibiotic to set up a small bowl to use as a hospital, complete with a land area and a light.

The "hospital" should be kept at 80 or 85 degrees. The same tank light you've been using should keep an ordinary kitchen mixing bowl that warm. Just lay it across the top.

Like all reptiles and most birds, turtles do not heal or recover from illnesses easily. If your turtle dies even though you have done everything you can to help it, don't blame yourself.

Crayfish

Crayfish are crustaceans, relatives of lobsters, crabs and shrimp. Interestingly enough, one relative, the giant spider crab, measures 12 feet from tip of toe to tip of toe, while another relative, a water flea, measures only one one-hundredth of an inch.

The eyes of a crayfish are mounted on stalks. It can see in any direction. The pinch of its claw is something to avoid—in relation to its size (only a few inches in length) the pinch is close to 30 times more powerful than the squeeze of a human hand.

Trying to catch a crayfish, even in a small tank, is an unnerving experience. When going about its daily business, the creature walks rather sedately; when faced with a net, it jerks its abdomen into a tight loop, propels itself backward at eye-blurring speed and usually winds up in an inaccessible crevice between rocks.

We have not included any information on crayfish illnesses because there is really so little known that an entry would not be very helpful.

A larger variety of crayfish are eaten and enjoyed, especially down South in various dishes.

Choosing a Crayfish

Fresh-water crayfish are sold in pet stores during the spring and summer, or you can look for one yourself in local ponds and slow-moving streams

Crayfish feel their way around with their antennas.

(page 40). Crayfish living in rushing streams often need more oxygen than you can provide.

Crayfish have a special value in an aquarium: they scavenge garbage. A couple of crayfish in a tank with any of the other creatures in this chapter clean up and eat most of the leftovers. The sex of your crayfish is unimportant, since they don't breed in captivity.

Housing

Crayfish like to lurk—behind rocks, in the weeds, in hollows in the sand—so it would be a pity not to provide lurking places for these miniature monsters. Any old aquarium set-up fitted with good hiding spots is fine, and crayfish aren't fussy about either temperature or light.

Food

If natural garbage like leftover fish or turtle food is not available, crayfish appreciate a bone to pick clean from time to time. An inch of chicken wing tip has just enough meat on it.

People who enjoy monster movies will no doubt love to watch crayfish tearing at the flesh with their sharp claws. If you find a dead fish or a tadpole, it will make one more ghoulish meal for the crayfish.

If the crayfish isn't able to keep up with its meals, remove the leftovers after three days so they don't rot and foul the tank.

Tadpoles

Tadpoles are among those animals we humans call "cute." I always thought so too. But guess what tadpoles are used for in laboratories? To pick bones clean so scientists can mount them as skeletons. When frog tadpoles grow up, they are frogs. Frogs are kind of cute too. Guess what's been found in bullfrog stomachs? Mice, birds, and even snakes. Oh well, cute animals can be deceiving.

Some tadpoles grow up to be salamanders instead of frogs. Salamander tadpoles are rather longer and slimmer in shape than frog tadpoles, and grow four small legs very soon after hatching. They have feathery external gills to either side of the head—a dead giveaway, as no frog tadpole has external gills.

Choosing a Tadpole

Bullfrog tadpoles make superior pets. They are the best to buy. You can start them as eggs if you find some (page 40), or try pet stores, which may sell bullfrog tadpoles in the spring.

Large tadpoles can share their home with any of the water animals in this chapter, except perhaps the turtle. Turtles may chase and nip them. Small tadpoles may be in danger of becoming dinner for a large goldfish.

Housing

No adjustments of any sort need be made in the basic aquarium (page 323)for a group of tadpoles.

Food

There is a myth that tadpoles don't eat, but live off their tails. The tails do in fact become absorbed as the tadpole undergoes metamorphosis into a frog. And like some other amphibians, tadpoles can go a long time without food. Tadpoles, however, aren't mud puppies and will starve to death if you don't feed them. On the other hand, no matter how much you feed them, the resulting frog will always be smaller than the tadpole was.

Tadpoles eat voraciously. They like salad greens (boiled very briefly to soften them), the algae that plagues tanks, or chicken bones with raw meat still clinging.

Goodbye Tadpole, Hello Frog

It's hard to predict how long a tadpole will stay a tadpole before it begins to turn into a frog. Even assuming you started with unhatched frog's eggs, the period of time could be from a month and a half to two years. Up to the time of the big change, the tadpole merely eats and grows bigger. Then the change called metamorphosis begins.

Metamorphosis is triggered by a body chemical called thyroid. A tadpole with its thyroid glands removed grows bigger and bigger. It becomes a super giant tadpole but never a frog at all.

The first thing you'll notice when metamorphosis begins is a tiny hind leg emerging. Within days, the second hind leg comes along. Next you can see a bulge just behind the tadpole's jaw—the front legs forming under the skin.

By the time the front legs emerge, the rear legs are beginning to grow longer and more froglike, while the tail is beginning to shrink. As soon as the legs grow large enough to walk and hop, the tadpole can climb out of the water, now considering itself a frog in spite of the fact that it still carries its tail about. Within the next few weeks the rest of the tail is absorbed until no trace of it remains.

Now it's time to let the frog go back to the pond it came from, or some pond nearby (if you got the tadpole in a pet store). It is very difficult to gather a proper live insect diet to keep a frog as a permanent pet.

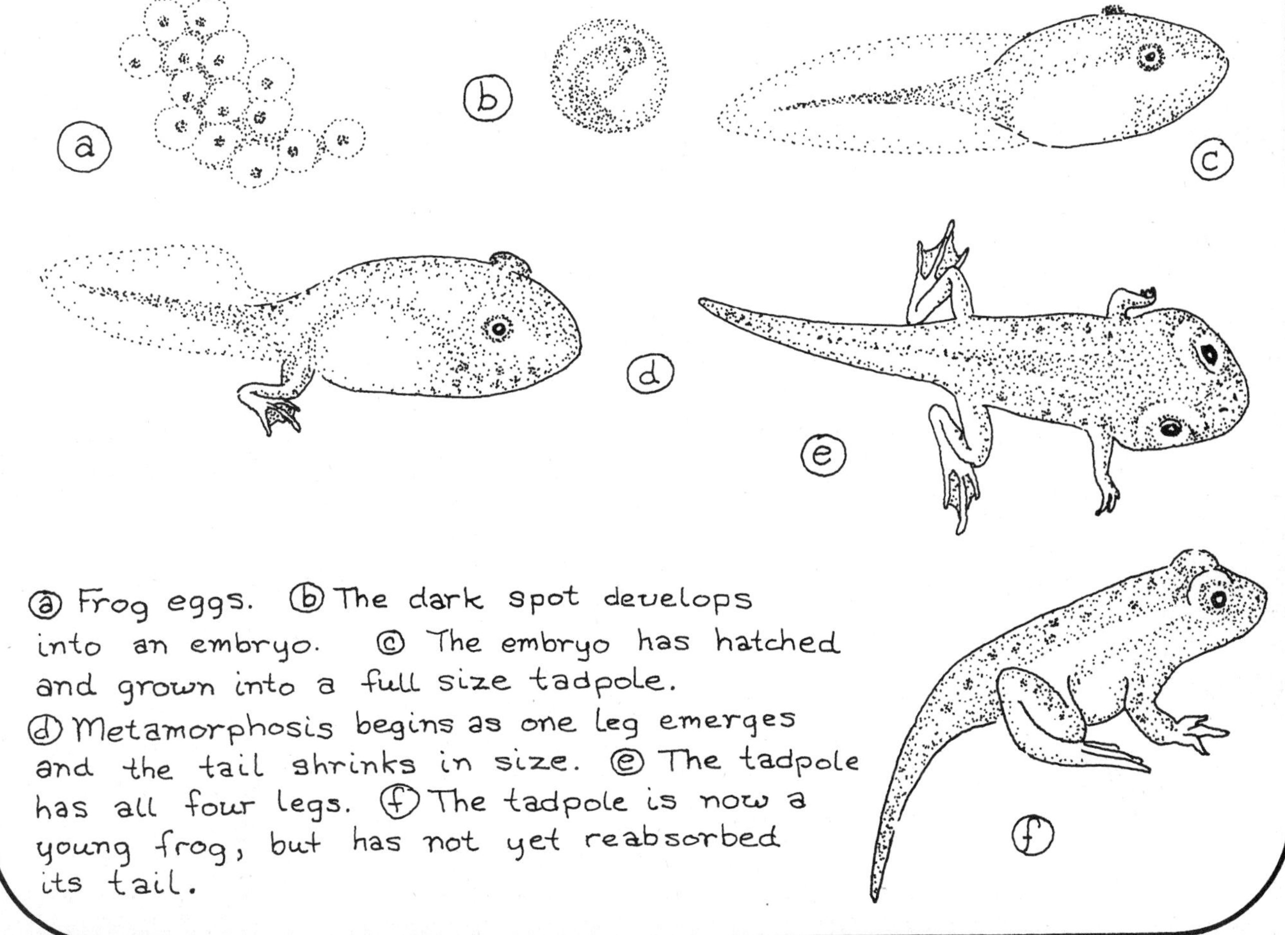

(a) Frog eggs. (b) The dark spot develops into an embryo. (c) The embryo has hatched and grown into a full size tadpole. (d) Metamorphosis begins as one leg emerges and the tail shrinks in size. (e) The tadpole has all four legs. (f) The tadpole is now a young frog, but has not yet reabsorbed its tail.

Water Snails

To have a snail or not to have a snail is a bigger question than you think. Just as land snails sit around and eat your tomatoes and lettuce, so water snails sit around and eat your water plants. If they could be trained to just eat the algae that forms on the sides of the tank, they would be the most useful of aquarium additions. But snails are no more trainable than bugs. Like goldfish, they are less likely to bother tough-leaved plants. We suggest trying one or two snails to live in the aquarium with any of the other animals in this chapter. No housing adjustments need be made, and no feeding is required.

As to the types of snail you might be able to get, pet stores may offer everything from tiny round brown snails about ¼ inch across to giant snails 1½ inches across. Choose a snail that you can see is moving rather than one lying about looking dead. Snails you find yourself in fresh water can be added to an aquarium too. Unfortunately, the more attractive salt-water snails would die in a fresh-water tank.

Rather frequently, adult snails produce baby snails. It's thrilling, but remember to watch out for your plants. As a reminder, turtles will eat small snails, so buy a large type if it is to be kept with a turtle. Should babies arrive, move them into a separate tank.

Serpentarium Pets

SERPENTARIUM PETS

SNAKES

Cost:

Rat snake		
	1½ ft./$15.00	3 ft./$25.00
Corn snake		
	1½ ft./$20.00	3 ft./$30.00
Common boa		
	1½ ft./$30.00	3 ft./$55.00
Rosy boa		
	1½ ft./$40.00	3 ft./$60.00
Indigo snake		
	1½ ft./$40.00	3 ft./$60.00

Housing:
For snakes up to three feet, 10-gallon tank, mesh top, incandescent light fixture, six-inch crockery water dish—$23.00
For snakes over three feet, homemade wood-and-plexiglass cage, light fixture, eight-inch crockery water dish—$48.50

Special Requirements:
Extra heat, extreme cleanliness.

Diet:
Live mice or other small rodents —50¢ to $1.00 per week (less expensive if you raise your own rodents).

Care:
Clean and refill water dish daily.
Feed once or twice a week.
Clean floor of cage when soiled, usually once a week.
Disinfect cage with chlorine bleach four times a year.

Tamability:
Become calm with handling. Enjoy warmth of skin. Not affectionate.

Life Span:
Up to 10 years, but many snakes die sooner for lack of proper care.

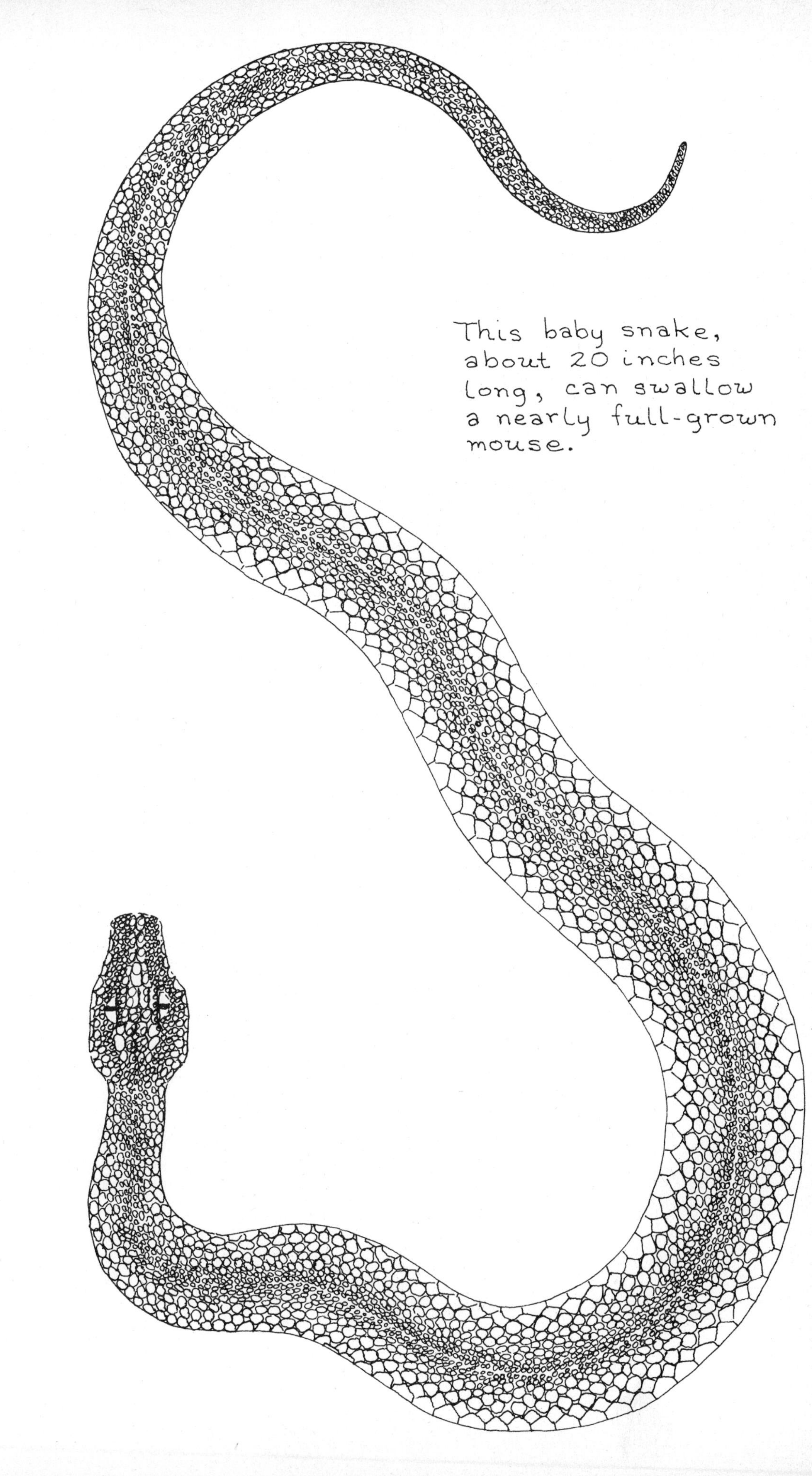

This baby snake, about 20 inches long, can swallow a nearly full-grown mouse.

Snakes are reptiles. Their ancestors, like other reptiles, had four legs. Today what remains of snake hips can still be seen on the skeleton of the python and the boa.

Snakes have developed several ways of getting about without limbs. The most common is called serpentine movement, in which each loop the snake forms with its long body pushes backward against uneven terrain, propelling the snake forward. A snake using serpentine movement can't get anywhere on a smooth surface like glass.

Less common is straight-line movement, typical of boas. Boas have rather loose skin and wide, raisable scales along their bellies. They raise up a group of scales, press the edges against the ground and push themselves forward. Groups of belly scales act in waves, so the boa appears to glide smoothly along with no visible effort. Our boa can straight-line himself along glass.

The rarest way for snakes to get around is by a method called sidewinding, and here the rattlesnake is the expert. It loops its body as though it were going to move in a serpentine pattern, but instead it moves sideways. It is actually stepping. Sidewinding is used in traveling across shifting sand where other forms of locomotion would be slow and arduous.

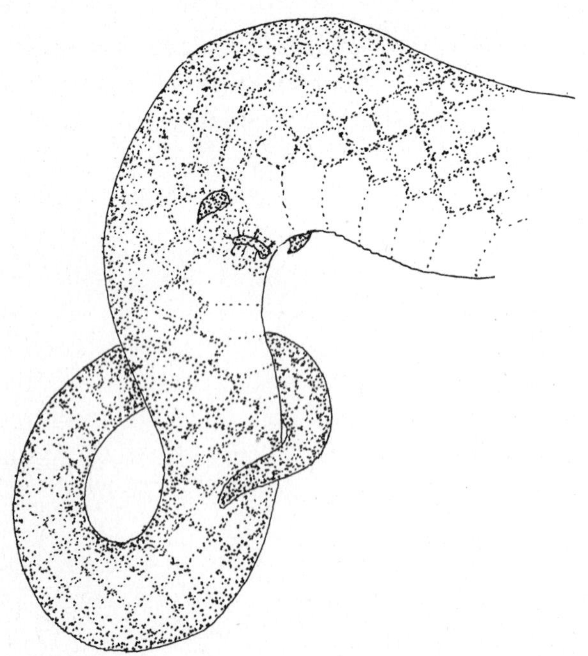

The males of some species of boa constrictor have a claw on each side of the cloaca. They are all that remain of what were once hind legs.

Snakes are cold-blooded, which doesn't mean their blood is cold but rather that they haven't a good mechanism for temperature control. Their bodies are no more than a few degrees warmer or colder than the air around them. In nature, snakes control their body temperature by seeking sun, warm rocks or cool burrows. Northern snakes hibernate in cold weather. Pet snakes that come from the tropics catch cold easily if they are not kept in heated cages. Even northern snakes need heat to be active enough to eat.

Many people have a particular horror of the snake's typically forked and flicking tongue. Some even confuse it with fangs, and think a snake is attacking when it flicks its tongue. A snake's tongue is a sense organ similar to our nose. As it flicks in and out, the tongue picks up scent molecules from the air or from surfaces and deposits them along a chemically sensitive area inside the mouth. A snake at rest doesn't flick its tongue; an exploring snake samples both the air and objects it comes upon in its travels. True, an aroused snake might flick its tongue in and out more frequently than a relaxed snake, but this is only the same sort of vigilance that a dog exhibits as it sniffs the breeze. Neither dog nor snake sniffs as a first sign of attack.

A snake's vision is quite good, its hearing quite bad. It may even be that snakes are deaf (can't detect air vibrations), though this is made up for by an acute sensitivity to vibrations received through the ground. Your snake might not hear you shout but can easily feel you sneaking about in stocking feet.

Another compensation for lack of well-developed ears is a special apparatus for heat detection. The rattlesnake, for example, has two special pit-shaped organs for heat detection on its face. A blinded rattlesnake can locate and catch a mouse six feet away simply by sensing the infra-red (heat) rays emanating from its prey.

Snakes shed their skins periodically. The next time you have a chance to look carefully at a snake skin, notice in particular the head section. You'll

A Little Light on the Subject

Our corn snake's tongue clued us in on an extraordinary fact about cold-blooded creatures. One winter day the light bulb in the snake cage blew out and the temperature dropped rapidly. By the time we discovered what had happened the corn snake was cold. His movements were slowed and weak, much as your hands would be if they got very cold. But even more dramatic, his tongue was flicking in slow motion. We could actually count the up and down flicks each time his tongue crept slowly out. We brought the snake into a warmer room and held him against our bodies to warm him gradually. As the snake warmed up, his tongue speeded up. It was like watching a thermometer rise. The full impact of cold-bloodedness hit us: a snake without heat is totally helpless. He can't even sniff.

see that each eye area is covered with a special sort of scale. The scale protects the snake's eye from damage, making both tears and eyelids unnecessary.

By saving and comparing skins each time a pet snake sheds, you can keep track of how much it has grown, although it isn't true that a snake sheds when its skin becomes too tight. Shedding is controlled by body chemicals called hormones, but no one is sure what conditions cause a snake to produce the hormones that allow it to shed. A snake can shed as often as once a month or as seldom as once a year.

Snakes have a hole at their rear ends called a cloaca. As in birds, this hole is for urine, bowel movements and reproductive purposes (see Breeding, page 131).The urine doesn't remain a liquid but solidifies when it hits the air into the same white stuff that you see in bird droppings. The dark matter is undigested animal remains, occasionally complete with teeth and bones and tufts of hair.

All the feared poisonous snakes have venom glands in the front of their mouth. They pump venom through grooved or hollowed fangs into their prey as they strike. Many snakes that we don't consider dangerous are in fact venom-producing. The venom glands of these snakes are located far back in the mouth, where the poison is squirted into the snake's mouth and must be mixed with saliva and chewed into well-torn prey before it can have any effect.

The major poisonous snakes in America are the rattlesnake, the copperhead, the cottonmouth and the coral snake. If you are ever in doubt about a snake you see in the wild, even if it is tiny, don't pick it up. Baby poisonous snakes are venomous from the moment they are born.

More varieties of snakes are now offered in pet stores than ever before. Unfortunately, many snakes offered are difficult to take care of. For instance, I've seen several varieties of water snakes for sale, as well as the common garter snakes. Water snakes must have water to swim in, necessitating a semi-aquatic tank which is much too large to be practical in the home.

Garter snakes emit a stinky smell when excited. Both water snakes and garter snakes can live on a diet of frogs, but frogs are hard to get in the winter. Many other snakes I've seen on sale require such foods as lizards, birds' eggs or even other snakes.

The best snakes for pets are boas, corn snakes, rat snakes and indigos. They are all rodent eaters and eat live mice.

If your family feels only lukewarm to the idea of a snake as a pet, here is some information that will calm their fears.

All the snakes this book recommends have been chosen because they tame easily. While snakes can bite and some can constrict hard enough to kill prey, once accustomed to handling these particular snakes rarely bite and won't tighten their coils around you.

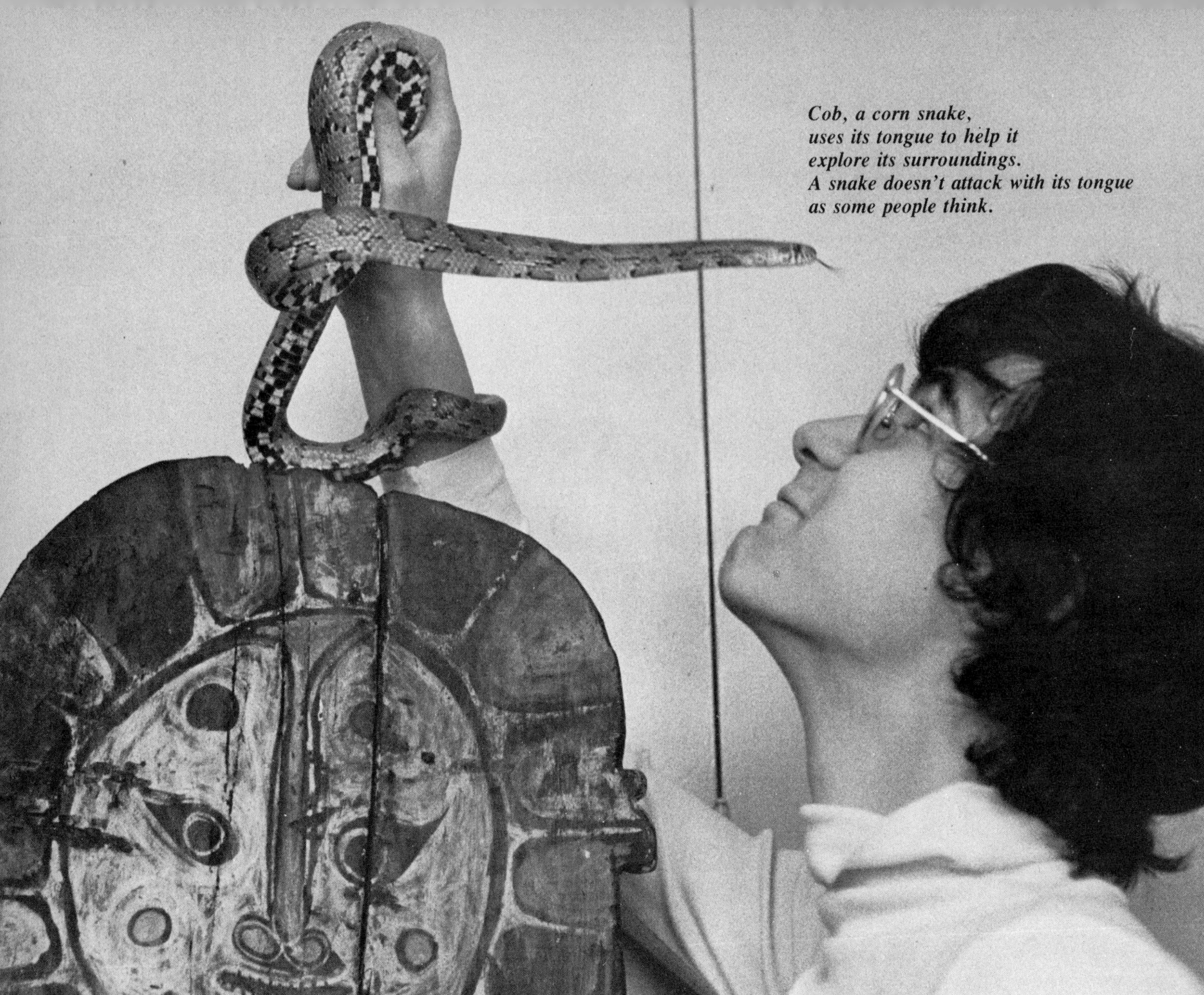

Cob, a corn snake, uses its tongue to help it explore its surroundings. A snake doesn't attack with its tongue as some people think.

The snakes suggested are neither terribly active nor terribly fast. Their movements are deliberate and their pace leisurely. A snake is not likely to slither from your grasp.

No snakes are slimy. They are dry and pleasant to touch, though cool rather than warm and cuddly.

Snakes can and do escape from their cages. They are not trying to go back to nature, but rather feel physically restless in cramped quarters. Care in building and fastening the cage can avoid escapes; and escaped snakes are usually found within a few yards of their cage.

Snakes are among the easiest pets to keep. They need to be fed only once a week and can go without food for a month (but they do need water to drink). Their cage has to be cleaned only once a week, and the bedding should be plain old newspaper. While they do need extra heat in captivity, an aquarium light is usually sufficient.

Now you are ready to pick the right snake for you.

Choosing a Snake

Snakes sold in pet stores seem rather high priced in relation to how common they are in nature. It's tempting to simply scout around for a free wild snake during the summer while they are not in winter hiding. This idea is workable only if you live in a location inhabited by one of the very few snakes that really make good pets. The problem with most snakes is twofold: aggressive dispositions that you won't like and prey that you can't provide. If you can't resist a baby ring-neck snake or a beautiful black snake, keep it as a temporary guest (see page 53).

Boa constrictors, either the common boa or the lovely rosy boa, are calm, rather slow snakes that adjust well to captivity. Of the other, somewhat faster snakes, good choices are the corn snake, the rat snakes, and the indigo, all native to America. Their more active natures are offset by the ease with which they adjust to handling and their reliability once they have become calm.

In nature, some of these snakes are active by day, others by night. In captivity, it doesn't seem to matter much either way. Our snakes eat whenever a mouse is available, no matter what time of day it is. Although they sleep (eyes open, body coiled), they awaken easily and become active with handling at any time.

The most important thing to find out about a snake is whether or not it is eating readily. Ask your pet dealer to keep the snake you have chosen without food for a week. When you return, ask the dealer to give the snake a mouse; it should strike within ten minutes. A snake that is not eating may not have adjusted to captivity, and perhaps never will. Or it may be sick. Breathing through the mouth can be a sign of respiratory illness but more commonly indicates mouth infection. Don't try to examine the mouth of a snake you don't know, especially the inside. Remember, the best proof of good health is a hearty appetite.

The next most important thing to find out is the snake's attitude toward people. Snakes, like other pets, have individual temperaments. Ask the pet dealer to take the snake out of his cage. Watch while he does it. The job should be as easy as picking up a piece of rope. Once out, a calm snake won't try to get away but will explore the dealer rather slowly, winding along his arms and shoulders, "sniffing" with its tongue.

Snakes ready to strike pull their bodies into a tense, tight configuration, with their head facing the hand that is reaching for them. Many snakes also vibrate their tails, a behavior the rattlers improved upon by keeping sections of shed skin on their tail ends. As a hand comes closer to it, an aggressive snake will strike out in a springing action, mouth open. If the dealer has the courage to pick such a snake up, it will thrash about and attempt to escape.

We bought a corn snake who acted that way. The pet store owner first explained that the snake must be hungry. So he threw it a mouse. The snake ate the mouse, and then struck at the pet dealer's hand again. The man said it was all very strange, as they handled the snake often and it had always been calm in the past. Disregarding common sense, I picked the corn snake up with a towel (a trick learned from handling ornery parrots) and took it home. To this day, we darn well wait until that crotchety snake is in a decent mood before trying to pick it up. The rule is: if you want to be sure of a tame snake at home, choose a calm snake in the store.

Housing

The 10-gallon serpentarium suggested on page 330 is large enough for a 2½-foot snake. Boas are tropical snakes and need a daytime temperature of 80 degrees; nighttime temperatures should not drop below 70 degrees. Northern climate snakes do best with daytime temperatures of between 70 and 80 degrees, but you can let the thermometer fall to 65 or even 60 degrees at night. Use the aquarium light suggested on page 327 with a thermometer taped inside the tank.

Newspaper makes a fine floor covering for a serpentarium. Tear it to the right size by placing the top of the tank onto four or five layers of the paper. Cut or tear the paper against the edges of the tank's top. You can also use a fake grass mat. It can be bought at most large discount stores.

Snakes can go for long periods without food, but fresh clean water must always be available. The water dish has to be heavy enough so the snake won't tip it over when it goes to drink, and big enough for it to soak in. A crockery dog-food dish works well and is available at pet stores.

Provide a branch for your snake to climb on and a cardboard box with a hole cut out for it to hide in. We supply a rock to aid in shedding but both our snakes seem able to shed perfectly well without it. Don't forget to line the edges of the mesh top with masking tape so your snake doesn't get a sore nose from rubbing against the wire. And don't forget to weight the top of the serpentarium with a rock to prevent escapes.

Snakes are known to be escape artists, one of the reasons parents might be reluctant to allow them as pets. Snakes object to close confinement, but they aren't long-distance travelers. Restlessness can be a sign that a snake needs larger quarters. The large wooden serpentarium on page 332 is big enough for two four-foot snakes. If you get two snakes very different in size, house them separately. Some snakes eat other snakes: we know of a nine-foot indigo who ate its five-foot boa companion. That's probably the record for the long swallow!

Serpentarium Care. Temperature control is the only frequent attention you have to pay to the environment in a serpentarium. Get in the habit of glancing at the thermometer from time to time during the day. In a smaller 10-gallon tank, you're in more danger of the temperature zooming up over 90 than dipping down below 60 degrees. After a while, you'll learn what conditions make it climb, so you can turn the bulb off before it gets too hot. In our large serpentarium we keep the light on most of the time, and rely on the snakes' judgment to move closer to the heat or further away.

The only daily care, other than temperature checking, is washing the water dish to prevent fungus and bacteria from growing there. Use soap or detergent, and very hot water. Rinse the dish thoroughly before refilling it with fresh water.

Your snake will probably only dirty its paper or fake grass once a week, and that's the time to change the newspaper or wash the grass mat. At the same time, wash the serpentarium itself with water to which Clorox® or another chlorine disinfectant has been added. Follow the disinfecting solution instructions on the package. Don't use disinfectants containing phenol or pine tar—both are toxic to snakes.

Your family will want to know where you are going to keep the snake while you clean its cage—a sensible question. Keep it in a pillowcase with the top closed with a rubber band. Plenty of air comes in through the cloth. If you ever have to take your snake anywhere—to school, on vacation, to the pet store to be boarded—carry it the same way so that it doesn't get injured.

Looking for Lloyd

As our boa, Lloyd, began to grow out of his tank, he spent nights restlessly rubbing his nose against the top until he learned to lift it. From then on he was more often escaped than confined. No problem. We always found him in the stereo amplifier. He has a larger cage now but we give him freedom too, for weeks at a time. A clumsy snake, he has fallen off rafters, knocked over plants, singed himself on light bulbs and gotten his head stuck in a hole in a cigar box. But snakes do learn. Now Lloyd knows the hazards of his territory, explores without mishap, and when the adventure's over, inevitably winds up in his amplifier.

Food and Water

In nature, snakes eat many kinds of prey, from birds' eggs, insects and frogs to other snakes. Mice are suggested for all the snakes we recommend as pets. They are a complete, nutritious diet.

A snake needs little more than his own weight in food each year. It can be fed once a week, twice a week, or not at all for as long as a month if you go on vacation. It must have fresh water daily. Use a crockery dish six or seven inches in diameter.

The size of the snake determines the size of the mouse you feed it. Start with small mice and go to larger ones as the snake grows. All snakes prefer their meat alive. If you want a pet snake you must face how you feel about this. Watching the kill is fascinating but not without an element of horror.

The mouse, on the other hand, doesn't seem to be the least bit afraid. Either pet store mice know

A snake in striking position.

nothing of snakes, or mice in general have failed to learn anything about snakes in the thousands of years they have been the snakes' staple diet. In fact, that's why you're not supposed to leave a mouse in with a snake for more than an hour. Because the mouse is unafraid he may sooner or later take a curious nibble from the snake, and you wouldn't want your three-foot snake to be bitten by a two-inch mouse. A mouse bite can get infected and cause real trouble; it's always best to stay around until your snake strikes at the mouse. A mouse will cheerfully walk along the snake's back, sniff at its nose, and sit right in front of its face, happily grooming itself. But if the snake is hungry you can see that it is poised, waiting for the right moment. It doesn't move a muscle in its body, but it keeps its head turned toward the mouse, watching constantly. Then, so fast that you really can't follow what is happening, the snake darts its whole body forward and strikes at the mouse. If the snake is a constrictor, it simultaneously loops its body around the mouse and squeezes. The mouse is dead within 10 seconds.

When the mouse has stopped moving, the snake begins to ingest it, usually head first. If you look at the size of the snake's head and the size of the mouse, you can see that it is clearly impossible for the snake to get that mouse inside. But it does. The snake's jaws dislocate so there is no attached bony structure to restrict the mouth opening. Its narrow throat is enormously elastic. The teeth point backwards like the barb of a fish hook. As the snake makes swallowing movements the mouse's body slides past the teeth but can't slide forward again. It takes about five minutes for the mouse to slowly disappear, head first, tail last. The bump that is the mouse then moves slowly down the long throat and comes to rest about a third of the way down the snake's body at its stomach, where it is digested over a period of days. Our boa digests it all—fur, bones, teeth. Our corn snake digests unnervingly less. Compared to the boa's solid, simple bowel movement, the corn snake's is flecked with tiny bones, bits of teeth, and fur.

Eager eaters who share a cage may run into grotesque problems, as when two pet snakes simultaneously strike at the same mouse. Neither will let go and both begin to swallow. So if you get two snakes, take one out while you feed the other.

Remember to give your snake fresh water every day. The snake will use the same dish to soak in, especially prior to shedding when it needs to soften its skin. As it grows, you will have to find a larger dish than the six- or seven-inch one mentioned before to fit its coiled body.

You can't tell a snake's age by its size. A snake's rate of growth depends on how much it gets to eat. Our three-year-old common boa, for

instance, is four feet long, whereas a local naturalist's three-year-old boa measures 10 feet—about the maximum for this species. If you raise your own mice for food and if you are willing to build large quarters for your snake, you can let it grow to its natural maximum within a few years. It won't object to frequent meals. One pet corn snake was observed to eat 13 mice in a single meal.

People who buy mice for 50 cents each prefer to keep their snake small. (Pet mice cost a dollar—they are customarily sold at half price for snake food.) Once you've made the decision to grow a giant snake, there's no going back on it. Big snakes keep their big appetites.

Illnesses

Kept in warm and clean tanks, most pet snakes do well. The problem is less the frequency with

Lloyd, a boa constrictor, eats mice. This series of photographs shows how he goes about attacking and devouring his food.

which they fall ill than the difficulty they have in recovering. Reptiles are incredibly slow to heal. A healthy snake can live in captivity for a very long time, the oldest known being a python who lived for 30 years. Ten years is more common.

The biggest medical problem with snakes, usually a fatal one, is an infection called mouth rot. The infection is picked up from dirty drinking water or dirty cages, or from other infected snakes. The first sign may be refusal to eat. If you examine the mouth by gently pulling it open, you may see white cottony patches on the gums, foaminess at the mouth edges, or red spots. Gradually, the condition permanently destroys gum tissue. The snake's mouth hurts. It continues to refuse food and ultimately starves to death.

Mouth infections are stubborn but curable if you work hard at it. Use Sulmet, a 25 percent solution of sulfamethazine made by Lederle. Wash the snake's mouth with it daily using an eyedropper.

A python makes a calm pet too, but you may be put off by the rate of growth. Four years ago, Satan, the python being held up by the 10 children, was an 18-inch baby. She (her sex was determined after she was named—how I

don't know) now measures 14 feet and weighs 150 pounds. Satan eats rabbits and roosters whole. The African python holds the world's length record—33 feet, much longer than the average living room.

Don't remove the white patches in the infected area, as they cushion the sore spots underneath and keep the infection from going deeper. They will fall off by themselves.

Thick as a snake's skin looks, it is easily injured. The most common injury is caused by a snake's nose rubbing against an unlined wire-mesh tank top or side. Snakes caged together may fight and once in a while a mouse will bite. Treat any skin injury with an antibiotic ointment applied three or four times a day. Ask a veterinarian's advice as to the best ointment to use.

Mites are another skin problem as common with snakes as with birds. They are such tiny creatures, one can't tell if the snake has them or not. You suspect mites on a bird when it scratches itself, but snakes don't scratch. Our answer to the problem is to place a Shell No-Pest® Insect Strip under the paper in the serpentarium for several weeks twice a year. It effectively kills the mites, who bite at night and retire into protected places during the day. A snake who goes under the paper can also be hurt by the strip, so when you use it tape the newspaper down really well with masking tape to prevent problems.

The other illnesses snakes in captivity commonly succumb to are a variety of respiratory diseases like pneumonia, bronchitis, and so on. Take note if your snake opens its mouth to breathe. It shows its nose is stuffy. Getting too cold is a common cause of sickness. Keep an eye on the thermometer in the serpentarium. This should certainly help prevent respiratory problems. Once the snake is sick, the only recourse is antibiotics injected into the large muscles to either side of the snake's backbone by a vet.

One last word. Although a snake may throw up his mouse if he is disturbed too soon after eating, we haven't heard of upset stomach problems in general. But snakes can become constipated.

Shedding

At intervals controlled by hormones and not by growth rate, a snake sheds its skin. The outermost

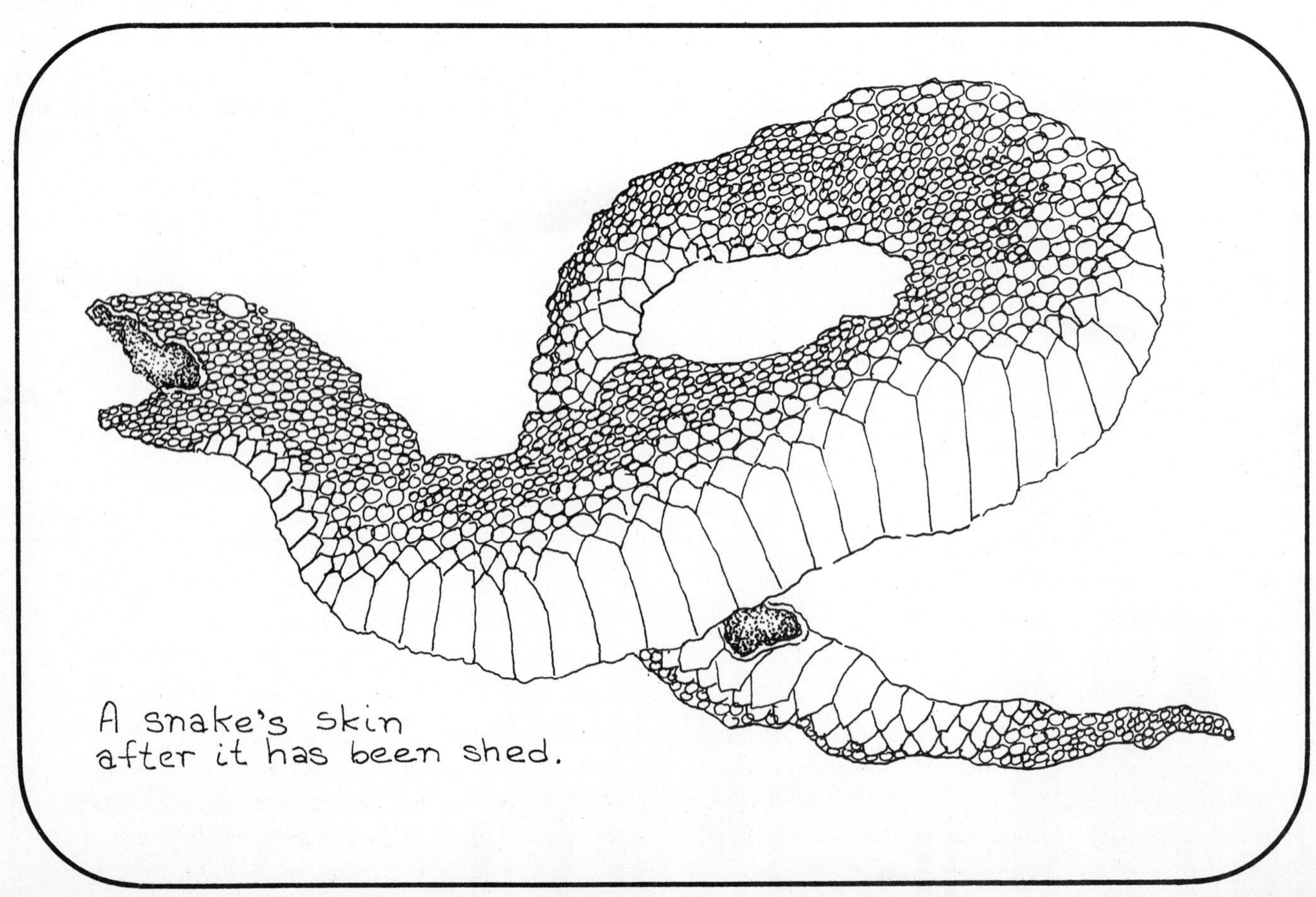

A snake's skin after it has been shed.

layer becomes somewhat opaque, giving the impression that the snake's color is fading. The specialized scales that ordinarily provide a transparent covering for its eyes become opaque too, so a snake about to shed looks like it is suffering from cataracts. It stops eating, and it may act jumpy or irritable—perhaps because it is nearly blind during this period. Shedding snakes are best left alone.

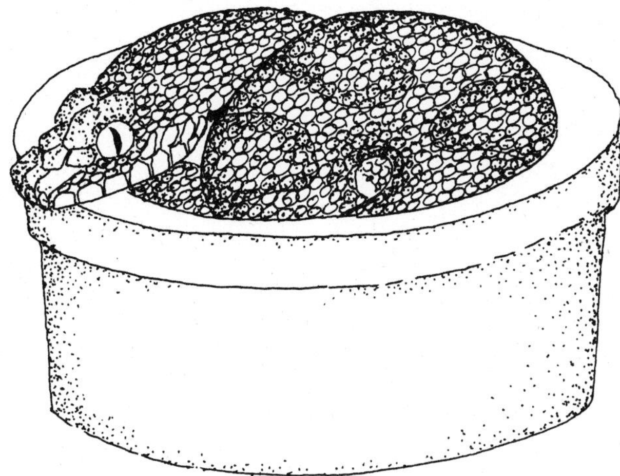

A snake soaking in its water dish.

The actual shedding process may be preceded by a few days' soak in the water dish. Sometimes with the help of a rock, and sometimes without, the snake then slips out of its skin. Both our boa and our corn snake detach their skin around the mouth and then peel it off from head to toe. It is rather like peeling off a sock. The shed skin is inside out and can be blown up like a balloon through the mouth opening. The snake's colors are at their most beautiful just after shedding.

Breeding

Snakes in captivity are reluctant to breed. Both males and females have the same coloring, so it will be almost impossible for you to tell what sex your snake is. Like birds, male and female snakes have no genitals outside their bodies, but the male does have a penis of sorts inside the cloaca where his tail begins. The organ is called a hemipenes and it has two prongs. When snakes copulate they twist themselves over one another, sometimes clockwise, sometimes counterclockwise. There is no telling in advance from which side the male will have to enter the female, so nature has provided him with an ambidextrous organ.

The female is entered through her cloaca. All the pets suggested here are egg-layers. Most female snakes lay leathery-shelled eggs in shallow nests made in loose soil or rotting leaves where the sun and the heat of decay helps keep them warm. The number of eggs varies from only two to over two dozen. Some snakes stay to guard the eggs and even to warm them with heat accumulated in their bodies from sunbathing. But none take care of the babies after they hatch. All baby snakes can take care of themselves.

When Baby Won't Eat

Now about problem eaters. Lloyd is our baby boa constrictor—about two feet long when we got him, four feet long now. Before we brought him home, we asked the pet store to watch and make sure he was eating readily when a mouse was put in his cage. They said he was. We brought him home with a spotted mouse. He wouldn't eat. Worried, we checked his mouth—no signs of mouth infection. We checked that the mouse was the right size. Lloyd wasn't big enough yet for full-grown mice, but this one was half grown, the size he was accustomed to eating.

We waited a few days, hoping Lloyd was just adjusting to his new quarters. Still no luck. We tried all the tricks. We waited a whole week to get him hungrier. We kept the mouse in a small box for an hour before it was to be served up so it would get nervous, sweat and smell better. We tried feeding Lloyd late at night in total darkness, in honor of the boa's nocturnal habits. We even left the house entirely so there would be no vibrations to distract Lloyd from his dinner. Nothing worked.

Finally we took the spotted mouse back and got another one; it happened to be brown. We put it in Lloyd's cage. We came back in an hour. The mouse was gone and a telltale bulge was already about halfway down Lloyd's long digestive system. Conclusion: some boas don't like spotted mice. We found out by trial and error that Lloyd didn't like white mice, light mice, or any sort of spots. Lloyd was a fussy eater.

Since Lloyd ate brown mice only and brown mice are scarce in pet stores, Lloyd's meals were few and far between. After four months, he hadn't grown enough to notice. All that changed after Lloyd's great escape.

We've said that snakes get impatient with confinement. They are also intelligent enough to follow their noses. If their noses just naturally lead over the top of the cage because someone forgot to weight it with a rock, snakes escape. Lloyd escaped. Or rather, he seemed to vanish into thin air. We boarded up the children's rooms so Lloyd couldn't get out under the door, and then took the place apart. We removed every book from every shelf, every baseball card from every drawer, every dirty sock from the floor. No snake. We left Lloyd's water dish out near his cage at night so he wouldn't perish of thirst.

Two weeks went by and we were into the third. Then, on a hunch, someone decided to take apart the phonograph amplifier that sits right next to Lloyd's cage. There he was; there he had lived the whole two and a half weeks. Boas aren't wanderers.

We figured Lloyd must be pretty hungry, so we offered him a mouse as soon as he was settled back into his cage. But he wouldn't eat—he was beginning to shed. Shedding takes a week of moping around and another three or four days of soaking.

By the time he was finished, Lloyd had been without food for a month. We rushed to the pet store for a fresh mouse. They had two choices: spotted or spotted. We took spotted. So did Lloyd. Lloyd wasn't about to starve himself for a principle. He is now cured of food fussiness. And wonder of wonders, he will even eat dead mice.

As Lloyd grew he began to eat regularly, Tuesdays and Saturdays. And then came our next problem. Lloyd became constipated. Lloyd usually went to the bathroom after each meal: one mouse, one mess. But now, somewhere inside that long body were the remains of four mice.

We were worried. We called around. Most people said not to worry (they didn't know the answer to the question). But finally a snake lover said that snakes get constipated from lack of exercise. We should take him from his cage every day, put a few inches of lukewarm water in the bathtub, and give Lloyd a 15-minute swim. There was some bickering as it was decided whose bathtub Lloyd was going to share, but once that was decided, Lloyd started his daily five times around the pool. He loved it and it worked. Now Lloyd is neither a fussy eater nor a constipated personality. We feel we have ironed out a few kinks.

Pet Birds

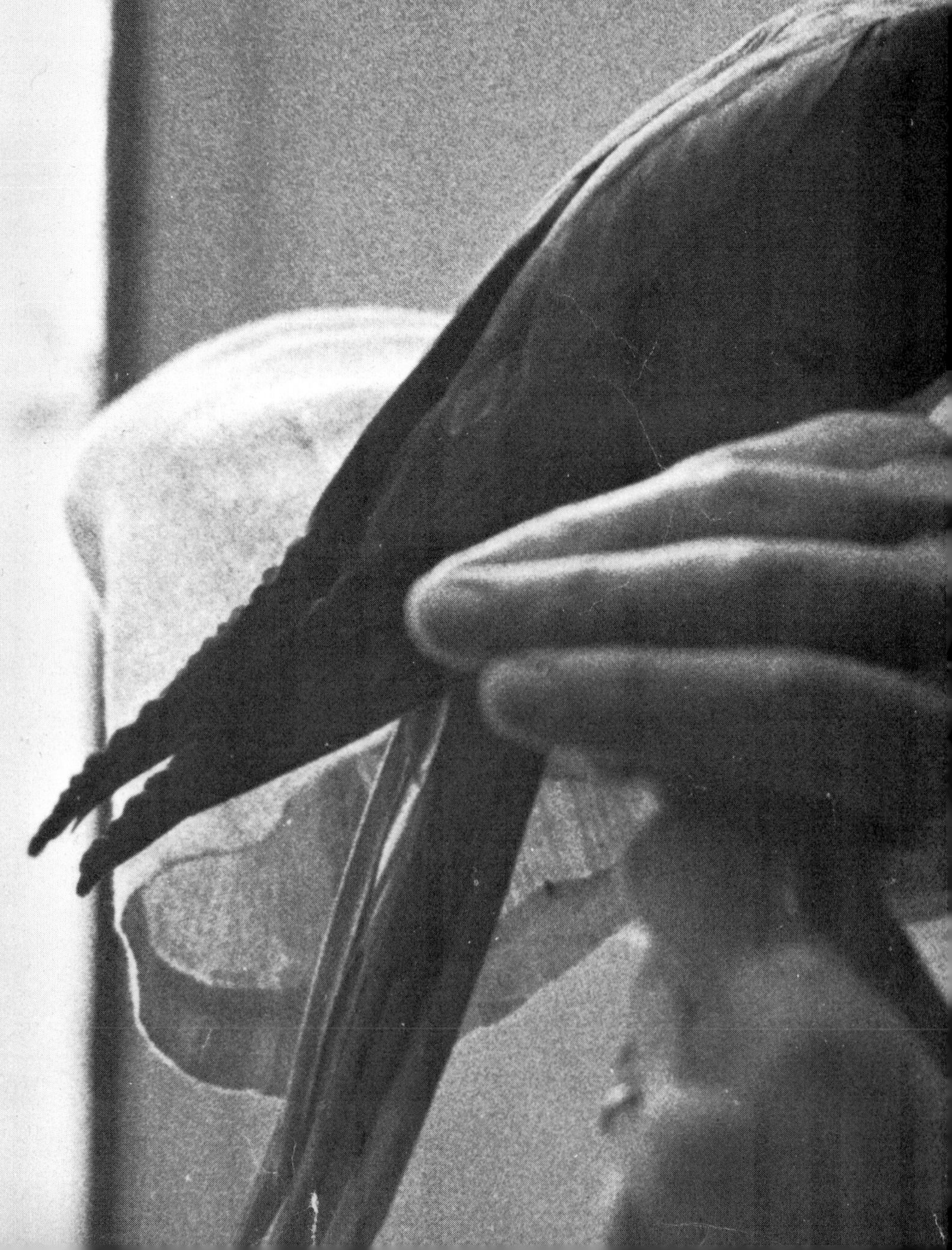

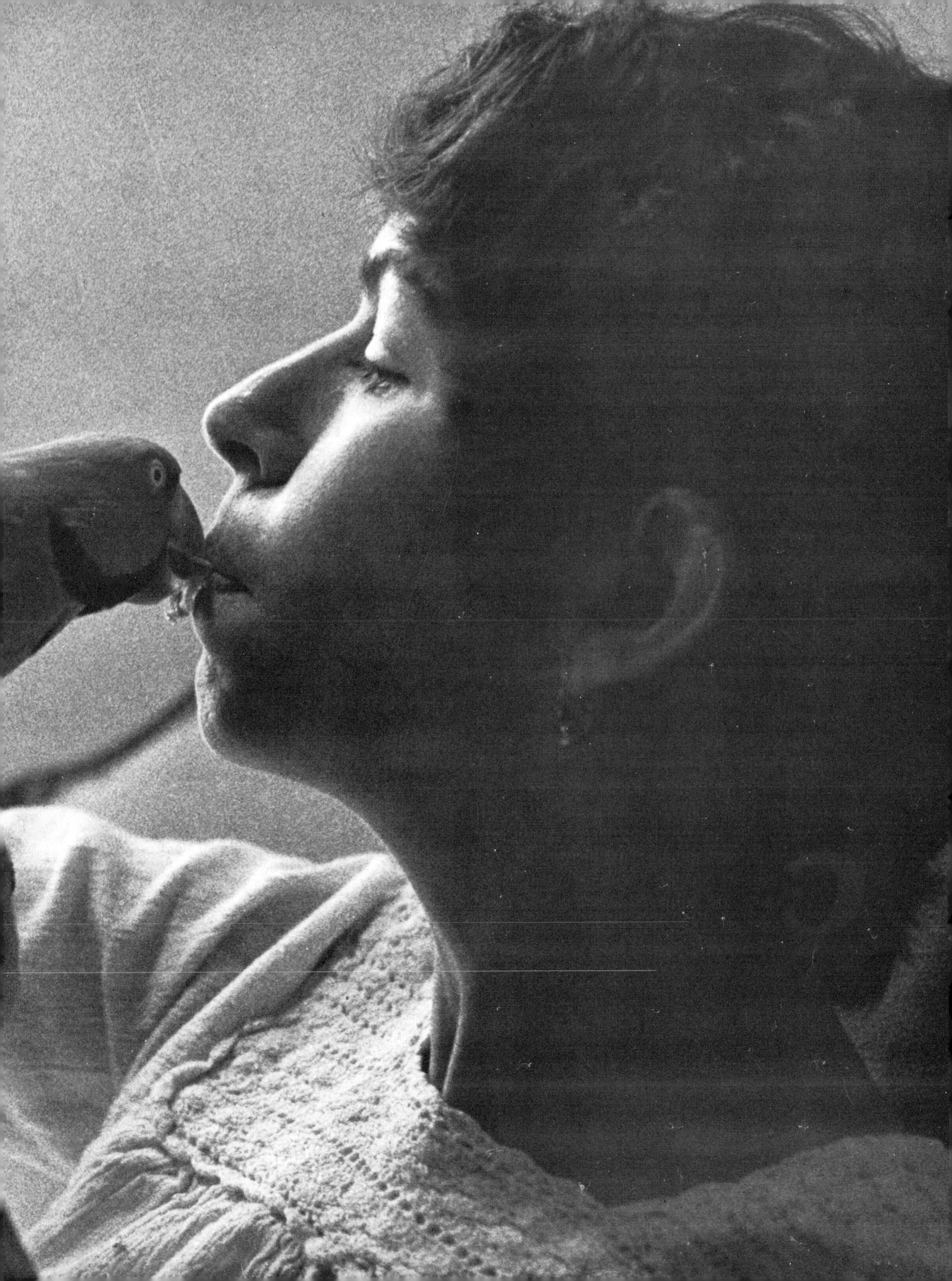

PET BIRDS

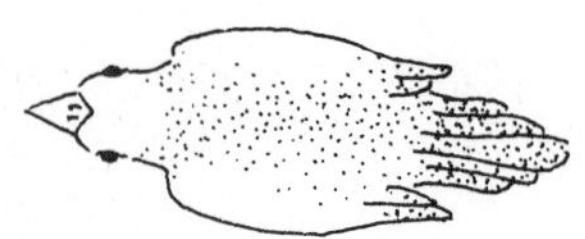

CANARIES

Cost:
Non-showbird quality choppers, rollers: Gloucesters, Border fancies and American singers—$40.00
Red factors—$50.00
(Prices for show-quality birds from breeders are higher.)

Housing:
Large homemade cakepan cage with seed and water containers and dowel perches—$12.00
Or small commercial birdcage—$15.00

Special Requirements:
Protection from drafts and direct sunlight. Wing clipping during taming period may be necessary.

Diet:
Boxed canary seed—20¢ per week.
Supplement with fresh greens or sprouted seeds.

Care:
Feed and replenish water daily.
Provide bath twice a week.
Clean cage floor once or twice a week.
Wash cage and perches monthly.

Tamability:
May become calm enough to perch on fingers and eat from hand.

Life Span:
Five to 10 years.

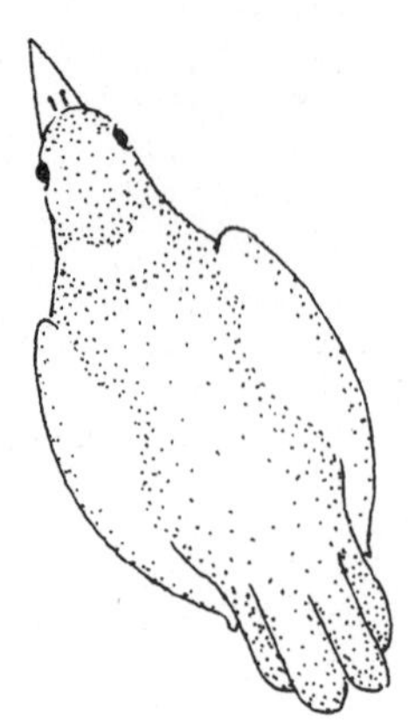

MYNAH BIRDS

Cost:
$250.00 (higher for a talking bird).

Housing:
Large commercial birdcage—$55.00 and up.

Special Requirements:
Protection from drafts and direct sunlight. Wing clipping during taming period may be necessary.

Diet:
Boxed mynah food—$1.00 per week.
Supplement with fresh raw fruits.

Care:
Feed, replenish water and remove leftover fresh foods daily.
Clean cage floor twice a week or more often, as necessary.
Provide bath twice a week.
Wash cage and perches monthly.

Tamability:
May become calm enough to perch on hand or shoulder. Mimic sounds, whistles and human speech.

Life Span:
40 years.

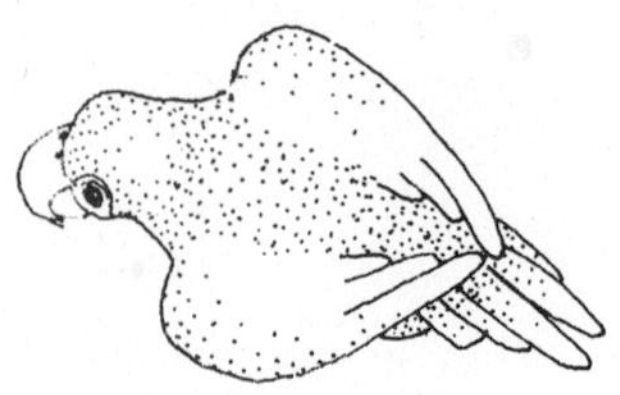

LITTLE PARROTS

Cost:
Grey cockatiel—$50.00
Pied cockatiel—$80.00
Albino cockatiel—$115.00
Green or blue parakeet—$15.00
Yellow or white parakeet—$15.00
Peach-faced lovebird—$35.00
Fischer's lovebird—$75.00
Bee bee parrot—$80.00

Housing:
Largest homemade cake-pan cage with seed and water containers and dowel perches—$12.00
Or medium-size commercial birdcage—$15.00

Special Requirements:
Protection from drafts and direct sunlight. Wing clipping during taming period. Toys.

Diet:
Boxed parakeet or parrot seed (depending on size of bird)—25¢ to 70¢ per week.
Supplement with fresh raw greens and fruits.
Supply bones or twigs to chew on.

Care:
Feed and replenish water daily.
Provide bath twice a week.
Clean cage floor once or twice a week.
Wash cage and perches monthly.

Tamability:
Become calm and affectionate.

Individuals may mimic sounds, whistles, or more rarely, human speech.

Life Span:
Five to 10 years for parakeets, 12 years for cockatiels, 20 years for lovebirds and bee bee parrots.

BIG PARROTS

Cost:
Ringneck parakeet—$80.00
Amazon parrots—$250.00
African gray parrot—$500.00
(Note: prices for tamed and talking parrots are higher.)

Housing:
Large commercial birdcage—$55.00 and up.

Special Requirements:
Protection from drafts and direct sunlight. Wing clipping during taming period. Exercise outside of cage. Toys.

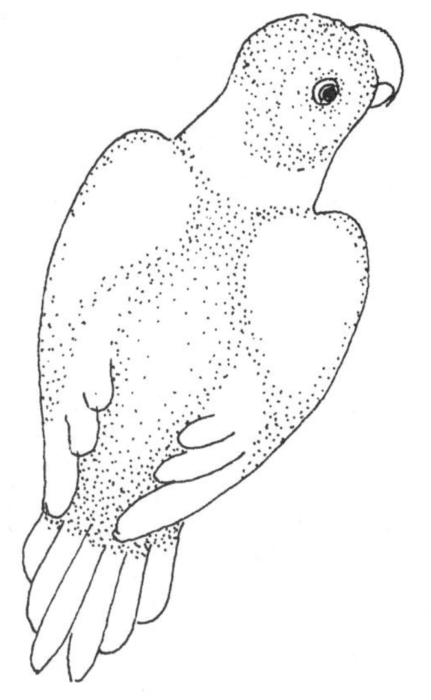

Diet:
Boxed or specially mixed bulk parrot seed—$1.50 per week. Supplement with fresh raw greens and fruits. Supply bones or twigs to chew on.

Care:
Feed and replenish water daily.
Provide bath once or twice a week.
Clean cage floor once or twice a week.
Wash cage and perches monthly.

Tamability:
Become calm, affectionate and devoted to owner and family. Mimic sounds, whistles and human speech.

Life Span:
20 years for ringneck parakeet, 25–50 years for other parrots.

Canaries, one of our most common cage birds, are similar to birds that have been kept as pets for centuries. Their close relatives, linnets, chaffinches and robins, were sold in the streets of ancient Rome and offered in the open markets of medieval towns. All these birds, and the mynah bird as well, are called "perching birds," or passerines.

Passerines are the best singers, the best nest-builders, and the most numerous of all birds. All the passerines share one trait in common—the structure of their feet. Three unwebbed, well-developed toes stick out in front. One toe sticks out behind. The toes are connected to the bird's legs by strong ligaments. When the bird perches, the weight of its body pulls the ligaments tight, closing the toes around any perch the feet are in contact with. Because the tightening does not require a conscious muscular grip, the toes stay tightly curled around a perch even when the bird is sitting head under wing, fast asleep.

All the other birds in this chapter are psittacines, or members of the parrot family. Their feet are quite different, with two toes in front, two behind. Parrots can use these feet like hands to hold food, pick up objects or climb along branches. When climbing, parrots use their beak as a third hand. Going downward, a parrot leans down, presses its beak onto a lower surface to stabilize itself, then climbs down one foot at a time. Going upward, it uses its beak as a hook, securing it to a higher surface and pulling its body up behind. A parrot can climb up a piece of fabric with ease, gripping the cloth above it with its beak at every step.

Parrot beaks are different from other bird beaks. Most bird jaws are similar to ours, hinged only at the bottom. Parrot beaks are hinged both at the top and the bottom, making a parrot yawn an impressive sight.

Officially parrots are well below passerines on the evolutionary scale. Their nests are sloppy, their behavior simple, and they do not sing songs of their own. Unofficially, however, they are superior as pets. The birdwatcher (ornithologist), stalking the forests with his field glasses, can appreciate the complex behavior of passerines, but in a cage the instincts that guide a bird's wonderful skills have little outlet. Caged passerines learn poorly, are unemotional with humans and unsurprising in their behavior. Parrots, on the other hand, are driven less by instinct. They learn things you teach them and devise tricks of their own. They become so emotionally involved with their owners that affections and jealousy can become a nuisance. And just when you think you have found out everything your parrot can do, it will surprise you once again with a brand-new trick.

Choosing a Bird

Birds are cheap to keep but not to buy. In order of cost, from cheapest to most expensive, these are the birds commonly sold as pets: parakeets, canaries, small parrots, mynah birds, and large parrots. Canaries are valued for their looks and song; parakeets and the small parrots like cockatiels, lovebirds and bee bee parrots become amusing and affectionate pets. The mynah is a wonderful mimic, both of sound effects and the human voice. The most common of the large parrots are the Amazons (there are many varieties) and the African gray. All the large parrots are very intelligent and loving pets. All of them can learn to "talk," and the African gray parrot is considered the best mimic in the world.

The healthiest birds are likely to be those raised in this country by breeders, rather than imported wild birds. Breeders' birds are recognized by a band on one leg which tells when the bird was hatched. All the smaller birds are available as breeder-raised youngsters. Mynahs and large parrots don't breed well in captivity—in fact mynahs won't breed at all. These birds are usually captured in the wild and imported into this country.

Sadly, many pet wholesalers do not take good care of either the birds they import or those they buy and sell to pet stores. Of the wild birds that survive the crowded and careless process of capture and shipment and a three-month quarantine period, many more become sick in the equally crowded and careless conditions at the wholesalers'. Your best bet is to buy a bird only after it has been at your pet store for two weeks. If it isn't sick by then, it is probably in fair shape.

Unfortunately, it is easy to misunderstand the symptoms of illness and buy a sick bird because it

Gloucester canaries have feathered caps.

looks cuter and tamer than the others. A sick bird feels cold, so it ruffles up its feathers. This makes it look cuter than the other birds. Because it has no energy, it doesn't fly in panic around its cage. This makes it look tamer than the other birds. Also look closely for deformities like crooked toenails and overgrown beaks. Check that the eyes are bright and fully open. Choose a bird in good feather, with no bald spots. Look under the tail—any dirt or droppings clinging to the feathers means the bird has diarrhea and may be sick.

All the small birds can share a cage with one of their own kind (particularly of the opposite sex), but may not get along with birds of different species. The larger parrots may or may not get along with one another, even if they are of the same species. Sometimes personalities clash. One cage is nearly always too small for two parrots anyway. All the parrots, both big and small, become less fond of their owner if they can shower their affections on a friend or a mate. Unless you want to breed your parrots, a single bird makes a better pet.

Housing

To stay healthy, a bird needs exercise. Small birds should be able to fly about their cages, large ones to flap their wings freely The illustration will give you an idea of the size to look for. Unfortunately most cages are smaller than these ideal sizes, so under each bird's separate listing you will find suggestions for providing extra exercise.

Cages come equipped with food and water dishes and with several perches made of wooden dowels. The dishes are well designed, but the dowel perches are not ideal. The reason for this is that a bird's toenails grow all the time, just like yours do. In nature, birds are constantly landing on and walking along rough branches. The bark keeps their toenails worn down to proper length. The wooden dowels are too smooth to do this. There are several ways you can keep bird toenails manicured properly even on a dowel perch. Wrap one of the dowels with fine sandpaper, using white glue to keep it in place; or smear white glue onto the bot-

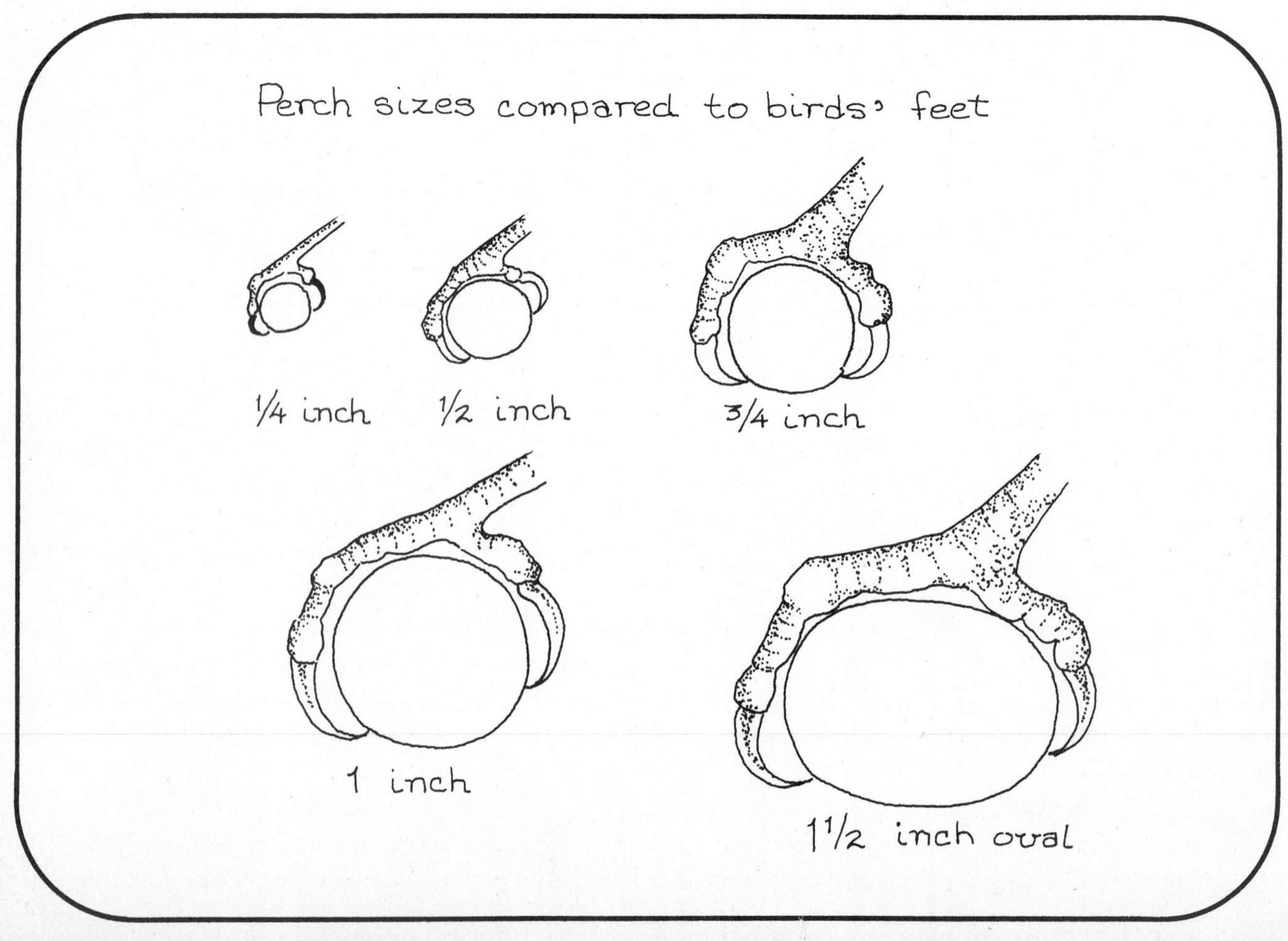

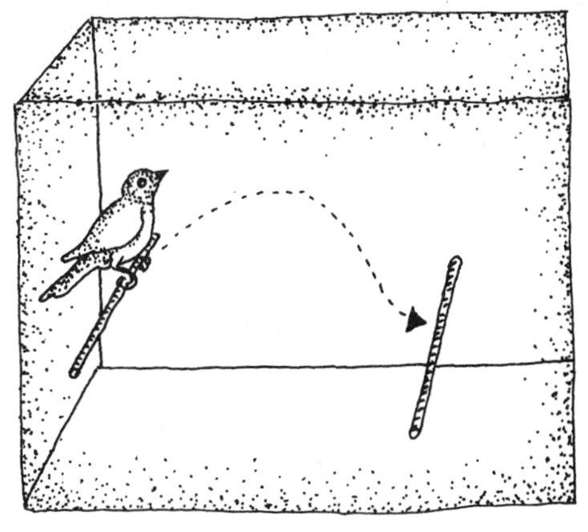

Small birds like canaries and parakeets should be able to fly from perch to perch. Mynahs should be able to hop from perch to perch. Large parrots should at least be able to flap their wings.

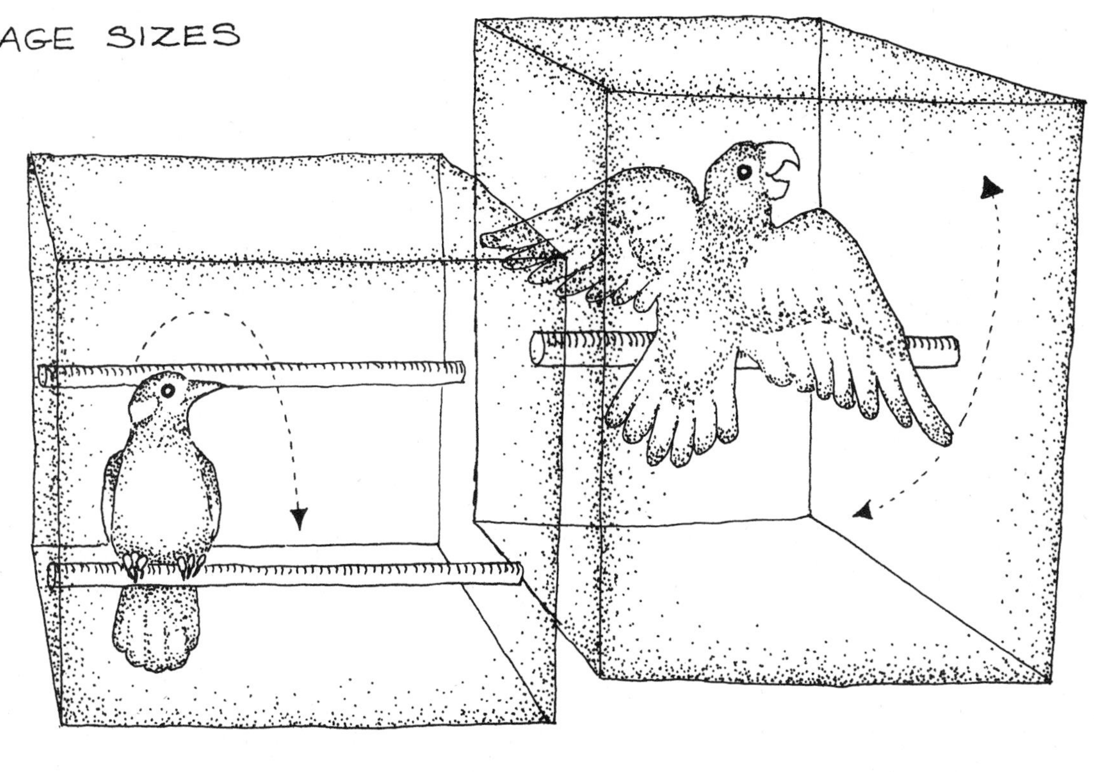

tom half of a perch and then dip it in fine sand. With the second method, nails are kept worn but the sandpaper can't injure the tenderer foot parts. There are also special perches sold at pet stores that are rough like sandpaper and may be substituted for one or more of the perches in the cage. Probably the nicest thing to do is to find a pretty branch to use instead of a dowel. It will be more interesting for you to look at and for your bird to perch on. You can wire it to the cage bars to keep it from slipping. And it's certainly easier to keep clean than sandpaper.

There is another advantage to a branch instead of a dowel. A dowel is the same diameter from one end to the other, whereas a branch is thick at one end and thin at the other. This lets a bird choose what thickness is most comfortable for its feet to hold on to. The dowels that come with cages are often too thin for the bird; its toenails wrap around it instead of hitting it, so even if the dowel is roughened its nails may grow too long and its feet may become deformed. For the largest birds, like parrots and mynahs, a hardwood tool handle, makes an excellent perch. The oval shape is comfortable for their feet. Parrots, who chew through most perches in short order, have trouble damaging these hardwood handles.

A bird's beak is covered with a thin layer of tissue similar to our fingernails. Although the bony beak underneath doesn't grow, the outside layer does. Birds manicure their beaks by either rubbing them against rough surfaces or by biting on hard objects.

For small birds like canaries and parakeets, equip the cage with a piece of cuttlebone (buy it in the pet store). The birds will rub their beaks on it and peck at it. A parrot does more biting than rubbing; it will chew the cuttlebone up in about five minutes. Give parrots twigs and bones to chew on in their cages but don't be surprised if they also chew their perches out from under them every few months. We gave one parrot a whetstone (knife sharpener) wired to his bars to rub his beak against. It was a good idea but it didn't work. He is an incurable perch-gnawer.

Commercial cages have a pull-out drawer bottom for easy cleaning and often come equipped with plastic side panels to prevent seeds from scattering outside the cage. If you find the side panels inadequate, pet stores also sell vinyl buckets that fit around the bottom of the cage to catch scattered seed. Neither of these devices is foolproof, and sweeping seed up from the floor is one of the cleanup jobs of a bird owner.

Newspaper is the best flooring material for covering the drawer bottom. Sprinkle medium-grit pet-store sand (gravel) over the newspaper. Birds need to eat grit to grind their food inside their gizzard (stomach). If the drawer bottom is covered with a wire floor like some of the larger cages, add the grit to your pet's food instead.

Pet stores also sell cage covers to fit the various shapes and sizes of standard cages. Covers serve two purposes: they cut off drafts at night and so protect your pet's health; and they are also used to quiet down a noisy bird in the daytime. A bird in a darkened cage will stop twittering, screeching or singing.

Cleaning Birdcages. Change the newspaper and sand at least twice a week for all birds except the mynah. Mynahs are fruit-eaters, whereas all the other birds mentioned eat seeds. A mynah's droppings are more copious, mushy and unpleasant than the droppings of seed-eaters. You may have to change the newspaper in its cage every day. Sprinkle fresh sand over the newspaper after each change. The perches should be scraped and washed, too. Dried droppings come off more easily if you wet down the perch and let the droppings loosen with moisture. A plastic scouring pad is better than a sponge for scrubbing. Wash the water dish with soap and water and rinse it well every day before refilling it. The seed dish should be washed whenever it looks soiled.

When the bars of the cage begin to get dirty—the length of time depends on the bird—the whole cage has to be washed with soap and water. Small birds that aren't tamable, like canaries, can stay inside their cages while you sponge the bars down. Tame birds, like any of the parrots, can be let out while you are cleaning.

Where To Keep the Cage. All the birds recommended here as pets are tropical birds. If they have been imported rather than bred in this country, they are vulnerable at first to cooler temperatures and may catch colds easily. When you buy an imported bird, do your best to find a place for its cage that is warm and without drafts. Since any window creates drafts at night, find a place away from a window. A towel over the cage at night is helpful. 70 degrees is an adequate temperature. You won't have to be this careful forever; after a while your bird will molt its rather poor covering of feathers and grow a heavier coat to suit its new climate. Though drafts are never a good idea, our parrots are healthy all winter at only 55 degrees night temperature—the usual lowest setting on a home thermostat.

Sunny locations sound nice, but birds in cages can't get out of the sun when it gets too hot for them. Bright light is fine, but avoid sun.

The only other problem to consider when you find a place for the birdcage is the seed scattering. Remember that it's easier to sweep seed shells from a bare floor than to vacuum them off a shaggy rug.

Food and Water

Canaries and the parrots mentioned here are all basically seed-eaters. Canary and parakeet seed mixtures come boxed at pet stores. Parrot seed mixtures are usually custom-mixed at pet stores from bulk seed in bins but there are several boxed brands

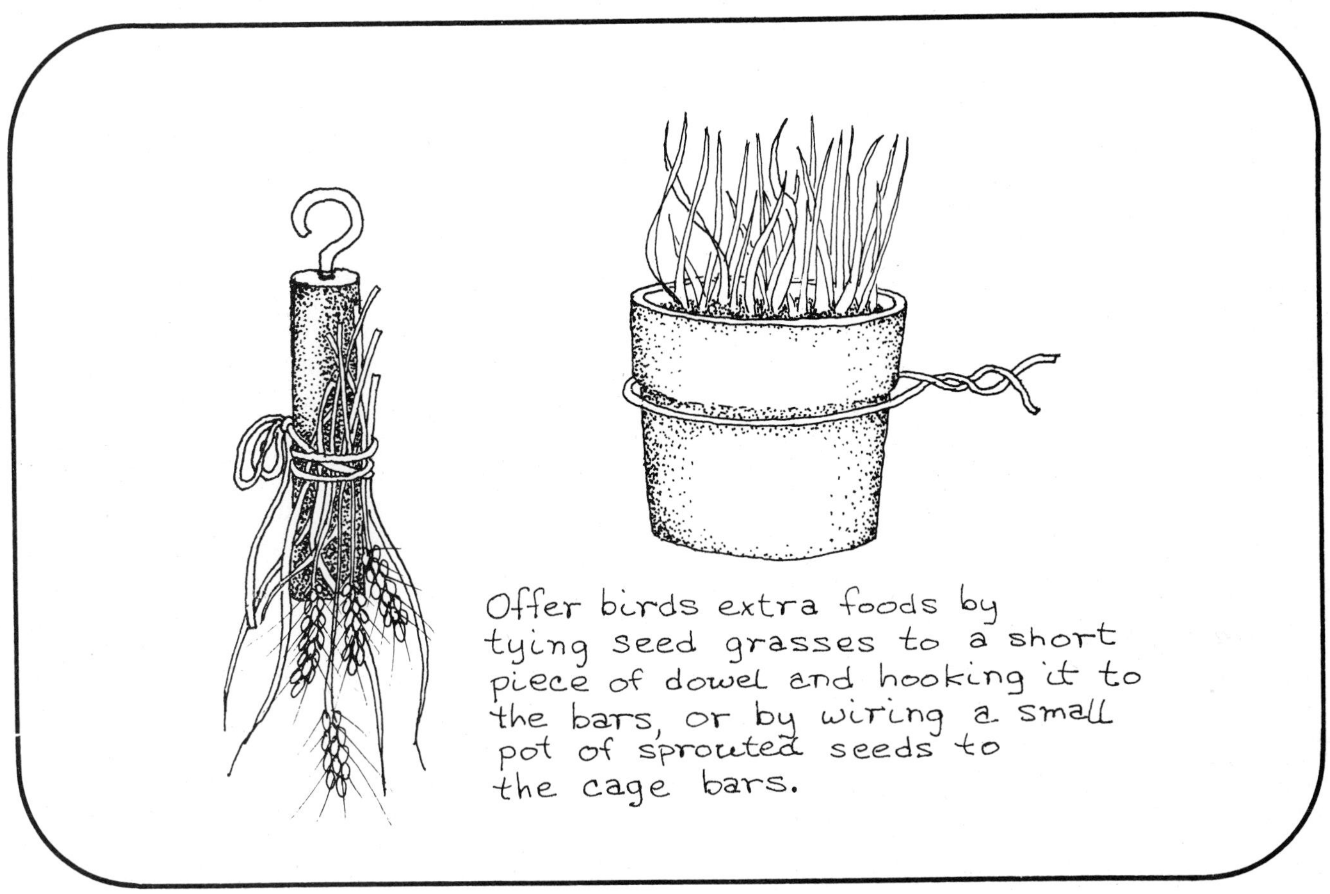

too. Small parrots like cockatiels and lovebirds require smaller seeds, while large parrots need larger seeds.

The mynah is a fruit-eater, and a pellet food containing dried fruit and cereal is sold for them in pet stores. This dry food helps somewhat to keep mynah droppings solid.

All the birds here, whether fruit- or seed-eaters, do best if offered some daily fresh fruits and vegetables besides their dry foods. In nature these birds occasionally need a high-protein diet that includes insects. Hard-boiled egg yolk, commercial high-protein biscuits (sometimes called conditioning food) and live mealworms are all good substitutes. Conditioning food and mealworms are sold in pet stores. Offer protein foods once a week, or every day if you are breeding birds.

Specific feeding advice is given under the discussion of each kind of bird. In general, when offering a new food put out only a little. New foods can cause diarrhea until the bird gets used to digesting them.

Birds have to be fed every day. They have a very high metabolism, which means they keep a high body temperature by burning up a great deal of food. Sometimes you will be fooled by what looks to you like a full dish of seeds. But examine it more closely and you will often find that the dish is filled with empty seed husks and that your bird really is out of food.

Fresh foods, fruit especially, rot quickly. Clean up leftovers every day. Birds also need to eat grains of medium-grit sand (gravel). It can be bought by the pound in pet stores. Some birds can bite with their beaks, but no bird can chew. Instead they swallow grit, which stays in their gizzard (stomach) and grinds the seeds up so they can be digested. Sand is usually served sprinkled on the cage floor.

The cuttlebone suggested as a cage fixture under Housing is a good source of calcium. Calcium is most important to young growing birds and to breeding females who need extra calcium to form the hard shells on their eggs. Besides cuttlebone, other calcium sources include crushed oyster shells (sold at pet stores), crushed eggshells and bone meal, all of which can be sprinkled in with the bird's food once a week. The large parrots enjoy nibbling on small bones, which are rich in calcium as well.

Fresh drinking water has to be provided for birds every day. Birds sprinkle seed into their water, drop their droppings into it and even bathe in it. You will have to make up for their lack of cleanliness.

Bathing

Birds will dirty their drinking water less if you give them a chance to bathe several times a week, outside of the water dish. Just among the parrots we keep, the cockatiel bathes by rolling about in wet lettuce leaves, the macaw splashes himself in a pan of water, the Amazon becomes ecstatic at the sight of a plant mister, and the ringneck will stand under the trickle of the kitchen faucet. It may take a while to discover how your bird likes its bath. First, try a glass pie plate filled with water on the floor of its cage each morning. Since birds are nervous about a new article you put in their cages or hold near them, your bird may shy from the dish at first or even fly about in panic. Offer it for a few minutes every morning for a week until the bird calms down, then put it there for a few hours each morning for another week. If it's not using it by then, try a plant mister. Again, just give the mister a moment's try each morning for the first week (not directly into the bird's face, but from above or behind). As a bird comes to enjoy a spraying, it will spread its wings and ruffle its feathers so the water can seep down to its skin. If it doesn't like the spray it will continue to try to get away from this mist. The alternative for a bird dead set against dish baths or spray is wet lettuce or cabbage leaves to roll in. If the bird can have a good bath every few days (or with larger parrots, once a week) it may give up taking baths in its water dish.

There is still another way that some birds like to keep themselves clean—dust baths. Unfortunately for our family, that's how our fifth parrot, an African gray, likes to bathe. If we put sand in his cage, he squats in it and kicks the sand up under his belly and wings, and about four feet in every other direction too. So instead of sand we keep newspaper in his cage. But African gray parrots invent new ways to annoy their owners. Our fiendish bird unfastens his water dish, drops it to the floor of his cage, lets the water soak into the newspaper, chews the newspaper into a mush and grovels in it.

Illnesses

Pet birds get sick less often and probably live longer than wild birds. The reason is simply that they don't have a lot of other birds around to catch things from. As a treat, people occasionally put a bird in its cage outdoors for a few hours in nice weather. But this is a real danger. Wild birds visit the cage, attracted by the birdseed. Diseases they harbor can be picked up by the caged bird, and often prove fatal.

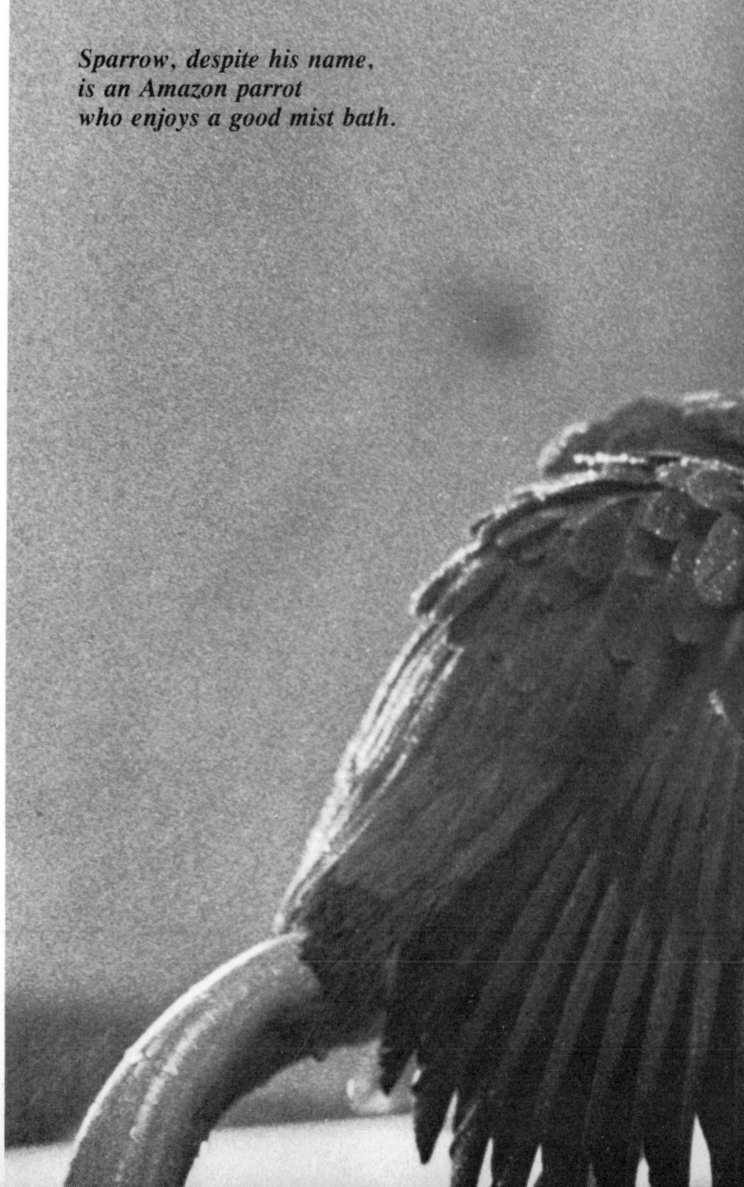

Sparrow, despite his name, is an Amazon parrot who enjoys a good mist bath.

Even without exposure to wild birds, pets may get sick or develop other physical problems. Colds and respiratory diseases like bronchitis and pneumonia are the most frequent problem, especially with newly imported birds. The symptoms of respiratory disease include a runny nose (a bird's "nose" is the nostrils at the top of its beak), ruffled feathers, quietness, a squatting position, a reluctance to eat, and sometimes breathing through the mouth. Birds also cough and sneeze. When a bird is quite sick, its breathing may become rapid and even noisy.

A sick bird dies much faster than another animal might. The important thing is to act fast. If you suspect your bird is sick, don't wait—it won't matter if you were wrong; the treatment can't hurt. Buy a bird antibiotic at the pet store. Most are tablets which you crush and add to the drinking water daily. If the bird isn't drinking water, force some drops of the medicated water down its throat. Wrap it in a handkerchief or towel and get someone else to hold it. Pull the bird's beak open with thumb and forefinger of both hands. Then the person holding it can drop in the medicine. Repeat the medication every three hours during the day. Cover the bird's cage with a blanket and put it near a heater to keep the temperature around 90 degrees. For little birds like canaries who don't chew on wires, you could instead hang a 40-watt light bulb right inside the cage.

Mites are a common parasite even in caged birds, but they are easily gotten rid of. If your bird seems to be scratching itself a lot, put a white cloth over the cage at night. In the morning, check the

inside surface of the cloth for tiny reddish spots. Those are mites. Buy a mite spray sold for birds in pet stores. Spray the bird thoroughly. Remove the newspaper from the cage floor and give the whole cage a good wet spraying before you put fresh newspaper in. Repeat the treatment once a week for three weeks.

Overgrown toenails and beaks seldom happen if you provide the right perch and a good beak-rubbing surface or chewing materials. But occasionally a bird has a defective beak that grows unevenly as a horny projection, or a bird might come to you with toenails or beak already very overgrown. In such cases you will have to help the bird out by clipping off the extra. Wrap the bird in a towel, and get another person to hold it belly-up. Extract one foot at a time, or the beak. Use fingernail clippers to do the clipping. Naturally a parrot will give you a good nip if you go for its beak, but there is a simple way to do the job safely: get a good hold on its upper beak—it can't possibly bite you while you are holding on to it. A nail file can be used to smooth the edges of the cut. Clip toenails only a little at a time to avoid hitting the blood vessel in the nail. Spread the job over several sessions so the bird doesn't get exhausted from fear. If you do hit a blood vessel, a styptic pencil like men use for razor nicks will stop the bleeding.

At intervals during the year, every bird molts (sheds) its feathers and grows new ones. Some birds molt most of their feathers all at once, usually only once or twice a year. The molting takes a month or less. Others may molt over a longer period, or lose only a few tail feathers, flight feathers or body feathers at a time. When a bird molts all at once, it can be a sorry sight and may worry its

If you want to be sure your mynah will be a talker, buy one you've already heard gabbing.

owners, especially because it will act rather quiet and perhaps not eat as well as usual. The larger parrots molt gradually; you will notice shed feathers on the cage floor but the bird will not look bedraggled or act dejected. Normal molting is nothing to worry about; it is the way birds replace old or damaged feathers, prepare for cold weather with a heavier plumage, or even change into bright colors for courting or for camouflage for different seasons. Your bird will be sleeker and more colorful with its new feathers.

Taming and Training

In general, taming a bird is mostly a matter of letting it get accustomed to you. Canaries become calm enough to perch on a finger and eat from your palm. One canary owner I know actually seems to have won her bird's affection. The canary sits on her head and grooms her hair by pulling strands gently through its beak. Mynah friendship is probably at about the same level as canary friendship. Only with parrots can you expect insane devotion, embarrassing displays of love, and violent jealousy. Parrots are emotional birds.

A baby bird calms down faster than an adult, but the taming method is the same. The first thing any bird has to get used to is your hand. Its idea of a hand at first might be "the thing that grabs and holds defenseless birds." You have to change its mind until a hand means "the thing that is pleasant to perch on and may contain treats." It takes patience to change a bird's mind. For the first week try to leave a new bird alone in its cage; then start becoming a part of its life. Talk to it whenever you're near. In nature, a predator doesn't announce

itself, so talking means you're not stalking. Rest your hand on the cage. Open the cage door. Rest your hand on the entrance and inside the cage. As long as your bird panics (or, rarely, tries to peck or nip at you) with every intrusion, don't try to go any farther. Just getting a bird used to hands coming near it can take several weeks. As its panic dies down, the bird will only move to avoid your hand rather than dashing about wildly. Now you can be more persistent. Put your hand next to the bird on its perch. When it moves to another perch, move your hand near again. If you play this game several times a day, most birds will remain calm within a week, even when your hand is quite near.

What, beyond calmness, you can expect from a bird depends on what sort of bird you have. Canaries and mynahs can be trained to perch on your finger and eat from your hand (pages 153 and 156 first in the cage, and then sometimes outside it as well. The smaller parrots may become affectionate as well as tame (page 161), and can perform little tricks like taking a sunflower seed gently from between your lips. The big parrots and the mynah birds can be trained to mimic human speech, whistles or even short melodies (page 156). And the parrots in particular can be encouraged to perform on command tricks they themselves have devised (page 168).

Taming or training outside the bird's cage is easiest if the bird's wing feathers are temporarily clipped to prevent flying until the bird is reliably calm. Some pet stores will clip a bird's wings for you when you buy it; vets will also clip wings. Once you are used to handling birds, the job is easy to do yourself with the help of one other person.

Breeding

Some birds are perfectly happy to court, mate, build nests, lay eggs and raise babies in captivity. Others are not. The mynah bird, for instance, has not been known to breed in captivity, though no one seems to know why. Most of the large parrots will breed, but only in very big outdoor aviaries. Apparently they need plenty of flight space to come into breeding condition. Canaries, parakeets, cockatiels and lovebirds, on the other hand, have all been bred in people's homes. Each bird needs a different sort of nesting place and different treatment to breed, so we will explain canary breeding just as an example. You should be able to get information on the other species at the library.

First be sure you have a male (cock) and a female (hen) canary. The cock can be distinguished by his song. The hen, who looks identical, doesn't sing. Check with the bird dealer or pet store to make sure that you are not buying hybrid birds. Many of the prettier canaries sold today are actually crosses between a canary and a finch, a process which adds pretty new colors and patterns to the offspring. They are pretty but they are unable to have babies of their own.

Canaries breed during late winter or early spring, anywhere from mid-February to the beginning of April. Breeders usually start to get the birds in breeding condition by the beginning of January. Birds breed when their bodies are in peak condition. In nature, they often change their diet to include more fresh greens or high-protein insects before the breeding season. You can accomplish the same thing by adding special high-protein foods to the canaries' basic seed and vegetable diet mentioned earlier in this chapter. Conditioning foods (either seeds or crushed biscuits) are sold by pet stores. They have varying ingredients but are all high in protein. Offer the conditioning food every day in a separate cup. By mid-February buy yourself a special breeding cage from a pet store. This cage has two compartments separated by two removable partitions, one made of wire and the other solid. Each side has its own food and water dishes.

Put the cock into one side and the hen into the other. Provide the hen with a nesting place, either a nesting bowl bought in a pet store or one made from a kitchen strainer with the handle cut off. Attach it in a corner of the cage using wire if necessary. Be sure the nest is low enough to allow the canaries to perch on the edge without bumping their heads on the cage top. Both parents will feed their young by perching on the nest edge and reaching their beaks down into the waiting mouths.

Over a period of a few days to a few weeks, the male will begin to court with bursts of song. Soon both birds call back and forth in a high-pitched whistle. At this point, remove the solid partition

Wing Clipping

It takes two people to clip a bird's wings. One person holds the bird, the other clips the wings. Use any comfortable scissors, but try them on cloth first to be sure they cut easily.

Wrap the bird up in a dishtowel or a terry-cloth hand towel. Turn it belly up, as this posture quiets birds and usually stops them from struggling. Keep a flap of towel over its face if it tries to peck or bite. While one person holds the bird in his or her lap, the other can extract one wing from the wrappings. Spread the wing out (by straightening the "elbow") and cut straight across the long flight feathers. Cutting feathers does not hurt the bird. Like fingernails, feathers are sensitive only where they grow inside the bird's skin, and you are cutting well away from there.

You need only clip one wing to prevent real flying. The bird will flutter along the ground but can't take to the air. The short clipped feathers will fall out during the bird's next molt, probably only a few months away. If it's tame by then, you can let its feathers grow in so it can fly again.

There are two other ways to clip wings that keep the wing looking more normal but are not as effective in preventing flying. Either, however, can be used with the larger birds who need nearly all their flight feathers to support their heavier weight.

The first method is to leave the first two or three flight feathers long and cut the rest of them off. You'll see the resulting gap when the wing is opened, but when the bird folds its wings, they will look nearly normal. The second method is to cut every other flight feather, starting with the second one. Even when the wings are fully spread, the evenly spaced gaps look quite natural. Both methods require that both wings be clipped.

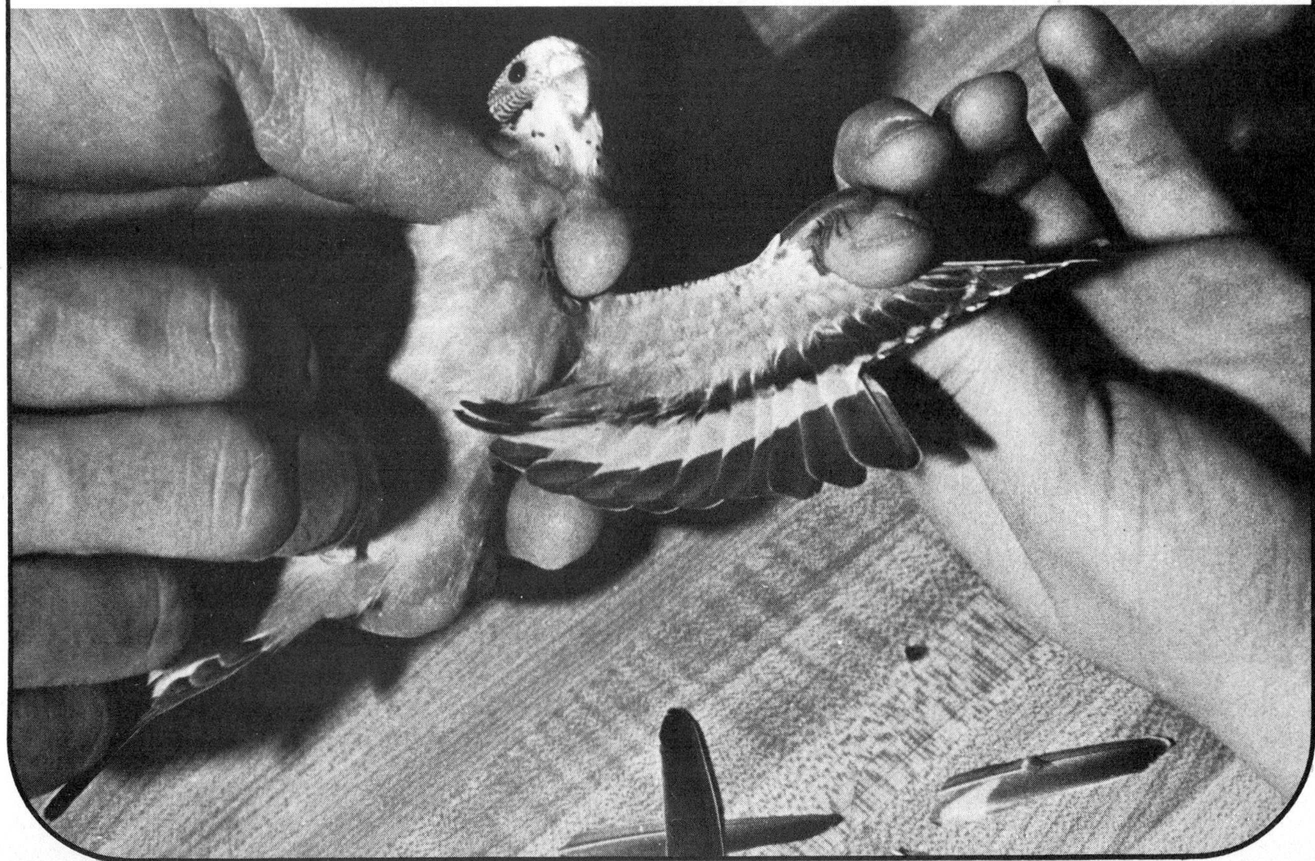

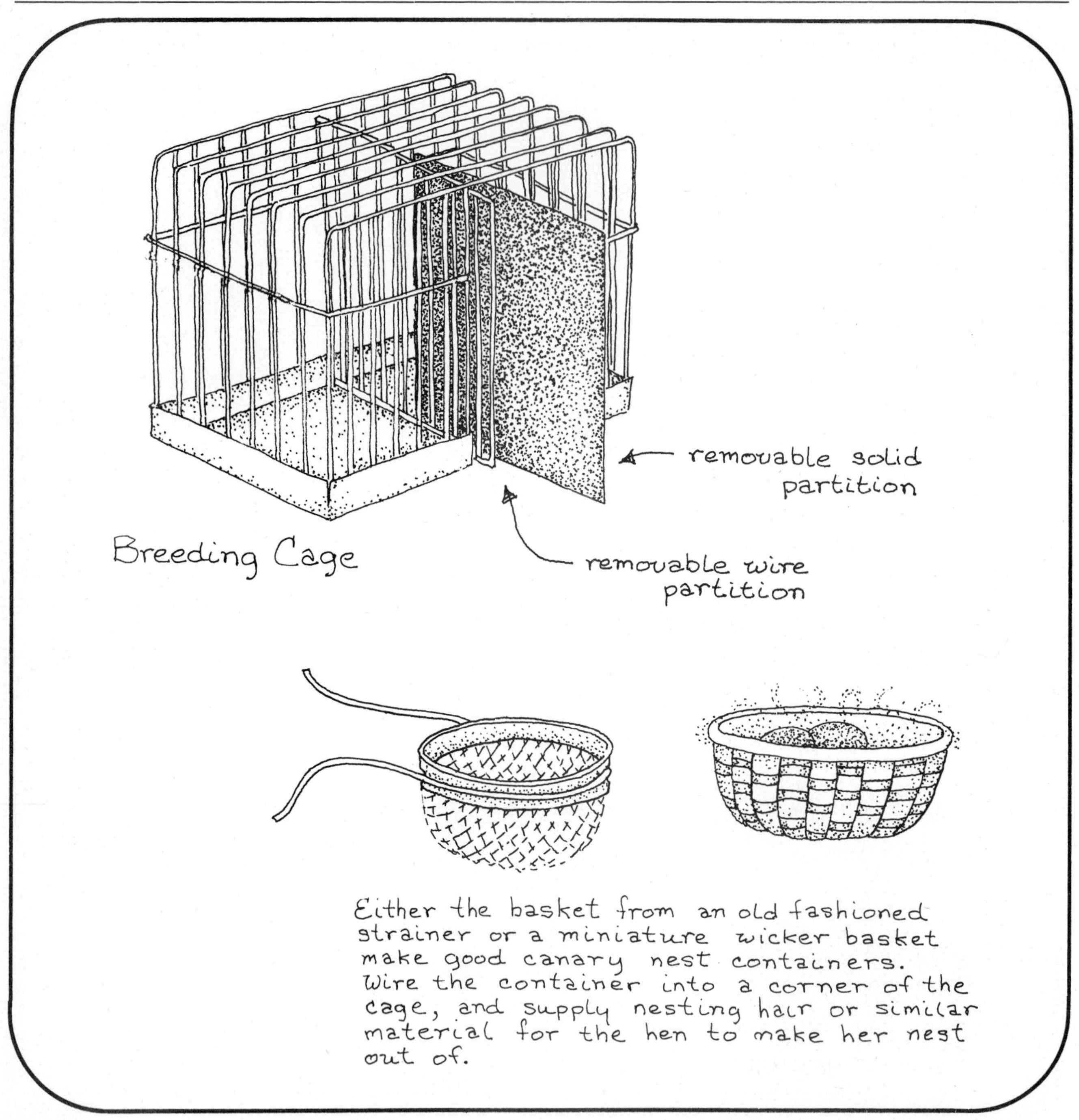

but not the wire one. Watch how the cock and hen behave together. If they squabble through the wires, they are not ready to mate and you should put the solid partition in again to give them more time. If the male feeds the female through the wires, you can remove the wire partition and expect the birds to mate.

Both male and female birds have a single opening at the base of the tail, called by biologists the cloaca (the same word used for the same opening in reptiles). In common language the hole in birds is called a vent. It is used for droppings, for laying eggs and for transferring sperm. Penises are rare in birds. Ducks and geese have them but canaries don't. To fertilize the hen's eggs, the cock canary must mount her back while she uplifts and spreads her tail feathers. Then he drops his rear end over hers until their two cloacas touch. Then sperm, swimming on their own, enter the hen's cloaca and move on into her oviduct, where her eggs are fertilized (joined to the sperm). This takes only a few seconds.

When the sperm reach the eggs, they are not yet covered with shell but are instead the pinhead-sized cells that are the actual eggs. Each egg cell has already been supplied with the yolk that will nourish it as it grows to be a baby bird, but everything else we think of as egg—the "white" (albumen), the thin membrane surrounding the white (allantois), and the shell itself—are secreted around the egg and its yolk as it travels down the oviduct.

While all this is happening, the hen will want to build her nest inside the container you have provided. You may notice her picking up bits of fluff or feather from the cage floor and beginning to arrange them in the strainer. At this point supply the hen with short pieces of yarn, bits of cotton, hair from your dog or cat, or commercial nesting hair that pet stores sell.

Once the eggshells are completed inside her body, the hen lays her eggs into her nest, one a day for three to five days. The shell is at first soft and leathery but soon turns hard and brittle. Inside the egg the tiny fertilized egg cell begins its growth into a baby bird. Blood vessels connect the embryo to the yolk from which it gets its nourishment. Fourteen days after laying, the first egg hatches. Each of the other eggs will hatch at the same one-day intervals at which they were laid.

Baby passerine birds are born nearly naked and with eyes sealed shut. They have two talents: they are usually able to back themselves up to the edge of the nest to drop their droppings over the side; and they are able to open their mouths and beg for food, which they do more or less continuously.

There is no reason to remove the cock canary when the babies are born. Both he and the hen will feed the babies and keep them warm. The parents are kept quite busy filling those mouths and should still be fed a supplementary diet of conditioning food and some greens.

Nesting birds are more nervous than usual and may be too upset to feed and care for their young when you are around. Don't show off the nest, eggs or babies frequently. Try to give the parents extra peace and quiet. By five or six weeks old, baby canaries are covered with fledgling feathers, their eyes are wide open and they are able to feed themselves. They should be started on soft foods—conditioning biscuit mixed with water to a mushy consistency. Special fledgling foods are sometimes available in pet stores too. As soon as you can see they have begun to eat adult canary seed, you can consider the babies grown up enough to leave their parents, either for larger quarters in your home or as pets for others.

Canaries

Canaries are a species of finch that have been bred as pets for close to five centuries. The canaries you see in pet stores would hardly recognize their olive-drab-colored forebears. Before Columbus discovered America, the sailors who discovered canaries in the Canary Islands brought them home for the sake of their singing. Since then, breeders have been of two minds. Some have bred canaries for their looks, so that there are brilliant yellow, slate-blue, orange, red, pink and patterned canaries that sing mediocre songs. Others have bred the singing canaries called choppers and rollers to achieve heights of song, but their feathers are rather plain. Choppers have a brisk, clear, high song, including elements called chops. Rollers have a much more varied but quieter song consisting of rolls, flutes, tours and warbles.

Male canaries do the singing. Female canaries only chirp and twitter. It is only lately that scientists discovered why male birds sing songs: they sing at break of day not to express their joy, but to announce their whereabouts. The song tells other male birds to keep out of their territory, and invites female birds to come into their territory. The song sparrow announces itself more often than a radio station: up to 2,305 times a day.

Some birds vary their song somewhat in tone and intensity, so that their mate can recognize them as individuals in dense foliage where they can't see one another. Strangely, even though a canary might vary the sequence of his song—rolling first and then fluting, or vice versa—birds don't recognize different sequences as different songs. If the elements are there, it's the same song no matter what order it's sung in. This is like saying you would recognize a piece of music no matter what order the individual notes were in, so long as all the notes were there. We have different minds than birds.

Choosing a Canary

The only guarantee for getting a "show bird" in either looks or song is to buy directly from a breeder. You may be able to locate a canary breeder in a big city phone directory or by asking your pet dealer. However, show quality canaries are expensive pets to buy. The canaries carried by most pet stores only approximate the following descriptions because they are often mixed breeds. But they are within most family's budgets.

The best singing canary varieties are the choppers and rollers. You have to buy a male if you want to listen to bird songs because only males sing. Because you can't tell the sexes apart by looking, pet store personnel are supposed to listen to the birds, choose the males after they have begun to sing, and guarantee the singing to you in writing. Female birds are much cheaper than males because they don't sing. When a store advertises "young unsexed canaries" at bargain prices, you can bet they are all females! Usually only breeders are interested in keeping female canaries, but they make good pets and look as pretty as the males. If the singing is not important to you, buy a female. She will at least twitter and chirp.

Of the fancy lookers, the Red Factors, Border Fancies, American Singers, and Glosters also sing passably. The Gloster canary has a round cap of feathers on its domed head that falls half over its eyes. The Red Factor was an astonishing event in bird breeding. For ages breeders have crossed canaries with other finch species in attempts to get new markings and new colors in the offspring. They especially wanted a red or orange bird. But although many closely related species can breed with one another, and many canaries sold are the results of such breedings, the hybrid (mixed) babies are usually sterile and can't have babies of their own. The mating of a female canary and a male red siskin produced the Red Factor—the rare case of a hybrid who can have babies.

All canaries you see should be banded. The band on the leg tells you the age of the bird. A male begins developing his song at about three months of age, can be accurately identified as a male singer by six months and has perfected his song by a year. At that age, you know what you are getting musically, and the bird is still young enough to become used to humans.

Only male canaries do the singing.

Housing

No special alterations to a standard birdcage are needed by canaries. However, if you want to control your canary's singing times, you can use a cage cover.

Since birds naturally sing at daybreak to announce themselves, canary fanciers use cage covers to trick canaries into conveniently timed bursts of song. The cage is covered—nighttime and silence; the cage is uncovered—daybreak and song. If you get a lightproof cover to fit your cage, you can even convince your canary to entertain you in the evening by covering its cage in the daytime.

Food and Water

Boxed canary food is usually a mixture of canary and rapeseed. Thistle seeds and millet make good treats beyond the basic boxed diet, but canaries ought to have fresh greens in their diet, too. Plant some millet seeds in a small flowerpot. When they sprout, wire the pot to the cage bars so your canary can eat the fresh greens. In the summer you can gather seed heads from grasses, dandelion greens or even lawn grass. Wash them well to get rid of insecticide sprays. Hang the greens in bunches tied with string inside the cage. In winter, small bunches of broccoli, watercress, parsley, lettuce or spinach make good snacks. Try a bit of apple or orange in your bird's seed dish too. The cuttlebone suggested for beak rubbing is also a valuable source of salts and minerals. Canaries won't bite chunks off like the parrots do, but they will peck at it. Don't forget gravel on the cage floor and fresh water every day.

Taming and Training

After your canary is calm enough to sit near your hand (page 147) you can finger train it inside its cage. Put your finger up under the bird's chest, just above its legs. Push slightly back against it. Your canary has three choices of what to do next: fall backwards off its perch, something any bird would try to avoid; fly away, something most birds do at first; or climb onto your finger, which it will ultimately do. Keep at it until it climbs onto your finger every time you push against its chest. Some people say you can couple the action with the command "Hop," so the canary learns to hop onto your finger on command. I don't believe it.

Unless a bird's wings are clipped, it is in real danger the first few times you let it out of the cage. All pet birds see both mirrors and glass as holes, similar to the gaps in foliage through which they fly in nature. Plenty of pets have killed themselves by crashing head-on into windows and mirrors. On top of that, caged birds have so little exercise and so little flying practice that they are inaccurate, have trouble landing and get very out of breath.

Don't feed your bird the day you're going to let it out. A hungry bird will be more likely to come to you for food when it is time to get it back into the cage. Choose a small room that has curtains on the windows. The kitchen is a bad choice. Birds can't learn not to land on hot pots and burners. Close the curtains; either take down mirrors or put sheets of newspaper over them. Close all the doors too. Put the cage down in the middle of the room. Put the seed box next to it.

Now you're ready; but you can't just let a bird out of a cage. Its cage is the only territory it knows, and it's not all that eager to leave safe ground. If you reach in and grab your bird, you're only ruining all that patient hand training. So put your finger in, let it perch, and see if you can very slowly move the bird out the door. This may not work; the manufacturers make those doors very small. A better alternative is to remove the tray of the cage and the metal sheet that is under it, and the food and water dishes. Then turn the cage slowly upside down. The canary will come out.

As the canary flies, you'll notice it may be having difficulties. It doesn't really know where to land, and it may get tired quickly. Pretend you are a birdfeeder. Sit next to the cage, pour some seeds into your hand and hold your hand out. The idea is for the bird to recognize your finger as a safe perch, see the food it's so hungry for, and eventually land on you, the birdfeeder. After a few minutes see if you can put the cage over your bird, and then slide the metal sheet back in to close it.

If the bird never comes to you, there's the problem of catching it to get it back in the cage. Its exhaustion now may prove helpful. Get a dishtowel. Each time it lands, shoo it into the air again. When you see the canary panting for breath and low enough for you to reach, just drop the dishtowel over it. Hold it gently through the towel with your hands; extricate it from its wrappings as you put it through the cage door. If you've had this much trouble, it means you should probably go back to more hand feeding and finger perching in the cage before you let the bird out again. Remember that wild birds learn easily to come to a birdfeeder; your canary will too.

The other way to let a canary loose is to first clip one wing so it can't fly (page 149). Either way, a canary given liberty ultimately has to learn to get about a particular room without bumping into everything, and to come to its human birdfeeder when it's time to go back in the cage.

Mynahs

The mynah is one of the best pet talking birds. It repeats a large variety of phrases and sound effects, as well as making astonishing and peculiar noises of its own. It can meow like a cat, gurgle like wine from a jug, click like a metal cricket toy, or plip-plop like pebbles tossed in a pool. Joe-Joe, the mynah who lives in our local pet shop, speaks with the clockwork sound of a cuckoo bird, which is so comical it causes the best mimic of all, the human race, to imitate him back. As a result, all the salespeople in the store sound like wind-up mynah birds.

The only mynah commonly on the market is the Indian hill mynah, a medium-sized (somewhat larger than a robin), very glossy black bird with a bright yellow beak and white eye markings. It is a relative of the common starling. A mynah is not as calm a bird as a parrot, spending much of its time hopping back and forth from perch to perch. Calming and finger training are possible, and a definite preference for one person in the family has been reported. I haven't heard of actual signs of affection, but you may get them by working with your bird often enough.

You may wonder why some birds mimic sounds. It is certainly not meant to amuse humans. I've wondered, and have come up with an idea. Many birds are territorial animals. They stake out their own place, then announce themselves to rival birds with a special song. The song is a warning only to their own kind and doesn't mean a thing to other species. The song of the robin doesn't keep out the titmice or the nuthatches—only other robins. But suppose a mynah came along who learned to mimic the robin, the titmouse and the nuthatch. Instead of keeping out only other mynahs, it might warn off three other species as well. Naturally, it would get that much more food and living space for itself. Logical as this idea sounds, I haven't been able to find out if it's true.

Talking birds aren't really talking, of course. They haven't the vaguest idea what they are saying. People have been fooled by birds who hear the telephone ring and say "Hello," or who hear the dog scratching at the door and say "Do you want to go out?" This "finishing out" a noise (telephone ring, "hello"; dog scratch, "do you want to go out?") is similar to duetting, in which a pair of birds alternates parts of the same song so cleverly that they sound like a single bird. Duetting keeps a pair of birds in contact where dense foliage prevents them from seeing one another. I have a parrot who consistently performs the first or last part of a wolf whistle and expects me to fill in the missing part. I'm a disappointment to her. I can't whistle.

Choosing a Mynah

Theoretically, male birds should be the better talkers. In nature they are the guardians of territory and the singers of songs. Both the male and female mynahs do talk, however. No one seems to know if the male learns more readily, and anyhow you're not going to be able to tell a cock from a hen mynah. If you want to be sure of a good talker, buy a bird who already talks.

As far as taming goes, a baby bird in pinfeathers is the best bet, but very hard to find. And of course babies don't talk yet. The best compromise may be a bird who has begun to talk and who doesn't panic when you move your hand towards its cage. Getting a calm talker several years old is fine—they live a long life, the record being 30 years in captivity.

Once trained, a mynah consents to perch on your arm.

Housing

The mynahs need large cages, larger than those available. So you must take your bird out regularly for exercise. Inside the cage, perches should be horizontally parallel so the bird can hop from one perch to another. Place them wide apart to accommodate the mynah's surprisingly long hops. The standard perches that come with the cage might be too small to keep the bird's nails down. See page 140 for larger perches to install.

Because of the mynah's messy droppings, you'll have to change the newspapers on the cage floor every day. Some of the larger cages come with a wire floor through which droppings fall onto the paper-covered bottom drawer. This keeps the bird's feet out of its own mess if it walks on the bottom, but mynahs prefer to stay on their perches and the extra wire floor is just one more thing to clean.

Food and Water

Mynahs are fruit-eaters who also eat insects when they can. The dry foods sold in pet stores are claimed to be a balanced diet, and definitely cut down on the moisture and messiness of the droppings. Fill the food dish with dry mynah food daily so it is always available. But you should be skeptical of the nutritional claims of this and most other packaged foods; your bird may need and will usually enjoy a supplement. Offer small bits of orange, apple, broken grapes and banana, but only a heaping teaspoonful once a day. Your mynah will probably like to eat live mealworms (available at pet stores) as a weekly snack, too. Mealworms are meat, but not the best quality. Try little pellets of raw hamburger as a snack. Don't forget the sand for digestion. Put some in the food dish, rather than down among the droppings.

Mynahs drink a good deal of water, and bathe frequently. Remember to change the water in their dish daily. To avoid the mess they make trying to get their too-big bodies into the water dish, try a plant-mister spray bath. Even better, let your bird get in the kitchen sink and putter around under a trickling faucet after it's calmed and trained.

Taming and Training

Calming and finger training a mynah can be done the same way you would for a canary. If your bird gets so nervous that it bats its wings or bangs its head against the bars when you reach into the cage, you might consider clipping wings (page149)and proceeding outside the cage as for a parakeet, which you will read about later in this chapter. Sit in the middle of an uncluttered room when training so that there are fewer obstacles for your bird to bump into. Extremes when training aren't necessary: the mynah's bite is no harder than a little pinch. Because of the mynah's nervousness and active nature, you'll need time (10 or 15 minutes every day) and patience to calm it. But it's worthwhile; you may know your mynah has only a bird brain, but when it perches on your shoulder and yacks at your friends, they will be impressed.

All the talking birds seem to learn new words and phrases best when the house is quiet and when you are not within view. A method often recommended is to cover the cage at night, then repeat the new word or phrase off and on for 15 minutes in the morning before you take the cover off. High-voiced women and children are imitated more readily than men, and training proceeds better if only one person is doing it. The method sounds logical—it comes closest to a bird in nature concentrating on the high-pitched bird song of a single species out of sight in the forest at dawn.

Little Parrots

Parakeets, lovebirds and cockatiels are all in the parrot family and they all make good pets. Many are bred in this country and therefore are more reasonable in price than the larger parrots that are caught in the wild. When people ask for a parakeet, they are usually thinking of only one particular kind of parakeet: the Australian budgerigar, or "budgie." There are other kinds of parakeets, some nearly as big as an Amazon parrot.

If you want any of these small parrots to become very attached to you, buy only one. Although two birds are fun to watch, they will be more affectionate with one another than they will be with you. Young budgies will be easiest to tame. Look at the forehead: babies have a scalloped pattern on the feathers of the forehead above the beak. The scallop markings will give way to solid-colored feathers by the time the bird is 10 to 12 weeks old.

Choosing a Little Parrot

Budgerigars. Budgies make calm, trustworthy and interesting pets. They like to play, and like all the parrots they can get very attached to a human. They are smart for small birds, but not as smart as the larger parrots. There is one thing disappointing about parakeets—most of them really can't learn to talk. Worse, there's no way of telling whether the parakeet you have chosen will happen to be one of the unusual ones that will learn or one of the usual ones that will never say a word. Whistling is a better bet, and if you set your sights on a wolf whistle or something equally easy, you may be pleasantly surprised.

Cockatiels. Cockatiels are also from Australia. They are a perky, crested bird with a long tail and graceful wings. The common ones are gray, the less common ones "pied" with white bars and dots, and the rarest is a white albino shading to yellow on the crest. Best of all, cockatiels have rosy cheeks; sometimes the orange spot on their cheeks is so perfectly round and bright it looks as though someone had painted it there. Males have a brighter cheek patch than females. The albino, sometimes called a moon cockatiel, shows off the orange cheek and shoe-button eyes best, making it

one of the prettiest birds you can buy. But they are expensive. There are reports of talking cockatiels, but this is most uncommon.

Bee Bees and Lovebirds. Of the miniature parrots, the common, least expensive, dull-colored bee bee parrot is among the best pets. There are many prettier birds—especially lovebirds—but the bee bee is calm, loving, and may become charmingly eccentric. Once you tame a bee bee it will do things like say "bee beee beeee" at you all through breakfast unless you share your toast, or develop a liking for pockets and creep into them, or steal cigarettes, or do something else no one has thought of yet.

The lovebirds come in soft rich colors. Some of the more common ones you're likely to see are the peach-faced and Fischer's. Lovebirds get their name from the way a devoted pair carry on with one another. Stores may try to convince you that a lovebird can only by happy with a mate, even at today's prices. That's great for their profits, but if you want a bird to love, groom and attempt to feed you regurgitated sunflower seeds, buy only one. Don't expect either the bee bee or the lovebird to talk; both have a rather shrill screech on occasion and chirp somewhat noisily.

Housing

A small parrot has enough room to fly a little in a canary-sized cage. But all of them, and the cockatiel especially, need some flying time outside their cage. Follow the information in the beginning of this chapter for setting up a cage home for your small parrot.

Food and Water

All the small parrots eat small-sized seed like wheat, millet and canary seed. Boxed parakeet mixtures are fine as a basic diet for any of them. As usual, you shouldn't trust a boxed food to be sufficient nutritionally. Offer fresh snacks of dark greens like spinach, romaine lettuce, parsley or watercress, plus fruits like oranges and apples. Since the small parrots can give a nasty bite for their size, use sunflower seeds for hand feeding.

Fingers make good parakeet perches.

No More Bored Birds

Scratching, screeching, feather plucking, or pacing can be symptoms of nervousness in caged birds, or they can point to another common problem—boredom. Boredom is more likely to afflict the intelligent parrot family than the less curious songbirds.

A sure sign of boredom is a bird who sits around looking stupid. In other words, if you find your bird bores you, this is because it's bored. After all, when you have to sit in school too much, you chew pencils, tip chairs, fiddle with your hair and doodle in your books. So give your small parrot some things to interest it.

Pet stores sell all sorts of cage toys for small birds. The toys use bright colors or are made of sparkly materials, or they jingle or jiggle. Some of them are climbable or swingable. Many of them have mirrors, but I don't think that's a good idea: birds react to mirrors because they think their image is a rival bird, so they ruffle up, bob their heads up and down and carry on a lot. It doesn't mean the bird is either amusing or admiring itself. It really means the bird is hopelessly confused and perhaps upset. Therefore a mirror is a mean toy.

Toys might be fun to make yourself. Here are some ideas: jingle bells on a wire loop; split rings attached to one another; split rings holding nuts and washers; paper-clip chain with buttons on the last clip; fancy dime-store metal rings; plastic Christmas-tree balls on a metal bead chain. You can make ladders from two lengths of wooden lattice strip with thin wooden dowel rings glued between. Pet stores sell swings, or you can rig your own with wire and a short piece of dowel.

Toys are a real problem with bigger parrots. They can bite through strong metals. They can untwist a paper clip in a moment, and undo even the largest-sized snap ring.

We've found only a few toys that last: padlocks locked on to the bars of the cage; large jingle bells attached to the split rings sold as key holders (or attach old keys instead of the jingle bells); the iron Indian bells available in some gift stores; and metal chain slip collars intended for dogs, held to the bars with either a padlock or the clip from a dog leash. Toys less sturdy are a waste of time and money.

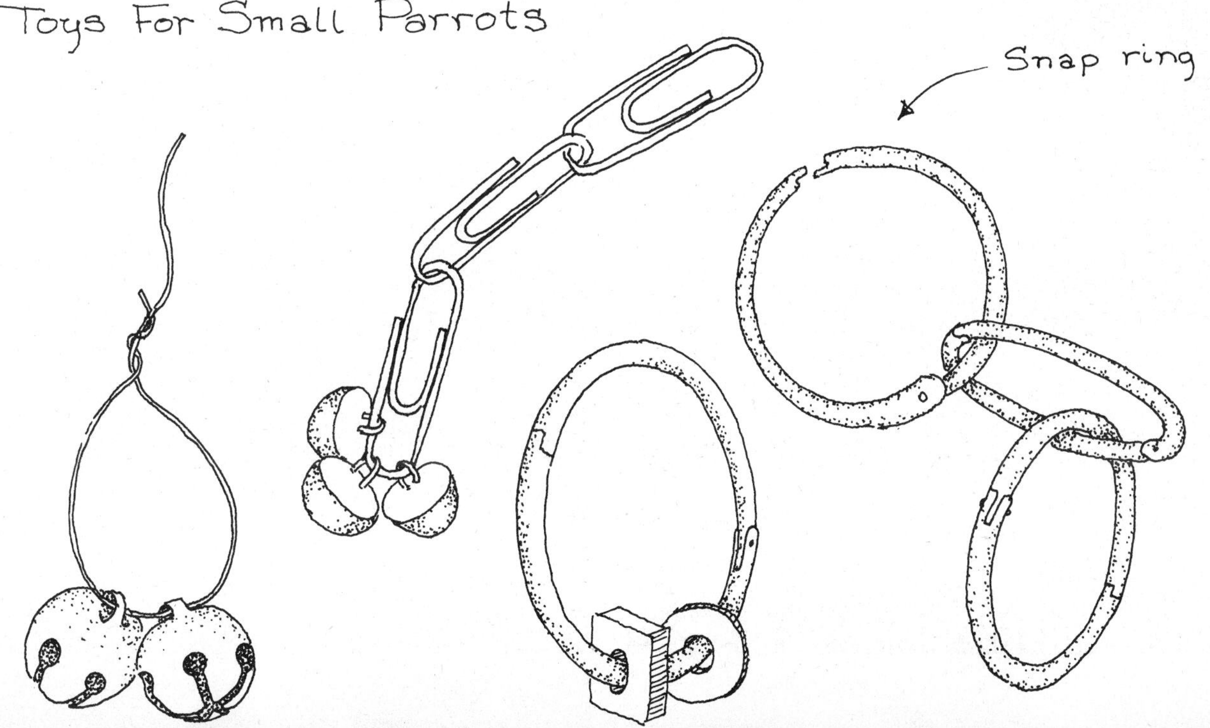

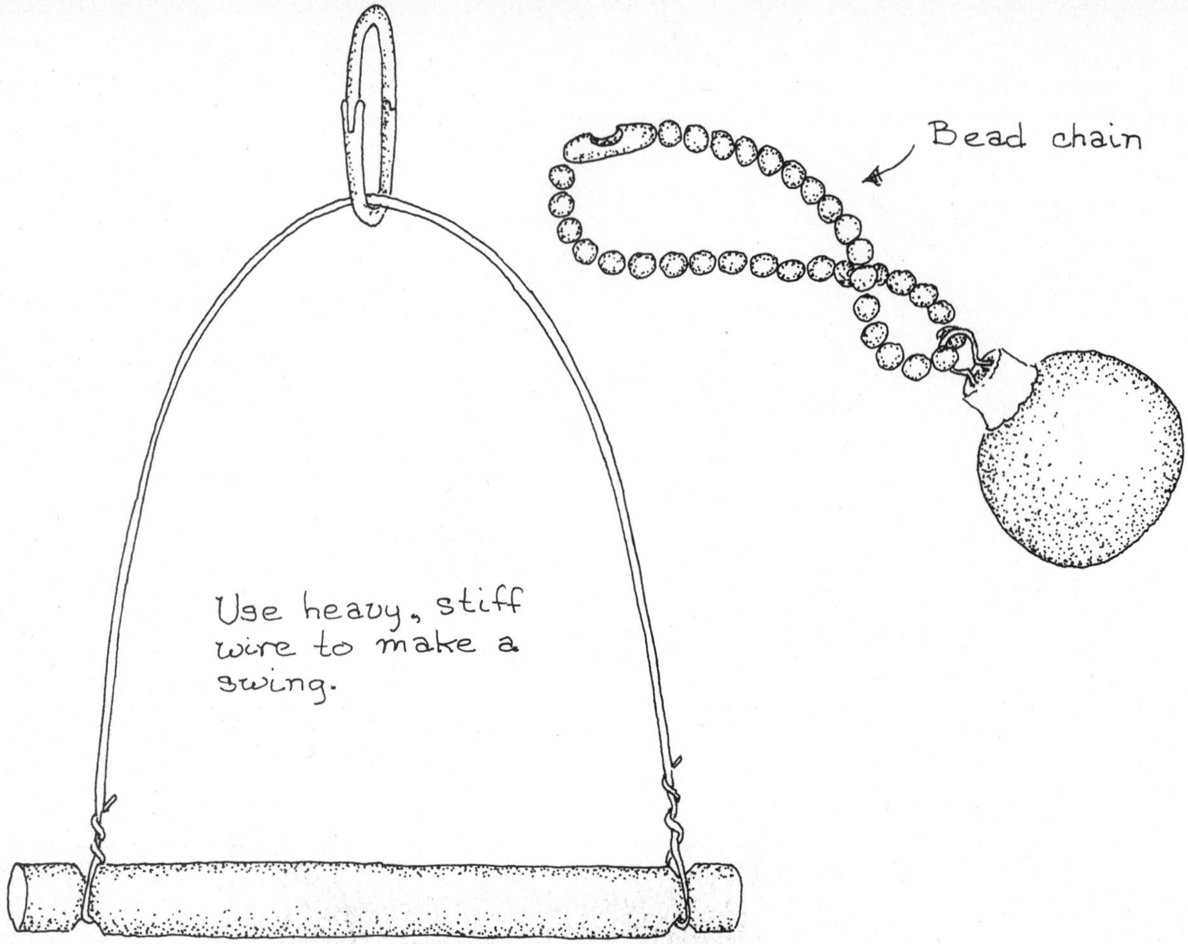

Bead chain

Use heavy, stiff wire to make a swing.

Toys For Large Parrots

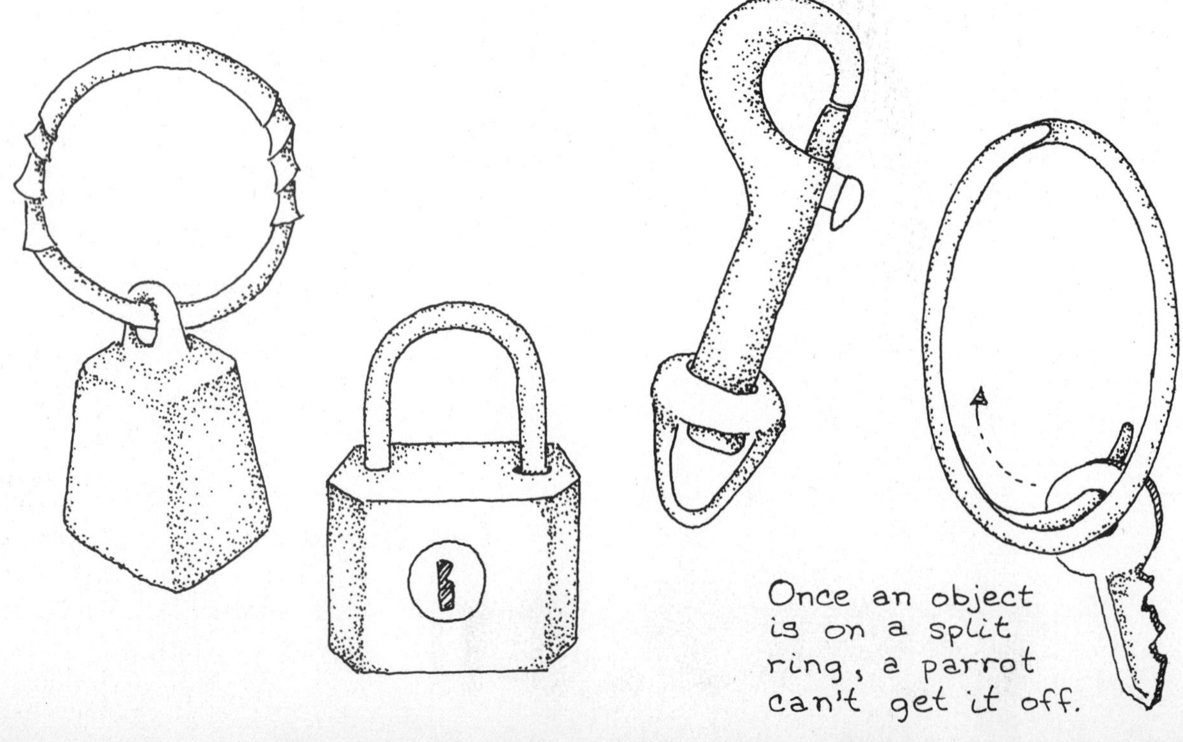

Once an object is on a split ring, a parrot can't get it off.

They're big enough so the bird can take them from your fingers without nipping fingertips. Save the sunflower seeds for treats. As a steady diet, they're fattening for caged birds.

Cuttlebone will give the small parrots something rough to nibble on to keep their beaks in shape, and also supply minerals not found in seeds. The cuttlebone won't last as long as it does with canaries. You might have to replace it every other week. Chicken bones serve just as well, and come free off the family dinner plates. A bit of meat left on the bones or an occasional mealworm will no doubt be appreciated too. Gravel on the cage floor or the bottom of the seed dish is a must.

Drinking water can be served in the cage dish, but some of these parrots can learn to drink from a water bottle instead. The kind to try has a metal spout with a ball bearing just inside the tip. Don't trust that your bird can use it until you see it drinking. The advantage to a water bottle is that you won't have to change it every day.

Once you're fed up with attempts by your little parrot to bathe in the water dish, experiment with the three other bathing methods: wet leaves, a plant mister or a shallow bath dish.

Taming and Training

People who try to tame a small parrot tend to stop short of achieving the singular devotion and real affection these birds are capable of. You really have to inflict yourself on your bird several times a day, every day, to get beyond mere calmness and finger perching. During much of the time it won't look like you're getting anywhere. But when love happens, it happens fast, and from then on the bird will be your friend for life.

Because much more handling is involved in taming a parrot than in taming a canary, you'll have to get your bird's wings clipped, or do it yourself (page 149). With clipped wings, a bird can walk or flutter only a short distance. You can train it outside the cage and yet easily retrieve it each time it tries to get away from you.

Once wing clipping is over, proceed as you would for a canary, resting your hand on the cage, and then putting your hand inside. At first your bird will flutter and screech at you, but after a week or so it should calm down. When the fussing stops, try bringing one finger up under its chest and lifting it slightly. Your bird may step on your finger or bite it.

If it steps onto your finger, you can start taking it out of the cage this way and sitting with it at a table or on the floor. Every time the bird hops off, put your finger in front of it again. It should soon learn that nothing awful happens when it sits on this new perch. Talk to the bird in a running stream. Offer it food from your fingers. As it gets used to you, try transferring it to your shoulder by holding your whole arm at a downward slant. The bird's response to the downhill position should be to walk upward to your shoulder. It can be taken down by putting a finger in front of its chest. The first sign of affection will be a gentle nibbling and pulling of the hairs at the nape of your neck. It is preening or grooming you as it would another bird.

If your parrot bites you, there is another method of taming which may at first frighten the bird more, but actually seems to work faster. Put on leather gloves. They may frighten the bird because it may have been roughly handled by gloved hands in the past. Take your bird out of the cage and sit on the floor with it. Put it on one gloved finger. The bird will get off right away. Pick it up (just put your whole hand around it) and try again. Keep doing it. Talk gently as you work with it, and each time it hops off be gentle as you put it back on. With this method you may be able to train your bird to sit on your hand in a single afternoon, but you will still have to win its love over weeks of talking, hand feeding, finger perching and shoulder climbing.

Big Parrots

A big parrot is a very permanent pet. A parrot lives so long that the bird you buy now may be your children's pet 20 years from now. There is a record for a pet parrot held by an African gray who lived to be 80, having been handed down through three generations of the same family, and a cockatoo who lived in a zoo died at 120 years of age. A big parrot becomes so attached to the family it lives with that it is a tragedy in its life if you sell it to strangers. And since a parrot can cost more than a purebred dog, it makes sense to be cautious in choosing one.

Choosing a Big Parrot

The best of all choices is a baby parrot, because it is the easiest to tame. But you probably won't be able to find one. Many times the dealer doesn't know how old the parrot is, but a pet store parrot is almost never that young. A real baby parrot looks like a baby—smaller than an adult, with fuzz and pinfeathers on top of its head the same as any fledgling. A young parrot, though full-grown and fully feathered, tends to have smooth flat scales on its legs and feet. As a parrot gets older, the scales become larger and coarser. Since a parrot lives so long, it doesn't really matter whether it is one or five years old so long as it is tame or tamable.

If no one is sure how old the parrot is, you will have to choose it by its behavior. Come up close to its cage, and watch how it acts. If it screams and growls at you, you'll have a rough time. If it just backs to the other side of the cage or climbs up higher on the bars, try putting your arm up next to it (no fingers through the bars, please!). If your parrot acts terribly frightened and bats about in a panic all over the cage, you are still going to have a hard time. If it simply acts nervous but a bit curious, you can probably tame it with little trouble.

If the dealer claims this parrot is already hand tamed, ask to be shown this. He or she should be able to feed the bird by hand and get it to climb on an arm if it is actually tame. A really tame parrot will lower its head to be scratched by the people it is used to, although it may act fearful or aggressive toward strangers until it has known them several weeks or even longer.

Sometimes things happen the other way around. We once found a parrot in a pet store that the dealer claimed had never been touched. He was sure the bird was wild and dangerous. But when we approached the cage and held our arms up, it seemed calm and curious. We believed our own eyes, and bought it. Sure enough, when we let it out of the cage, it climbed right to our shoulders and preened the hair on our necks lovingly. It was probably hand raised as a baby.

It is harder to judge a parrot's health by its plumage than it is with other birds. Feathers can look broken and dull even on a healthy bird if it has just come through immigration and quarantine, or if it's

been batting its feathers against the bars of a small cage. You can see, however, any of the signs of illness described at the beginning of the chapter. Some people say that if a parrot perches on one foot, it means the bird is sick. That isn't true; you might check that its feet aren't injured, but most likely it is just perching on one foot. Don't take a parrot that has bald spots unless it's been caged with another parrot, and it's the other parrot who has been plucking the feathers. A bird who plucks itself has psychological problems. Other nervous symptoms are pacing and screaming. These emo-

It took a lot of patience to stick train Looney, an African gray but he eventually got the idea.

tional ills may be incurable; it's wise to avoid such birds.

The personality of parrots seems to vary as much as the personality of dogs and cats, depending more on individual inheritance and personal experience than on species. The only exception is the African gray, which most people agree is more aggressive and more eccentric than other parrots. Since the African gray is also a better talker than any other parrot, it's worth extra patience in taming. The cost of macaws has put them just about out of sight financially, and they are now so depleted in nature that one shouldn't encourage their capture by buying them anyhow. Not all cockatoos are rare in nature, but I haven't seen one for sale in America for five years. Amazons are plentiful; all Amazons are basically parrot green with various brightly colored heads, facial markings and wing tips. The large Amazon family constitutes the bulk of the pet parrot selection. If you can find one of the larger parakeets, like the Indian ringneck, it makes an excellent pet as well.

Before you take an untamed parrot home, be absolutely sure its wings are clipped. This is not a job for you to do on a large parrot until you are friends with the bird. The job should be done at the pet store and considered part of the purchase price. We emphasize it because you'll have an awful time taming a parrot who can fly.

Housing

There are really no available cages large enough for parrots. If there were, they would probably be unaffordable. The best cage available is about two feet square and close to three feet tall, made of very stout wire with a wire floor over the drawer portion. It's large enough to allow an African gray, Indian ringneck, or Amazon to stretch, climb, and flap its wings; flying is impossible. Think of the cage as you think of your home: a place to live but not to stay in all the time.

Most parrots will chew on the perches in their cages. See the Housing information at the beginning of the chapter for suggestions about replacing perches as they are damaged.

Cages that are made with wire bottoms over the solid tray floor don't really have to be cleaned more than once or twice a week. You might want to use a half inch of sand in the drawer instead of newspaper. The wire floor prevents the bird from kicking the sand out. Each week, rake seed and droppings from the sand with a fork, remove the pile and add some fresh sand to the cage bottom. If the cage has no protective wire over the bottom you'll need to use newspaper and change it more frequently, especially if your bird likes to walk about on the bottom.

Parrots Out Of Cages. If you keep your parrot's wings clipped, and if it has a reasonable personality (which most of them do), you don't have to keep it in a cage at all. Sparrow, an Amazon parrot, lived on a branch in the kitchen (see pages 335 for instructions on how to do this).

If you keep the branch rather high, the parrot won't really want to plunge down off it. It knows it can't fly well with its wings clipped; the plunge is too much like falling. But we can't guarantee that every parrot will react as Sparrow did. Ringo, an Indian ringneck parakeet, felt unsafe up on a branch with clipped wings. Until his feathers grew back, he made his home under our stove. Every time we used the oven he would come out and scold us. The stove is not recommended as a parrot hole, in spite of Ringo.

Both Sparrow and Ringo prove a little-known point about captive parrots: they become attached to their own place. Sparrow was pleased to explore about the kitchen, but even when his wings grew back he rarely ventured from his branch for more than an hour or so. Ringo, when he could fly again, exchanged his hideaway under the oven for a perch above the stove. Now all our parrots live in an aviary off the kitchen. When the doors are opened, it may take as long as an hour before anyone decides to come out. And in all the ten years since we've had parrots, with all the liberty we give them, no bird has ever explored farther than the kitchen unless first given a free ride to other areas on a friendly (and safe) shoulder.

Food and Water

Parrot food does come mixed in boxes like other pet foods, but is often mixed specially from

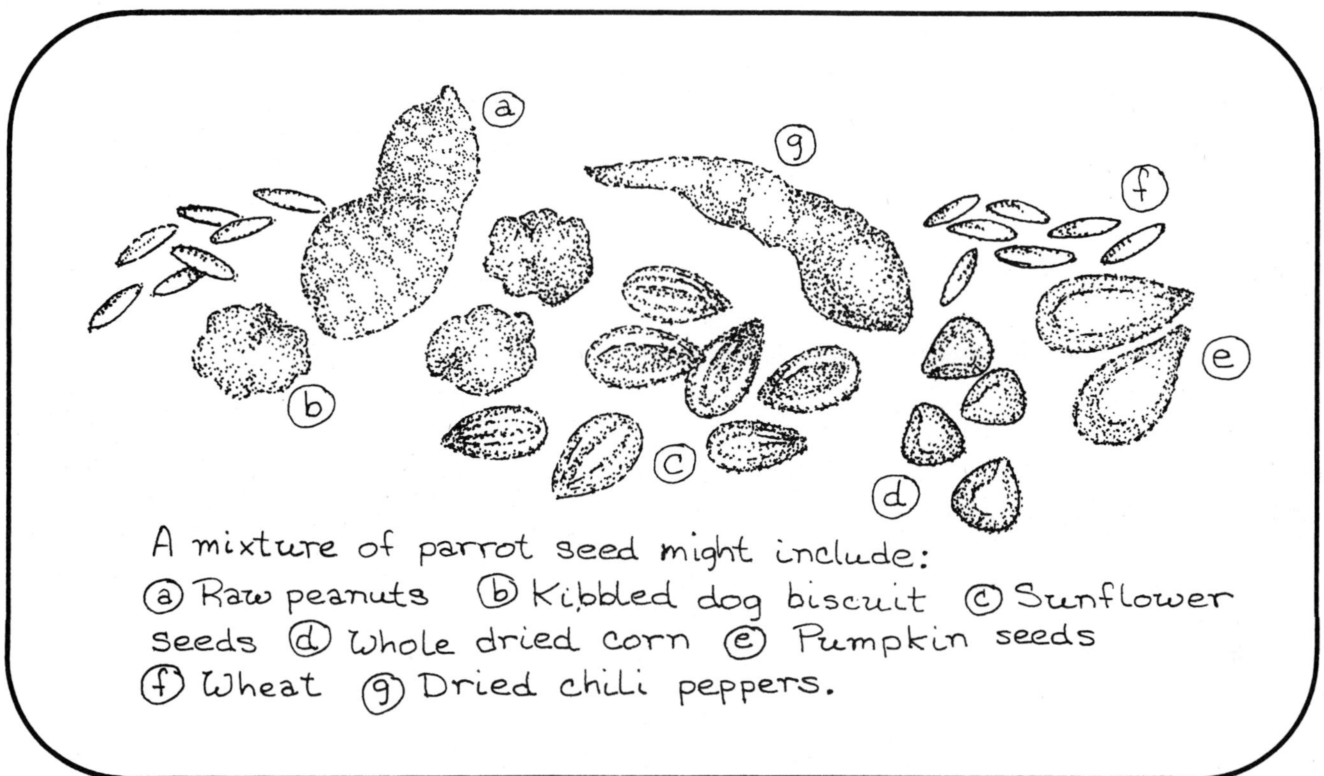

various sorts of seed and grain. The mixture we use contains kibbled dog food, wheat, corn, pumpkin seeds, dried red peppers, a high proportion of sunflower seeds, and a few raw peanuts.

The parrots love this particular mixture because it has so many peanuts and sunflower seeds in it —their favorite foods. However, peanuts and sunflower seeds are both very fatty foods, and the only reason it's okay for us to use so much is that our parrots live in an aviary large enough for daily flying, supplemented by kitchen liberty on weekends. A caged bird who is not allowed to fly would get too fat on this mixture and should have the proportions changed to include more kibble, corn and small seed. The dried peppers are supposed to keep a bird in good color, and I've heard Spanish people say they encourage talking. I don't believe either claim, and my parrots routinely remove the peppers from their seed dish. I only keep them in the mixture because they look so pretty.

Give the large parrots daily portions of dark-green leaves like spinach, watercress or romaine lettuce, and slices of apple or orange. Supply either green twigs or small bones for chewing. Cuttlebone won't last long enough to bother with, but bones supply the same minerals, as do eggshells. Pet stores may sell crushed oyster shell for minerals too. Sand is needed for digestion.

A parrot may be suspicious of foods inside its cage that it has not seen before. I once made the mistake of shoving a piece of pomegranate into a parrot's cage and leaving for the day. The bird was still cowering in the corner farthest from the innocent fruit when I got home hours later. If the bird is free to investigate on its own outside the cage, it is likely to sample any food that's around, including coffee, beer, spaghetti, scrambled eggs, lamb stew and pizza.

The dietary needs of different parrots must vary: our ringneck supplements his basic food with many stolen snacks. His favorites are fats like butter or bacon, and high-protein foods like raw meat, scrambled eggs and cheese. It seems best with pets whose nutritional needs are not exactly known to try many foods. Wild bird nutrition has not really been studied closely, and a pet's own preference when offered a delicatessen array may be the best guide.

Water requirements are no different than any other bird, except that I swear parrots dump newspaper scraps and apple skins into the water dish on purpose. Be sure to change that water daily.

Because of a parrot's size, it has trouble bathing in the water dish. A cake pan of water is fine, or a good misting, but both are rather wet propositions for a cage. It is less sloppy to get the bird used to taking a bath outside its cage. It can perch at the kitchen sink for a mist spray or splash in a pan on the kitchen floor. If you always give a parrot a bath on a certain day of the week, it might learn to tell the day. One of our birds perches on a certain chair and spreads his wings every Saturday morning to tell us it is spray time. Another paces up and down the kitchen counter flapping and clucking until his water pan appears.

Taming and Training

Let me explain parrot taming by explaining some of our experiences. Looney Bird is really a parrot, an African gray parrot. But he was such a crazy baby that the name landed on him, and stuck. A mad parrot is a very frightening critter. In spite of the fact that this one was still small, with fledgling fuzz and feathers sticking from his head like a lady in curlers, a beak too big for his puny wings and clumsy feet to match, he could nevertheless hold off the bunch of us. He growled, he screamed, he snapped. We kept our distance. But the idea of having a vicious parrot isn't appealing; Looney Bird had to be tamed. Looney couldn't be a better example of how to tame a parrot—if the method worked with him, it should work with any parrot.

Looney's cage was kept smack in the middle of the kitchen floor so he could get used to the bumps and yells of family life. We casually rested hands and feet on the cage and talked to him sweetly. He screamed. We opened the door of his cage. He growled and snapped. We offered him the end of a very long carrot with our fingers. He screamed, growled, snapped a chunk of carrot off and tossed it away. We offered it again. Scream. Growl. Snap. Toss.

We kept up the sweet-talk-and-long-carrot regime for a good month. Things began to get better. Once in a while, Looney would nibble on his piece of carrot for a moment before he dropped it. He screamed less often, but still growled. In another couple of weeks, he was eating the carrot, and we let it get shorter and shorter until he was taking the last bit very close to our fingers. Finally, we started to offer him small slices of carrot, apple and banana from our fingers. No screams, no growls, no snaps—as long as there was food between his beak and our fingers. When we had worked our way through peanuts, and finally to sunflower seeds, we knew we faced the big question—what next?

At this point the books say to put on heavy leather gloves, put your hand under the chest of the bird while it is still in its cage, and encourage it to climb onto your hand. In the case of the big parrots, the books are wrong, and this is why: when a parrot is caught in the wild the catcher wears heavy leather gloves. When a parrot is handled—mostly mishandled—in shipment, the mishandlers wear heavy leather gloves. When the parrot is removed from its cage and shoved into another cage for you to take home, the shover wears heavy leather gloves. All of these experiences have terrified the parrot. Big parrots have long memories. Heavy leather gloves terrify parrots forever and ever.

The books also say to do the taming inside the bird's cage. They are wrong again. The parrot's cage is its home, the place it feels safe—the place it will defend like a pioneer with a shotgun. Little birds may let you finger train them inside their cages, but if you want to tame a big parrot, you have to do it on your territory. The catch is, the parrot may have become attached to its place; it may not want to come out.

Now is the time to start leaving the parrot's cage door open. Offer it food very close to the door so it gets used to coming to the door when you open it. Sooner or later, the parrot's intelligent curiosity will get the better of its fears, and it will venture out—probably to sit on top of the cage. (Since its wings are clipped, the only way it can get anywhere but to the top of its cage is to waddle pigeon-toed across the floor—a vulnerable position that parrots prefer to avoid.)

Sweet-talk your parrot a lot and give it nice bits of food. After a while, it will climb back in through the door again to eat dinner and you can shut it in. When it is used to coming out of the cage and used to being fed by hand there, buy yourself a dowel stick the same thickness as the perch in the cage. Cut it in half so it isn't clumsy to use. Leave it on top of the cage.

Ringo, a passionate Indian ringneck parakeet eats seeds from his owner's lips.

Your parrot will be suspicious of the stick at first—it may start to scream again when it sees the stick there, or it may pick it up and angrily toss it. Persist, with patience. Pick the stick up and lay it on the cage again. Lay your hand on the stick innocently. Move it around a little. Keep it up for however many days it takes the parrot to decide the stick isn't going to attack. When your bird doesn't mind the stick and your moving it about, pick it up gently and rest it against the bird's chest just above its legs. If the parrot stays calm, lift the stick slightly and see if it will transfer its feet from the cage onto the stick. If your parrot doesn't the first time, it will sooner or later, and then you will be the proud possessor of a stick-trained parrot.

By now you may discover as we did with Looney that your parrot likes to be out of the cage, and is perfectly happy to live on top of it. The stick will become a great help because you can get the bird on its stick and transfer it in through the cage door to its own perch. When you try this, be careful to hold the stick so it is tilted upward. A parrot will always tend to climb up rather than down. If you tilt the stick down, ''up'' will be towards your hand and you may find your parrot sitting on your arm somewhat earlier in the game than you would have liked.

If your bird panics, refuses the stick, and won't go into the cage, there are two other methods: get a bath towel. Corner the bird and throw the large towel over it. Wrap the parrot in the towel; take it to the cage door and carefully manipulate it into the cage as you unwrap the towel. Or remove the bottom drawer and wire floor from the cage, and put the cage over the parrot. When it climbs up inside, you can slide the bottom parts back in the cage.

From now on the taming is largely up to your parrot. All you can do is feed it a snack by hand every time you come to its cage, let it sit on the stick you are holding, talk to it a lot while it is on the stick, and feed it more snacks. Believe it or not, your parrot will begin to like you. And when it does, the following will happen. One day Looney Bird was sitting on his stick, and we held out a sunflower seed for him to eat. He reached out his head to get the seed, but instead of taking it in his beak he made a little muttering noise, lowered his head, and ruffled the feathers on his scalp. We tried again, but he wouldn't take the seed. He just kept muttering, ruffling, lowering his head. At last we understood. It was an invitation—he wanted to be groomed. Looney was tame.

From that point on, the only problem with a parrot is how to get away from it. Once friendly, you can substitute your forearm for the stick, but then your bird will want to sit on you all the time; it will groom your hair and clean your fingernails; it will mutter and make eyes at you (by contracting them and dilating them in a provocative way—at least it is provocative to other parrots); it will more enjoy being gently petted than fed; and, most loving of all, it will bob its head up and down, then regurgitate seeds into any available opening, usually your open hand, but occasionally your open ear. If it could figure out your strange anatomy better, or if you behaved properly and opened your mouth, your parrot would feed its regurgitated seeds to you. This is a mark of great love and devotion among parrots.

The tamer your parrot, the more interesting and eccentric it is likely to become. Looney has reached the height of eccentricity. He now sleeps upside down, hanging by his toes like a bat.

Sometimes an eccentricity can be turned into a trick. Looney used to hang onto one side of his opened cage, and, holding the door in his beak, bang it noisily against the cage side. We began to say ''Bang your door'' each time he did it, and soon he learned to do his trick on command. One day, when Looney was making a nuisance of himself on the kitchen table, someone said, ''Oh, Looney! Go bang your door,'' at which command that brilliant parrot picked up the nearest spoon and proceeded to bang it against the tabletop. These days, Looney stays mostly in an aviary off the kitchen. Deprived of loose objects with which to bang, he has come up with still another way to satisfy the command. He stands at the glass, and knocks against it with his beak—surely the most literal way to bang his door.

Looney so enjoys attention that just getting everyone to look his way is enough reward for a trick. Rewards of food, especially favorites like peanuts and bits of apple, might work better in training parrots in general to perform their natural tricks on command.

As your parrot becomes tame and loving, you can let it out of its cage every day. But you must be prepared to keep careful watch on it. Parrots chew everything in sight, including electrical wires and the kitchen chairs. Looney likes to drop coffee cups off the edge of the table. Sparrow takes buttons off shirts. Ringo chews up pencils, dismembers ballpoint pens and leaves footprints in the butter. They all plop droppings on the floor. It's not their fault, so try to clean up cheerfully.

Sometime after you have tamed your parrot and it is used to walking about outside its cage, those clipped wing feathers will molt, and new flight feathers will grow in. At this point, your bird will learn to fly across the room, scattering papers from the table and ashes from the ashtray, and landing on you when you least expect it. If your parrot is not quite trustworthy yet, try the modified type of wing clipping suggested earlier. It will allow your bird to flutter for short distances but will discourage headlong dive bombing. By now your parrot should be tame enough for you to manage this clipping with a friend's assistance.

Don't be tempted, just because your parrot is so tame, to let it loose outdoors. This is especially true if you've let it grow all its flight feathers back.

Love a Parrot

You have to have several parrots to really appreciate parrot passion. Our most affectionate parrot is named Sparrow. (The name reflects the mood in which my husband greets any new animal in the house—the name is similar, for instance, to the cat he named Temporary.) Sparrow has taught us all we know about loving parrots. He has shown us that to pet him well we must pretend our fingers are beaks. As beaks, they can scratch between his ruffled feathers but they can't smooth his head the way a flat hand can pat a dog. And they can lightly pluck at individual feathers as a parrot's beak would do if he were grooming. If Sparrow wants his head groomed, he lowers it and ruffles; if he wants to be groomed under a wing, he lifts the wing. He enjoys scratching behind his jaw, but one must be careful of the delicate ear drum that is on the side of his head.

Sparrow grooms us back when we groom him. At his best, he will groom the hair at the nape of your neck gently, in a tickly fashion; or remove a breakfast crumb from your lip. At his worst, he will try to remove foreign bumps that you, as a bird, ought not to have. The bumps include buttons, glasses, earrings and ears.

On several occasions, Sparrow has gone into paroxysms of affection, leaning down from my shoulder, falling in a rolling fashion onto my chest, nudging around under my hands like a feathered pig in a mud wallow.

Since Sparrow was my first parrot, I didn't know much about them then. Because he was so tame, it seemed safe to let him loose outside so he could fly about a bit. What I didn't know is that parrots who aren't used to flying will fly up, but won't fly down. Also, parrots have little sense of direction. They get lost. Sparrow flew to a tree, then to a higher tree, then to a higher one. Each was farther away, and soon we lost sight of him in the woods behind our house. Thinking he would surely come back, we gave up the search after an hour.

It had been a warm June day, but that evening the weather turned raw and it began to rain. We sent word out through the neighborhood for everyone to keep their eyes open for a lost parrot. A week of awful, cold, wet weather passed and no one had reported him. At last the milkman, our best-traveled news carrier, reported that a family on his route had been "taking care of" a stray parrot for several days. We rushed over, only to find that the "care" had been to leave poor Sparrow out unprotected on the lawn with a soggy piece of bread in front of him. He could no longer eat; he could no longer move. He lay soaking wet, wings out flat, unable even to lift his head from the cold grass. We figured he would die within the hour.

We drove home with Sparrow lying limply in my lap, bravely muttering the sweet things parrots mutter to the people they love. We wrapped him in towels and held him next to a radiator. We thought of brandy, something people sometimes use to warm up. We had only vodka. We took a plastic dropper and squirted a shot of vodka down Sparrow's throat. He choked, gasped, picked up his head, took a few unsteady steps into my lap, and rolled about in ecstasy. It was either gratitude or drunkenness.

Pocket Pets

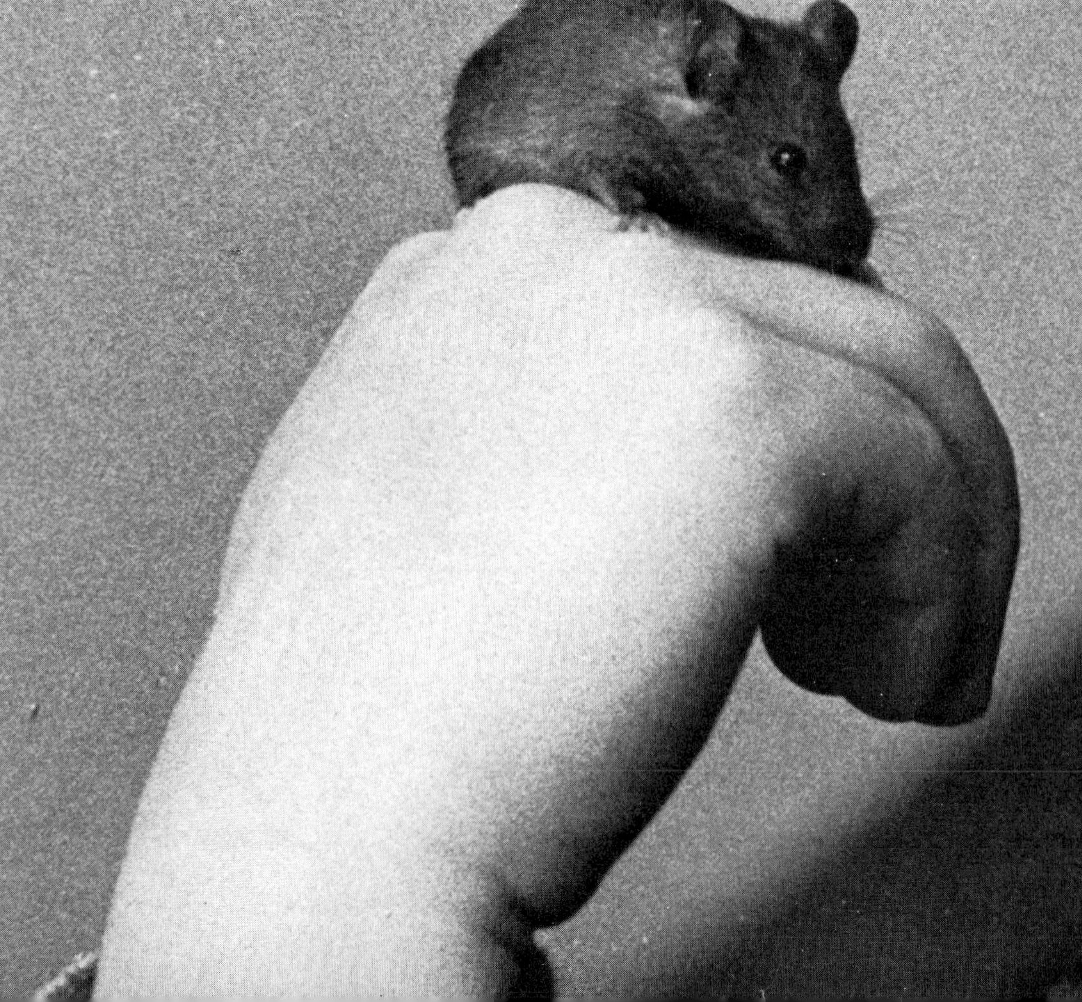

POCKET PETS

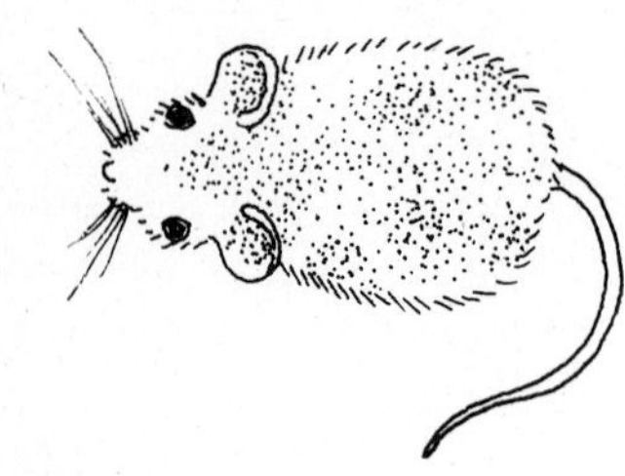

MICE

Cost:
$1.00.

Housing:
Small homemade cake-pan cage, water bottle—$8.00
Or 5½-gallon tank, water bottle, mesh top—$14.00
Wood shavings for bedding—20¢ per week.

Special Requirements:
Baby mice can squeeze through bars of commercial wire rodent cages.

Diet:
Lab chow sold in bulk—5¢ per week.
Or boxed parrot seed or gerbil food—20¢ per week.
Supplement with fresh raw vegetables, meat and cheese.

Care:
Feed, check level of water in water bottle, remove leftover fresh foods daily.
Clean cage once or twice a week.
Provide twigs or bone for gnawing once a month.

Tamability:
Calm down somewhat with handling, but remain nervous.

Life Span:
Two to three years.

HAMSTERS

Cost:
Golden hamster—$2.00
Teddy bear hamster—$5.00

Housing:
Medium homemade cake-pan cage, water bottle—$9.00
Or plastic hamster Habitrail®-type cage, starter set—$10.00
Or commercial wire rodent cage—$12.00
Or 5½-gallon tank, water bottle, mesh top—$14.00
Wood shavings for bedding—20¢ per week.

Special Requirements:
None.

Diet:
Boxed hamster food—35¢ per week.
Supplement with fresh raw vegetables.

Care:
Feed, check level of water in water bottle and remove leftover fresh foods daily.
Clean cage once a week.
Provide twigs or bone for gnawing once a month.

Tamability:
Become calm with handling, but tend to nip when sleepy or frightened.

Life Span:
Two to three years.

GERBILS

Cost:
$2.50.

Housing:
Small homemade cake-pan cage, water bottle—$8.00
Or commercial wire rodent cage—$12.00
Or 5½-gallon tank, water bottle, mesh top—$14.00
Wood shavings for bedding—5¢ per week.

Special Requirements:
None.

Diet:
Boxed gerbil food—35¢ per week.
Supplement with fresh vegetables and dried cereals.

Care:
Feed, check level of water in water bottle, remove leftover fresh foods daily.
Clean cage once a month.
Provide twigs or bone for gnawing once a month.

Tamability:
Become calm with handling.

Life Span:
Three to four years.

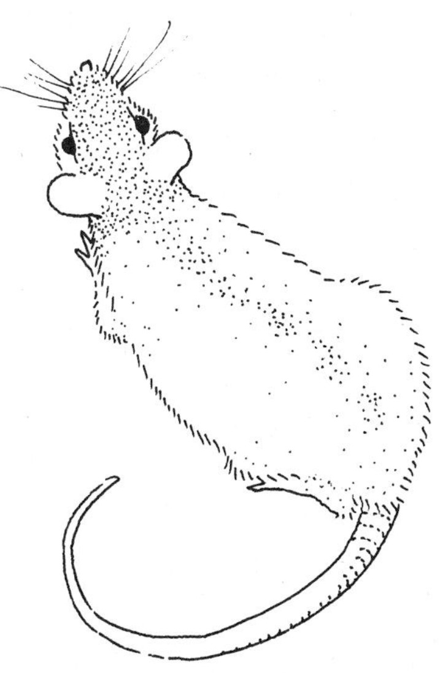

RATS

Cost:
$2.00.

Housing:
Medium homemade cake-pan cage, water bottle—$9.00
Or commercial wire rodent cage —$12.00
Or 5½-gallon tank, water bottle, mesh top—$14.00
Wood shavings for bedding—20¢ per week.

Special Requirements:
None.

Diet:
Lab chow, sold in bulk—10¢ per week.
Or boxed parrot seed or gerbil food—40¢ per week.
Supplement with fresh raw vegetables, meat and cheese.

Care:
Feed, check water level in water bottle, remove leftover fresh foods daily.
Clean cage once a week.
Provide twigs or bone for gnawing once a month.

Tamability:
Become very calm with handling. Enjoy exploring and being carried around outside of cage.

Life Span:
Three to four years.

This chapter is called "Pocket Pets" because it is about a group of animals that not only are small enough to hide in a pocket but love to. The animals are mice, rats, hamsters and gerbils—and they are all rodents.

The word "rodent" makes many people think of pointy snouts, sharp teeth, beady eyes and germs. Rodents like hamsters and gerbils aren't very pointy-snouted, but all rodents have sharp teeth; they need them to gnaw the hard foods that are their basic diet. Their eyes may gleam like beads, but I prefer bright-eyed as a description. For small animals, rodents are particularly smart. As for germs, rodents get them mostly from us. Well adjusted as they are to sharing human food—in the form of both stored food and leftover garbage—wild rodents pick up and carry about the germs our discards provide. But that is accidental, not vicious. Pet rodents don't get a chance to sample the local dump or live near sewers, so they are perfectly clean.

The rodents now sold as pets have come to us by way of the laboratory. They have helped scientists to understand, to treat and even to help prevent disorders as varied as cancer, diabetes and burns. They are very useful as lab animals for several reasons. Both rats and mice have dietary needs nearly identical to humans and so have helped us with all sorts of nutritional studies. All rodents breed early and often, so there is never a shortage. And they are easy to care for and to handle.

No doubt rodents are much easier to handle now than when the first ones were captured in the wild and bred for research. Natural selection has been at work. Annoyed by nips and exasperated by panicky coworkers, scientists probably bred their gentlest rodent specimens and ignored the wilder ones. The result over many generations is a rodent population gentle enough to find its way into the pet stores—and into your pocket.

As for pockets, the reason rodents like them so much has to do with their normal way of life. Mice, rats, hamsters and gerbils are all nocturnal (night creatures) and dwell in holes and burrows. Pockets are simply snug, dark holes—obviously safe places for short naps.

Choosing a Pocket Pet

Much as all rodents may seem alike to people who dislike them, as pets they are quite different from one another. Read each of the separate sections following before you decide which would be best for you. Gerbils, for instance, are the easiest to care for, but rats are the most intelligent and social. Mice are perhaps the sweetest-looking, but they are rather smelly; and hamsters are a bit more difficult to handle than their plump cuteness would imply.

Buy any rodent as young as you possibly can. Full-grown rodents will be hard to tame, whereas a rodent bought just after it has been weaned (about a month old) will become very reliable if handled often. As for health, look for plumpness, a sheen to the coat, and check under the tail for signs of diarrhea. There are differences in temperament between individuals, but this may be difficult to detect at the time you buy your pet. A good, calm, curious baby rat should certainly come to investigate your hand when you reach into the cage, but mice, gerbils and hamsters will all scramble away.

Mice, rats, and gerbils may be picked up by the tail and then quickly transferred to your free hand. Once your pet is used to you, it's best to approach it from its rear and quickly and gently scoop it up using two hands. Be sure it's awake first, so you do not surprise and scare it.

Since a hamster has such a short tail, you can't use it as a handle when picking it up. You can't pick up a hamster from the front either, since it will feel threatened and attack. So, use the two-hand scoop method right from the beginning, being sure you've woken it up thoroughly first.

Housing

All rodents require metal or hard plastic cages or covered aquarium tanks to live in. They chew through any other sort of home. The commercial hard plastic cages are not engineered to either fit together or come apart easily. They are attractive but frustrating. None of the commercial metal cages are really well-made either. The floor trays that hold shavings for the pet's bedding are too shallow and have sharp edges. Wire bars are too far apart for baby mice, who escape the first time you're not looking. And all the commercial cages I've seen have only one small door through which you're supposed to reach for your pet and drag it out to play. This is a good way to get bitten. A 5½-gallon tank makes a better home, big enough for a mouse family, a twosome of gerbils or hamsters, or a single rat. Pet stores sell wire-mesh tops to fit each size tank. The easiest cage to clean is the homemade cake-pan cage on page 338.This is also good for housing your pocket pet.

You will need a water bottle mounted on the side of the cage unless you want to change a water dish every day. You don't really need a food dish. A rodent is happy to find its food in the same corner every day, and the only advantage to a dish is that you will be able to tell more easily when it is getting short on rations. Both crockery and hard plastic dishes are sold in rodent size.

You'll need bedding made of wood chips to absorb urine on the floor of the cage. Individual rodents may be allergic to cedar shavings. Pine chips or chlorophyll-treated pine shavings are both good.

Any of these rodents feel more comfortable if they can make a nest to sleep in. You don't have to buy anything. Just put in an old sock, tissues, paper towels, a washcloth or any other soft material. The pet will do the rest.

The best exercise your pet can get is being let out to play. For more exercise, especially at night, you can buy an exercise wheel to fit its cage. Commercial cages often come equipped with a wheel, but free-standing ones are available for tanks and homemade cages.

Cage Cleaning. How often you clean depends on which of these pets you choose, but don't just let your nose be the guide. Urine-soaked shavings cause first a sort of diaper rash and then infection. All but gerbils need their shavings changed once a week. Gerbils, because they urinate so little, can go a month between changes.

Before you clean your pet's cage take out the animal; put it in the bathtub with the drain closed or into a tall can or jar. Gerbils, mice, hamsters and rats cannot get out of a bathtub. Hamsters, gerbils and mice can't get out of a coffee can or mayonnaise jar. Rats can. Empty all the bedding into the garbage, then wipe up any you have just spilled on the floor. Keep the nest unless it smells. Wash the cage out with dish detergent and water, rinse it well and dry it. Wash the water bottle and the food dish. Put in fresh bedding about an inch and a half deep. Add new nest materials if you have had to throw the old nest out. Put the cage back together. Don't forget to refill the water bottle and fill the food dish. For complete satisfaction at a job well done, add some of the snacks and toys that are recommended for each pet.

Food and Water

Mice, rats, gerbils and hamsters are basically seed- and grain-eaters—the historical scourge, in fact, of barns and granaries from the time agriculture was invented. But any old seeds and grains won't do as a diet for caged pets. In the wild, these animals eat from nature's remarkable delicatessen, which as well as the basic seeds and grains may include fresh vegetables, bark and assorted gleanings from garbage pails. The only balanced diet you can depend on for rats and mice is called lab chow, which consists of pellets specially formulated for these rodents. Unfortunately, it is hard to get lab chow. It is sold in bulk to laboratories but is seldom commercially packaged for pet stores. What packaged food is available in pet stores is intended for hamsters and gerbils only, and even then is not likely to be the complete diet the packages claim. The problem is easily solved by offering your pet a delicatessen similar to nature's—but from the leavings of your family dinners. Your pet's own body will influence its choices, just as it would have in the wild. You'll find details of what snacks to use to supplement the basic grain diet in the discussion of each kind of pet.

If a rodent does suffer from malnutrition, an early sign is hair loss. Add rodent vitamin drops to the water, following the instructions on the bottle. Pet stores carry the vitamins. But start offering the suggested variety of snacks too. By watching what your pet prefers to eat and continuing to feed it those snacks, you can keep it on a balanced diet.

A water bottle is the best way to keep drinking

water available. A water bottle has a slightly bent nozzle, and the best ones have a ball bearing behind the opening. The ball bearing closes the hole so water can't leak out. When the rodent licks at the end of the nozzle, it joggles the ball bearing and water seeps around it for the rodent to drink. You're more likely to find a ball-bearing type bottle labeled as a bird bottle! The bottle is held on the outside of a wire cage by a U-shaped wire or spring holder. It is held on the inside of a tank with a special metal bracket sold separately.

Check the food supplies daily and don't be fooled by what looks like a full dish—often it is only empty shells and there is really no food left. Rodents eat a high percentage of their body weight every day because their hot bodies and active natures require that much fuel. This means that a rodent can starve to death much faster than a larger animal.

A Ball Bearing Water Bottle

Illnesses

Besides malnutrition, rodents can come down with various viral and bacterial diseases. Luckily, caged animals rarely get sick. There are no other rodents around to catch the germs from. If your pet does get sick, pet stores sell antibiotics that might help. They are usually in tablet form, to be crushed and added to drinking water or sprinkled on food. Vets may refuse to treat rodents, and pet store personnel may not really know very much about them. So if standard antibiotics don't work, unluckily there may be nothing else you can do to help your pet.

Breeding

In nature rodents are the major food of a horde of animals from cats and snakes to hawks and coyotes. So rodents have to have plenty of babies if they are to escape extermination. Theoretically, one pair of rats can multiply to 800 within a single year, as they have babies, their babies have babies and so on. The number of mice and rats alone is greater than the human population of the world.

Breeding one of the pocket pets couldn't be easier. All of these rodents are grown-up enough to have babies by the time they are two or three months old. Pregnancy lasts about three weeks and a litter may range from two babies to as many as a dozen. In another three weeks the babies are old enough to leave their mother—fast work.

If you have a female but no male, ask around school or at a pet shop for an adult male. Arrange to introduce your female into his cage and let her live there for a week. That should be long enough to get her pregnant. Don't bring a male into your female's cage. She will not like a stranger on her territory. Instead, put her into the male's cage. The male rarely minds a female visiting him. To be certain they don't hurt one another, keep your eye on them for the first 15 minutes of their acquaintance.

You probably do not need to leave the two together for more than a week because the smell of a male will bring the female into heat (her eggs will become ready to be fertilized) within a few days. Be certain to remove the female to her own cage before the three weeks of pregnancy are up. Males don't act as fathers to their babies and may eat them.

If male or female starts to fight, you'll have to take your female out and put her back in her own cage. If this happens, keep the cages next to each other for a few days, then try again. This technique usually works.

By the time a female rodent is a week and a half pregnant you may already be able to notice her belly growing bigger. Feed her a variety of foods now—fresh vegetables for all the rodents, additional cheese and meat for mice and rats. Add vitamin drops to the water bottle. The label will tell you how much to use. Continue these extra foods after the babies are born until they are weaned.

Give the mother really nice nesting materials like yarn, cotton batting and facial tissue before the babies are born. Clean the cage often, because you may find the mother doesn't want to be bothered with you cleaning the cage during the three weeks she cares for her babies.

Rodent babies are usually born at night, and are kept in a round, ball-like nest until they can walk on their own. The mother may be irritable and bite if you put a hand near the nest. But of course you want to see the babies, so lure the mother out with a nice snack (a friend says peanut butter works beautifully), uncover the nest and gaze at the naked little critters to your heart's content.

Page186 gives you a detailed description of the birth and growth of a litter of rats, which is fairly typical of hamsters, gerbils and mice as well. But one warning: just when the babies get cutest, at about three weeks, start finding homes for them. If you wait too long, they will be rather old for other people to tame well and may become old enough to get pregnant on their own before you even notice which are male and which female. It's a good idea to take them to the nearest pet store if you haven't found enough rodent-loving friends by the time the babies are a month and a half old.

Recapturing Escaped Pets

The easiest way to recapture a lost rodent pet is with a Havahart® trap. The device is a wire tunnel with a trap door at each end. Bait (your pet's favorite food) is placed on the platform in the middle. The trap is placed in a corner or under a piece of furniture near where your pet escaped. When it comes for food, the platform triggers the two trap doors, which fall shut without harming the animal at all.

Put the trap, animal and all, into your pet's cage. Then lift the trap doors and let it come out in to its cage.

You can buy the smallest-size No.0 Havahart® trap in a hardware store for about $5.00.

Mice

ice, being the smallest of these pocket pets, are the cutest. White mice are most common but black, brown, apricot, gray and spots of all those colors are available too. At their tamest, mice are nervous, fidgety animals. They slip easily from hands or even jump. Once lost, they remain hidden and may be very hard to find.

Housing

The mouse cage can be the smaller homemade cage on page 338 or a 5½-gallon tank.

Of all the small rodents, mice leave the worst odor. It is more their urine than their droppings that smell. Chlorophyll-treated shavings work rather well. You may get by with a weekly cleaning if your nose isn't too sensitive. The mouse itself will not smell because it keeps itself clean by licking and grooming.

Mice particularly like cotton batting as nest material. A mouse will chew small pieces of the batting and build it into a round, hollow nest with a single entrance. It will add to the nest from time to time until it gets quite big. After a while you may not like the smell of the nest anymore, so remove it and give the mouse new materials. Another nest will appear in a single night.

Food and Water

Mice can survive very well on lab chow if your pet store carries it. If you can't find it anywhere, use gerbil food or even birdseed instead, but supplement with snacks of cheese, raw vegetable, peanut butter, meat or fat from meat, uncooked oatmeal, or nuts. If you always offer a snack with your fingers, your mouse will learn to come to your hand to see what you've got for it. It's an easy way to encourage it not to scramble away when you want to lift it from the cage.

Mice, like all rodents, have front teeth that continue to grow all through their lives. The only way they can prevent their teeth from getting so long that they can't close their mouths is by gnawing a lot. The gnawing keeps their teeth the right length, like running on rough ground keeps a dog's toenails the right length. If you don't give your mouse any choice, it will spend most of the night gnawing at the bars or mesh of its cage. That upsets nearby people: not only do they think your mouse is trying to escape (which it isn't), but it makes an awful racket. Give your mouse leftover bones and green twigs, which it will prefer to wire anytime. Both the bone and the green bark serve as food, too.

Breeding

A female mouse can be bred when she is two months old and will have babies three weeks later. Most of our litters have been between 10 and 12 babies. The pregnant or nursing mother has a voracious appetite, so be careful of sticking a finger in the cage in case it is mistaken for a snack and grabbed.

Hamsters

Hamsters have a fat and fuzzy look. They smell less than mice, move more slowly and act less nervous. They can, however, be grouchy, especially when they are woken from a sound sleep. Both of the hamsters we had nipped our fingers if they were handled roughly, if they were busy eating or if they were sleepy. They bared their teeth and squealed at us in warning if they had time.

Waking up a hamster sounds easier than it is. They are stubbornly nocturnal, but worse than that, their daytime sleep is best described as similar to a coma. We were once sure our hamster was dead, belly up, on the floor of his cage. We picked up his limp body and laid it on a table. He came to life about as slowly as a parent on a Sunday morning. Hamsters don't often sleep in that dead-looking posture but usually curl into a ball so tight you can't tell nose from rear. I've been told that if you get a hamster young enough and handle it a lot during the day, you can get it to switch to your schedule. The person who told me has a nursery school where the hamsters are played with constantly during school hours.

The original pet hamster, the one that still lives

in the wilds of Europe and the Middle East, is tobacco colored, with darker markings about the shoulders and pale grayish white underneath. All the millions of pet hamsters in the world are descended from one male and three females who were captured in the wild early in this century: they produced 150 babies by the end of their first year in captivity. Breeders have since developed albino strains, spotted hamsters, beautiful apricot ones, silver grays, and even a long-haired variety called a teddy bear hamster, which can come in any of these colors.

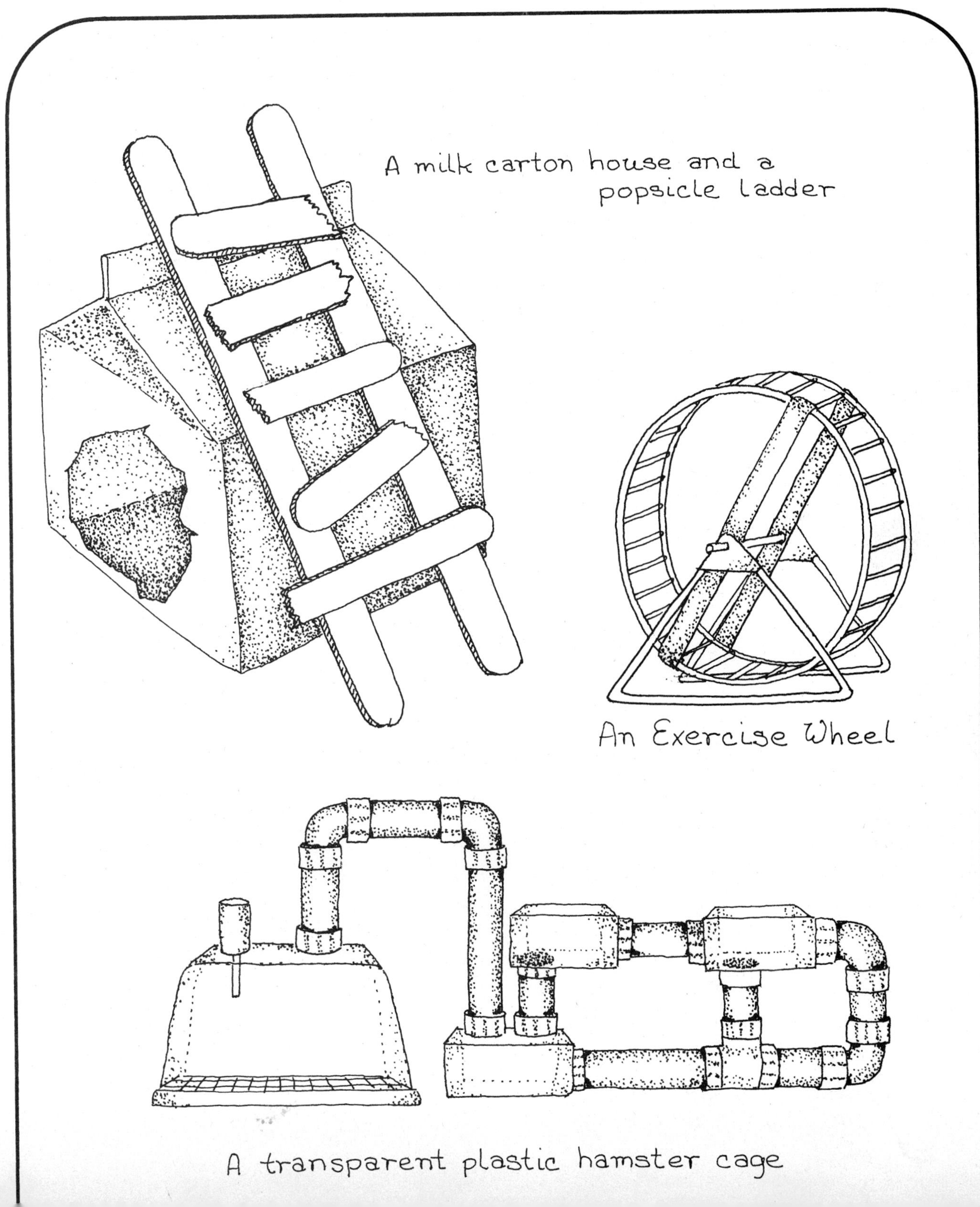

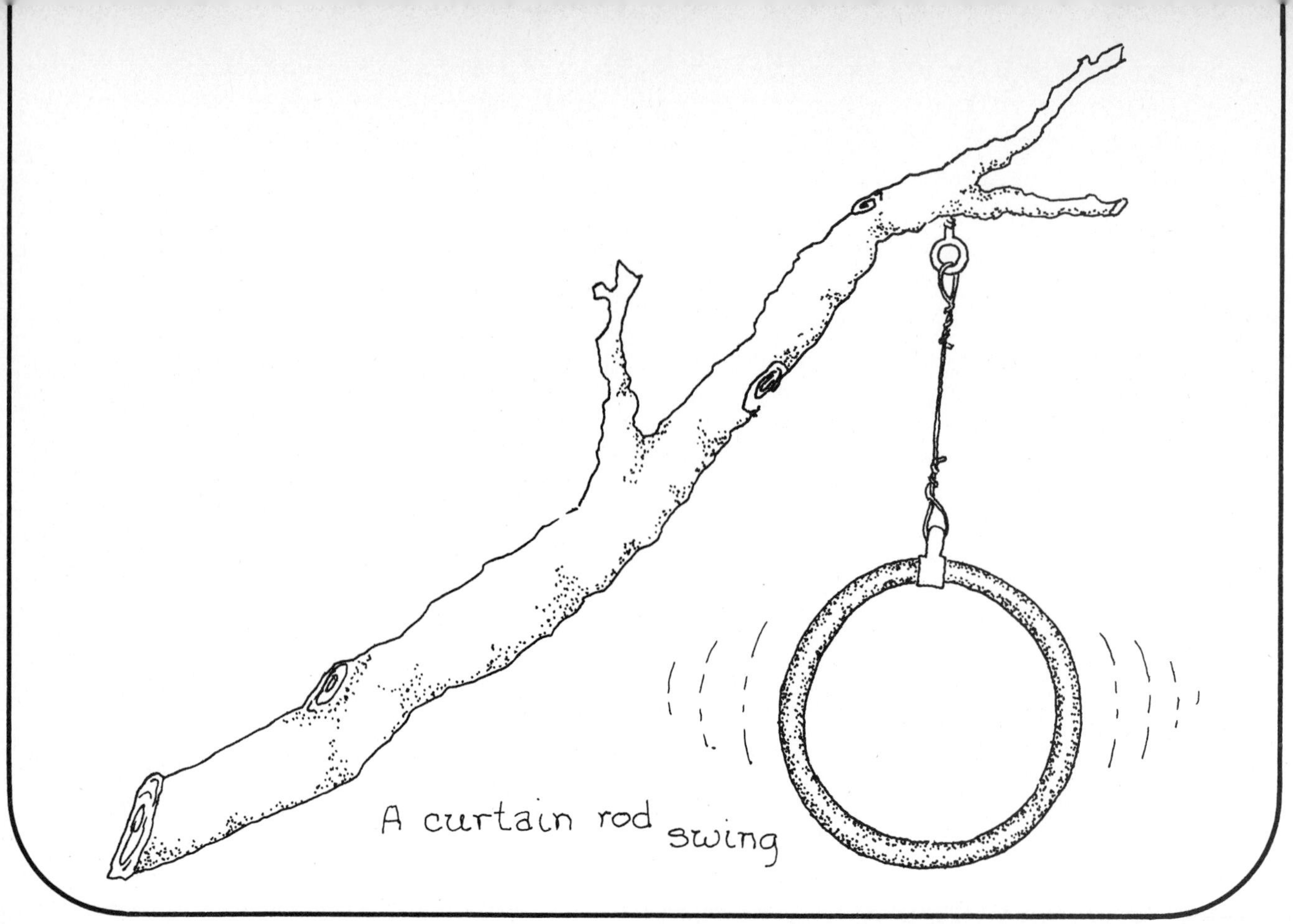

A curtain rod swing

Hamsters are active enough when awake but don't like having their sleep disturbed.

Housing

Lately an expensive but interesting plastic hamster cage has been available. It is made of transparent plastic rooms and tunnels that interconnect in lots of ways. Since the hamster is a burrowing animal, it is very pleased with these plastic burrows and is active, acrobatic and fun to watch, especially in the middle of the night. But otherwise the cage is a nuisance to clean and handle.

A hamster's plumpness is deceiving. Hamsters can flatten themselves to slide through astonishingly small openings. You'll have to check any cage you buy to be sure there aren't good escape places. One way hamsters often escape is by pushing out the tray that holds shavings in wire cages. Once the tray is pushed out an inch, there is a gap left beneath the wire that a curious hamster might squeeze through. For this reason alone, if not also for the expense of commercial hamster cages, I suggest the wire cage on page 338. It is foolproof. Or, if you prefer, try the 5½-gallon tank with a mesh top.

You can improvise your own playground for your hamster for much less money than the plastic tunnels cost. Lean a branch diagonally across the cage, screw a small eye screw into it near the top, and hang from this screw a big metal curtain ring attached with wire to act as a swing. Use a small milk carton with a hole cut in it for a room, and make a ladder out of ice cream sticks for the hamster to use to climb up to the top of the house.

Hamsters also appreciate old socks to burrow into and hide inside. Hamsters, like mice, chew to keep their teeth down, so many of the things you make won't last too long. But they are easy to make again, and you may get better ideas than these as you go along.

Hamsters have a habit of following their noses no matter where they lead—probably because they have an instinct to follow tunnels and tunnels don't require too many left-turn, right-turn, straight-ahead decisions. So you will find that if you keep putting one hand in front of the other, the hamster will keep running from hand to hand in the most senseless way. It doesn't seem to bother it at all that it is getting nowhere fast.

For this same reason, hamsters are tireless users of exercise wheels. Exercise wheels always seem to squeak, so use a stick of graphite to keep them running silently—except for the pitter-patter of tiny hamster feet.

Hamsters have been known to fall off table tops and shoulders rather easily. They are not climbers in nature, are not accustomed to heights, lack a sturdy tail with which to balance themselves, and are supposedly nearsighted as well. Since one bad fall can kill a hamster, keep careful watch over it when it is out of the cage.

Food and Water

Hamsters, like squirrels, store their food. They have pouches inside their cheeks that stretch to hold an amazing number of seeds. The pouches can hold half the hamster's own weight in food. The instinct to store is so strong that one common hamster, a guinea-pig-sized relative of the Syrian pet-store variety, was found to have stored 190 pounds of corn and potatoes in its burrow over a single summer.

Of course, hamsters don't need to store food in their cages, but they do it naturally. They will stuff their pouches and then empty them out, eat some of the seeds and stash the rest away in a hidey hole. To prevent decay, you will have to clean out the caches of stored foods every day.

Any pet store carries hamster food, a good basic combination of seeds and cereals with some dried vegetables added. A good diet for a hamster also includes snacks of fresh raw vegetables and fruits. Try spinach, lettuce, carrots and apples. Withhold fresh foods for a few days if your pet gets diarrhea.

Breeding

A female hamster can have her first litter when she is about two months old. She has the shortest gestation period of any mammal except the marsupials—her babies are born in only 15 days. She will usually have about eight babies per litter.

The introductory material at the beginning of the chapter discusses rodent breeding in general, but there is an additional caution with hamsters. Whereas the male is inhibited by instinct from ever biting a female, the larger and more aggressive female may attack the male and even kill him. The best safeguard is to raise a male and female together from babyhood so they already are good friends by the time they are ready to breed.

If you are introducing strangers, put their cages next to one another for a week so they know each other by smell. Then put the female into the male's cage and watch her behavior. Be sure you are wearing heavy gloves or mittens, because if the female attacks you will have to reach a hand in and take her out right away. Then repeat the whole procedure the following week. In either case, the male should be put into a different cage once the babies are born.

Gerbils

Gerbils were only brought into pet stores in this country about 10 years ago, and were such a rarity that they sold for $15.00 each. People soon found out that gerbils breed prolifically just like any other rodent, and so the price is now low. Gerbils are about the size of hamsters, but their fur is grayish brown and has a slight layer of oil on it which keeps them from looking fluffy. Their long tails are furred and have a tuft on the end.

When they're not sleeping, gerbils are almost as hyperactive as mice, but they don't seem to be as easily startled. I've seen panicky mice, but never a panicky gerbil. They aren't quick to bite, either. Our gerbil takes easily to daytime hours and calmly rides in a pocket for a full afternoon, peeking out at the world from time to time.

Housing

Gerbils are certainly the easiest rodent to keep—they are desert animals who have developed the ability to utilize almost all the water they take in at the front end, so there's very little left to come out the other end.

Gerbils have no smell (to people), and the cage has to be cleaned only once a month if it has a good layer of bedding about an inch and a half thick. It should be at least the size of the homemade cage on page 338, or if you prefer,substitute the 5½-gallon tank. The tank is good in that gerbils are diggers and their constant attempts to make holes in the bottom of a metal cage throw the bedding all over the place. A tank solves that problem. If you are using a mesh cage, cut down a grocery carton and place the cage inside it.

Photographing a Pocket Pet

The propensity of a gerbil to sit in a pocket for so long got us to thinking one day about snapshots. Obviously, a pocket's a good place to put a gerbil if you want it to stay in one place long enough to take its picture. You need a close-up attachment if your camera won't focus at less than three feet, and you need flash cubes to take the pictures indoors. Focus the camera and wait until your gerbil pokes its head out. Then snap its portrait.

What else works? Well, a toilet paper tube, for one thing. A gerbil can't leave a tube alone. It simply must go inside! Once in, it must poke a nose out. There's your picture. For the same reason, a small cardboard box with a hole torn in it makes a likable snapshot.

We experimented some more. Because they are fairly cautious about heights, a gerbil will stay on top of a milk carton or a wooden block for quite a while before it dares to jump off. It will stay in a toy car too if you put it on top of a block.

We found this height technique not only works for gerbils but for mice, hamsters and rats too. None of the pocket pets like to climb down from heights, all of them love tubes and pockets, and they're all so curious they must stick their cute noses out of holes so you can snap their picture.

We had a problem with our gerbil that may or may not be typical. He used his whole cage as a nest, rather than the neater corner arrangement our hamsters, rats and mice have built. The nest always grew to water-bottle height. Then the drops from the bottle would soak the whole nest and we'd start all over again. It was as though because he was unable to dig through the floor into a burrow, he was making himself a whole underground world instead. Finally it dawned on us to give him a burrow to make his nest in. We cut both ends off a dog-food can for the burrow. Sure enough, it took him only a couple of nights to move his shredded papers into the can, leaving the cage floor clean. When he goes into his burrow to sleep, he pushes his nest around inside the can until he has sealed up both entrances.

Food and Water

Gerbils eat commercial gerbil food, available at pet stores, plus snacks like raw oatmeal, peanut butter, dry breakfast cereal and popcorn. Ours began to lose patches of fur at four years old. He was cured in only two weeks by the addition of fresh spinach to his diet and vitamin drops to his water. This leads me to believe that some fresh vegetables should be offered to a gerbil. If it eats them, it probably needs them. Give gerbils things like twigs and bones to chew on too.

In the wild, gerbils need only the water from the vegetables they eat, but caged gerbils should have a water bottle to make up for the dryness of their diet.

Breeding

Beginning when they are nine to 11 weeks old, gerbils have litters of from one to seven babies. There is no particular difficulty in breeding them, so just follow the general procedure discussed at the beginning of this chapter.

Rats love exploring this easy to construct playground.

Rats

Rats make by far the best pets of any of the small furry rodents: they are calmer, friendlier, more intelligent; they don't smell bad like mice do; they don't kick their shavings around like gerbils; they don't slither out of your hands like hamsters.

Wild albino Norway rats were domesticated long ago for use as laboratory animals. Their descendants, sold in pet stores today, are smaller, far less aggressive and probably not as bright as the original wild rats. Besides the albino, there are now black strains, cream-colored ones and a particularly nice white and black combination called a hooded rat.

Unfortunately, although rats are very common in laboratories, many pet stores don't carry them. Too many people think of rats as horrid dirty things. This is true of wild rats, who are vicious, large, scurrying, and as germ-laden as the garbage they eat. But laboratory rats represent hundreds and hundreds of generations of mild-mannered cage-contented pets. They have forgotten their beginnings. Many people also object to the rat's long tail. There is nothing you can do about that but keep the rat to yourself.

Many people think of rats as only larger mice. Anatomically that's close to the truth, but their behavior is very different. Compared to the fearful, cowering mouse, the rat is a brave, curious, friendly giant. If your pet store does not carry them, the manager might be able to get one for you from a distributor. If you have a choice, a female rat is more alert and less lazy than a male. They are also prettier.

You can give a pet rat baths and let it swim in the bathtub. You can carry it with you in the sleeve of your sweater; it will not be jumpy. It will be contented in a plain cage; it will be curious about a new environment. It is a good acrobat; it is the only rodent you can really play with. For example, the rat I had as a child went to school with me almost every day, happily riding in a sweater sleeve or calmly staying in my gym locker or a school desk. The teachers never even knew. The same rat went to camp with me in the summer and took a morning swim with me in the lake each day. Running loose in my room in the evenings, she would explore about, climbing up on the bed from time to time to sit on her hind legs and beg for a snack.

Housing

Most of the cages sold in pet stores are too small for a rat. You'll be better off with the larger homemade cake-pan cage on page 338. The cage needs nothing extra in it but the water bottle and food dish, some bones to gnaw on and some paper towels for your rat to chew up for nest building. If you choose a tank instead, weight the wire-mesh top down with a rock or two.

You can let a tame rat out of its cage to wander around your room for hours at a time—it won't escape because it doesn't want to. But you do have to watch what the rat is up to. Wild rats have been known to eat through lead pipes and gnaw through concrete. I know from experience that a pet rat can bite a good-sized hole in a one-inch-thick wooden desk drawer, and neatly sever every lamp cord in sight. Rat-chewing damage in the United States alone amounts to billions of dollars each year. That's not eating, that's just chewing.

Give your rat some exercise by allowing it out to explore your room a few times a week, or build a playground for it to play in.

Food and Water

Lab chow is a totally balanced diet for rats. If it's not available in your pet store, use gerbil food or birdseed mixed equally with rabbit or guinea pig pellets. Offer plenty of snacks from the same food groups humans need. Given a choice, a rat knows what to eat to avoid malnutrition. We give our rats, Eliza and Marjorie, meat, cheese and raw spinach along with a mixture of seeds and Dog Chow® they share with the parrots. On top of all this, they are forever begging for food as we walk by their cages. So they get bits of peanut-butter sandwiches, potato chips, grapes and just about everything else.

The Breeding and Birth of Rats

Breeding of rats is very similar to the breeding of any of the pocket pets, so you can use this step-by-step description to help you if you'd like to substitute hamsters, gerbils or mice instead.

If one of the reasons you want to have a rat is to see it have babies, be sure you are getting a female. You can tell the sex of a rat after it is six weeks old. Lift the rat up by its tail and look for testicles. If you don't see any, you have a female. Of course you will then have to buy a male rat too, unless you can find someone who will lend you one. If you don't want to buy one perhaps you can board your female rat with a male at the local pet store when she is old enough to breed. It's worth asking.

A rat is grown-up and able to breed at only three months old. From then on she has eggs ready to be fertilized every four days. It takes only 21 days of pregnancy until the babies are ready to be born. The mother can mate again the following evening.

As the time of birth grows near, the mother will want to build a particularly fine nest so give her lots of materials to work with. Rats tend to give birth between midnight and 4:00 A. M. *It takes only an hour or so for a rat to give birth to a litter of half a dozen or a dozen babies. If your rat goes into labor while you are watching, you will notice that she is stretching out her body and that her sides are heaving. But she will go inside her nest to give birth, so open the nest roof to get a good view. She'll repair the roof later.*

As each baby is born, the mother first removes the transparent wrapping (amniotic sac) that is around the baby. Then she bites off the umbilical cord, which connected the baby to her placenta and through which the baby was fed when inside the mother's womb. She eats it and the placenta, and thoroughly licks the baby clean. The licking and handling stimulate the baby to breathe and get its blood flowing well.

A few minutes pass and the next baby is born. The babies are a bluish pink, with skin so transparent you will be able to see blood vessels underneath. Their eyelids are still fused shut over their eyes and their ears are still fused flat to their heads. They are hairless and quite helpless. They can't walk yet, but they can pull themselves along with their front legs. And they squeak to call for help when they find themselves no longer touching the other babies or their mother. Much of what they say is lost to our ears, though; rats talk in ultrasound—high squeaks only your cat can hear.

When the last baby has been born, the mother will pick up in her mouth any baby that has crept away or rolled from the nest and carry it into the baby heap inside her nest. If there is a baby that she shoves aside or ignores, you can be sure there is something wrong with it. It is either dead or will die soon. A mother rat's mind is made in such a way that if a baby does not act like a baby—move, squeak, feel warm, smell right—it is not a baby at all. Sooner or later she will eat it as she ate the other nonbaby stuff, the cords and placenta. If this is too horrifying to you, remove the dead baby and bury it, or wait for the sick one to die and bury it. You will not be able to save its life.

There is a myth that giving a rodent meat will get her in the "habit" of eating her babies. That's just plain silly. If it were true, we wouldn't have mankind's old rat and mouse problems; since both eat meat in nature, they would long since have turned cannibal and eaten themselves into extinction. The commonest reasons for cannibalism are crowding, when there are many mothers trying to nest in a small area, and nervousness, caused by disturbing the mother, the nest or

the babies. Cannibalism can also be caused by malnutrition. To be sure of a good diet, we have always fed our pregnant rats and mice extra foods like cheese, vegetables and meat. Liverwurst is a great favorite.

The babies have only one talent at this point: sucking. They can barely get to the nipples of their own accord, pulling themselves shakily along and falling often on weak and uncoordinated legs. The mother helps. In fact, she spends a great deal of time in the nest at first, letting the babies nurse almost constantly, day and night. Within a week a sheen of fur is already sprouting from the babies' naked skin. In five more days their eyes have opened, their ears stick out from their heads, and they are furry.

Like all babies, their heads look big, their bodies small, and their feet a size too large. They are adorable. The mother weans them the easy way: by the time they are about three weeks old she just gets up and walks away whenever she is sick of nursing. The babies, disagreeing as most babies do with the need to be weaned, hang on to her teats for dear life but tumble off in the end. In their less babyish moments, though, they are getting interested in grown-up food and giving it a try. As they try to do the grown-up things—getting into the food dish, washing their backs, climbing the mesh—they totter and tumble like toddlers. At this point, be sure to lower the water bottle to their level. They have to drink too.

Now you are the happy owner of seven rats, or maybe fourteen. What next? Well, you could keep them, but with just one male rat in the litter, you could have 100 rats in less than three months. In a well-stocked, catless granary, a rat population can double every two months. Unless you want to go into the rat business, it's best to find homes for them. Ask among your friends—you may be able to get one or two adopted that way. Give the rest to a lucky pet store.

Unusual Apartment Pets

UNUSUAL APARTMENT PETS

RABBITS

Cost:
Dutch rabbit—$6.00
Lop-eared rabbit—$25.00

Housing:
Homemade indoor hutch—$13.00
Or commercial hutch—$15.00
Or homemade outdoor hutch—$20.00
Crockery food dish and large water bottle—$6.00

Special Requirements:
None.

Diet:
Rabbit pellets—20¢ per week.
Supplement with discarded vegetable peelings and outside leaves of salad greens. Offer extra salt.

Care:
Feed, check level of water in water bottle daily.
Change newspaper under indoor hutch twice a week.
Move outdoor hutch once a month.
Groom every few days during periods of heavy shedding.

Tamability:
Become calm with handling; may seek attention and affection. Some individuals can be housebroken.

Life Span:
Three to five years.

GUINEA PIGS

Cost:
Smooth-haired—$5.00
Abyssinian—$8.00
Peruvian—$12.00

Housing:
Homemade indoor hutch—$13.00
Or commercial hutch—$15.00
Or homemade outdoor hutch—$20.00
Crockery food dish and large water bottle—$6.00

Special Requirements:
None.

Diet:
Guinea pig pellets—20¢ per week.
Supplement with discarded raw vegetable peelings and outside leaves of salad greens, or with lawn grass.

Care:
Feed, check level of water in water bottle daily.
Change newspaper under indoor hutch twice a week.
Move outdoor hutch once a month.
Groom long-haired varieties weekly.

Tamability:
Become calm with handling. Squeal at owner for food.

Life Span:
Four to six years.

SKUNKS

Cost:
$25.00 to $50.00.

Housing:
Cardboard carton with old towels inside (no cost).
Or wicker sleeping basket—$15.00
Or homemade plywood cage—$25.00
Crockery food and water dishes—$4.00

Special Requirements:
Veterinary examination and inoculations—$16.00 to $30.00, depending on local fees.

Diet:
Canned cat food, apples, raw carrots—$2.00 per week.

Care:
Feed, replenish water dish, change newspaper in "bathroom" corner daily.

Tamability:
Become affectionate, devoted to own family. Aloof with strangers. Easily housebroken.

Life Span:
10 to 12 years.

FERRETS

Cost:
$25.00.

Housing:
Homemade plywood cage—$25.00
Water bottle—$3.50
Optional plastic litter box—$2.50
Clay litter—$1.00 per week.

Special Requirements:
Veterinary examination and inoculations—$16.00 to $30.00, depending on local fees.

Diet:
Canned cat food—75¢ per week. Or raw hamburger, beef heart or kidney, supplemented with powdered animal vitamins—75¢ per week.

Care:
Feed, check level of water in water bottle, change newspaper or pick droppings from litter box daily.
Change litter in optional litter box once a week.
Wash cage as necessary.

Tamability:
Playful and friendly, but tend to revert to wild if allowed freedom outdoors as adults.

Life Span:
10 years.

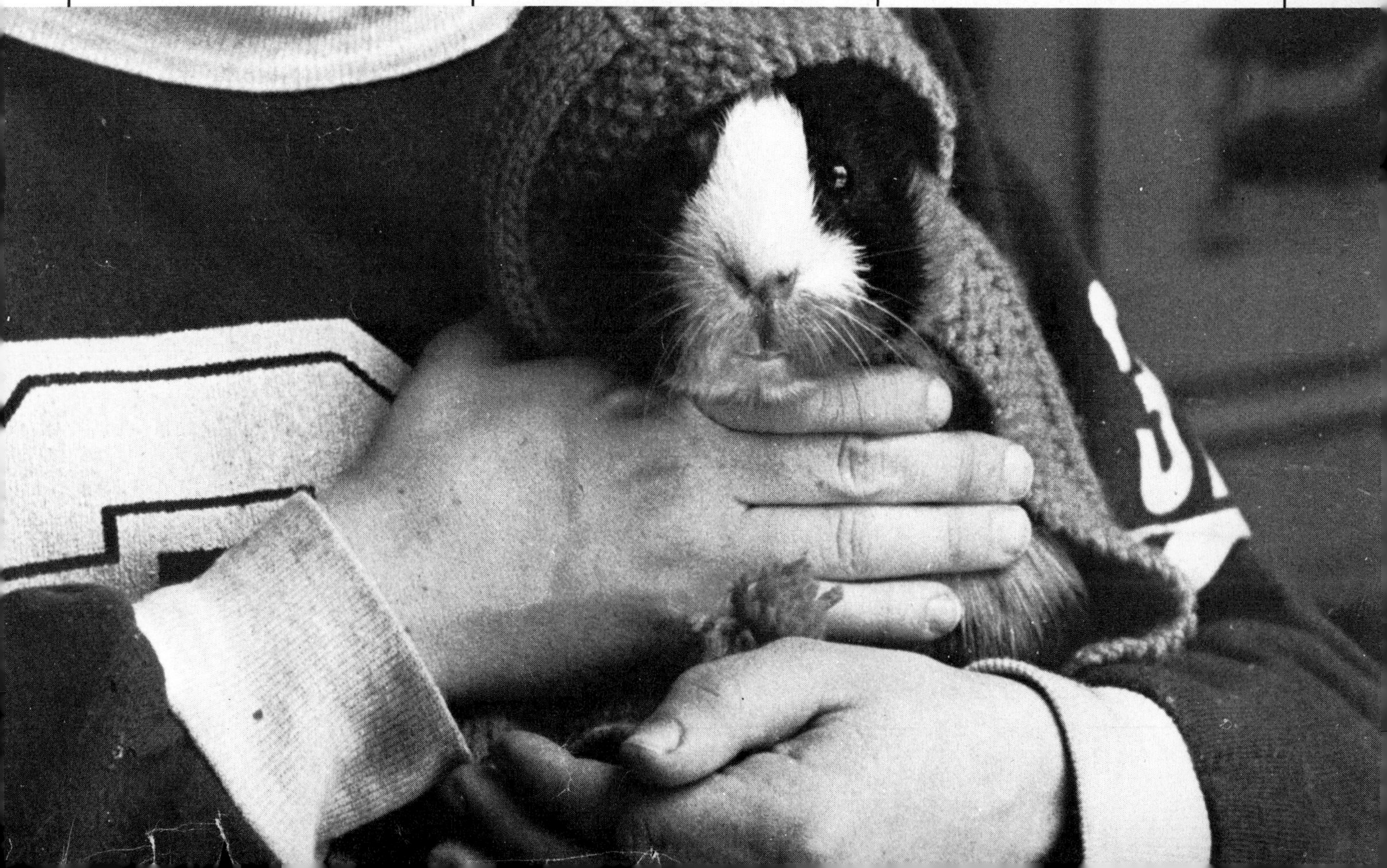

The four animals in this chapter—rabbits, guinea pigs, skunks and ferrets—satisfy the "medium-sized furry pet that is not a cat" requirement. All four need similar-sized housing, make fine apartment pets, and demand less of you emotionally and physically than a cat. Otherwise, they don't belong together as a group. Some people think of rabbits as big rodents, but they're not. Others don't think of guinea pigs as rodents, but they are (the biggest rodent of all, the 110-pound capybara, looks like a giant guinea pig). Ferrets are carnivores who would spend their lives happily hunting rabbits and guinea pigs if they had half a chance. And who would have thought that a garbage-eating skunk is the ferret's kissing cousin?

Rabbits

A rabbit comes close to the ideal pet for people who are absent-minded about caring for pets, always thought rabbits were cute, soft and friendly, and like to play with an animal loose in the room or yard.

Rabbits don't need daily care. Their hutch is constructed of wire to allow their droppings to fall through onto newspaper, and although the newspaper can get pretty messy if you forget to clean it, the cage stays healthy. Rabbits, like rodents, can drink from a water bottle, so you don't have to change the water every day. And you can

buy a food dish large enough to carry you over several days without refilling.

Cute, soft and friendly animals, many rabbits raised from babyhood will follow you about the house like puppies and hop into your lap to be petted. A rabbit who has been accustomed to handling while young is not scared of humans and can be let loose in the house. It doesn't panic easily or run off or try to hide. More surprising, it can be housebroken.

The small Dutch rabbit, usually the only variety sold in pet stores, is probably the most popular because of its size. The albino Dutch rabbit is sold at Easter time, but the same small rabbit comes in black, "wild" brown (called agouti), golden tan, lovely grays, and spotted versions of all the above. But the Dutch rabbit, cute as it is, looks ordinary next to the incredible breeds rabbit breeders have developed.

Pet stores will not be able to help you much with fancy breeds. The place to go is a rabbit show. If you don't know of any rabbit shows near you, write to the American Rabbit Breeders Association, Ed Pieter, Jr., Box 426, Bloomington, Illinois 61701. Mr. Pieter will be able to supply the information. There is almost undoubtedly a show somewhere within driving distance.

Once there, you can expect to be treated to a view of fluffy Angoras, the huge Belgian hare (who must have been a model for Br'er Rabbit), rabbits colored and shaded like Siamese cats, and so on. The most wonderful rabbit of all is, unfortunately, too big and too expensive for most people to keep. It is the French Lop-Eared rabbit, a huge, plump

These very distinguished rabbits look as if they've eaten too much dinner.

bunny with great wide ears that flop down like a stuffed animal's instead of standing stiff like other rabbits'. The French Lop weighs in at 15 pounds, while the Dutch is more likely four pounds.

The breeders at these shows do not kiss, cuddle or whisper to their rabbits. Most of them are raising rabbits for meat and for their fur. (Hunting rabbits for meat gave way to breeding rabbits for meat as early as the first century B.C. But it took the taxonomists until the mid-20th century to realize that rabbits are not big rodents. They are a separate group called lagomorphs that developed at least 60 million years ago. If rabbits are related to rodents, their common ancestor would have had to live in the Age of Reptiles, at the time that the dinosaurs were becoming extinct.) Breeders will not mind, however, selling a baby rabbit for a pet. In spite of their superior coats and colors, most breeds of fine rabbits are no more expensive than pet-store rabbits.

Wild rabbits, even if taken as babies, don't eat well and often die in captivity. It's a pity, because it would be fun to own a Western jack rabbit who can leap 20 feet at a single bound and outrun any predator except a cheetah.

Choosing a Baby Rabbit

Rabbits are weaned and ready to leave their mother at eight weeks. There are two ways you can pick up a rabbit when examining it. Grab the scruff of its neck firmly with one hand, just behind the ears, and place your other hand under its rump. Or instead, grab the scruff with one hand and the skin over its rump with the other. Neither method sounds comfortable to us, but if you try to pick up a bunny as you would a kitten or a puppy, you'll see it feels unsupported, kicks, jumps and often falls.

A healthy baby should have thick, somewhat glossy fur, and a solid, not too skinny feel in your hands. Look under its tail; if its rear is messy, it probably has diarrhea. Check the baby's eyes and nose to see that neither is runny. If you notice a baby that is calmer than the others, it would be your best bet as an apartment pet. Males (bucks) and females (does) make equally good pets, but in general, adult rabbits don't get along well together. Unless you are intent on breeding, a single rabbit is advised.

Housing

Rabbit houses are called hutches. You can buy hutches in most pet stores, especially at Easter time. The usual ones, and the cheapest, are made of wood and chicken wire, with a heavier hardware cloth mesh on the bottom and a sliding masonite top. The smallest size, about two by three feet, is large enough for one Dutch rabbit, but the larger breeds should have a hutch four by four feet unless the rabbit is only using the hutch to sleep in at night. If someone in your family is willing to help, you can make a better hutch yourself. Instructions appear on page 340 .

Rabbits are more sensitive to heat than to cold. Breeders don't heat the sheds where they keep their rabbits but do cover them with plastic sheeting or similar protection when the weather is windy or bitter. If you have an outdoor area—under a porch or in an open shed—where there is protection from rain and the hot sun, you can keep the hutch outdoors most of the year. Apartment dwellers lucky enough to have a terrace, balcony or roof can keep the hutch outdoors too. Remember that it's illegal to keep any obstacle on a fire escape.

Newspapers spread beneath an indoor hutch will catch droppings and urine. Spread it six sheets deep. Change the paper twice a week, or more often if you'd rather. Wash the whole hutch with water from the hose or in the bathtub every couple of months.

Your rabbit can live outside a hutch in a small room if you wish. Keep its food and water dishes in the same place, and check the section on Taming and Housebreaking.

If your rabbit will be living in your backyard, you could make the outdoor hutch instead. It has a sloping roof to keep out the rain. A hutch made this way can simply be moved from spot to spot when the ground beneath gets covered with droppings. The droppings can be left to disintegrate and fertilize the lawn.

Food and Water

The best basic diet for a rabbit is rabbit pellets. Most pet stores carry them. Use a crockery dish that the rabbit won't be able to tip over and keep it

Lop-eared rabbits make very comfortable surroundings.

filled with pellets. Rabbits, who are grazers in nature, eat all day long. A rabbit can get overweight if it is caged all the time, but it would be better to provide it with freedom to exercise than to ration its food.

Your rabbit will enjoy snacks, too. Try grass that has not been sprayed with insecticide, or hay, lettuce and carrots. Rabbits need more salt than many animals, so breeders often keep a salt disk around in the hutch for the rabbit to lick. Pet stores usually carry salt disks, but if you can't get one put some table salt in a dish every once in a while to see if your rabbit wants it. If it does, offer salt in a dish or sprinkle salt on the food once or twice a week.

Rabbits need to drink a lot of water. They can drink either from a water bottle or from a dish. If you use a dish, it should be crockery so it is heavy enough not to tip, and you must change the water every day. A water bottle is easier. Change it only as the water gets low. Large water bottles that hold several days' supply can be bought at pet stores. The best ones have a ball bearing inside the tip of the spout to prevent leaking.

Illnesses

Rabbit diseases are rather complicated, but fortunately pet rabbits do not get sick very often. If your bunny seems to have something wrong—stops eating, breathes noisily, moves jerkily—take it to your veterinarian. A rabbit can live for up to five years, and most pet bunnies die of old age.

Rabbits who go outdoors can get fleas. Use a cat flea powder to kill them, following the instructions on the label.

Taming and Housebreaking

Rabbits need to be handled for frequent but short five- or 10-minute periods in order to get used to humans. Handling doesn't mean hauling your rabbit all over the place and subjecting it to the kinds of play a puppy would enjoy. Pick it up, pet it for a few minutes, put it down and let it come back to you in its own time. As the rabbit gets older and more used to you it will become calm and even affectionate—especially if you offer it snacks from your hand when you come to see it.

Many rabbits can be housebroken, but there is no guarantee that every individual is trustworthy. This is the way to do it: let your rabbit loose in some room that you hope will be its home—your bedroom, or your kitchen if you can keep the door shut, or a playroom, or even the whole basement if it isn't very large. You'll notice that the rabbit tends to leave its droppings in only one or two corners. Put a regular cat litter box in the corner (or each of the two corners) it uses. It will probably accept the box as its bathroom and you will have a housebroken rabbit. A rabbit loose in a room will nibble on furniture, so you may prefer to keep it in a hutch when no one is around.

If you choose to let your rabbit live in a hutch all the time, you may be able to avoid the nuisance of newspapers. One family we know keeps a mixing bowl under the mesh of their rabbit's bathroom corner. It drops its droppings there and they clean the bowl every couple of days.

Grooming

Rabbits, like dogs and cats, have periods of shedding. The heaviest shedding starts as the weather warms up, but there is some shedding all the time. The fluffy hair floating around sticks to things and is hard to vacuum off of rugs and fabrics. Some people are allergic to rabbit hair, and even nonallergic people can get an itchy nose.

Walking Your Rabbit

You can also take a rabbit out on a leash, not as part of the housebreaking but just for exercise and the fun of it. City streets may be too confusing for most rabbits, but a city park or the suburbs or country are fine. The kind of harness that is used for cats is just right for a rabbit. You may have to take your rabbit with you to the pet store to fit it properly.

When your rabbit is very tame and comes to you easily in the house, you can risk letting it loose for a few minutes at a time outdoors. It will love to nibble the grass and will not be interested in running away. Be careful of dogs, though. If a dog comes up to it suddenly, your rabbit may be startled and bolt away. Or the dog might try to kill it. If you have a fenced yard to keep dogs out, a rabbit can live free outdoors all summer long. In fact, we once had a small gray rabbit named Toby who wouldn't run away no matter what we did. We lived in a house where the landlord threw a tantrum one day and banned all pets. The house was in the country, so we figured it would be an easy thing to just let Toby go. We let him go. He stayed. Perhaps he liked us—he would hoppity-hop up to us every time we went outside and stand on his hind legs pawing gently at us for a pat. Or perhaps he liked the flowers that grew in the landlord's garden—he ate them up. The landlord wasn't pleased, so we took Toby for a drive and deposited him in a less civilized area about a mile away. Two days later, Toby poked his head up from the midst of the ruined flower bed, very pleased with himself. We moved to a different house—with Toby.

Loose hair in the rabbit's coat can get matted and messy. There is also some danger that the rabbit, who grooms itself by licking, will swallow enough hair to form a mat in its intestines. A bristle dog brush will get the loose hair out easily. If that seems clumsy to use, try the finest-toothed metal combs that are sold for dogs. A weekly brushing or combing should be enough during most of the year, with more frequent grooming if the rabbit is shedding heavily.

Breeding

The rate at which rabbits breed is legendary, but actually rabbit breeding is not all that easy. The babies are born extremely immature—eyes shut, bodies naked and with poor temperature control. The mothers must keep them warm as well as nurse them. But with litters they are nervous: if they or the babies are disturbed, they may abandon their offspring and leave them to die.

Professional rabbit breeders provide specially constructed nesting boxes and are careful of the doe's diet as well as her peace of mind. Still, it is common for several babies in a litter to die.

If you want to give it a try, the 4-H club in your area can tell you where to purchase a nesting box and how to go about introducing the doe to the buck. Rabbit copulation must be one of the fastest known—breeders advise leaving the doe in the buck's hutch no more than five minutes. No one mentions rabbit courtship—there probably isn't time for any preliminaries.

Guinea Pigs

Guinea pigs are not pigs—they are rodents, tailless relatives of rats and mice. They don't come from New Guinea either. They are native to the Andes Mountains of South America, mainly Peru, where they are raised for food. Some people think they were named "guinea" because to the English the word once meant any strange, faraway land. Everyone agrees they are called "pigs" because of the oinks, honks, snorts and whistles they produce. If a regular pig could produce that much noise in proportion to its body size, it would be terrifying. Among the more charming noises guinea pigs can make are rattling purrs which they reserve for their mates or for any human who will scratch them behind the ears. Knowledgeable people skip the nickname of guinea pig and call them by their native Peruvian Indian name: cavy.

Cavies are nearly as cute as rabbits, certainly as tame if handled a lot, but dumber. Don't expect them to seek affection, to follow you around the house or to come when called. Don't expect housebreaking either.

The ordinary cavy has short glossy hair that lies flat to its body. It comes in a variety of colors including pure white, deep black, bright ginger, pale gold, and the "wild" agouti brown. Guinea pig fanciers often look for special patterns of color combinations, like tricolor stripes, a black spot over each eye, or a white "cape" over the shoulders. The next fanciest breed is the Abyssinian cavy, who has silly looking whorled cowlicks in illogical places like its rear end. The fanciest breed of all is the Peruvian cavy, who has some cowlicking, but since its hair ordinarily grows to five or even eight inches long it looks like a dust mop with feet. There are reports of Peruvians growing three-foot-long coats. No doubt it gets difficult to locate the eight-inch pig underneath. The colors of the two fancy breeds are as varied as the smooth-haired varieties.

Choosing a Guinea Pig

Nearly every pet store carries guinea pigs from time to time. They may offer both babies and

Another name for guinea pig is cavy.
Tamed cavies don't mind being dressed up.

adults. The adults look so tame that many people are happy to buy them. Actually, though guinea pigs certainly won't bite you, they can be very skitterish if they're not handled a lot while they are young. Look for a three- to four-week-old baby, the calmest one you can find. A baby that kicks and squeals when it's picked up may have a nervous temperament, though all babies will scamper away as you reach for them. A cavy that is well socialized purrs when you scratch behind its ears.

As you pick up each cavy to determine its temperament, examine its body too. It should feel solid and heavy, not light and skinny. Its fur should be thick in all of the varieties, and glossy if it is smooth-haired. Check its rear end for signs of diarrhea and its front end for signs of runny eyes or nose. You may notice what look like splits or tears in the ears. These are not old, healed wounds but normal cavy ears.

If you want more than one cavy, have the salesclerk check their sex carefully by feeling for testicles under the skin at the rear of each animal. You can't keep more than one adult male in a hutch, but you can keep females together, with or without a male. If you do have both sexes, they will surely have babies.

Housing

A guinea pig can live in the same sort of hutch as a rabbit (page 340), and will drop about as many droppings, usually in two or three of the four corners of the hutch. For some reason, though, guinea pigs are incredibly wetter than rabbits. Why guinea pigs must drink so much only to puddle so often is a mystery we have not been able to solve. Change the newspaper at least twice a week, and scrub down the hutch when it gets messy looking.

Guinea pigs enjoy a perch in their hutch. A brick will do if you don't want to go to more trouble. It would be nice, though, to get a small, corrugated carton, cut the sides down low enough so that your pet can climb onto it, and then cut a door in one side as well so it can crawl under. The cavy won't soil this perch or the home inside it.

Like rabbits' homes, a cavy's hutch can be kept outdoors if protected from wind, rain and sun. Bring it in during the coldest winter weather.

A cardboard carton serves as both a burrow and a perch.

Apartment balconies are a perfect place to let a cavy loose for exercise. You can let your guinea pig loose outdoors in the country too, but only if you have a wide-open space where you can keep an eye on it. If there is anything remotely resembling a burrow, it will be down it or under it faster than you thought its plump, short-legged body could go. If there's nothing to scramble under, your guinea pig will concentrate on munching its way through the grass.

Food and Water

Guinea pigs are more interested in food than you can believe. They will eat their way in a straight line through almost any vegetation you put in front of their faces. We have watched one of our pigs eat his way lengthwise in one sitting through three whole carrots laid end to end. Try it. Ours also eats cabbage, apples, spinach, beets, cauliflower, corn, lettuce, bark, seaweed, flowers, grass, hay, leaves, and peanut butter sandwiches. He doesn't appreciate jelly.

The basic diet should be guinea pig pellets, left daily in a dish in the hutch to be nibbled on all day. Guinea pig pellets look exactly like rabbit pellets but are actually composed of different foods in different proportions. Pet stores usually carry rabbit pellets, insisting they are fine for guinea pigs too—but they aren't. Be insistent, or be prepared for malnutrition. If you have no way of getting the right pellets, add vegetables like spinach or romaine lettuce to your cavy's diet, and vegetables like carrots, and fruits like apples that are high in vitamin C. Offer fresh foods only a little at a time to be sure you don't set off a bout of diarrhea.

In nature a guinea pig grazes on grass and other vegetation, but it also chews on twigs along the way. The twigs help to keep its teeth short enough. In captivity a guinea pig's teeth, like those of rats and mice, will grow too long if it is given only soft foods like vegetables. The pellet food helps keep its teeth worn down, but twigs may be needed too.

In the summer, if you have plenty of grass and hay available for your pig, that plus some green twigs for chewing is an adequate diet. Offer salt or a salt disk.

Like rabbits, caged guinea pigs can get overweight, but again it is not from overeating. Not enough exercise is the reason, so try more freedom and not less food.

Don't worry about forgetting to feed your guinea pig. It will remind you. A cavy feels so passionate about food that if it so much as hears your footsteps when it is hungry it will whistle and honk at you until you bring something to fill its belly.

Provide water in a large water bottle to avoid the mush of sodden pellets and droppings that guinea pigs manage to get into water dishes.

Any container looks like a hiding place to the guinea pig.

Illnesses

The commonest thing that can go wrong with guinea pigs is vitamin deficiency. They are particularly apt to get scurvy, caused by too little vitamin C. The first symptom of malnutrition you'll notice is thinning hair along the center of the back. You'll be able to see skin under the hair. The moment you notice thinning hair start adding vitamin drops to the guinea pig's water. The instructions on the bottle from the pet store will tell you the proportions. Re-examine the diet you've been using. Try to get back on a balance of guinea pig pellets, raw spinach and carrots.

Other diseases in guinea pigs are rare when you keep them as pets, and their life span is quite long—about five years, occasionally even eight.

Grooming

Smooth-haired guinea pigs stay neat and clean, but the Abyssinians and Peruvians can get droppings stuck to their fur or knots of matted hair. They require grooming and sometimes a bath too.

You can give guinea pigs baths with warm water and mild soap if their fur has gotten messy. They don't seem to mind it. Rinse well and dry with a towel afterward.

A fine-toothed metal comb or a small bristle brush is handy for grooming. Short-haired cavies will not need grooming often, but you may want to brush or comb out loose hairs if your pet is shedding. The shedding is never as heavy as with rabbits and the hair is not as itchy-feeling. The long-haired cavies, especially the Peruvians, need grooming. Their own licking can't get out the mats and tangles that form in the fur. If mats form that are too hard to get out, cut them out with a pair of scissors. The hair will soon grow back. It's impossible to keep long-haired guinea pigs in good coat if they are not in separate cages. Natural affection among guinea pigs is expressed in fond hair nibbling.

Breeding

Guinea pigs are easy to breed. Their babies are born looking like miniature adults—completely furred, eyes open, able to walk about and even to eat solid foods. Because they are so mature at birth, the gestation period (how long it takes before they are born) is long—about three months. Usually only one to three babies are born in a litter. To breed guinea pigs, you have only to leave a boar (male) and a sow (female) (remember they are named after pigs) together in one hutch. Sooner or later, usually by the time the sow is six months old, she will get pregnant and have her babies. You don't have to remove the father as you do for other rodents, because guinea pigs live well together in family groups. You will find them to be very affectionate with one another, and the father will not harm his young babies.

A baby nesting box with hay on the floor.

If you are breeding it might be a good idea to use vitamins in the water and to pay special attention to diet. Even when you are very careful, the mother guinea pig will lose much of her hair and look pretty scrawny until some weeks after the babies have been born. In the wild, guinea pigs keep their babies in burrows. To make your sow happy, put a box with a door inside the cage and put some hay or grass inside it as bedding for the babies. The sow may pull out some of her own hair to add to the nest. She will nurse her babies for about three weeks, even though they are eating for themselves during the same time. A three-week-old guinea pig is old enough to sell to someone else as a pet.

If you plan to keep the babies, remove the young boars before they are a month old. You can tell they are males by feeling for their testicles under the skin at their rear ends. The father boar will be pleased to have a harem for his very own, but he will fight and kill rival boars as they grow up even if they are his own sons.

Skunks

We have never really had a pet skunk ourselves. We had one for three days, but she was fat, sullen, sleepy and smelly. We thought skunks didn't make good pets. Now we know Eugene, a skunk belonging to Igor, a friend of ours. Igor's father says of Eugene, "If he was a person, he'd be the sort that would hand you an exploding cigar and then laugh his fool head off." He lays in wait for their dog and their cat and then dashes up from behind and pounces on them. They don't appreciate practical jokers.

With his own human family, Eugene is likably playful and even affectionate, climbing into laps and sprawling for a good petting. He's pigeon-toed, clumsy and waddles when he walks. The fact that he tries to look dignified at the same time makes him a natural clown.

Eugene, like all skunks, is shy of strangers. When guests visit, he nobly mounts the stairs, tail up in disdain, to retire to his basket. The raised-up tail is not to be feared in descented skunks, but you'll still get some skunk smell out of a frightened or annoyed pet even after the operation to remove scent glands. All the mustelines, ferrets and skunks included, exude scent from glands in their skin when they are upset. Naturalists have observed, but not explained, how reluctant skunks are to spray. Before a skunk lets loose, it ups its tail, bows forward, and sometimes even stands on its front legs, balancing like an acrobat. The warning is usually enough for any animal that has had experience with skunks; the encounter usually ends without spraying.

No doubt everyone you know says skunks stink. Tell them that in tests where the smell was at low concentration and the subjects weren't told what it was, most people found skunk smell pleasant. Very little children rather like skunk scent in normal concentration. Musk, a substance taken from the anal glands of musk deer, is the "turn-on" smell in our most expensive perfumes. On a direct hit, however, the spray of a skunk can damage eyes to the point of blindness.

Choosing a Skunk

Like all animals in this chapter, you must get a skunk young to socialize it sufficiently. Often there is no way to tell the exact age of a young skunk if it was caught in the wild. If it was raised by a breeder, try to get it when it has just been weaned. Eugene was bought as a caught-in-the-wild baby at a pet store, both descented and altered, but we have seen only one other skunk for sale in a pet store. The wild animal farms that advertise in poultry magazines sometimes sell baby skunks. We've found that people take less advantage of you if you have talked with them personally rather than just mail-ordered from them. The additonal expense of a long-distance call may assure you a just-weaned baby.

Housing

Because skunks are nocturnal, you can trust them to stick to their own quarters during the day and join the family in the evening. This makes them perfect pets for working families, since no one has to worry about what the skunk is up to when no one is at home. In the evening your pet is awake and ready for company. Skunks are not terribly active at any time, which makes them ideal for small apartments.

This type of woven dog bed is perfect for a skunk.

Skunks enjoy munching an apple whenever they can get one.

Eugene spends much of his time, by choice, in a small bathroom. He has not been caged and doesn't seem to need to be. He has a cavelike basket to sleep in (sold as a dog basket in pet stores) and a piece of newspaper in a corner to use for his droppings. There is no difficulty in housebreaking a skunk. First observe which the skunk's preferred corner is and then leave newspaper there.

Food and Water

Skunks thrive on canned cat food as a basic diet. Because they are omnivorous in nature, living best of all on the thrown-out leftovers of balanced human diets, they need fresh vegetables like carrots and fruit like apples besides meat or fish. Feed your skunk once each evening when it wakes up.

In nature skunks go into a very deep hibernation, similar to bears. During the late summer and the fall, when the eating is good, they stuff themselves to the point of extreme obesity. We've heard that you have to put pet skunks on a diet during this time of year. The theory is if they get too fat, they will try to hibernate even if they live in a warm house. Igor says this is not true of Eugene. He is not fat, but the skunk we tried to keep one November was awfully fat—and cranky. We think she was trying to hibernate.

Eugene, of course, is kept on a strict diet all year long. Instinct propels skunks to eat greedily while they can in preparation for that all-winter nap during which, in the wild, they would have to live on accumulated fat for about four months. It's impossible to predict how large the evening meal should be. If your skunk begins to put on weight, cut down the quantity of food it gets. Wait and see if the new amount keeps it at a stable weight. When you have it right, stick to that amount.

Illnesses

We have not heard of any particular health difficulties with skunks except fatness. They should be inoculated by a veterinarian for feline and canine distemper, and rabies.

If a skunk does get sick, try getting advice from your vet first. If he is unsure what to do, call nearby zoos or nature centers which may keep skunks. Their experience is often helpful with unusual animals.

Ferrets

Ferrets are small, weasellike animals domesticated from the wild polecat. They hunt snakes, rodents and other animals for food, and are by nature quick, bright, aggressive and sharp-toothed. Many people think ferrets are wild animals who can be tamed much like a skunk or a raccoon. There is one wild polecat species called a ferret—the black-footed ferret of North America, which is nearly extinct. But the domestic ferret is no more a wild animal than our domestic cat. Ferrets have been domesticated for over 2,000 years, so long that no one is sure which of the many wild polecats they were originally bred from. Some scientists even think the wild forebear is now extinct. Ferrets and polecats look almost exactly alike and can be bred easily with one another. But domestication has made the ferret less touchy, less agile and less nocturnal than its wild relatives.

Domesticated ferrets have been kept during all these centuries as hunting animals. Let loose from time to time around barns and homes, they can kill as many rats, mice and snakes as a cat can. But mainly ferrets have been trained as rabbiters. Their narrow foot-long bodies are made to fit through holes. Equipped with either a tiny muzzle to prevent them from eating bunnies in their burrows or a collar of jingle bells to warn their prey, they chase the rabbits from the warren (the large underground communities European rabbits live in). The hunter then kills the rabbits and rewards the ferret with rabbit liver. A preference for livers, kidneys and hearts is still typical of ferrets. Ours gobbles chicken hearts and beef kidneys the way kids gobble cookies.

Ferrets are of the family of carnivores called mustelines, who are not only the most primitive of all meat-eating animals but also the stock from which all other meat-eaters evolved. Mustelines include skunks, who have developed to a fine art the musteline trademark of musk-producing glands at the base of the tail. Male ferrets have a slight musky odor all the time, and females also smell if they are angry or frightened or in heat. Our female ferret only smelled objectionable the first few evenings she played with our overenthusiastic 90-pound puppy, and the one morning when she had accidentally gotten locked into the clothes dryer for the night. These days she smells less strong than a wet dog or a dry mouse.

Choosing a Ferret

Ferrets are available from wild animal farms and sometimes from mink breeders. You will find ads for them in poultry magazines. Some states require that a ferret be registered as a wild animal. Your vet should be able to find out if this applies to you.

It is extremely important to get a ferret just after it has been weaned, when its eyes aren't even fully opened and it can barely get around on its unsteady legs. If it's any older your chances of really taming it diminish. If you choose a male, he should be altered by your vet to reduce the chance of him wanting to escape and revert to wildness as an adult. The vet can remove the anal glands at the same time to reduce the musky odor.

Since you'll have to order your ferret by phone or letter, you can't check on its health ahead of time. Also, whatever its condition when it leaves the animal farm, it may suffer a difficult journey by plane to your airport. Open the crate as soon as possible and offer food and water to the ferret. Even if it seems in good shape, ask the vet to check it over—it should have its shots (page 207) right away.

Most domesticated ferrets are albinos with white

Pest, a female ferret, is not much on picture posing.

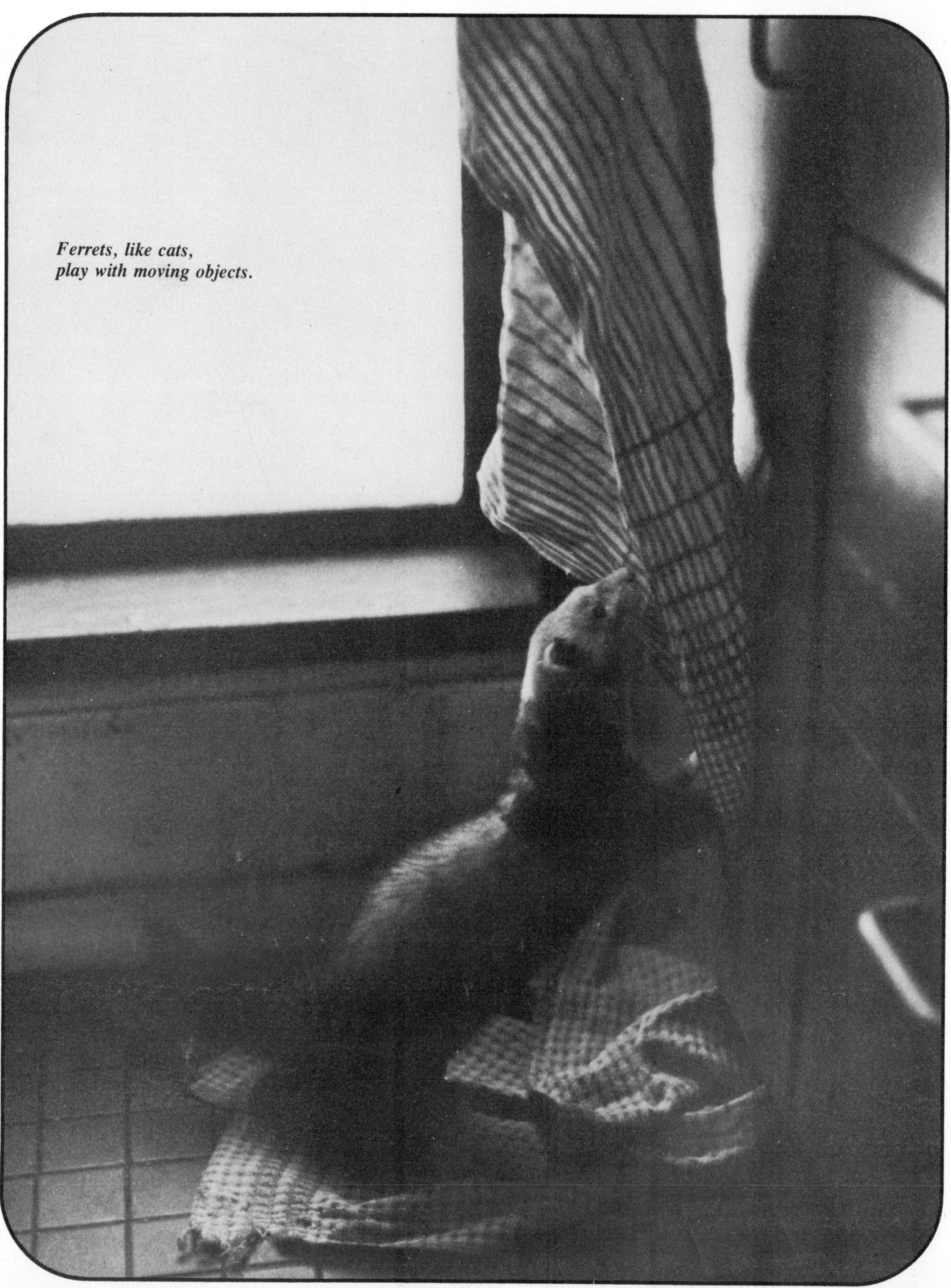

Ferrets, like cats, play with moving objects.

fur and red eyes. There are also nice brown ferrets and crosses between the two. The crosses are the prettiest, having white fur on the belly and sometimes on the paws. The rest of the body is tan, tipped with brown, with an almost-black tail. Our albino-brown cross turns quite pale and frosted-looking in the winter and a warm brown in summer. She has a white marking on the top of her head and white toes all year.

Housing

When you first bring a ferret home it is advisable to cage it so that you will always be able to find it. The cage on page 343 is made of wood and wire mesh, with newspapers spread on the floor. It is shown equipped with a den, a nearly closed off area where no one can spy. The den is absolutely necessary. Ferrets sleep very heavily, sometimes requiring several minutes to wake up even with much joggling and prodding. Somehow ferrets must be aware that deep sleepers need safe places for snoozes.

Our ferret is named Pest and her quarters are built into a cupboard at floor level, constructed much like the drawing on page 344. Since Pest is housebroken, we no longer latch the door. She is left entirely free, and while she sleeps in her den at night, she often naps in other nooks she has found around the house.

Pest's den is just a closed-off portion of her cage entered through a corner cut out of the plywood partition. She has a supply of rags with which she both makes her bed and plugs her hole at naptime. The plywood partition is removable so we can take out the pieces of meat she sometimes drags inside for midnight snacks.

You'll find your ferret will use the darkest and most private corner of its cage for a bathroom, but never its own den. As soon as it's decided which corner to use, put a small box of kitty litter there. Ferrets are as neat as cats and like to cover their messes up. A box inside the cage is the beginning of box training for uncaged ferrets.

Cage Cleaning. Change the litter in the litter box and the newspaper every few days. Ferrets have a way of backing themselves into a corner to go to the bathroom, so you may have to scrub the corner walls each week. If you don't like scrubbing, tape a folded sheet of newspaper into the corner behind the litter box. Then any mess will be on the paper, which is easily taken down and changed.

Once your ferret knows how to use its litter box, it will be easier to train it to use a litter box outside the cage.

Food and Water

A ferret is an easy pet to feed, happy with raw hamburger (and not too much of it), canned dog or canned cat food, or fish. Beef kidney is cheap and much appreciated.

Cat food is a balanced diet for ferrets. If you prefer other foods, sprinkle powdered dog or cat vitamin supplement on the meat to supply the calcium and phosphorus contained in cat food and in the mouse bones they would eat in the wild. The vitamins are available in pet and drug stores.

Keep a crockery water dish filled with fresh water for your pet ferret to drink. If you like, you can train it to drink from a water bottle instead. Buy the size sold for rabbits in a pet store. Deprive it of water for a day, then keep touching its lips with the tip of a filled water bottle until it begins to lick. A few lessons will get the point across.

Our ferret steals milk from our glasses whenever she gets a chance. It invariably gives her diarrhea.

Illnesses

Ferrets are hardy, healthy animals, needing protection only from hot sun and subzero temperatures. But they can get any of the diseases a cat can, and should be inoculated by your vet with regular cat pneumonitis, distemper and influenza shots. If your ferret is allowed outdoors on a leash, it should have a rabies shot as well. Take a stool sample to the vet to check for worms. Fleas can be treated with cat flea powder or spray; apply it every three days for three or four weeks in order to kill new fleas as they hatch during treatment.

Bathing and Grooming

Our ferret enjoys bathing in water from time to

time. We set out a roasting pan filled with water at room temperature. She dives in the water, head and all, and comes up shaking like a puppy. Since a ferret's bathing style requires much leaping in and out of the water, put the pan on the bathroom or kitchen floor so you can mop up afterwards. Or you could put the pan in the bathtub or the kitchen sink.

For a long time we couldn't figure out why our ferret always looked so neat and clean. We never saw her grooming herself. Then one night she settled down to sleep under the covers of my bed. Judging from the movements of her humpy body for the next hour, I knew she was grooming herself thoroughly. But every time I lifted the covers to watch, she stopped. I assume ferrets, like some humans, prefer to groom themselves in private.

Taming and Housebreaking

Pest is not the first ferret we have had as a pet. Puck, a male and half grown when he arrived, came before her. He was unaccustomed to handling and had not been altered. He was untamable and eventually ran away.

We decided to try again. This time we ordered a female and insisted she be no more than six to eight weeks old. At this age a ferret has just been weaned and has not yet formed a firm opinion as to the sort of life it will lead. Pest arrived by air from the

animal farm where she was born, well-crated and in good shape. She was still too young to really walk; her belly more or less followed her front paws as she pulled herself about. Her eyes, just opened, were sleepy, and in fact she could stay awake only for about 15 minutes before collapsing into a comalike snooze. She didn't bite at all, although she nibbled fingertips in a cuddly way, and she wasn't ready yet for playful antics.

We handled Pest constantly. She got her belly rubbed and her neck petted, sampled food from our fingers and slept in our laps. This time it worked. Pest is now a thoroughly socialized, delightful, amusing, reliable, affectionate pet. When we leave her, she runs after us, muttering a ferret tune that sounds strangely like a laugh. When she's tired she climbs into our laps and sleeps in the crook of an arm, sometimes rolling belly-up as though she were in a hammock on a summer afternoon. When we stop petting her, she opens her eyes and nudges for attention like a dog. When she plays, it is a dance—around and around and pop into the air, as though the floor under her toes were too hot to touch. Legs stiff, back humped, eyes shining, she circles, pops, and POUNCE! she's got a toe. Her nip is not a bite but a tickly nibble (what is known to scientists as an inhibited bite), and then she's off in her dance again. The only time we could complain of her teeth is when we accept the challenge of her dance and roll her about with our hands as you do with a kitten. Then she will hang on to a finger and kick her legs against our hands in mock fierceness. But still she tries to be careful with her teeth and has never really hurt us.

Ferrets don't seem to fear much—even animals bigger than themselves.

Box training our ferret was quite easy. Pest goes to the bathroom after she eats and after she wakes from a nap. At first, we gave her a chance to use her box before we let her out of her cage. Then we could trust her not to mess around the house for several hours. As she began to run loose for longer and longer periods, we found she had chosen a corner of the kitchen under a projecting cabinet for a downstairs bathroom. So we put a litter box there too.

The larger the area in which a ferret runs free, the more litter boxes it will need. If you have a large house, your ferret is likely to choose more spots than you want to supply with boxes. The answer is to keep your ferret loose in a smaller area. We keep doors shut to confine our ferret to the two areas of the house that are convenient to her two litter boxes. Small-apartment dwellers may get along with only one box.

A ferret's instincts tell it to do a few things that have nuisance value in a home. Ferrets are burrowing animals and would as soon burrow in a flowerpot as elsewhere. Beware also of letting a ferret inside your pants' legs or under your shirt. Their claws are sharp, and shirts and pants are like burrows to the ferret. Burrows, of course, start out as holes. A ferret will go into any hole, including wastebaskets, dog-food cans, shoes and milk cartons.

Ferrets don't climb well but can cling to a shoulder.

Pup and Pest

Ferrets are known to be totally unafraid. That means they don't jump when you drop a book two inches in front of their faces, and they don't run away from anything. Unfortunately, that means a pet ferret won't run away from a dog.

You can't have a houseful of more or less free animals without letting them learn to deal with one another; but our sheepdog pup is both energetic and clunky, and we figured one good bam with a paw or one excited snap at Pest and it was all over. We let them play for a few minutes a night until we felt the pup was calm enough to be trusted.

One evening we turned and saw that our worst fears had come true. Pest lay dangling from the puppy's whiskery mouth. But no, not quite! Pest was hanging in midair, all right, but on her own steam. She had clenched the pup's whiskers in a death grip. The pup had no idea what to do next. She just stood there blinking, dangling a determined ferret. Within a few days, the puppy did begin to carry her pet ferret around in her mouth. Ferrets can get used to anything.

Two weeks later, we heard Pest screech. Now, we thought, it's happened. Pest lay prostrate on the stairs, the pup standing over her pawing at her body as though it were a rag. Pest was hissing at her, and this was the first time we had heard that warning noise. We picked up the limp body. Pest shut her eyes and collapsed. We rushed her to the vet wrapped in a towel. Broken leg? Internal bleeding? Injured spine? Brain damage? We opened the towel. Out popped Pest, performed a little dance, plucked at the vet's fingers, attacked the stethescope and pounced to the floor. Entirely normal, for a ferret. Ferrets, the vet explained, are hypoglycemic animals. They tend to use up their available body sugar rapidly when they are very excited or are exercising very hard. Moral: feed your ferret before you play. And by the way, Pest loves ice cream, honey and homemade butterscotch sauce.

We take Pest out on a leash. She wears the smallest-size cat harness and a light leash. It was a kicking scramble to get it on at first, but now she is used to it and no longer objects.

Breeding

Ferrets can have several litters of a half-dozen or so babies each year, but breeding is best left to professional breeders. Pregnant and nursing ferrets are ill-tempered, and unaltered males don't remain attached to the home.

Pet Cats

PET CATS

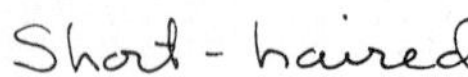

Long haired

CATS

Cost:
Domestic short-hair (alley cat) —usually free.
Mixed short- or long-haired breeds—usually free.
Persian—$125.00
Siamese—$125.00
(Show quality and rare breeds are more expensive)

Housing Equipment:
Food and water dishes—$3.00
Litter box for indoor cats: open type—$2.50
covered type—$8.00
Litter—$1.00 per week
Optional leash and collar or harness—$3.00
Brush and comb for long-haired cats—$3.00

Special Requirements:
Veterinary examination and inoculations, probable worming—$30.00 to $80.00, depending on local fees.
Optional altering: male—$25.00
female—$50.00

Diet:
Kitten or cat chow and canned cat food—$1.25 per week.

Care:
Feed and replenish water, clean droppings from litter box daily.
Clean and replace litter in litter box once a week.
Groom long-haired cats weekly.
Groom any cat as necessary during heavy shedding periods.
Take to veterinarian for checkup and booster shots once a year.

Tamability:
Need introduction to litter box or to outdoors, but no housebreaking.
Individuals may learn a few commands and to follow their owner on walks.
May become aloof or very affectionate and responsive, depending on treatment as kittens.

Life Span:
10 years.

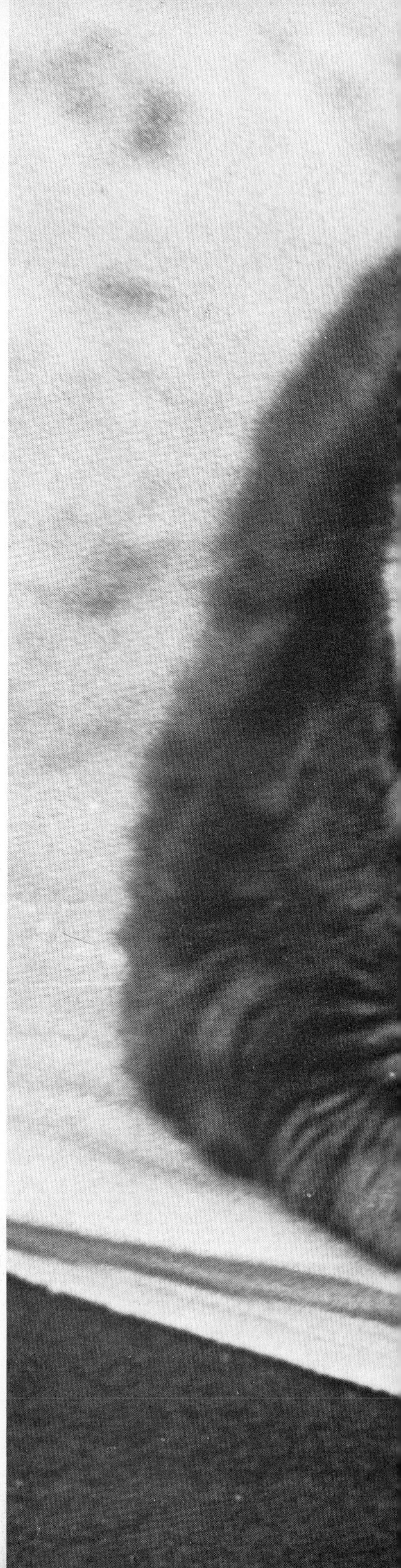

For such a small animal, no bigger than a bunny really, the cat carries a heavy load of superstition. The ancient Egyptians thought cats were gods. Anyone who killed a cat was treated like a murderer, and executed. When a cat died, it was made into a mummy. Three hundred thousand cat mummies were once found in Egypt, all buried in the same place. In the Middle Ages, people thought cats were witches and burned them at the stake. The cats of Germany and England were just about wiped out by that superstition.

There are still superstitions existing today. In America, black cats are bad luck. In England, white cats are bad luck. And my mother-in-law once warned me that cats smother babies.

Of course all this is nonsense. But it makes me wonder—what is it about cats that has made so many people imagine so much for so long? I don't know the whole answer but I can understand some of it. Cats make me uncomfortable. They stare at me. They don't let on what they're thinking. They don't let me love them when I feel like it. They rub against me when I don't feel like it. And when things don't go their way, they simply move in with someone else.

The cat is like it is because, of all our common domesticated animals, it is the only one who in the wild would live by itself. Wild dogs live in packs, geese in flocks, and cows in herds. Cats are solitary. The cat in Kipling's "Just So" story said it straight out: "I am the cat who walks by himself. . . ." No creature who lives in a group can afford to act aloof. It needs its family and friends; it had best be nice to them. But a cat can live with no love from anyone and reminds us of it rather too often.

The wild Kaffir cat of Africa was first domesti-

cated in Egypt 4,500 years ago, much more recently than the dog or even the ox. At that time, the Egyptians had launched a program to try to domesticate and find a use for all sorts of animals. They even tried the hyena. The use they found for the cat was as a bird hunter and retriever. Except for the fact that I never saw a cat go hunting and retrieving for its master, our domestic cats of today have changed little in thousands of years.

The Natural Hunter. Hunting is an instinct in cats and you can't teach yours not to do it. Domestic cats survive well in the wild as long as there is sufficient prey to eat. Dogs, who hunt and live in packs, have years in which to learn hunting skills from adult dogs. Cats don't. A mother cat deserts her kittens shortly after they are weaned. They are on their own as half-grown kittens, using extraordinary senses and instincts to fill their bellies.

Hunting is made up of three steps—the stalk, the pounce, and the killing bite. The steps are automatically triggered by slight movements or rustling sounds. Jiggle your toes under the blanket in bed or make a scratching sound on your sheet. Your kitten will crouch and begin to creep toward the sound and movement. That's stalking. Then it pounces, its hind feet landing first, its front paws free to sink their claws into your foot. Then comes the killing bite, if you haven't pulled your foot away.

Of the three steps, only the killing bite must be learned. The bite is given in the back of the neck. A canine tooth is used to feel out the space between two neck vertebrae through which the spinal cord can be severed. Instinct tells a kitten to aim its bite roughly where the body of an animal narrows for a short space—the neck. (That explains why kittens bite ankles.) The direction of fur or feathers may aim its mouth toward the spot too. But to learn the

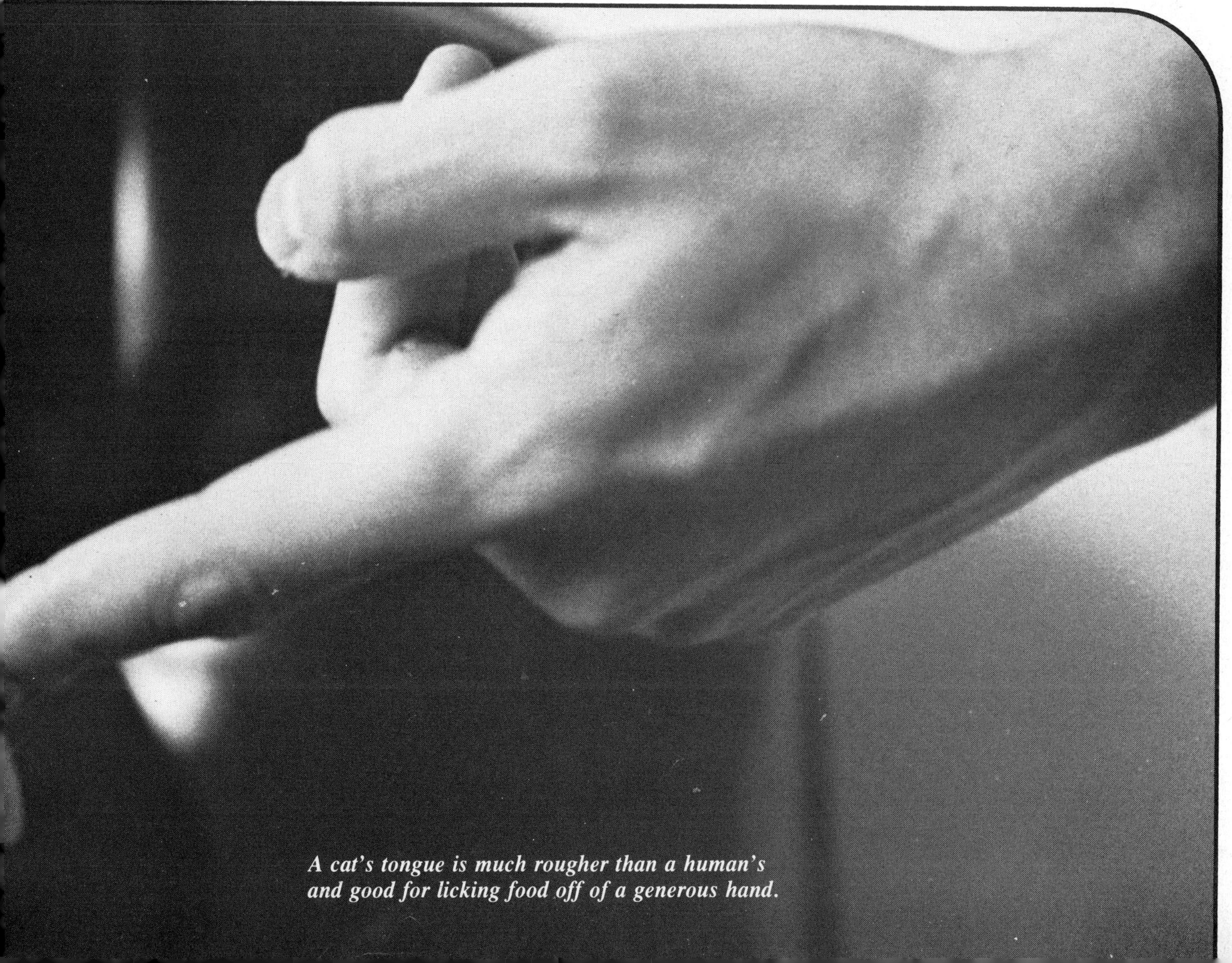

A cat's tongue is much rougher than a human's and good for licking food off of a generous hand.

art of feeling out the vulnerable spot with the canine teeth and severing the cord, a kitten needs two kinds of experience. First, it must see its mother kill prey. Second, during a critical period of early kittenhood it must be brought live prey to practice on. Mother cats who are allowed to hunt first bring home dead prey for the kittens to eat.

From that experience the kittens learn what is their proper food. A kitten taught to eat only mice will be slow to bother birds, and vice versa. Then the mother begins to bring home live prey, first killing it in demonstration herself, then letting her kittens practice killing their own dinner.

Kittens raised with mice or rats will not hunt them. They have not been taught to see them as prey. Kittens raised by nonhunting mothers will go through the first two steps of hunting but may not be able to kill their prey. This is sometimes the reason for what looks like cruelty to us: the cat that seems to tease its prey. This is not the cat's fault; it is short-circuited. Lacking the last step in the sequence, it lets the prey go; but then the prey moves, makes a noise, and the first two steps are automatically triggered all over again.

Both sight and hearing in cats are specially developed for hunting. A cat's ears are tuned to ultrasound, like the high-frequency squeaks of mouse talk that are inaudible to human ears. Naturally it's helpful to a cat to hear the mice talking behind the baseboard. The cat's automatic reaction to rustling sounds comes from a built-in sensitivity to the faint stirrings of leaves and grass that might betray a mouse or a bird.

A cat's eyes are like colored bicycle reflectors, flashing back even small amounts of light in devil red, ghost green or ghoul yellow. The Egyptians thought that cats kept the sunlight in their eyes overnight, and it was this sunlight glowing out that explained why cats can hunt in darkness. Actually, a cat in a really pitch-dark room can't see any better than you can. But nighttime darkness is not pitch-black at all, except to our poor eyes; for a cat, there is plenty of light available.

In the dark, a cat expands its large pupil to let the most possible light hit the extremely light-sensitive area at the back of the eye. In bright light, it contracts the pupil to a mere slit. To watch it happen, use a penlight in a dark room. With the cat in your lap, shield the light so you can just barely see its eyes, then gradually point the light at its face. The pupils will contract slowly enough for you to watch.

Cats don't use their noses to sniff along a trail as dogs do. Birds leave no trails and a mouse's trail ends in a hole the cat can't enter. Instead, a cat stations itself in a likely spot and waits for telltale sounds and movements. An experienced hunter will wait three and four hours, motionless but for its twitching tail, for a mouse to venture from a hiding place.

As the cat waits, it sees but does not notice grass blades, twigs and leaves—until they move. This is not really a strange skill. We do it all the time when we fail to hear anything that is going on around us until someone speaks our name. Our brain blocks out what is unimportant to us and notices only what we want to hear.

When cats bring home their prey, dead, alive or mutilated, it is not a ''gift'' for you at all. It is only a not very hungry cat bringing its prey home for future dining. The behavior becomes appropriate when a mother cat is caring for her kittens. Lacking kittens and not allowed to hunt, one frustrated female was even in the habit of bringing her two catnip mice to her dish each night. When animals are run by instincts but don't need to use them, some of the things they do seem crazy.

There are several explanations for a cat's whiskers, all having to do with hunting. The whisker area is supplied with an abundance of nerve endings, so there's little doubt that whiskers are a sense organ of some sort. They could be wind-detectors, telling the cat which way the wind is blowing so it can locate its prey better; but since any animal can feel which way the wind blows without whiskers (and cats don't use their sense of smell much in hunting), this doesn't seem enough of an explanation. For a while the most popular theory was that whiskers warn a cat whether a hole or crevice it is trying to squeeze through as it hunts is really big enough.

When a cat falls, it swivels its tail for balance as it turns its body to land feet first.

That made sense for cats with long whiskers which would really be able to feel out the size of a hole, but short-whiskered cats would be out of luck. Then someone discovered that if you touch a cat's whiskers, it blinks. Try it. Whiskers acting as a trigger for a blinking reflex makes sense. A cat stalking through shrubbery at night with its eyes wide open could get some nasty pokes in the eye from twigs. But if whiskers brush the twig first and trigger a blink, such accidents would be neatly avoided.

Cats get up trees with ease by gripping the bark with hooklike claws. On the ground, long curved claws that stuck out from toes would break in no time. They would also go clackety-clack along the ground, warning all the rodents in the neighborhood. So cats' paws are made with sheaths into which they can retract their claws completely. When a cat's claws are retracted, its velvety pads are noiseless.

Choosing a Kitten

Cats need good mothering, play with their littermates and handling by humans if they are to be friendly, happy pets. They especially need all three kinds of friendship between four and eight weeks of age. That means often an orphaned kitten will not act like a normal cat, a stray will be scared of people and even a kitten raised without littermates may be neurotic when it grows up.

The healthiest kittens are usually home-raised kittens. Often pet stores and pounds have no idea how a kitten has been treated during the first months of its life. So it makes sense not to get a kitten from either a pet store or a pound. There is another reason not to get a kitten from a store or a pound: they are too often the best possible places for a kitten to pick up diseases. Look in the classified section of a newspaper for ads for kittens that

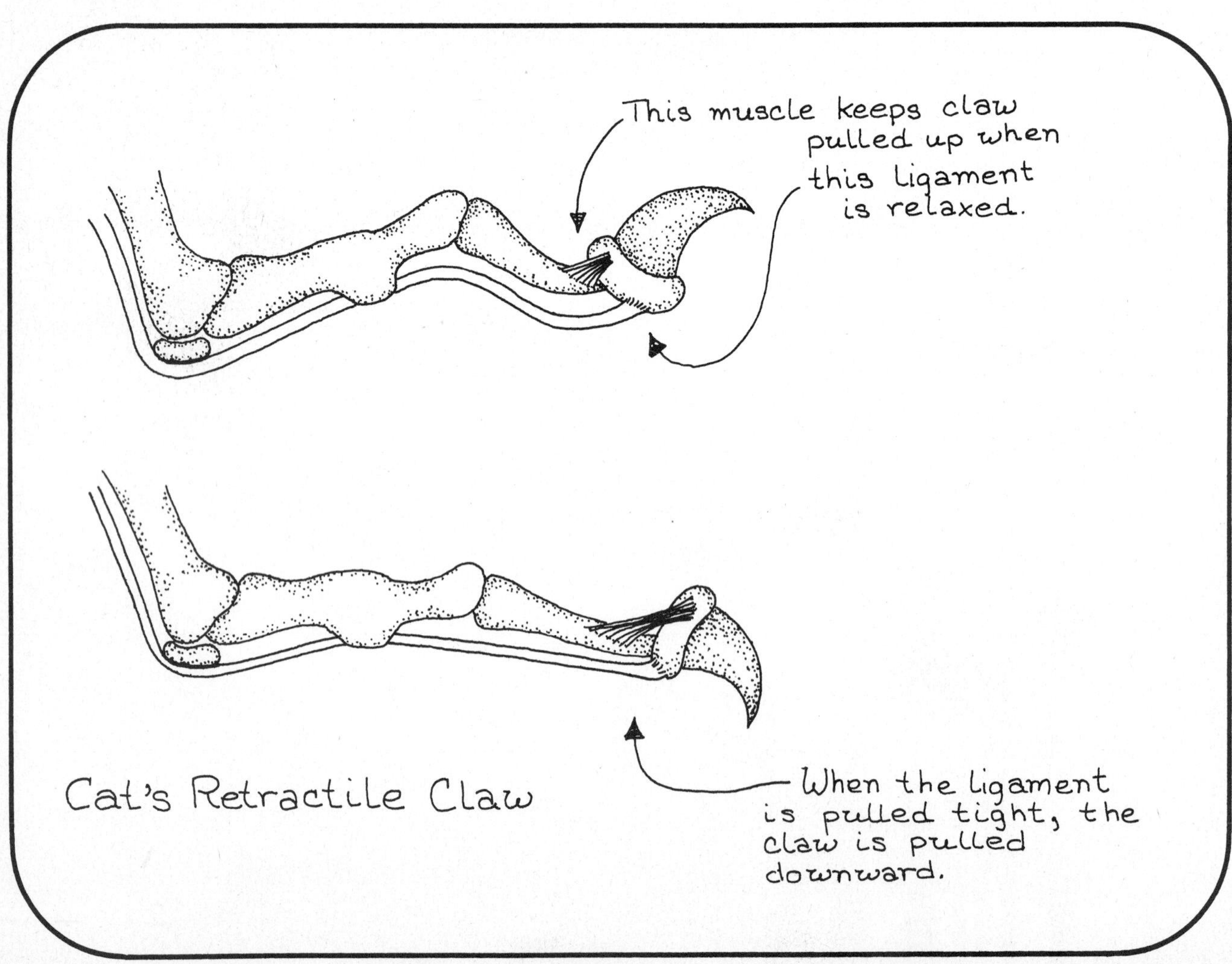

Cat's Retractile Claw

This cat is listed as the fattest in the world by the 1976 Guinness Book of World Records.

have been home-raised. The domestic short-haired kittens (alley cats) are almost inevitably free. Purebred kittens, varying in price, are offered by ad too.

Try to visit the kittens when they are six weeks old. Ask to pick them up. Healthy kittens have thick coats. They don't have pot bellies. They don't have runny eyes or noses. They aren't skinny. Feel a kitten's skin and look at its tummy to check for rashes, bald spots, scabs and fleas. There's no sense starting out with skin problems.

No matter what the owner promises you a kitten's disposition is going to be, you have to do some testing of your own to choose a good kitten. First ask to see the mother cat. If she's very shy and nervous, the kittens are likely to have inherited her timidity. Perhaps her jumpy behavior also affects the kittens. There's no sense even bothering to go further with a litter from a timid cat.

If the mother is calm and friendly, here are some tests to try. Watch while the mother nurses the kittens. Some will act aggressive, pushing other kittens out of the way to get to their accustomed nipple. (Each kitten chooses and keeps its own nipple soon after birth.) Others will be timid—the last to claim their nipple. Neither the most timid nor the most aggressive are good choices for a house pet.

When the kittens have finished nursing, pick up the one you have your eye on. At first, it will cling to your hand with its claws out; its body will feel tense. Pet the kitten. If it has been handled enough it should relax in your hands, sheath its claws, and stop clinging. If it hasn't been handled enough to know that petting is relaxing and pleasurable, it won't learn now. And it will most likely never make a good pet.

Last, ask to take the kitten into a room by itself. Put it down. The kitten should attempt to explore the room a little. If it just freezes and doesn't show any curiosity, it's too timid to develop well. After you've given the kitten a chance to explore for a few minutes, go near it and clap your hands hard or slam the floor. If it is a normally curious kitten, it should recover quickly from its startled reaction and go back to exploring. Crumple a little paper and toss it a bit to see if the kitten attempts to play. A relaxed kitten will, a tense kitten won't. A kitten who has been well mothered and handled enough by people should have a strong desire to follow you. Stand up and call the kitten to you. Back off. If the kitten makes no move to follow after you something has gone wrong with its socialization and it will not make a good pet.

This series of suggested tests are pretty rigid and even the sweetest, most social kitten would find it hard to get straight As. But it is important for a kitten to do well on most of them before you decide to make it your pet.

When you've chosen a kitten, arrange to bring it home when it's two months old. Bring a carton with a lid with you to carry it in.

Housing

Many cat breeders recommend keeping cats as strictly indoor pets. Although we have always allowed our housecats to come in and out at will, there is no doubt that the big outdoors is dangerous. Besides cars and dogs there is another hazard: a friendly kitten may strike a passerby as a "poor little stray" and be innocently kidnapped.

If you have an inside cat you will need a litter box for its droppings. There are a variety of litter boxes on the market, from simple pans to a two-piece affair with a rim that prevents the cat litter from being scratched out onto the floor.

There are different sorts of litter too, all based on some material that absorbs and supposedly deodorizes. The best litters resemble crushed clay. Odor is the problem with cats. In fact, "odor" is probably too nice a word. Like the smell of skunk, cat smell is difficult to get rid of.

The litter in a cat's box has to be changed and the box washed with soap and water every couple of days. Even if you could stand the smell, cats don't like to use their boxes after they are dirty and will find other places instead. The only time one might leave a bit of dirty litter in a box is as a reminder to a kitten.

If your home has a fireplace, you might have to cover the front with an impenetrable screen. Cats use ashes for droppings as readily as litter boxes. Some cats use bathtubs. Perhaps cats see the bathtub drain as a hole in which to hide their droppings (although they always seem to miss it).

Maybe that explains the occasional story of a cat who uses the toilet, too. It is, after all, a hole.

Food and Water

Mother cats wean their kittens when they are between six and eight weeks old. At this age, they need to be fed three or even four times a day. Gradually reduce the number of meals as the kitten grows. Grown cats can eat once a day but often bother you for a second meal.

The most nutritious food for your cat is dry processed chow for cats rather than canned meats and fish. Meat and fish alone may be a cat's favorite but a solid diet of these foods causes malnutrition and even kidney and bladder problems. Some people give a chow for two days, then canned meat or fish for one day. Others mix the meat or fish into the chow for every meal. Either way, the proportions are two-thirds chow, one-third meat or fish. Only a vet should advise a change in diet if your cat doesn't do well on this one.

Cats and kittens need a water dish left out for them all the time so they can drink as they need to. Kittens should have milk served separately at each meal but grown cats can live without it. Use fresh or dried milk, or evaporated milk diluted with an equal amount of water.

If your cat gets finicky, firm steps are necessary. A cat who eats its meat but won't touch its chow is only going to hurt itself. The same is true of pampered pets who have been led to believe that if they are stubborn enough, someone will finally offer canned salmon, raw beef, calves' liver or filet of flounder. The firm step for problem eaters is temporary starvation. You may feel nasty, and it's annoying because the cat will rub against you and meow for the two or three days of treatment. But starvation will get a cat to eat what's offered and in the long run keep it healthy. Two or three days without food won't hurt it a bit.

Cats can chew on small bones but not those from fish or chicken. They tend to splinter and stick in the cat's throat.

Illnesses and the Vet

Every kitten should be taken to a veterinarian after you get it home. It should be examined, inoculated, and checked for worms. Roundworms are passed as larvas through the mother's placenta to even the healthiest of kittens. Tapeworms are carried by fleas and the eggs may be ingested when a kitten eats a flea. Both kinds of worms are very common.

Bring a sample of the kitten's droppings with you in a small bottle or a plastic sandwich bag so the vet can check it under the microscope for worm eggs. Worms are gotten rid of by a poison that kills them without harming the kitten. The medicine is a pill, which is best administered by the vet to save you the unpleasantness of the diarrhea the medicine causes within a short time after taking it, and the worms themselves.

Many kittens die of feline distemper, influenza and other diseases that could have been prevented by inoculation. Find out from the previous owner if the kittens were started on their series of shots, and if so, when. Then your vet can either start or complete the series for your kitten. Cats that will be allowed outdoors should be inoculated against rabies, too.

The vet should check for any signs of malnutrition or other problems that would require a special diet. As the vet uses his stethoscope to listen to your kitten's heart, you may be shocked to see him slap your pet. He has to slap it to get it to stop purring. You can't hear heartbeats over the amplified buzz of a purring kitten.

While you have your kitten there, talk to the vet about spaying and neutering. Unless you really want your female kitten to have babies—and are sure you can find homes for them with the present overpopulation of cats—she should be spayed. Females come into heat as early as seven months, and continue at intervals of six weeks through most of their adult lives. Unlike dogs, who may take it in stride, a female cat in heat yowls, screams, groans, rolls, rubs, and pushes her rear end in the air. While she's inside the house driving you crazy, the howling, fighting tomcats are outside the house driving you even crazier. The operation of spaying should be done when a kitten is between four and six months old. The kitten's ovaries are removed under anesthesia and she must stay at the hospital overnight. Spaying does not make the cat lazy, fat or stupid. Spaying often does keep her more social and friendly than she might have been.

Unless you are a breeder, you should neuter a male kitten. Unneutered tomcats are propelled by their hormones to wander, to fight, and to spray urine all over your home. Scientists used to think spraying urine was a way of marking a territory. They thought each spray of urine on a tree trunk or rock was a KEEP OUT signal. But now researchers in animal behavior think spraying is more like a calling card, which states who the cat is and when he passed the spot. Since most cats in the wild are solitary creatures, these calling cards politely help them avoid the discomfort of meeting one another, or help to arrange meetings between male and female. A tom will mark his home regularly unless he is neutered as a kitten.

Unneutered tomcats can't be stopped from wandering or fighting. A tomcat regularly comes home from his prowls with split ears, nasty bites and bloody gashes. He may stay home to lick his wounds for a few days, but then he's off on the prowl again.

Neutering is a less complicated operation than spaying. It is done when the kitten is between four and six months. The glands inside the kitten's testicles that would ordinarily produce male hormones are simply disconnected. The vet doesn't remove anything; the cat's testicles look entirely normal. The operation requires anesthesia, but the kitten can come home the same day.

Housebreaking

When you read an ad for kittens in the paper that says "adorable kittens, housebroken," it's a good come-on but inaccurate. No one has to housebreak a kitten. Cats cover their feces and urine by instinct. As long as they are offered a place in which they can dig and bury, they will use it as a bathroom. The only training involved is showing a kitten where the litter box is and keeping it where the kitten can get to it.

A sure-fire method for getting the point across quickly is to wait until a kitten has eaten a meal, take it to its box, and move its front paws in a scratching motion in the litter. Since eating stimulates the kitten's bowels and it already knows what the pawing motion is all about, chances are you'll have success. Once the kitten's own smell is in the box, it will come back to it of its own accord.

The same method is used to teach a kitten to go outdoors when it needs to. Open the door for it after a meal so it learns the way out. Take the kitten to the spot you want it to use and scratch its paws in the soil. If you have a sandbox, beware. No cat can resist the easy digging possible in sand.

Both cats and dogs may express displeasure or depression by soiling on rugs and furniture. The only cure I know of for this purposeful soiling is to give the cat more love and attention no matter how mad you are. Cats aren't reasonable. You can lock a cat in a bathroom when you have to go out as a safe measure, but it's not guaranteed to help.

To get the smell of urine or feces out of rugs, clothing or furniture, wash the area with a commercial preparation sold in pet stores. This is probably better than the traditional remedies like baking soda or vinegar.

Taming and Playing

To raise your eight-week-old kitten into a really friendly pet, you have to force yourself on it. A puppy will demand love and attention even if you ignore it, but a kitten, remember, is made to live on its own. It will ignore you if you ignore it; it will grow into an aloof cat. If that's what you want, fine. But if you want a cat who really seeks out your affection, you have to work at socializing.

Hold the kitten often so it gets used to the slight restraint of your hand. Let it sleep in your lap and on your bed too, as often as you can. Pet it while it's eating. Let other people handle and pet it

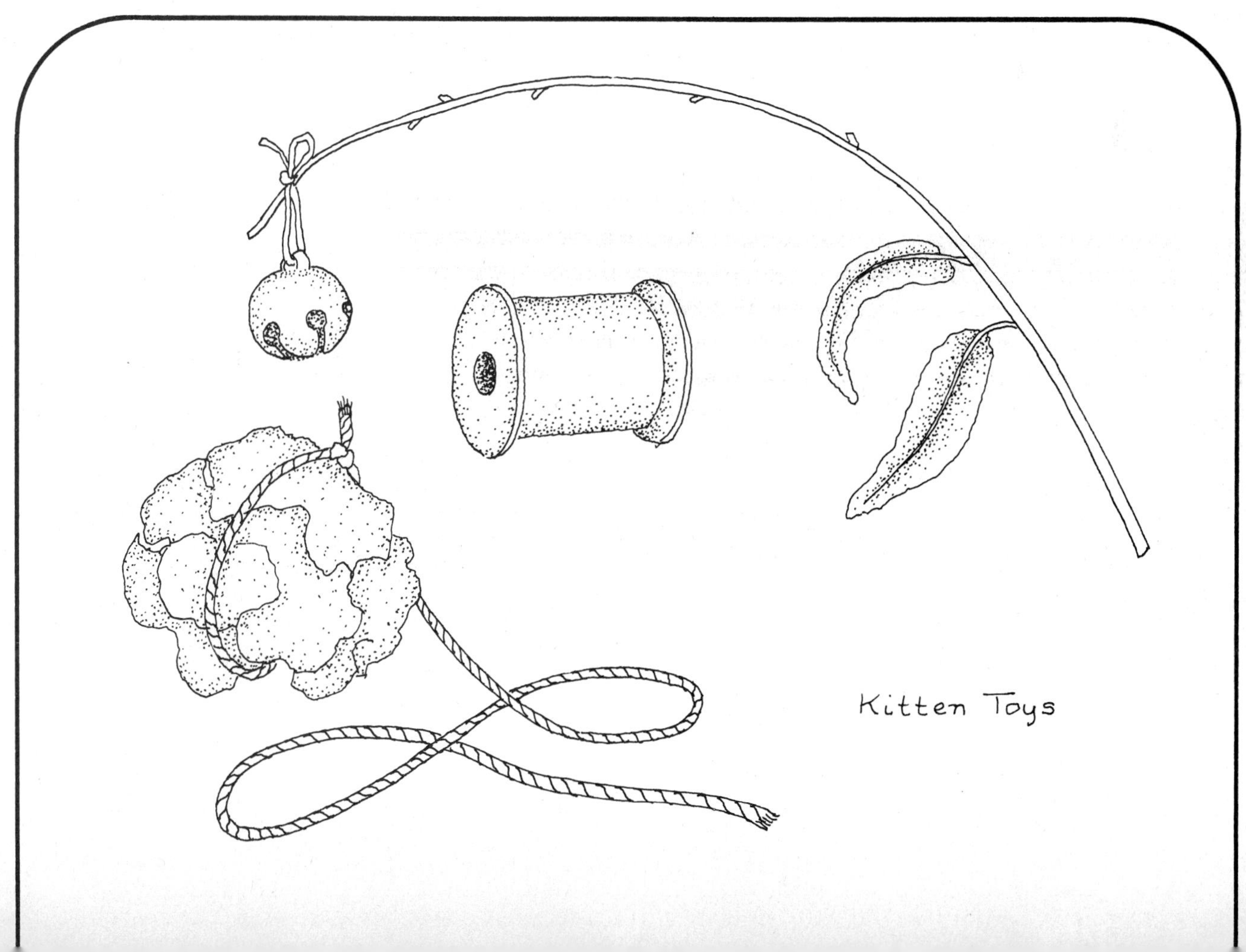

too—guests, relatives, friends and neighbors. The more people a kitten gets used to, the friendlier its attitude will be toward people in general.

Play with your kitten at every opportunity. Crawl after and chase it and let it chase you back. Try the game called "kill the foot." It's played when you're in bed, dying to go to sleep but unable to keep a toe from twitching under the blanket. The kitten waits for the twitch, pounces, grabs and bites viciously. Another way to play this game without limping the next day is to lay a blanket or quilt out on the floor. Tie a toy (spool, catnip mouse, baby's rattle) to a long string, put it under the quilt, and yank the string to make the toy move. As the kitten begins to attack the lump under the blanket, you can cleverly move it about by pulling the string from side to side.

You can get a kitten to play at hunting with any toy that jerks and rustles. A crumpled piece of paper or cellophane makes a great victim. Try tying a paper ball or a bell on to a long string; then pull the ball slowly and jerkily along, flicking it in the air sometimes for the kitten to leap at. Most kittens enjoy this game.

The branch of a weeping willow tree, sometimes called a willow whip, makes a super toy. Tie a paper ball or even a jingle bell to the end of the branch to provide the noise. As you start to play

Kitten's are fascinated by string.

you'll find the suppleness of the branch lets the toy bob and jump about, but you will have better control of the action than you would with a string.

Any small thing that rolls is a good chasing toy. If you can find a wooden spool, that would be perfect; but most spools today aren't and some are styrofoam, which will get chewed to bits in no time. Ping-pong balls are a kitten's favorite, although the small rubber balls with a jingle bell inside specially sold as cat toys are nice also. The thin rubber toys with a squeaker attached are fun for cats, but the squeaking can be annoying once a kitten gets over some initial caution and starts using it a lot. A little wind-up car is a good toy too.

Still another way of involving yourself in your kitten's life is to set up adventures for it. Put it up on the kitchen counter and turn the water faucet on to a mere trickle. Put your finger in and out of the water until it can't stand your having all the fun and tries it too. The result will be a funny conflict between the kitten's curiosity about water and its dislike of having wet paws. Games like this one are not a way of teasing, since you are not frustrating it by interfering with what the kitten wants to do.

Body Language

The result of all this playing and petting will soon be evident. The kitten will begin to follow you about the house. It will invite you to play by pouncing out from behind the drapes, stiff-legged and puffy-tailed. It will greet you with its tail up straight, head bowed low, and rub against your ankles. It will leap into your lap and nuzzle into your armpit, contracting its eyes to mere slits as it purrs.

All of these attentions are, of course, in cat body language. Hair raising on body and tail is very common in mammals. It is meant to make the animal look very big to its enemies and scare them off. Even humans raise their hair. When you feel your scalp or the back of your neck prickling from getting "the creeps" it is a remnant of puffed-up human attempts to bluff enemies by a false impression of size. Cats not only raise their fur but hump their backs, stand on tiptoe, and turn sideways to the "enemy" to look as enormous as a smallish animal can.

Coming toward you with the tail held straight up, bowing, and rolling over on one side are all friendly greetings. The greetings started as kittens' signals to the mother cat to tell her that they needed to be cleaned and nursed. They are held on to as simple "hello, friend" messages in adult cats.

I used to think cats rubbed people's ankles to annoy them. My own reflex makes me kick at anything that unexpectedly brushes my ankles. As it turns out, when a cat rubs its face against you or brushes its tail along you, it is marking you with a friendly-smell message. A cat has scent glands distributed along its lips, behind its ears, and at the base of the tail. When it leaves its scent on you, you are supposed to be appreciative.

Cats enjoy our smells too. Even a grown cat will sniff, nuzzle, and push its paws rhythmically against you, purring all the while, as though it were still a kitten nursing at its mother's belly.

The pupils of a cat's eyes express emotions. So do ours. When humans fall in love, they dilate their pupils at one another. Cats do the opposite. If a cat dilates its pupils at you, this means it's scared or angry. A contented, loving, purring cat contracts its pupils in pleasure.

Rubbing is one way a cat leaves its mark on a friend.

Open out a paper bag on the floor for your kitten to investigate. A cat in a bag can get pretty funny too. Get a cardboard carton from the grocery store and cut windows and doors into it with a sharp knife. A kitten can have fun exploring, and with the addition of a towel for a mattress it might adopt the little house as its bed too.

A family we know got such a kick out of their kitten's exploring new structures that they now feed their cat on a constantly changing contraption out on the porch. One day their cat discovers he has to climb a ladder to his dinner, then the family adds a swinging door the cat has to get through, then a narrow catwalk, or a seesaw or a tunnel. If you have enough space and spare lumber, you can invent your own cat contraption. This kind of exploring not only keeps a cat amused and involved with you, but actually makes it more intelligent. Trickling water, paper bags and swinging doors, after all, give even a kitten pause for thought.

Irresistible Catnip

Catnip toys are always winners. Although the chemical in catnip that gives such pleasure to cats has been identified, no one yet knows why it makes cats behave so strangely. But it's no myth: catnip excites cats and even fills them with ecstasy, causing them to roll, rub, and make noises of pleasure. You can buy catnip toys in pet stores or departments or you can make them yourself.

Dried catnip is sold in many health-food stores. Cut a rectangular piece of cloth from any scrap that's around. Fold it in half and sew up two sides. Turn it inside out, stuff it with catnip, then turn in the edges of the third side and stitch the edges together. Use the illustrated pattern to make a catnip mouse toy for a special pet treat.

Even more fun for a cat than a catnip toy is a whole bed of catnip. Herb nurseries and many garden centers carry packets of catnip seeds during the spring. Choose a sunny place but one out of the way, since catnip is an ugly weed. The cat will find the catnip bed for itself and spend hours at a time rolling and sunning in it. If you have no yard or if you keep your cat confined to the house, plant a pot with catnip to keep your kitten happy. Late in the summer you can harvest the potted or outdoor catnip crop and dry it. Pull the plants up and hang them upside down in small bunches tied with string in any dry room. The dried catnip will give you a winter supply for toy stuffing.

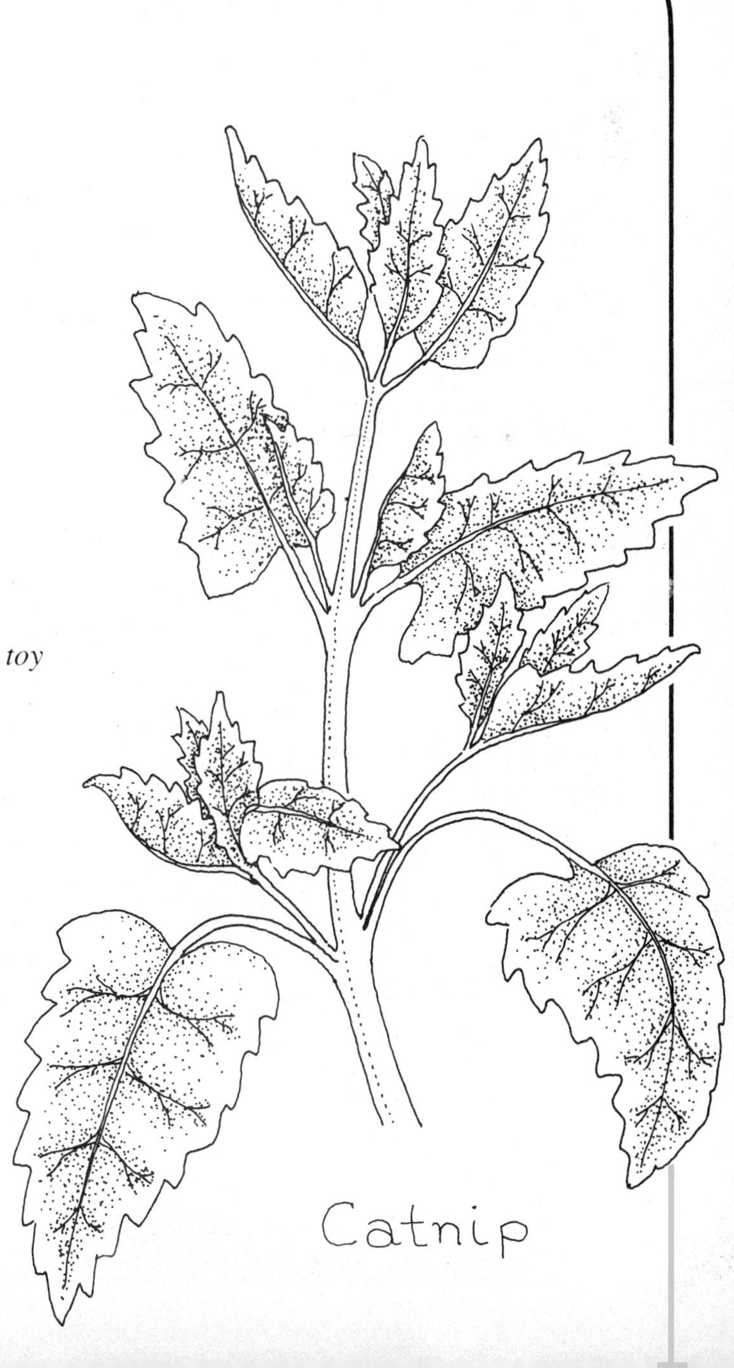

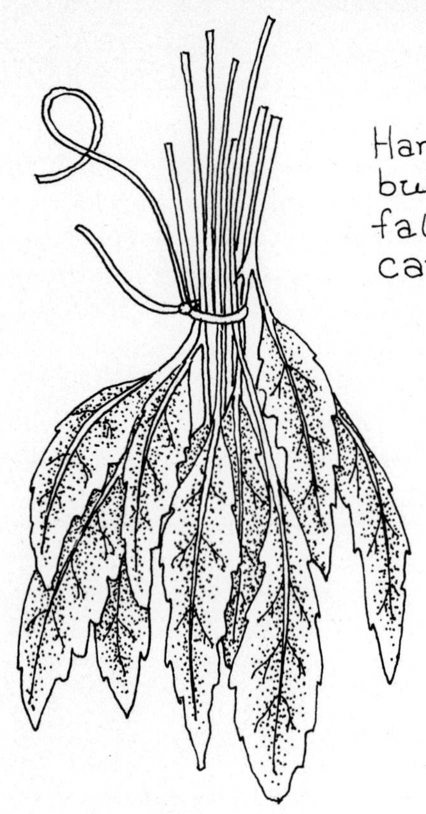

Hang catnip in small bunches to dry in the fall. Use it for stuffing cat toys.

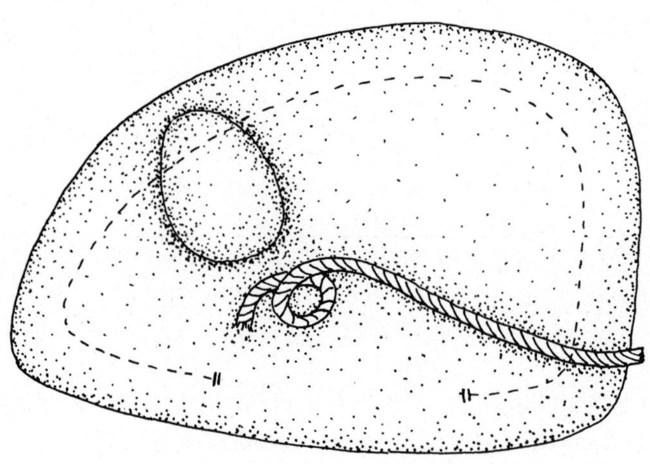

To make a catnip mouse:

1. Cut two mouse-shaped pieces from any scrap of cloth.
2. Cut two ear-shaped pieces from felt.
3. Cut a four inch piece of string.
4. Lay both ears and the tail on one mouse-shaped piece as shown.
5. Lay the other mouse-shaped piece on top; pin in place; stitch along dotted line.
6. Turn inside-out; stuff with dried catnip; sew up gap.
7. Draw on eyes with marking pen.

Catnip Mouse

Training

If a kitten has been socialized by plenty of petting and playing, it can be trained—slightly. Don't expect a cat to be like a dog. Dogs are made to be taught. In nature they learn survival skills like hunting and social skills like manners from their elders over a long period of time. Cats aren't made to be taught. In nature their mother teaches them to kill prey, then leaves them on their own. A dog knows what you're talking about when you say NO. A cat may just stare at you—not with disdain, just bafflement.

Start training by taking advantage of things kittens do naturally. Kittens naturally follow people they like, so some can be trained to follow you on command. When you see your kitten hold its tail straight up in the air and begin to follow you, encourage it in a high, catlike voice. You can reward it with tiny snacks along the way too, first indoors and then outside if you have a place to walk that is safe from both dogs and cars.

If your cat won't follow—and only some will, even with the most patient training—you can try leash training. Get a lightweight collar or a harness and let your kitten wear it around the house. Tie a crumpled-up piece of paper to a string two feet long and attach the other end of the string to the harness or collar when the kitten stops trying to scratch and rub it off. At first, just the slight weight of the paper will be enough for the kitten to get used to. If

Cats don't always take to leashes.

it plays with the paper, all the better. After the first couple of times, you can begin tugging gently at the string while you dangle the paper for it to grab. Call the kitten at the same time you tug. When the procedure doesn't bother it anymore, substitute a light leash. Let the kitten drag it around and play with it. Then start the tugging and calling. After a few more days, try this outdoors for a few minutes at a time, encouraging the kitten with tidbits and calling it to follow you.

Cats have also been taught to beg for a snack and to fetch a toy. Hold a snack in your closed fist just over your kitten's nose and see if you can get it to sit up to sniff at your hand. Say BEG if it does. Repeated several times a day every single day, you may get to the point where you can just say BEG and your kitten will sit up. But you will probably always have to reward your cat with a snack to keep it doing the trick. Unlike dogs, cats don't do things just to please you.

Some kittens chase a toy and carry it back to you, and some don't. A catnip mouse is more likely to become a good fetch toy than others. If your kitten brings a catnip mouse to you, take the mouse from the kitten, say FETCH, and throw it for the cat to retrieve. The reward here is play rather than food, so even if your kitten learns what the word means, it will probably only fetch when it's in the mood for play.

For bad behavior like biting your hands or jumping on the dinner table, it's useful to teach your kitten the word NO. Say NO first, then cuff the kitten across the nose with a flick of your finger. A mother cat disciplines a kitten with a cuff. Each time the bad behavior is repeated, say NO, then cuff. Sooner or later the kitten will begin to pause

when it hears the command NO. Then you can stop cuffing and just use the word.

There are other habits cats have that can't be stopped by discipline. Scratching is one, chewing another. Kittens and cats rake their claws against rough surfaces like rugs, furniture and drapes. Though the scratching probably does keep the tips of the claws in shape, sharpening and cleaning don't seem to be the only purposes. A wild male cat leaves his urine mark at the base of a tree, then reaches up as high as he can to claw at the bark. The scratch marks clearly tell other cats how big he is.

You can't stop a cat from scratching. Pet stores sell carpet-covered scratching posts which may or may not work. Get one early in your kitten's life. When it claws at something it's not supposed to, try saying NO and cuffing its nose with your finger. Then take the kitten to the scratching post and show it what it is supposed to do by moving its front paws against the post. If the kitten won't use the post it might prefer a rough log nailed in an upright position to a plywood stand.

If all else fails, you can have a cat declawed. Declawing is removal of the whole nail from each toe on the front feet only. It must be done by a vet, since it is a real operation and requires an anesthetic. If you declaw a cat, you must keep it indoors from then on. A declawed cat can't climb trees to escape from dogs, and can't fight back if it gets cornered. Sending a cat out into the world with its major defense removed is a death sentence.

Most dogs only chew things up when they are puppies, but cats may do it all their lives. They favor wool, probably because it still smells like animal to them. Cats that hunt are seldom problem

chewers. Nonhunting cats probably develop the habit out of a frustrated urge to chew up furry prey. Cats that don't get a chance to hunt should have chop bones or sparerib bones to chew on and toys made of real fur, like a rabbit-fur mitten or a bit of sheepskin. Some cats deprived of hunting animals attack and bite ankles instead; fur toys may help get rid of this bad habit too.

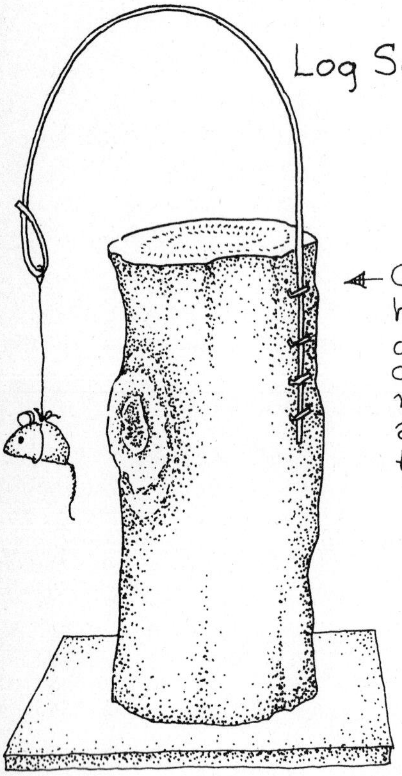

Log Scratching Post

Opened out coat-hanger wire or other heavy wire can be added to make a springy arc for hanging toys.

Hammer nails up through plywood base into log.

Some cats chew up house plants. There's a reason for everything. Cats are frequent grass-eaters; deprived of grass, they chew up plants. You may wonder at that, since cats are supposed to be exclusively meat-eating carnivores. So are dogs, but they also eat grass. Both wild dogs and wild cats eat the stomach of their prey, complete with whatever's in it. Their prey are mainly grass- and grain-eating animals like rodents, birds and rabbits, whose stomachs are full of grass and grain. Neither cats nor dogs digest this roughage well. As you've probably noticed, they throw it up or let some of it pass all the way through their digestive system to come out in their droppings. It's possible the periodic eating of roughage helps to keep the dog's or cat's digestive system clear of parasites, indigestible food, and hair they've swallowed while grooming themselves.

An obvious solution to the problem of plant-eating house cats is to give them what they really want. Plant grass. Fill a disposable aluminum pan with soil, sprinkle grass seed on it, rake it in lightly with a fork, and water it. If you keep it moist the grass will sprout within a week or so and grow well in a sunny window. Your cat will probably find the treat by itself and feel all the better for thinking it has discovered the best house plant of all behind your back.

Grooming and Bathing

Grooming a cat is important. Cats shed a little hair all the time, and a lot when the seasons are changing from warm to cold or cold to warm. Long-haired cats can't get out their own tangles, and even with a short-haired cat the hair gets all over the furniture and upsets whoever has to do the vacuuming. A bristle brush is all you need to groom a short-haired cat, but a metal comb and blunt scissors may be necessary to cut and untangle mats in long-haired cats.

Start getting a kitten used to grooming right away. Keep the brush handy; wait until the kitten is drowsy and relaxed in your lap. Then use the brush as though it were your hand, gently stroking down the kitten's head, neck, back, and sides. Forget its belly for now; belly tickling sets off a clawing and wrestling response in any kitten. Stroke the brush the same way the fur lies. Brushing against the lay of the fur irritates cats and may cause them to bite the brush, a game which you may never be able to end.

A long-haired cat's fur will mat unless brushed and combed at least once a week. You will most likely need an adult's help with the job. Don't cut mats straight off, as that leaves temporary bald spots. Instead, use a *blunt* scissors to make several cuts straight into the mat (but not the skin!). Then gently comb the loose hair, a little at a time, from the mat. Most cats will struggle or even try to bite or claw as you tug at the mats. When the job is finished, you might decide you never want to go through it again; your cat came to that conclusion long before you did and is probably hiding by now. When you can get hold of it again, trim the hair shorter under its legs, beneath its tail or wherever else the worst matting occurs. You'll still have to groom but mats will take longer to form.

As your kitten begins to relax during grooming, gradually begin to include the belly hair.

Long-haired cats pick up a lot of fur on their tongues as they groom themselves. They swallow the hairs, which form into indigestible wads or strings in their stomachs and intestines. The hair wads cause vomiting (although vomiting doesn't get the wad up) and sometimes sickness and even death. A good precaution is a half teaspoonful of mineral oil once a week, mixed directly into the cat's meal. The oil coats the wad and lets it slip out through the digestive system.

There are times when the cleanest of cats may need a bath. An interlude with a rotten rabbit can be the occasion, or a close investigation of the oily underside of a car, or a naïve attempt to approach a skunk. Cats don't like being wet, but if a bath is necessary always use lukewarm water (lukewarm means the same temperature as your skin—you can hardly feel the water because it is neither warmer nor cooler than your hand).

Fill the kitchen sink with the lukewarm water. Put a piece of rug or towel in the bottom so your cat won't slip around and panic. Get someone else to hold it firmly while you do the bathing. Use a plastic pitcher to pour water over the cat, and baby soap, baby shampoo, or unperfumed adult soap for sudsing. Try not to get soap in its eyes. Rinse your cat very well so it doesn't feel itchy from soap afterward. Dry it with a regular bath towel.

The Witch—A Breeding Lesson

If you want your unaltered female cat to have kittens, put her outside when she's in heat; she'll come home pregnant. Instead of telling you what ought to happen next, I'll tell you a story about a scrawny, sway-backed cat called the Witch.

The Witch was a cat I had given my mother for her birthday. The first time this cat was pregnant we made her a perfect nesting box—a low carton, towel-lined—and placed it in a closet under the eaves. Cats supposedly prefer to keep their kittens private. The night the Witch came into labor, she followed my mother all over the house, obviously straining but just as obviously unwilling to let a kitten drop. My mother kept taking her to her nest, the Witch kept climbing out and jumping on the bed. We got the message. She had her kittens in bed, like any proper lady.

Now that the kittens were comfortably on the bed, the Witch decided that's where they should stay. She and my mother worked out a compromise in the form of my mother's middle bureau drawer. All went well for about two weeks. But then the Witch was ready to go hunting again. One by one, she picked up each kitten and placed it next to my mother in her bed. Then she climbed out a window and disappeared for the night. She had found her first babysitter. My mother babysat that litter, and the next, and the next. But then a better solution came along in the shape of the Witch's daughter, called Daughter.

As often happens when females live together, both cats came into heat together. They delivered their litters within hours of each other. The Witch took the time to clean her kittens as they were born. Then she picked each one up and deposited it in Daughter's nest. Daughter from then on managed to nurse twelve or thirteen kittens each time a double litter came along. The Witch took over the only part of child rearing suited to her temperament: bringing home the mice.

The Witch regularly took the kittens hunting too, and we noticed her doing something quite strange. She would tempt the kittens into a rousing chase. Then she would leap onto a tree and climb quite high. The kittens would follow her, clawing their way up the trunk. She would let them come up only a foot or two, then she'd back down toward them, forcing them to the ground. Each time she let the kittens climb higher. Each time she forced them to back down. She was teaching those kittens how to get down out of trees. When you think about it, it's perfectly logical. How in nature could a tree-climbing animal survive if it was not *able to get down? There are no firemen in the wild.*

That experience should have made me less naïve with my latest episode with a cat. It was winter and bitter cold. The wind was howling and the trees were creaking when we heard a blood-curdling noise coming from the woods. There, high up in an oak tree, yowled a huge, lanky white cat. Filled with admiration for his size and sympathy for his predicament, my children and I hoisted a long aluminum extension ladder a good two stories high. My eight-year-old volunteered to climb up and fetch the cat, who gratefully met him at the top of the ladder and melted into his arms.

We fed the cat and stroked him, and decided we liked him a lot. We waited impatiently for my husband to get home so he could help us think up a name. He did. The name was Temporary.

That night, Temporary ate our hamster. The next morning he was gone. By afternoon he was one house down, yowling in a tree. Rescued again by our neighbors, he stayed at their house for a meal and a warm bed. Then he worked his way down the road to the next house-with-tall-tree-and-sympathetic-people. No doubt something had gone awry with his early socializing. But I'll bet you anything he knew darn well how to get down out of trees.

A mother cat nursing her young.

Pet Dogs

PET DOGS

Small Dog

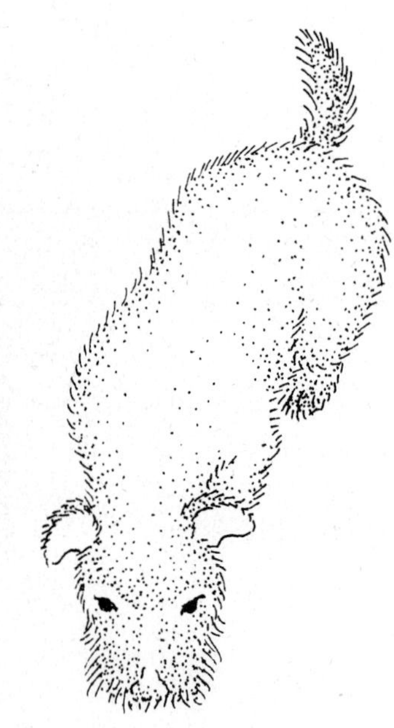

Medium dog

DOGS

Cost:
Mixed breeds (mongrels)—free, or occasionally $10.00 to $20.00. Purebreds (depending on breed and quality)—$75.00 to $200.00. (Large breeds, rare breeds and show quality of any breed are more expensive.)

Housing Equipment:
Food and water dishes: small dog—$4.00 large dog—$12.00
Brush, slicker or metal comb—$2.00
Slip collar and leash—$2.50

Special Requirements:
Veterinary examination and inoculations, probable worming—$30.00 to $80.00, depending on local fees.
Optional altering: male—$50.00 female—$60.00 to $150.00, depending on size.

Diet:
Puppy or dog chow, flavored with canned meat:
small dog—$1.00 per week.
medium dog—$1.75 per week.
large dog—$2.50 per week.

Care:
Feed and replenish water dish daily (more often for puppies).
Walk four times a day (more often for puppies).
Groom once a month to twice a week, depending on type of coat.
Bathe as necessary.
Take to veterinarian for checkup and booster shots once a year.

Tamability:
Must be housebroken.
Need basic obedience training to be well-behaved.
Become exceptionally affectionate, devoted and responsive.
Learn to play several games and perform tricks.

Life Span:
10 years.

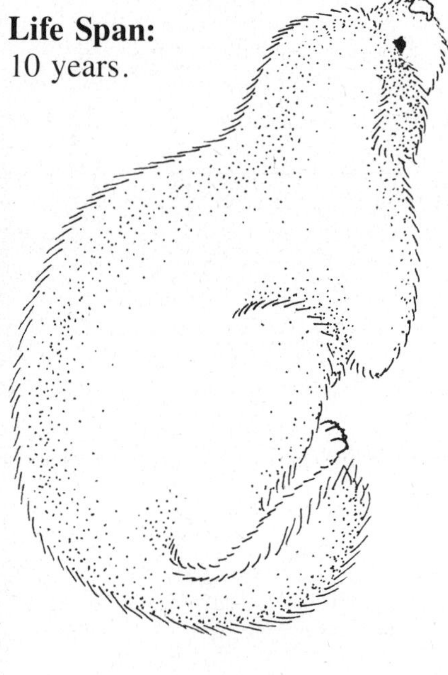

Large Dog

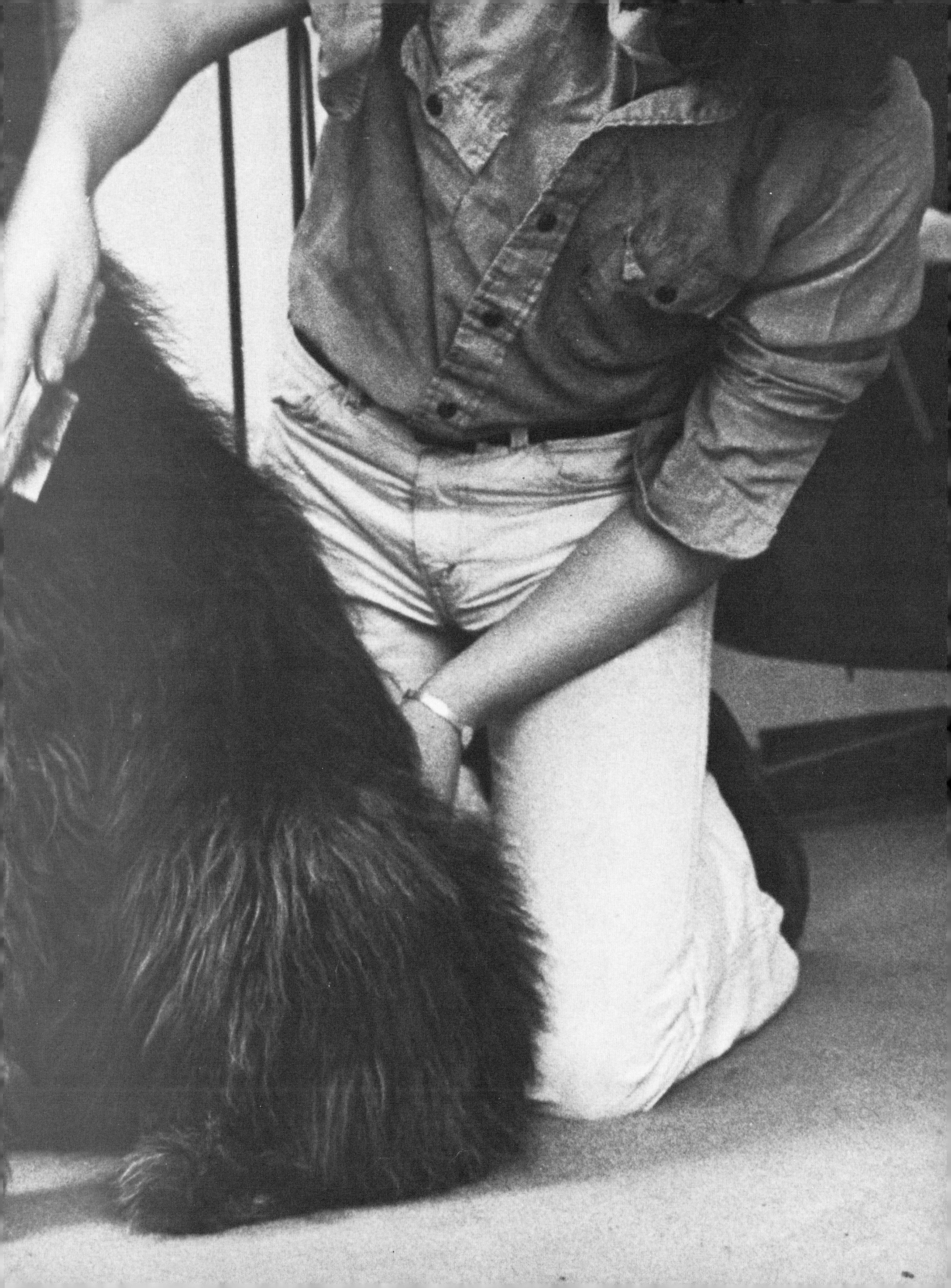

If you have decided you want a dog more than anything else in the whole world, you will find that the first step in getting one is to convince everyone else in your family that it's a wonderful idea. You will say, "Please, can I have a puppy?" and someone will say, "Well, I don't know," or "Who will take it out?" or "Dogs are smelly." And then you will say, "I promise to take it out, I promise to give it a bath every week," and then someone will say again, "Well, I don't know."

Convincing everyone can take rather a long time—from months to several years. To get through it, try to remember that the adults are right: dogs can be a nuisance and do require care; you will not do all the things you promised to do; adults will have to help you. Training and caring for a puppy is probably the hardest, most time-consuming job you have ever taken on. You will start fewer arguments and receive fewer lectures if you admit these facts in the first place and then try to settle on who can do what. The four main jobs are feeding, grooming, taking the dog out, and training it, all explained later on in the chapter.

Feeding is the easiest job, followed by taking the dog out and grooming. Training, including housebreaking, is by far the most difficult job of the dog owner. Plan to get a puppy as close to the beginning of summer as you can. You will be home to do the work, and the pleasant weather will make housebreaking easier on you. Read through these sections before making promises you may not be able to keep.

Choosing a Puppy

Choosing a puppy who will make a good family pet means satisfying everyone at least a little. It's too much to expect different people to all love St. Bernards or chihuahuas. And people look at the same dog from different points of view too—yours may be size, your father's the food bill. You may look for cuteness, while your mother looks at the hair on the rug. Luckily, there are hundreds of breeds of dogs and millions of mongrels—all different. First decide the basics, like small, or large, or in between. Then get everyone to contribute their reservations—small but not yappy; big but not bouncy; any size, so long as it doesn't shed! Try to build a composite picture, the kind the police make of suspects, then go to the dog books to see what fits the description. There are several good dog encyclopedias offered by most libraries. The American Kennel Club describes the 118 breeds they recognize in *The Complete Dog Book* (Howell Book House). In such books you'll discover that there are large dogs who wouldn't think of bouncing, small dogs who wouldn't dream of yapping, and all sorts of wire-haired and woolly dogs who hardly shed at all. By the way, you will find the descriptions quite exaggerated (they are written by the breeders). That's exactly why they are helpful. Each kind of dog breeder has a fantasy about what a "perfect" dog should be like; even if an individual dog falls short, the breed in general has probably been the breeder's wish come true. If the ideal dog described is about the same as yours, that's probably the breed you want.

Besides reading dog books, you may learn a lot by talking to dog owners—friends, a vet, breeders and even strangers out walking their dogs in the morning. Any information you can get will help, not only in choosing a purebred dog but also in choosing a mongrel. For instance, ads in my local papers recently have advertised golden retriever crosses, spaniel crosses, labrador crosses, collie crosses, poodle crosses and terrier crosses. Often the owners know for sure if the mother is a purebred dog. They may or may not be sure about the father.

After you have an idea of what kind of dog you want, you are faced with choosing the puppy who will grow up to be a good pet. This is not the same as choosing an adorable puppy. All puppies are adorable. Not all puppies grow up to be good pets. My husband once lovingly hand-raised and fed a boxer puppy whose mother could not give him enough milk. Once grown-up, the dog fought other dogs and killed cats. He knocked people down when he greeted them. He pulled them down when he was on the leash. He had to be kept penned. He was not a pet.

Twice I took in stray puppies from the pound. Both grew up to chew rugs, steal food and bark incessantly. When scolded they cringed and dribbled urine. They were pathetic dogs, but they were not pets either. Pet dogs should not act this way. If they do, something is wrong with them—they are "crazy." Usually what went wrong happened during the dog's first weeks of life. It was deprived of its mother, its littermates or human companionship.

To be normally social—well-behaved and trusting with other dogs and humans—puppies need certain relationships during the early critical months of their lives, particularly from six to 14 weeks of age. They must be fed, nuzzled, and finally weaned and disciplined by their mothers. They must play with and sleep next to other puppies, and they must be handled and spoken to by humans. In practical terms, this means most puppies offered through pet stores and pounds are in some way socially damaged. Often they are weaned and taken from the mother and littermates at six weeks. Caged, they miss out on a critical period of human handling. Strays are usually unsocialized by humans; orphans unsocialized by other dogs.

At first you may have difficulty noticing the symptoms of the damage that has been done, but once you do you will not be able to cure it. Deprived puppies grow up to be nervous and snappy, or overly boisterous and uncontrollable. They are unsure of themselves with other dogs, which makes them grovel when there is no threat or fight when there is no challenge. They are unsure of humans, too. They are too nervous to train, or too resentful, or too obstinate. Such dogs may adapt to a childless home in which few demands are placed on them. But family life is full of surprises; it takes an emotionally healthy dog to handle it. Don't adopt a stray. Don't take in an orphan. Don't get a puppy at the pound or from a store.

This advice may be strong medicine for you to swallow. The puppies in the pound or in the petstore window look awfully cute and are certainly in need of homes. Orphaned puppies and strays are terrible temptations, too. But a dog lives for 10 or 12 years. If you are 11 years old now, you'll still have this dog when you're 21. It's no fun to spend that decade with an untrusting cur or an uncontrollable beast. The best age to get a puppy is three and a half months old; the best place, the home where the pup has been raised with its mother and with littermates.

If you have decided to buy a purebred dog, write to the American Kennel Club, 51 Madison Avenue, New York, N.Y. 10010. Tell them the name of the breed you are interested in and ask them to send you the name of the secretary of that breed club. If you then write to the secretary, she or he will let you know which breeders in your area have puppies available. Even with the secretary's recommendation, avoid breeders who raise litters out in the kennels. Ask if the pups were raised in the home.

If you have decided to get a mongrel, look at ads in the classified section of your newspaper for home-raised puppies.

You may want to decide before you look at puppies whether you want a male or female. There is a difference in both personality and behavior. Male dogs—called dogs—tend to wander. Beagles and labradors are famous for it, but other breeds wander too. Female dogs—called bitches—are more likely to stick to home territory. Dogs fight more frequently than bitches. They may have a more unpleasant "doggy" smell.

Male dogs may be altered (by closing off their supply of male hormones) at about six months, or whenever your vet recommends. Altered dogs still tend to fight or wander if that is behavior particular to their breed-type. Dogs may be somewhat more difficult to train than bitches and may end up more exuberant than gentle, more aloof than sensitive.

On the other hand, a bitch who has not been altered attracts a gang of dogs when she is in heat (ready to become pregnant) and can present you with a litter of puppies. Unless you plan to breed your bitch (and are sure you can find homes for the puppies) she should be altered (an operation in which the vet removes her ovaries) after her first heat when her body is fully mature. After the operation she will neither attract dogs nor become pregnant. It is not a serious operation and will not change her personality at all.

Usually the earliest you will be looking at puppies is six weeks old. This is a good time to get to know a litter in general, but for individual personality, eight weeks or even 10 would be much more helpful. Remember that it's healthiest for the puppy, even after you have chosen it, to leave it with its mother and littermates until it is over 12 weeks old.

Go to look at several different litters if you can. Ask to see the mother and decide if you like her; her puppies might take after her. Ask what sort of mother she has been. If she hasn't had enough milk or if she's been reluctant to care for the puppies, it's a bad sign for their future temperament. Ask to handle the puppies so you can check them close up. A healthy puppy is plump, smells good, has shiny eyes and thick fur. It should not have runny eyes, a cough or smelly ears (the smell is from an ear infection). It should not be skinny, have scabs or a dusty, dull coat. These are not necessarily signs of fatal illnesses but they are signs of neglect. Neglect of any sort affects personality.

There are a few tests you can use to see which of the puppies are most sure of themselves. Sit on the floor. Puppies who are used to handling should come to you of their own accord. Puppies who hang back, whimper, keep their tails between their legs, or retreat when you reach for them are too shy to make good family pets. Notice if the puppies who do come to you stay upright as they approach, or fall over on their backs, squirming and letting out a few drops of urine. That fall-over-and-wet signal means more fear than you want in a pup. When the pups are near you, slap the floor hard. The noise will probably startle the pups or even send them scrambling, but the bold, curious ones should recover quickly and come back to investigate the sound.

Get up and walk a short distance from the puppies. Lean over, clap your hands and call to them in the high voice puppies seem to respond to best. They should come to you. Walk backward away from them. They should want to follow you. Again, the ones who don't show signs of following may not be sure of their relationship with humans.

Sit back now and watch the puppies at play or while they're fed. Watch for what could become annoying habits—the pup who whines a lot or yaps will usually be a whiner or a yapper when it grows up. A puppy who growls at the others at feeding time will growl and snap at you when you try to get things from its mouth.

After you have chosen a puppy, there are arrangements to make with the breeder. First, be sure the breeder understands you want that particular puppy, no other. When I was ten, my parents let me proudly go by myself to choose a pup from the litter my poodle had fathered. I knew how to choose puppies, so I chose the best one. When it came time to bring the puppy home, the owner had sold him to someone else. No doubt he thought I was just a dumb kid and any pup would do.

Next, be sure you understand what the price, if there is one, includes. The price should include all vet bills for any reason (including possible ear cropping and tail docking) up to the time you bring the puppy home. You can't force a family blessed with mongrel pups to have the litter checked by a vet, but a purebred breeder should certainly have had the pups checked for worms and protected by the first shots in the inoculation series. The owner should be asked what shots remain so you understand what you will be responsible for.

With any puppy, make sure the breeder guarantees the puppy's health in writing. The piece of paper should give you one week after you take the dog home to get a checkup at the vet. If the vet finds a disease or defect, you should be able to return the pup in exchange for another or for your money back.

Last but not least, set a date to pick the puppy up; then go home and get things ready.

Housing

Many families think they have solved the problems of the dog owner by deciding on an "outside" dog. For the small additional expense of a doghouse or a bed in the garage, they will be spared the nuisance of shedding, muddy feet, strewn garbage and puddles on the rug. This is true, but they will not have a pet either. Outside dogs make good watchdogs and sporting dogs, but only the house dog really learns the ways of humans. A dog has to be around when you have an awful headache to understand there are times it should fade into the background. A dog has to be around when you have friends over to understand whom to welcome, whom to threaten. A dog has to be around all the members of a family most of the time to learn that different people like dogs different ways—bouncily or quietly, clownishly or with dignity. That sort of sensitivity is not learned in the doghouse.

The New Puppy

Before you pick up your puppy and bring it home, get ready all the things you'll need. Buy a too-big woven slip collar (give the breeder a call to find out the size, which is a head rather than a neck measurement, and then buy two sizes too big). Buy an inexpensive leash (it will get chewed) and two dishes, one for food, one for water. There are lots of dishes to choose from. Puppies have the least trouble with heavy dishes that don't slide along the floor. Buy a processed chow made especially for puppies, and canned dog meat.

Prepare the puppy's den and its bed. Call the vet to make an appointment for the puppy's checkup some time during the first week.

If you have to travel in the car to pick the puppy up, get ready to deal with car sickness: bring a roll of paper towels and a plastic bag. If the trip is long you might need newspaper on the floor of the car for a bathroom. And if the weather is hot bring a bottle of water and a water dish. Holding an unhappy puppy in your lap for anything over an hour can be tedious. A towel-lined carton may be helpful.

The bouncy puppy you chose will no doubt act bouncy until you get it into the car. At that point its eyes will roll, its tail will tuck, and it will tremble and whine. Happy as you are to get it in your arms at last, it is not about to share your joy. A puppy who has just left its home, mother, brothers and sisters is inconsolable. Expect a new puppy to be miserable for two days and a few more nights; expect it to cry and even howl most of the night; expect it to urinate frequently; expect it to eat poorly; expect it to have diarrhea; expect it to smell doggy. Not all these things may happen—maybe none of them will—but you should be prepared if they do.

There are ways you can help your puppy through its first few nights. Make its sleeping place soft, even if it means adding a pillow under the towel. Warm the sleeping place by tucking a hot water bottle under the towel. If it still cries all night, some people say it helps to wrap a ticking alarm clock in a towel near it—this is supposed to sound like its mother's heart beating nearby.

It may help to bring the puppy from its den into your room to sleep next to you (not on the bed or it will wet it). Keep it on the floor with plenty of newspaper, and on a leash so it can't get off the papers. Warning: sleeping near you may be habit-forming.

For a puppy who has diarrhea that first week, feed it boiled rice and cooked hamburger instead of the diet recommended later in the chapter. If that doesn't work, call the vet and ask what dosage of Kaopectate® to use. Don't ever withhold water. Keep fresh water out all the time.

If your puppy won't eat at all the first day or so, don't worry. Keep water available. At feeding time, offer only a spoonful of food and take it away if it's not eaten. Try again the next feeding time. We've never heard of a pup starving itself to death. It will eat by the third day for sure.

For a puppy who dribbles urine when you approach, just be as gentle as you can. Don't try to get it to play yet. Don't act excited with it; just move slowly, talk quietly. If you chose a bold puppy, the symptom should be temporary—a week or less. All puppies safeguard themselves when frightened by a belly-up-and-wet signal. In the wild, the act identifies them as babies who should not be hurt. Even the most vicious dog in the act of attacking is inhibited by the puppy urine signal. Watch a dogfight some day if you can stand it—the loser signals its defeat by rolling belly-up. Grownup that it is, it still lets loose a couple of drops of urine. The attacker stops fighting on signal and walks off from the battle.

A doggy smell is another sign of nervousness. No doubt dogs, with their far better noses, can read a whole paragraph in the message. For us it says one thing: scared pup. It, too, will pass.

During the whole first week, a new puppy will fare best with gentle petting, plenty of talking and only as much playing as it initiates. Before this week is out take your puppy to the vet for its checkup and shots. Besides the routine checkup outlined on the next pages, ask any questions that have come up in your mind (why the puppy threw up, scratches a lot, has bad breath). If no problems are found, it's polite to let the breeder know. If the vet does find problems, discuss the advisability of returning the pup.

A puppy's corner with box, hook, leash and collar, newspapers and water dish.

Inside the house, a puppy needs a smaller place of its own where it can stay during most of the day while being housebroken. The reason that dogs can be housebroken at all is that they are housebroken in nature. Wild dogs do not mess their dens. The trouble is that your house is much bigger than a den and most puppies seem to think that while part of it is "home," most of it is "outside." This is an important trick in housebreaking: Give a puppy a small enough "den" of its own and it will try very hard not to soil it.

An old playpen makes a good den for a small puppy. A larger puppy might need a small bathroom to itself instead. Tying a puppy up works too, but only if you have some place that is far from table legs and chairs so the puppy doesn't get itself tangled up. A hook can be screwed into a wall about two feet from the floor to hold the leash. If

Dogs need to be scolded when they make mistakes. This pup is being reminded not to wet on the carpet.

your puppy chews its leash, you may have to tie it with a chain. If you're going to tie your dog, find a place near where people gather so it will not be lonely.

Put newspaper down everywhere the puppy can reach—not to "paper train" it, which is an unnecessary step, but just so you can clean up easily.

Make the puppy a bed to go in its den. For a small pup, cut down the side of a corrugated carton and line it with old towels to make the bed soft. For a larger dog, fold an old blanket or several towels into a bed. Place the bed to the rear of the den area—in the corner or against the wall. For now, this den is where you will feed the puppy and where you will leave its drinking water. You'll be confining it to the den whenever you can't keep an eye on it and whenever it wants to sleep.

As the puppy becomes housebroken, you can dispense with newspapers and leave only the dog's bed. By the time it is a year old, you may have to move the bed. Find a place that is not underfoot, but is on the fringe of family life. Even fast asleep, dogs like to be where they can have a sense of the comings and goings of their family.

Food and Water

It is not true that puppies only need canned dog meat to eat. Nor is it true that they need very complicated diets. You can feed a puppy a chow moistened with water. Add a spoonful of canned dog meat for flavor. Puppy chow, Purina® or other brands labeled specifically for puppies, is specially formulated to contain all the basic nutrition—vitamins, minerals, carbohydrates, and protein—that growing dogs need. Unless a vet advises it, milk, extra calcium, extra meat or other protein foods and powdered vitamin supplements are not necessary and may be harmful. Under some circumstances a vet may suggest moist canned puppy foods (meat plus grains and other nutrients) instead of chow, but usually chow is considered preferable.

An eight-week-old puppy needs four meals a day, usually breakfast, lunch, afternoon snack, and dinner. If there's one meal it barely touches, it only needs three meals a day. By the time it is six months old it needs only two meals a day, and by the time it is a year it needs only one meal a day. All these meals can be identical—chow, moistened with water and flavored with a little canned meat. The younger the dog, the moister the food should be. As it grows, it will begin to prefer its food crunchy rather than soggy.

There are all sorts of charts and measurements that tell you how much food to feed your puppy at each meal, but there's no reason this need be so complicated. Start out with a half cup for a little puppy, a cup for a bigger one. Then let the dog judge the quantity for you. If it doesn't finish its meal, you're offering too much food. If it finishes the food, try more next meal. If it finishes its meal every time and is getting fat, you've gotten a dog with poor judgment and you'll have to cut down on meals. A dog is too fat when it's hard to feel any ribs or backbone, and too skinny when ribs and backbone feel sharp under the skin. Some puppies may be so active they stay skinny no matter how much they eat. They begin to put on weight at about a year old. A puppy puts on weight and loses weight quickly, so you won't have to wait long for signs that quantities need adjusting.

When your dog is a year and a half old, it can change chows from puppy to dog. An adult dog does not need any food other than the chow. It contains everything a dog needs, and it is the cheapest way to feed your dog too. Dry chow is important for another reason: it is crunchy, and as the dog chews it, its teeth are scraped clean. A dog fed only on soft foods or on chow softened by too much liquid can develop bad tooth decay. However, there are two problems with chow. One, people think chow is too boring and feel sorry for the dog. Two, dogs think chow is too boring and feel sorry for themselves. You can try switching brands, or keep flavoring the chow with canned meat, or start spicing it up with table scraps and gravy. Some dogs like leftover vegetables, too. But no matter how you fancy up the chow to make it delicious, remember that it should still be the basic diet. Dogs in the wild eat the same diet all the time, and over the ages their digestive systems became accustomed to not expecting surprises. Change a dog's diet and its surprised intestines will give it diarrhea.

When you feed your dog, take its dish away as soon as it wanders off. It's nice to have a dog eat fast and get the dish cleaned up before flies and babies get into it. It's also best to train a dog not to eat bit by bit, since it will spend half the day growling at anyone who comes near its leftovers. By the way, if your pup does growl at you while it is eating slap it hard on the rump and shout NO! Then start staying with it while it eats; touch the dog, take food away, give it back, and in general make it perfectly clear that dinner is not private. Dogs who protect their food are dangerous to people.

Dogs learn how to inform you that they are hungry, but it's less easy to notice when they are thirsty. Keep water available to your puppy day and night, changing it morning and evening. As your dog gets bigger, it will undoubtedly find its own supply of water in the toilet. Whether you allow the dog to drink from the toilet is up to you and your family; it won't hurt the dog.

Vets prefer puppies not have bones to chew. They advise any of the nylon or rawhide substitutes sold in pet stores. If you still wish to offer your pup a bone, vets suggest only beef shin or knuckle bones (sometimes called marrow bones) which do not splinter readily.

Illnesses and the Vet

During a puppy's first few months it needs one

or more inoculations to protect it from distemper, hepatitis and other serious or fatal dog diseases. Vets differ as to the sort of vaccines they use, so the number and frequency of shots differ too. Every dog needs a single rabies shot at six months. And any puppy almost undoubtedly needs a deworming. Depending on the breed of dog and your own preferences, the puppy may need several visits to the veterinarian for procedures like ear cropping, altering, dewclaw removal and so on. During the rest of its life, it will need booster shots every year. Count on at least another visit each year for cuts, broken bones, intestinal problems, infected ears, rashes and assorted illnesses. If you are the one taking the dog to the vet, it will help you to understand what is expected of you, what the doctor is doing, and why.

Always make vet appointments in advance, unless it's an emergency and you must bring your pet in immediately. Your dog must be on a leash, and should not be brought up to meet any other dog (some are sick; some are hurt and in a nasty mood about it; most are scared and don't want anyone to bother them). You're expected to lift your dog up onto the examining table unless it's too big for you, and to hold the dog's head for the doctor, help to calm the dog, and not make a fuss.

If you have a new puppy, bring in a stool (bowel movement) sample on the first visit so it can be checked for the roundworms almost every puppy gets. The sample can be small—put it in an empty medicine bottle or just in a plastic sandwich bag.

The breeder should have given you inoculation information: what vaccine was used, the date it was given, and when any further shots are needed. Give this information to the vet.

In an ordinary examination, the veterinarian takes the dog's temperature—rectally, with an ordinary rectal thermometer. The normal temperature of a dog is 101 degrees. Watch how it's done. You may need to check it yourself someday if your dog is acting sick. Then the doctor checks your dog's abdomen. He puts his hands on both sides and presses them up to feel if the dog's belly is tense (which would mean it hurts), if there are any lumps that shouldn't be there, or if the liver or kidneys are too large or are sore. He'll check the puppy's eyes and inside its ears, and will run his hands over the dog's bones and joints, pressing down hard on its rear end to see if its legs are strong. He'll check teeth and gums and listen to your dog's heart. And if the puppy needs one of the inoculations the vet will give the shot. Most shots are given subcutaneously, which means the needle is stuck inside a fold of skin on the dog's shoulder or rump. The needle is small and barely hurts. Many dogs don't notice it.

If you have brought your dog in because you think it is sick, the doctor will ask you questions. He'll ask if the dog has been eating well and if its bowel movements have been normal; if the dog is active, or has been acting unusually quiet; when you first noticed something was wrong, and what you noticed.

Your dog will obviously need medical treatment for gaping wounds, collapse or convulsions. Less obvious reasons for medical attention include:

Unresponsiveness. The dog stays in one place, doesn't want to move, may wag its tail quietly when you call to it but doesn't leap up enthusiastically. Often people wait a day or so to see if anything more specific develops. Don't. Dogs can be very sick and complain little. Unresponsiveness is a frequent sign of being very sick.

Smelly ears or lots of head shaking. That means the dog's ears hurt or itch and something is wrong.

Constant scratching. This may mean fleas, dry skin or an allergy, but find out.

Chewing and licking at one particular spot. Look under the fur—you may see a wound you didn't know was there or a patch of eczema that needs treatment.

Loss of weight in spite of normal eating. This can be a sign of worms, or something worse.

Vomiting. This is only unusual if it's over a period of hours, since dogs normally vomit up anything that isn't digestible.

Diarrhea. Dogs get diarrhea from almost any change in diet and often from any change in routine, like when you go on vacation or even on a long car ride. It is only worrisome if it occurs over a period of days or if you see blood in the diarrhea or worms or bits of mucus. Don't worry about weird colors appearing. They are not unusual.

Medical attention is also necessary if your dog refuses to eat for several days; cries in pain, even if you can't see where it hurts; cries when you touch it somewhere; or limps.

Puppies aren't usually afraid of the vet but they dislike being left alone to go through strange and painful things. So try to stay with your pet.

If your dog has been sick and hospitalized, it may still need medical treatment after being released. Ask the vet to demonstrate to you exactly how to care properly for the dog. There's a special way to give dogs pills, liquid medicines, and ear, eye and wound medications. Most of the methods are easy, but frankly, giving pills only looks easy. If you can't do it the way the doctor does, stick the pill into the middle of a small piece of liverwurst rolled into a ball and give it to your dog for a snack.

Grooming

Grooming means brushing and/or combing a dog. Short-haired dogs like dachshunds need a good brisk brushing once a week to remove dust and loose hair. Woolly dogs that tangle badly—poodles, English sheepdogs—are often groomed twice a week. For other dogs, use your judgment. As long as your dog's coat looks and feels fine, don't bother. If a coat gets full of burrs or begins to tangle, it's time to groom. If a dog is shedding, groom often.

Get your dog used to grooming, if only for two minutes at a time, while it's still a baby. An older dog isn't going to like this new procedure suddenly sprung on it. Just give your pup a minute or so of brushing every once in a while in your lap as a playful introduction.

Puppies may sound like they're being murdered when you first try to brush them. Even a calm adult dog will startle and yip and begin to struggle when you pull a tangle too hard or when you get to the parts that are tender—muzzle, ears, tail, belly and feet. When a puppy yips and starts to scramble

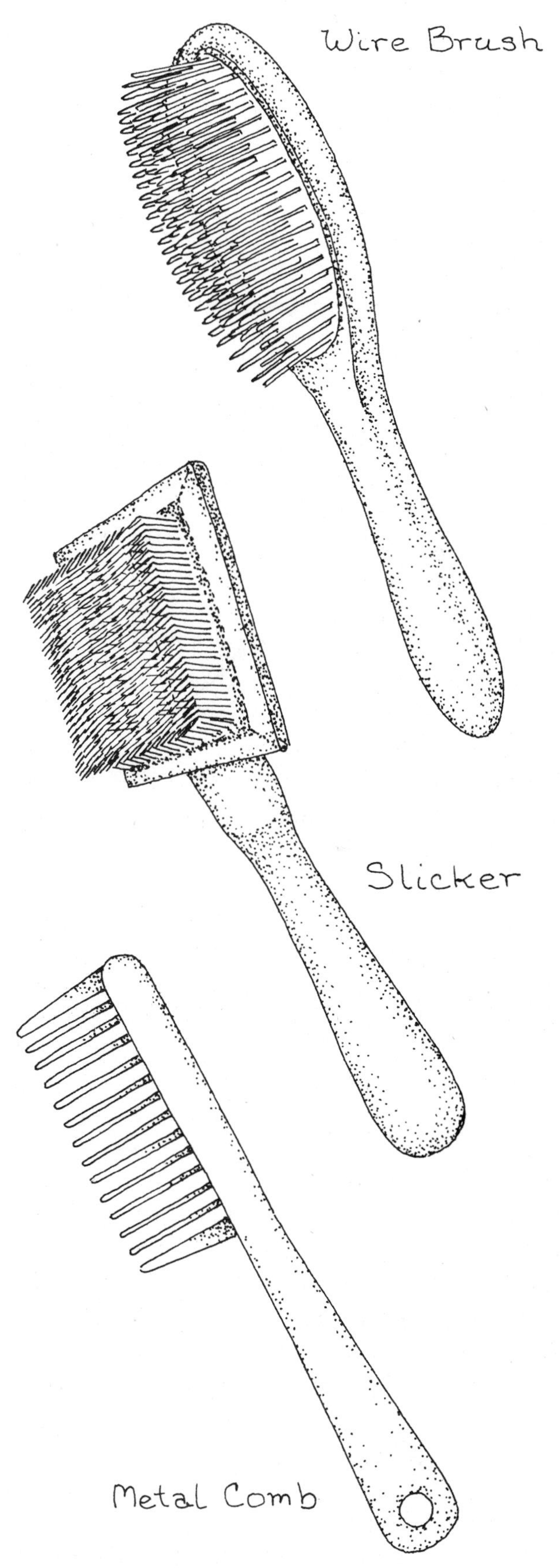

away or bite the brush, most people get mad, yell back and hit. Don't. Instead, when the puppy first complains, act as though it wasn't you that hurt it. Say, "Oh, you poor thing, did the brush get you? Well, you good, good dog, I'll take care of you." Pat your dog as you act sorry for it and then start brushing again. Your puppy will think that you are trying hard to protect it in a situation fate has brought about.

Dogs, especially puppies, will chew on the hand that brushes them. And if they tire of that game, they will simply leave. The trick to getting a dog brushed is to rig things so it can't turn its head and can't walk away. The requirements are met with a leash, a slip collar and two people to do the job instead of one.

First, put a slip collar and a leash on the dog. The slip collar, which tightens on the dog's neck, will help you control it. If it's small, lift it up onto a steady table (the dog will get panicky if the table jiggles or rocks). If it's big, leave it on the floor—or you could do the job outdoors if you live in the country. Move the collar up until it's just behind the dog's ears. Get the second person to hold the leash straight up, with just a little pressure. This keeps the dog's head from turning and holds its front end up. It doesn't hold its rear end up. To do that, the person who is brushing has to keep one hand up under the dog's belly just in front of its back legs.

There are several kinds of brushes and combs sold for dogs. Which kind you get depends on the kind of dog you have. A slicker is a brush made of thin, stiff wires set into a rubber base. Each wire is bent backwards at its tip so it can grab hold of loose hair and pull it out. Use slickers for dogs like collies when they are shedding their undercoat in the spring; or poodles, to get the mats and tangles out of their fur; or scotties, whose wiry coat is too thick for an ordinary bristle brush to get through. Slickers come in small to large sizes, just like the dogs they are intended for.

The next most useful brush is made of natural bristles, wire bristles, and sometimes both. Some have handles and some don't. You might find one with a handle easier to use. This kind of brush is good for short-haired dogs like dachshunds and beagles who just need a vigorous brushing to get out loose hair and dirt. It is also fine for long-haired dogs if their coats are not very thick—an Irish setter, for example, or a cocker spaniel.

Most dogs don't need combs. The ones who do—poodles, woolly sheepdogs and really long-haired dogs like the Maltese and Yorkshire terriers—will be best off with one of those steel combs that are rather sharp so that you can get all the way down to the skin. Metal combs can be bought with fine or more widely spaced teeth, depending on the coarseness of a dog's coat.

Before you start grooming, get out a paper bag to empty hair into as it accumulates in the comb or brush. Start brushing or combing along your pup's back and sides where it won't mind it much. Work down each leg. Save the tender areas—ears, belly, inside the legs, and face—until last.

As you work, feel along the dog's skin. You may find burrs. Pull the hair apart around them, then comb them out. You may feel a fingertip-sized lump, a tick filled with blood. Part the fur, take a look, and if it is a swollen, pinkish-brown tick, pull it out and get rid of it down the toilet. Dark gritty crumbs down near a dog's skin are flea droppings. Even if you can't find the fast-moving fleas themselves, a treatment with dog flea powder or dog flea spray is in order. Follow the directions on the container. (Don't use flea collars. They work, but too many dogs are allergic to them and develop nasty rashes on their necks.)

Big lumps of fur are called mats. Look for mats between the toes, under the legs, and under the tail especially. If a mat isn't in a visible area, you can just cut it off with blunt scissors (baby nail-scissors work well). If the bare spot would be noticeable, cut the mat straight down towards the dog's skin in several places, then tease out the loosened hair with a metal comb. It may still look a bit funny but it won't be a bald spot.

If you find any other skin problems—rashy areas, sores, lumps, cuts—it's best to ask the vet about them.

When the brushing is finished, vacuum up the hair from floor and table, put your clothes in the laundry, and if you itch, take a shower.

The last task of grooming is toenail clipping. Dogs who walk concrete pavements or scramble over rocks wear their own toenails down. But un-

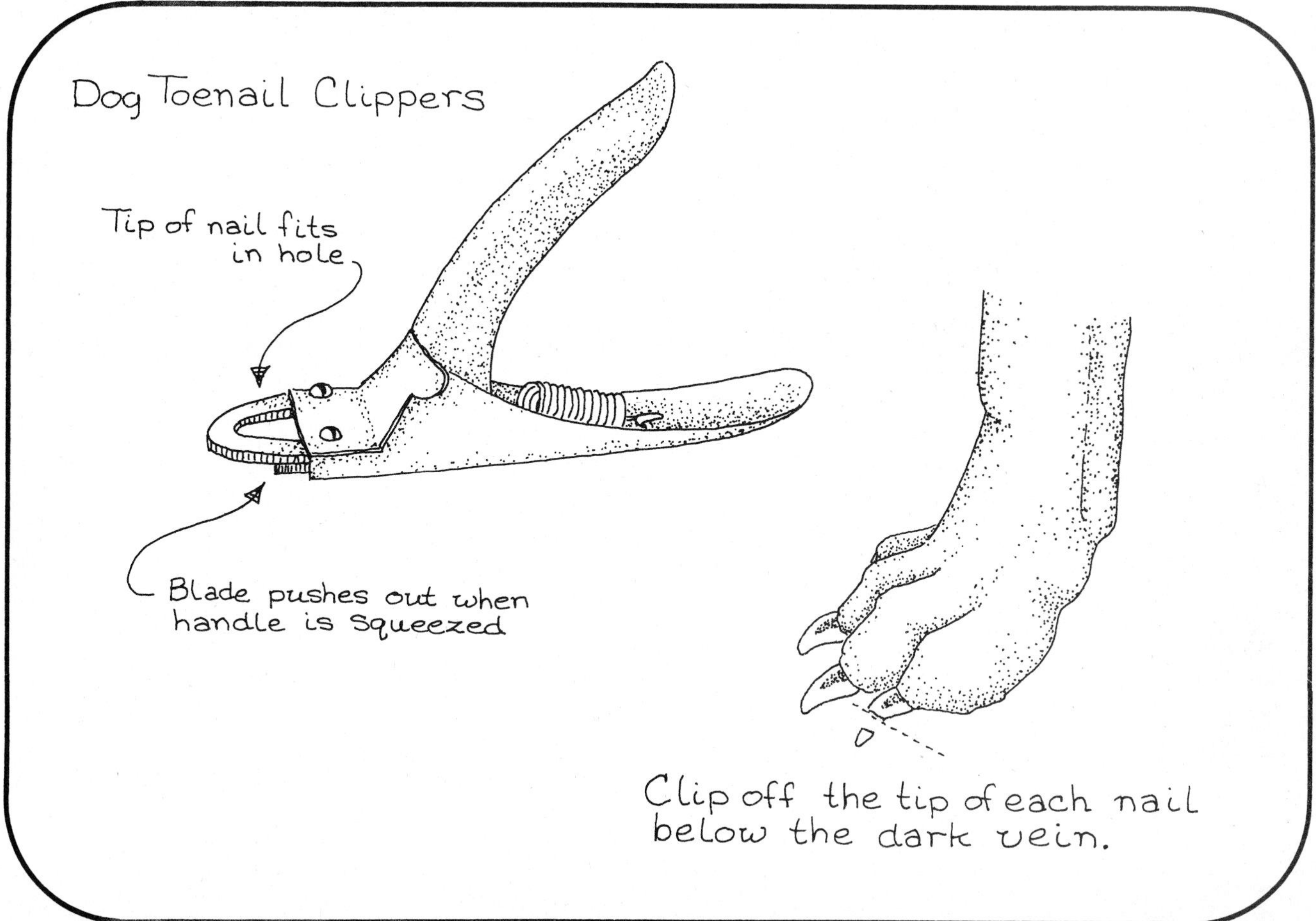

fortunately, dogs with dewclaws (the extra claw up high on the foot) always need the dewclaw trimmed, and dogs that walk mostly on grass need all their nails taken care of.

When a dog's toenails clackety-clack across the floor, they are too long. When a dewclaw begins to curve inward like the letter C, it is too long. Dewclaws can curve themselves right into the dog's skin. Long toenails push the dog's toes up and back, eventually causing sores and deformed feet.

There is a special kind of clippers available at pet stores made for clipping dog toenails. You hold the dog's foot, slip the clippers over the first eighth of an inch of nail (below where you can see the vein if your dog's nails are light enough to see it), and snip. Many dogs don't mind the procedure at all. Other dogs scream, bite, jerk their paw away and escape. Their fear may be caused by having a paw held firmly, because the cutting itself doesn't hurt. If your dog makes such a fuss about it, you will have to have it done by a professional dog groomer or a vet.

Bathing

Puppies, particularly new ones, may get messier and smellier than grown dogs. Because they have always been covered with fur, dogs have never had to develop the tough skins most humans have. Most of us can get soap on our skins every day without itching—a dog can't. Luckily for grown dogs, they don't need baths often, and some dogs don't need baths ever. Besides smelly pups, the kinds of dogs that need baths most often are white ones that live in sooty cities, dogs like Airedales with oily coats that hold on to dirt so that brushing doesn't clean them, and dogs with woolly hair that also doesn't shed dirt well. Some dogs have a doggy smell and need a bath once a month just for that reason. Probably the most any dog would ever need to be bathed is twice a month, and that would only be a white poodle in a city like New York.

Use plain soap to wash a dog or a puppy. The plainest are baby soaps or nonperfumed adult

Bathing a big dog is not always easy even when you join it in the tub.

soaps. Baby shampoo or castile shampoo is gentle too. Fill a bathtub or sink with warm water. Put an old towel or a rubber mat in the bottom so the dog won't slip and panic during the bath. Get a plastic pitcher or freezer container to pour water from. Put a slip collar and leash on your dog and find somebody who will hold the leash (unless there is a towel bar above the tub which you will be able to tie the leash to). If your dog is pretty big, get just about completely undressed because your clothes will get very wet. Lift your dog up by holding it under its chest and its rear end, and put it gently into the tub or sink. If you bathe your dog in the tub, sit on the edge of it with your feet inside; if in the sink, stand on a stool if you need to. Whoever is holding the leash should hold it straight over the dog's head and keep pressure on it all the time to discourage the dog from taking a step anywhere. If you're using the towel bar, tie the leash taut for the same reason.

Start pouring water over your dog's head and then soaping all around its neck, ears and the top of its head. It won't like this, but neither will any fleas that happen to be around. If you don't wash your dog's head first, the fleas will scurry up its neck and into its ears to ride out the storm and will emerge happily after the bath is over.

Your dog will absolutely hate having its muzzle washed, and since it will leap and struggle, save washing this for last to keep most of the bath as calm as possible. After its head and neck are soaped, rinse carefully and try not to get any soap in your dog's eyes. (Or you could put a few drops of mineral oil or vegetable oil in its eyes with a plastic eyedropper before you start the bath to protect them from soap.) Then you can pour water over its body and get that washed. Lift its legs one at a time to wash them. With a large dog, you'll find that you're all the way in the tub by this time. That's why you took your clothes off.

You will find the bathwater is now gray, scummy and disgusting. It is obviously not clean enough to use for a good rinsing, so pull the plug and get rid of the water.

Rinsing well is harder than washing well. There are several ways. In the kitchen sink, a hand spray is best if you have one. In the bathtub, you could keep the drain open, turn on the faucet and just use your plastic pitcher to rinse the dog. This works for small dogs, but takes rather a long time for larger ones and it's awfully hard to rinse bellies that way anyhow. What seems to work best is to rinse the best you can with the pitcher and then refill the tub or sink and rinse again, splashing water up onto the dog's belly and chest. A shower terrifies most dogs and seldom works.

When the rinsing is finished, let the water out. Pull the shower curtain shut, or shield the dog with a towel. Step out of the way because sooner or later your dog will shake. It should still be on the leash, and whoever is holding it should be as shielded as possible. Let it shake a few times before proceeding. When the dog has gotten the worst of the water off, dry it with a large towel, including its feet. It will still be wet, of course, but now when you at last let it out of the tub or sink it won't soak the room from floor to ceiling. Dry it again with another towel before you let it out into the rest of the house.

No dog will consider your drying job adequate. The moment you let it free, it will scramble in circles like a maniac, rubbing its face along carpets and furniture, rolling and kicking and acting a little crazy. If mayhem ensues and somebody yells to let that crazy dog out, it will continue to dry itself in the dirt and you may find that you should have kept that leash on longer.

There is one more step to bathing a dog, and that is cleanup. Be sure not to forget it.

Housebreaking

Often the first annoyance with a new puppy is the first puddle on the living-room rug. Confining a puppy to its den when you can't watch it is the best way to avoid messed-up rugs and floors. It is also the best way to start housebreaking. When the newspapers get wet or dirty, just fold them up, put them in a plastic bag and put the plastic bag in an outside garbage pail. Spread several layers of fresh newspaper in the puppy's den.

When the puppy wets or messes off its paper, clean it up right away. Soak up puddles with paper towels. If the puddle is on the bare floor, wipe the spot with a damp floor sponge. If it is on a rug or fabric, soak the spot with a cup of water to which a quarter of a cup of white vinegar has been added. The vinegar prevents bleaching. Let the spot soak for a few minutes, then wipe again with paper towels. Pick up bowel movements with paper towels, and clean the spot with a damp sponge and a very little bit of liquid detergent. Diarrhea and vomit can be scooped up with an old dustpan and paper towels. The spot will need a good scrubbing; use rug shampoo if it is on carpeting, detergent if it is on bare floor.

Besides confining a young puppy to its den for much of the day, early housebreaking also includes taking it out frequently. You can expect a puppy to need to go each time it wakes up from a nap; after every meal; very early in the morning, probably before you usually get up; and in general, every half-hour all day long.

Take your puppy outside the moment it stirs in the morning. It will have to be on the leash unless you live very far from streets or roads, or unless you have a fenced yard. Puppies have no sense at all about cars. If your puppy has already wet and messed before you get up, get an alarm clock and get up earlier. Carry the dog outside or it will let loose before you get to the door. If you possibly can, take your puppy out when it wakes up from every nap, too. After a successful half-hour of play-without-mess, either take it out again or take it to its den.

When you let a new puppy loose in the house, you'll have to watch it every minute. If you catch it in the act of soiling or puddling, you can scold and punish it by grabbing the scruff of its neck and giving it a good shake. Forget anything you've heard about rolled-up newspapers, rubbing its nose in the mess and so on. By the time you get the newspaper and roll it up and chase the pup around the house, it's not going to remember what you're scolding it about. Noses in messes make no sense at all to a dog. In fact, there's no proof that scolding a dog for messing works unless you catch it while it's making the mess. Dogs are not as smart as people think.

Try to notice how your puppy behaves just before it soils so you can get it outside in time. Some puppies pant as a sign of discomfort, some just wander off to find a private place. Almost all hold their heads low to the ground and circle a bit just before they go to the bathroom.

You can see that housebreaking is quite hard.

But if you confine your dog to its den when you are not with it and watch it to prevent accidents when you are, and take it out very often so it does most of its business outdoors, you will notice progress. Nature is on your side too. As your puppy grows, it has to urinate less often. And as you get to know the dog, you will be able to notice signs that it is about to go off and puddle or mess.

The biggest problem with housebreaking is that the dog often knows what's expected of it before its people understand the signals. For instance, if you find your dog has chosen private places in the house to mess—like in an upstairs bathroom or basement laundry room—but not in the more public parts of the house like the living room or kitchen—then your dog is housebroken but you're not. The poor cuss is looking for the most "outside" place inside the house. But somehow you're failing to notice the signs that show it needs to go and you're not taking it out. When and if you get to this stage, begin by keeping all the doors to those rooms shut so the dog can't use them as private bathrooms. And stop letting the dog loose so often. Then try to figure out what times of day you're missing the boat. Often it's during the night—are you taking your pup out for the last time late enough? Are you getting it out early enough in the morning? Have you stopped tying it during the night too soon? If it happens after the pup's after-meal walk, wait longer to walk it next time it eats. Don't bring your puppy back from its walk until it has done something. Watch more carefully for "having to go" signs—walking off from you, sniffing the floor, circling around, disappearing into the next room.

No matter how hard you are working at housebreaking, you can't possibly expect a dog to be housebroken until four months, and not reliably so until six months. Many dogs have lapses until they are 10 months—especially small dogs, who can take a long time to become trustworthy.

By the time your puppy is six months old, it may get along on four walks a day—first thing in the morning, at noontime, at about three or four o'clock in the afternoon and at about nine o'clock at night. Stick with that leash—even among adult dogs, the number one cause of death is car accidents.

Taming and Playing

A new puppy graduates from pathetic to pain in the neck in about one week. The puppy who wouldn't eat at all is into the garbage pail. The puppy who cried those first nights now leaps at you and rips your clothes. The puppy who wouldn't budge from behind the couch is all over the house now, chewing as it goes.

All this is bad behavior. If you think stealing, biting, leaping and destroying belongings is just puppy high jinks which the pup will outgrow, you'll wait forever.

A mother wolf or wild dog plays with her pups, but she doesn't stand for nonsense. When she's fed up with them, she gives a warning growl—like a low-voiced NO. When they still bother her, she cuffs them—like a slap against the nose. When you discipline your puppy with a growl or cuff, just as when you let it kiss your ear or play its puppy games, you are speaking its own language. The better you learn your puppy's language, the better it will one day learn yours. The longer you wait, the worse it gets. Tap (or even slap) a pup with the flat of your hand right up against its nose when it bites you or your clothing. Say NO in a deep voice and loud enough to startle. Do it every time. If the puppy jumps on you, be just as stern. For a big puppy, bring your knee up hard against its chest when it jumps. For a small puppy, slap your hand against its nose.

Put the garbage pail up on the counter while the puppy's around and keep an eye on your sandwich. Keep your shoes, socks, underpants and toys where they belong. You're not just saving your family's temper with either of these precautions: puppies chew up and swallow just about anything—splintery chicken bones, sharp plastic, electric wires and dangerous pills. An Airedale puppy of ours once ate a whole bottle of decongestant pills similar in effect to pep pills. The poor critter chased hallucinated rabbits around the house for 24 hours, in spite of a sedative injection that was supposed to knock him out.

You have to exercise a certain balance in discipline. If you hit and scream at a dog all day, you're going to make a wreck of both of you. One growled NO when you catch it doing something is all it

Some dogs will do anything for a little attention.

takes. Instantly, put on a happy smile and act like nothing happened. Pet your pup, invite it to play. This is not being phony. It just takes account of the fact that puppies have short memories of past crimes, even five minutes past.

Try to substitute a legitimate game for a criminal action. For the pup who tugs and rips your clothes, play tug of war. You can buy rubber and rawhide tugging toys at pet stores, or you can knot an old rag or a piece of rope instead. Vicious as they act, most puppies aren't as strong as you, so let the dog do the pulling until you get the feel of how hard it can pull. Then pull back.

Nature prepared pups to chew a lot so they would get enough to eat. The fact that we invented tender tidbits instead of tougher meals doesn't change the instinct. For the dog who chews everything up, provide plenty of things to chew. Rawhide bones, available at pet stores, are fine. They get nice and gushy as the dog works at them. Nylon bones are chewy in a different way. Soupbones, bought at supermarkets or gotten free from friendly butchers, are for hard, serious chewing. Any other kind of bone splinters and is dangerous.

For puppies who chase and pounce on you too much, try weaning them to a good game of ball. The best balls for dogs are solid, hard rubber (not sponge rubber). They don't get chewed up and swallowed. Pet stores carry solid rubber balls.

From these descriptions it sounds as though you are substituting human games for a puppy's play. Not at all. It is you who are learning to play dog. For instance, when your puppy greets you as you come home it jumps on you. If you lean down to it, it licks your mouth—or rather your muzzle. Why? Wild dogs and wolves don't carry home prey to their young like wild cats do. Instead they regurgitate freshly swallowed meat for the pups to eat. That muzzle licking is a begging gesture—the way a pup gets an adult to regurgitate food. You don't have to allow the jumping, you don't have to get your mouth licked and you certainly don't have to throw up. But you'll find if you turn your face to the side as you lean down to greet your puppy, it will be delighted to lick your ear: this feels good, and you're learning to play dog.

When your puppy's in the mood for play, it may let you know by bouncing about, bowing and paw-

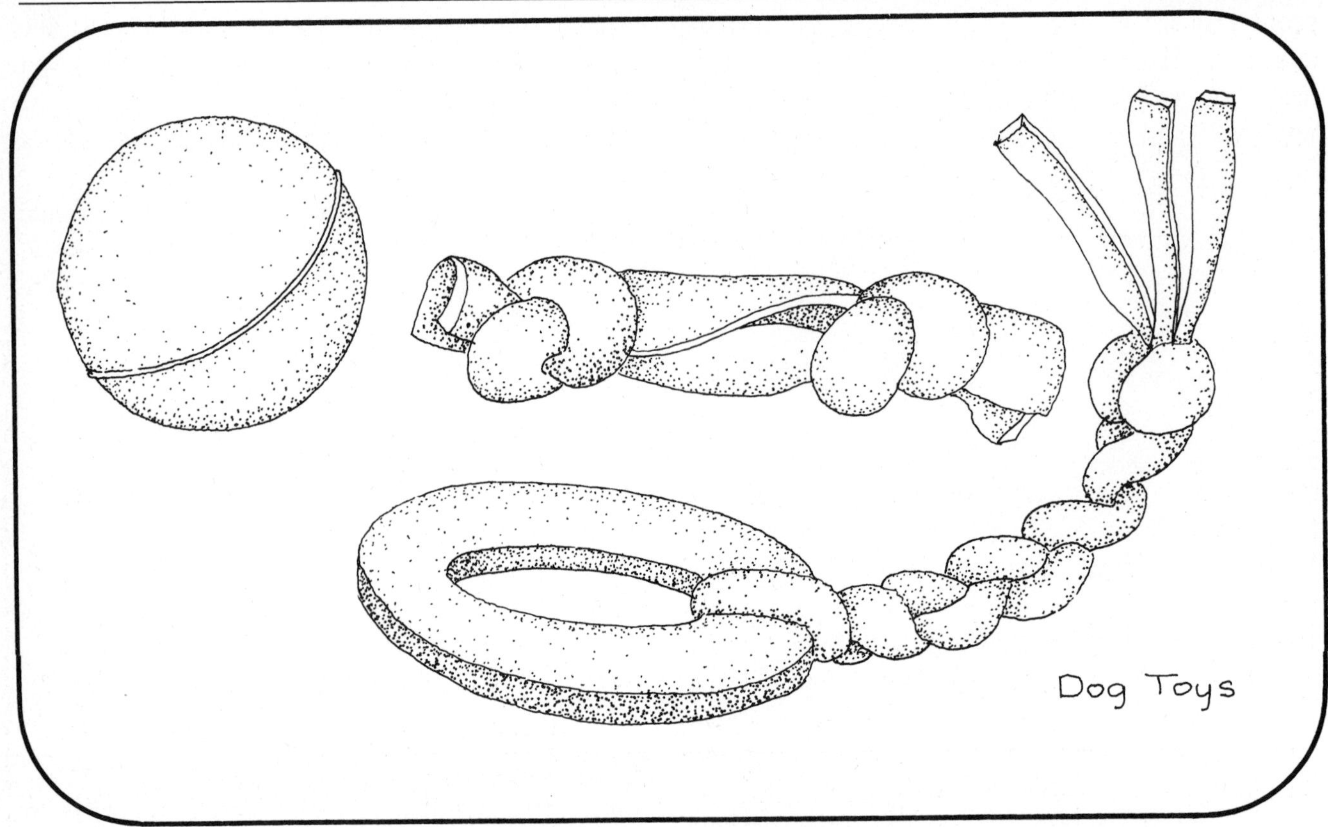
Dog Toys

ing at you. In adult wild dogs, this is an invitation not to play but to hunt. For 10 minutes or more, the hunting males bow to one another, paw, muzzle-lick, bounce and make short dashes away, only to start the procedure all over again. It's like a pep rally before a football game. Each dog is encouraged by the enthusiasm of the others until, when the cheering has reached a peak, the dashes become a headlong run and the dogs are off to the hunt. Try bowing, pawing and making short dashes. Your puppy will understand the invitation.

Puppy play is itself a training ground for the moves of hunting. The crouch, with rear end wiggling, gets the pup set to move whichever way the rabbit (or the ball) goes. Then comes the chase, the pounce, the grab. Try the same game with something limp like a knotted rag and you'll understand the tug of war game too. After the grab, the rag is shaken—if it were a rabbit that shake would break its back. Playing dog this way is only what any pup would do to practice for the hunt with friends.

Part of learning a puppy's language is noticing when it is miserable. Signs of misery are harder to notice than signs of joy. For instance, you can't read a tail by its wagging. You have to notice where the tail is as well. When your puppy greets you, it holds its tail high as it wags. When it meets a stranger, watch the tail—it may still wag, but it is held lower. The lower the tail, the more frightened or worried a puppy is feeling. When a dog tucks its tail beneath its rear end (even though it may still be wagging!), it has probably done something for which it expects to be scolded and is very worried.

Ears show fear too. The unafraid dog holds its ears up—or pricked if it has drooping ears. The more frightened it is, the lower it lays its ears back along its head.

As you play with your puppy, pay attention to what it is saying with ears and tail. If a game gets too rough or if it is being scolded, it will tuck its tail and flatten its ears. That's the time to stop scary playing or let up on the scolding. It may also flatten its body towards the ground, turn its head sideways and even roll onto its back. Even in a grown-up dog these gestures mean "Don't hurt me, I won't hurt you." When it was a baby, your puppy "groveled" like that to its mother. In return, she licked its turned-up belly (to stimulate digestion and elimination), turned on her side and let it nurse. It's against social rules when playing dog to continue to scold a dog who grovels for you. It has already admitted it is "only a pup." At the same time, it has admitted you are the boss. A pat or two from you will acknowledge that you understand the gesture and appreciate it.

There is one more dog meaning you should learn. When your puppy flops down, closes its eyes and falls asleep, it means "For heaven's sake, let me sleep." Puppies need as much sleep as babies. Don't wake them up.

Preventing Bad Habits

Bad habits should be stopped when they start, not after everyone is having temper tantrums about "that darn dog."

Jumping on people. *Every single time your puppy jumps up on you, push it down hard. If it's big, bring your knee up hard into its chest. If it's small, bring the palm of your hand up hard under its snout. Do both hard enough to get a whimper out of your dog. If you fool around with jumping games, there's no way in the world that pup is going to figure out that while you like jumping, other people may not. Show it another way to say an excited hello. Before it jumps, stoop down to its level and pet it a lot.*

Jumping on furniture. *Whack the puppy hard on the rump and drag it off every single time you see it on furniture. If you're allowed to have it on your bed, a dog is smart enough to learn there is a piece of furniture it can sleep on and others it is never to go on. What it can't learn is that sometimes you're in a good mood and will let it on the couch and sometimes company's coming and you won't. Since dogs long for soft beds, get a dog pillow or bed for your dog to sleep on and keep it where it most enjoys sleeping.*

Taking food. *Puppies are not sneaky about stealing food. They come right up to you and grab your sandwich out of your hand. When that happens, grab the dog just as fast. Say NO! Whack it hard. And above all, extract the sandwich from its mouth so it doesn't get to eat it. Now trick your dog. Put the sandwich on the chair where it can be reached. As it goes for the bait, grab and spank it. Now put the sandwich on the floor next to the dog. If it reaches for it, spank the dog again. Tempt it in every way you can, but punish it each time it goes for the food.*

On the other hand, when you offer it something to eat, either its dinner or a snack from your hand, the floor, the chair or anywhere, say OKAY, then let it eat. The point is that the dog should take no food at all unless you say it's okay. This is not just to teach your dog politeness, but to be sure that it does not steal food out of garbage cans or off the kitchen table, pick up rotten food from the gutter or the poisonous food that is sometimes around.

There are some bad habits that seem impossible to break. These are digging holes, wandering and chasing cars. If a dog keeps digging a place to lie in the cool earth at the roots of its favorite bush, and the bush is dying, you can fill the hole and put a big rock on top of it. The dog will of course find another place, but you have saved that bush. A dog that wanders simply has to be tied or penned or watched or taken out on a leash. The same goes for a dog that chases cars.

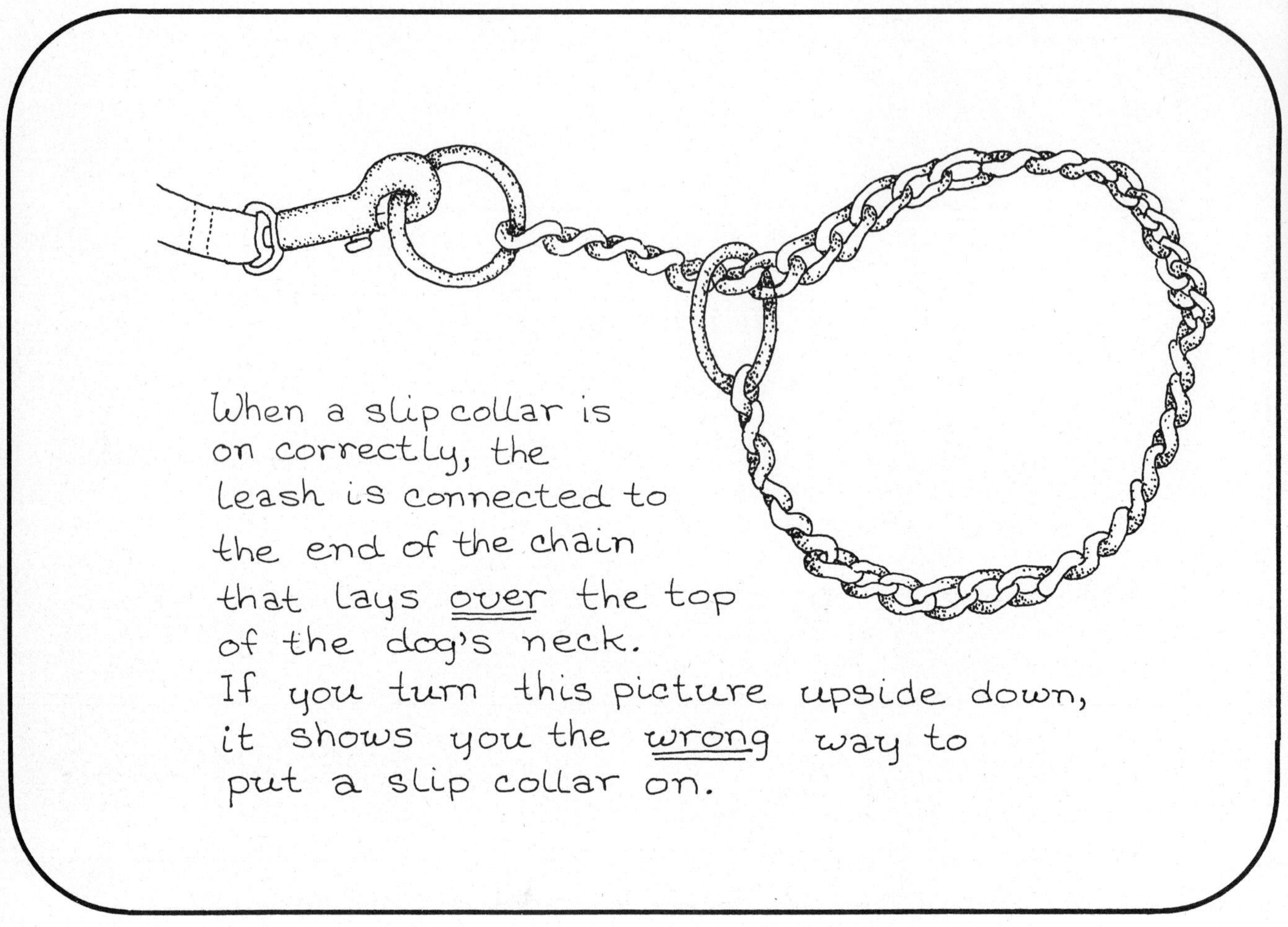

Simple Commands

Once you have become familiar with dog language by playing dog, you can begin to teach your dog human language by training it. You can start to train a dog when it is four months old, but you can't expect much until it is six months old. Even if you have put training off for years, you can still train your dog. It is not true that an old dog can't learn new tricks.

Dogs love best the person who trains them. Somewhere between six months and a year, your dog will choose its master. Its master will be the person the dog has come to listen to best and who understands it. The best way for man and dog to learn how to listen to each other is by working together. Training is that work.

The minimum a dog has to learn to be likable is to walk on a leash without pulling, to sit and to lie down when it is told, to stay, and to come. The method for training a dog for obedience trials can be found in dog training books. The method we are using here is less rigid but easier. All training is done on a leash and with a slip collar. You'll need a six-foot web lead and a slip collar that just goes over your dog's head without too much extra length. A slip collar, made of either webbing or chain, is often misunderstood. People think it is choking the dog all the time and that this is a cruel way to train it. Some call it a choke chain. The whole point of a slip collar is that you don't choke a dog with it because you never let it pull against the collar. You only use it to jerk your dog as a signal. It tightens around its neck for a moment but then you must let it go slack again. You should never pull a dog by its slip collar or let it pull you.

First, get the collar on the right way. Look at the picture. The collar has been put on the correct way for walking the dog to your left so that your right hand is free. If you're left-handed, you might want to reverse the collar and walk your dog to your

Teach a dog to lie down by saying LIE DOWN and showing it what to do with its legs.

A firm push on a dog's rear end will help it learn the command, SIT.

right. When the collar is on right it will tighten as you tug the leash; when you release pressure the weight of the collar will pull downward, making the collar slacken right away. Put the collar on the wrong way and see what happens. When you tug and then slacken, the collar doesn't respond. And if the collar doesn't respond, your dog isn't getting a clear signal.

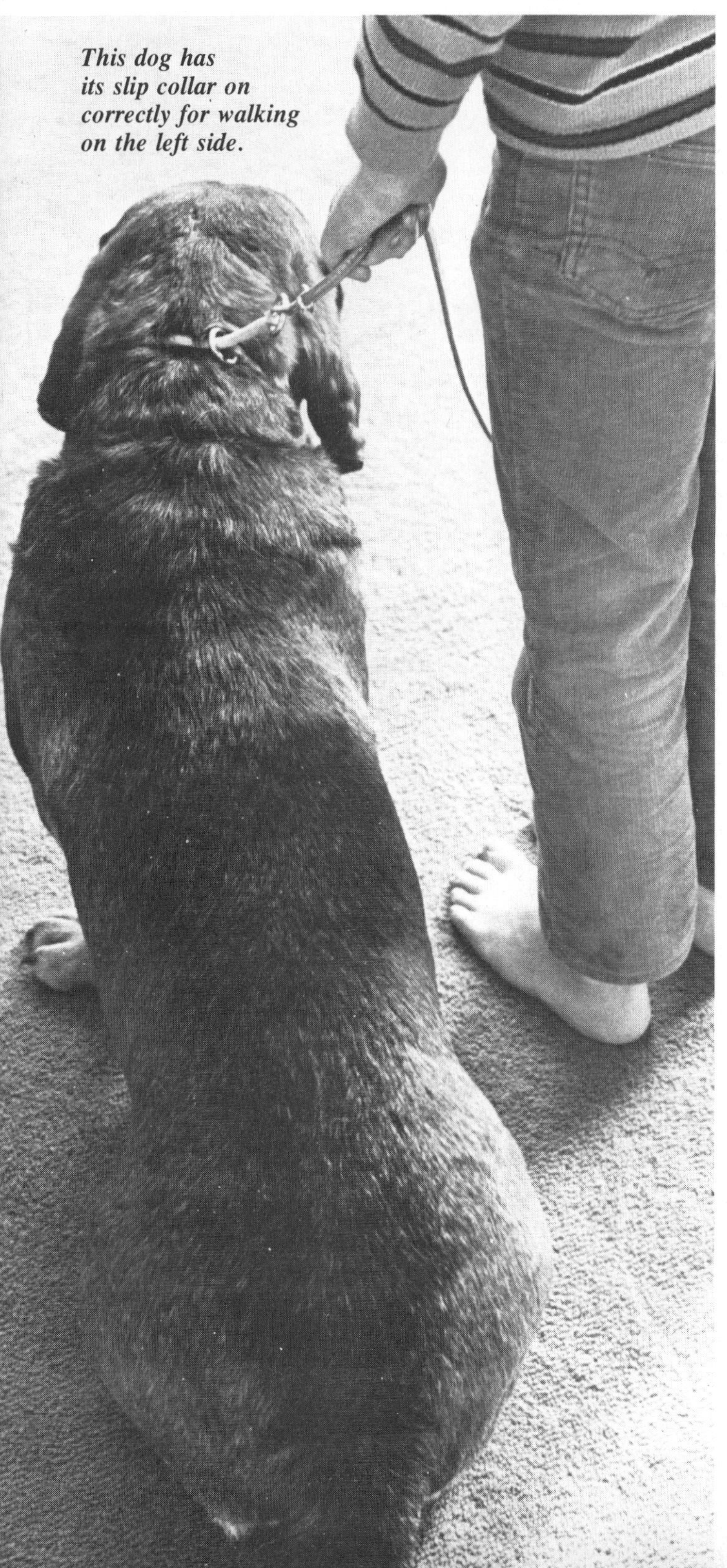

This dog has its slip collar on correctly for walking on the left side.

The Leash. Teaching a dog to walk on a leash without pulling you has a simple logic behind it. One dog trainer described it this way: if a dog is running headlong toward a wall and crashes into it, it will learn very quickly not to run into walls. If a dog wearing a slip collar runs headlong next to you and pulls ahead and you give it a jerk backward, it will learn very quickly not to run ahead of you.

Put your dog on the leash (check to see that the collar is on correctly). Hold the leash close enough to the dog so there is only about six inches of slack. You can hold the extra length in your other hand, or bunch up the leash and hold it all in your left hand. The slack allows you to jerk the dog instead of pulling. Most people are tempted to hold the leash rather close, keeping a little pull on the dog's collar all the time. But that just confuses it, because then there isn't enough difference between how its neck feels when it's walking in the right place and how it feels when it's walking into the wrong place.

Heel. A dog should feel absolutely nothing when it's heeling (walking level with you) and a really hard jerk when it gets out of place. If the dog moves ahead, you raise your left hand a little and bring it back to your side fast. If the dog moves behind, you move your hand backward and give a sharp tug forward. It's not allowed to move out from you either—move your hand away from your side and bring it back sharply. If your dog moves into you and bumps your leg, give it a bump with your knee (or your foot if it's little). Say your dog's name and then tell it what it's supposed to do—for example, FIDO, HEEL! As you say HEEL, start walking and give a quick jerk on the leash. If your dog pulls ahead, jerk hard as you say HEEL again, but always slacken the leash right away. If it pulls to the side, do the same thing. And if it trails behind, do the same thing. You are never pulling on that leash. You are only giving a sharp, hard tug and letting the leash go slack again.

When your dog has learned that there's only one place it can walk comfortably (because it gets a big jerk when it walks anywhere else), show it that the pace can be fast or slow. Walk at a normal speed, then start to trot. Jerk the dog up if it lags behind. Then suddenly slow down. Jerk if your dog gets ahead. This may seem too hard on the dog, but it isn't at all. It can see to the side of its head better than you can, so it always has a glimpse of what you're up to unless it isn't paying attention.

Now teach your dog how to turn while heeling. Walk in a straight line, hold the leash tightly, keep your left arm absolutely stiff and straight at your side, and suddenly make a right U-turn until you're facing the opposite direction. Try a left turn. There's no way you can give your dog a jerk with the leash when you're turning toward it, so a different method has to be used. Walk along normally and without warning make a sharp left turn, pivoting on your left foot. As you pivot, your right foot will bump into your dog unless the dog has been alert enough to notice the turn. If it wasn't the first time, it will be soon.

All the time you're training your dog, keep bending down to pat it and tell it how good it is. There is never need to scold it for a mistake. If you keep up the training, your dog will learn that if it doesn't pay attention when it is out walking with you, uncomfortable things happen. When it is alert, it is pleasantly rewarded.

What if your dog needs to go to the bathroom? Every once in a while when you are heeling say DOG (your dog's name), OKAY, and give it a push on the rump to get it out of the heel position. It won't take it long to learn it can wander to the leash's end when you say OKAY.

When your dog has learned to heel at a fast and slow pace and goes through right turns and left turns with fairly good accuracy, you can begin to teach it other polite things like sitting, staying, lying down, and coming when it's called.

Sit. Pull the leash straight upward (not jerking it now, just firmly taut) and say DOG, SIT! At the same time, push down on its rump with your left hand. You have to lean awfully hard on a big dog, by the way. When you've managed to wrestle it into a sitting position, tell it how wonderful it is. Now walk with it a few steps and say SIT again. Sooner or later, your dog will catch on.

Stay. When it will sit on command, you can teach your dog STAY. Get it sitting first. Then hold the palm of your hand in front of its face and tell it, DOG, STAY! It will instantly get up. Move your palm up quick for a good tap under the chin. Get it sitting again, repeat the words DOG, STAY, and try again. Chances are sooner or later the dog will figure out that that hand just happens to come up to slap its chin every time it makes a move forward. It will begin to stay. When it will stay for a while, try backing off, then circling around (still holding the leash, of course). Every time the dog gets up, go through the whole deal again.

Come. Your six-foot leash will be important for teaching your dog to come—you can get six feet away from your dog without it getting away from you. When your dog will sit and stay even when you back off the whole six feet of leash, you can teach it to come. Walk ahead of it the full six feet. Face it and say DOG, COME! and pull the leash in, hand over hand, as fast as you can to drag your dog to you. Act as though the dog came to you of its own free will and congratulate it. Sooner or later, it will leap to you before you get a chance to pull it in.

Down. To teach a dog to lie down, you have to get it lying down. This is very hard. A big dog has muscles superior to yours. Even a small dog resists pressure to force it down. Any dog tends to panic when it feels someone tackle it to the ground, and so would you. You have to gently trick a dog into a lying-down position so that it is lying down before it knows what is happening. First get your dog to sit. Then say DOG, DOWN! as you pull its front feet slowly out from under it and to one side, so as not to cause alarm. The dog will now be lying on its side. Pat it calmly while it is lying down and say how good it is. Then let it get up before it panics. Needless to say, wait until your dog is in a relaxed mood to start teaching it to lie down.

By the way, dogs have trouble learning that DOWN means one thing one time and another thing another time. Or that two different people use different words to mean the same thing. For instance, if you use the word DOWN to mean "Get

Puppies are wonderful to cuddle.

off the couch,'' and also to mean ''Stop jumping up on me,'' and also to mean ''Lie down,'' you're going to get nowhere fast. If you like, you can use LIE DOWN so the dog won't get confused, or OFF for getting off furniture.

Dogs also have trouble finding a key word they're supposed to listen to if you have surrounded it with a bunch of other words. If you say, ''Now listen, dum-dum, I said DOWN and I mean it,'' your puppy will wag its tail and wonder what is going on. Limit commands to one or two words. If the dog is at least six months old, and you practice daily, it shouldn't take you longer than a month or so to train. Remember the training order: dog's name first, command second, hard jerks only on the leash, no scolding, lots of patting.

Teaching a dog to dance is easy if the dog can balance well on its hind legs.

Consider training an everyday, all-day thing rather than a special lesson. That is, your dog should HEEL *all the time* it's on the leash, except when you say OKAY. It should SIT any time during the day when you'd like it to sit. It should STAY when it's convenient for you to have it stay—indoors or out. You have to do these things all the time with your dog, anytime you think of them. Training isn't a thing you do once. It's a relationship developed between dog and master.

Fancy Tricks

The principle behind any trick from fetching to begging is to manipulate your dog into the right action as you say the words, and then pat it enthusiastically as though it had done the action all by itself. Scolding only confuses the dog. Since it doesn't know yet what it is that it's supposed to be doing right, it certainly doesn't know what it did wrong. If you use food as a reward, you won't be able to show off wherever you go unless you have some goodies in your pocket. Patting works almost as well.

Begging. Get your dog into a corner and get it sitting down with its rear snugly into the corner. Say DOG, BEG! as you lift its front end up into the right position. Hold it for a moment and then tell it how wonderful it is. Dogs are upset when they think they are falling over backward, so try not to push it too far. If you have a very floppy sort of dog and its bottom seems to be coming out from under it whenever you try to get it sitting up, you may not be able to teach this trick.

Shaking Hands. Most dogs sooner or later paw at you for attention, so the gesture of shaking hands is half done for you by nature. Get your dog to sit, pick up a paw while you say DOG, SHAKE HANDS; then pat it a lot. If your dog learns this without too much trouble, it may be the sort who can learn an impressive variation that will astonish your friends. Hold your hand slightly to its left side. Say "Shake your LEFT hand" (and pick up that paw). Do the same with its right paw, holding your hand more to that side. People will think it is highly intelligent for a dog to know left from right. The fact is it doesn't—the position of your hand is simply the signal to the dog to give you the nearest paw.

Playing Dead. Playing dead means the dog must roll onto its back, belly up, and stay there for a while. Dogs will do this trick quite enthusiastically if they get their bellies rubbed in the bargain. Like other tricks, you have to manage to get the dog into the play-dead position while you say DOG, PLAY DEAD. It has to be lying down first—then just roll it over. Rub its belly right away. Later, when the dog is more or less doing what you want, wait before you rub. It will learn to stay waiting belly-up for the rubbing it knows is coming.

Rolling Over. This trick is hard to teach big dogs because they're so heavy and clumsy to roll. If you can roll your dog over, then you can teach the trick in the same way as all the others. Say DOG, ROLL OVER as you roll it; then give it a cuddle.

Dancing. Big dogs must feel as silly as they look when they try to stand on their hind legs. Trying to teach them this trick usually makes them suffer. For some reason, smaller dogs often prance around on two legs naturally (possibly they are trying to reach up to where the action is), so they are much easier to teach. There is no doubt that food is the best reward for this trick. If you don't use food you will have to get your dog up on its hind legs by holding its paws, and any dog will pull away from anything holding its paws. If your dog will stand or jump up on its hind legs for even a moment for a bit of food, however, you can then stick the front part of your arm under its foreleg for support, to give it the idea that you would like it to stay in that position for a while when you say DOG, DANCE. Don't hold the food up above its nose, because it will jump all over. Close your hand over the food and hold it right next to its nose while you hold it up for a few seconds. Let the dog down again before you give it the food. When it stands with good balance for 10 seconds or more you can teach the dog to actually dance (even though this is the word you've been using all along, so far it's really just been balancing). Just move the hand holding the food slightly forward so the dog takes a step or two. Even later, you can teach it to dance around in a circle by moving your hand in a circle.

Saying Please. A dog who never barks to get your attention is not a good candidate for SAYING PLEASE. But if your dog even occasionally makes noises when it wants a bit of your sandwich, it can be taught this trick. Tempt it with a piece of food. (Liverwurst throws most dogs into a frenzy of excitement.) Keep saying DOG, SAY PLEASE, and follow the command with your best rendition of a small bark—WRUFF! The moment any sound comes from its throat, give it the snack and praise its intelligence. As soon as it SAYS PLEASE every time, you can teach it to surprise people even more. Tell it to say a LITTLE PLEASE (and use a soft voice); give it the snack no matter how loud it is. Then tell your dog to say a BIG PLEASE (use a big voice). Don't give it the snack until it gets very excited and gives a good loud impatient bark. Before long it will take its clue from your voice, and finally from the actual words you use (at which point you can give the command in a perfectly normal voice).

Fetch And Drop It. Luckily, all puppies run after and pick up a favorite toy if you throw one. Sooner or later, all puppies come up to you with the toy in their mouths. Take advantage of the situation by saying DOG, FETCH every time you toss something to your pup. Then do not move a muscle! If you go after your dog you will be teaching it a game of tag, not a game of fetch. Just sitting

Shaggy Dog Stories

The stunts—good ones and bad ones—a dog thinks up all by itself can be quite eccentric. Because I've never figured out whether dogs are awfully dumb or awfully bright, I leave you with these three stories to figure out for yourself.

Sheevra, an Airedale who learned everything in this chapter and more, was terrified of thunderstorms. At the first rumble, she would dash into the bathroom, leap into the tub and frantically try to dig herself into the only hole in our city apartment: the bathtub drain. After 10 years and 200 thunderstorms she never saw the ridiculousness of the situation.

My old French sheepdog, Amber, loved the water. She could be found in the summertime stretched full-length in a roaring brook, her head supported on a rock. In the winter, every time I drew myself a hot bath she stepped sedately into the tub and sat there, grinning, panting, snuffling up the steam as it curled about her whiskers. I was certainly surprised to have that sweet old dear accused by neighbors of being a thief. They complained she stole their garden tools, their children's toys and their husbands' dungarees fresh off the clothesline. Of course I didn't believe them. Then came spring, and the snow at the bottom of the yard melted. Gaily waving her plumed tail, Amber took me to her cache: 30 feet of garden hose, a rake, a child's truck and bulldozer, and the dungarees.

Most startling is a greeting ceremony invented by my wolflike, one-eyed mongrel bitch, Greta. Greta's fierce devotion pushed her to unusual feats—like jumping a seven-foot fence to escape from the vet's exercise yard and trekking home cross-country over five miles of completely unfamiliar terrain. In Greta's early years, an impolite brown poodle lived next door to us. Each morning at 7 A.M. he appeared at the ridge of a rock that separated our boundaries, trotted down the slope and deposited a bowel movement on our front-door step—a shocking disgrace to dogdom. Greta took to chasing the crude fellow away with a nip on the butt, egged on by me and the whispered command "Get 'im!" As the months passed, nipping the poodle's rear end became such a roundly applauded stunt that Greta lived with her eye to the boundary ridge. The moment the poodle appeared, she was off up the rocks to try to get a nip in before he made it to the safety of his own territory. Gradually the ceremony became a way of greeting me when I returned from work. Whether the poodle was there or not, Greta would dash up the rock, make a show of investigating for poodle intruders and then dash back to me to say hello.

More years passed and the poodle died. But the ceremony had become a ritual. As Greta grew old, we got an Airedale pup. The pup learned the ritual. Greta died, but the dash up the ridge and back did not. The poodle dash, performed as our car pulls in the drive, is a dog-to-dog tradition in the family, unbroken now for several generations of pups to whom it can make no sense at all.

doesn't look like a promising romp to your puppy and chances are it will flirt with you and the toy for a few minutes, and then carry the toy back to you in its mouth. Now, tell it it's terrific, but don't play around. As you pat your dog and make a fuss, manage to get a good hold on it, and as you say DOG, DROP IT, extract the toy calmly from its mouth. Wait a minute before throwing the toy again as you say DOG, FETCH. (If your dog does not calmly give things up, keep smiling; stick your fingers down behind what it's holding, pull it from its mouth and then say how wonderful it is to be so generous about giving up its toys.) Since this is no game at all for your dog until it brings the toy back to you and drops it, it will probably learn to fetch and drop pretty fast. When your dog loves the game and does it well, you can encourage it to swim by playing fetch near water. At first throw the ball just to the edge of the water, then a little farther out. Be careful or you may lose your ball should your dog not want to swim after it.

Incidental Tricks. Most dogs, in their efforts to communicate with you, develop their own expressive ways. A pup, in its enthusiasm for dinner, might once pick up its dish in its mouth. Or a dog might drag its leash around, hoping someone will take it out. Or stand up at the window and look out because someone it likes has just left the house. If you reward the dog right away and put words to what it is doing, it will soon have another trick in its collection. Say what comes to your mind, like DOG, DINNERTIME! if it picks up its dish (and feed it right away), or DOG, BRING YOUR LEASH (and take it out right away), or DOG, SEE WHO'S THERE (and go and look with it and pat it a lot). It seems to be a rule that the more a dog has been trained to understand words, the easier it can learn new words and the actions that go with them. It still doesn't speak your language, but it has generalized the principle that your sounds have meaning.

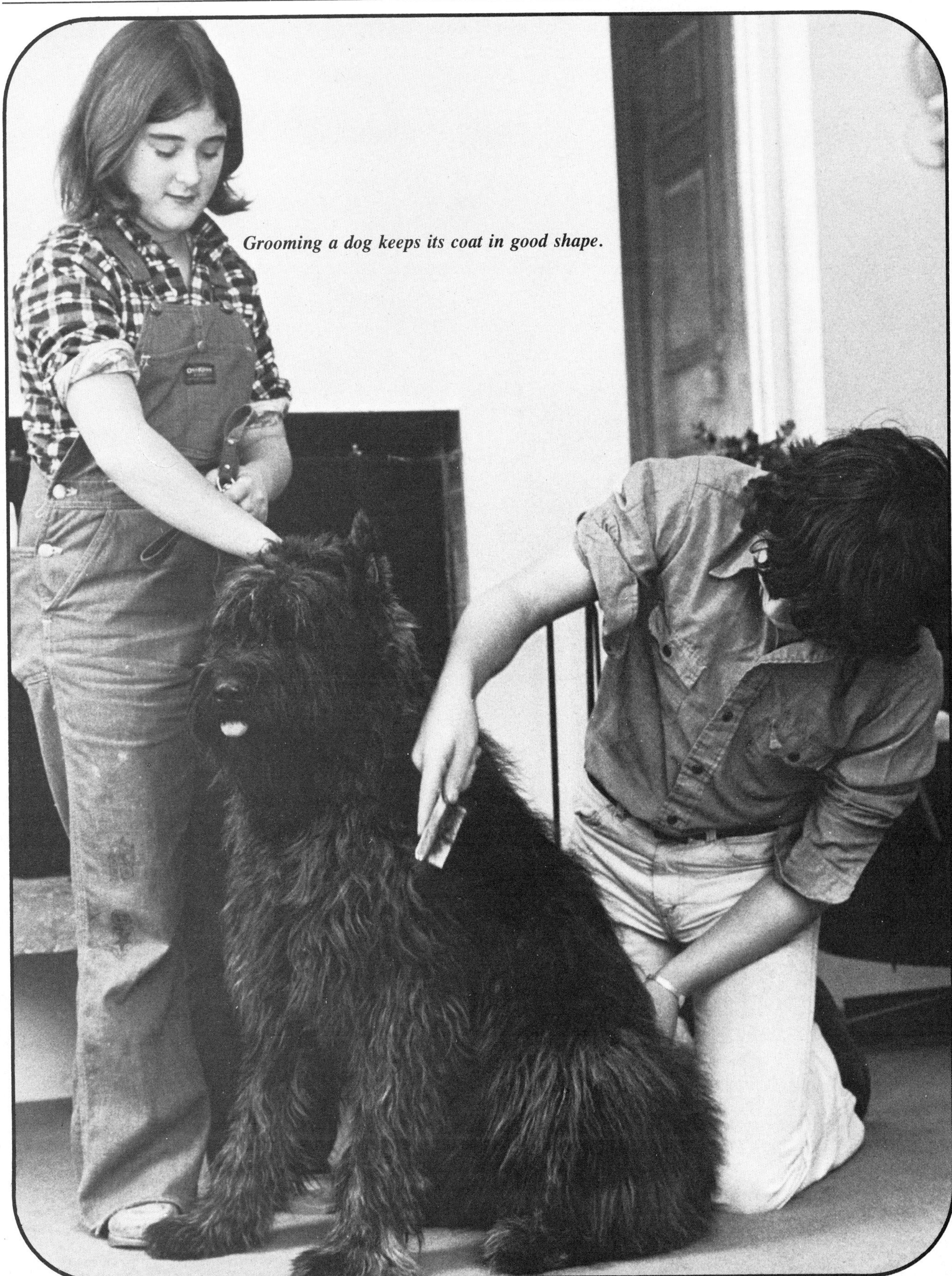

Grooming a dog keeps its coat in good shape.

Backyard Pets

BACKYARD PETS

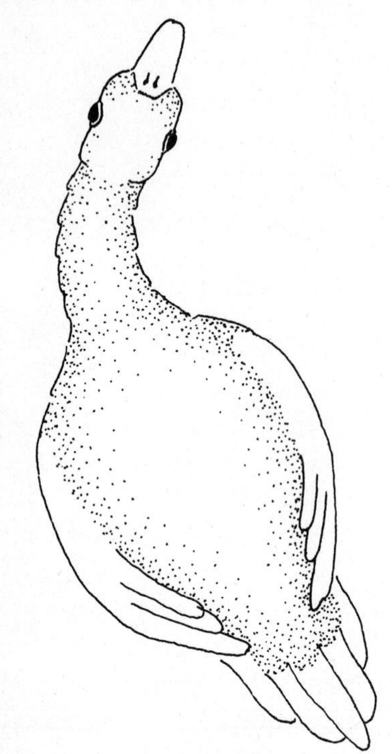

GEESE

Cost:
Goslings—$2.00 to $2.50 each
Older geese—$5.00 to $12.00 each
Mated pair—$50.00

Housing:
Natural shrubbery shelter (no cost).
Or homemade plywood poultry shed—$20.00
Optional mesh door and floor—$12.00
Water bucket—$2.00
Bedding hay for shed—10¢ a week or less.

Special Requirements:
None.

Diet:
For goslings, gosling or duck mash—20¢ per week.
For geese, during the summer, grass (no cost); during the winter, whole dried corn—50¢ per week.
Supplement with discarded outside leaves of salad greens, vegetable peelings, and stale bread or leftover cereals.

Care:
Feed, or allow to graze, refill water bucket daily.

Tamability:
Follow owner about, enjoy human company, defend family from strangers.

Life Span:
15 to 25 years, but could be longer with excellent care.

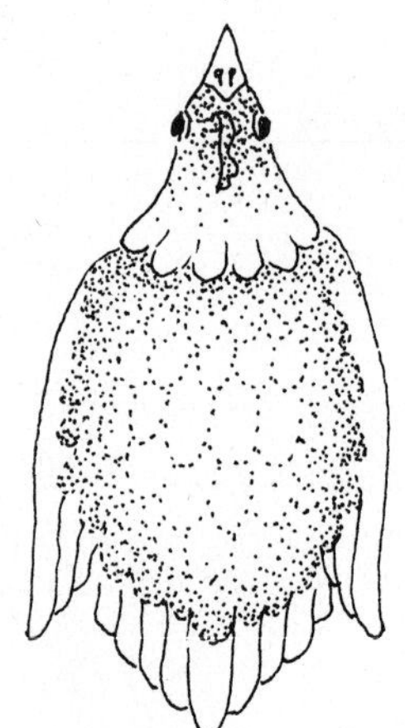

CHICKENS

Cost:
10¢ each, or $2.50 for 25 one-day-old chicks.

Housing:
Natural shrubbery shelter (no cost).
Or homemade plywood poultry shed—$20.00
Optional mesh door and floor—$12.00
Optional homemade nesting baskets—$2.00
Water pan—$1.50
Hay for bedding and nesting in shed—10¢ per week.

Special Requirements:
Newborn chicks require extra heat for first three weeks of life.

Diet:
Chicks, chick mash—2¢ per chick per week.
Older chickens, chicken feed—5¢ per chicken per week.
Supplement with discarded outside leaves of salad greens, vegetable peelings, stale bread or other leftover cereals, and bone meal.

Care:
Feed, refill water pan daily.
Gather eggs daily if they are to be eaten.
Rake bedding from shed floor weekly, and replace with fresh bedding.
Or, for mesh floor, rake droppings from under floor monthly.

Tamability:
Come for food at signal. A single chicken can become devoted to its owner.

Life Span:
Three to four years.

PIGEONS

Cost:
High flyers, tumblers, rollers, or any common "fancy" breeds—

$5.00 to $20.00 a pair, depending on quality.
Homers (racing pigeons)—$25.00 a pair.

Housing:
Homemade plywood coop—$35.00
Water and feed dishes—$3.00
Gravel for coop floor—10¢ per week.

Special Requirements:
Confinement of new pair for first few weeks. Dusting with bird insecticide to prevent lice during hot weather.

Diet:
Pigeon feed—15¢ per week per pair.
Supplement with bone meal.

Care:
Feed, refill water dish daily.
Rake and replenish gravel weekly.
Provide bathing water twice a week.
Scrape and wash inside of coop three or four times a year.

Tamability:
Learn to come for food at signal, and eat from owner's hand. Learn to fly free, and return home each day.

Life Span:
Six to eight years.

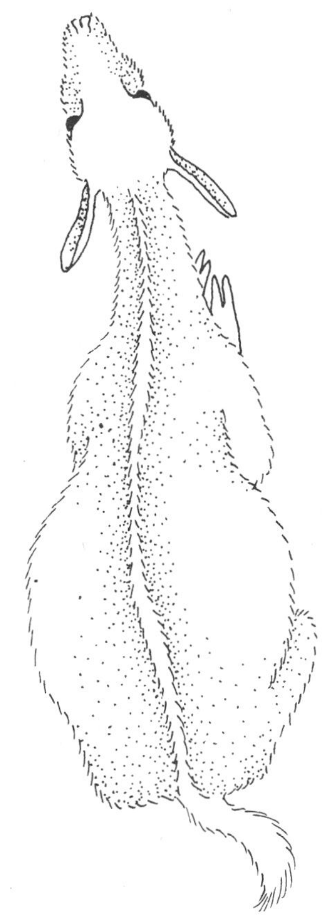

GOATS

Cost:
Male kid—$15.00 to $25.00 (price may or may not include altering, which costs $10.00).
Female kid—$35.00 to $75.00 (cost of the best purebred milkers may be as high as $125.00).

Housing:
Stall in garage or other existing building—$35.00
Or homemade goat shed—$170.00
Optional goat yard attached to shed—$90.00
Stake or hitching ring, chain and collar—$9.00
Feed and water buckets—$4.00
Bedding hay—60¢ per week.

Special Requirements:
Must be staked or fenced to prevent damage to plantings. May have to be dehorned by veterinarian.

Diet:
For kids under three months, cow's milk, calf-starter grain, green hay—$2.00 per week.
For goats over three months, goat grain or chow, green and grass hay—$1.80 per week.

Care:
Feed and water daily.
Spread fresh bedding hay daily.
Stake or fence outside shed or stall daily in good weather.
Clean stall or shed twice a year.

Tamability:
Extremely friendly, devoted and affectionate.
Too obstinate for any training.

Life Span:
12 to 15 years.

Domesticated animals, like a farm cow, and pet animals, like a pet cow, are two entirely different things. A farm cow will remain aloof and dignified, while a pet cow will trot after you mooing for a glug of soda from the bottle you are carrying. A farm goat will lower its horns to a stranger, while a pet goat will case his or her pockets for a cigarette to munch. A farm rooster will cock-a-doodle-doo at sunrise and then go about its own business, while a pet rooster will be into your business, from the vantage point of your shoulder, all day long.

When you consider keeping a backyard animal, better consider whether you want a farm temperament or a pet temperament. The difference is in how you raise it. If you take a partially grown animal and simply care for its creature needs, it will think you are a kind human and leave it at that. Such a relationship is appropriate for those who want goats for goat milk or geese for dinner. But if you take a really young animal and fuss over it, feed it by hand and carry it about, it will think you are the same kind of animal it is—or it is the same kind of animal you are. Either way, you may be in for a more intense relationship than you bargained for.

Backyard Pet Blues

Madeline was a three-week-old Nubian nanny goat, still drinking from a bottle, still small enough to carry in your arms. Who could resist her? Not us. And the fact that she was adorable was, we were told, nothing compared to her utilitarian virtues. She would mow our lawn for us; she would decimate our poison ivy; her droppings, we were advised, made excellent fertilizer.

We took Madeline home in the car. Collar and leash weren't necessary. She followed us eagerly into the car, onto the front seat. She followed us out of the car, in the front door, up the stairs and onto my bed. Madeline was home.

We told Madeline that she had gotten it wrong: indoors was our home; outdoors was her home. She never did get that straight. All of us learned to sidle snakewise in through the door and slam it fast behind us. If we weren't quick enough, she'd be inside and bounding from chair to table to bed to sink. No one had told us how well goats leap and climb.

We felt we could adjust to the situation—after all, who can fail to love so loving a baby. We weaned Madeline from the bottle (well, sort of—she never did grow out of grabbing baby bottles from unwary toddlers) and introduced her to grass and leaves. Then we settled down to await the disappearance of our poison ivy, the neat cropping of our lawn. Madeline started on the flowers.

That was our first lesson—devoted baby goats don't run away from home, but they do eat everything in sight, so they have to be confined. We staked Madeline out on a chain during the daytime when we couldn't supervise her eating. Other times, she was free to follow us on walks along the road and into town for shopping. She never needed a leash. She followed us so reliably, in fact, that we came up with a bad idea.

By now it was fall, and Madeline, true to her Nubian background, had grown small straight horns in her forehead. Jet-black, goatlike, horned and cloven-hoofed. Remind you of something? The Devil! Aha! Halloween! The children decided costumes were not necessary. All they had to do was wait until it was very dark, let Madeline follow them on their round of the neighborhood, ring doorbells, hide to one side, push the goat devil to the forefront and laugh their heads off.

They rang the first bell. They hid to the side of the door. They heard footsteps coming. The hand on the knob. NOW! Madeline leaped into the house, bounded onto a table, snatched what candy she could and disappeared off into the rest of the house.

That was Madeline's last trick-or-treat.

Now we settled down to the serious business of how to keep a pet goat happy outside of family and neighborhood life. We built a six-foot fence around her shed. She leapt it. We put her back on a chain. She broke it. We got a stronger chain and sunk an iron stake far into the ground. She cried—baa baa baaaaaa—to be with us. And that was how we came to know the awful responsibility we are trying to explain to you now: if you take a farm animal and make a pet of it, you become its family. Like a child, it will want to hang around you all the time.

And it isn't only goats. A woman who raised a baby pig in her kitchen has to replace the screen door every time the by now full-grown, milk-cow-sized sow walks through it to visit her home and family. A tiny Easter chick who grew into a rooster tried to spend all his waking hours on his owner's shoulder. A goose and gander, when they grew up, protected their "family" by hissing and making threatening gestures at postmen, meter readers, garbagemen and guests.

If a backyard animal as part of the family doesn't appeal to you, avoid the emotional strain by getting an animal that has been raised in an ordinary farm situation, in an animal family of its own; and get one that you consider a young adult rather than a little baby. The physical care of these animals is the same whether you choose to raise them as pets or as farm animals. As for Madeline, she will always need human company.

Geese

Geese are the all-round best backyard pet. They look terrific, keep the lawn clipped, chase off strangers, companionably join the family at picnics and ball games, and require next to no care. They can live to the ripe old age of 50 years. Geese are considdered to be the most intelligent of the barnyard fowl, and are certainly the most emotional. Geese fall in love—suddenly and often at first sight—long before they are old enough to mate and raise families. A female goose is called a goose, but a male is called a gander. Their babies are goslings. A married goose and gander stay together faithfully until one or the other dies. A widowed gander or goose will search long and sadly for his or her lost love, mourning for months or even years before he or she recovers sufficiently to choose another mate. Both mother and father take care of eggs, nest and goslings. In fact, a goose family is aware that it is a family. All through life adult brothers, sisters, and parents greet one another enthusiastically with stretched necks and noisy gabbling.

Around the yard, one pair of geese—gander walking boldly in front, modest goose behind—will follow you about for sheer company. When you sit down, they'll settle down next to you. When a stranger comes along, the gander will stretch his neck threateningly, hiss and even nip if his threat is not taken seriously. Quite sensibly, however, geese learn to recognize routine visitors, and though they may hiss and threaten, they seldom nip people they know. Occasionally a stranger may get a goose nip, but it is only a pinch at worst.

Choosing Geese

It's cruel to buy only one gosling. Geese are social animals and must have at least one friend to share their love with. The friend need not be of the opposite sex, since two males or two females will become devoted to one another, too. This is fortunate because you can't tell a boy from a girl gosling, and you can only tell a goose from a gander by watching who takes the lead when they walk along, or who is courting whom. The gander both leads and courts. Through ads in poultry magazines, breeders sell by mail order either unsexed goslings or paired young adults who will probably breed the following year. Naturally, goslings are cheaper.

A "married" pair of geese will be more likely to mate and raise goslings of their own if they live in a group rather than by themselves. But there are no hard and fast rules and you may well get a batch of babies every year from a lone pair.

The typical "old gray goose" is either a graylag goose or its larger, plumper descendant, the Toulouse goose. The white Embden is another big variety.

Housing

Two geese, bold as they are, can still fall prey to dogs. A flock of six geese could no doubt keep a dog at bay. If dogs are no problem where you live, or if your yard is fenced, the only construction your geese need is a nesting place (if they are a married pair), and you can use the small shed on page 346. Clean hay is fine for the floor.

If you can't protect your geese from dogs, plan on either a sizable flock that will protect itself, or a fenced-in poultry yard (page 352). If you fence in your geese, however, they will not have enough grazing space and you'll have to feed them either whole dried corn and leftover household greens or grass daily.

Housing itself isn't necessary because geese will find all the shelter they need at the base of whatever shrubbery or hedges you have. Covered as they are in goose down, they are perfectly comfortable in the coldest weather, and fine in the summer too as long as they can settle in the shade when they wish.

Food and Water

Feed newly hatched goslings either commercial gosling food or duck mash bought at a feed store or a mash made from stale bread crumbs and milk mushed together. Within weeks, goslings will be eating grass on their own. From then on, lawn grass is a perfect diet and you have no more feeding problems until winter. During the winter, the geese will still eat dry grass until it becomes covered with snow, but their diet should be supplemented every day with whole dried corn (buy it at feed or pet stores) and leftover greens from your dinners. Stale bread, particularly whole wheat, is healthy, too. It is no myth that geese will weed your garden; it's true, but they will eat the newly sprouting vegetables as well. A fenced garden is suggested.

Geese need a deep container from which to drink, because they plunge their whole head in to fill their bills. Use an ordinary bucket; rinse and refill it daily.

Geese don't have to have water to swim in. The varieties suggested here all live happily out on the lawn, just with the bucket to drink from. That doesn't mean a goose doesn't want to have water to swim in. Our geese met their end at a neighbor's pond, where they had traveled, I believe, to investigate a lakeside nesting area. The neighbor's dog had long since given up on catching wild geese, who simply fly away. But our two fat Embden geese, unable to fly and accustomed to our dogs, hadn't a chance on a strange dog's turf. It's best not to allow your geese to wander.

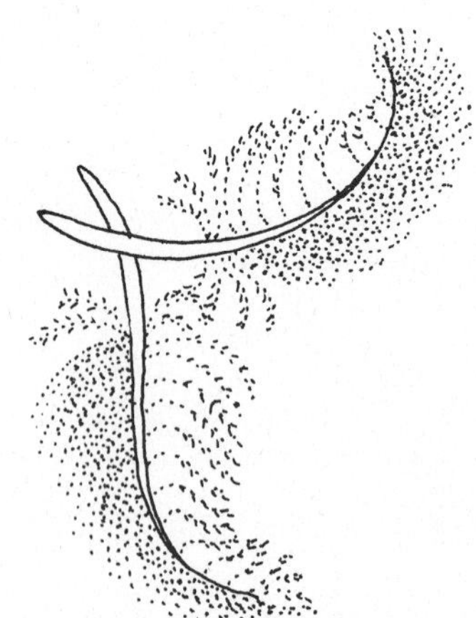

A shed like the one on page 346 will encourage geese to nest. If your geese do nest there (or in some other spot of their choice) and lay eggs in the spring, don't bother the couple while they are incubating (keeping warm) their eggs. If they are disturbed, they may decide they have chosen a dangerous spot and abandon the nest, eggs and all. Once the half-dozen or more goslings hatch, you will see them in a matter of hours following their parents about the lawn in single file. Give them their own lower water dish to drink from, as they won't be tall enough to reach into the bucket. A large crockery dish is fine. Give them gosling feed or bread-and-milk mash until you can tell for sure that they are eating grass.

Illnesses

Geese are among the hardiest of birds. They seldom get sick and quite frequently live to be 25 to 50 years old. If your geese do get sick, only country vets, trained to care for farm animals, will be much help. However, the 4-H Club, which has chapters all over the country, is very helpful in locating someone who can tell you what to do. If you can't get help right away, confine the sick goose in a closed bathroom or in a large carton indoors. Put bird antibiotics (available at pet stores) into its drinking water daily, following the instructions on the label.

If your goose is injured by a dog or breaks a wing or leg, any vet, city or country, can treat it.

Chickens

It was not until this century that chickens (adult females are called hens, adult males cocks or roosters) were mass-produced as food. For 4,000 years prior, chickens were bred for just about everything except meat. The Egyptians first learned how to incubate the eggs of the jungle fowl, ancestor of all our chickens, in nests of heated brick. Necessity was the mother of this invention: all those men working on the pyramids occasioned the need for mass-produced food. So from that time until this century, chickens were raised for their eggs. Of course, excess cocks and old hens (whose laying days were over) were stewed down for food. But what we now know as tender fryers and succulent roasting chickens, both of whom are mere babies (or pullets), were rarely eaten.

The roosters of many of the breeds of chickens have been used through all those centuries for cockfighting, the most universal sport known to man. In spite of the fact that cockfighting is against the law in most of the United States, there are still cockfights every day even in the most unlikely places—for example, in New York City apartments.

After egg production had been perfected, chicken breeders veered off in an exotic direction: show birds. The Japanese bred a rooster with such long tail feathers he had to be kept on the top of a flagpole-high roost so his 30-foot plumes stayed neat. State fairs still give an opportunity to see chickens with extraordinary fluffy hats, chickens decorated with perfectly round white polka dots, chickens of metallic gold or silver hues and scalloped patterns, chickens with fuzzy pantaloons, chickens covered in curls, and chickens whose feathers are so fine they look like hair.

Hens seem to be quarrelsome creatures. When you watch a group of hens choosing a place to roost in the henhouse or deciding who gets to eat first, it appears as though everyone is pecking at someone. Actually, a group of hens arranges itself socially in very strict ways. The bossiest, strongest hen (the most dominant) can and does peck at all the other hens. She pecks them out of her way at mealtimes, at the water dish, and in the roosting area. The second bossiest hen may not peck her, but can and does peck all the others under her. And so it goes to the bottommost, weakest (most subordinate) hen, who is pecked by everybody but may peck no one in return. This social structure is called, logically, a "pecking order."

Roosters don't behave quite the same way as hens. The dominant rooster chooses a big area that belongs to him (his territory) and surrounds himself with the hens of his choice (his harem). He fights off any rooster who enters his territory or bothers his hens. The boldest rooster has the biggest territory and the most hens. He advertises himself and his possessions by crowing. The least of the roosters has no territory and no hens. In fact, his status is so low that he is that most pitiful of barnyard sights: the henpecked rooster. You can see why it is difficult to keep more than one rooster with your flock of hens. The roosters will fight and will probably refuse to share the small winter quarters you have provided.

Choosing a Chicken

An incredible number of chicken breeds are advertised and sold through poultry magazines like *Poultry Journal*. You can even buy the real genuine original—the beautiful jungle fowl, with its rust-red feathers and metallic green and blue tail and neck feathers. For pets, most poultry breeders recommend the pygmy chickens called bantams. They're small, they're cute, they come in many colors and they lay a lot of eggs. Unfortunately, the minimum order for mail-order day-old chicks is usually 25. They are shipped in cartons by airmail, to be picked up at the post office.

Day-old chicks are cheap to buy. Some will grow up to be hens, some roosters. Roosters don't lay eggs and do fight a lot. Practical people avoid inevitable cockfights by killing off the roosters at about five months, when they can be distinguished from the hens by their large combs and wattles. Others save one rooster so they can get more baby chicks without buying. And some are understandably too soft-hearted to do any killing, but simply let the chickens form a natural society running loose in the yard.

You can also buy just hens (again, 25 of them), but they will be pullet-sized instead of cute little yellow fluff balls, and they cost more. At five months, pullets are sort of gangly and adolescent looking.

If you wish to buy less than 25 chicks, you'll have to hunt around at local farms, find neighbors with extra chicks or look in pet stores around Easter time.

Housing

Day-old chicks must be kept warm for at least three weeks before they can be allowed outdoors. Keep them in an uncovered cardboard carton with

The Henpecked Rooster

To be henpecked was the fate of a chicken I once raised from a hatchling. It was one of those Easter chicks sold in pet stores in the spring. Not knowing that poultry of any sort was against the law in the city where I lived, I raised the chick in a cardboard pen in an apartment. He grew up to be a large white insanely devoted rooster who followed my every move from either under my feet or on top of my head. Besides that, he crowed every morning at dawn and was not a good pet for a city apartment.

We decided that during his first summer we would ease him into a more natural life on a farm in the country. But—and this is what I mean about the difference between a pet and a farm animal—he had only lived with people, so he thought he was a human. That poor rooster knew nothing of chicken life. He was attacked by everyone, rooster or hen. Even adolescent pullets pecked him. He would have been killed if we had not found him another human family to live with in the country.

newspaper on the bottom. Big toilet tissue or paper towel cartons from the supermarket are large enough. Cut the sides down to about 18 inches. Provide a shallow pan for chick feed, and another dish for water. Small glass pie plates work well. Sprinkle grit (coarse sand) on the paper. Change the paper, grit, food and water every day.

The box should be kept at 95 degrees the first week, 90 degrees and then 85 degrees the second week, 80 degrees and then 75 degrees the third week. In this way the chicks are gradually accustomed to outdoor temperatures of about 70 degrees. The easiest way to adjust heat is with either the clamp-type light that is used by auto mechanics or a gooseneck lamp. Tape a household thermometer two inches from the floor inside the carton. Adjust the amount of heat by moving the clamp light up or down the side of a chair or table leg near the box, or by bending the gooseneck light up or down. If a regular 40-watt light bulb doesn't heat the box enough, use an infra-red heat bulb instead. The chicks will tell you when they are in distress from either too much heat or too much cold. A contented chick chirps quietly. Distressed chicks peep loudly and shrilly. If they are peeping because they are too cold, you'll probably find them crowding toward the heat source. If they're too hot, you'll find them crowding away from the heat source.

After they are a few weeks old chickens may be left loose outdoors both winter and summer. They have enough sense to seek shelter from rain under shrubbery and to stay close to home where the eating is good. In winter, a simple shelter like the one on page 346 is sufficient for a dozen bantam hens. Keep the floor covered with dry hay. Rake it out once a week and replace with fresh hay. Or use the wire floor on page 349 and rake droppings out from under it every month.

Dogs, cats, and wild animals like foxes and coyotes are more danger to chickens than rain and snow. If you suspect you will have trouble with these animals, build a small poultry yard of four-

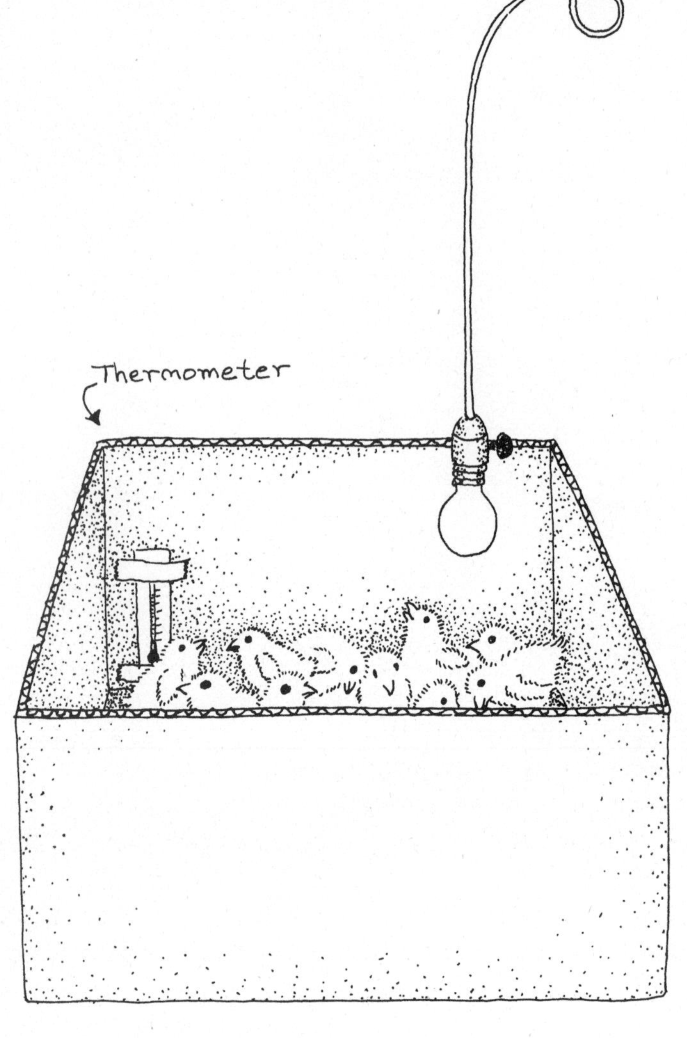

Keep day old chicks warm in a corrugated carton heated with a 40-watt light bulb.

Be sure to hang the light from a chair back or table edge, or by any other method that will keep the hot bulb several inches away from the cardboard.

foot-high chicken-wire netting. The yard needn't be larger than six feet by six feet for a flock of a dozen chickens.

Food and Water

I've seen chickens raised in the rural South without benefit of any commercial food at all. They call them scavenger chickens. Besides the worms, insects, weeds and grass these chickens find for themselves during the summer, they are given the family's leftovers, including meat scraps, bread and vegetables, both cooked and raw. Chickens even eat eggs—cooked and not in the shell.

To be certain of a balanced diet, however, feed baby chicks daily with commercial chick mash, available at feed stores and some pet stores, until they are a month and a half old. Then switch to adult chicken feed, still feeding every day. Once in a while, sprinkle bone meal in with the feed to give extra calcium. Offer fresh raw greens like lettuce when you have them available, and from time to time bones and meat scraps, too. None of the food need go in a pan once the chickens are outdoors. Chickens really prefer to peck their food out of the dust and dirt, and this lets them peck up some natural grit too. The grit is kept in their gizzard (stomach) to help them grind up hard bits of food.

Keep a shallow pan of water out for the chickens. If they are loose in the yard, the easiest place to keep the pan is next to the garden hose, so you can simply rinse it out and refill it every day without troubling yourself too much.

Chickens do take baths, but not in water. They bathe in dust. If you don't provide your chickens with a nice dust patch, they're quite likely to make one for themselves in a flower bed. An ideal bathing area would be a shallow depression about three feet in diameter, filled with fine sand from a pet store or lumberyard. The bathing place won't prevent chickens from pecking about in the garden for juicy worms and beetle grubs, but it may stop them from scooping out bathtubs there.

A nesting box can be built of 8-inch board cut just long enough to make a snug box for the hen. The box doesn't need a floor, but line it with hay.

Egg Laying

Hens begin to lay by the end of their first year during February and March, slacking off during the following winter. The average number of eggs is something over 200 per year, laid at one- or two-day intervals. If you build the small shelter on page 346, you could add two or three wooden boxes to serve as nesting areas. The boxes should be filled with hay. Otherwise, look for eggs under porches, shrubs or any other protected area around your house. Egg hunting is the more exciting way to get your breakfast.

Hens lay eggs whether or not a rooster is available. But without the rooster, the eggs can't hatch into chickens. If you have kept a rooster, all the eggs are likely to be fertile. Kept warm by the broody hens, they will hatch into chickens. If the eggs are to be eaten, you have to get to them fast before the chicks begin to form. A fertilized egg will develop a small red spot on the yolk within 24 hours. The spot is the beginning of the network of blood vessels that will bring nourishment from the yolk to the chick, and the beginning of the chick itself.

For those interested in raising a small flock of chickens for eggs and meat, get in touch with a local chapter of the 4-H Club, your county or state extension service, or a state agricultural college.

Illnesses

Chickens are subject to a large variety of diseases, but these are troublesome mostly to commercial chicken farmers who keep hundreds or thousands of chickens under rather crowded, often indoor, conditions. To prevent disease, farmers include daily doses of antibiotics in the chicken feed—a practice that the medical profession is beginning to doubt the wisdom of (it seems to force bacteria to develop antibiotic-resistant strains, not only in the chickens but eventually in the humans who consume traces of the antibiotics along with the meat they eat). A few chickens living outdoors are less likely to get sick. If a chicken does seem ill, seek advice from a local chicken farmer or feed store or give treatment as for geese.

Pigeons

No doubt pigeons found man before man had bothered to find pigeons. Wherever grain is scattered, whether as bread crusts in the park or oats in the barnyard, flocks of pigeons gather to feed. If there is a loft, a ledge or even a fair-sized windowsill nearby, pigeons move in to stay. Each morning the flock gathers itself together from its night's roosting. A pigeon takes flight, wheeling in circles about the roosting area. Another joins it, and another, until the whole flock—a handful or a hundred—is wheeling in larger and larger, higher and higher circles in the sky. Within a few minutes they choose a direction to a known feeding ground and are on their way to breakfast. The flock spends the morning eating, the noontime resting, and the early afternoon eating some more. By midafternoon, the wheeling flight begins again. When all the members of the flock have joined, they all fly home.

Choosing Pigeons

Pigeons are bought as young mated pairs. They choose mates at four or five months, and shouldn't be over a year old when you get them. Each pigeon should have a leg band that will tell you the date it was hatched. To make it easier for you to train pigeons to come home, buy only one pair at a time.

Pigeon breeders advertise in poultry magazines like *Poultry Journal,* or you might be able to locate breeders through your local 4-H Club. It's a good idea to find a breeder close by, so you can look at what you're getting. A healthy pigeon is active and its feathers look smooth, clean and solid. Signs of illness are ruffled feathers, runny nose or eyes, and inactivity.

There are dozens of breeds of domestic pigeons, all originally descended from the blue rock dove. If you want your pigeons to fly free in a flock during the day and come home again in the afternoon, the best breeds for you are flights, rollers or tumblers. The names describe the birds on the wing: flights fly a lot, rollers roll over and over as they fly, and tumblers tumble downwards in flight—all apparently for the fun of it.

The highest flying pigeons are logically called high flyers. They wheel higher and higher in the sky until they look no bigger than specks. The best homers, of course, are called homers. Each of these pigeon breeds looks somewhat different than

An Internal Homing Device

All pigeons can find their way home from at least several miles away, and in the case of homing pigeons, from hundreds of miles. A pigeon close to home probably finds its way by landmarks, but landmarks are no help when a pigeon is released 300 miles from home in an area it has never seen before.

The mystery of homing is only now being solved. A pigeon, it seems, has a remarkable sense of time, an internal clock more accurate than most watches. In its home area, at a particular time of year and at a particular time of day, the sun is always at a certain spot in the sky. When a pigeon is released away from its home area, its internal clock tells it the right time but its eyes tell it the sun is in the "wrong" place. The pigeons sets its course in a direction that will take it to where the sun "looks right" for that time of day.

the others; some have slimmer bodies, longer necks, smaller heads, shorter beaks or different markings of black or gray on white bodies.

If you are looking for a fancier breed, you can also buy pigeons with feathery leggings, curled plumage, and crests on their heads. You can leave many of these fancy pigeons loose too, not because they always come home, but because they seldom leave home. Most of them have wings too small for long-distance flying. Before you buy, however, check with the dealer as to whether he or she recommends leaving a particular fancy breed free. Any of the varieties of pigeons can share the same quarters.

Housing

The coop on page 350 is large enough for six pairs of pigeons. But pigeons don't roost on the ground like chickens. They will only roost and nest up off the ground, so the shed must be mounted up about five or six feet and the bottom covered with a wooden floor. The illustration on page 351 shows how to mount the shed onto the side wall of a garage or house, with the door facing south. You could also mount a pigeon coop on a tree, like a small treehouse, or even up on a post, like a large birdhouse.

Cold temperatures will not hurt pigeons, but drafts will. Face the coop opening toward the south to get the sun and avoid the wind. If the weather turns windy or bitter in the winter, the wire door should be temporarily covered with burlap, canvas, or plastic sheeting. Use a staple gun to attach it.

The inside of the coop has to be fitted with shelves for roosting and for nesting. Pigeon breeders have rather fancy ways of fixing up the inside of a coop with separate roosting shelves, special nesting boxes and nest bowls. But pigeons can manage with a plain 10-inch board shelf, to which is glued a lattice strip so eggs can't roll off (page 350).

Cover the floor of the coop with a layer of sand. Each week, rake off the droppings and sprinkle fresh sand over the floor. Three or four times a year, scrape droppings from the shelves with a paint scraper or a pancake turner. In the spring, brush all the old sand from the coop and completely replace it.

Food and Water

Pigeon feed, available at feed stores, makes a good diet for pigeons. It is a mixture of whole dried peas, whole dried corn and an assortment of other grains. Like any other bird, pigeons need grit in their gizzards to grind the grain. If you let your birds loose, they'll find their own sand or gravel. You should still sprinkle crushed oyster shell, bone meal or eggshell in with their food once a week to supply minerals.

Serve the pigeon feed in a shallow pan once a day. Usually pigeon owners open the coop and let their birds fly loose early in the morning without feeding them breakfast. Pigeons tend to come home more faithfully if they are a little hungry. The daily meal can be at three or four o'clock in the afternoon, when pigeons naturally settle back at their roosting area. Experiment with the amount, starting with only a handful, until you find a quantity that is finished in about 15 minutes. When the pigeons have young to feed, increase the amount of food.

Instead of filling their beaks and then tilting their heads back to swallow like most other birds, pigeons actually suck up water like horses. Keep a pan of water two inches deep so they can stick their beaks in far enough. Wash and refill the water pan every day. A loaf cake pan is a good shape, because it can be kept under a roosting shelf where it is least likely to be soiled with droppings.

Except when the weather is very cold, put out a roasting pan filled with bathing water in front of the coop several times a week. Pigeons who can't bathe are miserable. Bathing is important for another reason too. When the birds are sitting on their eggs, the moisture from their feathers after a bath moistens the eggshells and softens them somewhat. Without the moisture, the babies can't peck their way out of the hard shell.

Illnesses

Pigeons, while subject to a range of germ-caused diseases, are more likely to be troubled by them in overcrowded conditions rather than in a small flock. Check the illness section under Geese (page 281) for treatment.

In warm weather pigeons routinely get lice, which live both on their bodies and in their nests. To check a pigeon for lice, pick it up and turn it over, belly-up. Stretch out one wing; this is quite easy after a little experience. Lice tend to gather on the undersides of the long wing feathers. They are very small and white. Kill the lice by dusting the pigeon with an insecticide dust intended for birds and available at pet stores, sprinkling the powder on its belly and under its wings, then ruffling the feathers to work the powder down to the skin. Sprinkle the powder in the nesting areas as well.

Flies may become a nuisance in the coop and can really bother newly hatched babies. Hang a Shell No-Pest® insect strip in the highest portion of the coop where pigeons will not peck it.

Another fact of pigeon life is hawks. No matter where you live, even in civilized suburbs or cities, from time to time hawks may dive down and grab one of your pigeons as it emerges from the coop, even if you are standing right there. You can't do a thing about it.

Our smaller hawks—chicken hawks and sparrow hawks—are common birds. And even though pigeons cock their heads to scan the sky for hawks before they take off, they are still caught unaware by the sudden, swift dive. Once in the air they are safe, as pigeons can outfly hawks in ordinary flight.

Breeding Pigeons

Pigeons can (and sometimes do) lay eggs and rear their young throughout the year. But sensible pairs, perhaps understanding that cold temperatures kill pigeon squabs (babies), are most likely in colder climates to lay their eggs during the spring—from March to about June or July. This doesn't mean they only court in the spring. Among the many birds who mate early and remain faithful to one another for life, courtship behavior serves as a bond to remind them they are married. It's about the same as reminder kisses, compliments and candy between human husbands and wives.

Before nesting time the male has found a roost for himself in the coop. He may have had to battle other cocks for the right to his own roost, but once he has it, his property rights are respected. Only his

Pigeons have a homing instinct which allows them to fly free without getting lost.

hen can share his roost with him.

As nesting season approaches, the cock looks for a suitable nest site. In large coops, separate boxes are provided on a different wall from the roosts. In your simple coop, the cock will have to settle for an area of the same shelf on which he has roosted. He and his hen mate only after they have agreed on the nest site. You can usually tell that mating is about to take place when the birds "bill." Billing describes how the hen puts her bill inside the cock's bill to receive a snack of regurgitated grain.

After mating the cock goes out in search of twigs and straw for the nest. He drives his hen to the nest site, where she squats to receive each twig he brings and arranges it to form a circle around her body. Pigeon nests are not works of art. They are only a crude gathering of twigs or grass, but they serve to keep the eggs from rolling.

When the nest is ready, the hen lays exactly two—no more, no less—eggs in her nest. Both parents take turns sitting on the eggs for the two and a half weeks it takes them to hatch. The pair of squabs that hatch are very ugly and very hungry. They will double their weight in 48 hours. Unlike any other birds, pigeons feed their young on "milk," a mixture of partially digested grain

Each pigeon cock finds a roosting place within the coop for his hen and himself.

mixed with nutritious secretions manufactured in their crops (a swollen part of a bird's throat that acts as a sort of stomach). Both hen and cock produce pigeon milk for the first few days, after which both gradually substitute a higher and higher proportion of regurgitated grain. The squabs greedily beg for food by jamming their heads down their parent's throats. As the squabs grow, the cock takes over their care more and more, while the hen lays another set of eggs in a second nest and begins to sit on them. She can repeat the whole process every few months for at least the warm seasons of the year.

By the time the first babies are six weeks old, fully feathered and following their father about the coop, old Dad decides he's had enough of the greedy beggars and begins to fly away from them as they approach. Surprised, the squabs watch him, wondering what to do next. He drinks, he eats; they watch and catch on. Within days the babies are eating and drinking for themselves.

As you can see, young healthy flocks can grow by doubling, tripling or more each year. What do you do about it? This small coop of yours will run out of roosting and nesting space quickly, and the result will be fights, trampled eggs and fallen squabs. You can either build larger quarters or give the young pigeons to friends or a pet store.

Training Pigeons

Each new pair of pigeons has to learn that the coop you built is home. When you buy a new pair, keep them in the coop together for a month. If you already have other birds flying free, you'll have to confine the new pair in the coop inside a temporary cage. The cardboard cage illustrated here is strong enough, and is set up with food and water dishes of its own.

Male and female pigeons, like most birds, are called cocks and hens. You can't tell male from female by their colors; you can only tell by their behavior. The male puffs his throat, coos and struts. He eats and drinks more aggressively than the female. He may be larger, and his neck looks thicker (because he is puffing it) than the female's neck.

Supply yourself with a commercial wire cage, a wire milk carrier or even a large wire bicycle basket. After the month, reach in the temporary cage and grab the hen. Grab fast, using both hands to wrap around the hen's whole body. As long as your hands are around her wings, she can't hurt herself

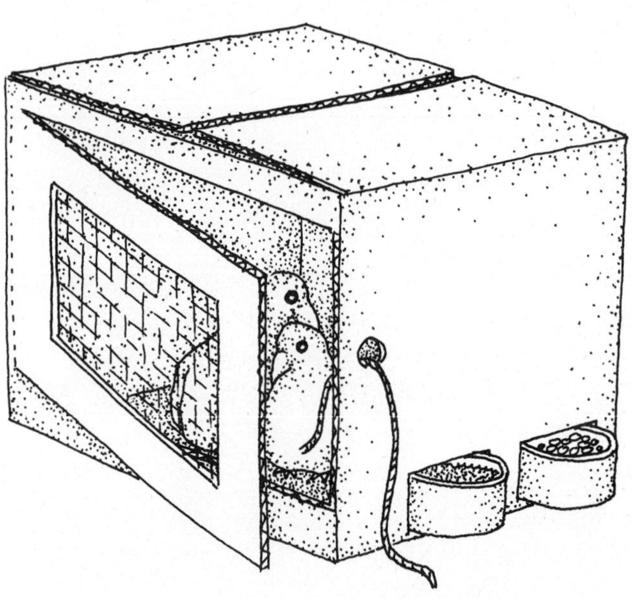

A Temporary Cardboard Pigeon Box

1. Glue the flaps closed. Cut the door in one side of the box. Staple hardware cloth over the cut-out portion. Tie the door shut with string as shown.
2. Cut snug slots for food and water dishes and slide them part way through so they don't tip over.
3. Cover the floor with newspaper or with sand.
4. To make this box last longer, spray or brush on three coats of varnish inside and outside.

by struggling. Put the hen under the wire basket or in the wire cage on the open ground in front of the coop. Let the cock fly out of the coop. A cock pigeon is very reluctant to lose sight of his hen. He's not likely to go far—he'll probably sit on a tree or roof nearby or even on the coop, so he can keep his eye on his hen. When you want him to come back into the coop, put the hen back inside and he'll fly in to join her. After a week of repeating this routine every day, both the cock and the hen can be let loose to fly, as by now their attachment to home is very strong, and the cock has had a chance to learn some local landmarks.

Pigeons easily learn to recognize their owner and even to come to his or her whistle. As often as you have the time, feed your pigeons by hand instead of putting their grain into the grain pan. At first, sprinkle the food on the coop floor near you. Gradually sprinkle less and less on the floor and keep more and more in your open hand. The bolder cocks will probably be the first to come to your hand, but the hens will soon follow. Each time you feed your birds, whether from your hand or in the pan, whistle to them as you arrive with dinner. They will associate the whistle with feeding time, and eventually you will be able to call your flock from the sky. They will all swoop down and settle about you and on you, eating without fear from your open palm.

Goats

Smaller goats are better for backyards than larger ones. Even a small goat is very strong and can leap high. But goats are not that easy to find, and you may not have much choice as to breeds. If you do, most people find the prettiest goat to be the Nubian, the only breed with long pendulous ears and a delicate Roman nose. The Alpine and the Toggenburg are both rather large goats with upright ears and dish faces (curved in instead of out). A hard-to-find but wonderful pet goat is the African pygmy, a dwarf breed that is usually shades of warm brown and beige.

Choosing a Goat

If state fairs are held near you, by all means go to see these breeds and others. The breeders will be happy to talk to you about buying a baby. Another way to get in touch with breeders is through a local 4-H chapter, an agricultural college or the American Dairy Goat Association. (This association changes its address with each new president. The other organizations can give you the latest address.) Local farm-zoos may sell extra baby goats in the spring. Many of them raise the African pygmy.

Goats are ready to be weaned onto grass and grain by about one month old. A nanny goat is a nice pet and will give milk for most of the year if she is bred each winter.

Far cheaper is the billy goat, whom no one wants. Goat farmers only keep one or two billy goats for breeding purposes. They smell bad and act mean. Those that aren't kept are usually killed. Once castrated, these otherwise doomed babies make excellent pets and can be had for little more than the cost of the operation. Although castrating assures they won't be aggressive adults, there will still be some billy goat smell.

If you're able to spend a lot of time with a pet goat, it's all right to have just one. But goats so crave companionship that you may feel unable to live with one lonely goat's plaintive bleating. Better to have two, so they can keep each other company when you're too busy for them. Sex doesn't matter—two castrated billy goats, two nanny goats, or one of each will be friends.

Housing

People have kept goats in everything from oversized dog houses to basements. Assuming a goat spends time outside, it needs no more than a space four feet by five feet to eat and sleep in. Page 353 suggests a scheme for building a stall for one goat in a garage, and page 354 gives instructions for a free-standing shed large enough to house two goats.

Goats have a thing about getting wet—they hate it. Put the shed on a high and dry bit of land. The open front faces south for sun, the closed back protects the goat from wind. No heat is necessary. The floor can be dirt, but sand drains better.

Spread hay on the floor for bedding. The hay will trap and absorb urine, and the small, dry goat droppings will work their way down under the bedding. Each day, cover the old hay with a fresh layer. As time goes by and you keep adding layers of dry hay, the floor will get higher and higher. Within six months, the floor will have grown to nearly two feet high. Then it's time to clean the goat shed.

Rake out all the old bedding until you're down to dirt or sand or the garage floor again. The old bedding, left outside in a heap to finish decaying, will make good compost for the garden next season. Add a layer of dry hay to the shed floor and begin the process over again. You can see that a goat shed is easy to care for, since cleanup time comes only twice a year.

Confining a goat is more difficult than housing one. A goat can't live in a shed all the time. It needs exercise. But on the loose, goats are destructive eaters. There are two solutions. One is to chain a goat; another is to build a goat yard.

If you have just one goat, you can chain it to the doorway of its shed. This way it can decide whether it wants to be outside exercising or inside resting in the shade or warmth of the shed. See page 296 for instructions for chaining.

When you stake your goat in an open area, you'll have to remember to bring it out in decent weather and put it back inside when it rains. In very cold weather, goats prefer to stay in the stall or shed.

I know one goat that has learned not to get himself wound about the tree he is chained to. Provided you keep your eye open at first for trouble, you could try a tree instead of a stake. If you have more than one goat, you will have to stake them at a distance from one another to prevent tangling, or build the goat yard on page 361.

Food and Water

When a kid is a month old—the time you are likely to buy one as a pet—it may still be drinking milk. The milk can be cow's milk, and two pints of milk a day are enough. Heat the milk in a saucepan to 103 degrees (use a household thermometer) and serve it to the kid either in a dog's dish or a bowl, or from a baby's bottle equipped with a crosscut nipple. A bottle is really not necessary, but it's fun to feed a kid that way. The rest of the kid's diet can be a calf-starter grain, sold at feed stores, and hays like timothy and alfalfa, too. A kid's stomach is still very small, so offer three or four small meals a day to be sure it eats enough.

Milk isn't needed at all by the time a kid is three months old; now it can go onto a steady diet of goat grain mixes and hay. Good nutritious hay is greenish in color and has a variety of leaves in it. In other words, it's not just dry yellow stalks, which goats won't even bother to eat. The best hays are legume crops like clover, alfalfa and soybean. Roughage is necessary to a goat's digestion, so hay is the staple diet of goats when they can't browse in a meadow. Goats prefer to nibble their food from high places—like leaves from a bush. They do a more thorough job of eating their hay if it's kept up high off the floor of their shed.

A simple way to manage this if you don't want to build a fancy manger (hay feeder) is to buy a big wire bicycle basket, mount it on the shed wall and put an armful of fresh hay into it every morning. Goat Chow® or a goat grain mixture—about a pound or a coffee can full each day—can be served in a small bucket hung from a hook screwed into the wall.

A bucket is a convenient way to serve water too. If you just put the bucket on the shed floor, the goat will promptly knock it over. Put a stout hook into the wall to hold the bucket handle. The hook

For anyone with enough space, Nubian goats make affectionate pets.

should be just high enough from the floor so that the bucket rests on the floor but can't tip.

If you let them, goats eat anything that is basically vegetable. That includes paper (made from trees) and cigarettes (made from leaves). They don't eat tin cans, but they do nibble the paper labels from them. They adore roses and other flowers, ornamental shrubbery, fruit trees and garden vegetables. If this were not misfortune enough, they also haven't the sense to keep away from an array of poisonous plants, any of which can make them sick or even kill them if they eat enough of them. A partial list of poisonous varieties includes: buttercup, cowslip, lily of the valley, foxglove, laurel, rhododendron, bracken fern, dry or wilted wild cherry or oak leaves, delphinium and yew. Feel free, however, to let your goat eat up all the poison ivy and poison oak around. We used to lend Madeline out to friends for a day's nibbling on their ivy patches. But beware of your own reaction to both plants: the poison oils left on your goat's skin are enough to cause a rash on your skin.

You may be interested in getting delicious milk from your nanny goat. It really is nice, and you can get two quarts a day per goat for about nine months of the year for far less than you pay for cow's milk. You can also make several cheeses, especially a soft pot cheese, quite easily. Of course, neither cows nor goats produce milk unless they have babies every year. For more information about this practical side of goat owning, write to your own state or county extension service, your state agricultural college or a local 4-H Club.

Illnesses

Goats don't need any inoculations and suffer from few diseases. A vet that has been trained to care for farm animals can help you if anything does go wrong. Again, the 4-H Club can usually tell you which vets in your area have had experience with farm animals.

Worms are fairly common and can be detected and treated by any vet if you give him some fresh goat droppings to check under the microscope.

Flies are a nuisance in warm weather, but using an insecticide to get rid of them is worse. Goats will nibble on flypaper and spray-soaked wood. The insecticides in these are poisonous. Better to clean out the goat shed or stall weekly in the summer if the flies get unbearable.

Some goats are naturally hornless, but most have to be dehorned. Madeline kept her horns with no disasters, except that playful butting was occasionally misinterpreted by nervous mothers. Even in play a horn could hurt, and two goats kept together might hurt each other. Dehorning is not a job for the amateur. Ask for a dehorned goat, or try to find a vet who knows how to do it. The operation is done with the most success and the least pain during the kid's first weeks of age.

How to Chain a Goat

Unless you build a goat yard, you will have to chain your goat when it is outside its stall or shed. If you have more than one goat, they will have to be chained at a good distance from one another so they don't get tangled up.

You can chain a goat to the wall of its shed or another convenient building, or to a stake in the ground. The area you choose should be free of shrubs, trees or any projections your goat could get caught on. If you decide to chain your goat to a building, use a hitching ring that is attached to either a bolt or a plate. If you will be chaining your goat out in an open area, use the spiral stakes sold for tying dogs outside.

Measure your goat's neck around the narrow portion behind its head. At a pet store, buy a flat, wide leather dog collar to fit; then buy a dog leash clasp, two S-hooks, 10 to 12 feet of twisted chain, and a hitching ring or stake at a hardware store.

Put the stake into the ground, or secure the hitching ring to the building. Attach one end of the chain to the stake or ring with an S-hook. Close the S-hook tightly with pliers. Attach the swivel-type dog leash clasp to the collar, and then to the free end of the chain with another S-hook.

Check to make sure your goat can't pull its head out of its collar, and then chain it up. Stay around at first to watch your goat, making sure it can't get its chain tangled anywhere.

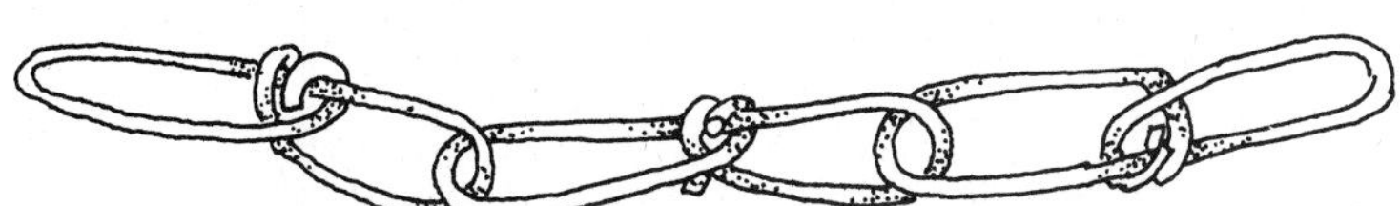

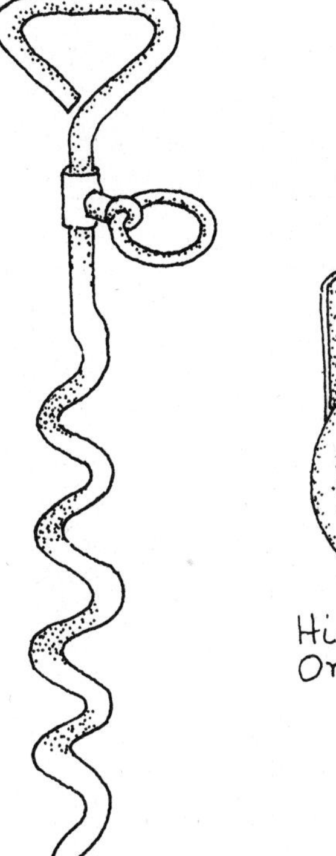

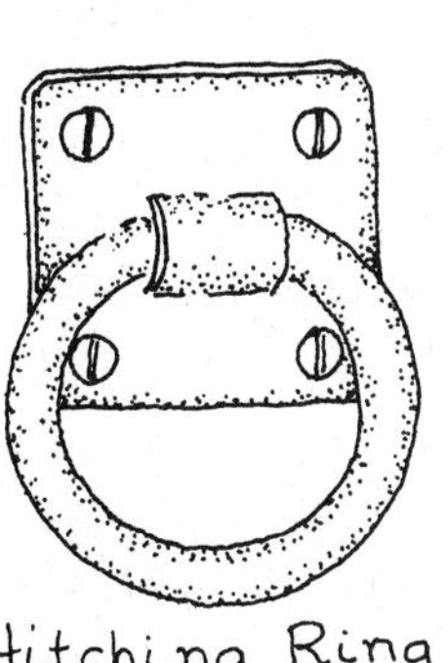

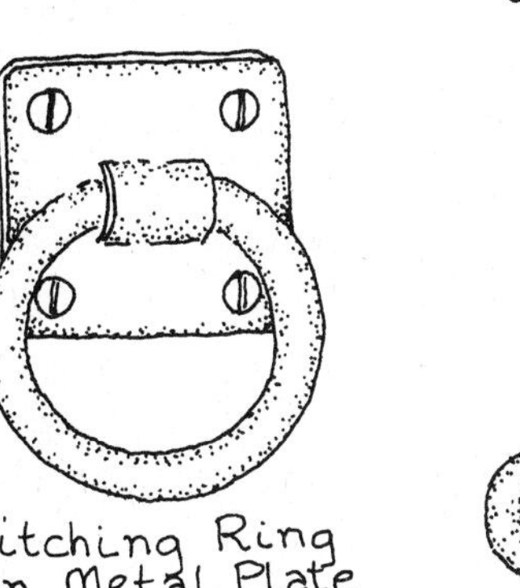

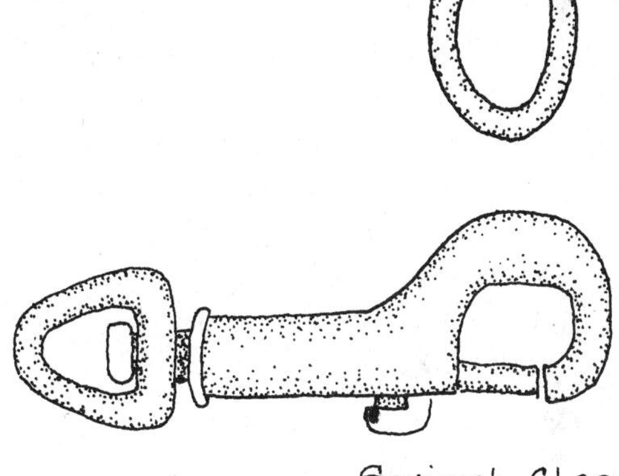

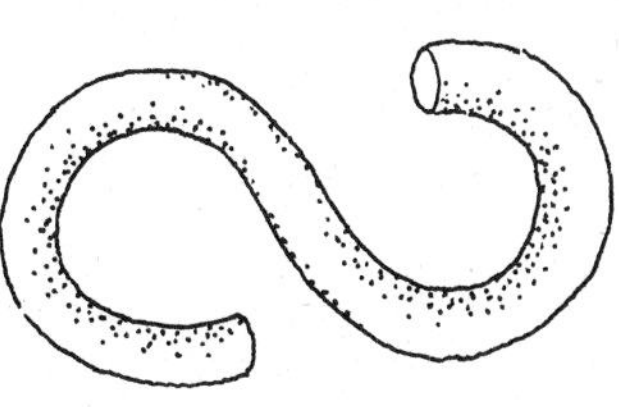

Ready Homes Construction

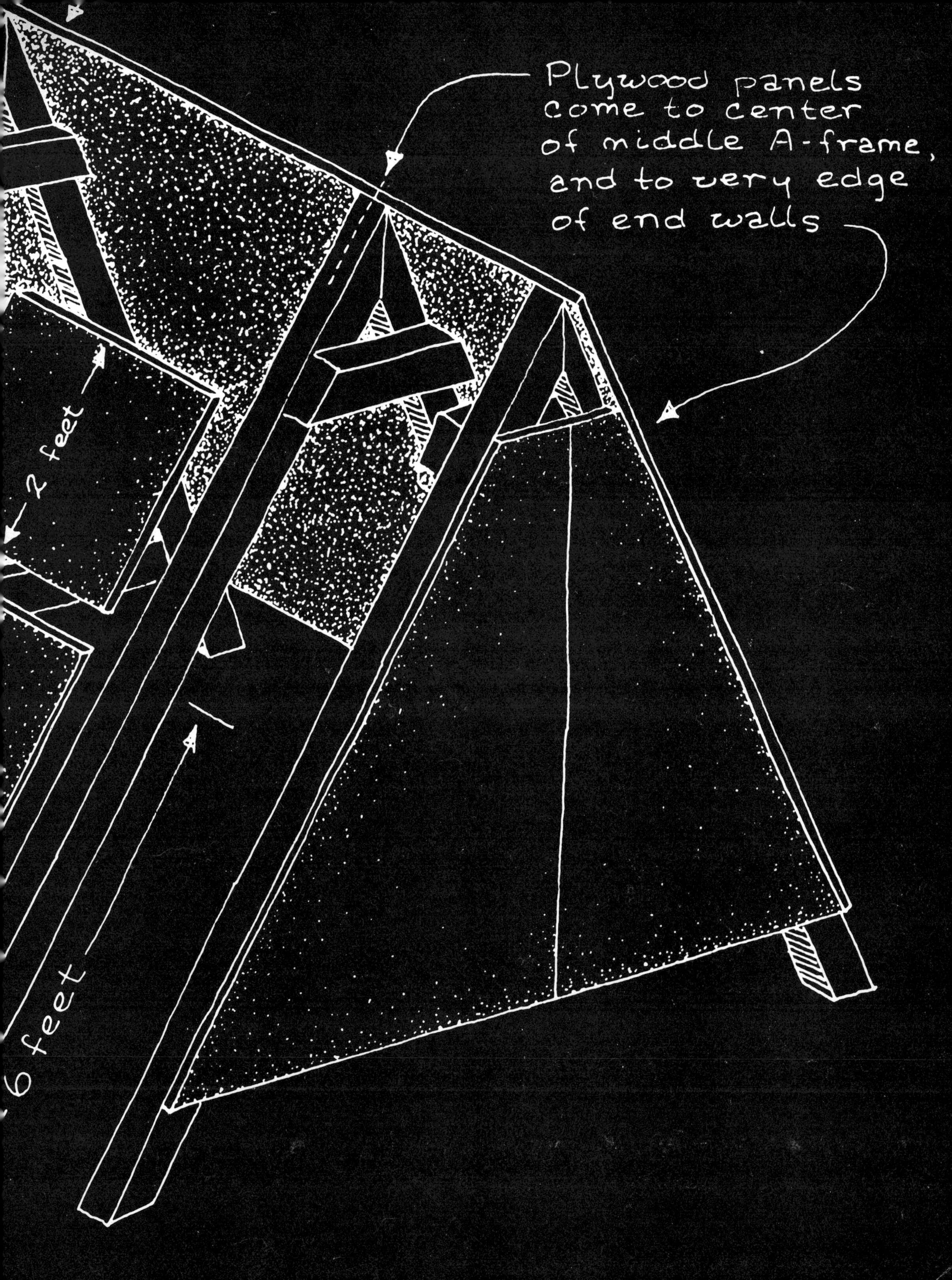
Plywood panels come to center of middle A-frame, and to very edge of end walls
2 feet
6 feet

Ready Home Construction

CHART: COSTS

Lumber:

¾-inch interior-grade plywood 4 by 8 feet — $19.20 per sheet
¾-inch exterior-grade plywood 4 by 8 feet — $20.00 per sheet
½-inch interior-grade plywood 4 by 8 feet — $14.56 per sheet
½-inch exterior-grade plywood 4 by 8 feet — $15.36 per sheet
¼-inch (nontempered) Masonite 2 by 4 feet—$1.68; 4 by 4 feet—$3.36
¼-inch pegboard 2 by 4 feet—$2.28; 4 by 4 feet—$4.56
6-inch shelving—31¢ per lineal foot
8-inch shelving—41¢ per lineal foot
10-inch shelving—51¢ per lineal foot
2-inch lattice stripping—13¢ per lineal foot
1-by-2-inch lumber (spruce)—5½¢ per lineal foot
1-by-3-inch lumber (spruce)—7½¢ per lineal foot
2-by-4-inch lumber (spruce)—22¢ per lineal foot
½-inch dowel (36-inch piece)—28¢
¾-inch dowel (36-inch piece)—62¢
Round fence post (8-foot, spruce or hemlock)—$3.30 each
4-by-4-inch fence post (8-foot)—$4.72 each
Tool handle (hardwood, grub-hoe length)—$3.40

Hardware:

6-foot steel posts—$2.25 each
1-by-2-inch galvanized welded wire fence (4 feet high)—75¢ per lineal foot
36-inch chicken (poultry) wire, 25-foot roll—$7.15; 50-foot roll—$13.70
6-inch T-hinge—$2.65 a pair
3-inch straight hinge—$2.65 a pair
Hook and eye closure—29¢
Galvanized roofing nails, ⅞ inch—67¢ per pound
Common nails (from 1 to 5 inches)—75¢ per pound
2-foot wire window screen—44¢ per foot
36-inch hardware cloth (¼- or ½-inch mesh)—$.90 per foot
48-inch hardware cloth (¼- or ½-inch mesh)—$1.20 per foot
Window glass—75¢ per square foot (price increases with size)
¼-inch plexiglass—$2.75 per square foot
Double aluminum sliding track (cost includes entire assembly)—$3.50 per foot
Cheesecloth—59¢ per small package
Sandpaper—30¢ per sheet
2-inch brush—$1.00
3-inch brush—$1.80
Creosote—$1.59 per quart
Shellac—$1.79 per pint
Exterior enamel paint—$4.99 per quart
Masking (freezer) tape, 1 inch wide—$1.00 per roll
Friction tape, 1 inch wide—80¢ per roll
White glue—39¢ per small bottle
Epoxy glue—$1.09 per tube
Silicone glue—$2.69 per tube
Soft wire—79¢ per spool
Asphalt shingles—$7.75 per bundle (covers 33 square feet)

Roofing paper—$9.85 per roll (covers 432 square feet)
12-by-18-inch roasting pan—$2.79 each
8½-by-8½-inch cake pan—$1.20 each
8-by-12-inch cake pan—$1.59 each
Door pull handle—29¢ each
Metal utility shelf—$2.59
5-inch angle irons—40¢ each

Pet Store Equipment (Also found in some feed stores, plant departments, etc.):
5½-gallon tank—$8.00
10-gallon tank—$10.00
18-gallon (tall) tank—$22.00
Mesh top for 5½-gallon tank—$3.50
Mesh top for 10- or 18-gallon tank—$4.00
Incandescent light for 5½-gallon tank—$6.50
Incandescent light for 10- or 18-gallon tank—$7.50
Fluorescent light for 5½-gallon tank—$17.00
Fluorescent light for 10- or 18-gallon tank—$20.00
Vita-Lite® bulb for 5½-gallon size—$4.00
Vita-Lite® bulb for 10- or 18-gallon size—$5.00
Glass top for 5½-gallon tank—$3.00
Glass top for 10- or 18-gallon size—$3.50
Inside corner filter box—$1.00
Outside filter box—$4.00
Plastic tubing—10¢ per foot
Air pump—$4.00
Bone carbon charcoal—$1.50 per pound (or 1 lb. box)
Filter fluff—99¢ per 4 oz. package
Fish net—50¢
No. 0 grade gravel—10¢ per pound
No. 1—No. 5 grade gravel—15¢ per pound
Dyed (colored) gravel—39¢ per pound
Tank thermometer—$1.00
Thermostatically controlled tank heater—$3.00 and up
Bubble stone—39¢
Chlorine remover—79¢ per bottle
Siphon (rubber-bulb type)—$2.00
Water plants: Vallisneria—10¢ each or $1.00 a bunch
Brazilian sword—$1.50 each
Anachris, Creeping Charlie—79¢ per bunch
Banana plant—59¢ each
Lead water-plant weighting wire—39¢ per package
Decorative rocks—25¢ per pound
Driftwood—$4.00 per piece
Crockery dishes, 3-inch—$1.00; 4-inch—$1.50; 6-inch—$2.00; 8-inch—$2.50; 10-inch—$3.50
Water bottle: small size for rodents—$2.00; large for rabbits—$3.50 (Both are ball-bearing type.)
Tube-shaped bird food and water containers—79¢ each
Metal bucket—$2.00 each
Pine shavings—79¢ per bag
Dog-leash swivel hook—$1.00
Hitching rings: bolt type—$1.00; plate type—$1.00
Twisted chain—20¢ per foot
Corkscrew dog (or goat) stake—$1.50
Flat leather goat collar—$4.00
Plants—69¢ per 2-inch pot
2-inch plastic pots—45¢ each
Sterilized potting soil—$1.29 per small bag
Plant mister—$1.50

Often the obstacle to owning a pet is not how to get the animal, but what to keep it in. In some cases, excellent commercial cages are available in pet stores. This chapter will tell you how to set them up with all the comforts of home. In other cases, the basic containers are available—glass-walled tanks, for instance—but you will need to know how to transform them into suitable environments for the many different needs of the pets they can house. In still other cases, there are no commercial cages available, or the ones that are could stand great improvement. This chapter gives instructions for a variety of homemade cages that are as inexpensive, simple and practical as possible.

The simplest homes are ones that house pets only temporarily. They are an assortment of containers that can be kept on hand to take care of pets you will keep for a night or so, and then let go.

Permanent homes for pets who have few special needs are cheaply and easily made. These include cake-pan homes for rodents, hutches for guinea pigs and rabbits, and some of the tank homes. Other permanent pets have special needs that require rather expensive lighting and heating equipment, though the setting up or construction is still easy.

A few homes require both expensive materials or equipment and hard, sometimes skilled work. Homes for backyard pets in particular need accurate construction and may run up a substantial bill at the lumberyard.

Stay with the simple projects until you get used to measuring accurately and handling tools. Before you get to homes that require carpentry skills, there is much to learn.

Measuring

Accurate construction with lumber requires special measuring techniques. You can't precut all the pieces before you start to build. Instead, cut and build only the outside frame or basic shape of the house. When that's done, any pieces of lumber that are to be added—such as shelves, floors, bracing pieces, doors—must be held against the place where they are to fit, and marked with a pencil. Then they can be sawed along the pencil line and nailed in place.

There are two reasons for using this method. One is that no matter how well you measure the basic pieces that make up the frame of your construction, you will never saw absolutely accurately. Sawing just a hair to one side or another of your pencil line will change the overall dimensions of your building. If, for instance, you had precut a shelf that was to fit inside that building, the shelf could easily turn out either too long or too short to fit snugly.

The other reason is that the dimensions of lumber vary from one part of the country to another, from one lumberyard to another, and even from one shipment to another. The nominal dimension of a piece of lumber—a 2 by 4(two by four inches), for example—is not the same as the actual dimension, which may be 1⅝ by 3⅝ inches, or slightly less, or slightly more.

Another note on measuring and marking lumber: if you are using a yardstick, check it first along the edge of a sheet of plywood or some other surface you are sure is straight. Many yardsticks are warped and will give you a curved pencil line instead of a straight one. Long steel rulers are more accurate than yardsticks, and if anyone in your family knows how to use a chalk line, this is the most reliable tool of all for long, perfectly straight marking.

Cutting

A few projects, like birdhouses and hutches, may be made from scraps of lumber to save the cost of buying large plywood sheets or long boards. If you can't find large enough scraps around your home ask at lumberyards. Some keep a scrap bin of pieces that could be used for these projects. You may be able to find just what you need and not have to cut at all. Also, most lumberyards will cut lumber for you at an extra cost of only a few cents per cut.

If you do your own cutting, narrow lumber—shelving or 2 by 4s—is not too hard to cut along a pencil line with a handsaw. It is very hard to cut plywood straight with a handsaw, no matter how well you have marked it. The job should be done with an electric circular saw, but only by someone who has experience using this dangerous tool. If no one in your family feels comfortable with the work, or if you have no saw, a neighbor might help. Once the measuring is done, the sawing itself goes quickly.

Nailing

To be sure pieces fit before they are permanently attached, tack them together with nails that are hammered only part of the way in. Then check the tacked-together piece against the basic construction. If the fit is good, hammer the nails all the way in; or if the instructions call for gluing, remove the nails and apply the glue before renailing. If the fit isn't right, you can make adjustments before you glue and nail permanently.

Use nails that are two and a half to three times longer than the thickness of the wood you will be hammering through. All the following animal homes use what are called common nails, unless

Nail through thinner piece into thicker piece of wood

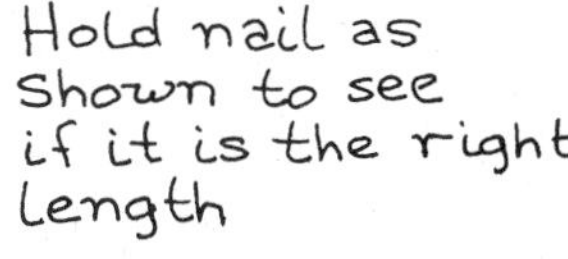

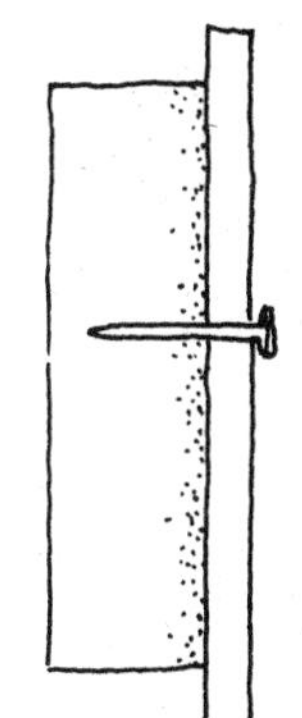

otherwise specified. Common nails are sold by the pound: there are 150 2¼-inch nails in a pound, fewer longer nails, and more shorter nails. A quarter of a pound of nails is enough for a birdhouse, about a half-pound for any of the small sheds, and a whole pound for the goat shed.

Materials

The plywood for any outdoor housing must be what is called exterior grade. The layers (laminations) of interior-grade plywood will become unglued and split apart after a few rains. Shellac your buildings before you paint them, both to protect the wood and to seal it so the paint covers it more easily.

Some of the animal housing calls for hardware cloth (wire mesh) attached to wood. The easiest way to attach it is with a stapling gun, which can be rented inexpensively by the day from many lumberyards. If possible, an adult should do the stapling, as these guns force the staples out under great pressure, and can be quite dangerous if carelessly used. Before starting on a project requiring a staple gun, make sure you can rent or borrow one easily.

Hardware cloth is sold by the foot from rolls 36 inches wide or wider. It is available in hardware stores and lumberyards. For small projects like the ones in this chapter, you must be sure the cloth is not warped before you ask the clerk to cut it. Many home tool chests don't contain the big wire shears needed to cut hardware cloth. Since shears are expensive, try to borrow some, or ask the clerk to cut the piece you are buying to the right dimensions for your project with his or her shears while you are in the store.

Hardware

Some of the roofs and all of the doors in these projects are attached with hinges. Be sure to leave enough space between the two pieces of wood so the hinge works freely. Take your time installing hinges, because any crookedness at all makes the hinge bind instead of swinging easily. The screws are much easier to put in if you first make a hole smaller than the screw with a nail or drill. The same is true when installing hooks and screw eyes, which are used to close all the cage or house doors in these projects.

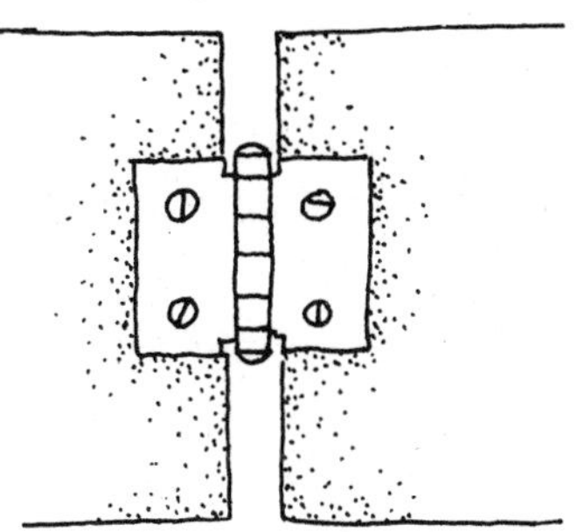

Leave space between the two pieces of wood when installing hinges

Posts

Some of the projects call for putting posts or stakes into the ground. This is a hard job. For wood posts, use 4-by-4-inch lumber or round fence posts. Paint the bottom two feet with creosote, a natural tarry substance which protects the wood from moisture and kills the bacteria that might otherwise rot the post bottoms. Common steel posts come prepainted for weather protection, and have hooklike protrusions for attaching wire fencing. For any post, dig the hole two feet deep. While a friend holds the post upright in the hole, you wedge it firmly in place with rocks. Then fill in soil around the post and stamp it in hard with the heel of your shoe.

Quantities

We have tried to give you accurate estimates of how much lumber, hardware cloth and other materials you will need to complete a job. For some of the smaller projects, like a birdhouse or a bug house, it would be wasteful to buy whole sheets of plywood or long lengths of lumber or window screening. Instead, try to find scraps that will fit the pattern. Many lumberyards keep a box full of small leftover pieces of lumber, or often neighbors who are building something in their home will have scraps of materials they really don't want. Bigger projects list the materials you will need in terms of standard dimensions—4-by-8-foot plywood sheets, for example, or 8- or 10-foot lengths of board and lumber, or standard roll widths of hardware cloth. In these projects, there will be some unavoidable waste of materials.

Costs

The biggest problem to us has been to give you an accurate idea of what each project will cost. Prices may be higher or lower where you live, and they may differ from month to month. Also, we don't know if you have on hand many of the common materials that are needed—masking tape, wire, white glue, nails and so on. The approximate cost we have given you for each project includes all the lumber (even if some could be waste scraps) and all the other materials (even though you might not have to buy everything in the list). Costs also include all necessary accessories such as water bottles and feeding dishes. Optional accessories are listed separately in charts. If some of the items in the list are already in your home, the cost of the project will be lower than our estimate.

The estimates don't include tools. If you don't have the tools that are necessary for a job, try to borrow them. Buying new tools would add a lot on to the cost of each job.

Attracting A Pet In The Wild

The best way to attract pets in the wild is with food. But for the most part there is no reason to build shelter or feeding stations for wild animals—a garbage can or a garden suits them fine. The exceptions are some songbirds, who appreciate the shelter of a birdhouse during nesting time, and the convenience of a feeding station during the winter.

Birdhouses ($10.00)

Wild birds will enthusiastically nest in a birdhouse you build. They don't see the building as a house, only as a safe, dry nook (much like a hollow tree) in which to build a nest. Birds only live in nests during the few springtime weeks when they are laying eggs and raising their young. But a birdhouse looks pretty even when it is unoccupied.

You can design a birdhouse in any shape you want so long as the entrance hole is the right size, a perch is provided, and the house is located properly. Parent birds will be too disturbed to care for their young if the house is placed where people are always coming and going. You can put a birdhouse close by or even attached to a human home, but don't put it near a doorway, path or gate.

This plan is for a basic pitch-roofed house that is

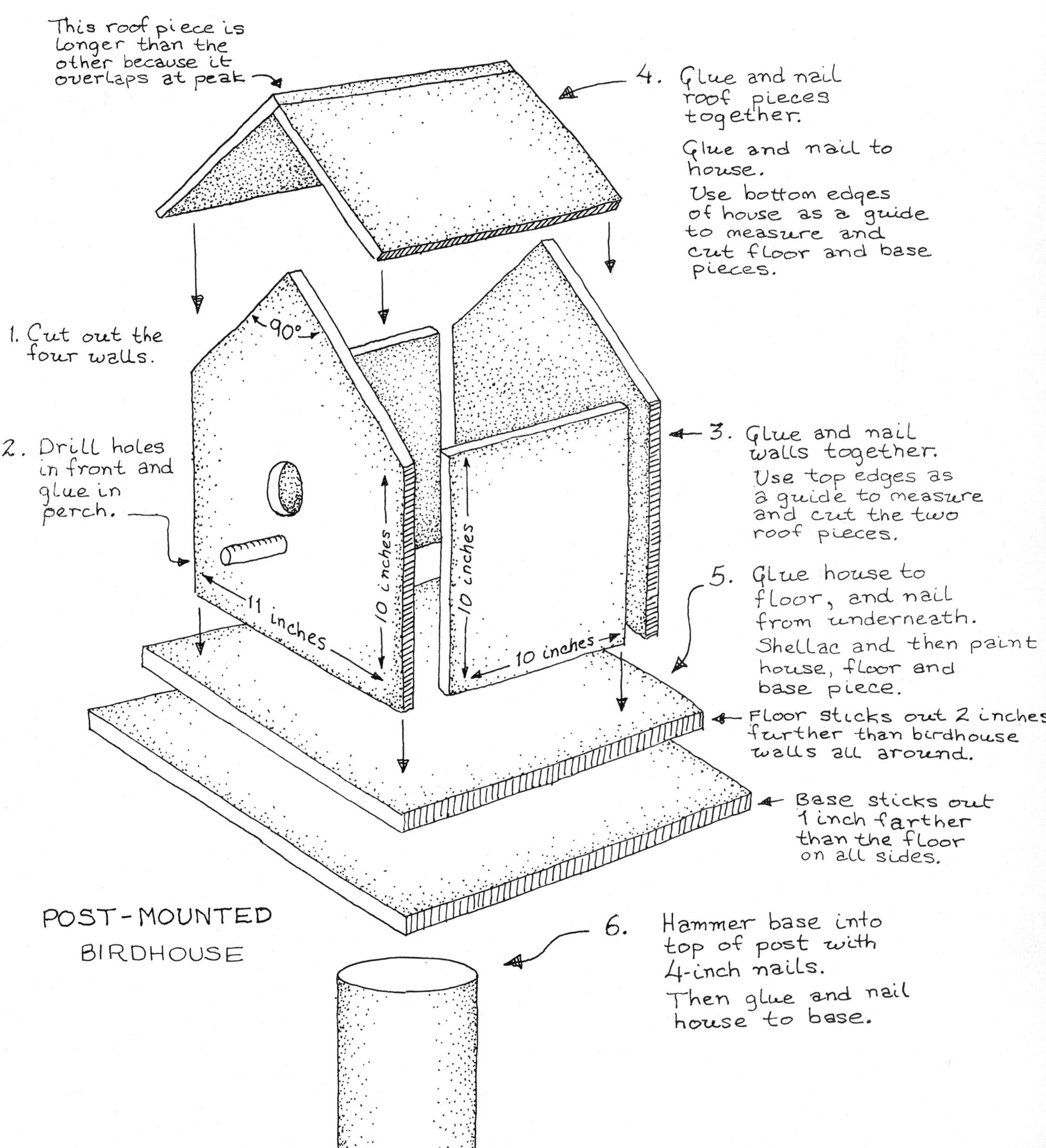
This roof piece is longer than the other because it overlaps at peak
4. Glue and nail roof pieces together.
Glue and nail to house.
Use bottom edges of house as a guide to measure and cut floor and base pieces.
1. Cut out the four walls.
90°
2. Drill holes in front and glue in perch.
3. Glue and nail walls together.
Use top edges as a guide to measure and cut the two roof pieces.
10 inches
10 inches
11 inches
10 inches
5. Glue house to floor, and nail from underneath.
Shellac and then paint house, floor and base piece.
Floor sticks out 2 inches further than birdhouse walls all around.
Base sticks out 1 inch farther than the floor on all sides.
POST-MOUNTED BIRDHOUSE
6. Hammer base into top of post with 4-inch nails.
Then glue and nail house to base.

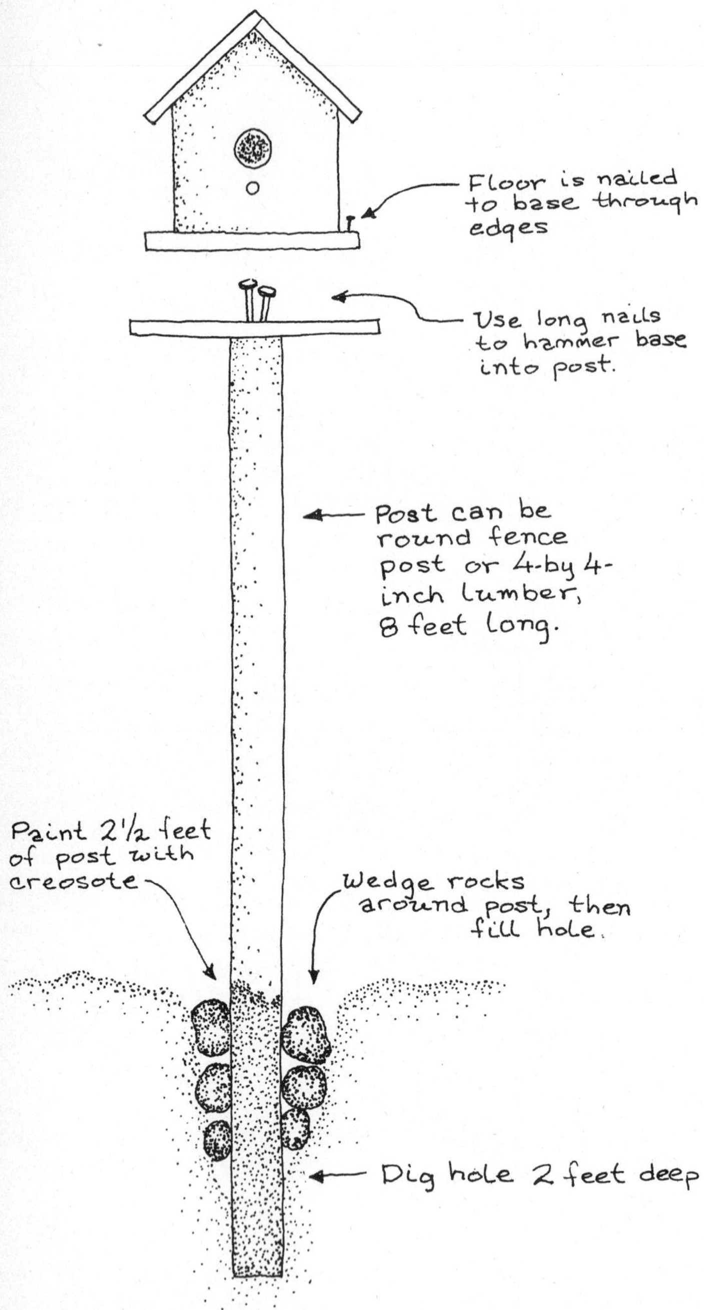

the right size for many common songbirds. You can probably get large enough scraps of wood to fit the pattern from the scrap bin at a lumberyard.

YOU NEED:

MATERIALS:

Exterior-grade plywood or board scraps to fit the pattern
½-inch dowel, 3 inches long
White glue
Common nails (the length depends on how thick your scrap lumber is)
Pint of shellac
Leftover exterior enamel paint
Fence post, either a 4-by-4-inch or a round post, 8 feet high (or you could mount the birdhouse on an existing post or a building wall)
Quart of creosote, if you are sinking a post

TOOLS:

Yardstick
Handsaw
Drill with 2-inch and ½-inch drill bits
Hammer
Paintbrush
Shovel or spade, if you are sinking a post

ACCESSORIES:

4-by-4 inch lumber, small piece
Four ¾-inch dowels
Lattice strip, about 2 feet long

A birdhouse is usually set up on a post six feet off the ground, but you can also nail a birdhouse onto a house or garage wall, if you check with your parents first. Before you cut any pieces out, decide which way you will mount the house, as the patterns are a little different. Then follow the illustrations to construct the house.

There are people who so enjoy the coming and going of nesting birds, or who so love to make birdhouses, that they end up with a bird village of a half-dozen or more houses, each different. The richer birds live in colonnaded mansions, the bird minister in his church, and others may inhabit barns, schools, firehouses or chalets. You can add a porch to countrify a house, or add a steeple to make it look like a church. You can nail in balconies and paint on windows, tack on chimneys or even attach a weathervane. None of these additions bother the birds, and all of them tickle humans. The supplies you need for these additions are listed under Accessories.

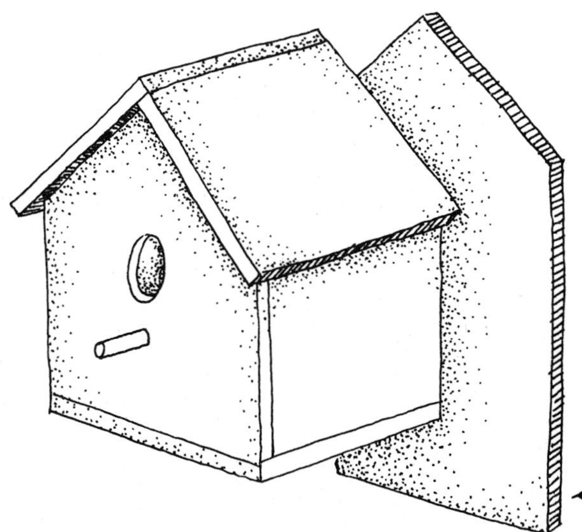

To make a birdhouse that can be mounted on a wall, cut the back wall 8 inches higher than the front wall.

Cut the floor to fit even with the walls instead of sticking out.

The roof can stick out in the front, but is even with the back wall.

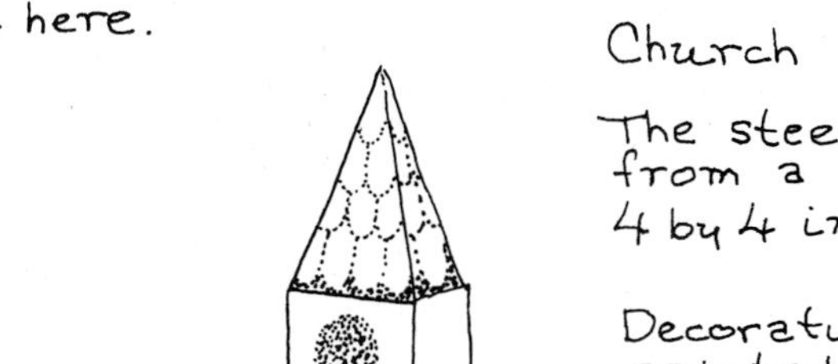

Church

The steeple is cut from a piece of 4 by 4 inch lumber

Decoration is painted on.

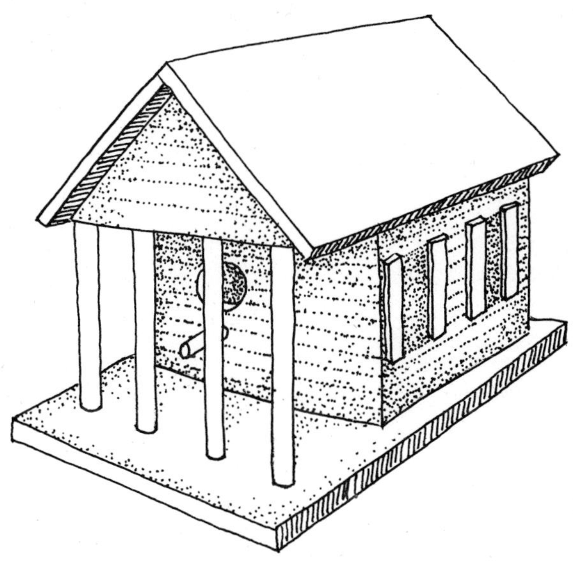

Mansion

The roof pieces are cut 6 inches longer to overhang the porch, and a triangle is cut for the front.

The floor piece is 6 inches longer too.

Columns are 3/4 inch dowels, and shutters are made of lattice strip.

Other decoration is painted on.

Birdfeeders

Since birds live in houses only during the spring, the way to keep them around in other seasons is to feed them. Feeding attracts the most birds during the winter, when wild foods are scarce.

Many birds seek high-energy fatty foods during the cold winter months—wild foods like larvas and grubs, or ones you can provide, like suet and peanut butter. The easiest fat feeder is a nylon net bag filled with lumps of suet—the crackly dry fat from beef. You may be able to get it free from a butcher, but if not, it is inexpensive even in the supermarket. The birds will cling easily to the netting, pecking through to get to the suet.

Any other sort of leftover fat from cooking will be appreciated too. Use grease that hardens at room temperature, like bacon fat. A milk or ice cream carton makes a good container. Wait until the fat has cooled a little so it won't melt a hole in the container. Pour it in, mixing it with birdseed if you wish. After the fat has hardened, cut holes in the container with a sharp knife, stick twigs through to serve as perches, and tie three strings to the top so you can hang the feeder up. The birds will get at the fat by perching on the twigs and eating through the holes. Peanut butter mixed with birdseed is delicious too, but more expensive.

Feeding stations that contain seed will attract many kinds of birds. The feeders don't have to be fancier than a flat tray that you sprinkle the seed on every morning. If you want something fancier, here is a drawing of a coffee-can feeder that you won't have to refill too often, and another even nicer one made with a plastic gallon milk container and filled with sunflower seeds.

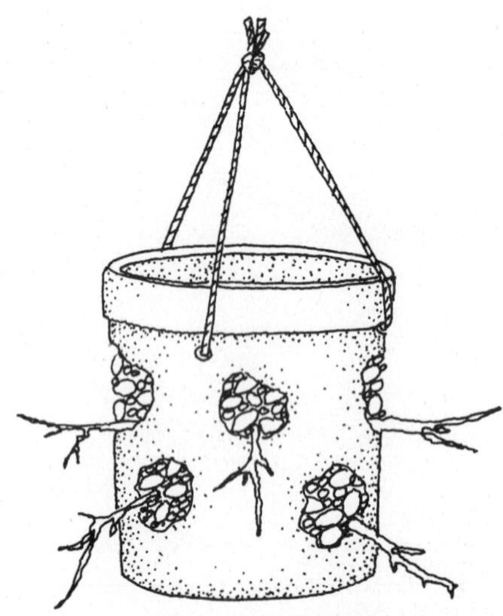

An ice cream carton packed with birdseed in bacon grease

The holes are cut after the grease has hardened, and twigs are stuck in for birds to perch on.

A gallon milk jug filled with sunflower seeds.

Cut holes on opposite sides of jug. Stick dowels through for perches.

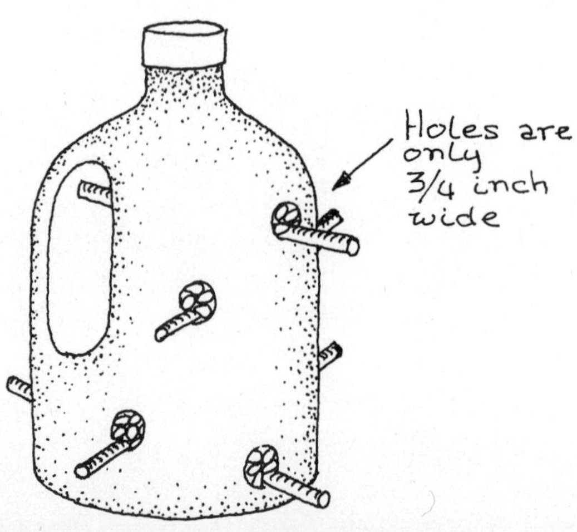

You can hang the jug by its handle.

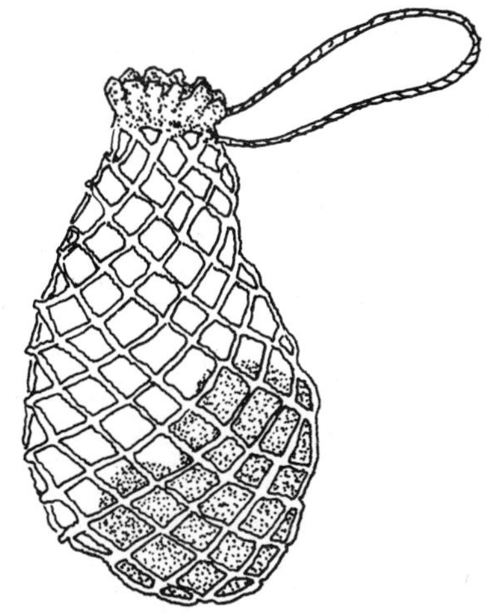

A nylon net bag holds lumps of suet (beef fat)

Birds can perch on the netting easily.

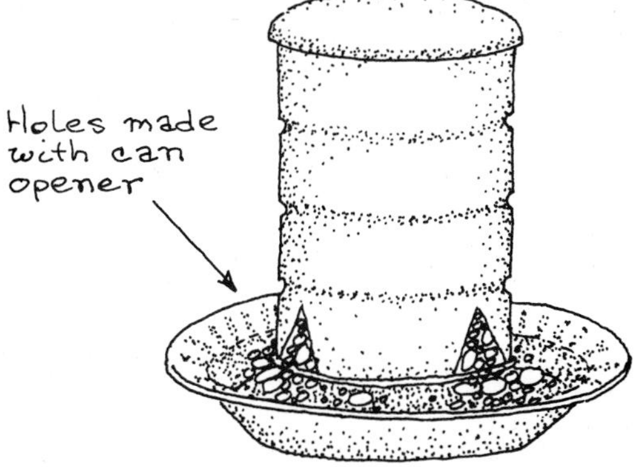

A coffee can filled with birdseed and placed on a pieplate. As seed is eaten, more spills out from holes around the bottom.

Keep covered with the plastic top.

How To Hang A Birdfeeder

People who live in the country don't usually have much difficulty figuring out how to attach a birdfeeder somewhere. It can be hung with string from a tree branch near a window, or nailed into a wooden window frame or fence post, or simply placed on a terrace wall. People who live in apartment houses in the city may have a hard time figuring out how to attach a birdfeeder outside a window. Here are two possibilities. One is a shelf, which can be glued to a masonry surface with special masonry glue, or nailed into concrete walls with masonry nails. Both the special glue and nails are sold at hardware stores. The other possibility is a hanging birdfeeder, which can be hung from a bracket screwed into a small piece of board. The board is attached to a masonry wall the same way the shelf is. Of course, be sure to check with your parents before you fasten anything to a wall of your house or apartment.

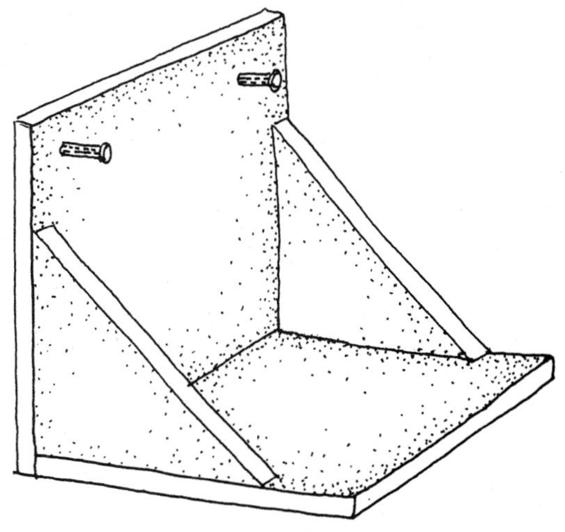

Shelf to hold birdfeeder

Nail into wood wall. Use masonry nails for brick or concrete walls, or buy masonry glue at a hardware store.

Shelf braces can be wood triangles or angle irons.

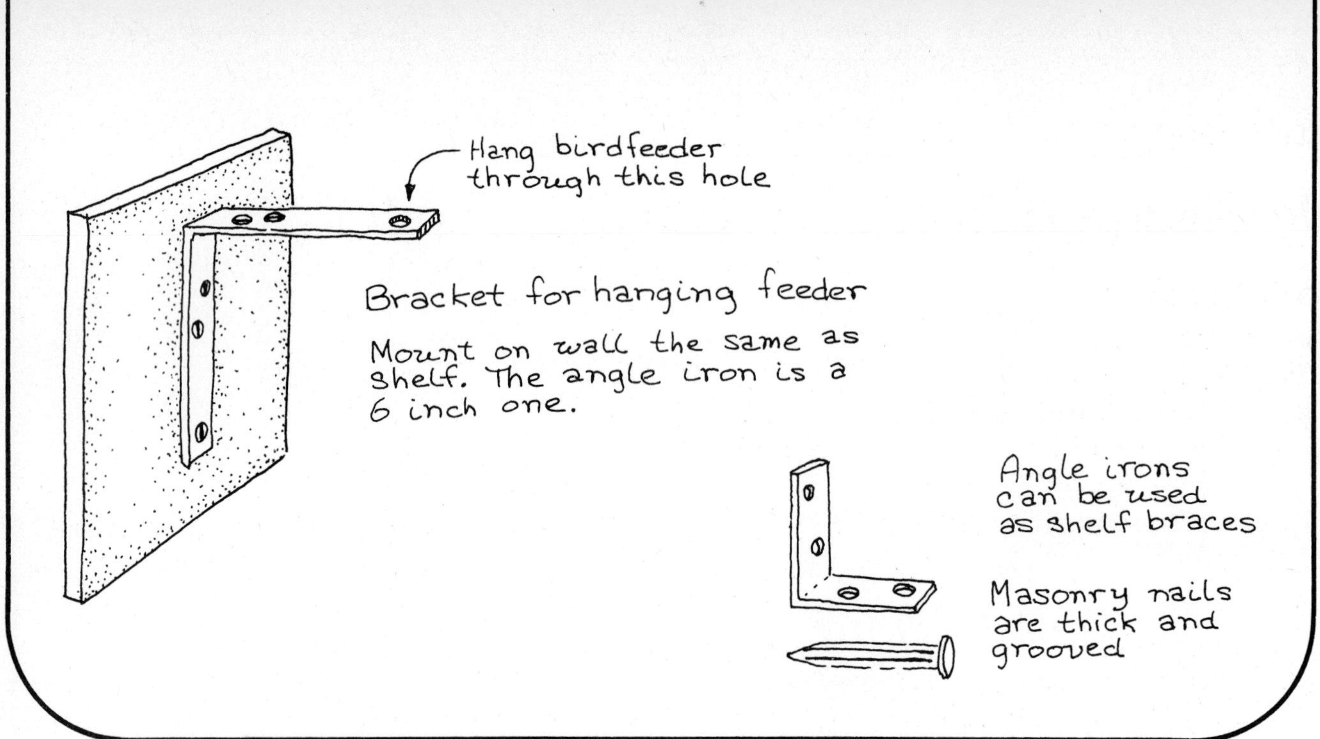

Overnight Pet Houses

Overnight pets—the ones you keep for only a day or so—tend to turn up unexpectedly before you have a home ready for them. It rains, and suddenly you find an adorable salamander walking on the lawn—but you have no cage to keep it in. At last a baby deer mouse is discovered in the bottom of the dog-food bag—but no home is ready for it. Rather than miss these opportunities, keep on hand the following ready homes, each of which costs from nothing at all to only a few dollars.

Tank Home ($5.00)

YOU NEED:

MATERIALS:

5½-gallon tank. The tank can be a leaky one bought cheaply at a thrift shop or garage sale.

Wire-mesh top, made according to instructions under Desert Vivarium

Rock to weight the top

Several layers of newspaper to cover the tank floor

Two small crockery dishes

Empty can

Use this tank without the can or dishes for temporary pets like large toads, large lizards, snakes, land or water turtles. For overnight rodents like a mouse or a chipmunk, provide water and birdseed in the two small crockery dishes. Add the empty can to serve as a hiding place.

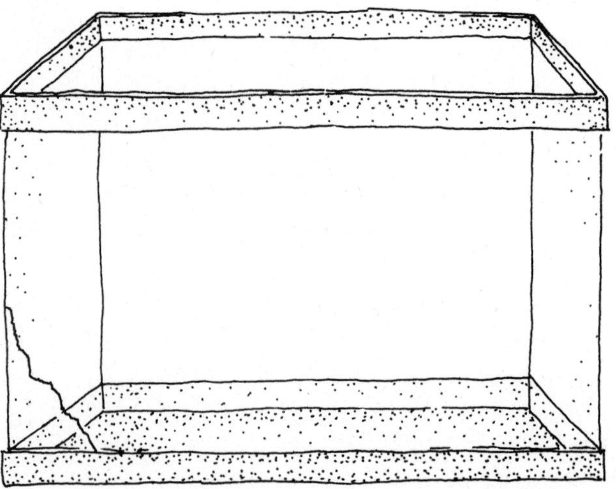

A tank with a crack in it or a leak in the seams may cost only a dollar.

Jar Houses ($1.00)

YOU NEED:
MATERIALS:
Cheesecloth
One quart-size wide-mouthed jar
One gallon-size wide-mouthed jar (pickle and mayonnaise jars come in gallons)
Wide rubber bands to fit jar mouths
Paper towels

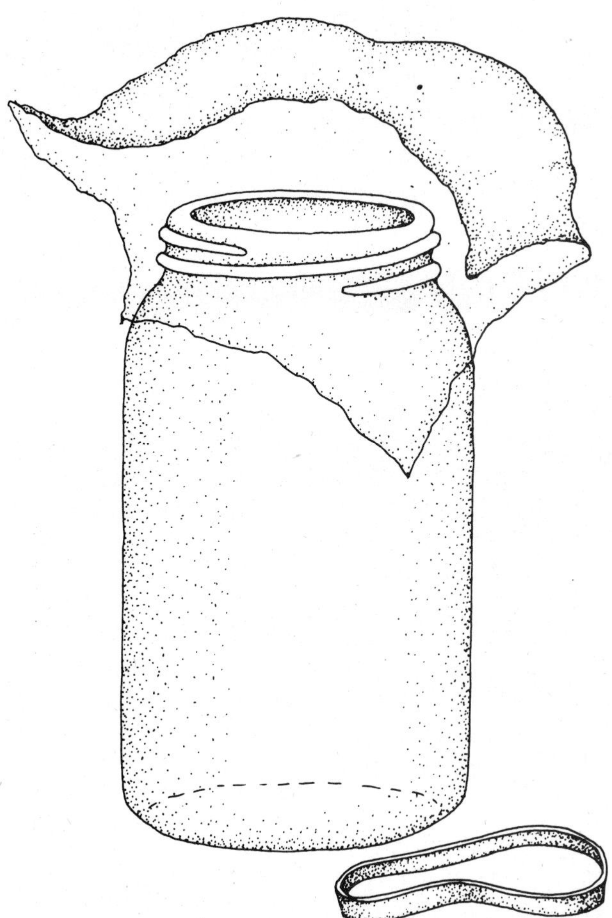

Use a rubber band to keep the cheesecloth in place

Cut a square of cheesecloth to fit over the mouth of each of the jars. Hold it in place with a rubber band. Use the small jar as is for land snails, cocoons, insect and spider eggs, small toads, small lizards and baby snakes. To keep moisture-loving pets like salamanders and tree frogs overnight, add a layer of moist paper towels to the bottom of the small jar. Use the large jar filled with the right kind of water as temporary quarters for water pets—salt-water ones like starfish and crabs, or fresh-water ones like frogs, baby water turtles and crayfish.

Bug Cage ($1.00)

YOU NEED:
MATERIALS:
Wire window screening, at least 9 by 14 inches
Two empty, clean tuna fish cans, the family size, each with one lid removed
Soft wire, about a foot long

TOOLS:
Ruler
Scissors
Wire cutters

With scissors, cut out a 9-by-14-inch rectangle of screening. Stand the screen on one of its nine-inch ends, and curve it into a cylinder that fits snugly inside the tuna cans. Weave the overlap together with the soft wire. This cage is good for larger insects like grasshoppers, crickets, katydids, walking sticks, caterpillars, moths, fireflies and beetles.

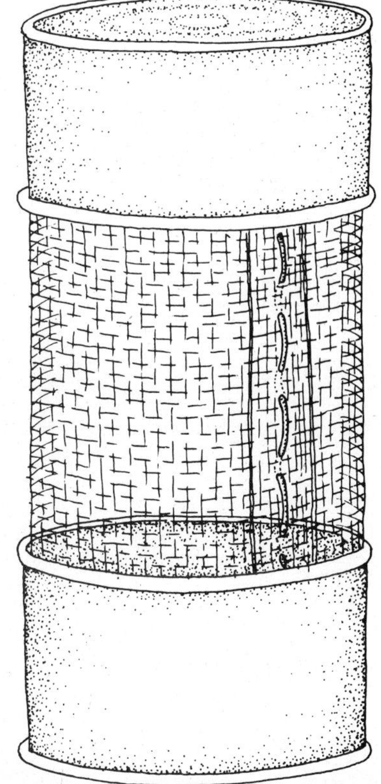

Lace the overlapped screening with soft wire to hold it closed.

Emergency Homes

If, in spite of all warnings to the contrary, you still find yourself with a potential pet and no place to keep it, these are some emergency measures that should tide you over the time it takes to build a more substantial home.

For insects, small snakes, toads and salamanders: use a jar with any piece of cloth over the top, held on with a rubber band. Holes punched in the metal top of the jar really do not let enough air circulate.

For moisture-loving animals like salamanders and tree frogs: add a wet piece of paper towel around the inside of the jar so the animal can stay moist. Don't leave the jar in the sun; it acts like a greenhouse, heating up and killing the animal inside it very quickly.

For snakes: a pillow case, closed at the top with a rubber band.

For water animals like crayfish and tadpoles: the largest container you can get, like a plastic pail, filled with water from the pond or stream where you found the animal. Again, don't leave it in the sun to heat up.

Emergency use of bathtubs: turtles, snakes, mice and other small rodents, large beetles, salamanders, toads, frogs (except tree frogs, who can cling to the sides), and most other animals can be put in the bathtub, with or without water, depending on what sort of animal you have. The sides are too steep and slippery for them to escape. Be sure to close the drain first, and be sure to clean the bathtub afterward.

A Snake In A Pillowcase

Vivariums

Small animals with special needs are kept in glass homes that provide climate control or mini-environments. For instance, salamanders, tree frogs and other amphibians need to keep their skin moist. A covered glass tank planted as a woodland keeps the air damp enough for them. Other creatures, such as land tortoises and desert lizards, need to be kept quite warm. A heated glass container keeps their environment warm enough. Homes that suit these special needs are called vivariums.

Although each vivarium is basically a tank, the accessories you need vary so much from one animal to another that there is no such thing as an "average" cost. Look up the animal you intend to house in the Vivarium Pets chapter in this book. Check all the accessories—special lights, lids, dishes—that you will need. Then add up your costs by using the chart below. When adding up, remember you can save on these costs, which are based on new and store-bought equipment, by buying secondhand and collecting decorative accessories in the wild.

TANK SIZE	5½-gallon	10-gallon	18-gallon
Tank	$8.00	$10.00	$22.00
Incandescent light	$6.50	$7.50	$7.50
Fluorescent light	$17.00	$20.00	$20.00
Vita-Lite® bulb	$4.00	$5.00	$5.00
Glass top	$3.00	$3.50	$3.50
Commercial screen top	$3.50	$4.00	$4.00
Homemade wire-mesh top	$2.00	$2.00	$2.00
Tank thermometer	$1.00	$1.00	$1.00
Bone carbon charcoal ($1.50 per pound)	$2.25 (1½ pounds)	$3.00 (2 pounds)	$3.00 (2 pounds)
Grade No. 0-3 gravel (fine to coarse sand, 15¢ per pound)	$1.50 (10 pounds)	$2.25 (15 pounds)	$2.25 (15 pounds)
Grade No. 5 gravel (pebble-sized, 15¢ per pound)	$1.50 (10 pounds)	$2.25 (15 pounds)	$2.25 (15 pounds)
Potting soil, smallest bag	$1.29	$1.29	$1.29
Crockery dish, 3-inch size	$1.00 per dish		
Crockery dish, 8-inch size	$2.50 per dish		
Plant in 2-inch pot	70¢ to $1.00 per plant		
Store-bought decorative rocks	25¢ per pound		
Store-bought decorative driftwood	approximately $4.00 per piece		
Plant mister	$1.50		
Bubble Stone	39¢		

Desert Vivarium

Land tortoises, desert iguanas, anoles and tarantulas may all be kept healthy in a hot, desertlike environment. The common iguana needs more humidity, but this is supplied by equipping a dry vivarium with a large dish of water for bathing set into the sand. You should figure on getting a 10-gallon tank to provide enough room, but it can be a secondhand leaky one. For desert iguanas you will need an 18 gallon tall tank.

YOU NEED:

MATERIALS:

10 pounds No. 3-grade gravel (sand)
Pail or bowl for washing sand
10-gallon tank

ACCESSORIES:

Screen or hardware-cloth top
Incandescent tank fixture, or 40-watt bulb, socket and extension cord
Fluorescent tank fixture
Vita-Lite® bulb
Tank thermometer, and masking or cellophane tape to stick it in place
Plants like cacti and succulents, or a leafy plant
Plant mister
Driftwood or climbing branch
Decorative rock
Small square of wood (to brace leaning rock)
Epoxy glue
3-inch crockery water or food dishes
8-inch crockery bathing dish
Fork and spoon for cleaning vivarium

Wash the sand by putting it all in a pail and running water into it, letting the water overflow until it looks clear. (The reason for this is to get rid of dust which might bother pets when they breathe.) Pour the water out slowly. The sand will

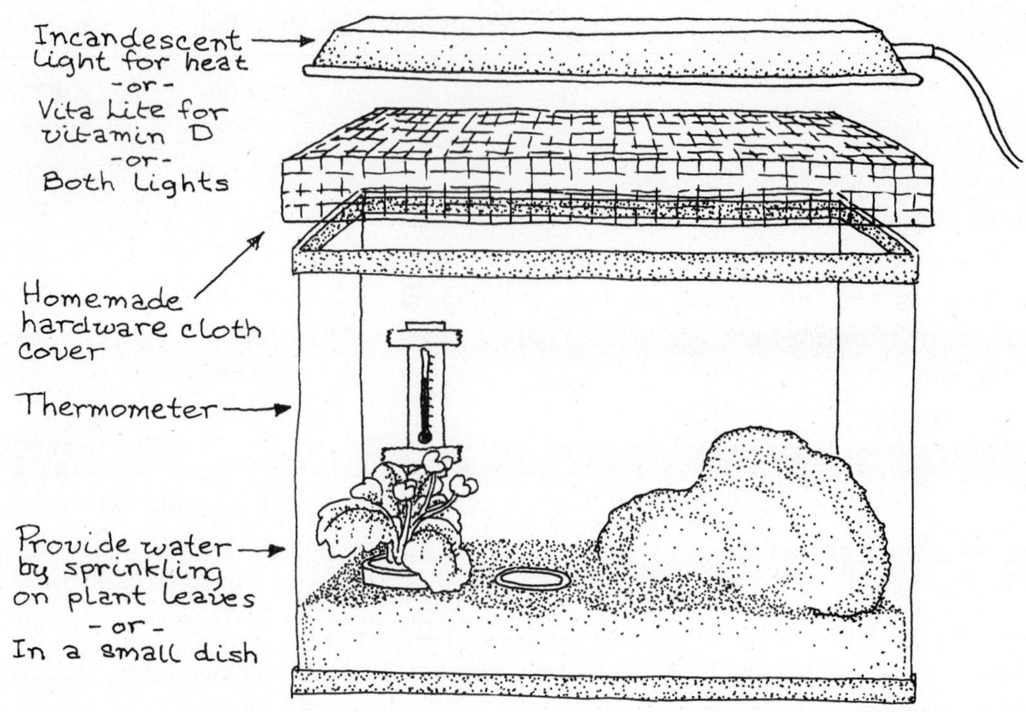

Set-up for hot, dry desert environment

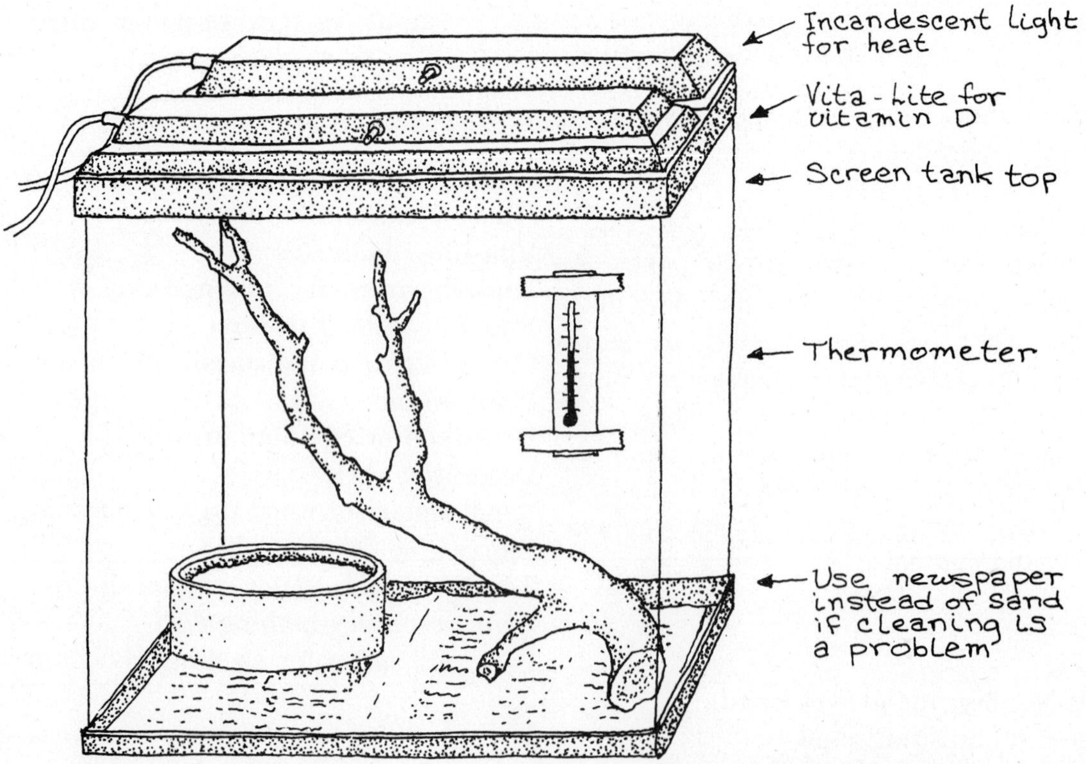

Set-up for a hot, humid but well-ventilated environment. This is an 18-gallon "tall" tank - good for an iguana. The dish is large enough for bathing. Plants could be added too.

remain on the bottom of the pail. Spread the sand out on newspaper and let it dry for a day or two in the sun. Or dry it for a few hours in a roasting pan in the oven at the lowest setting. Spread the sand in the bottom of the tank.

Tortoises can't climb out of a tank, but lizards and spiders should have a top. Make one from hardware cloth, or buy a commercial screen tank top.

Any local lizard, spider or tortoise can no doubt do without special heat in this vivarium. If your home or apartment is air-conditioned in the summer, however, even a locally captured pet will need daytime heat. The least expensive way to heat the tank is to let a 40-watt light bulb (screwed into a socket on an extension cord) hang over the side of the tank or lie on the wire top.

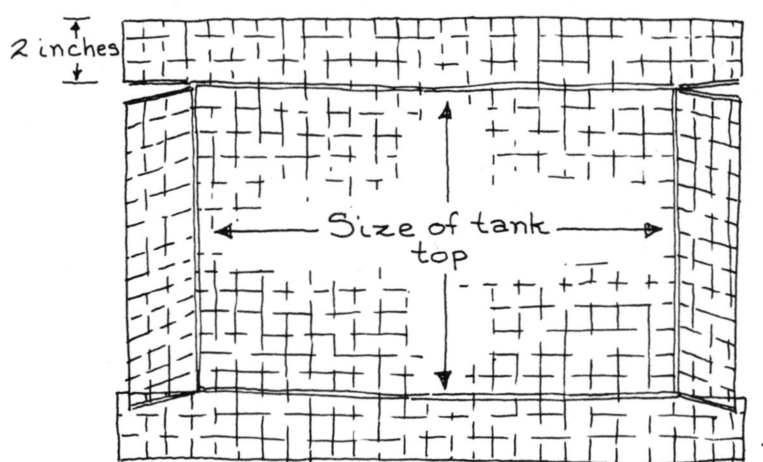

1. Cut a piece of 1/4-inch mesh hardware cloth 2 inches larger than the top of the tank on all sides.
2. Snip 2 inches into all four corners as shown to form four flaps.

Flap

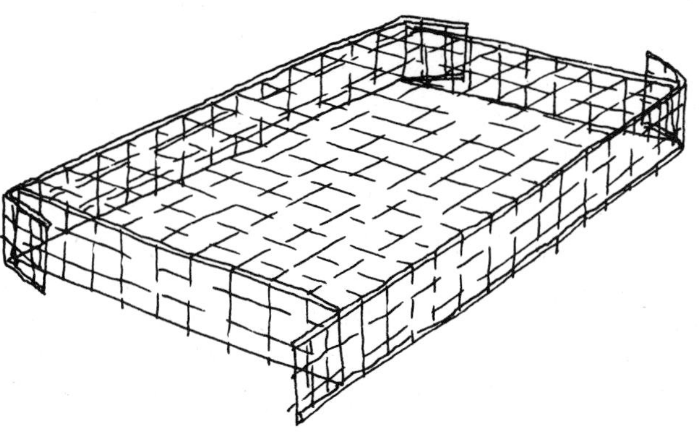

3. Put the hardware cloth on the tank and bend the edges over so the top fits snugly. Bend the flaps around the corners.

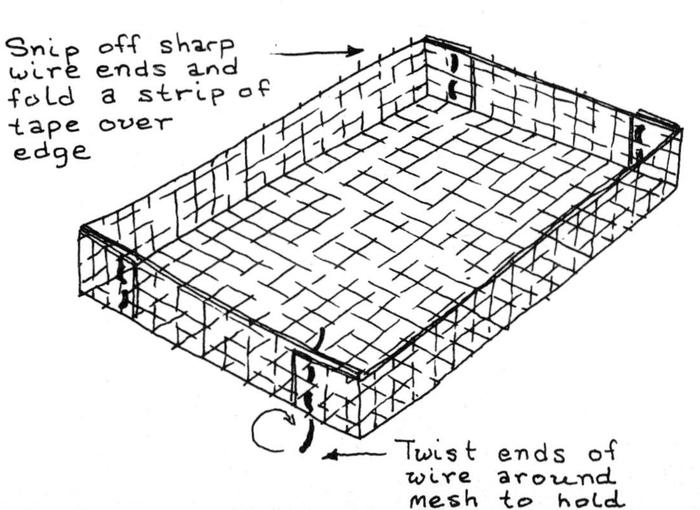

4. Take the top off the tank and weave the flaps closed with soft wire.

If the edges of the top are sharp, snip the wire ends close and fold a 1-inch wide strip of tape over the edges. Use freezer, adhesive or friction tape.

Pets imported from desert areas will need a better heat source, and in some cases ultra-violet light as well. Heat alone is best provided by an incandescent tank fixture designed to fit the top of your tank and sold in pet stores. More expensive, but necessary for tortoises and lizards who must bask in sunlight to manufacture vitamin D, is a fluorescent tank fixture outfitted with a special kind of bulb called a Vita-Lite.® Sunlight shining through windows or glass tank walls is of no use to basking animals. The ultra-violet rays they need are filtered out by glass. The fluorescent fixture may come with a plastic tank lid, but this lid prevents adequate ventilation and shouldn't be used. Both light fixtures can sit on top of the tank itself or on the hardware-cloth top.

It's useful to tape an aquarium thermometer to the inside of the tank so you can check on the temperature. They come bent over at the top to hang on the tank edge, but measuring the temperature so close to the source of heat won't tell you how hot or cold your pet is down at the bottom of the tank. Straighten the bend out, and tape the thermometer inside the tank close to the bottom. The Vita-Lite® will keep a 10-gallon tank over 80 degrees during the daytime, and over 65 degrees at night, even in the winter. Incandescent lights are hotter, so they should be checked often to prevent overheating (over 90 degrees for most animals). When a tank overheats, snap the light off. Sunlight may also overheat a tank. If your vivarium is temporarily empty, by all means keep it in the sun for the benefit of the plants. But while it is occupied, keep the tank away from sunlight. The plants will manage on artificial light.

If the vivarium is to be used for small lizards, you might want to plant cacti and succulents. Most of them come in two-inch plastic pots, which can simply be sunk into the sand wherever they look right. Anoles need a leafy plant rather than a cactus type, because they drink water droplets from its leaves. Water cacti and succulents every two weeks; spray the leafy plant with a mister every day, water once a week. Don't bother with plants for tarantulas or tortoises. Spider webs are hard to remove from the plants, and tortoises knock plants over.

A piece of driftwood or an interesting rock will help make this vivarium a convincing desert as well as provide shade and hiding for pets. Add a branch for climbing pets like lizards. A rock that leans against a corner forms a good cave.

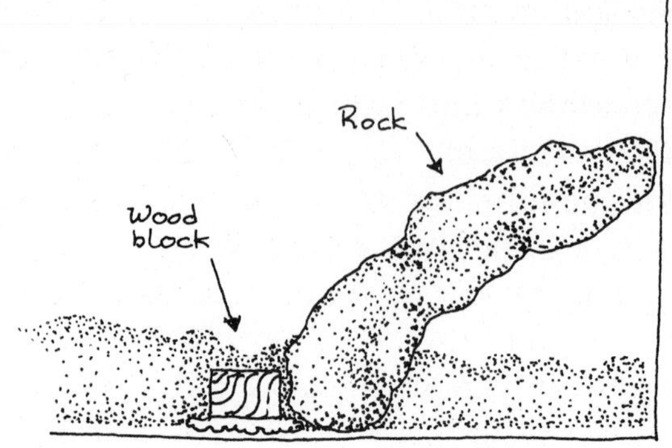

Wedge a leaning rock in place with a small block of wood glued to the tank floor with epoxy glue.

Cover block with sand so it is not visible.

Every pet except the anole needs a water dish. The common iguana needs one six to eight inches across for bathing; a three-inch dish is fine for all the others.

A dry desert vivarium is easy to clean. With a fork, rake the surface of the sand so all the debris is in a pile. Pick up the pile with a spoon, and dump it in the trash. From time to time, sprinkle on more sand.

Moist Woodland Vivarium

A vivarium can be kept as a moist, humid environment by planting it with moisture-loving (usually woodland) plants. This vivarium looks pretty all the time, even when you're not housing pets in it. It stays damp enough for small salamanders, tree frogs and land snails.

YOU NEED:

MATERIALS:

Large glass container (a gallon-size jar or a round fishbowl) or a tank. The smallest tank is

the 5½-gallon size. The most useful for permanent pets is the 10-gallon size. The tank can be secondhand and even leaky.
Bone carbon charcoal, available in pet stores (check the label, as other cheaper kinds are ineffective in preventing decay)
No. 5-grade gravel (pebble-size), available in pet stores; or you can use clean driveway gravel
Soil, either the smallest bag of potting soil or soil you collect from the same place you find your plants
Plants, bought or collected
Stones or twigs
Plant mister
Paper towels or sponge

ACCESSORIES:
Trowel and plastic bags, if you are collecting your own native plants
Lid for vivarium. The lid can be glass, screen or cheesecloth, depending on the type of container and the pet you are keeping. A glass lid to fit a tank can be cut by a glazier or lumberyard.

Wash the container out well. Put a two-inch layer of bone carbon charcoal in the bottom, and then a thinner layer of well-rinsed pebbles over the charcoal. The charcoal keeps stagnant moisture in the bottom clean and fresh smelling, and the pebbles provide a drainage area so soil doesn't get soggy.

The next step is to plant your vivarium with small plants and mosses to copy a woodland environment. If you live in the city, you can buy potting soil and moisture-loving plants like baby's tears, a fern, or an African violet. Baby's tears will spread nicely to form a woodland floor. Spread three inches of soil over the pebble layer. Transplant the plants into the soil, or bury the pots in the soil and other layers so only the plants are exposed.

If you live in the country, you can collect your own plants and mosses from the woods, planted in soil collected from the same area. Supply yourself with a trowel and several plastic bags. Since this vivarium is to be a moist woodland environment, find a moist woodland for your plant collecting.

The plants you are looking for are not babies of plants that will grow larger—they would grow too big for your vivarium too fast. Look instead for naturally miniature plants like the ones shown here. Field guides to ferns and wildflowers are helpful in identifying your finds.

When you have found an area that has plants you

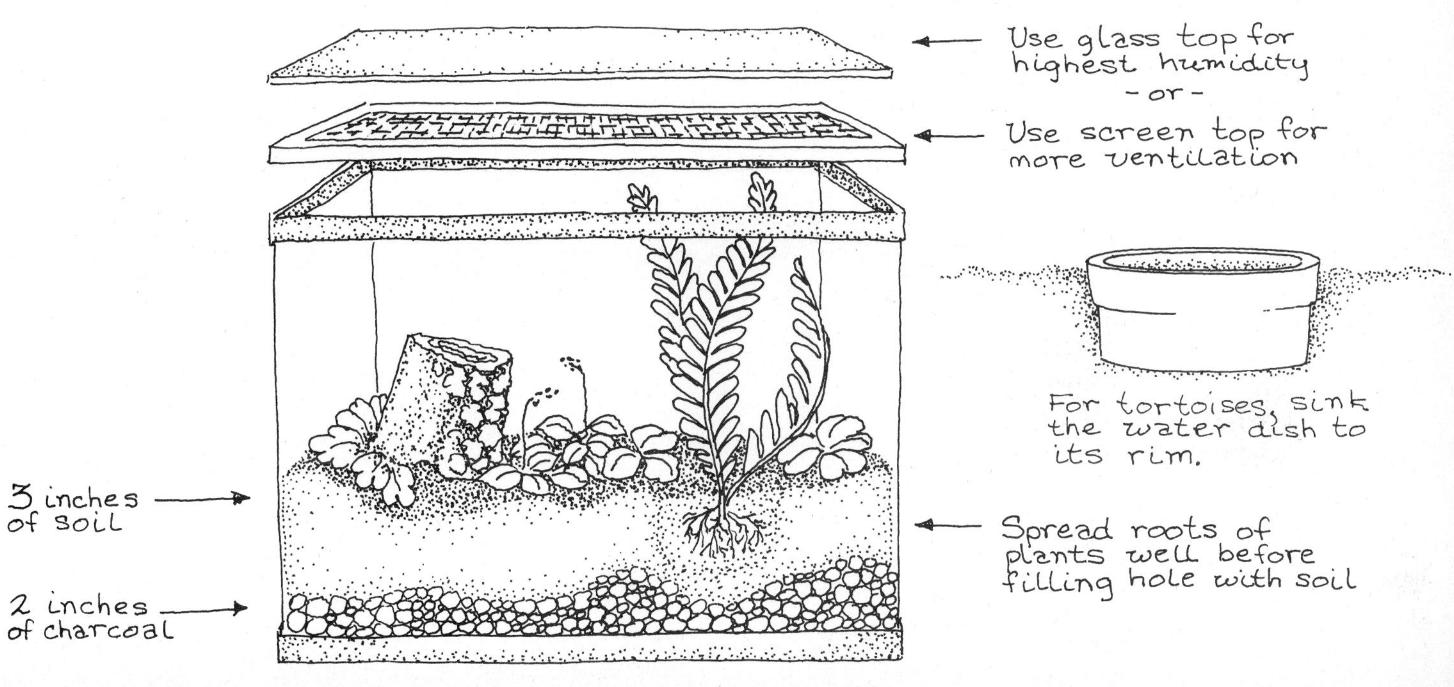

Set-up for a moist woodland environment

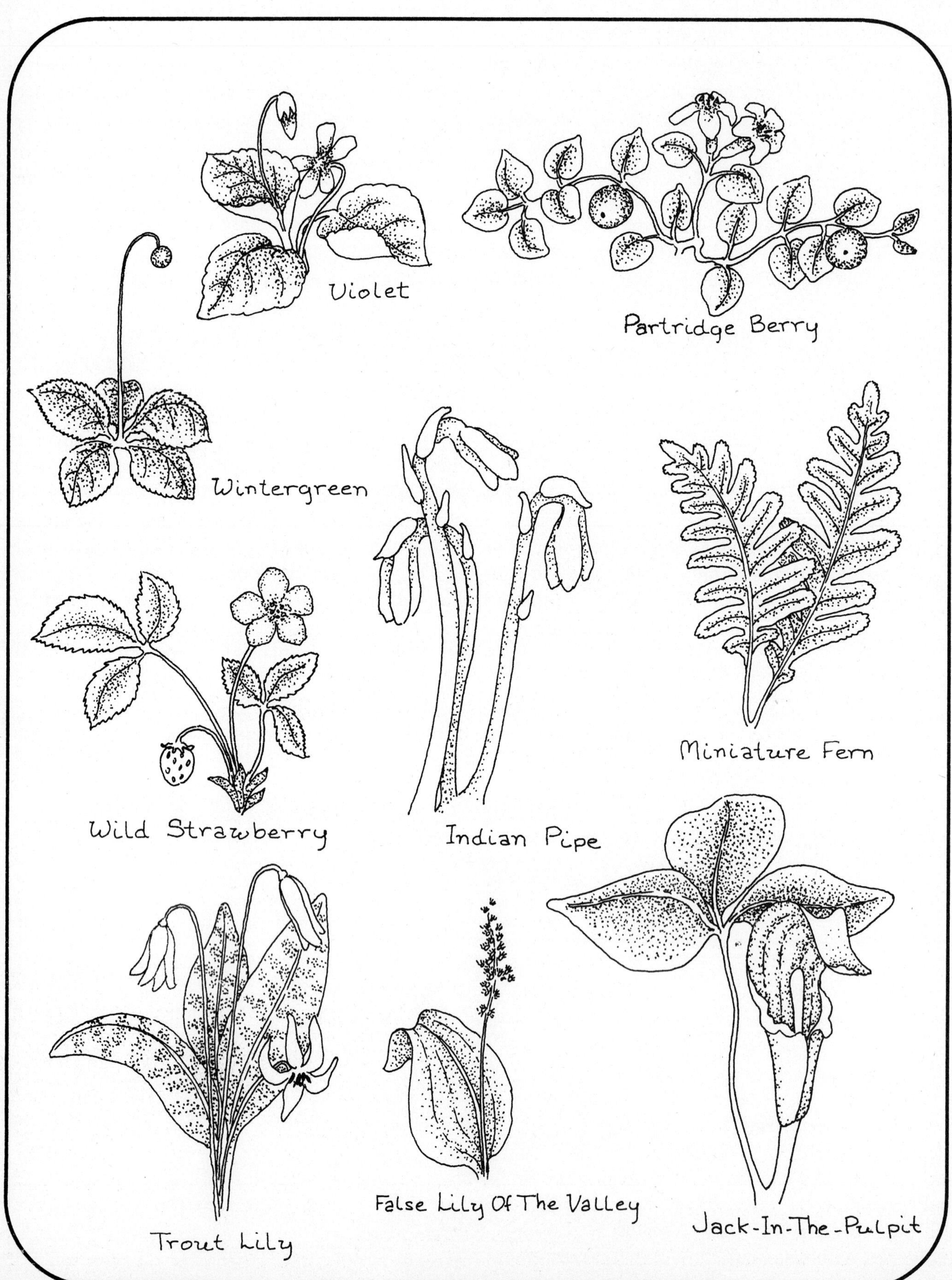
Violet
Partridge Berry
Wintergreen
Miniature Fern
Wild Strawberry
Indian Pipe
False Lily Of The Valley
Jack-In-The-Pulpit
Trout Lily

like, start collecting what you need in this order: collect soil first, then some mosses, then a stone or a bit of bark or twig with interesting fungus or lichen on it, and then the plants, last of all. As you carefully dig out a plant (digging out plants in woodland is not easy), try to injure the roots as little as possible by digging around the plant first to loosen the soil. Don't try to just pull a plant out. As soon as you have a plant, put it in its own plastic bag to keep it moist. When you get home, put the plants to soak in a bowl of water, roots and all, while you put three inches of soil in your container. Then dig holes, spread the plant roots well in them, and tamp soil firmly around them. Water the plants once they are in the soil. Put the moss down to make a pretty forest floor, and set the rock or twig anywhere you like. Clean the sides of the terrarium with a paper towel.

Keep a woodland vivarium in bright light—bright enough to read by—but not in the sun. Watering is best done with a plant mister. How often you mist depends on the size of the container and on whether or not it is covered. A mayonnaise jar, for instance, needs no lid because it has a relatively narrow mouth which cuts down on evaporation. Jar containers won't need misting more than once a week. An open tank would probably need misting once a day, but if you fit the tank with a glass cover, once every other week is sufficient.

When you add pets to the vivarium, you may need a top of some sort to prevent escape. Glass cut to size is fine for either tank or jar, provided you lift it once a day and ventilate the vivarium by fanning fresh air in with a piece of cardboard. Better ventilation is provided by a cheesecloth top for a jar (hold it in place with a rubber band) or a screen top for a tank. Pet stores sell screen tops to fit both the 5½-gallon and the 10-gallon tank. The homemade mesh top suggested for the desert vivarium has holes too large to contain small woodland creatures like tree frogs.

Extra heat isn't necessary in woodland vivariums. The animals that live here are too small to make a noticeable mess, so no cleaning is necessary, either. The exception is the land snail, who can leave mucous trails on the glass walls. These can be cleaned off with paper towels or a sponge moistened with water—but not cleaning solutions.

Semi-aquatic Vivariums

A few animals require both land and water to simulate their natural environment. Water turtles may spend much of their time on land, but must eat in the water. The large salamanders and most frogs need to have a swimming or soaking pool. There are three alternative ways to set up a semi-aquatic vivarium; at least a 10-gallon tank must be used for all of them. Look up costs in the chart at the beginning of the Vivarium section.

Sunken-dish Semi-aquatic Vivarium. This is by far the easiest to set up, as well as the easiest to keep clean. But because the water area is rather small, it is only appropriate for a large salamander, small frog or very small water turtle.

YOU NEED:

MATERIALS:

10-gallon tank set up as a moist woodland environment

6-to-8-inch shallow crockery or glass water dish with sloping sides. (You may find this dish

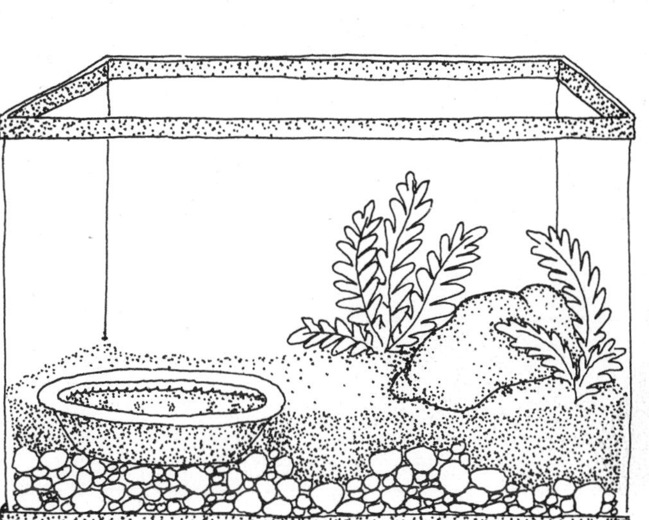

Sunken dish semi-aquatic vivarium can be planted in any way you wish.

Use a shallow dish with sloping sides. Lift it out to clean it.

disguised as an ashtray or masquerading as a cookware item.)

ACCESSORIES:

Glass top cut to fit the top of the tank by a glazier or lumberyard, if fruit flies are what you feed your pet; or commercial screen top

Fluorescent light fixtures and Vita-Lite® bulb

Dig a hole to fit the water dish. Sink the dish in the soil up to its rim. The dish has to be removed at least once a week for washing and refilling (more often for a turtle), but otherwise this vivarium is no different in either construction or maintenance from a woodland one.

If you are keeping a small water turtle in this vivarium, you will not need a lid, but you must have a fluorescent light fixture with a Vita-Lite® bulb resting on the top of the tank.

Sloped-incline Semi-aquatic Vivarium. This arrangement is not hard to set up, but does require a tank without leaks. It is more work to keep clean than the sunken dish arrangement, but supplies far more water. It is a good set-up for a water turtle.

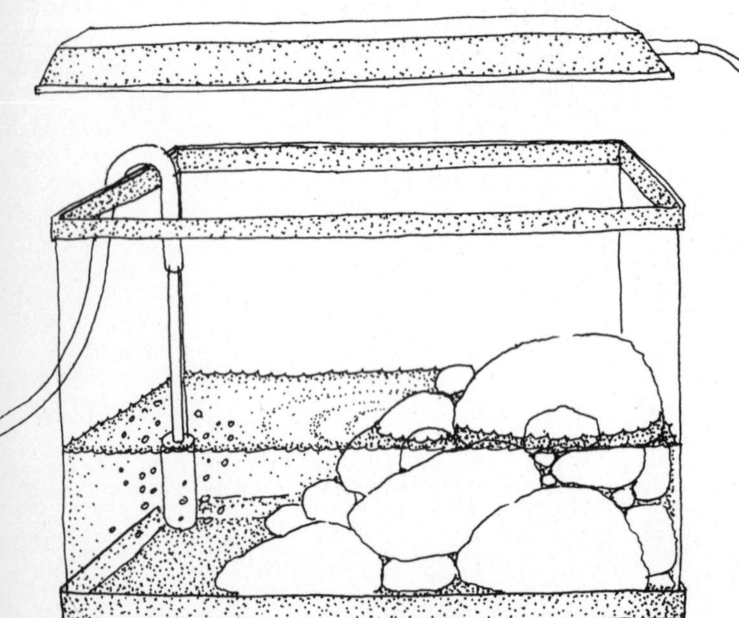

Sloped incline semi-aquatic vivarium is made by building a gradual hill of smooth stones, or by leaning a log or piece of bark against one end of the tank.

A bubble-stone aerates the water to retard decay between cleanings.

YOU NEED:

MATERIALS:

Smooth rocks or a small log or piece of bark cut to fit diagonally across the length of the tank

Scrub brush

10-gallon leakproof tank

Bubble stone and a pump to run it (both available at pet stores)

Several feet of plastic tubing to connect bubble stone to pump

ACCESSORIES:

Glass top cut to fit the tank, or a commercial screen top

Fluorescent light fixture and Vita-Lite® bulb

Wash the stones, or scrub the log or bark with a brush under fresh water. In the tank, build the stones up into a gradually sloping hill, eight inches high at the highest part; or fit the bark or log into the tank at about the same incline. Add fresh water to a height of six inches. It is important that the last two inches of land area are perfectly dry, especially for turtles, who may suffer from fungus infections if they cannot dry off completely between swims. Add whichever top is needed by the pet you are going to keep—or no top at all for turtles. The fluorescent light for turtles rests on top of the tank.

Connect the bubble stone to the pump with the plastic tubing, and let the stone rest in the deep end of the water. The bubble stone, while it doesn't actually clean your tank, will help to slow down decay of leftover food or droppings. It does this simply by bubbling air into the water. Aerated water, rich in oxygen, is a discouraging environment to bacteria.

Nevertheless, this tank must be taken apart and cleaned thoroughly once a month. Even if you pick up leftover foods as you notice them, bits will accumulate under the wood or between the stones—and you will begin to smell the results. As soon as the tank begins to smell or the water looks murky, take everything out of the tank, wash the tank and everything in it with salt and water, rinse well, and replace.

Split-tank Semi-aquatic Vivarium. This is a very practical set-up for water turtles and large salamanders that provides plenty of water space, but some construction is required.

YOU NEED:

MATERIALS:

Piece of plexiglass cut to fit exactly across the width of the tank by a glazier or lumberyard. The exact height will depend on the height of the filter.
Shortest possible inside-tank filter, a pump to run it, filter fluff and filter charcoal
10-gallon leakproof tank
Silicone glue
Bone carbon charcoal
No. 5-grade gravel (pebble-size) or clean driveway gravel
Soil
Moss, grasses or other plants

ACCESSORIES:

Sloping rock
Glass or commercial screen top
Fluorescent light fixture and Vita-Lite® bulb

Before you get the plexiglass cut to size, measure the height of the thicker tube that juts out the top of the filter. The filter will not work unless water level in the tank is higher than this tube—which means the plexiglass partition must be higher too. The filter we measured would need a seven-inch-high partition to keep the water level high enough.

Have the plexiglass cut for you at a lumberyard or glazier's; if necessary, bring the tank with you to be sure the piece fits well. Using plenty of silicone glue so you're sure there's no leakage from the water to the land side of the tank, glue the partition into place about one-third of the way across the tank.

Prepare and plant the larger area the same as a moist woodland vivarium. Fill the smaller area with water nearly up to the height of the partition. Prepare the filter according to directions on the package, connect it to the pump with the plastic tubing, and place it in a corner of the water area. If a turtle is going to live here, add the sloping rock to help it climb ashore. Add a top for large salamanders or a light for turtles.

Take care of this tank according to directions for aquariums (page 323).

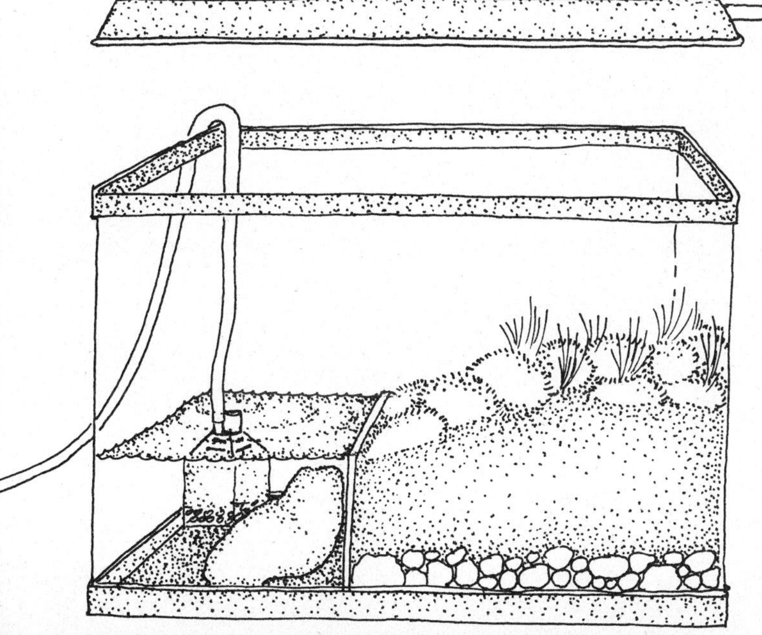

Split-tank semi-aquatic vivarium is made by gluing a piece of plexiglass inside to confine water to a third of the tank. Plexiglass must be 1 inch higher than the top tube on the filter box.
(Buy the shortest filter you can)
Add a sloping rock to help your pet climb onto land. This land area is planted with moss and grass.

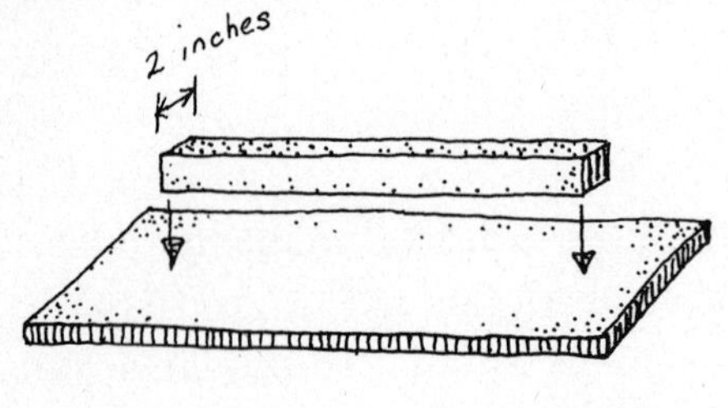

1. Glue bottom piece along center of the plywood or board base, 2 inches in from each end. Nail from underneath.

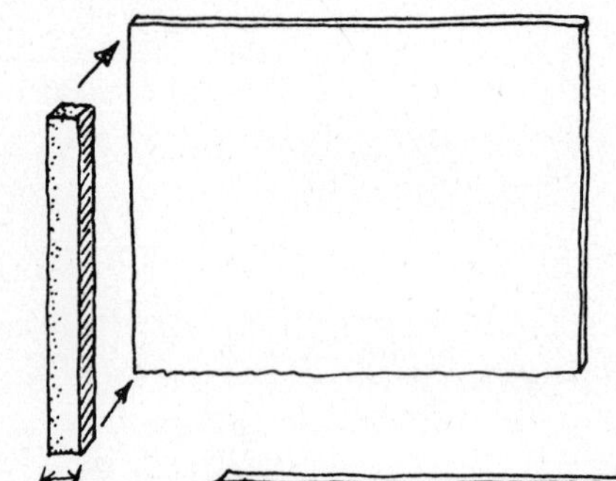

2. Glue side piece to glass.

ANT VIVARIUM

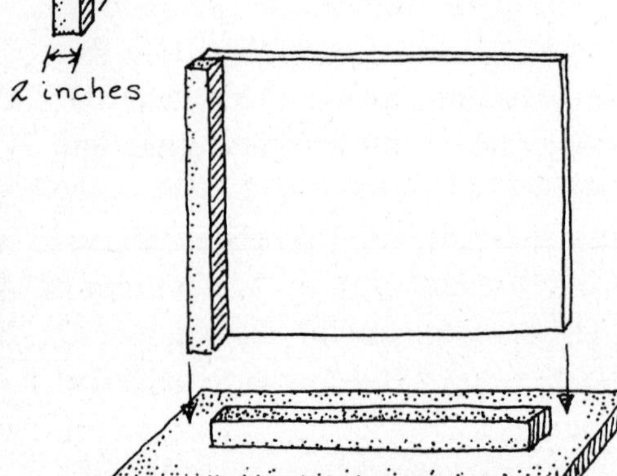

3. Glue glass with side piece to bottom.

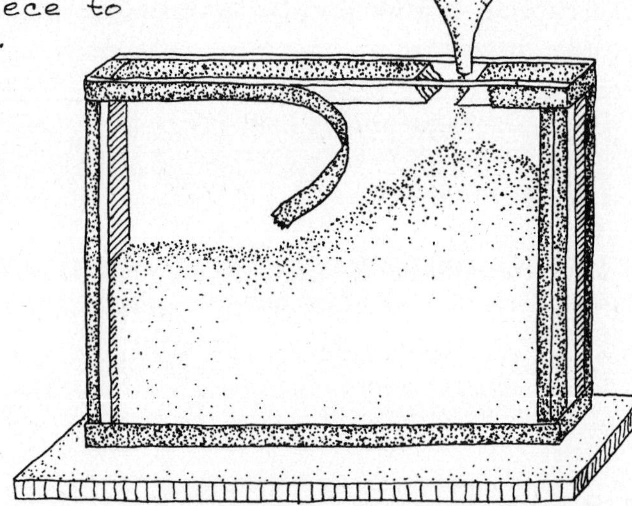

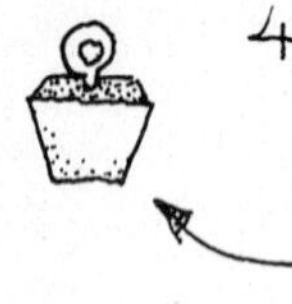

4. Cut 2-inch wedge from top piece near one end.

   Put eye screw in wedge for handle.

8. Tape side edges with 1-inch friction tape.

   Tape around top and bottom.

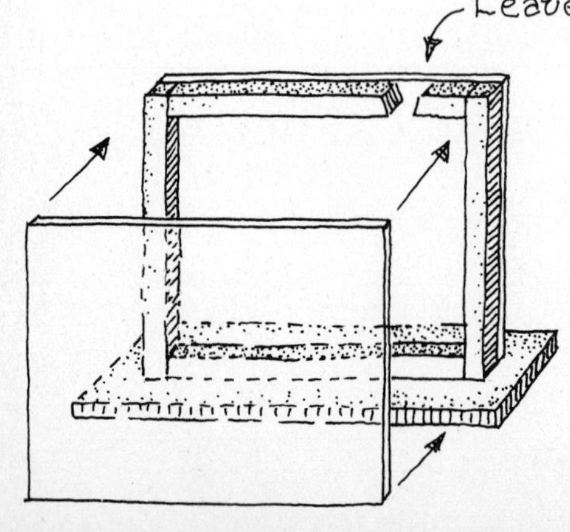

5. Glue other side piece and both top pieces in place. Do not glue wedge.
6. Clean the inside of both pieces of glass with plain water and a paper towel.
7. Glue second piece of glass in place.
9. Use funnel to pour in loose sandy dirt from near anthill.

   Close with wedge.

Ant Vivarium ($4.00)

Ants need a very special type of vivarium if you want to enjoy watching them at work underground. Commercial plastic ones are available. This homemade one is built of wood and glass. The narrowness of the structure lets you see the whole complicated network of tunnels and rooms that are ordinarily hidden in the soil beneath an ant hill. Because it is an unusual type of vivarium we are listing its price separately from the chart prices at the beginning of this section.

YOU NEED:

MATERIALS:

1-by-2-inch lumber, 4 feet long
Two pieces of window glass, each 10 by 12 inches
Scrap of plywood or board, about 6 by 14 inches
Common nails, 1½ inches long
Small eye screw
Masking, friction or adhesive tape, 1 inch wide
Paper towel
Loose, dry soil from the area in which you collect ants

TOOLS:

Handsaw
Epoxy glue
Hammer
Kitchen funnel

You can precut all the pieces of this vivarium before you begin construction. This is how to measure them accurately: mark two 10-inch-long side pieces on the 1-by-2-inch lumber, using the side of the glass as a guide. Cut the two side pieces. Lay the two side pieces on the edges of the glass with the 1-inch side against the glass. Mark the top and bottom pieces on the 1-by-2-inch lumber, using the space between the side pieces as a guide. Cut the top and bottom pieces. Check that all the pieces fit well by laying them out on the glass. They should form a neat frame that just comes to the edge of the glass all the way around. If the pieces fit, assemble the ant vivarium according to the illustrations. If the fit is not good, make adjustments before you start to glue.

You will find it is easiest to assemble this vivarium if you lay it out on a table, with the base sticking over the edge so the glass lies flat.

When the vivarium is finished, pour loose soil from where you are collecting your ants into the space between the two panes of glass. If you have no funnel, you can pour from a creased sheet of paper. Fill the vivarium to within two inches of the top.

Aquariums ($20.00)

An aquatic vivarium, usually called an aquarium, is not a tank of water, but an environment no less complicated than any other vivarium. A good aquarium must supply oxygen for the animals and light for the plants, and must filter out waste materials produced by both. The chart below lists the costs of the accessories you may want for you aquarium.

TANK ACCESSORIES

Store-bought decorative rocks, per pound . . . . .25¢

Water plants, per plant or bunch . . . . .50¢ to $1.50

Plastic pot, per pot . . . . .45¢

Lead plant weights, per package . . . . .40¢

Potting soil, smallest bag $1.29

Chlorine remover, per bottle . . . .80¢

Siphon $2.00

Fish net . . . . .50¢

Fluorescent light fixture $17.00

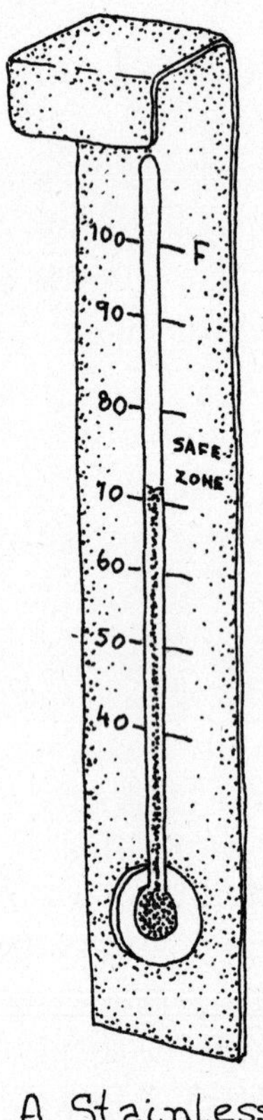

A Stainless Steel Tank Thermometer

Inside- or outside-tank filter, charcoal and filter fluff
Kitchen strainer
Air pump
Several feet of plastic tubing to connect filter to pump
Several gallon plastic jugs for storing extra water

ACCESSORIES:
Chlorine remover, if your water is chlorinated
Decorative rocks or other decorations
Water plants

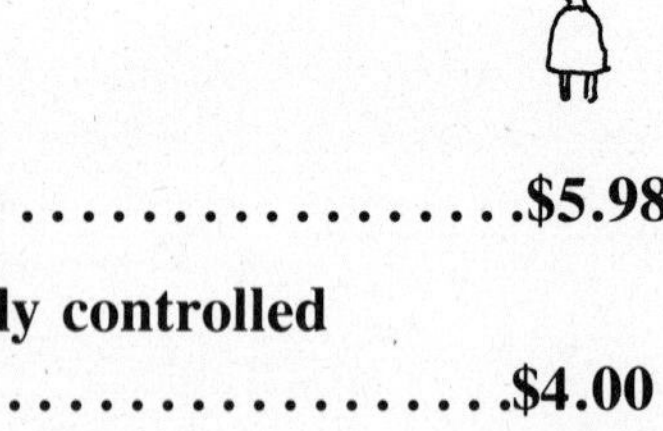

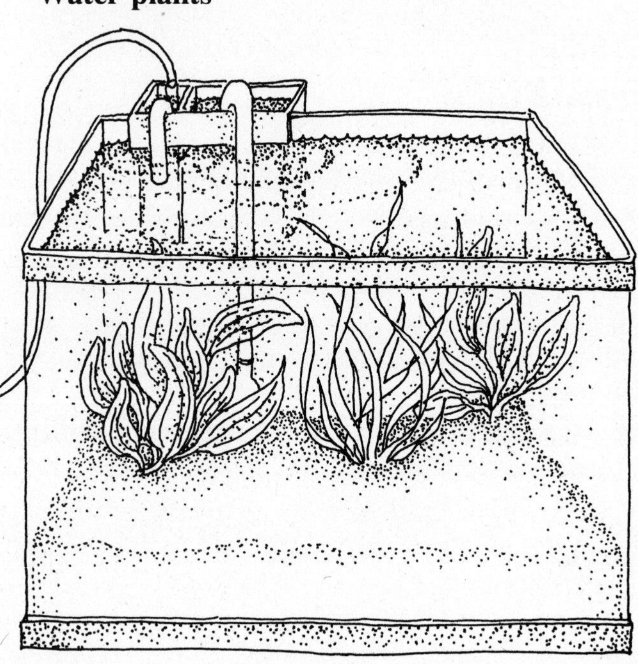

Aquarium set up with an outside tank filter box and air pump. Plants hide the two tubes.

Water level has to be up to 1/2 inch from the top for an outside filter.

Gro-Lite® bulb $5.98

Thermostatically controlled heater $4.00

Thermometer $1.00

YOU NEED:

MATERIALS:
10-gallon tank, preferably new
10 pounds of No. 3-grade gravel, natural or colored (Don't use glass gravel, because the sharp edges can cut the mouths of pets like goldfish, who pick it up in their search for leftover food. Avoid fine terrarium sand too; pretty as it is, it is difficult to keep clean.)
Large pail
Fluorescent light fixture and Gro-Lite® bulb
Heater
Siphon and bucket for occasional cleaning

Rinse the tank so it is free of dust. Put the gravel in a pail and run fresh tap water (it doesn't have to be dechlorinated) into it. As you let the water run and overflow, stir the gravel with your hands. When the water looks clear, the gravel is clean.

Pour off the extra water and spread the gravel in your tank.

Before you put water in the tank, find a non-sunny location to keep it, where temperatures won't vary much. A filled tank is terribly heavy to move. Avoid bedrooms where windows are open on cold nights, or rooms where air conditioning might lower the temperature rapidly. The creatures who will live here can get as cold as 60 degrees and as hot as 85 degrees, but will die from rapid temperature change.

There are other problems to be aware of before you fill the tank with water. In cities and many towns, and even in some private water-supply systems, water is chlorinated to kill bacteria. The chlorine is a lethal poison to water creatures. Pet stores sell a liquid chlorine remover that works instantly and makes chlorinated water perfectly safe. A few drops to a gallon is all it takes. Read the instructions on the bottle to be sure you are accurate.

Other chemicals are equally lethal. Dissolved copper, present in the water when new copper pipes have been installed in a home, kills many water animals. If new plumbing work has been done in your house, get your water from a neighbor until the new pipes have been in use for six months.

Fill the tank and install the filter and air pump, following the directions on their packaging. The instructions on the filter package tell you how much charcoal and fluff to use and where to put them. The instructions may neglect to say that you have to rinse the charcoal to remove its black dust before you use it. It's easiest to rinse it in a kitchen strainer under running water.

Aquatic environments need nothing more than this, but decorating a tank is almost irresistible. Watch out for tank decorations that may contain harmful chemicals, though. Shells, corals and some rocks contain lime. Lime makes water too alkaline (the opposite of acidic) for fresh-water creatures. Copper minerals, of course, act the same way as new copper pipes. Stones from the seashore and artistic driftwood make water too salty. To be safe, stick to petrified wood, fresh-water driftwood, slate, quartz, granite or basalt.

If your school, community or artistic neighbor has a kiln, you can make your own tank decorations. Use moist clay, either terra cotta or boneware—the kind you have to fire, not the kind that is self-hardening or is baked in a home oven. Caves are fun, especially for crayfish who will lurk appropriately. Tall thin clay pieces can look like corals. Of course, you can make monsters and mermaids, too. The pieces can be left plain, or glazed. Lead glazes, which can be lethal to humans, don't hurt water creatures at all.

There are dozens and dozens of water plants with which to decorate an aquarium, but few of them do well at room temperature. Before you buy, ask whether the plant you like is a tropical plant that will only grow in a heated tank. Plants come two ways: in bunches without roots, and as individually rooted plants. Bunch plants are cuttings—pieces of stem cut from a "mother" plant. Eventually, almost all of them will sprout roots near the bottom of the stem and can be established as rooted plants. Some bunch plants, like cabomba and anachris, are bought mostly as food for hungry goldfish, turtles and tadpoles. They are slow to root and quick to break and decay. You can keep bunch plants like this in a jar of water and put a sprig at a time into the tank for snacks. If you want to root a bunch plant, take off the rubber band that holds the stems together. With a razor blade, slice each stem above where the band probably crushed it. Put the cuttings into a jar of water and keep them in a sunny window. Change the water daily, and cut off any portions of the stems or leaves that begin to rot. When roots appear, you can plant the cuttings, following the suggestions below for rooted plants.

If this method of rooting plants sounds like too much trouble, you can just remove the rubber band, slice the stems above the crushed area, hold the bunch together with a lead plant weight (bought at the pet store), and shove the stems down into the gravel. If the weight isn't enough to keep the plants from floating upwards, plant the bunch with the roots bent sideways and put a rock on top. The tops of the stems will soon turn upwards, and at least some of the stems will root into the gravel.

Some of the plants that come with roots are ones that grow in sand or soil at the bottom of the tank. A native water plant of this type that you may be able to collect yourself is wild watercress. Others,

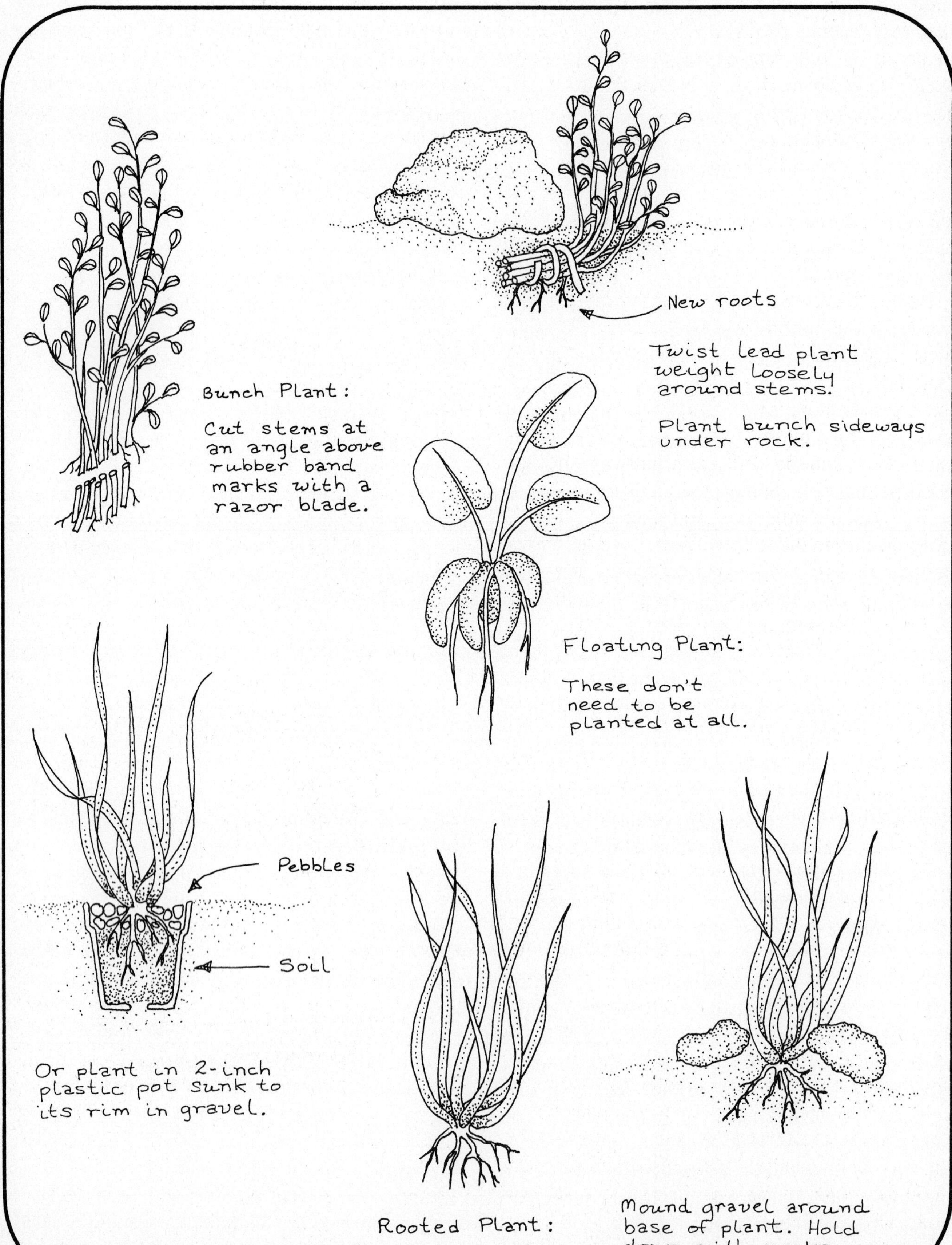
New roots
Twist lead plant weight loosely around stems.
Plant bunch sideways under rock.
Bunch Plant:
Cut stems at an angle above rubber band marks with a razor blade.
Floating Plant:
These don't need to be planted at all.
Pebbles
Soil
Or plant in 2-inch plastic pot sunk to its rim in gravel.
Rooted Plant:
Mound gravel around base of plant. Hold down with rocks.

though they may send roots to the bottom eventually, are floating plants which don't need to be anchored in soil. Among the floaters is a funny plant called a banana plant, which floats on bladders that look like a tiny bunch of bananas. Another is a native temperate-zone plant called duckweed, which you can collect yourself. You may see it nearly covering ponds with its tiny green leaves during the summer. Duckweed will probably do so well in your tank that you'll have to keep removing it by the handful.

Rooted plants get some nutrition from animal wastes at the bottom of a tank, but most will do better if they have a nutrient soil to grow in rather than the sterile gravel you are using as a floor. No one wants mud on the bottom of a tank, so here's a trick: buy tiny plastic flower pots, the kind baby cacti often come in. Fill them halfway up with a good potting soil. Spread the plant roots over the soil. Sprinkle a little more soil over the roots. Fill the container to the top with coarse gravel or small pebbles to hold the soil in place and match the ground in your tank. Soak the pots thoroughly. Now sink the potted plants (*very* slowly) into the gravel in your tank bottom. The pots will not be visible, the plants will get good nutrition, and when you change your mind about where the plants should go, moving the pots is easy.

The pets who are going to live in this aquatic vivarium don't need light, but the plants do. They would all love some sun, but any sun at all will encourage algae—a green plant that bedevils the tank owner by covering everything with green fuzz. There is no perfect solution for getting healthy plants and no algae, but the closest thing to it is to use a fluorescent lighting fixture that fits snugly on top of the tank. The fixture should be equipped with a special Gro-Lite® bulb, available to fit 5½- or 10-gallon tank fixtures in either pet or garden stores. The Gro-Lite® is a balanced fluorescent lamp that provides the ultra-violet light plants need without the intense light algae love and the heat many water creatures hate. Six to eight hours of light is recommended. If algae nevertheless get a foothold, compromise. Cut the light hours down to four, and see what happens.

Temperature is maintained in a tank either by just keeping it in a room that stays about the same temperature all the time (no air conditioning, windows not opened on freezing winter nights) or by a thermostatically controlled heating system. Heated tanks are necessary only for tropical fish. The heater and its controlling thermostat are available in pet stores and cost from $3.00 and up. Tropical fish are complicated to keep, so the aquatic animals we suggest in this book are all ones that remain healthy without a heating system.

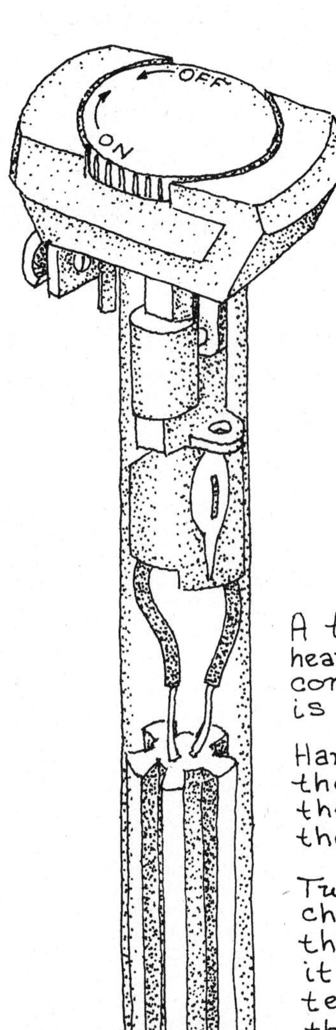

A thermostatic tank heater looks complicated, but it is not hard to use.

Hang the heater on the tank rim with the glass tube inside the tank.

Turn it on. Keep checking the tank thermometer until it reaches the desired temperature. Turn the thermostat slowly until you hear it click off. From now on, the thermostat will click on again whenever the water temperature falls below that point.

Maintaining An Aquarium

Theoretically you could keep an aquarium clean by siphoning off a third of the water from the bottom every week and replacing it with fresh water. In practice, siphoning is a long, messy, inefficient job, and is not recommended. You could also theoretically establish a balanced environment of plants and scavenger animals, which would function much like that of a stagnant but livable pond. In practice, this is best left to ecologists who know exactly what they're doing. For most people, a filter system is definitely the best way to cope with keeping a tank clean.

The filter system performs various functions: it traps particles of algae (tiny green water plants), waste products and leftover food in the fluff, keeping the water clear. It filters the water through charcoal, which removes some chemical waste products. And it provides oxygen by bubbling air through the water.

A filter must be cleaned every week. Read the instructions that come with the filter to see how much charcoal and filter fluff your filter needs. Unplug the pump and pull the filter up out of the water. Detach the plastic tube from the filter box. Take the filter to the sink, take the top off, and throw out the dirty filter fluff balls. Rinse the charcoal at the bottom under running water, and replace the dirty fluff with new fluff. Every other week, replace the old charcoal with fresh, well-rinsed charcoal. When a filter box feels slimy or looks dirty, wash it out with salt and rinse it well. Never use soap or detergent, because the residue you don't notice can kill your pets.

Each week, replace the water that has evaporated with water (dechlorinated if

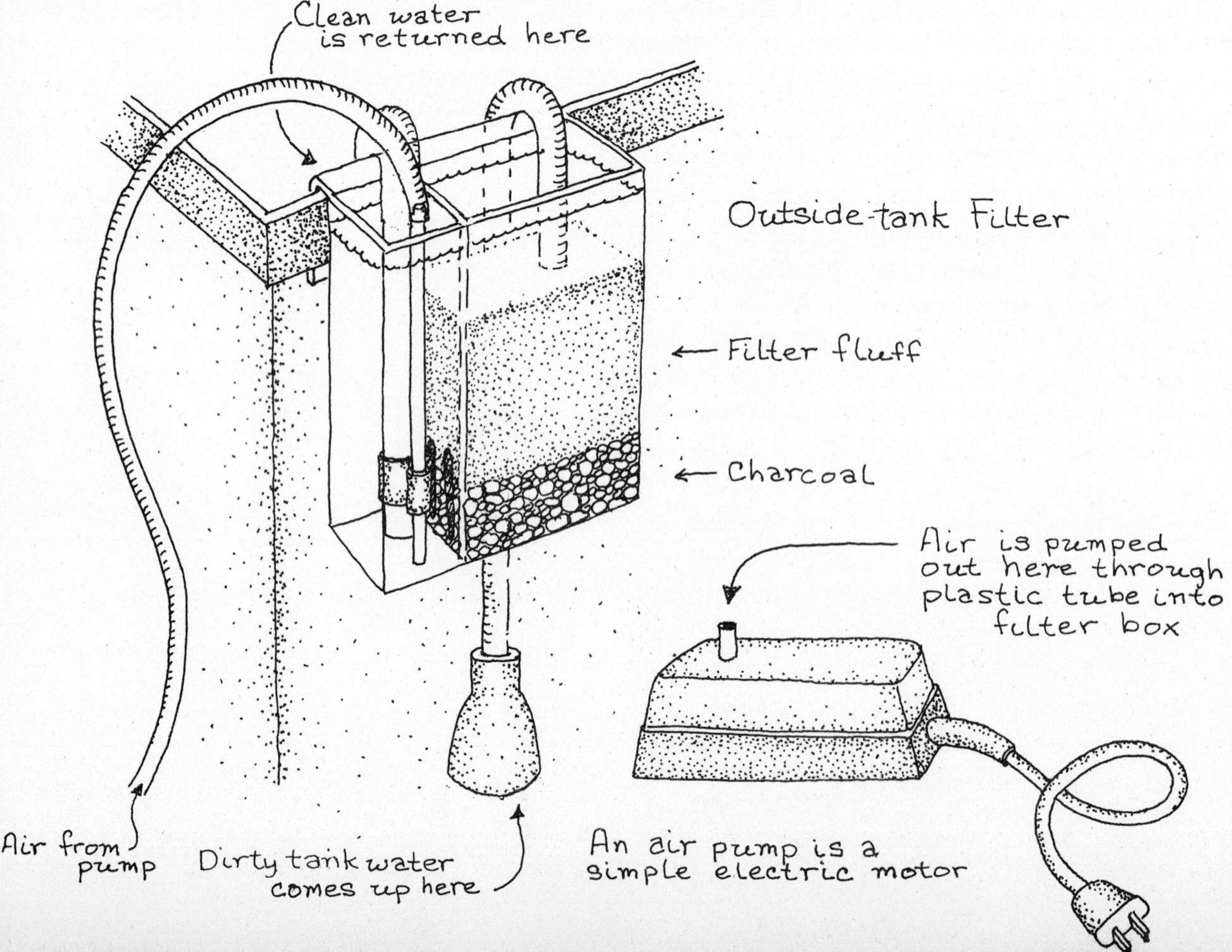

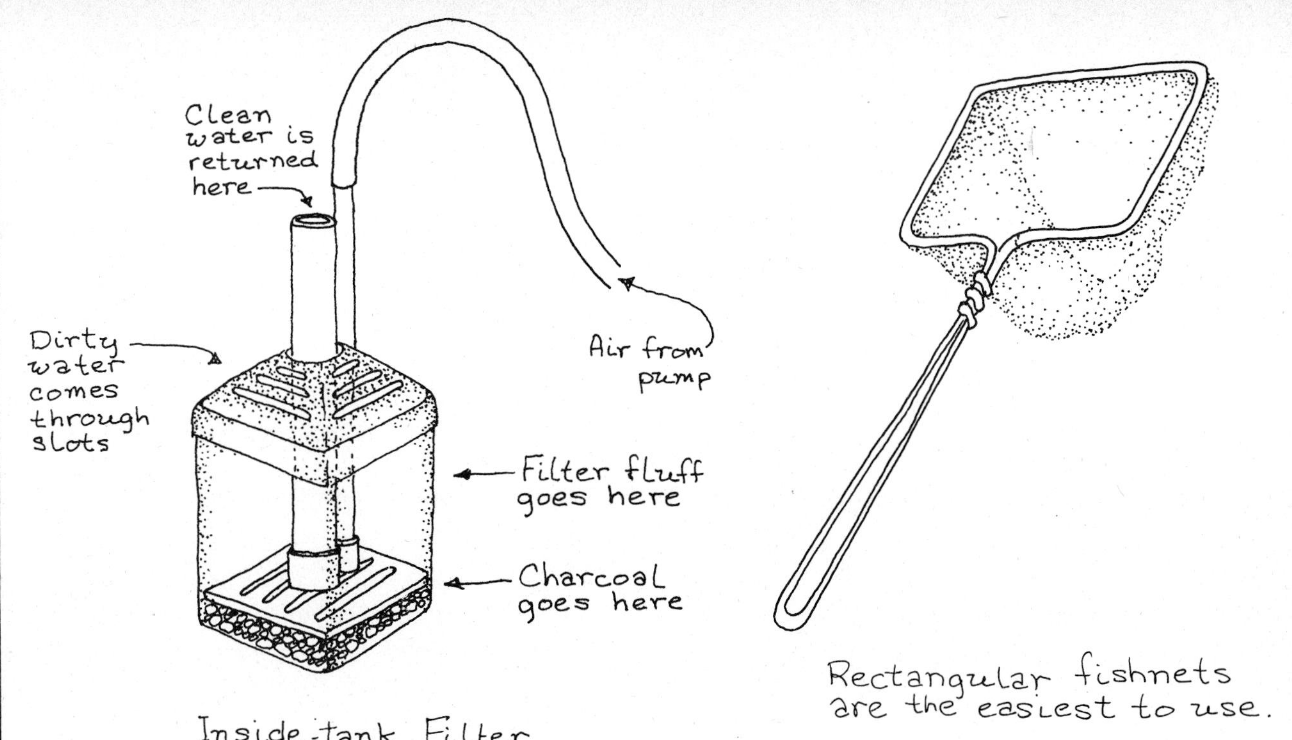

Inside-tank Filter

Rectangular fishnets are the easiest to use.

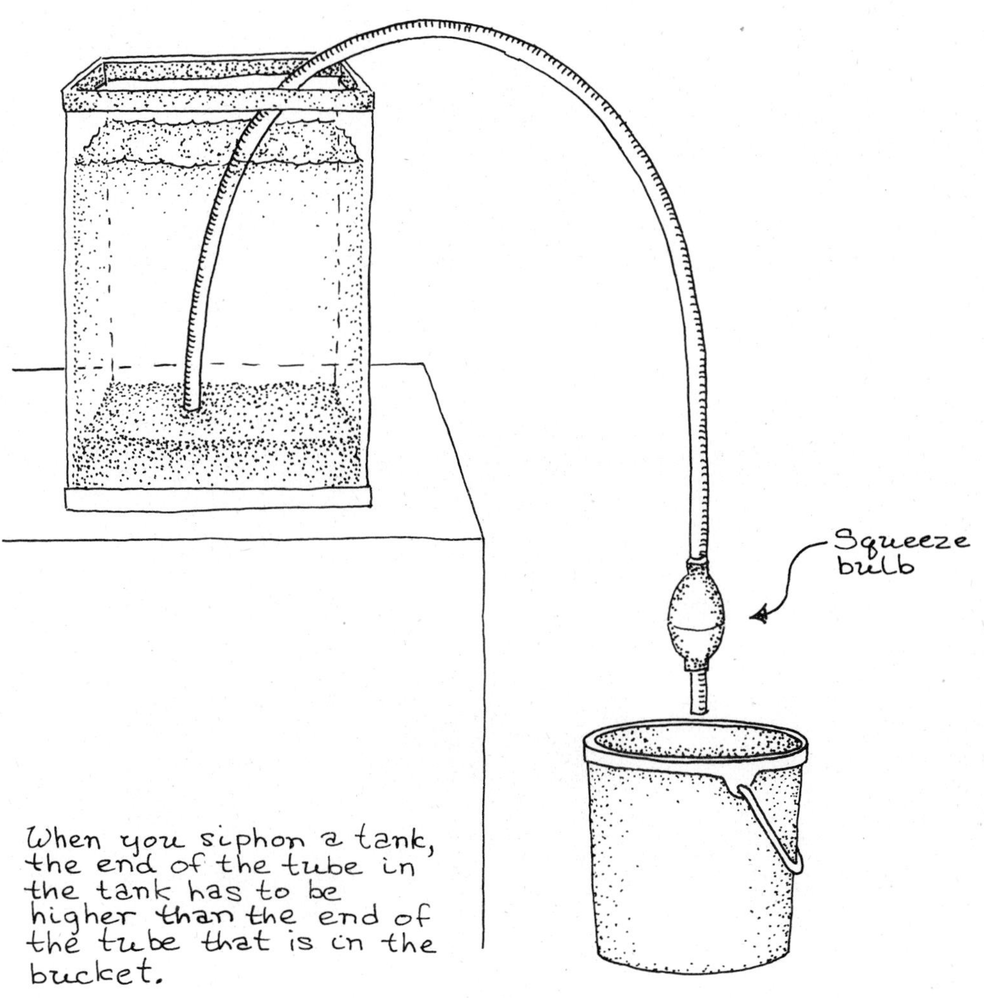

When you siphon a tank, the end of the tube in the tank has to be higher than the end of the tube that is in the bucket.

necessary) and left to sit at least two days earlier so it is the same temperature as the tank water. Keeping two-gallon jugs (milk bottles) of prepared water handy all the time makes the job easy.

Three times a year, replace a third of the

water in the tank with new water. This is to remove accumulated wastes the filter can't handle. Prepare the water two days beforehand so it's the same temperature as the water in the tank. You'll need almost four gallons for a 10-gallon tank. Siphon off a third of the water; refill with the fresh water.

Siphons these days are made with a bulb device at one end. The bulb may be rubber (the best kind) or molded right along with the tube itself (not very good). The principle behind siphoning is that any continuous stream of water will flow towards its lowest point. Gravity sees to that. A siphon is simply a way of connecting the water in your tank in a continuous stream with a lower point so that it will flow downward. This sounds easy, but there is a catch to it. First you have to get water up into the tube. That's what the bulb is for. Stick the bulb end down into a pail on the floor. Put one finger over the bulb end and squeeze the bulb; that forces air from the tube. Still holding your finger over the bulb end, release the bulb. Water flows into the tube. Now you can take your finger off the end, and water will start flowing from tank to pail in a continuous stream.

If you ever have to completely empty and clean a tank—because it's been neglected or is full of algae—use salt to scrub it, not soap or detergent. Of course, salt has to be rinsed out well, but a slight residue is not lethal.

Serpentariums

Baby snakes up to two and a half or three feet long can live in a serpentarium that is nothing more than a tank with a screen or mesh top. Large snakes over three feet long need larger quarters. Restless rubbing against the top of a tank may be a sign that a snake is seeking more space. You can either buy a larger tank—they come up to about five feet long—or build a wood and plexiglass serpentarium yourself. Neither is cheap.

Tank Serpentarium ($22.00)

YOU NEED:

MATERIALS:

10-gallon tank
¼-inch mesh hardware cloth, 18 by 36 inches; or commercial mesh top to fit tank
Masking tape (freezer tape), 1 inch wide
Several feet of soft wire
Heavy rock

TOOLS:

Yardstick
Wire shears
Wire clippers or pliers that cut wire

ACCESSORIES:

Incandescent tank fixture to fit tank top
Tank thermometer
Newspaper or plastic grass matting to cover floor of cage
Crockery water dish
Climbing branch and rock

Have a 10-gallon tank ready to house your snake. Line the inside perimeters of a commercial screen top with masking tape to protect the skin on your snake's nose when it rubs against it. Or build the homemade mesh top illustrated here, fastening the corners with soft wire. Lay an incandescent light fixture across the top for warmth. Tape a tank thermometer to the inside of the tank with masking tape. (If you don't want the tape to show, fold it into a ring, sticky side out. The sticky sides will hold to both the tank wall and the back of the thermometer.)

Serpentariums must be kept very clean. Gravel may look pretty, but it invites bacteria and can't be

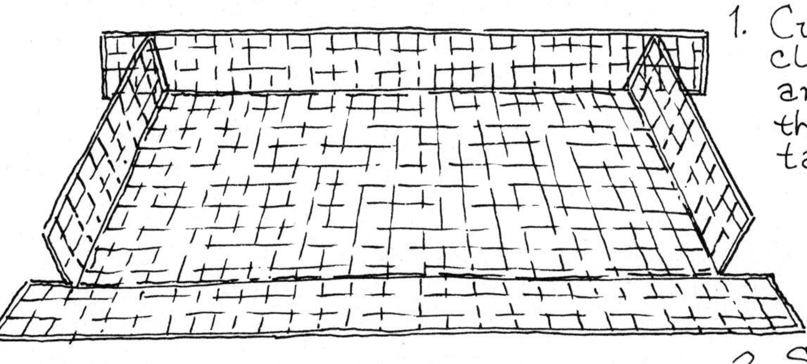

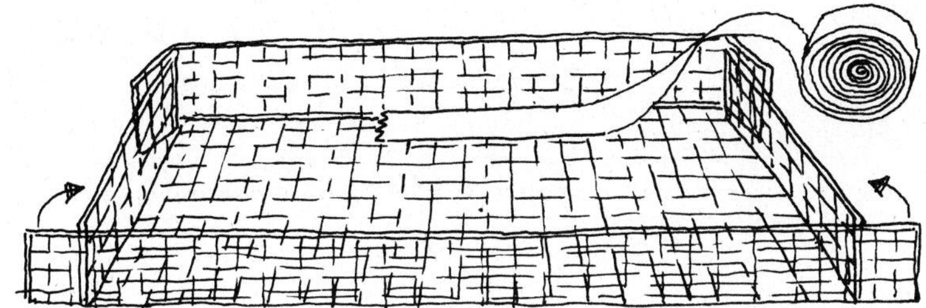

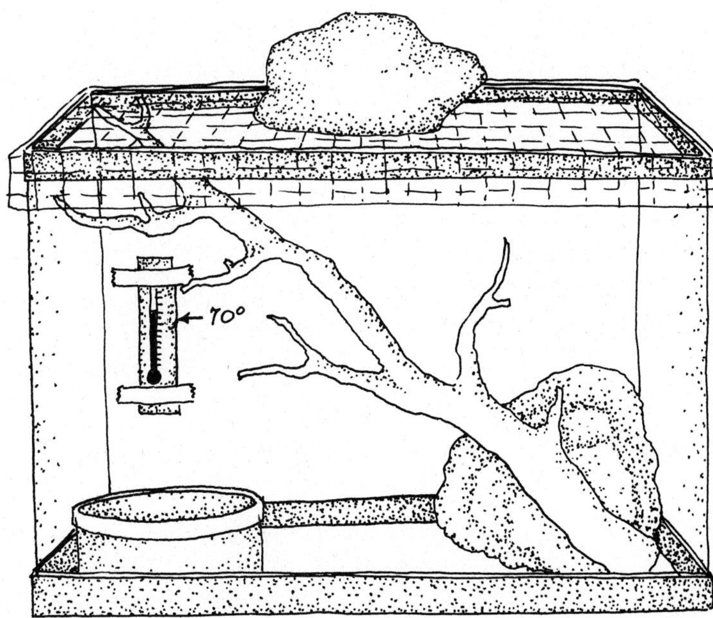

washed well enough. Use newspaper or plastic grass matting for flooring material. The newspaper can be changed each time it gets soiled, and the plastic grass can be washed off.

Add the crockery water dish. Your snake will use it for both drinking and soaking, so the dish should be large enough for the snake to submerge all but its nose in it. A rock to hide behind and to rub against at shedding time is welcomed. Another nice addition is a branch propped diagonally from one side of the tank to the other, for resting and climbing.

Wood Serpentarium ($45.00)

A wood serpentarium is basically a plywood box, opening at the front. The opening is fitted with two sliding plexiglass doors that move along a standard aluminum track. Wire mesh is not a good substitute for the plexiglass, as you will not be able to protect so large a surface with masking tape. Don't buy either the track or the plexiglass until you have finished building the rest of the serpentarium. Once you know the exact dimensions of the front opening, a glazing company can cut the track and plexiglass for you, and tell you how to install the doors.

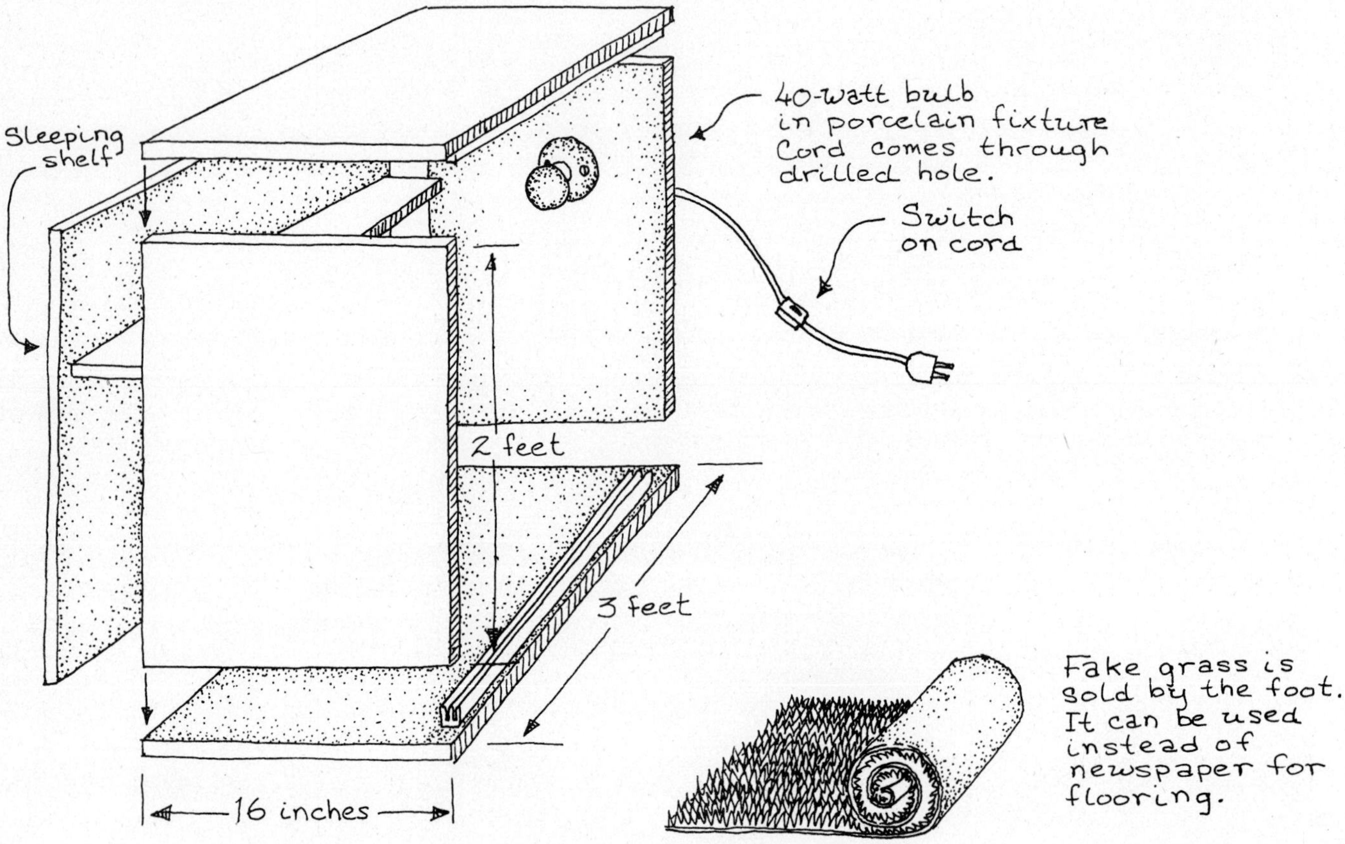

Sleeping shelf

40-watt bulb in porcelain fixture Cord comes through drilled hole.

Switch on cord

2 feet

3 feet

16 inches

Fake grass is sold by the foot. It can be used instead of newspaper for flooring.

1. Cut two side pieces that measure 2 feet by 16 inches. Cut top and bottom pieces that measure 3 feet by 16 inches. Use ½-inch plywood.

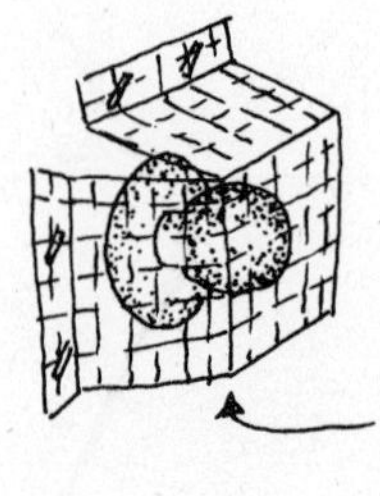

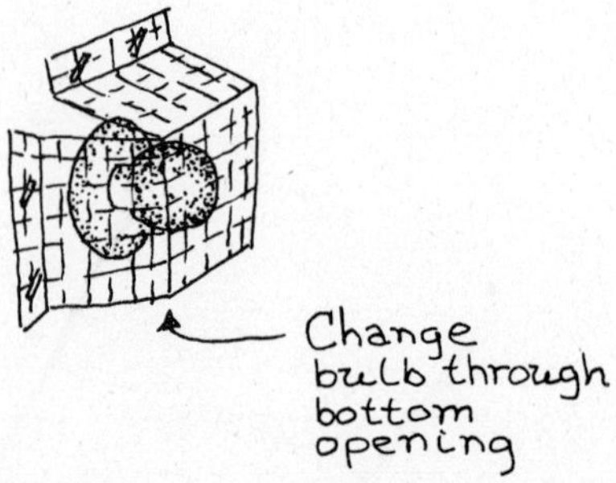

Change bulb through bottom opening

2. Glue and nail top, bottom and sides together. Use the assembled box as a guide to mark and cut the back wall so it is even with the edges all the way around.

   Glue and nail back wall in place.

3. Measure for the 8-inch sleeping shelf. Glue and nail in place toward top of back wall.

4. Drill 1-inch hole for light cord two-thirds of the way up the middle of one side. Screw the fixture in with the cord emerging through the hole.

5. Measure front opening carefully so glazier or lumber yard can cut track and plexiglass to fit. Install track and doors according to their instructions.

Shellac inside of serpentarium

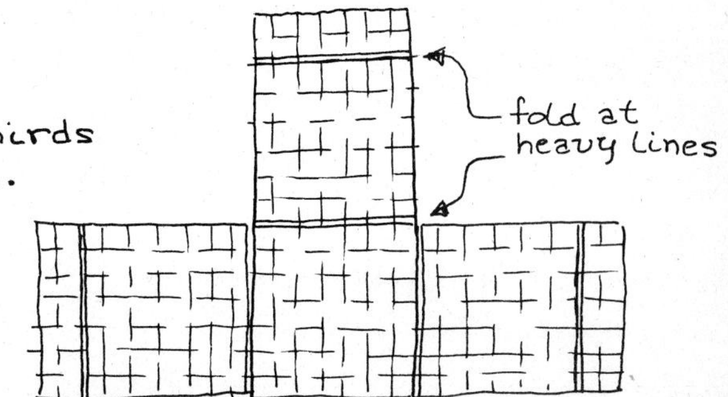

A hardware cloth guard can be added to protect snake from hot light bulb. Cut and fold as shown. Staple in place.

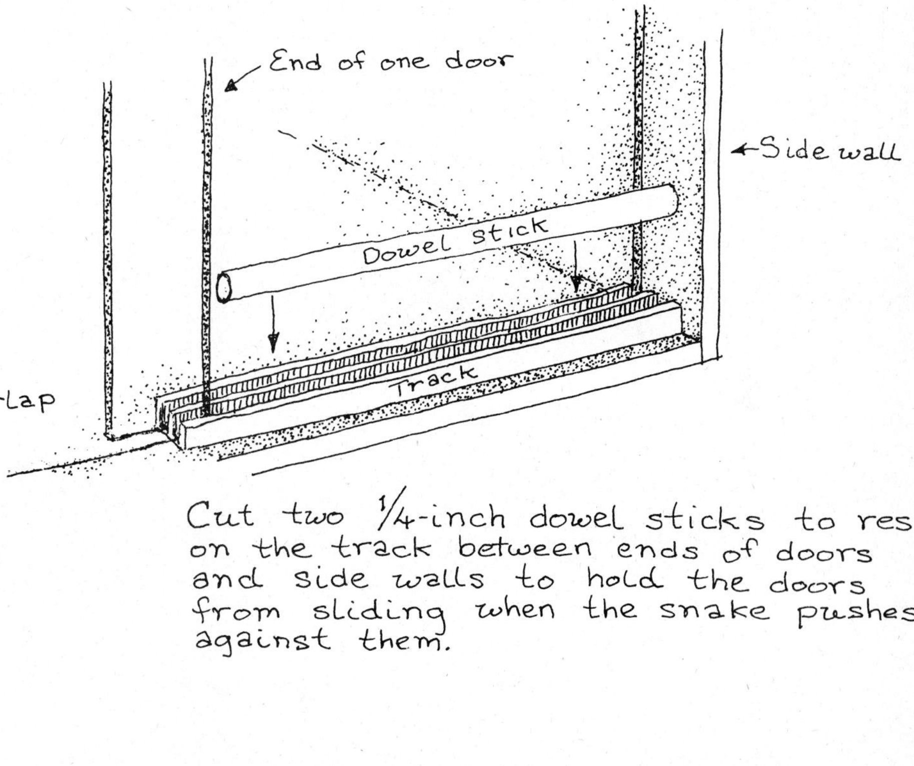

End of one door

Side wall

Dowel stick

Track

Cut two 1/4-inch dowel sticks to rest on the track between ends of doors and side walls to hold the doors from sliding when the snake pushes against them.

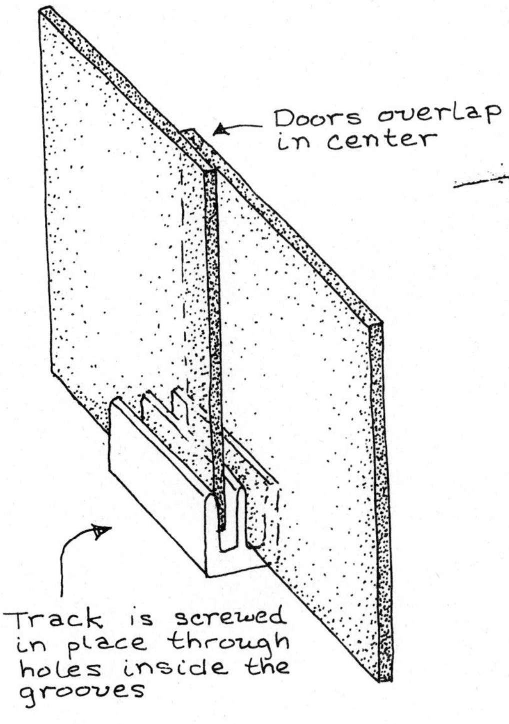

Doors overlap in center

Track is screwed in place through holes inside the grooves

Double aluminum track is installed at both the top and the bottom of the front opening to hold sliding plexiglass doors.

YOU NEED:

MATERIALS:

½-inch interior-grade plywood, one 4-by-8-foot sheet
White glue
Common nails, 1¼ inch long
8-inch shelving board, 3 feet long
Porcelain light fixture
Electrical cord, plug, cord switch and 40-watt light bulb
Double aluminum sliding track, cut to fit top and bottom of front opening by glazier or lumberyard
Two plexiglass sliding doors, cut to fit front opening by glazier or lumberyard
Pint of shellac
½-inch dowel, 36 inches long

TOOLS:

Yardstick or long ruler
Circular saw
Handsaw
Hammer
Drill with 1-inch bit
Screwdriver
Paintbrush

ACCESSORIES:

Hardware-cloth bulb guard
Tank thermometer
Newspaper or plastic grass matting to cover floor of cage
Crockery water dish
Climbing branch and rock

Follow the illustrations to assemble the serpentarium. When it has been put together, measure the front opening accurately. Bring this measurement with you to a glazing company so they will be able to figure out the exact sizes of track and plexiglass to cut for you. Bring this book along too, if you think it would help to show them the picture. Since installation differs with the kind of track the glazing company carries, ask them for installation instructions.

A determined snake will force its way out where the two sliding doors overlap in the middle.

There's probably a sophisticated method of preventing this, but we just use a piece of masking tape. If your snake learns to slide a door open by pushing against it with his nose, a piece of dowel can be cut to the right size and placed in the groove between door and side of cage, as shown in the illustration.

Interior fixings might include a shelf as well as a branch for the snake to rest on, a large crockery water dish for drinking and soaking, and a rock for shedding. A cardboard box with a hole in it serves as a burrow—a luxury that most tanks are too small to hold. This cage is sized so that you can easily cover the floor with standard newspapers (not opened out, but overlapped as shown).

Birdcages *($12.00)*

It is very difficult to make a birdcage as well designed and practical as a commercial cage. However, the cakepan cage assembled on page 338 can be made larger to serve small birds like canaries or parakeets.

YOU NEED:

MATERIALS:

Two roasting pans, each 12 by 18 inches
½-inch mesh hardware cloth, 19 by 66 inches
Several feet of soft wire
Small branches for perches
Tube-shaped water and seed dispensers, available at pet stores

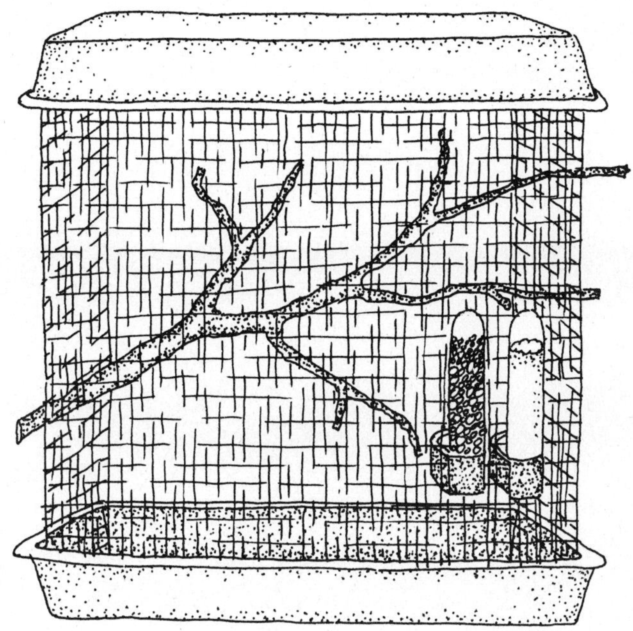

A cake-pan cage can be made to suit small birds.

Cut hardware cloth several inches higher than plan on page

Poke a branch through mesh to serve as a perch.

Snip wire as needed to make holes large enough to take these tube-shaped or other food and water containers.

Use newspaper or sand as flooring.

Several layers of newspaper, or sand for flooring

TOOLS:
Wire shears
File
Pocketknife for cutting perches
Wire clippers or pliers that cut wire

Follow the illustrations on page 338 to construct the basic cage. Stick branches through the mesh from one side of the cage to the other to serve as perches, prying open holes if necessary so the branches fit through. To insert the tube-shaped seed and water dispensers, use wire clippers to cut out whatever area of wire is necessary to make a hole large enough to accommodate the dish part of the containers. Spread sand or newspaper for flooring.

To clean this cage, simply lift the cage off the bottom pan. The bird will perch inside the rest of the cage while you empty and wash the bottom pan with soap and water and change the newspaper or sand.

Parrot Perch ($8.00)

If you wish to keep a parrot outside a cage, here is a perch set-up that works for one who has had its wings clipped.

YOU NEED:

MATERIALS:
Large screw-in hook, 4 or 5 inches long
12 feet twisted chain, or the same length of heavy galvanized steel wire
Three S-hooks, if you are using chain
Three eye screws, about 1½ inches long
Thick, forked branch, about 3 feet long
Metal utility shelf that bolts into wall
Expansion bolts for attaching shelf
Crockery food and water dishes to fit in shelf
Newspaper

TOOLS:
Hammer
Drill with bit to suit screw-in hook
Wire clippers
Pliers

Choose the spot where you would like the perch to hang. Locate a ceiling beam behind the plaster or wallboard by gently tapping with a hammer until you find a spot that does not sound hollow. Drill a hole into the beam somewhat narrower than the large screw-in hook; then screw the hook into the hole.

You can follow the illustration to see how to

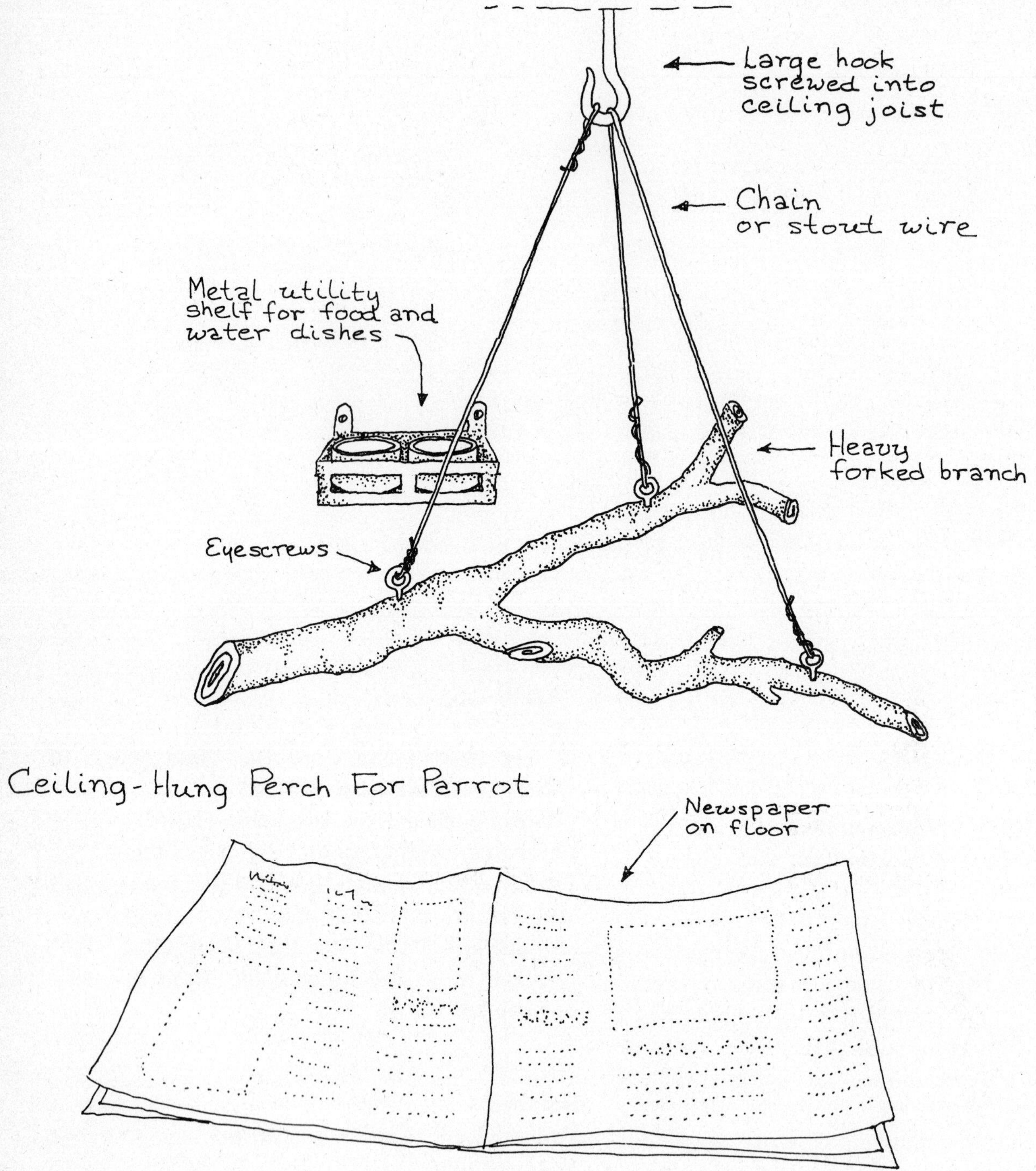

Ceiling-Hung Perch For Parrot

finish the perch, but before you cut the final lengths of wire or chain, adjust them until the perch hangs steadily and parallel to the floor. Use the S-hooks for attaching the chain to the eye screws. Locate the utility shelf within reach of the perch so your bird can get to its food and water dishes. A sheet of newspaper on the floor, changed every day, catches droppings and seed.

Mynah Perch ($11.00)

A mynah can be kept outside a cage on an easy-to-make wooden perch set-up, which includes a tray to catch droppings and seed. The bird will stay there simply because, with its wings clipped, the floor looks very far away.

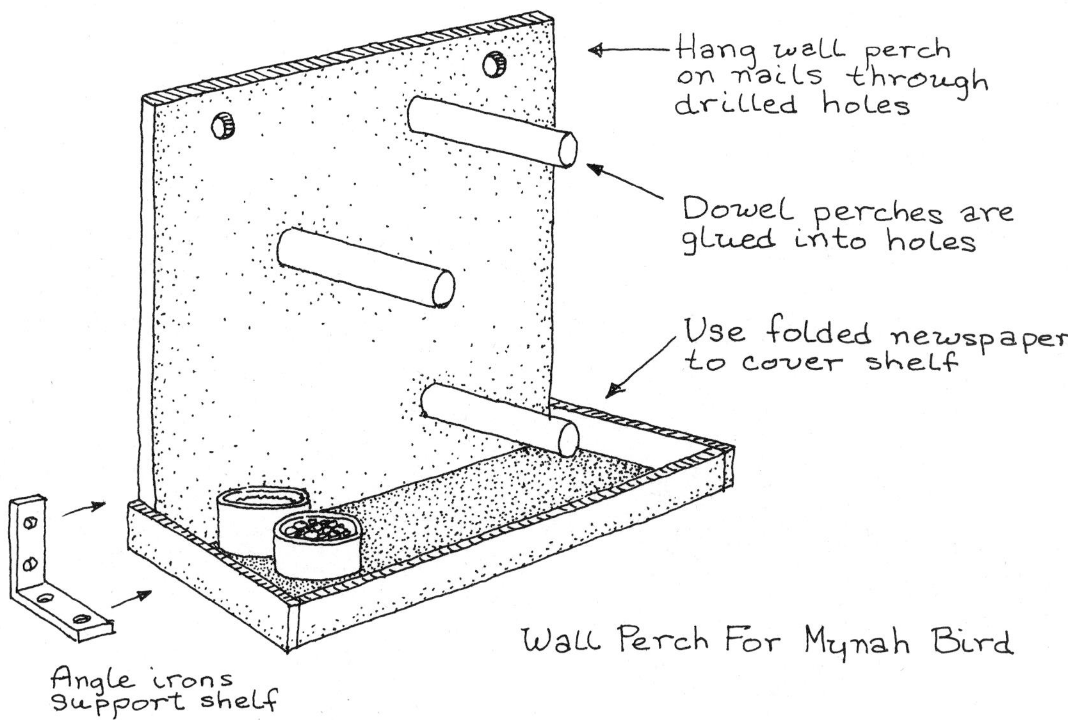

Wall Perch For Mynah Bird

YOU NEED:

MATERIALS:

¾-inch interior-grade plywood, two pieces
White glue
Common nails, 1½ inches long and 4 inches long
Two angle irons, 2 or 3 inches long and enough screws, ⅝ inch long
2-inch lattice strip, 4 feet long
¾-inch dowel, 36 inches long
Pint of shellac

TOOLS:

Hammer
Screwdriver
Yardstick
Handsaw
Drill with ¾-inch and ½-inch bits
Paintbrush

ACCESSORIES:

Crockery food and water dishes

Try to find scraps of plywood at the lumberyard the right size to make this perch. Glue and nail the two plywood pieces together in an L-shape, as shown in the illustration, and reinforce them with angle irons screwed to the inside corners.

Measure, mark and cut the lattice strip so it fits the edge of the shelf as shown. Glue and nail it in place, using the smaller nails.

Drill three ¾-inch holes in the back wall of the perch to accept the dowels. Space them with your mynah bird's hopping distance in mind. Cut the dowel into three equal pieces for perches, and glue the perches into the holes.

To attach the perch to a wall, you will have to locate studs to nail into. Find them the same way you found ceiling beams for the parrot perch—by tapping until you get to spots that don't sound hollow. Studs are usually 16 inches apart. Hammer two four-inch nails into the studs about five feet above the floor. Measure the distance between them, and then drill ½-inch holes that distance apart in the back wall of the perch so you can hang it.

Give the wood several coats of shellac. Cover the shelf area with folded newspaper, and put the food and water dishes in place.

Cake-Pan Rodent Homes

($6.00 for small, $7.00 for medium)

Gerbils, hamsters, mice and rats are all rodents—and all gnawing animals. Gnaw-proof commercial metal cages are available, but this cake-pan cage serves very well. Because the top removes for getting at the animal and the bottom removes for washing, it is a more convenient cage than the commercial ones. And it is just as gnaw-proof.

YOU NEED:

MATERIALS:

½-inch mesh (for mice, ¼-inch mesh) hardware cloth, 36 by 10½ inches for the small cage, 42 by 13½ inches for medium-sized cage
Two aluminum baking pans of the same size. For a small cage, square pans 9 by 9 inches; for a medium-sized cage, rectangular pans 8 by 12 inches
Several feet of soft wire
Rock to weight the top

TOOLS:

Wire shears
Wire clippers

ACCESSORIES:

Newspaper or wood shavings
Nesting materials (toilet paper, yarn, cloth)
Water bottle and wire bracket

Examine the roll of hardware cloth before the salesperson in the hardware store cuts it. If the mesh is warped, don't buy it. Warped mesh will make it impossible to construct anything but a jiggly cage.

The hardest part of making this cage is cutting the hardware cloth. The person in the hardware store may do the rough cutting for you, but he or she will leave the cloth with sharp ends sticking up from it. You will have to trim these off. You can use either wire shears or a wire cutter. When all the spikes are trimmed, put one end of your piece of hardware cloth in the pan, and give it a bend where it meets the first corner. Take it out again and crease the corner up to the top edge. Repeat the process of bending and creasing for each corner, as shown in the illustrations.

Your piece of hardware cloth is long enough to

1. Bend the hardware cloth to fit inside the bottom pan.

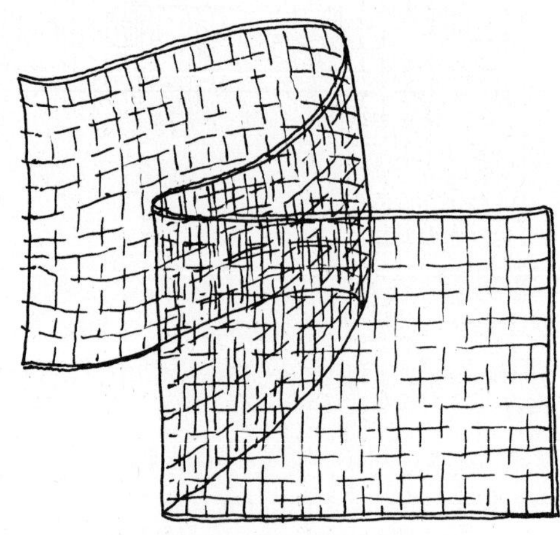

ⓐ First bend

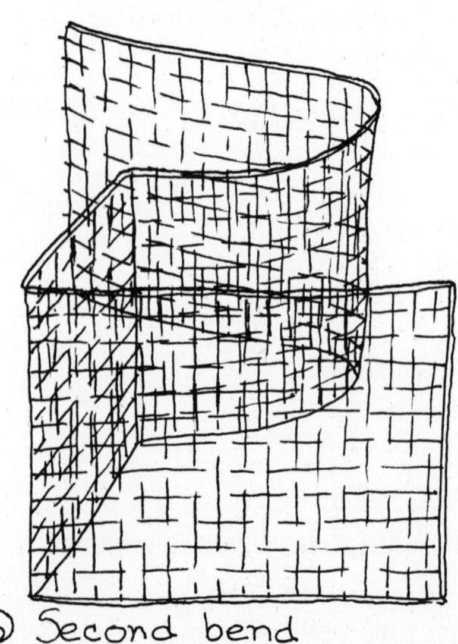

ⓑ Second bend

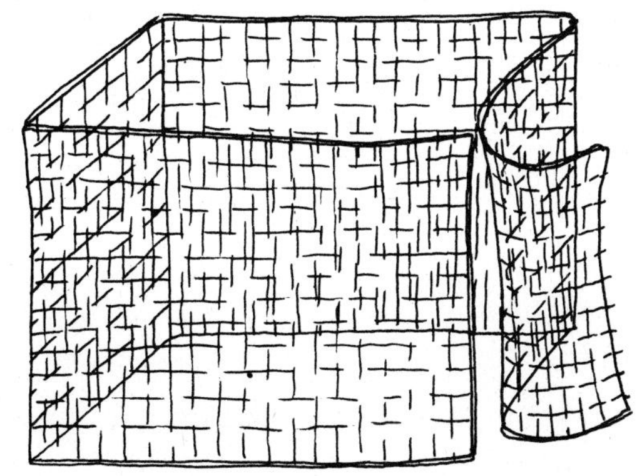
Ⓒ Third bend

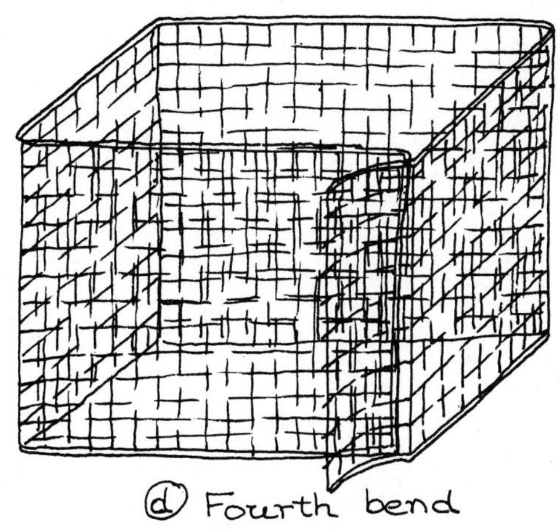
Ⓓ Fourth bend

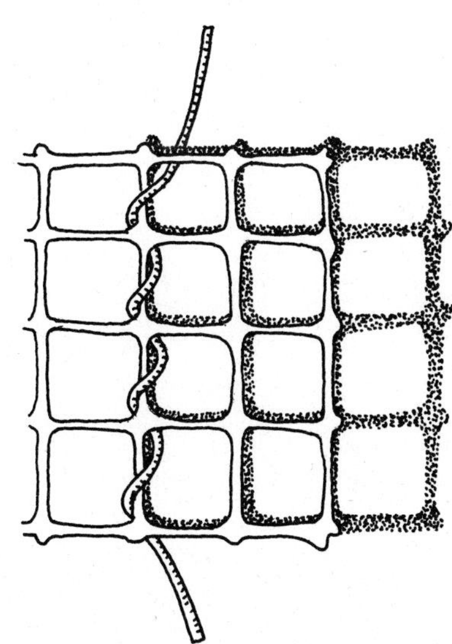
2. Trim overlap neatly to 1 or 2 inches. Line up mesh. Lace together both edges with soft wire from top to bottom of cage.

form a two-inch overlap. Check that the creases fit neatly into the corners of the pan, and then weave the overlap together with soft wire. Put the other pan on top, and weight it with a heavy book or rock.

Set up any rodent cage with 1½ inches of wood shavings on the floor as bedding material. Add soft materials like toilet paper, cotton batting, yarn or cloth for nesting materials (the rodent will make its own nest from it). A food dish is not necessary, but attach a water bottle to the side of the cage, as shown. If your water bottle didn't come with a wire bracket, the illustration here shows you how to shape a bracket out of heavy wire.

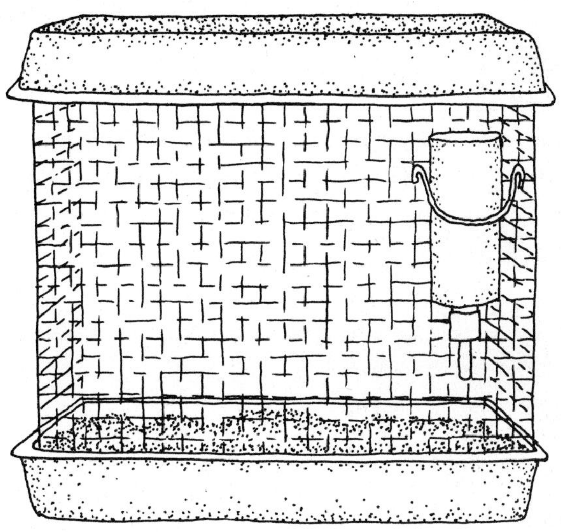
3. Finished cage with water bottle and bedding.

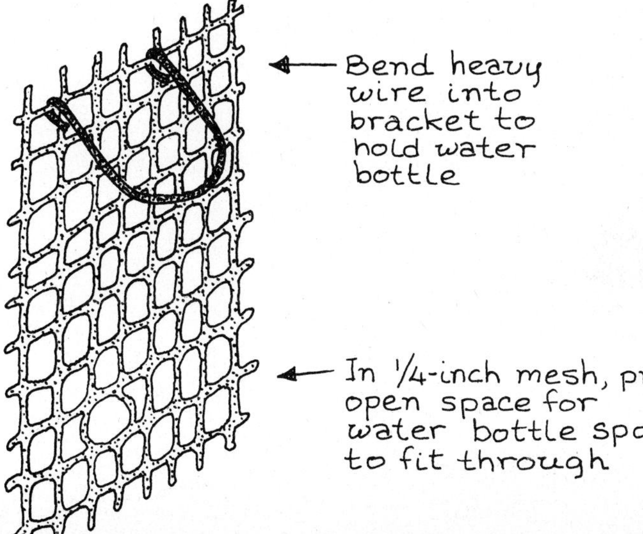

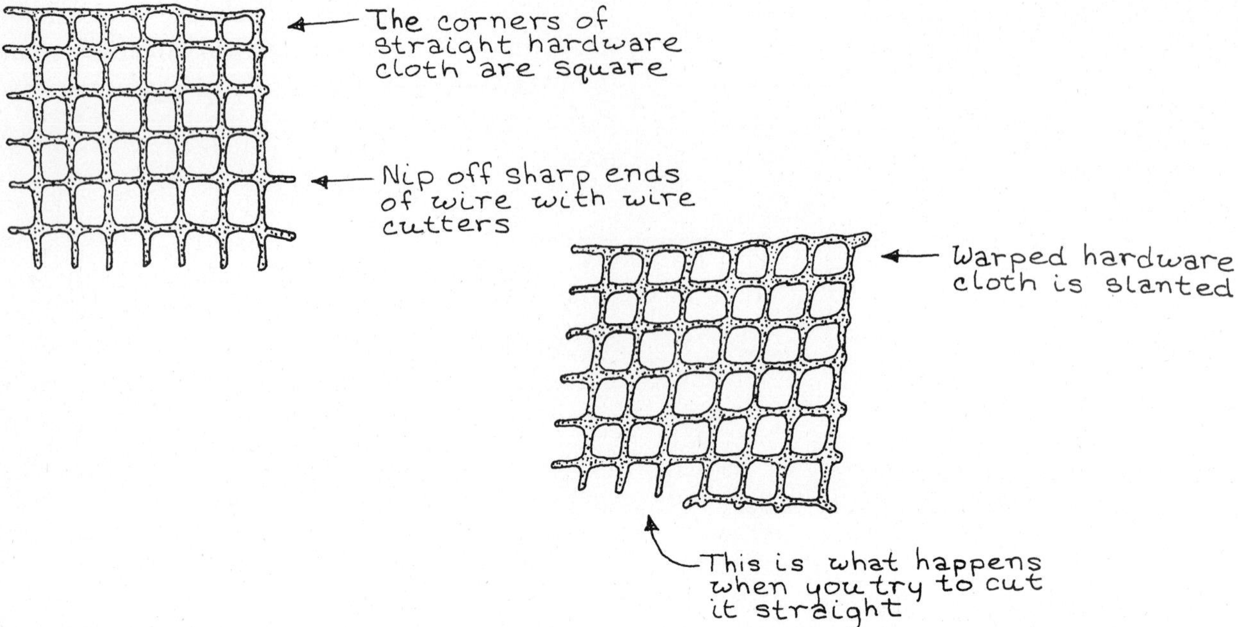

Rabbit Or Guinea Pig Hutches

Around Easter time, pet stores may sell hutches. Since they are neither cheap nor well made, you're probably better off with a homemade hutch. A hutch is a wire and wood cage with a mesh floor that is raised a few inches from the ground. Your rabbit or guinea pig's droppings will fall through the holes in the mesh onto a sheet of newspaper indoors, or the ground outdoors. Instructions are included here for both an indoor and an outdoor hutch.

Indoor Hutch ($13.00)

YOU NEED:

MATERIALS:

¾-inch interior-grade plywood, 16 by 32 inches
½-inch mesh hardware cloth, 36 by 54 inches
Pegboard or Masonite, 16 by 30 inches
2-by-4-inch lumber, 36 inches long
Heavy rock to weight top

TOOLS:

Yardstick or long ruler
Circular saw
Wire shears
File
Staple gun and wire staples

ACCESSORIES:

Water bottle and wire bracket
6-inch crockery food dish
Newspaper

Trim the 36-inch-wide hardware cloth to 30 inches before you start. It's a good idea to carefully trim the spikes off the cut edge so you don't scratch yourself as you work. When the hardware cloth is ready, follow the steps in the illustration. When the hutch is finished, cut the 2-by-4s in half, and set the cage up off the floor on the two pieces as shown. Cover the area under the cage with six layers of newspaper.

1. Cut two 16 by 16 inch squares out of 3/4-inch plywood.
2. Trim a 54 inch length of 1/2-inch mesh hardware cloth to 30 inches wide.
3. Fold over the first 2 inches and staple the cloth to the two squares as shown.
4. When you get to the last side, bend over the cloth where it meets the top, leave 2 inches for the fold, and trim off the excess.
5. Cut a piece of Masonite or pegboard 16 by 30 inches for the top.

Set hutch up off the floor on 2-by 4-inch pieces of lumber. Add water bottle, food dish, and rock weight.

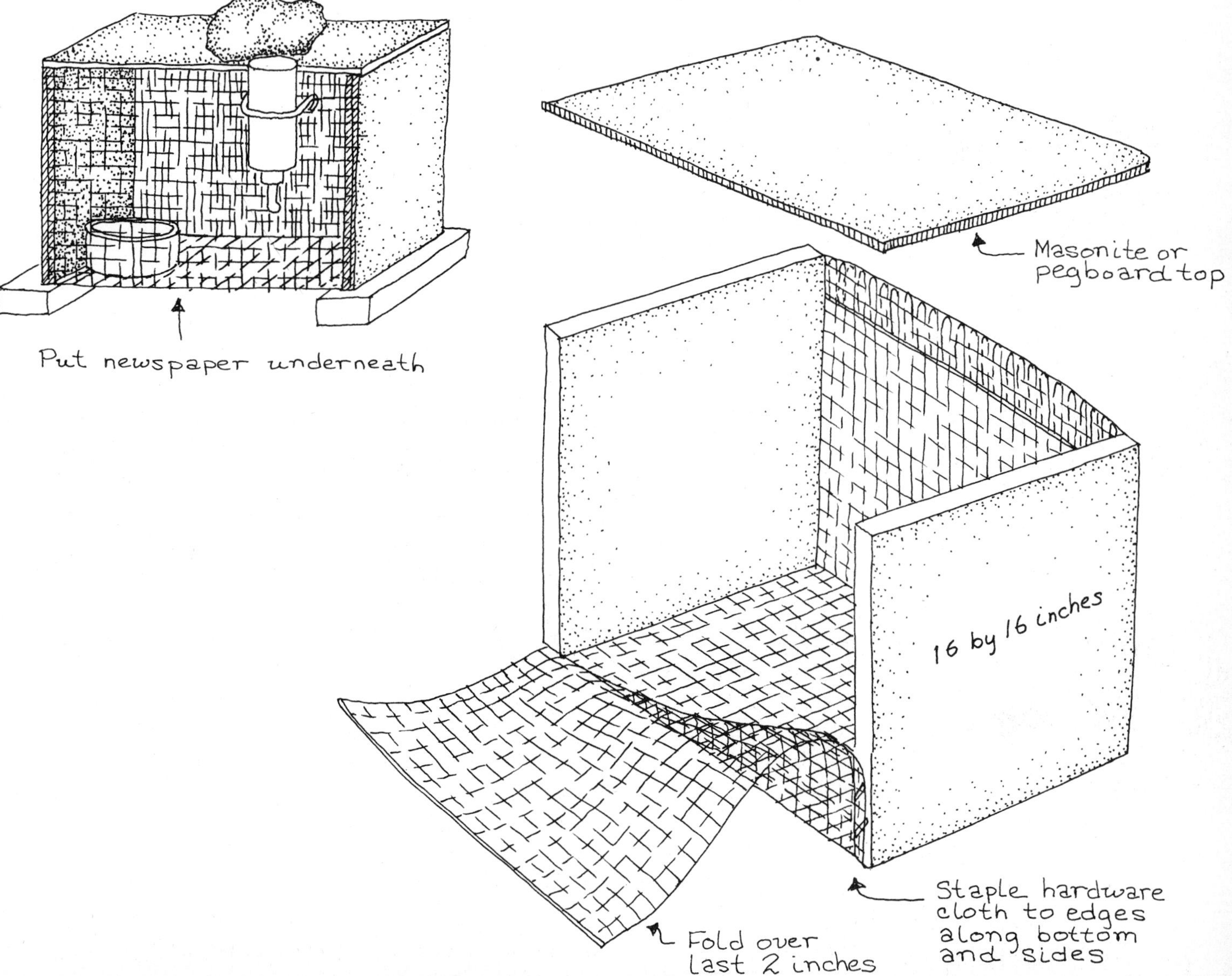

Outdoor Hutch ($20.00)

YOU NEED:

MATERIALS:

¾-inch exterior-grade plywood, 16 by 40 inches
½-inch mesh hardware cloth, 36 by 54 inches
6-inch shelving board, 30 inches long
Common nails, 1½ inches long
½-inch exterior-grade plywood, 18 by 32 inches
Two 6-inch T-hinges
3-inch screw-in hook
Pint of shellac
Quart of exterior enamel paint
2-by-4-inch lumber, 36 inches long; or four bricks

TOOLS:

Yardstick or long ruler
Circular saw
Wire shears
Staple gun and wire staples
Screwdriver
Paintbrush

ACCESSORIES:

Water bottle and wire bracket
6-inch crockery food dish

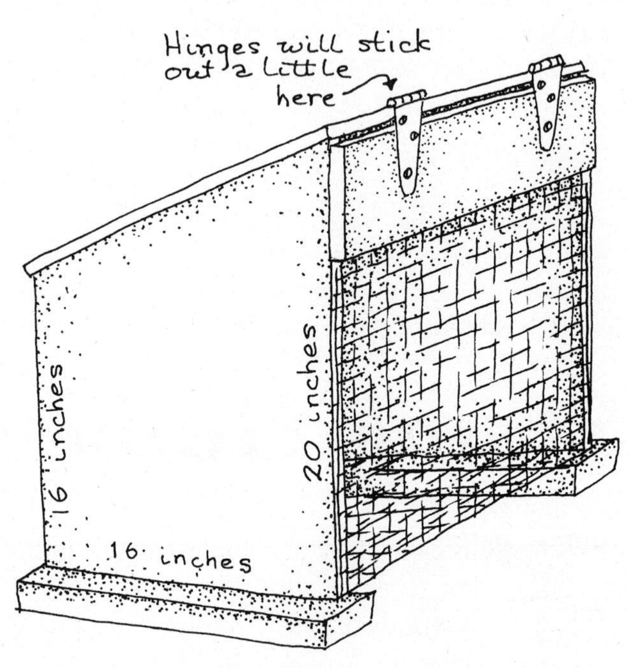

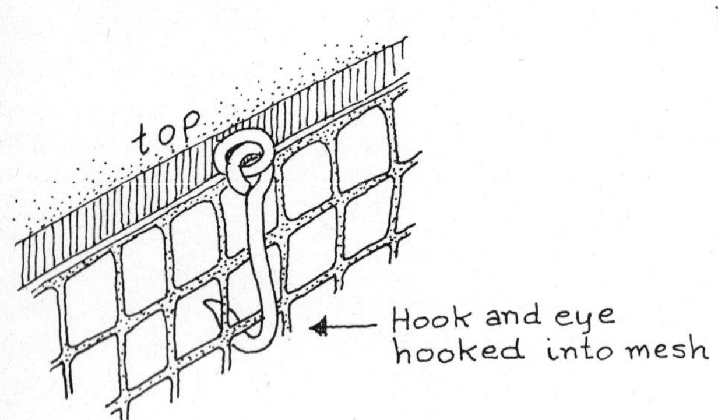

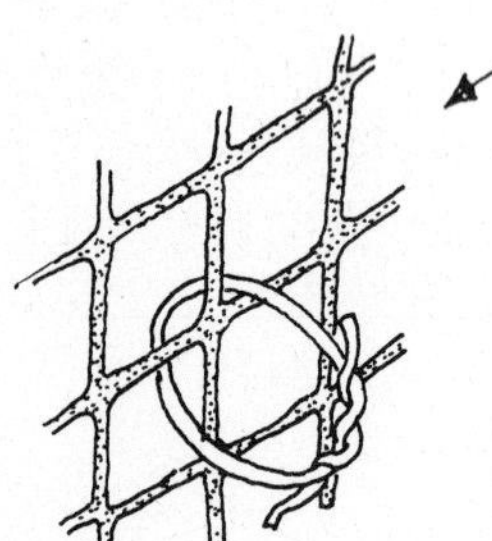

Hook and eye could be hooked into wire ring instead.

Use ¾-inch exterior grade plywood for the slanted sides of an outdoor hutch, and ½-inch exterior plywood for the top.

Begin stapling the hardware cloth from the low front of the hutch, bending the first two inches as for the indoor hutch. You don't have to bend the cloth over at the high back of the hutch.

Nail the board in place as shown right over the hardware cloth.

Attach the top to the board with 6-inch T-hinges. They won't fit just right but it doesn't matter. Screw a hook and eye into the front edge of the top. The hook can be hooked into the mesh below or into a wire ring in the mesh to hold the top closed.

Shellac the inside and outside with several coats of shellac. Paint the outside of the hutch with one or two coats of exterior enamel paint.

The roof of this outdoor hutch is sloped down so it will shed rain. Cut the two sides as shown in the illustration, then proceed as for the indoor hutch, starting the wire mesh at the low front end of the hutch. You don't have to bend it over at the high end, because it will be covered by the board. Hold the roof in place while you screw in the hinges. The roof will overhang one inch on each side. Screw the hook into the front edge of the roof. You should be able to hook it down into the wire mesh to hold the roof closed. If you have trouble getting the hook to stay put, attach a small S-hook or wire ring into the mesh for the hook to grab onto.

Give all the wood two coats of shellac inside and out, followed by two coats of exterior enamel paint on the outside surface only. Put the hutch up on the two halves of the 2-by-4, or on the four bricks.

In bad rainstorms and temperatures below 20 degrees, you can throw a tarpaulin or a heavy plastic drop cloth over the hutch for better protection.

Ferret or Skunk Home *($25.00)*

This cage is made complete with a private den separated from the rest of the cage by a sliding panel. Remove the panel to clean the den if it becomes necessary. For a ferret, the triangle you saw off the den panel to make an entrance hole should be quite small, as ferrets like sneaking through small spaces. You will have to cut off a larger triangle to accommodate the bulkier skunk.

YOU NEED:

MATERIALS:

½-inch interior-grade plywood, one 4-by-8-foot sheet
White glue
Common nails, 1¼ inch long for nailing plywood, and 3½ inches long for nailing door frame
1-by-2-inch lumber, 14 feet long
Corner braces
Screws
½-inch-mesh hardware cloth, 36 by 18 inches
Two 6-inch T-hinges
Hook and eye
Pint of shellac, and paint if you wish

TOOLS:

Yardstick or long ruler
Circular saw
Hammer
Handsaw
Screwdriver
Wire shears
Staple gun and wire staples
Paintbrush

ACCESSORIES:

Water dish or water bottle and bracket
Newspaper to cover floor or litter box
Silicone gel

Follow the steps in the illustrations to cut the basic pieces of plywood and to assemble the cage.

You can mount a water bottle through the wire door on this cage just as you do for a cake-pan cage or a hutch. Spread newspaper on the floor outside the den area, or use a small litter box, as discussed in the ferret section of unusual apartment pets. You might add some rags, in case your pet wants to pull them into its den to make a bed.

Change the newspapers or box when soiled, and wash the inside of the cage with soap and water when necessary. To clean the den area, pull the panel out, using the rear corner opening as a handle to get it started. If the panel is hard to slide, a silicone gel (available in hardware stores) can be squeezed into the grooves as a lubricant.

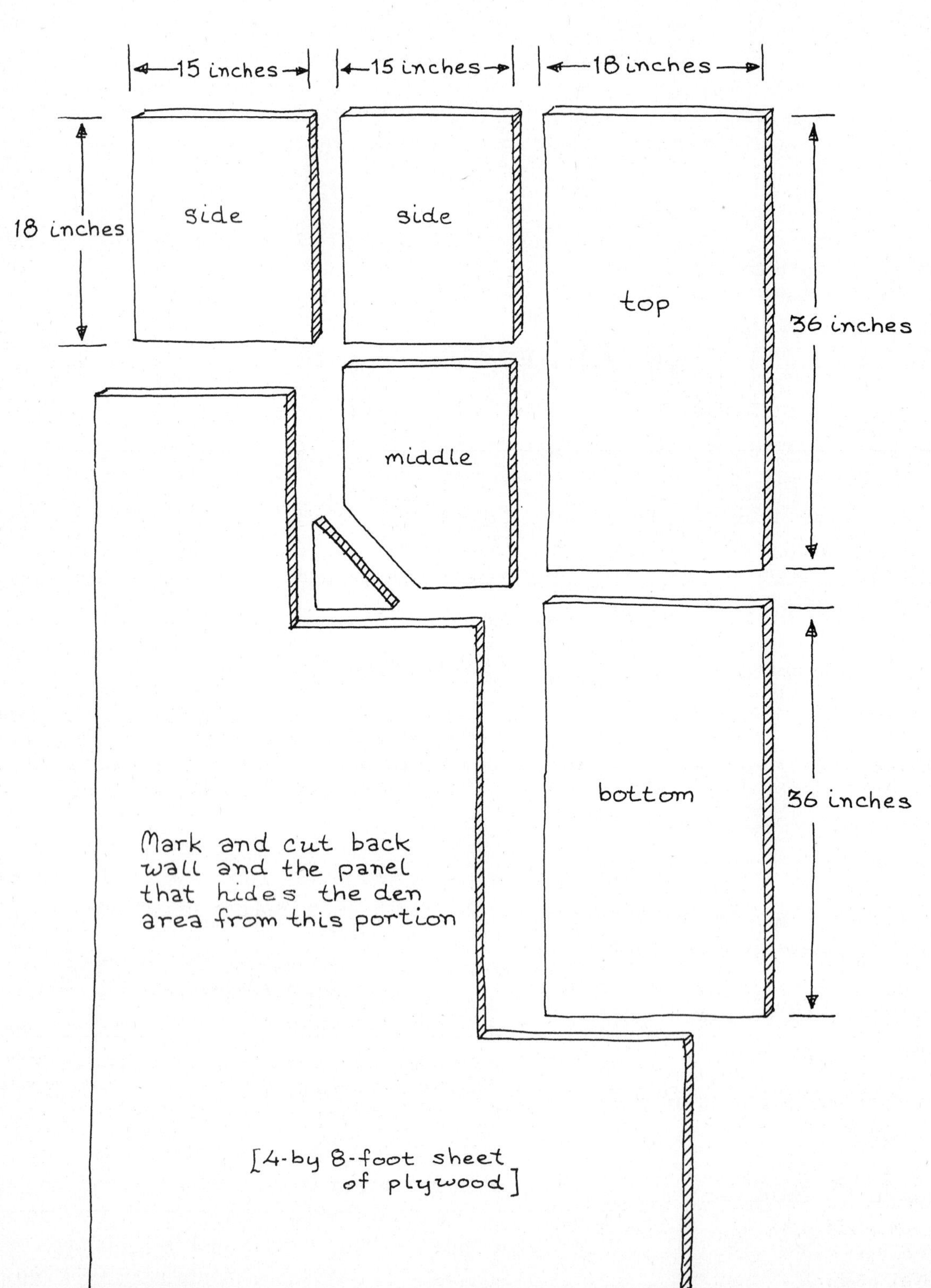
1. Cut two sides, top, bottom and middle den piece from a sheet of 1/2-inch plywood, as shown.
15 inches
15 inches
18 inches
18 inches
side
side
top
36 inches
middle
bottom
36 inches
Mark and cut back wall and the panel that hides the den area from this portion
[4-by 8-foot sheet of plywood]

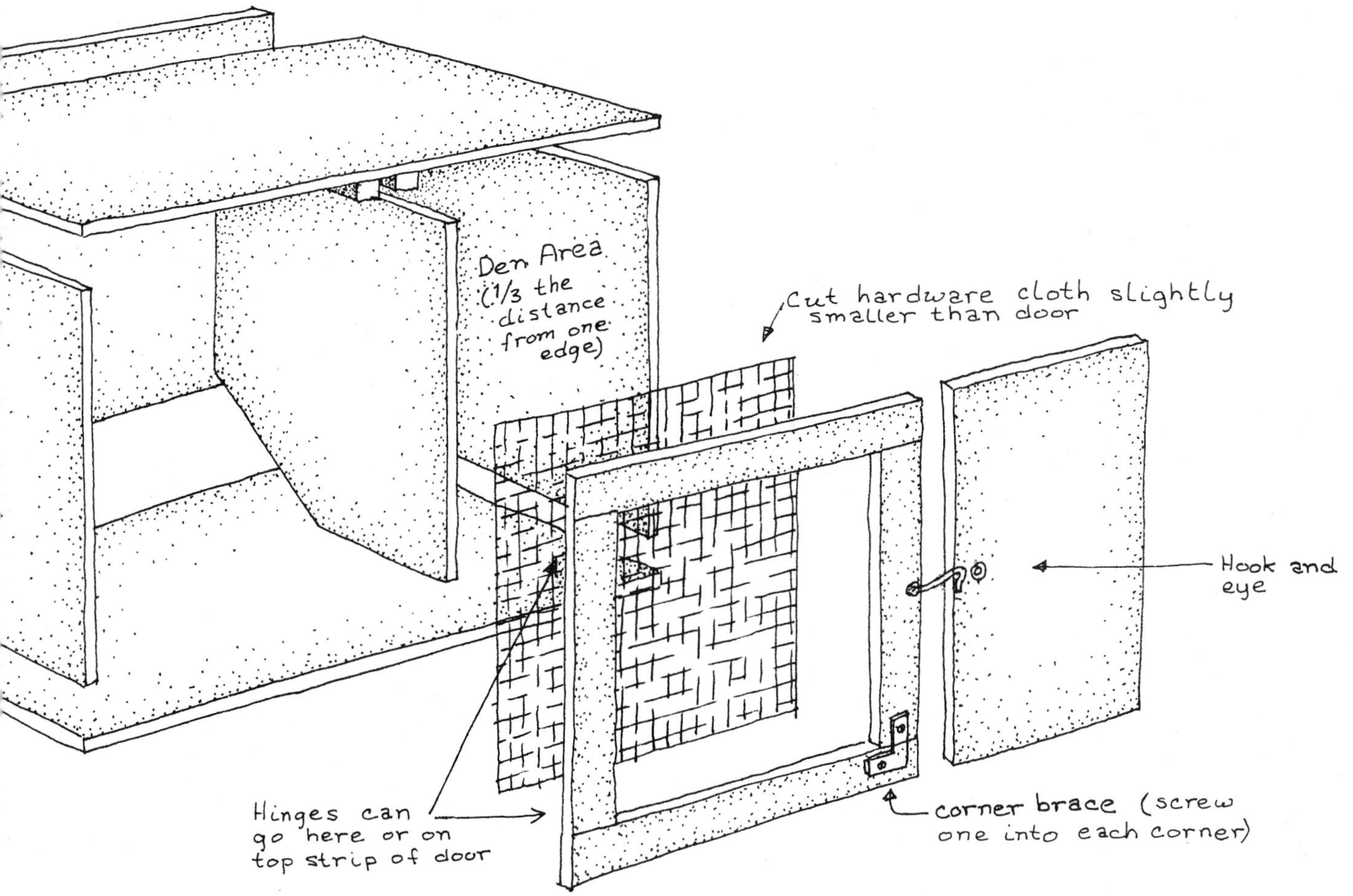

2. Glue and nail two sides, top and bottom.
3. Use assembled box as a guide to measure and cut back wall.
4. Glue and nail back in place
5. Position middle panel about 1/3 of the way from one side to make a small den area. Mark position on inside of top and glue two 1-by 2-inch strips of lumber to either side of mark as shown.

   These strips are to hold the den panel in place. Glue strips to the bottom too if the panel is too loose.

6. Measure carefully for the 1-by 2-inch lumber door pieces. Door should line up with side wall, and extend just beyond the den panel so the panel can slide out when the door is open.

   Brace door corners with corner braces. Cut 1/2-inch mesh hardware cloth to fit and staple to inside of door.

7. Measure and cut plywood panel that covers den area. Glue and nail in place.
8. Attach door with T-hinges at either top or side. Close with hook and eye.
9. Shellac inside surfaces with three coats. Paint or varnish outside as you wish.

Poultry Sheds ($20.00)

A shed is a lean-to type construction—three walls and a simple, one-piece roof. This shed, the size of a small doghouse, can house six chickens, a pair of geese, or with some adjustments, a dozen pigeons. In cold areas, sheds facing the south offer enough protection for the birds, but their drinking water may freeze. Special electric drinking-water heaters are available at feed stores and can be connected to your home with an extension cord.

Locate the shed on dry, raised ground, with the open side facing south. Put a thick layer of hay on the floor. Unless you want to confine your chickens or geese, you don't really need to build more than this basic shed.

YOU NEED:

MATERIALS:

½-inch exterior-grade plywood, one 4-by-8-foot sheet
White glue
Common nails, 1¼ inch long
Exterior enamel paint
Pint of shellac

TOOLS:

Yardstick
Circular saw
Plane
Hammer
Paintbrush

ACCESSORIES:

Water container
Hay for bedding

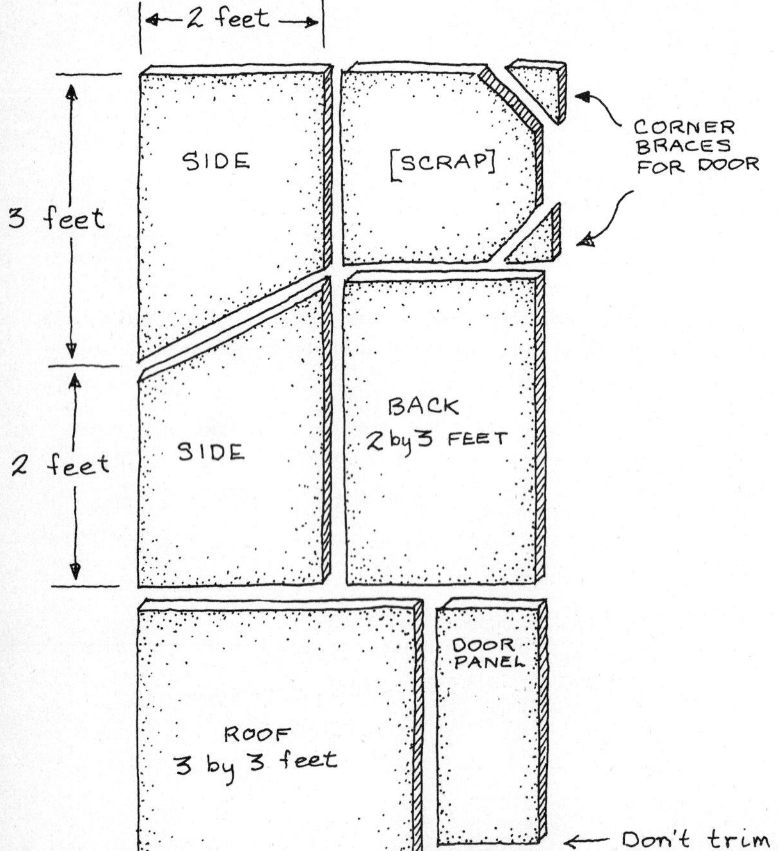

1. Cut a 4-by 8-foot sheet of plywood as shown.

2. Glue and nail pieces of coop together as shown. The roof is even with the side walls, but hangs out over the front and back.

   Shellac inside and outside with several coats of shellac.

3. Paint the outside with exterior paint. If you want a door or a floor, wait until they are finished and do all the painting at once.

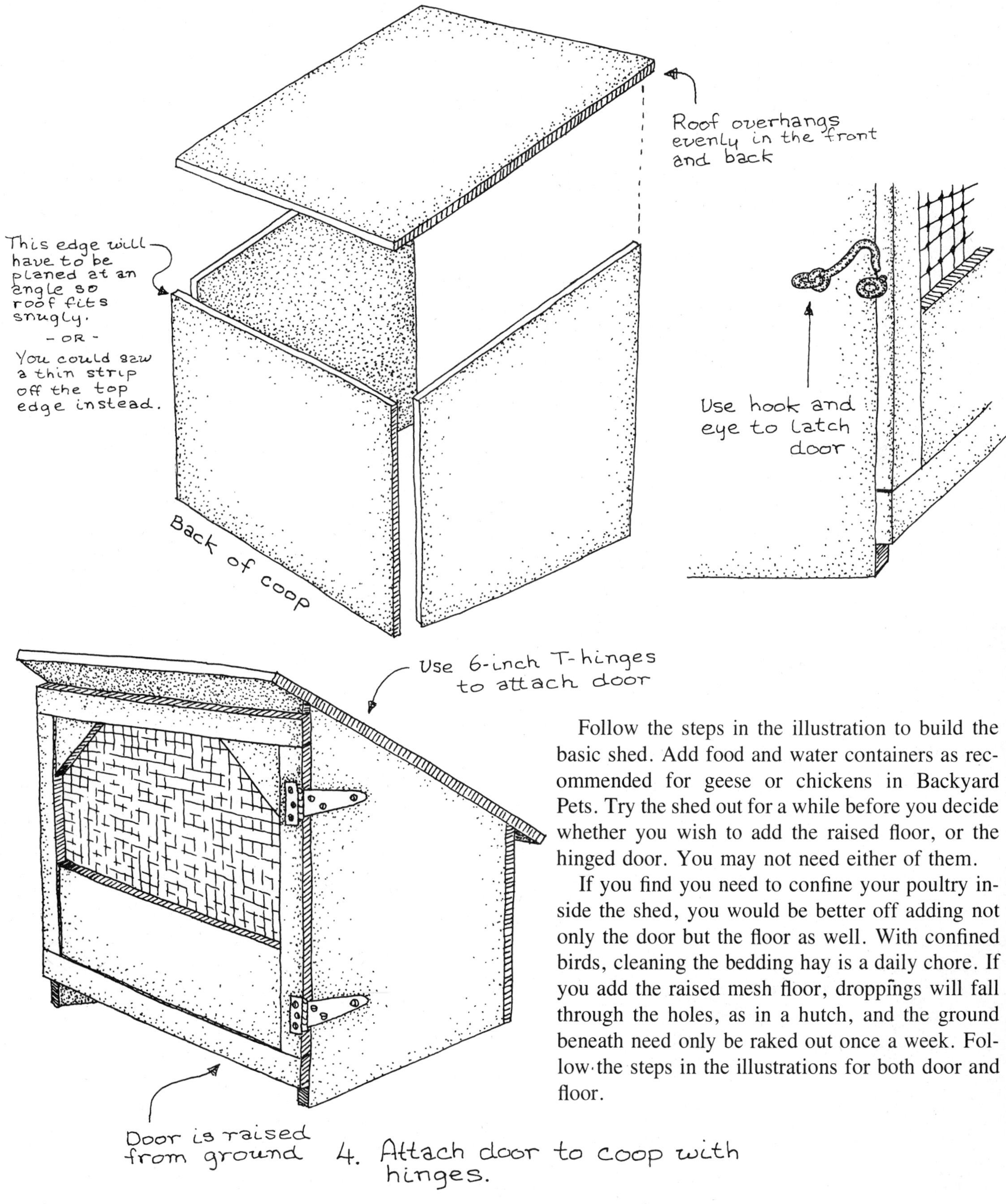

Follow the steps in the illustration to build the basic shed. Add food and water containers as recommended for geese or chickens in Backyard Pets. Try the shed out for a while before you decide whether you wish to add the raised floor, or the hinged door. You may not need either of them.

If you find you need to confine your poultry inside the shed, you would be better off adding not only the door but the floor as well. With confined birds, cleaning the bedding hay is a daily chore. If you add the raised mesh floor, droppings will fall through the holes, as in a hutch, and the ground beneath need only be raked out once a week. Follow the steps in the illustrations for both door and floor.

Poultry Shed Door ($6.00)

YOU NEED:

MATERIALS:

1-by-2-inch lumber, 12 feet long
½-inch plywood panel left over from building shed or cut from scrap
Two ½-inch plywood triangles cut from scrap, each 6 inches on the short sides of the triangles
White glue
Common nails, 3½ inches long
½-inch mesh hardware cloth, 24 by 36 inches
Pair of 6-inch T-hinges
Hook and eye
Shellac
Same paint used for shed

TOOLS:

Yardstick or long ruler
Handsaw
Hammer
Wire shears
Staple gun and wire staples
Screwdriver
Paintbrush

1. Cut pieces of 1-by 2-inch lumber as shown, measuring each piece against the actual coop before sawing.

   The dimensions given here are only approximate.

2. Glue and nail the door together, checking for fit before hammering nails all the way in.

3. Cut hardware cloth to fit inside door. Staple in place.

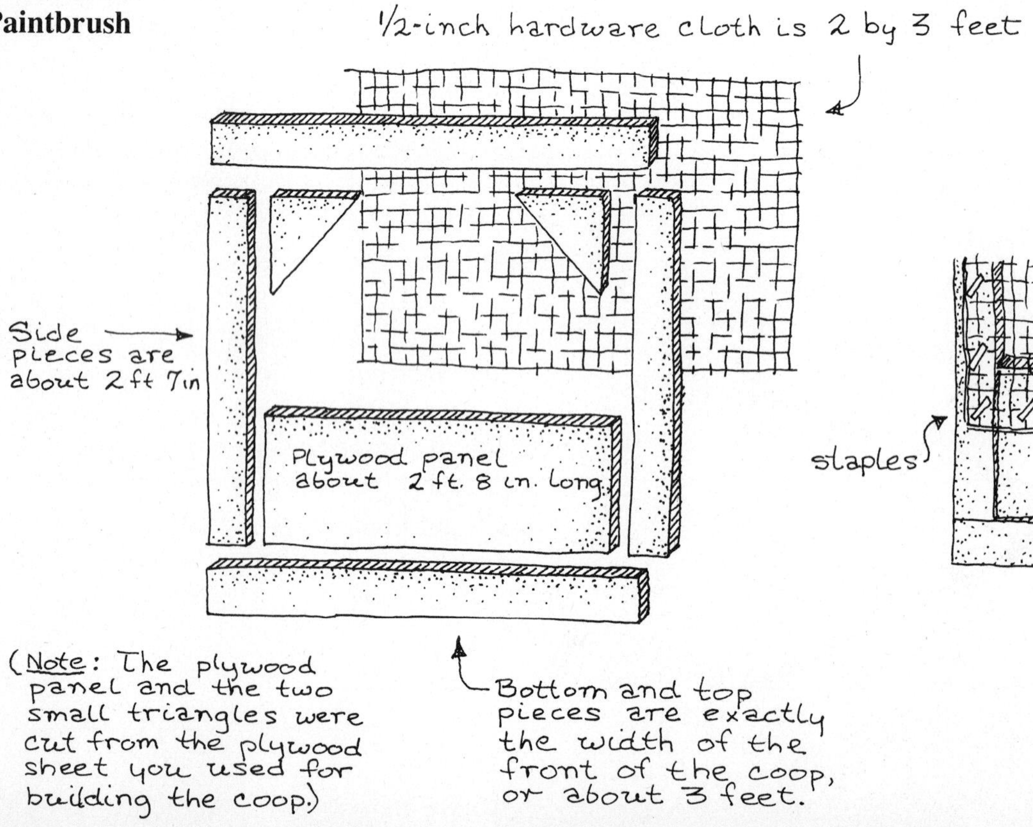

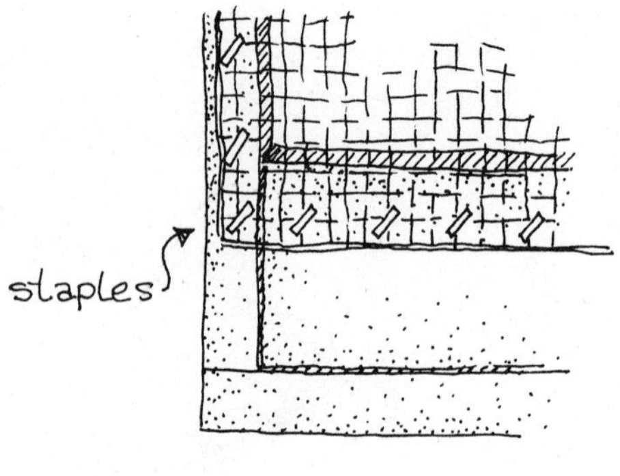

Poultry Shed Floor ($6.00)

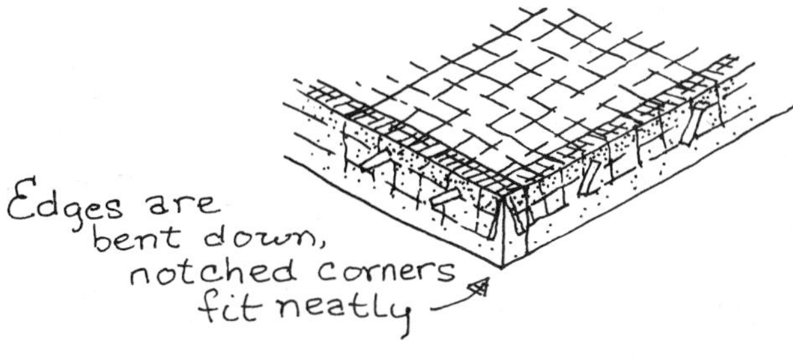

YOU NEED:

MATERIALS:

1-by-2-inch lumber, 12 feet long
White glue
Common nails, 3½ inches long for nailing floor together, and 1½ inches long for nailing floor to coop
½-inch mesh hardware cloth, 36 by 42 inches
Pint of shellac

TOOLS:

Yardstick
Handsaw
Hammer
Wire shears
Staple gun and wire staples

1. Cut front and back pieces from 1-by 2-inch lumber first. Cut both 1/4 inch shorter than the inside dimension of the coop to allow for thickness of hardware cloth.

2. Hold the front and back pieces in place inside the coop to measure for the three cross pieces. Cut cross pieces 1/4 inch shorter than your measurement.

3. Assemble floor frame as shown, gluing and nailing pieces together. Shellac wood.

4. Cut hardware cloth 3 inches wider and 3 inches longer than the floor frame. Notch corners in 1½ inches. Staple in place.

5. Nail floor inside coop, hammering from outside the walls and back. Floor should be 4 to 5 inches off the ground.

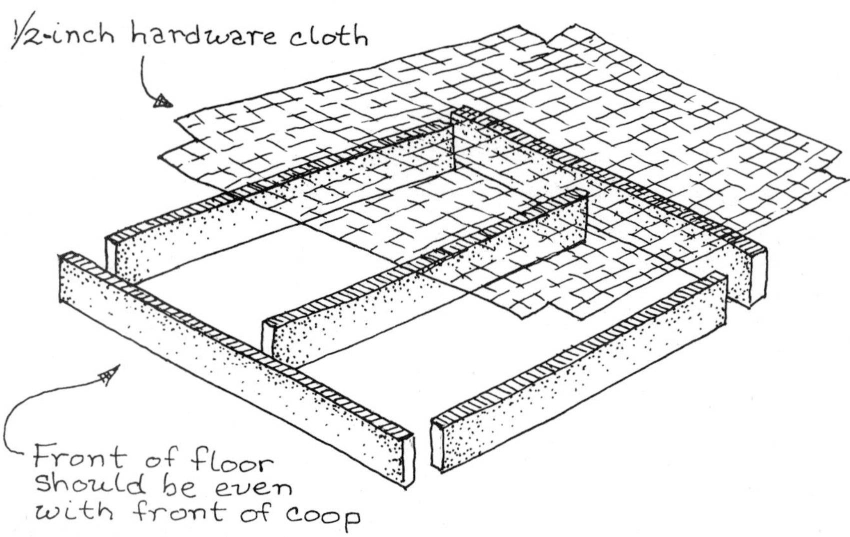

1. Measure 10 inch shelving against inside of coop. Cut to fit. Cut 2-inch lattice strips the same length as the shelves.
2. Mark the inside of the back wall of the coop with three straight lines at 6-, 10- and 8-inch intervals. Continue the lines a little around the sides too.
3. Hold each shelf in position against a line and nail in place from outside the walls.
4. Glue and nail lattice strip edges to shelves. Seal wood with several coats of shellac.

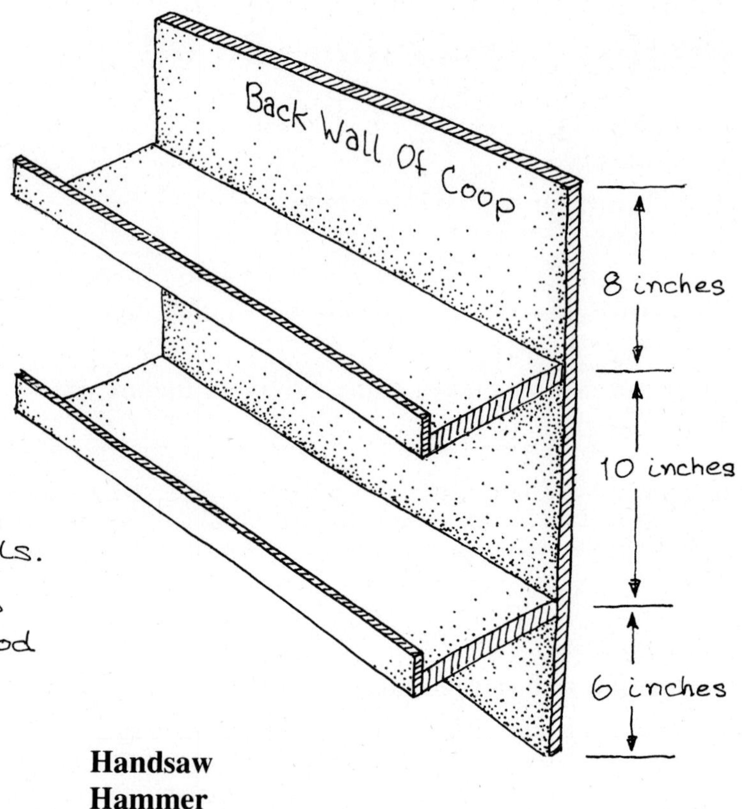

Pigeon Coop ($35.00)

The pigeon coop shown here is only a variation of the poultry shed. The floor is solid instead of mesh, roosting shelves have been added, and the whole coop is mounted up on a building wall so the pigeons, who are not ground birds like geese and chickens, can roost up high where they feel they belong.

YOU NEED:

MATERIALS:

Start with basic poultry shed equipped with door
10-inch shelving board, 6 feet long
2-inch lattice strip, 6 feet long
White glue
Common nails, 1½ inches long for nailing shelves and for adding floor, 4 inches long for nailing braces together, and 5 inches long for nailing braces into house wall
Pint of shellac
½-inch exterior-grade plywood, 2½ by 3 feet
2-by-4-inch lumber, 16 feet long
Same paint you used to paint shed

TOOLS:

Yardstick or long ruler
Handsaw
Hammer
Circular saw
Paintbrush

ACCESSORIES:

Feed and water dishes

Once you have completed the basic shed, follow the steps in the illustrations to make the shelves and nail them in place. Add the plywood floor, and make the braces as shown. Now select a place for the coop, about five feet up off the ground on a building wall. To get the coop to fit flat against the wall, you will have to cut off the rear overhang on the roof. This is not hard with a properly adjusted circular saw.

You will have to locate studs inside the wall for nailing the braces into. Tap along the wall with a hammer until you find a spot that does not sound hollow. Tap above and below that spot, to be sure you have found a vertical stud. The next stud over should be about 16 inches away, and the next after that another 16 inches, making the first and third studs 32 inches apart. The braces will support the coop well if they are about that same 32 inches apart.

Once the braces are nailed firmly into the two

1. Add plywood floor to coop. Measure it against coop bottom, adding an extra 6 inches in front for a landing ledge.
2. Saw off roof overhang at back of coop. Roof edge should be even with the back wall.
3. Construct two braces from 2-by 4-inch lumber. The top piece measures 2 feet. Measure the back piece so that the back of the brace is also 2 feet. Mark and cut the diagonal piece carefully. Shellac and paint the braces.
4. Nail braces into studs in building wall 5 or 6 feet from the ground. Nail coop onto braces, centering it first.

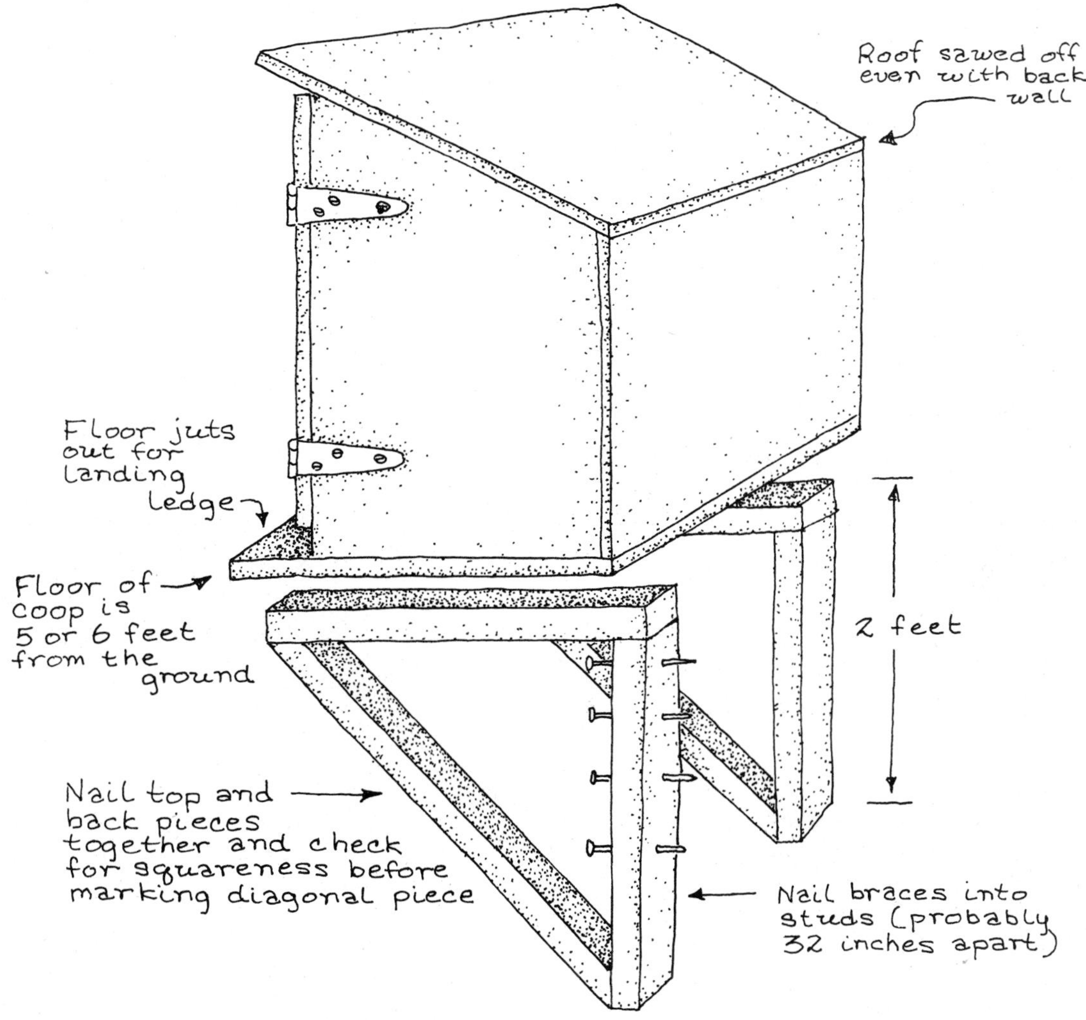

studs with long nails, lift the coop up onto them. If you want, you could drive a few nails through the coop floor into the braces, and a few more through the back wall of the coop into the stud that is between your two braces. Probably neither is really necessary, and it's not a bad idea to be able to lift the coop down when you want to give it a good scrubbing.

Chicken Yard *($8.50)*

To confine chickens, build a small yard from poultry wire and wooden stakes. Chickens don't need a lot of exercise, so you can make this yard as small as 6 by 6 feet.

YOU NEED:

MATERIALS:

4-foot stakes made either of 1-by-2-inch lumber, made pointed at the bottom with a hatchet; or 1-inch bamboo or similar round poles (you may be able to cut your own stakes from alder or other brush in your area). Plan on stakes placed no more than three feet apart.

25-foot roll of poultry wire

TOOLS:

Stapling gun

Wire cutters

Hammer

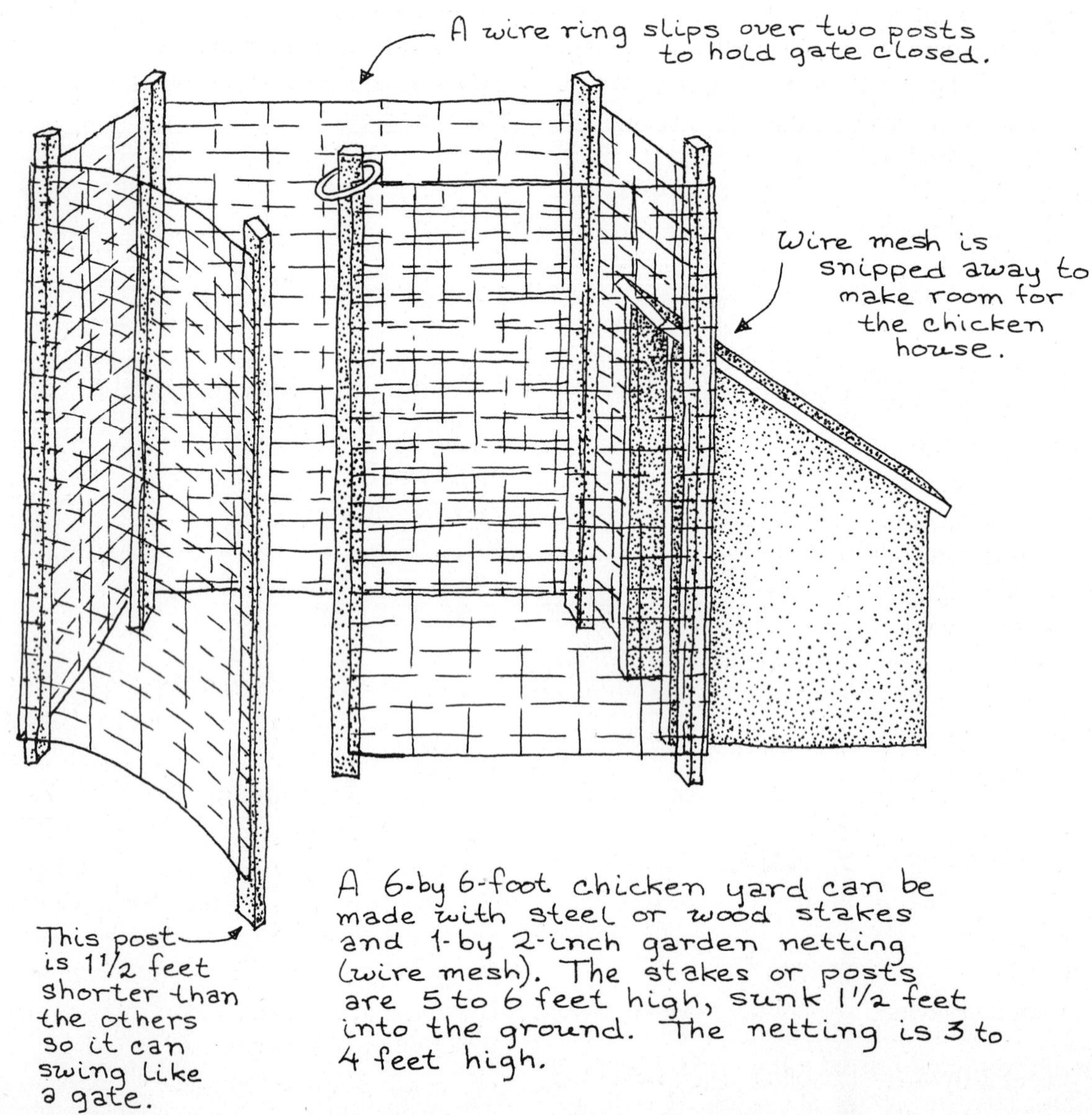

A 6-by 6-foot chicken yard can be made with steel or wood stakes and 1-by 2-inch garden netting (wire mesh). The stakes or posts are 5 to 6 feet high, sunk 1 1/2 feet into the ground. The netting is 3 to 4 feet high.

Figure out where you want the stakes before you begin. Plan on one stake to either side of the poultry shed, then a stake every three feet or less. Staple the wire onto the stakes at the planned intervals, leaving a foot of stake free at the bottom for sinking into the ground. When the wire is all stapled to the stakes, hammer the stakes into the ground where they belong. This fence is short enough to step over, so you don't really need a gate. If you want a gate, you can make one as shown in the illustration: cut the wire next to one stake, staple the free end onto a shorter pole, and hold it closed with a wire ring placed over the gate pole and the stake you are joining it to.

Home For a Goat

For most people, a simple stall in a corner of the garage is the easiest way to keep a goat. This stall is fairly easy to build. However, instructions are also included here for those ambitious people who have always wanted to build a goat shed. Either way, goats have to be confined all the time, unless you want to live in a desert devoid of leaves, grass and flowers. Goats are formidable eaters, and are stubborn besides.

To confine a goat outdoors you need either a collar, chain, and stake in the ground, or a fenced area. The fenced area is something the shed builder might be interested in. Others can use a stake.

A goat stall need be no bigger than four by six feet. The sides are built of 2-by-4s and plywood, but an exact design can't be given, since you'll be using whatever walls or rafters exist in your garage to support at least part of it. All we can give you here is a scheme for using a corner of a typical stud-wall garage interior. It's not complicated, since two walls already exist.

Goat Stall ($35.00)

YOU NEED:

MATERIALS:

½-inch interior-grade plywood, two 4-by-8-foot sheets
Four pieces 2-by-4-inch lumber, each 8 feet long
Common nails, 3½ inches long for nailing framework, and 2 inches long for nailing plywood to framework
Two 6-inch strap or T-hinges
Hook and eye

TOOLS:

Yardstick or long ruler
Circular saw
Hammer
Screwdriver

ACCESSORIES:

Hay for bedding
Wire bicycle basket for holding hay
Feed and water baskets

Since the construction depends on what the inside of your garage is like, use the illustration here as a guide only—in other words, don't cut anything until you have figured out how big it should be.

When the stall is finished, cover the floor with hay. Add a little hay over the surface every day. Goat droppings and urine don't smell much, and goat keepers only clean the bedding and floor twice a year—spring and fall. The daily layer of hay keeps the goat clean and dry. Of course, the floor gets higher and higher, but it will all make excellent compost in the long run. The 2-by-4 behind the door keeps the bedding in the stall.

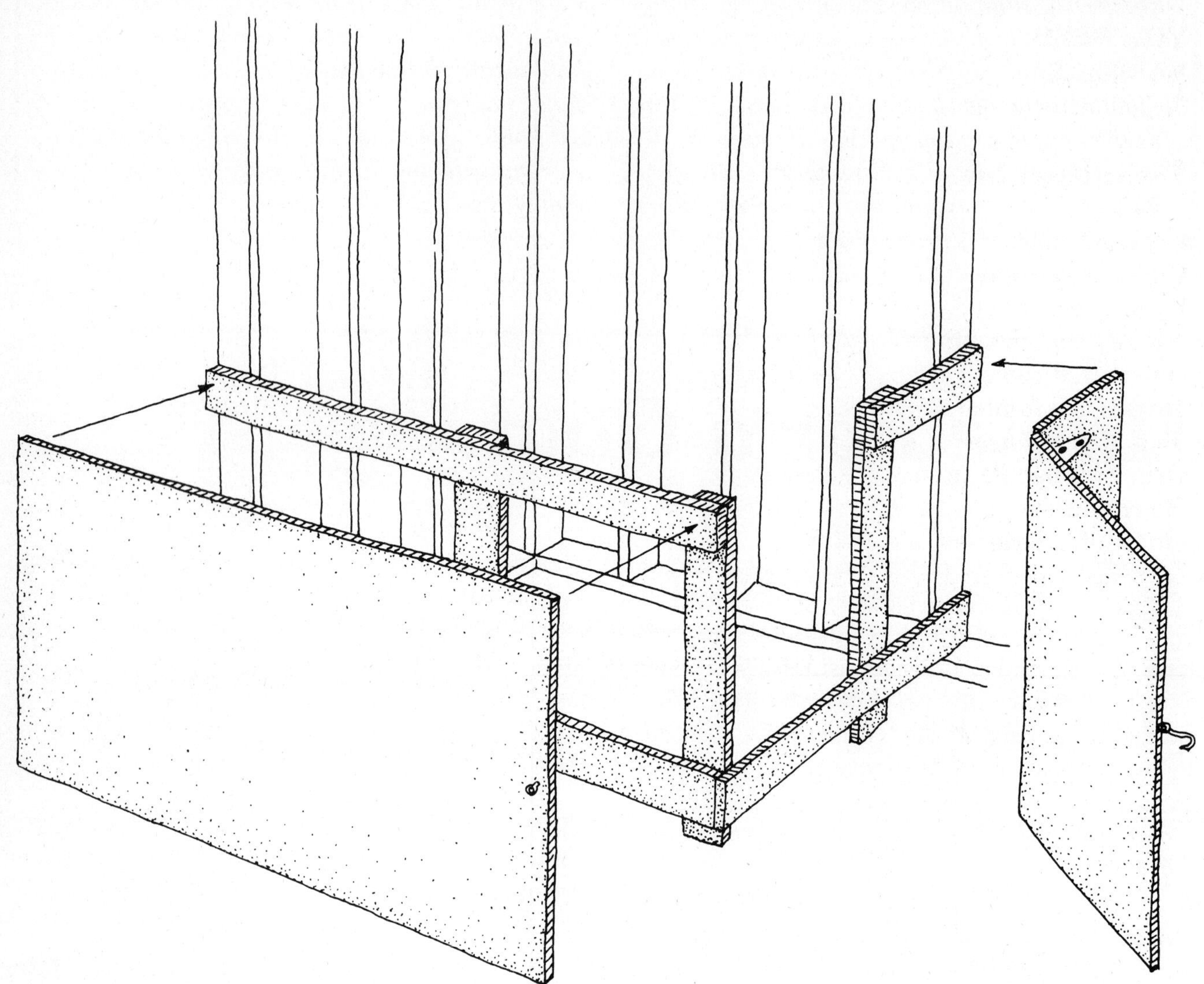

Use existing stud walls in your garage to build a goat stall into one corner. The framework is built of 2-by 4-inch lumber; walls and door are ½-inch plywood. The stall should be about 4 by 5½ feet, with walls about 4 feet high. Use strap hinges for the 2-foot door, and close it with a hook and eye.

Only the new lumber you have to add is shaded in this drawing.

Goat Shed ($170.00)

This goat shed is by far the hardest and most expensive project in this book. Even though it is an A-frame—one of the easiest-to-build and strongest shapes in construction—the job requires two or perhaps three people just to hold frames up while the plywood walls are nailed in place. Before you begin building, make sure you have chosen a good site. The door of the shed should face south. The area should be level and on high dry ground, as goats object to any dampness underfoot. If you intend to add a goat yard onto the shed, measure to make sure you have room for it.

YOU NEED:

MATERIALS:

- ¾-inch exterior-grade plywood, five 4-by-8-foot sheets
- Twelve pieces 2-by-4-inch lumber, each 10 feet long
- Common nails, 3½ inches long
- Quart of creosote
- Roofing paper, one roll
- Asphalt shingles, three bundles
- Galvanized roofing nails, ⅞ inch long
- 1-by-3-inch lumber, 2 feet long
- Two 3-inch hinges
- Door pull handle (no latch necessary)
- Hook and eye
- Quart of exterior enamel paint

TOOLS:

- Yardstick or long ruler
- Circular saw
- Hammer
- Paintbrush
- Staple gun and wire staples
- Matte knife
- Screwdriver

ACCESSORIES:

- Hay for bedding
- Wire bicycle basket for holding hay
- Feed and water buckets

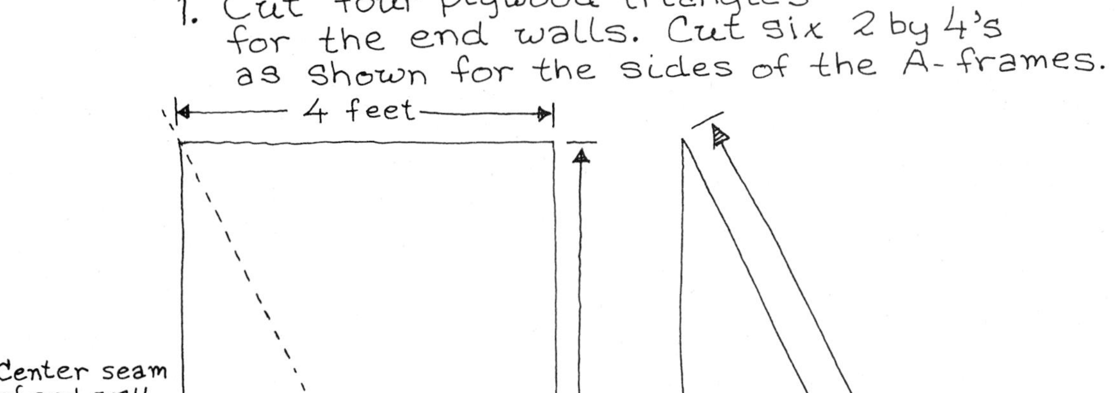

Ⓐ Cut plywood panel diagonally. Each triangle is half an end wall.

Ⓑ Measure longest side 8 feet down from tip; cut excess off straight at bottom.

Look at the drawings and read the instructions very carefully before you take each step. If something confuses you (or comes out wrong), ask advice of someone who has experience with carpentry before you go any further.

When you are finished with the building, either add the fenced-in goat yard as shown, or plan to chain your goat to the shed or to a stake in the ground (page 295). Cover the shed floor with hay the same as for a stall. If you decide on a goat yard, sand is a good dry flooring for it, and is easy to rake clean.

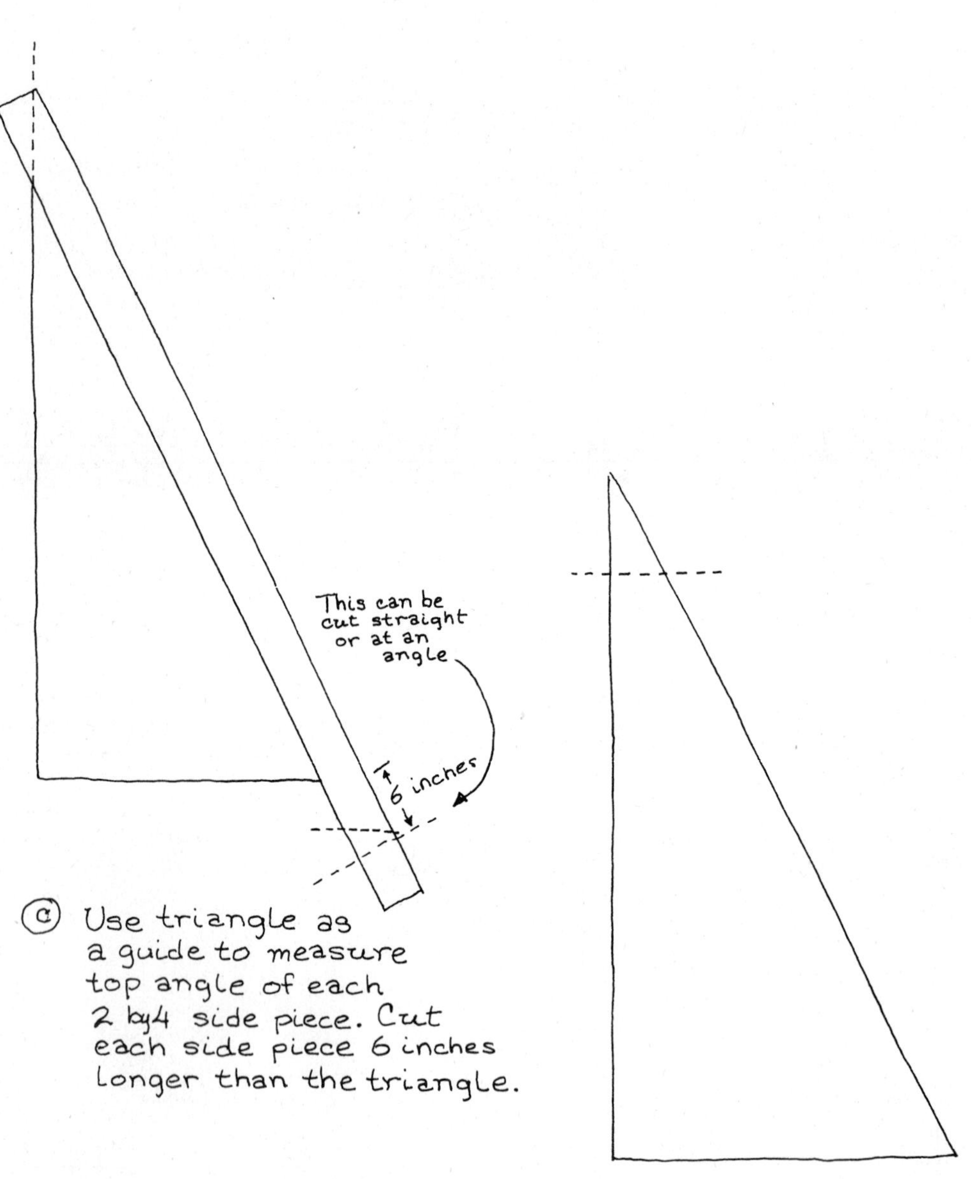

ⓓ Cut about 10 inches off the top of each triangle.

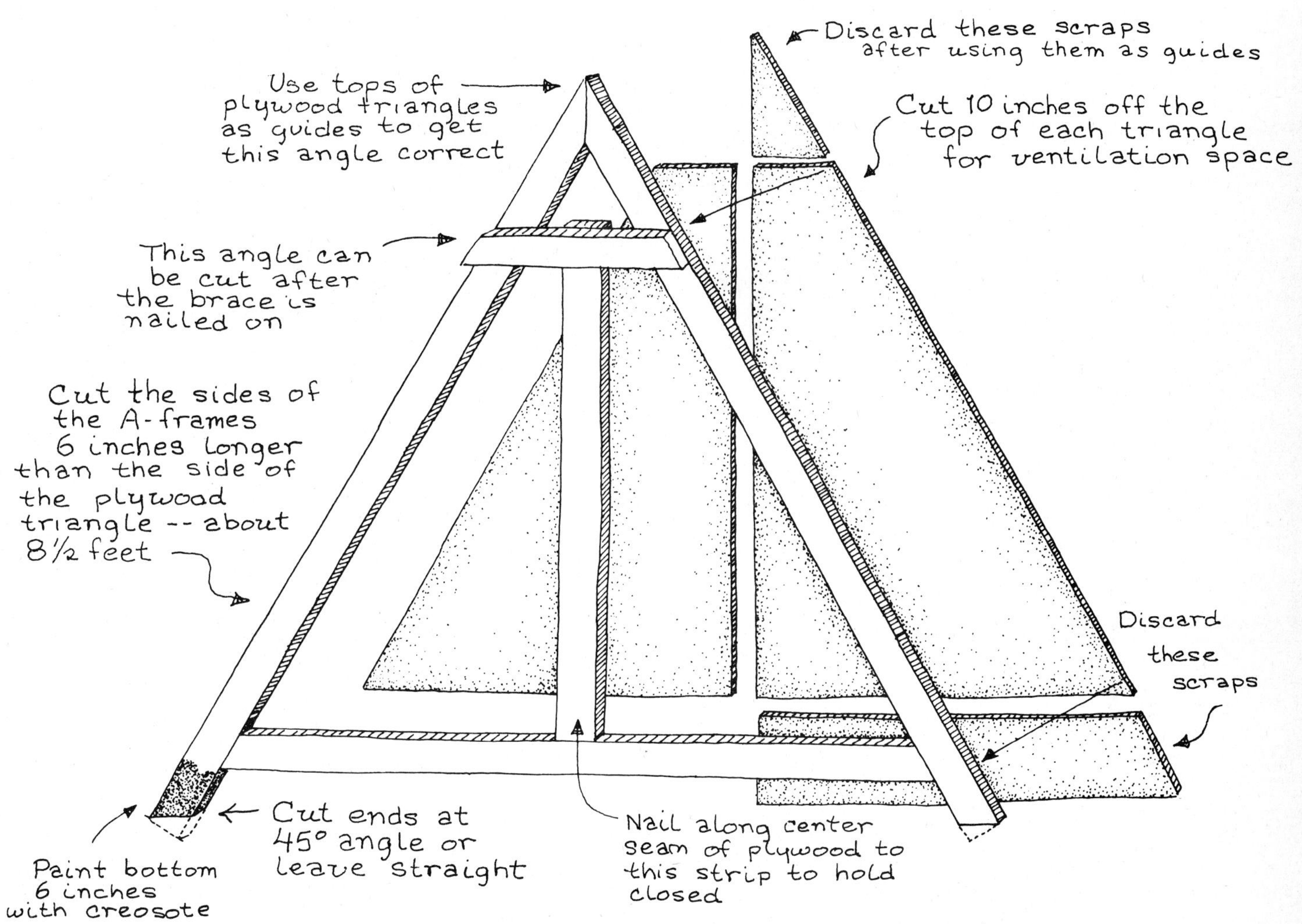

2. Assemble both end walls as shown. Nail triangles onto side pieces first. Then use the shape of the whole end wall as a guide for cutting the three bracing pieces inside each frame. The bracing pieces are cut from 2 by 4's.

3. Assemble the middle A-frame, leaving out the bottom brace and the vertical brace. The top brace will hold it together for now.

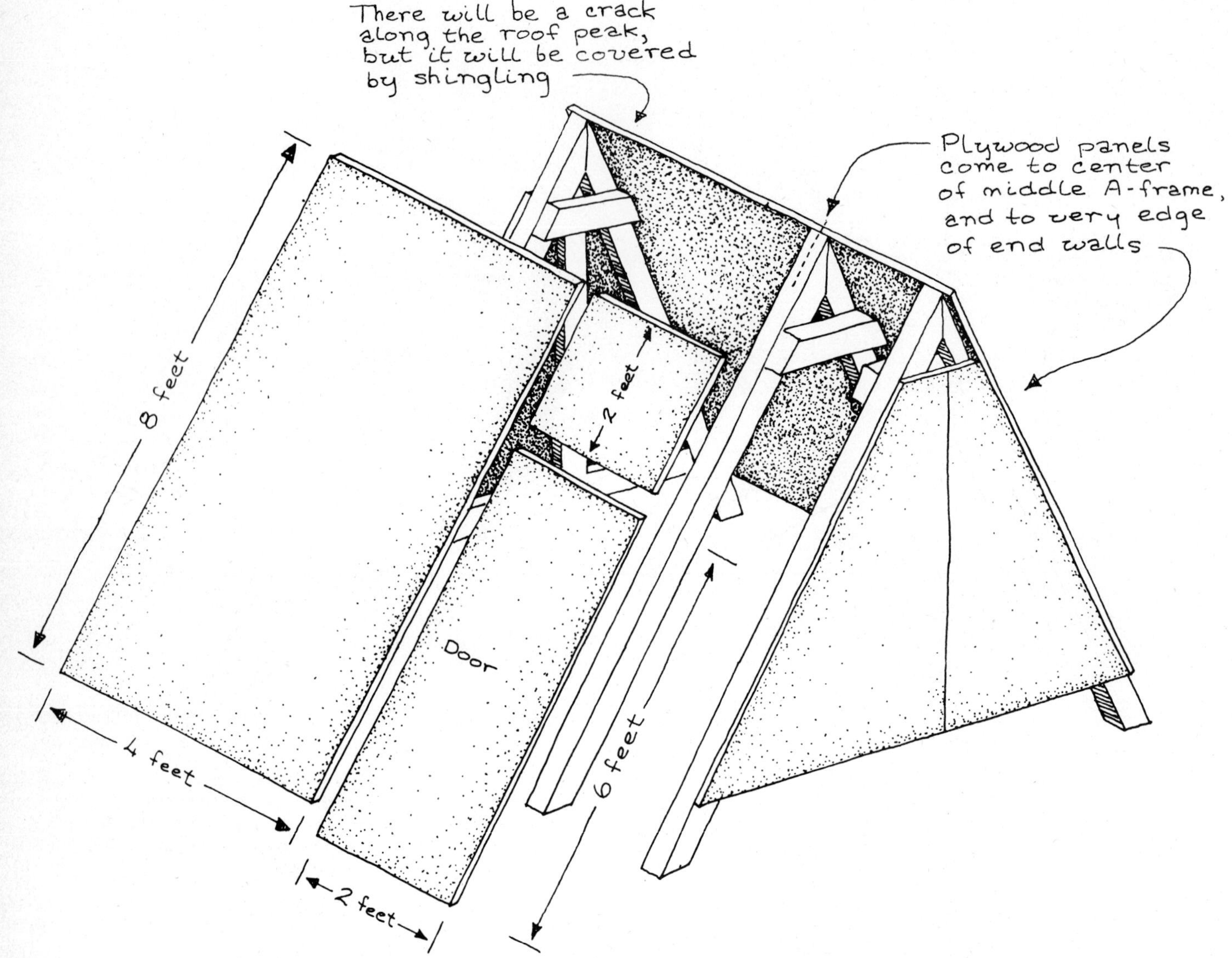

4. Cut one of the three remaining plywood panels in half lengthwise. Cut a 2-foot piece off one of the halves as shown to make the door.

   Don't cut the last two plywood panels at all.

5. Nail the two whole 4-by 8-foot plywood panels in place between one end frame and the middle frame. Then nail the 2-by 8-foot panel in place between the middle frame and the other end frame. Nail the 2-by 2-foot panel in place over the opening where the door will go.

   Don't nail the door on.

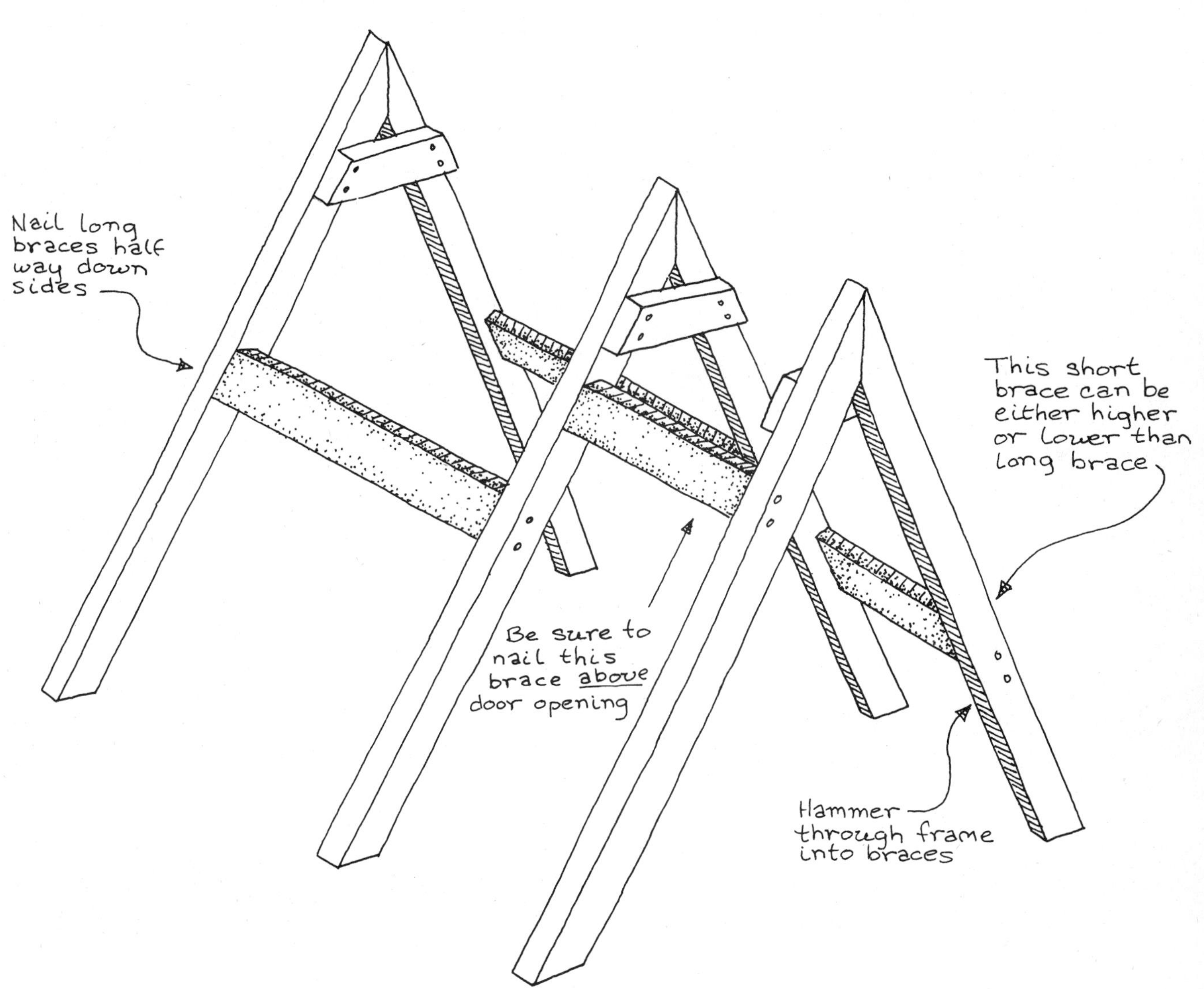

6. Add horizontal 2 by 4 braces between the frames inside the shed after the plywood is all nailed down. (Plywood is not shown in this drawing).

Measure for each brace individually.

7. Staple roofing paper to shed roof. Lay asphalt shingles from bottom to top in rows 6 inches apart (15 rows). Nail with 3/4-inch galvanized roofing nails.

See detail of shingle flap before roofing over doorway.

Finish top of roof with shingles from which the flaps have been cut, overlapping them along the peak as shown.

8. Install door with 4- or 5-inch hinges. Screw in handle and hook.

Paint door and end walls with several coats of exterior paint.

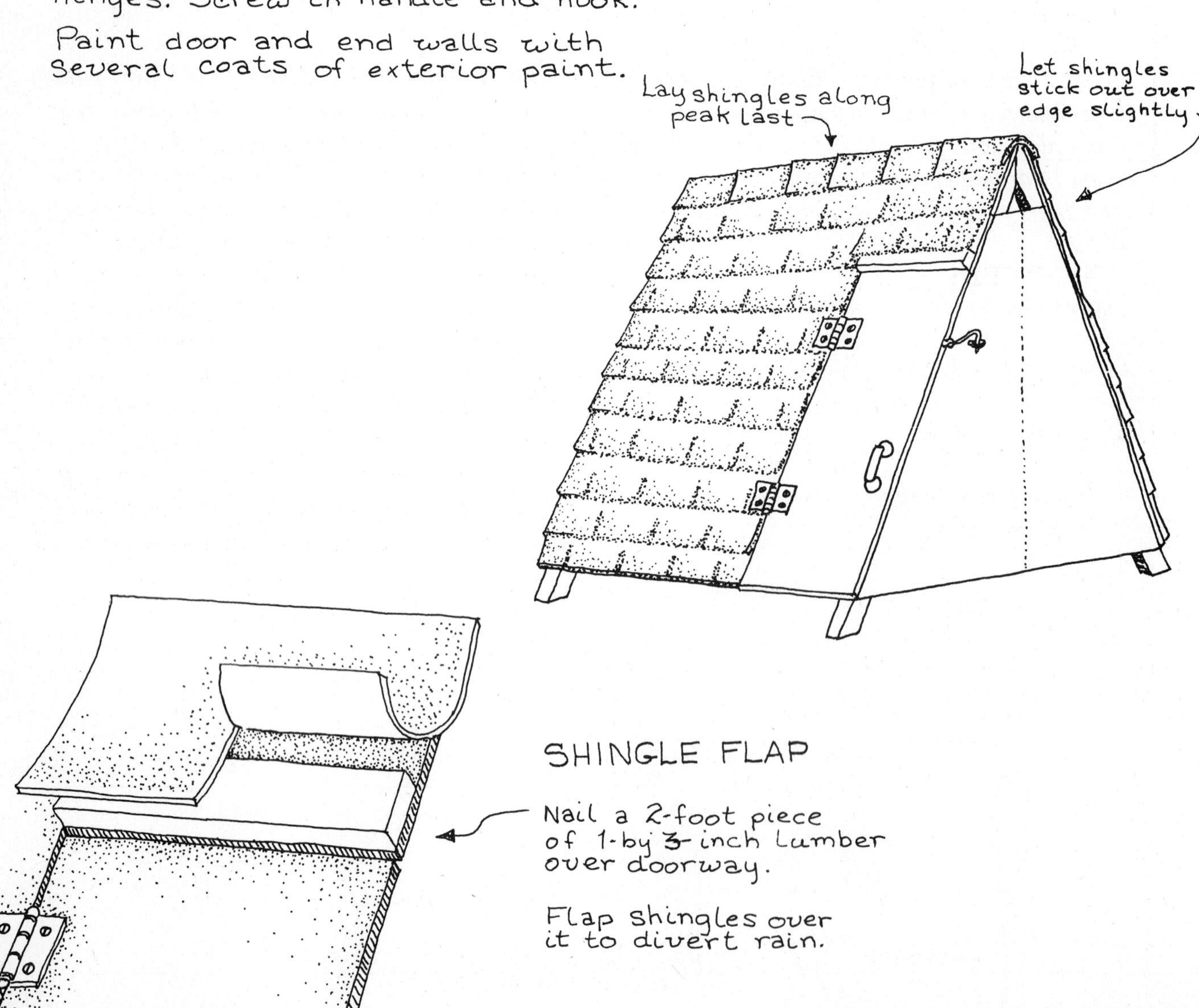

Goat Yard *($90.00)*

If you have more than one goat, a fenced yard is a more practical way to confine them than staking. A goat yard is usually attached to the shed so goats are free to come and go as they wish when the shed door is open. Sand is the best flooring. Water drains from it easily and it can be raked clean of droppings from time to time. Commercial gates are available, but their cost is out of proportion to the yard and shed itself. You might prefer to improvise a gate by stapling fencing to a wood frame, or just cutting one from a piece of plywood. Either gate can be attached to the wood fence posts with hinges. This plan calls for a four-foot fence; if your goat is a jumper, you may have to use higher fencing—and of course a higher gate.

YOU NEED:

MATERIALS:

Six 4-by-4-inch wood posts, each 6 feet high
Quart of creosote
34 feet of 1-by-2-inch-mesh galvanized welded wire fencing (sometimes called garden netting)
Piece of plywood 2 by 4 feet for the gate
Pair of 3-inch straight hinges
Hook and eye to close the gate
100-pound bag of sand

Brush
Shovel
Staple gun
Wire cutters
Screwdriver
Rake

Paint the bottom 1½ feet of each post with creosote. Starting three feet out from the rear corner of the door side of the shed, dig a hole for the first post 1½ feet deep. Place the next post another three feet out for a corner post. Continue around the side of the yard with posts at three-foot intervals until you come to the front corner. The gate will be hinged to this post, and hooked to a post two feet from it. The last post can be centered between the gate post and the front corner of the shed.

Begin stapling the fencing to the rear wall of the shed. Continue stapling it around the posts until you get to the front corner post,

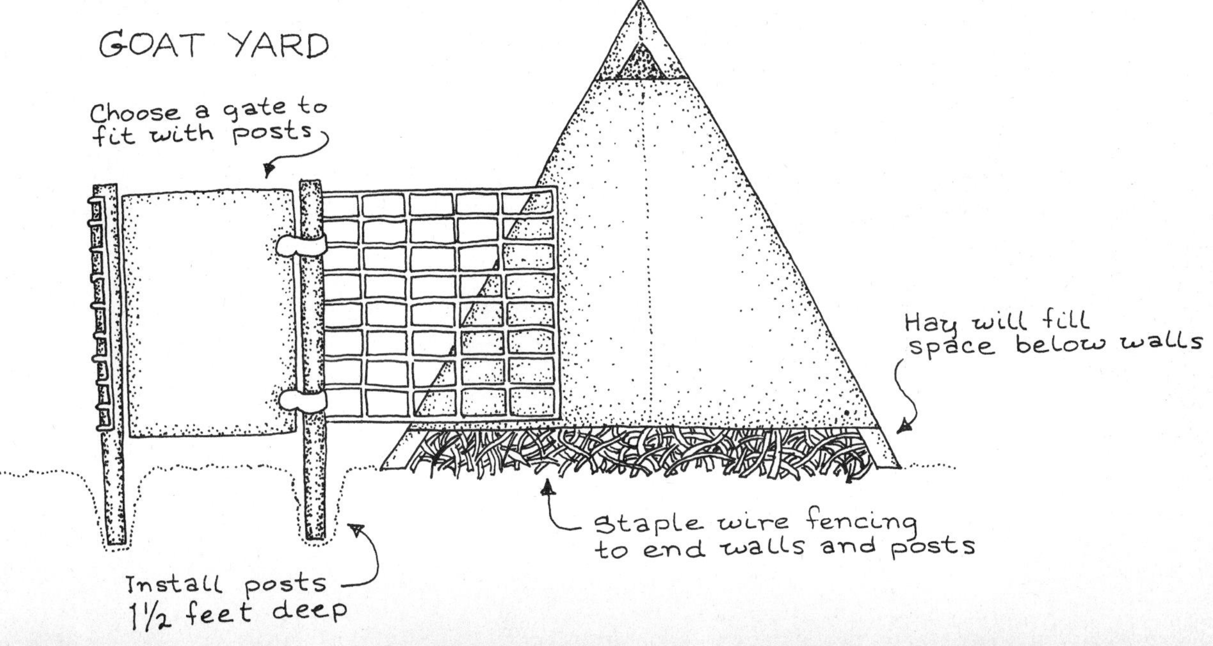

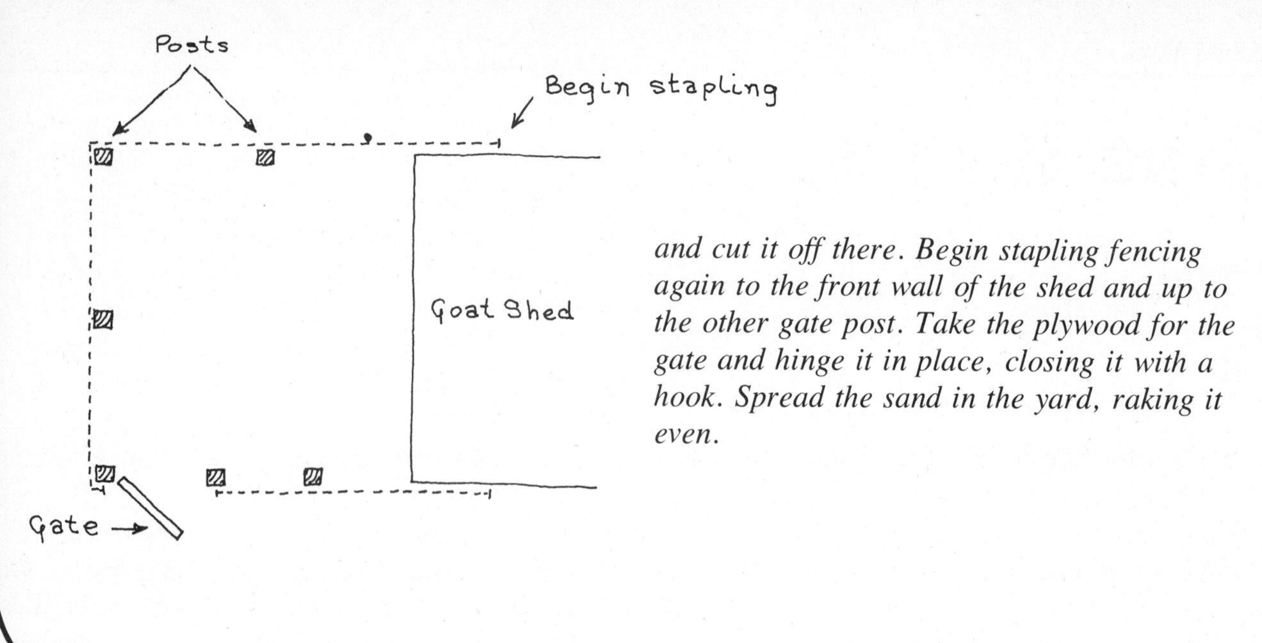

and cut it off there. Begin stapling fencing again to the front wall of the shed and up to the other gate post. Take the plywood for the gate and hinge it in place, closing it with a hook. Spread the sand in the yard, raking it even.

Last Words

These last words are important. They are about some of the troubles the owner of any sort of pet has to go through. One trouble is vacations: how to you get away without taking your pets with you? Another trouble is escapes: how do you find a lost pet? And the last trouble is death. Sooner or later, every pet dies.

As for vacations, many of the animals in this book can get along for a few days without you, provided you leave a larger amount of food and water than usual. Any reptile, bird, amphibian, insect, mollusk, spider, fish or crustacean can be left over a long weekend.

For longer vacations, you have three choices. If most of your animals are temporary ones like salamanders, tadpoles, garter snakes and grasshoppers, you could let them go and start all over again when you return. If most of your animals are small, caged, permanent and portable, like pet turtles and fish, a pet store may board them, usually at a reasonable price. Many veterinarians board cats and dogs, though the cost is not cheap. If permanent pets include nonportable members like geese and goats, or if you have many pets, you will have to hire a pet sitter. It is cheapest to find a child who has always wanted to keep pets to do the sitting, rather than hiring an adult. The price is up to you and the pet sitter. Estimate the time it takes to do daily cleaning and feeding, add up the total number of hours, and settle on something like 75¢ an hour. Chances are this rate, even for quite a few pets, won't run more than $2.25 a week. Be sure to start showing your sitter how to take care of things well ahead of time, though, and let him or her go through the whole routine once or twice before you leave so any questions that come up can be handled. Written instructions are helpful too. Be sure to leave enough food for the whole time you will be away. And leave a way to reach you, just in case.

Escapees and runaways are a bigger problem. There is no such thing as a cage that prevents an animal from ever escaping. Not because there is anything wrong with the cage, but because you will forget to close it correctly, or will think the animal can't climb or jump or squeeze as well as it really can. And some animals will run—or perhaps only wander—away from home.

The first thing to do is control your own behavior. Don't panic and carry on. Adults will be sorry they ever let you have a pet if it's going to cause all this fuss. Don't make a joke of it, either. People don't think a garter snake in the closet is funny, and the garter snake doesn't think it's funny either.

For small lost animals, make the search easier by shutting everything that can be shut—doors, windows, boxes, closets, drawers, cupboards. Start looking. The most likely place for an escaped animal to be is close to its cage, in the nearest natural hiding place. For instance, a snake that was "lost" for two weeks was found exactly 12 inches from his cage, curled up inside an amplifier. A mouse that was gone for days was hidden in a school bag that was kept right next to his cage. He took three trips to school and back before anyone noticed him.

In other words, animals seldom really try to escape. But once they have made the mistake of leaving their cages, they simply try to live as conveniently as they can. Do your searching methodically, starting right next to the cage. Strip beds and lift mattresses. Remove books from shelves. Go through drawers, and then shut them. Take everything off the closet floor and search each shoe and boot. If you can't find your pet this way, try leaving the cage open with some food in it for a few nights. Stay up for a while in the evening and watch. The animal might come during the night to eat. If it does, slam the cage shut once it's inside.

If your pet is not in hiding near its cage and refuses to come back of its own accord, it may still turn up within the next few weeks. For rodents there is one other technique—trapping. A Havahart® animal trap is specially designed to catch small animals like rodents without harming them. Bait the trap with your pet's favorite food and put it in an out-of-the-way spot. If your pet really is nowhere near his cage, the next most likely spot is the kitchen, so you might try placing the trap under the sink, behind the garbage can, or anywhere you have seen wild mice come to eat. Keep trying for at least a few weeks.

So much for animals that escape indoors. Animals that escape outdoors are in greater danger, both from cars on the street and from neighboring dogs. Before you dash around, think through the animal's habits. Most animals head for logical places—a goose to water, a goat to the nearest flower bed. Chickens are most likely to be close by, happily pecking for worms. Rabbits are most likely to be just as close by, nibbling grass. Guinea pigs, however, go into hiding under shrubbery, in woodpiles or under porches. They can be hard to find.

If you don't see your pet in a logical place on your own property, start calling neighbors. Word of stray goats and tame bunnies gets around fast. We've found the milkman to be helpful too. Milkmen know everything. Mailmen often do too. And garbage men.

Once you've located your pet, the next problem is getting it back into its proper home. Herding seems to work better than catching for geese and chickens, and often for rabbits. Get someone to help you. Start the animal in the right direction, then crowd it toward home calmly and quietly. Goats will no doubt come to you for food. Put a rope or a leash around the goat's neck and drag it home. Guinea pigs probably should be caught with your hands, or under a carton or wastebasket.

For runaway or lost cats and dogs, each community has its own finding methods. Some local radio stations broadcast descriptions of lost and found animals at specific times each day. Call the stations near you and find out if they have such a service. Any newspaper will run classified ads for lost or found pets, the cost of the ad depending on the number of words you use. And there is always the ASPCA and other animals shelters who accept lost pets. You have to call them as soon as you notice your cat or dog is missing, since many of them will keep a cat or dog only three days before they "put it to sleep" (kill it by a painless injection). If all else fails, put notices up on bulletin boards or in windows of local stores, veterinary offices or wherever your neighborhood allows such free ads.

If a lost pet isn't found within a week or two, you will wonder if it is dead. That depends on the pet. Lost reptiles, unless they are native to your area, will probably not survive without your care. Rodents, on the other hand, can usually get along on their own unless there is a native population of rats nearby, who may kill any other rodent intruding into their territory. Birds who escape outdoors in warm climates will be fine, but none of the pet birds in this book can survive cold weather. Escaped rabbits, guinea pigs, skunks and ferrets may get along for a while, but are often too domesticated to keep out of the way of dogs. Runaway cats have probably run away on purpose, in a snit about something. They tend to find a home sooner or later, or even get along without humans in the wild. Dogs—especially the wandering types like hounds—may also adopt a new family (no one knows why). The greatest worry about a dog or cat is whether it has been run over. You can check this possibility out with the highway department, since they are responsible for picking up animal carcasses from the road. It's a sad thing to have to do, but it is better to get an answer one way or the other.

Death is the hardest thing of all. When you find the limp corpse of your pet gerbil, who only yesterday munched its lively way through life, your heart sinks, your fingers are reluctant to touch. Worse, you feel guilty, as though there were no way your pet could die without you being in the wrong. Plenty of pets die from old age, not mistreatment. Old age for a mouse, after all, is only a couple of years; for a cricket, a winter's span. Plenty of other pets die from sicknesses you could not have cured even if there had been a way to notice them. But of course pets may die from mistreatment, too. Anybody who has had a lot of pets has killed some by not caring for them well enough, by not understanding all their needs, or by not protecting them from enemies. We were responsible for the death of a rat by not cleaning its cage often enough, of a tortoise by not understanding its need for warmth, and of a hamster by not securing its cage from the cat. Those deaths were our fault. There are other deaths for which you might have to accept responsibility. If you want to keep a tarantula or a boa constrictor alive, you must be ready to take on responsibility for the killing of crickets and mice, both of which might have become pets themselves. A woman once asked one of my children whether he didn't feel sorry for "those poor defenseless mice'' when he fed his snake dinner. He asked her if she felt sorry for ''those poor defenseless cows'' when she fed herself dinner. Responsibility for certain deaths is a fact of life that everyone must face.

When any pet dies, whether you had anything to do with it or not, you will feel awful. You will feel even worse if you get rid of the body—down the toilet, in the garbage or by burial—without formalities, and without farewells. Whether your pet is a tiny salamander or a dear big old dog, you will need a way to acknowledge death and say goodbye the way humans have always done it—with a funeral.

If your pet is small, find a box that its body will fit into nicely, or find something soft to wrap your pet in. It might feel right to you to wrap a hamster in the sock it loved to burrow into, or nestle a turtle into moss or leaves, or wrap a cat in a soft old towel. People often feel better if they put a little food or a favorite toy in with their pet too, even though they know it will not eat or play anymore.

A funeral is not a hard thing to do. Everybody we think will care about the pet's death comes together. We talk about the pet. We say nice things we remember; we apologize for things we feel bad about; we say we will miss our pet. If we have a place to bury it, we put a stone or flowers on the grave. If we don't—if the veterinarian must take care of it, or the garbage man—we have still said goodbye in sad, proper, ancient human fashion.

INDEX

Page numbers in italics indicate illustrations.

whirligig beetles, *94*
wild animals, *12*–31, 204, 304
wild songbirds, 21
wild strawberry, *318*
wild watercress, 325
wintergreen, *318*
wolf spiders, *77*
woodpeckers, *21*
worms (illness), 224, 244, 250, 296

Z